Anonymous

Abstracts and results of magnetical and meteorological

observations

Anonymous

Abstracts and results of magnetical and meteorological observations

ISBN/EAN: 9783337713270

Printed in Europe, USA, Canada, Australia, Japan

Cover: Foto ©ninafisch / pixelio.de

More available books at **www.hansebooks.com**

ABSTRACTS AND RESULTS

MAGNETICAL & METEOROLOGICAL

OBSERVATIONS,

AT THE

MAGNETIC OBSERVATORY,

TORONTO, CANADA,

FROM 1841 TO 1871 INCLUSIVE.

TORONTO:
PRINTED BY COPP, CLARK & CO., 67 & 69 COLBORNE STREET.
1875.

COPP, CLARK & CO., PRINTERS AND PUBLISHERS, COLBORNE STREET TORONTO.

MAGNETICAL OBSERVATIONS.

CONTENTS.

	PAGE
Introduction	ix
Remarks on Magnetical Observations	11-30

LIST OF MAGNETICAL TABLES.

TABLE.

I.—Monthly and yearly means of Absolute Westerly Declination 33

II.—Monthly mean Declination for each of the three groups, with the corresponding corrections for secular change 34

III.—Monthly mean Declination for each group, corrected for secular change, together with the means of the three corrected groups................ 34

IV.—Annual variations of Declination 34

V.—Monthly and yearly means of Absolute Inclination 35

VI.—Monthly and annual means of the Absolute Horizontal Force.......... 36

VII.—Monthly and annual means of Total Force 37

VIII.—Aggregate amount of the disturbances of Declination, Horizontal Force, and Vertical Force, in different years ending 30th June, with the ratios expressing their relative amount in each year as compared with the mean of all years 38

IX.—Containing, for the Total Force and Inclination, numbers analagous to those of Table VIII, together with certain other ratios 38

X.—Aggregate values of the disturbances of Declination in the several months, with the ratios of the aggregate values of the disturbances of the several elements to their respective mean annual values 39

XI.—Containing, for each Magnetic element, the ratios of the amount of Disturbance, in each of the twenty-four hours, to the mean amount of the Disturbances at all hours, Disturbances of an opposite sign being taken jointly as well as separately............................... 40

XII.—Shewing the aggregate effect of the disturbances of Declination, Total Force, and Inclination on the Solar diurnal variations of these elements, together with their average effect in one day 41

XIII.—Solar diurnal variations of Declination for each month, for the two half years, and for the year, derived from the five years ending 30th June, 1848, after the separation and omission of the larger Disturbances 42

XIV.—Solar diurnal variations of Horizontal Force for each month, for the two half years, and for the year, derived from the five years ending 30th June, 1848, after the separation and omission of the larger Disturbances. 43

XV.—Solar diurnal variations of Vertical Force for each month, for the two half years, and for the year, derived from the five years ending 30th June, 1848, after the separation and omission of the larger Disturbances. 44

XVI.—Semi-annual and annual means of the Solar diurnal variations of Total Force and Inclination, derived from those of the Horizontal and Vertical Forces 45

CONTENTS.

TABLE		PAGE
XVII.	Semi-annual inequalities of the diurnal variations of the Magnetic elements for each hour, with the signs proper to the half year, April to September inclusive, derived from the five years ending 30th June, 1848.	46
XVIII.	Aggregate values of the Disturbances in the different years, each ending 30th June, and derived from six observations each day	47
XIX.	Solar diurnal variations of Declination for each month, at the ordinary six observation hours, after the separation and omission of the larger Disturbances, and derived from different groups of years	48
XX.	Solar diurnal variations of Horizontal Force for each month, at the ordinary six observation hours, after the separation and omission of the larger Disturbances, and derived from different groups of years	49
XXI.	Solar diurnal variations of Vertical Force for each month, at the ordinary six observation hours, after the separation and omission of the larger Disturbances, and derived from different groups of years	50
XXII.	Solar diurnal variations of Total Force for each month, at the ordinary six observation hours, after the separation and omission of the larger Disturbances, and derived from different groups of years	51
XXIII.	Solar diurnal variations of Inclination for each month, at the ordinary six observation hours, after the separation and omission of the larger Disturbances, and derived from different groups of years	52
XXIV.	Comparative view of the semi-annual and annual inequalities of the Solar diurnal variations of the Magnetic elements, at the six observation hours, as derived from different groups of years	53-54
XXV.	Dates (Astronomical time) at which unusually large disturbances of Declination occurred at the ordinary observation hours, with the amount of abnormal variation of each such disturbance. Declination, abnormal variation not less than 15'. The (+) sign indicates an easterly disturbance, and (−) a westerly disturbance	55
XXVI.	A selection of dates (Astronomical time) at which extra readings of the Magnetic Instruments were taken, in consequence of prevailing large disturbances, with the amount of abnormal deviations ($\Delta\Psi$) of Declination, ($\Delta\theta$) of Inclination, and $\dfrac{\Delta\phi}{\phi}$ of Total Force	56-59

INTRODUCTION.

The Toronto Magnetic and Meteorological Observatory is situated in the grounds of the University of Toronto, in latitude 43° 39'.4 N., longitude 5h. 17m. 33s. W., 108 feet above Lake Ontario, and 342 feet above the level of the sea.

Prior to the spring of 1853, the Observatory at Toronto, in common with those established at the recommendation of the Royal Society of London, at other colonial stations, was maintained by the British Government, and was under the general control of Major, now General, Sir Edward Sabine, of the Royal Artillery.

The first Director, Lieut. Riddel, R. A., arrived in Canada in the summer of 1839, accompanied by the following non-commissioned officers as assistants:

Messrs. JOHNSTON (1),
" WALKER (2),
" MENZIES (3).

(1.) Now Assistant Secretary to the Canadian Institute.
(2.) Deceased in June, 1865.
(3.) Now Senior Assistant at the Observatory.

After examining various sites, Lieut. Riddel finally gave the preference to Toronto, where a grant of 2½ acres belonging to the University of Toronto (then the University of King's College), was made by the Council of the University, with the sole condition that the building to be erected should not be appropriated to any other purpose than that of an observatory, and should revert to the University if the Observatory should be discontinued.

The first observatory building was completed in September, 1840, the observations prior to that date having been carried on in a barrack in Bathurst street.

Lieut. Riddel was succeeded early in 1841, by Lieut. Younghusband, R. A., who finally gave up his charge to Lieut. Lefroy, R. A.,* in the autumn of 1844. The latter officer continued to be Director till the spring of 1853.

---

* Now General Lefroy, and Governor of Bermuda.

Further details concerning the early history of the Observatory, including the circumstances which led to its establishment by the Imperial Government, are given in the introduction to the first volume of the observations, published under the superintendence of General Sabine, which, together with the second and third volumes, contain the magnetical and meteorological observations from 1840 to 1848.

From the spring of 1853, when the observatory ceased to be an Imperial establishment, it has been maintained by and under the control of the general Government of Canada.

It is intended in the present volume to give a very brief summary of the principal results derived from the magnetical and meteorological observations from the establishment of the Observatory to the end of 1871, together with tables of the daily observations from 1863 to 1871, both inclusive. Unless it is stated to the contrary, it must be understood that discussions of observations prior to 1853 have been abridged from the publications of General Sabine.

As details regarding the several instruments and their adjustments are described at length in the three first volumes (1840 to 1848), and in the three volumes, 1853-62, they are omitted here.

MAGNETICAL OBSERVATIONS.

ABSOLUTE DECLINATION.

In Table I. are given the monthly and annual values of the declination in every case in which they could be procured.

The series may be divided into three principal groups: from 1845 to 1851; from 1856 to 1864; and from 1865 to 1871.

Secular change.

According to General Sabine, the monthly determinations in the first group furnish 84 equations of the form $\psi = \psi' + ay$; in which ψ is the most probable declination at the mean epoch, July 1st, 1848; ψ' the observed declination in any other month; (a) the interval in months between the date of ψ' and July 1st, 1848, (a) being regarded as positive for dates later than the mean epoch; and (y) the monthly secular change.

From these equations were obtained $\psi = 1° 34'.91$; and $y = 0'.1627$, or $12y = 1.952$, the mean annual increase of west declination.

Probable error of the monthly determinations.

From the 84 equations the following are derived:

$$\psi'_1 = 1° 34'.91 + 0'.1627\, a_1,$$
$$\psi'_2 = 1\ \ 34.91 + 0'.1627\, a_2,$$
$$\&c., \quad \&c., \quad \&c.$$
$$\psi'_{84} = 1\ \ 34.91 + 0'.1627\, a_{84},$$

as the most probable values of the declination in the several months in the group. From the differences between these and the observed values, the probable error of a single monthly determination was found to be $\pm 0'.75$, and the probable error of the mean determination $\pm 0'.08$. The probable errors include the effects of disturbance and of mean annual variation.

By a method similar to the one described above, the mean monthly increase of westerly declination, derived from the 108 equations furnished by the monthly determinations in 1856 to 1864, was found to be $0'.2606$; the probable error of a single monthly determination was $0'.74$; and the probable error of the mean of the group, ($2° 10'.04$,) corresponding to July 1st, 1860, was $0'.071$.

Again from the 84 equations, similarly derived from the later group, 1865 to 1871, the mean monthly increase was found to be 0'.3127; the probable error of a single monthly determination was 0'.99; and the probable error of the mean, (2° 34'.62,) corresponding to July 1st, 1868, was 0'.109.

Annual variation.

The process of computing the annual variation of the declination is exhibited in Tables II., III., IV.

Table II. gives the monthly means of the observed declinations derived from each of the three groups, 1845-51, 1856-64, and 1865-71, together with the corrections for secular change, needful for reducing them to their respective mean epochs, July 1st, 1848, 1860, and 1868. In Table III., the monthly means are reduced to the mean epochs; and, finally, in Table IV., are shown the annual variations, obtained by subtracting the annual mean of each group from the several reduced monthly means.

INCLINATION.

The monthly and annual means of inclination, from 1841 to 1871, are given in Table V.

From 1841 to 1852, the annual variation was shown to be approximately expressed by a formula which, when modified so as to harmonize with the notation adopted further on, is as follows:

Annual variation $= 1'.11 \sin (n \times 30° + 122°)$;

where (n) is the time measured from January 15th, the unit being the twelfth part of the year.

Making $n = 0$, $n = 1$, &c., &c., $n = 11$, the mean annual variations for the several months are as follows:

Jan.	Feb.	Mar.	April.	May.	June.	July.	Aug.	Sept.	Oct.	Nov.	Dec.
+0.94	+0.52	—0.04	—0.59	—0.98	—1.11	—0.94	—0.52	+0.04	+0.59	+0.98	+1.11

This series shows a maximum in December and a minimum in June, with a range from one solstice to the other of 2'.22.

* When the years 1853-54-55 were incorporated with the preceding twelve years, the conclusion arrived at respecting the annual variation of inclination was that, after the elimination of secular change, the inclination in June or July is lower than in the previous January and the succeeding December, by an amount which may be taken approximately as 1'.71. In

---

* The investigation, including 1853-55, was made by Sir E. Sabine.

subsequent years the irregularities in the inclination, whether occasioned by disturbances or by other causes, are sufficient to mask the annual variations which are so distinctly marked in earlier years.

Annual variations and secular change of Inclination in the years 1858-71.

From the fourteen years we find the mean inclination to be 75° 20'.88, which would correspond to January 1st, 1865, if the inclination were assumed to decrease uniformly. Combining this mean and the several yearly means, fourteen equations were constructed of the form $ax = d$, where (x) is the most probable annual decrease; (a) the intervals in years or fractions of a year from the mean epoch, January 1st, 1865, (a) being positive for dates prior to the mean epoch, and (d) the excess of the corresponding yearly mean above 75° 20'.88. The fourteen equations give $x = 0'.704$; whence the approximate mean monthly secular decrease is 0'.059.

Also the probable error of a single annual mean is 0'.52, and the probable error of the mean for January 1st, 1865, is 0'.14.

In the following Table are shewn—

(1.) The monthly means of inclination in the fourteen years uncorrected for secular change;

(2.) The corrections for secular change;

(3.) The *minutes* of the monthly means corrected for secular change; the degrees (75°) being omitted to save space;

(4.) The annual variations from the preceding line.

	Jan.	Feb.	Mar.	April.	May.	June.	July.	Aug.	Sept.	Oct.	Nov.	Dec.	Mean.
Mon. means 14 years....	75° 20'.99	75° 21'.06	75° 21'.35	75° 21'.41	75° 21'.24	75° 20'.54	75° 20'.21	75° 20'.56	75° 20'.76	75° 20'.99	75° 20'.74	75° 20'.68	75° 20'.88
Cor. for secular change....	−.32	−.26	−.20	−.14	−.08	−.02	+.02	+.08	+.14	+.20	+.26	+.32	
Cor'd monthly means......	20.67	20.80	21.15	21.27	21.16	20.52	20.23	20.64	20.90	21.19	21.00	21.00	
Annual variations......	−0.21	−0.08	+0.27	+0.39	+0.28	−0.36	−0.65	−0.24	+0.02	+0.31	+0.12	+0.12	

From the third and fourth lines of the Table just given, it is obvious that the annual variation cannot be expressed by one circulating term. In fact, the actual variations in the fourth line are given by the following formula, in which the coefficient of the second term is double that of the first:

Variation $= 0'.18 \sin (n \times 30° + 74°) + 0'.36 \sin (2n \times 30° + 265°)$
$+ 0'.09 \sin (3n \times 30° + 139°) + 0'.04 \sin (4n \times 30° + 284°)$
$+ 0'.07 \sin (5n \times 30° + 188°)$
$+ 0'.02 \sin (6n \times 30° + 270°).$

If all the terms but the two first be omitted in the above formula, the variations of the dip in the several months will be as follows:

Jan.	Feb.	Mar.	April.	May.	June.	July.	Aug.	Sept.	Oct.	Nov.	Dec.
−0.19	−0.03	+0.28	+0.41	+0.16	−0.28	−0.53	−0.38	+0.02	+0.31	+0.25	−0.03

ABSOLUTE HORIZONTAL FORCE.

The monthly and annual means of the horizontal force are shewn in Table VI.

The methods by which they were obtained were precisely the same as those described in Vol. III. of the early series of Toronto observations; but subsequent to July, 1858, the determinations were from observations in two days in each month, two sets of vibrations with deflections at two different distances being taken in each day. The coefficient of induction (μ) was determined by experiments similar to those employed by Mr. Welsh, of Kew, and described in Vol. III.

The partial determinations, after being reduced to the mean Bifilar reading of the day, were afterwards reduced to the normal mean of the month.

Secular change.

According to Sabine, the mean annual secular change of horizontal force from 1845 to 1852 was −.00371 ±.00091. From a recent investigation it has been found that the mean *monthly* secular change, obtained from 84 equations which are furnished by the seven years, 1845-51, was −.00022, and the probable error of a single monthly determination .00274.

By examining the column of annual means, it is evident that the progressive change was converted into an increase during the latter part of the series.

From the fourteen years, 1851 to 1871, the mean annual increase was .00148.

Annual variation of horizontal force.

From the provisional determinations of horizontal force, from 1845 to 1851, (see p. xci. of 2nd volume,) Sabine inferred that the annual variations could be expressed by the formula:

$$\text{Variation} = .002 \sin(n \times 30° + 312°),$$

(n) being the months or parts of a month reckoned from January 15th; and that the horizontal force had a maximum in June, and a minimum in December, with a total range between the solstices of .0038.

The annual variations have been also deduced from the monthly means of the fourteen years, 1858-1871, by the process shewn below:

TORONTO MAGNETICAL OBSERVATIONS.   15

	Jan.	Feb.	Mar.	April.	May.	June.	July.	Aug.	Sept.	Oct.	Nov.	Dec.	Mean.
Mon. means in 14 years..	3.4897	3.4895	3.4893	3.4900	3.4945	3.4938	3.4949	3.4929	3.4914	3.4895	3.4907	3.4915	3.4915
Cor. for secular change.....	+ 7	+ 6	+ 5	+ 3	+ 2	+ 1	− 1	− 2	− 3	− 5	− 6	− 7	
Cor. monthly means......	3.4904	3.4901	3.4898	3.4903	3.4947	3.4939	3.4948	3.4927	3.4911	3.4890	3.4901	3.4908	
Annual variations.......	−.0011	−.0014	−.0017	−.0012	+.0032	+.0024	+.0033	+.0012	−.0004	−.0025	−.0014	−.0007	

The corrected monthly means exhibit considerable irregularity, and the variations deduced from them can only be approximately expressed by two terms of the general formula. The expression is,

Variation = .0022 sin $(n \times 30° + 290°)$ + .0014 sin $(2n \times 30° + 127°)$.

The annual variations deduced from the monthly means of General Sabine are expressed more nearly by the introduction of a second term, namely, .001 sin $(2n \times 30° + 165°)$.

TOTAL FORCE.

The mean monthly values of total force (φ) deduced from $\varphi = X \sec \theta$, (where X and θ are the corresponding values of the horizontal force and inclination,) are given in Table VII.

Secular change.

From the years 1845-51, Sabine inferred that there was an annual secular increase in the total force of .0052. A cursory examination will shew that, on the whole, the subsequent change has been a decided *decrease*.

If the whole series be divided into groups of four years each, we find the means and the changes to be as follows:

Years.	1845-48.	1849-52.	1856-59.	1860-63.	1864-67.	1868-71.
Means............	13.9218	13.9356	13.8566	13.8113	13.7998	13.7803
Change...........		+.0138	−.0790	−.0453	−.0115	−.0190
Change in one year		+.00345	−.01129	−.01132	−.00287	−.00475

From the fourteen years, 1858-71, the mean annual change found by least squares was — 0.0049.

Annual variation.

Assuming the mean *monthly* change in the last fourteen years to be — 0.0004, the monthly means for this period, with the same means corrected for secular change are shewn below:

	Jan.	Feb.	Mar.	April	May.	June.	July.	Aug.	Sept.	Oct.	Nov.	Dec.	Mean.
Mon. means 14 years....	13.7978	13.7981	13.8018	13.8059	13.8209	13.8069	13.8066	13.8041	13.8010	13.7972	13.7979	13.8006	13.8032
Cor. for secular change....	— 23	— 18	— 14	— 10	— 6	— 2	+ 2	+ 6	+ 10	+ 14	+ 18	+ 23	
Cor. monthly means......	13.7955	13.7963	13.8004	13.8049	13.8203	13.8067	13.8068	13.8047	13.8020	13.7986	13.7997	13.8029	
Annual variations.......	—.0077	—.0069	—.0028	+.0017	+.0171	+.0035	+.0036	+.0015	—.0012	—.0046	—.0035	—.0003	

These monthly means show considerable irregularity, and in fact their variations cannot be expressed with precision except by the employment of six terms of the usual formula. The variations are given approximately by the expression,

Annual var. = .0065 sin ($n \times 30° + 302°$) + .0040 sin ($2n \times 30° + 197°$).

SEPARATION AND DISCUSSION OF THE LARGER MAGNETIC DISTURBANCES.

In the following investigations the magnitude of a disturbance or abnormal deviation of a magnetic element is expressed by the amount by which its value differs from the normal proper to the day and hour.

A disturbance is regarded as large where it equals or exceeds a certain limit. The limits employed by Gen. Sabine in the third Toronto volume, and adopted in subsequent reductions, were 5′ for the declination, 1′ for the inclination, ·0012 for the horizontal force (or ·0012 of the whole horizontal force), ·0026 for the vertical force, and ·0004 for the total force.

To estimate the magnitude of a disturbance it was necessary to adopt for each instrument a series of normal readings proper to each hour, and comparable with the observations made at that hour in a group of days sufficiently near together to be inappreciably affected by annual variations or secular and instrumental changes.

The normal scale reading for each observation hour was calculated by taking the average of all the readings at like hours, in a month or more suitable group of consecutive days, omitting those days in which the readings differed from the normal *finally adopted* by an amount equivalent to the limit determined on for the element under discussion.

Before this process could be applied to the force instruments, their readings were reduced to a uniform temperature of 55° by the application of the proper corrections.

The temperature corrections applied to the scale readings were in every case derived from the observations made with the instrument, by comparing the change of scale reading with the accompanying change in the attached thermometer.

The following was the mode of obtaining the temperature corrections. Let t_1, t_2, t_3, be the mean temperatures of three groups of days (as shewn by the attached thermometer,) each group consisting of three or four days, and so selected that t_1-t_2 and t_3-t_2 may have the same signs. Also, let R_1, R_2, R_3, be the corresponding mean scale readings of the instrument. Then the change in the scale reading corresponding to a change of one degree in the temperature, or $\frac{\varDelta R}{\varDelta t}$, will be approximately equal to

$$\frac{R_1-2R_2+R_3}{t_1-2t_2+t_2}.$$

The approximate scale equivalent will also be given by an expression of the same form, where t_1, t_2, t_3, are the mean temperatures of three equidistant quarters, in order of time; t_1 and t_3 being the temperatures either of two quarters of the same name, or of a spring and autumn quarter, and t_2 the temperature of the quarter midway between the other two.

Applying the same process to several similar combinations, the scale value equivalent to 1° of Fahrenheit is found finally by an expression of the form $\frac{\Sigma (R_1 - 2R_2 + R_3)}{\Sigma (t_1 - 2t_2 + t_3)}.$

The disturbances of the horizontal and vertical components of the force being found, the corresponding abnormal deviations $\frac{\varDelta \varphi}{\varphi}$, of the total force φ, and $\varDelta\ \theta$, of the inclination, were calculated by the formulæ:

$$\frac{\varDelta\ \varphi}{\varphi} = \cos^2\theta\ \frac{\varDelta\ X}{X} + \sin^2\theta\ \frac{\varDelta\ Y}{Y};$$

$$\text{And } \varDelta\ \theta = \tfrac{1}{2}\sin2\theta \left(\frac{\varDelta\ Y}{Y} - \frac{\varDelta\ X}{X}\right);$$

where $\frac{\varDelta X}{X}$ and $\frac{\varDelta Y}{Y}$ represent the contemporaneous abnormal deviations of the horizontal and vertical components of the force, where one or both of them were disturbed.

Of the resulting values of $\frac{\varDelta \varphi}{\varphi}$ and $\varDelta\ \theta$, those were retained as disturbances which equalled or exceeded the limits determined on for φ and θ, namely ·0004 for φ, and 1' for θ.

The discussion of the disturbances of the hourly observations in the five years, 1st July, 1843, to 30th June, 1848, are abridged from the third Toronto volume, published by General Sabine.

Disturbances of Declination.

The number of disturbed observations amounted to 2,172 in the five years of hourly observations ending 30th June, 1848, being about 1 in 17 of the whole.

The aggregate values in minutes of arc in the different years, are shewn in columns 1, 2, 3 of Table VIII., where (2) contains the easterly disturbances, (3) the westerly, and (1) the two combined.

Expressing the annual sums in terms of their respective means for five years, 3944.5, 2213.4, and 1731.1, we obtain the ratios given in columns 4, 5, 6.

The total aggregate of easterly disturbances in five years was 11066.9, and of westerly 8655.4; shewing that the general effect of the larger disturbances is to decrease the westerly declination, and that the easterly values preponderate in the ratio 1.28 to 1.

Table X. is computed by a process analogous to that just given. The columns 1, 2, 3 contain the aggregate sums of the disturbances, and of their easterly and westerly constituents, during the five years in each of the twelve months, and 4, 5, 6 contain these sums expressed in terms of the means of the twelve monthly sums.

From column 4 it is seen that September and April are the months of greatest disturbance of declination, and January and June the months of least disturbance, and that the progression from the maxima to the minima, and from the minima to the maxima, is continuous.

From columns 5 and 6, it is seen that the same general law prevails in both easterly and westerly disturbances, when viewed separately as when viewed conjointly; the equinoxes are the epochs of maximum, and the solstices of minimum disturbances.

The ratios which give the preponderance of easterly over westerly disturbances, shew a tendency towards a maximum at the June solstice, and a minimum at the December solstice. This is seen from the following table containing the ratios of the easterly to the westerly values :

May .. 1.29 ⎫
June.. 3.82 ⎬ 2.17
July .. 1.41 ⎭

Aug... 1.96
Sept... 1.29
Oct. .. 1.21

Nov... 0.77 ⎫
Dec. .. 0.74 ⎬ 0.93
Jan. .. 1.29 ⎭

Feb.. 1.27
Mar... 1.40
Apr... 1.04

In Table XI. the ratios shew the aggregate sums of the disturbances in the five years in each of the twenty-four hours, expressed in terms of the means of the twenty-four hourly sums.

Referring to column (1), from 10 A.M. to 7 P.M. inclusive, the ratios are invariably below unity, and from 8 P.M. to 9 A.M. inclusive, as invariably above unity. The hour of least disturbance is 1 P.M., and of greatest 9 P.M. The progression during the days is uninterrupted to and from the minimum at 1 P.M., but is much less regular during the night.

Referring to columns (2) and (3), the easterly disturbances are below the average during the day, or from 5 A.M. to 5 P.M., and above the average from 6 P.M. to 4 A.M.; the westerly are below the average from noon to midnight inclusive, and above the average, with a single exception (at 3 A.M.), from 1 A.M. to 11 A.M. inclusive.

The easterly have a maximum and the westerly a minimum at 9 P.M.; the westerly have a maximum at 8 A.M., and the easterly have minima nearly equal at 9 A.M. and 1, 2, 3 P.M. Excepting from noon to 5 P.M., when both easterly and westerly disturbances are small, and from 1 A.M. to 5 A.M., when they are both large, there is a systematic tendency to a diminution of easterly disturbance when westerly disturbance prevails, and *vice versâ*.

In Table XII, columns (1) and (2) contain the aggregate sums of the easterly and westerly disturbances at each of the twenty-four hours, being the numbers from which columns (2) and (3) of Table XI are derived. Column (3) gives for each hour the excess of easterly disturbance over westerly, or of westerly over easterly, in the aggregate values of the five years; and column (4) the mean effect at each hour, obtained by dividing the accumulated excess in the five years in column (3) by 1552, the number of days of observation. Column (4) exhibits, therefore, the *mean diurnal* variation produced on a general average by the disturbances amounting to or exceeding 5′ of arc, and which is superimposed upon the more regularly occurring diurnal variation derivable from the great body of the observations, after the disturbed observations have been separated.

It is seen from this column (4) that the general effect of the greater disturbances is to produce a maximum easterly deflection of the magnet of 0′.87 at 9 P.M., and a maximum westerly deflection of 0′.52 at 8 A.M., the intermediate progression either way being continuous, and only interrupted by a few slight irregularities in the afternoon, when the disturbances are fewest and of least amount.

Disturbances of Horizontal Force.

The number of the Bifilar observations, in which the amount of disturbance reached the limit .0012 in the five years, was 2968, being about 1 in 12 or 13 of the whole body of the observations.

From Table VIII., columns 7, 8, and 9, the numbers in which are obtained in a manner precisely similar to that employed for columns 4, 5, and 6 for the declination, we find a progressive increase in the annual value of the disturbed observations from the year ending June, 1845, to the year ending June, 1848. The aggregate value in the year ending June, 1844, was slightly greater than in the following year, in consequence of the substitution of the observations of 5 months, Oct., 1842, to Feb., 1843, for the 5 months, Oct. 1843, to Feb., 1844, when the vertical force magnet was dismounted.

Dividing the aggregate values into disturbances which increase, and those which diminish the force, it appears that the ratio of the disturbances decreasing the force to those which increase it, was on the average of 5 years, 6.4 to 1.

Comparison of the disturbances of Horizontal Force in the different months.

From the ratios in column (7) of Table X., it is seen that April and September are the months of maximum disturbance, and January and June of minimum disturbance. The amount of disturbance at the Equinoxes (April and September,) is to that at the Solstices (January and June,) in the ratio of between 3 and 4 to 1.

Comparison of the disturbances in the Horizontal Force in different hours.

From column (4) of Table XI., the amount of disturbance is seen to be systematically greater at all the hours from 10 P.M., to 10 A.M., inclusive, than at any hour from 11 A.M. to 9 P.M., inclusive. The ratios are equal to or above unity from 10 P.M. to 10 A.M., inclusive, and below unity from 11 A.M. to 9 P.M., inclusive. The maximum is at 2 A.M., and the minimum intermediate between 2 and 6 P.M., during which latter hours there is little variation in the amount. There is also a secondary maximum about 7 or 8 A.M., preceded by a secondary minimum about 5 or 6 A.M.

From columns (5) and (6) of Table XI., shewing the corresponding ratios when the disturbances at the different hours are separated into those which increase, and those which diminish, the force, we learn that, while the disturbances which increase and those which diminish the force are governed in amount by periodic laws depending on the solar hours, the laws are different in the two cases.

The disturbances which increase the force have a maximum at 4 P.M., and a minimum from 2 to 4 A.M.

From 10 A.M. to 8 P.M., inclusive, the ratios, with one exception, are above unity, and from 9 P.M. to 9 A.M., inclusive, without an exception below unity. It is in the hours of the day, consequently, that the disturbances which increase the force have their greatest prevalence; while the hours of the night are comparatively tranquil. The converse law holds in regard to the disturbances which decrease the force; from 10 P.M. to 9 A.M., the ratios exceed unity at every hour, and from 10 A.M. to 9 P.M., they are uniformly less than unity. The maximum is at 2 A.M., and the minimum at 4 P.M.

Disturbances of Vertical Force.

The number of the vertical force observations in which the amount of disturbance reached the limit, .00026, of the vertical force, was 5220, or about 1 in 7 of the whole.

From Table VIII., column (10), we find a progressive increase in the annual amount of the disturbances from the year ending June, 1845, to the year ending June, 1848; and from columns (11) and (12) it appears that this is also true with respect to the disturbances of contrary signs. Dividing the aggregate values into disturbances which increase, and those which diminish the vertical force, we find that the disturbances which diminish the vertical force are to those which increase it, in the ratio 1.4 to 1 nearly, on the average of the five years.

Disturbances of the Vertical Force in the different months.

From the ratios in column (7) of Table X it is seen that April and September are the months of maximum disturbance, and January and June the months of minimum disturbance. The progression from the maxima to the minima, and *vice versâ*, is continuous, with the exception of December, caused by excessive disturbance in December, 1847.

On the whole in the disturbances of the vertical force, as in the declination and horizontal force, the maxima occur about the equinoxes, and the minima about the solstices, the former being to the latter in the ratio of nearly 3 to 1.

From columns (9) and (10) of Table X, in which the monthly values of the disturbances which increase the force, and those which diminish the force, are expressed in terms of their respective mean monthly values, we find the same general law prevailing as in column (8): the equinoxes being the epochs of maxima, and the solstices of minima.

It has been stated that on the average of the year the disturbances which diminish the vertical force preponderate over those which increase it in the ratio of 1·4 to 1 nearly. This preponderance, however, is subject to a periodic variation, and to have a maximum about the northern solstice, and a minimum at the winter solstice. The comparative preponderance is shewn by the ratios in Table X, column (11), which are the monthly values of the disturbances which decrease the vertical force, expressed in terms of those which increase it.

From the comparison of easterly and westerly disturbances of declination made in page xxvii of Vol. II of Toronto Observations, evidence is shewn of an analogous periodic variation. In the north solstitial months, easterly disturbances preponderate, and in the south solstitial months westerly disturbances preponderate.

Disturbances of Vertical Force in the different hours.

From Table XI, column (7), the aggregate disturbance in the five years has a maximum at 3 a.m. and a minimum at 11 a.m., with a secondary maximum at 5 p.m. and a secondary minimum at 9 p.m. There is therefore a double progression; and between the successive maxima and minima, the progression is continuous. From 8 a.m. to 11 p.m., except from 4 to 7 p.m. inclusive, the ratios are less than unity; and from midnight to 7 a.m. the ratios exceed unity.

From columns (8) and (9) of the same Table, wherein the ratios are derived respectively from the disturbances which increase, and those which diminish the vertical force, we find that in the disturbances which increase the vertical force the values are highest from noon to 10 p.m.; they exceed unity or the mean hourly value from 1 to 9 p.m., and exceed twice that value from 4 to 7 p.m. The hours of maximum and minimum are *approximately* 5 p.m. and 5 a.m. In the disturbances which diminish the force the values are least from 10 a.m. to 9 p.m. inclusive; the ratios are below unity from 9 a.m. to 10 p.m. inclusive, and above unity from 11 p.m. to 8 a.m. The maximum is well marked at 3 a.m.; and the minimum, which is not so well marked, occurs in the afternoon. When the ratios are highest in the disturbances increasing the force, they are generally lowest in those which decrease the force, and *vice versâ:* but the periodic laws in the two cases are not strictly the converse of each other.

Disturbances of the Total Force.

The aggregate values of the disturbances in the different years, each ending 30th June, together with the aggregate values respectively of those which increase and those which diminish the force, are given in columns 1, 2 and 3, of Table IX. Expressing these in terms of the means of the five years given at the foot of the respective columns, we have the ratios in columns 4, 5 and 6.

The general effect of the disturbances is to decrease the total force, the ratios of the disturbances decreasing the force to those which increase it being on the average 1·94 to 1.

The values of these ratios in the several years are given in column (7) of Table IX.

Distribution of Disturbances of Total Force in the different months.

The aggregate values of the disturbances of total force in the several months, expressed in terms of the mean value for the twelve months, are shewn in column (12) of Table X, in which columns (13) and (14) contain the corresponding ratios when the disturbances are separated into those which increase and those which diminish the force.

The ratios in columns (12) and (13) show an exception to the law observed with reference to the annual distribution of the disturbance of declination, namely, that the maxima and minima occur respectively at or near the equinoxes and solstices.

This exception is due to the anomalous character of December, 1847; for if the year ending 30th June, 1848, be omitted, the ratio for December becomes less than unity for the disturbances which increase the total force, as well as for the disturbances considered without regard to sign. As the excessive disturbances in December, 1847, were chiefly those which *increase* the total force, the progression in the disturbances which diminish the force from a maximum to a minimum, and the converse, is continuous and uninterrupted.

Distribution of the Disturbances of the Total Force at the different hours.

The ratios which express this distribution are contained in columns (10), (11), and (12) of Table XI.

In the case of the disturbances, without regard to sign, shewn in column (10), it is seen that from 8 a.m. to 11 p.m. inclusive, the disturbance at every hour is less than at every hour from midnight to 7 a.m. inclusive. It is a minimum at 11 a.m. and a maximum at 3 a.m. From the maximum at 3 a.m. to the minimum at 11 a.m. the progression is continuous and uninterrupted; from the minimum at 11 a.m. to the maximum at 3 a.m. the progression suffers a slight interruption from 5 p.m. to 9 p.m.; but from the latter hour to the principal maximum at 3 a.m. the progression is continuous.

In columns (11) and (12) it is seen that the disturbances which increase the force, and those which diminish it, are so related that, for the most part, at the hours when the one augments in value, the other diminishes in value, and *vice versâ*.

To determine the mean effect produced in the total force by the disturbances at the different hours, the aggregate amount in five years of the forces of opposite signs are collected in columns (5) and (6) of Table XII. In column (7) are shewn for each hour the preponderance of the disturbances of either sign, or the *whole* effect in the five years. Finally, in column (8) we have the mean daily effect.

From this column we learn that the law of that part of the diurnal variation, which is due to disturbances, is as follows:—

From 11 a.m. to 9 p.m. inclusive, the disturbances augment the force.
From 10 p.m. to 10 a.m. inclusive, they diminish it.
The hour of greatest augmentation is 5 p.m.
The hour of greatest diminution is 3 a.m.
The greatest diminution is nearly twice as great as the greatest augmentation.
The hours of most rapid change are from 7 to 8 a.m. and from 11 p.m. to midnight.
From the greatest diminution at 3 A.M. to the greatest increase at 5 P.M., the progression is continuous; and from 5 P.M. to 3 A.M., it is also continuous, with the exception of a small interruption at 7 P.M.

Disturbances of Inclination.

The aggregate values of the disturbances of Inclination in the five years, each ending 30th June, when taken together, and when separated into those which increase and those which diminish the inclination, are shewn in columns (8), (9), and (10), of Table IX.

Dividing the several values in (8) by the mean, 1318.1, at the foot of the column, we have the ratios in column (11). The ratios in columns (12) and (13) are found in a similar manner from (9) and (10).

The general effect of the larger disturbances is evidently to increase the inclination, the ratio of those which increase the inclination to those which diminish it, being as 5.6 to 1, on the average of the five years. The analogous ratios in the separate years, which shew the relative preponderance of the disturbances, which increase the inclination, are given in column (14) of Table IX.

Disturbance of Inclination in the different months.

The ratios shewing the aggregate amount in each month, compared with the mean of the twelve monthly amounts, are given in Table X., column (15). December is the only exception to a periodical variation, which has its maximum at the Equinoxes and its minimum at the Solstices; this apparent anomaly being occasioned by unusual disturbances in December, 1847.

Disturbances of Inclination at the different hours.

The ratios of the aggregates at each hour to the mean hourly value, or average of all hours, are given in column (3), Table XI. The hourly disturbances of the inclination exhibit a double progression. From 7 A.M. to noon, and again from 7 P.M. to 2 A.M., inclusive, the values exceed the mean hourly value: and from 1 P.M. to 6 P.M., and again from 3 A.M. to 6 A.M., inclusive, they fall short of the mean hourly value.

In columns (14) and (15), of Table XI., are shewn the disturbances which increase the inclination, and those which diminish it, expressed in the usual manner.

The disturbances which increase the inclination have two epochs of maxima and two of minima; the principal maximum is at 1 A.M., and the secondary maximum at 7 A.M. The principal minimum is at 4 P.M., and the secondary at 5 A.M.

The disturbances which decrease the inclination are comparatively small at all the hours: they exhibit, however, a systematic tendency to be greater during the day than during the night: their maximum is at 2 P.M., and their minimum at 2 A.M.

The disturbances which increase the inclination preponderate greatly at *all hours*. The inclination differs in this respect from the declination and total force, for both of which elements there are certain hours in which disturbances of one sign preponderate, while at other hours the preponderance is of an opposite character.

Effect of the Larger Disturbances on the Diurnal Variation of Inclination.
To ascertain this effect, the aggregate values, at the several hours and of contrary signs, are collected in columns (9) and (10), of Table XII. The differences shewing the preponderance in five years of the disturbances which increased the inclination over those which diminished it, are given in column (11); and finally, by dividing the numbers in column (11) by the total number of days of observation in the five years, are obtained the mean daily effects at each hour, as shewn in column (12).

SOLAR DIURNAL VARIATIONS OF THE MAGNETIC ELEMENTS.

The solar diurnal variations obtained directly from the observations consist of two parts, of which one is that due to the disturbances. In column (4) of Table XII, the mean effect of the disturbances on the diurnal variations of declination is given at each hour, those disturbances only being taken into account which equal or exceed 5'.

When the diurnal variations are derived from the whole of the observations, the march of the north end of the magnet towards the east, which is continuous from the extreme westerly position between 1 and 2 P.M. to the extreme easterly position between 7 and 8 A.M., is interrupted by a small westerly retrogression between 9 P.M. and 4 A.M.; but if the effect of the larger disturbances be deducted, this westerly retrogression is considerably diminished both in amount and continuance.

Again: if it be assumed that the aggregate effect of the *smaller* disturbances be equal and similar to those already separated, and if these effects be also deducted, we have the residual diurnal variation as follows, in which the westerly retrogression is almost wholly obliterated:

Toronto Astron. Time.	0	1	2	3	4	5	6	7	8	9	10	11
Diurnal Variation.	3·01 W	5·01 W	4·78 W	3·75 W	2·39 W	1·25 W	0·66 W	0·46 W	0·34 W	0·35 W	0·09 E	0·18 E
Toronto Astron. Time.	12	13	14	15	16	17	18	19	20	21	22	23
Diurnal Variation.	0·30 E	0·28 E	0·35 E	0·55 E	0·97 E	1·95 E	3·27 E	4·40 E	4·06 E	4·09 E	1·54 E	1·38 W

The mean Solar diurnal Variation of Declination will thus be approximately as follows:

The chief variations are when the sun is above the horizon. The motion of the north end of the magnet towards the east, which during the night was slow, quickens between 4 and 5 A.M., and reaches its eastern extreme a little before 8 A.M. It then returns rapidly towards the west, and attains its westerly extreme about 20 minutes after 1 P.M., the amplitude being about 10′. After reaching its western extreme, the north end of the magnet returns again towards the east at a nearly uniform rate of about 1′ per hour, until about 6 P.M., when the slower motion proper to the night begins; a motion which, on the average of the ten hours from 6 P.M. to 4 A.M., is about 0.16′ per hour.

In Table XIII are shewn the solar diurnal Variations of Declination for every month, for the two half-years, from April to September, and from October to March, inclusive, and for the year, the larger disturbances, namely, those which equal or exceed 5′, having been eliminated.

In Tables XIV and XV are given the corresponding Variations of Horizontal Force, and of Vertical Force.

In Table XVI are shewn the annual and semi-annual means of the solar diurnal variations of Total Force and of Inclination.

In Table XVII are given the semi-annual inequalities of the Declination and Inclination for each hour, with the signs proper to the half-year when the sun is mostly north of the equator. For the other half-year, the signs must of course be changed.

The numbers in the table are taken from Tables XIII to XVI, by subtracting the annual from the semi-annual means of the diurnal variation proper to the half-year, April to September inclusive.

LUNAR-DIURNAL VARIATION.

The existence of a lunar-diurnal variation in one of the magnetic elements, namely, the declination, was discovered in Austria by M. Kreil, from observations taken at Milan and Prague; but Toronto was the first station at which the numerical values, at every lunar hour, of the lunar-diurnal variations of the three elements were published.

The lunar-diurnal variation of each of the elements is a double progression in the 24 lunar hours, having epochs of maximum and minimum symmetrically disposed. In character, therefore, it differs from what might be expected to take place if the Moon were a magnet, *per se*, and accords with the phenomena which might be expected to follow, if she were magnetic only by induction from the Earth. On the other hand, it is believed that the amount of the variation very far exceeds what can be imagined to proceed from the Earth's inductive action reflected from the Moon.

The observations employed in the investigation were the six years of hourly observations of the declination, from 1st July, 1842, to 30th June, 1848, and the five years of hourly observations of the horizontal and vertical forces, commencing 1st July, 1843, and ending 30th June, 1848, but having in the first year of the horizontal and vertical forces, the months of October, November, December, 1842, and January and February, 1843, substituted for the corresponding months in the following year, during which the observations of the vertical force were suspended.

The larger disturbances of each element having been marked for omission, and the hourly normals (excluding the observations so marked) computed, the retained observations were characterized in reference to their lunar relation by small figures signifying the lunar hour to which each observation most nearly corresponded.

In preparing the lunar tables, instead of the scale readings, the *differences* at each hour between these readings and the normals at the same hour, were employed; by which process the diurnal and other variations, depending on the period of the year and the hour of the solar day, were in great part at least eliminated. The means were then taken in every month, at every lunar hour, the signs being regarded: the monthly means were then collected into yearly means: and finally, the means of the yearly means were expressed by the usual formula of sines and cosines.

In this way the variation in the declination was found to be very nearly represented by the formula.

$\Delta X = 1''\cdot05 \sin(a + 168° 52') + 19'' \cdot 186 \sin(2a + 271° 21')$

a (+) sign indicating an easterly deflection of the north end of the magnet.

The following is the table of the deflections at the several lunar hours calculated from this formula.

Lunar Hours.	Deflections.	Lunar Hours.	Deflections.	Lunar Hours.	Deflections.	Lunar Hours.	Deflections.
22	9·29 to the west	4	9·19 to the east	10	10·67 to the west	16	10·77 to the east
23	15·02 "	5	15·89 "	11	17·30 "	17	17·78 "
0	18·95 "	6	18·14 "	12	19·38 "	18	20·21 "
1	16.46 "	7	15·34 "	13	16·31 "	19	17·43 "
2	9·54 "	8	8·20 "	14	8.86 "	20	10·19 "
3	0.14 "	9	0·42 to the west	15	1·04 to the east	21	0·42 "

Comparing these values with the actual deflections, the probable error at each observation hour was found to be ± 1·"37.

In addition to the foregoing formula, three other formulæ were calculated from the means taken for three periods, each of two years, namely,

July 1842 to June 1844, July 1844 to June 1846, and July 1846 to June 1848. These formulæ agree very nearly with one another, and with that obtained from the six years. The number of observations employed in the investigation was 40,543.

Horizontal Force.—The lunar-diurnal variation in the horizontal force may be represented in parts of the whole force by the formula.

$\Delta X = \cdot 0000187 \sin (a + 353°.6) + \cdot 0000289 \sin (2a + 13°.5)$.

The number of observations employed was 34,303.

Vertical Force.—The lunar-diurnal variation in the vertical force may be approximately represented by the formula.

$\Delta Y = \cdot 0000377 \sin (a + 182°) + \cdot 0000312 \sin (2a + 330°.)$

The number of observations employed was 31,773.

Formulæ were also constructed for the variation in both the horizontal and vertical forces, from the means taken over shorter periods; and in each case the results agreed very nearly with the above formulæ.

Inclination and Total Force.—If from the variations of the horizontal and vertical forces, the lunar-diurnal variations of the inclination and total force are calculated, it is found that they follow the same general law as those in the horizontal and vertical forces.

General Conclusions.—The three magnetic elements concur in shewing that the moon exercises a sensible magnetic influence at the surface of the earth, producing in every lunar day a variation in each of the three elements. The westerly maxima of the horizontal deflection of the north end of the magnet synchronize with the moon's superior and inferior passages of the meridian, the easterly maxima with the lunar hours of 6 and 18. The maxima of the increased magnetic force due to the moon's action occur about the lunar hours of 3 and 16; and the minima about the hours of 9 and 20. The maxima of the inclination occur about the lunar hours of 3 and 14, and the minima about 9 and 20. The extent of the variation in the lunar day, or the range between the extremes that are widest apart, is in the declination 38″.33, in the inclination 4″.4, and in the total force ·000012 parts of the whole terrestrial magnetic force at Toronto.

ON THE LARGER DISTURBANCES AND THE SOLAR DIURNAL VARIATIONS IN 1854 AND THE YEARS FOLLOWING.

The observations which form the groundwork of the previous remarks relating to the magnetic disturbances and the solar diurnal variations, were taken at every hour (Sundays excepted) during the five years ending 30th June, 1848.

The observations have been discussed in a very complete manner by General Sir E. Sabine, in the third volume, containing the Toronto observations for the years 1846 to 1848, and published under his superintendence in 1857. Persons interested in such discussions should, if possible, consult that valuable work; but as it is probable that there are many who cannot obtain access to it, the principal facts brought out in the discussions of General Sabine have been reproduced in a condensed form; the arrangement of the tables having been altered for the sake of brevity.

The disturbances in the years from 1854–'62 were discussed in a manner similar to that employed by General Sabine, and were given in a volume published in the year 1863. The results, as far as they went, were generally confirmatory of the conclusions previously arrived at; but as they were based on observations made only six times in each day, the distribution of the disturbances in the different months was of a less distinct character than in the earlier series. The epochs of maxima and minima were slightly changed and the range diminished in amount.

As the observations in and after 1854 were made *six* times only in each day; in order to compare different years it was necessary to separate the aggregate of disturbances at the same six hours from the general aggregate in the early series. The results are given in the volume published in 1863, and are also printed in Table XVIII of this volume.

For the years 1863 to 1871, the annual sums of the disturbances of Declination only, and without reference to direction, have been separated and are given in the following table, together with the annual sums derived from the same six hours in previous years.

TABLE, shewing the aggregate values of the disturbances of Declination, without reference to direction, in the years 1844 to 1871, inclusive; the disturbances being limited to those which were separated from observations made at the hours 6 A.M., 8 A.M., 2 P.M., 4 P.M., 10 P.M. and midnight.*

Years	1844	1845	1846	1847	1848	1849 to 1853	1854	1855	1856	1857	1858	1859
Sums	614'	702'	771'	1373'	1582'	*	1494'	*	366'	423'	961'	1200'

Years	1860	1861	1862	1863	1864	1865	1866	1867	1868	1869	1870	1871
Sums	1608'	1465'	1118'	1760'	1672'	1614'	1988'	1200'	1046'	1941'	1364'	1750'

* In 1849 to 1853 the disturbances were not separated, and in 1855 the observations were partially suspended.

The aggregate sums in this Table for later years certainly do not support the doctrine of a secular periodicity.

The solar diurnal variations of the magnetic elements in the six observation hours from 1856 to 1871 were computed as follows:—

(1.) For each instrument monthly normals were found in the usual way for each of the six hours.

(2.) Corrections deduced from Tables on pp. 90-92 of Vol. III, Toronto Observations, were applied to the means of the six normal in each month, whereby approximate values of the mean normals proper to twenty-four hours were obtained.

(3.) These twenty-four hourly normals being then subtracted from the monthly normals for each observation hour, the remainders reduced by the scale co-efficients, were taken as the diurnal variations at each hour.

In Tables XIX to XXIII are given the means of the monthly diurnal variations deduced from several years, collected into groups; those from the earlier years being taken from pp. 90-92 of Vol. III, Toronto Observations.

In Table XXIV is given for each element, a comparative view of the half-yearly and yearly means of the solar diurnal variations as derived from the observations in three groups of years; namely from 1844-1848, 1856-1862, and 1863-1871; the winter half-year being understood to extend from October to March, and the summer from April to September. By subtracting the annual means from those of the half-year, April to September, we obtain also the semi-annual inequalities for each of the three groups of years.

Table XXV contains a synopsis of those instances of extraordinary disturbance of declination, when the reading at the *ordinary hours* of observation differed from the normals proper to those hours by at least 15'.

Table XXVI contains some examples of continued disturbance. The numbers in the column headed $\Delta \varphi$ are the differences of the actual declination from approximate values of the normals proper to the instant of observation.

The analogous differences of the horizontal and vertical forces, being obtained in a similar manner, the corresponding deviations of the inclination and total force were computed from them in the ordinary way, and are entered in the columns headed $\Delta \theta$ and $\dfrac{\Delta \varphi}{\varphi}$.

TORONTO MAGNETICAL TABLES.

TORONTO MAGNETICAL OBSERVATIONS.

TABLE I.
Monthly and Yearly Means of Absolute Westerly Declination.

Years.	Jan.	Feb.	Mar.	April.	May.	June.	July.	Aug.	Sept.	Oct.	Nov.	Dec.	Year.
	° ′	° ′	° ′	° ′	° ′	° ′	° ′	° ′	° ′	° ′	° ′	° ′	° ′
1841	1 11.9	1 11.6	1 12.6	1 13.7	1 13.7	1 16.6	1 15.8	1 15.6	1 15.2	1 14.6	1 14.6	1 15.2	1 14.3
1842	1 14.6	1 18.0	1 18.4	1 18.7	1 19.1	1 20.4	1 18.4	1 18.4	1 19.2	1 21.5	1 21.5	1 21.5	1 19.1
1843	...	...	...	...	...	...	...	...	...	...	...	...	...
1844	...	...	...	...	...	...	...	...	...	...	...	...	...
1845	1 26.0	1 24.4	1 28.5	1 29.8	1 30.3	1 29.2	1 29.1	1 28.6	1 30.9	1 32.2	1 29.9	1 31.3	1 29.1
1846	1 31.5	1 29.4	1 29.1	1 30.0	1 29.9	1 28.8	1 31.8	1 30.5	1 32.1	1 31.7	1 32.3	1 32.1	1 30.8
1847	1 32.2	1 33.1	1 32.0	1 33.2	1 32.2	1 32.3	1 32.3	1 32.7	1 34.2	1 34.8	1 34.7	1 35.1	1 33.2
1848	1 34.5	1 35.0	1 34.6	1 35.6	1 34.6	1 35.2	1 34.6	1 36.4	1 35.7	1 37.3	1 36.2	1 35.1	1 35.4
1849	1 38.4	1 35.2	1 36.8	1 35.4	1 37.0	1 36.1	1 36.1	1 35.7	1 37.2	1 37.2	1 38.5	1 39.1	1 36.9
1850	1 36.5	1 37.5	1 38.5	1 37.5	1 37.1	1 38.1	1 36.2	1 39.9	1 40.4	1 41.2	1 40.7	1 39.5	1 38.6
1851	1 39.5	1 41.4	1 39.6	1 40.5	1 40.9	1 41.0	1 40.0	1 41.7	1 42.3	1 41.6	1 40.1	1 41.3	1 40.9
1852	...	...	...	...	...	...	...	...	...	...	...	...	...
1853	...	...	...	...	...	...	1 44.8	1 48.1	...	...	...	...	...
1854	...	1 44.9	1 48.6	1 47.2	...	1 48.0	...	...	...	...	...	...	...
1855	...	...	...	...	...	...	...	1 51.9	1 51.9	1 53.3	1 55.0	1 55.0	...
1856	1 54.3	1 55.3	1 55.2	1 56.3	1 56.1	1 56.1	1 56.1	1 54.4	1 58.5	1 57.1	1 58.5	1 57.0	1 56.3
1857	1 58.5	1 58.8	2 00.6	1 59.7	1 58.8	1 58.9	1 59.8	2 01.9	2 01.6	2 01.7	2 02.5	2 03.7	2 00.5
1858	2 02.8	2 03.8	2 04.4	2 04.0	2 03.7	2 03.5	2 04.3	2 06.3	2 05.4	2 05.3	2 04.8	2 05.5	2 04.5
1859	2 06.4	2 06.9	2 06.7	2 06.6	2 06.8	2 06.9	2 07.2	2 07.4	2 08.8	2 08.5	2 08.5	2 08.3	2 07.4
1860	2 08.5	2 09.3	2 09.5	2 09.6	2 08.9	2 08.9	2 10.4	2 11.4	2 10.8	2 13.9	2 13.3	2 12.6	2 10.6
1861	2 12.4	2 13.3	2 13.2	2 11.2	2 13.2	2 13.9	2 14.3	2 14.7	2 15.2	2 15.0	2 15.7	2 17.2	2 14.4
1862	2 15.7	2 12.0	2 13.9	2 13.8	2 14.4	2 16.7	2 16.2	2 15.9	2 17.1	2 17.4	2 17.6	2 17.2	2 15.7
1863	2 17.4	2 18.0	2 17.9	2 18.1	2 18.5	2 18.9	2 19.9	2 19.9	2 20.2	2 19.7	2 20.9	2 19.7	2 19.1
1864	2 20.7	2 21.3	2 21.2	2 21.0	2 21.2	2 22.6	2 23.2	2 22.7	2 22.3	2 22.3	2 22.2	2 21.9	2 21.9
1865	2 22.7	2 23.6	2 22.5	2 24.3	2 23.5	2 24.3	2 24.0	2 25.8	2 25.8	2 27.4	2 27.6	2 26.4	2 24.8
1866	2 27.1	2 27.8	2 27.0	2 27.1	2 27.4	2 27.0	2 27.2	2 27.7	2 27.8	2 28.6	2 28.6	2 28.2	2 27.6
1867	2 28.6	2 29.3	2 28.9	2 29.7	2 29.1	2 29.1	2 29.0	2 31.1	2 30.7	2 30.3	2 31.0	2 31.2	2 29.8
1868	2 30.7	2 32.0	2 32.0	2 32.8	2 32.9	2 31.6	2 34.6	2 33.8	2 34.6	2 34.0	2 34.5	2 35.2	2 33.2
1869	2 35.4	2 35.3	2 36.6	2 36.6	2 37.3	2 37.1	2 37.6	2 36.7	2 37.3	2 38.3	2 38.1	2 38.5	2 37.1
1870	2 40.1	2 40.3	2 40.2	2 41.6	2 40.8	2 39.8	2 40.4	2 42.7	2 42.6	2 44.9	2 44.8	2 44.2	2 41.9
1871	2 46.1	2 45.6	2 45.6	2 46.3	2 46.9	2 47.6	2 48.0	2 48.7	2 49.7	2 49.9	2 50.3	2 49.9	2 47.9

TORONTO MAGNETICAL OBSERVATIONS.

TABLE II.

MONTHLY MEAN DECLINATION FOR EACH OF THE THREE GROUPS, WITH THE CORRESPONDING CORRECTIONS FOR SECULAR CHANGE.

Years.	Jan.	Feb.	March	April	May.	June.	July.	Aug.	Sept.	Oct.	Nov.	Dec.	Year.
	° ′	° ′	° ′	° ′	° ′	° ′	° ′	° ′	° ′	° ′	° ′	° ′	° ′
1845-51	1 34.09	1 33.71	1 34.16	1 34.57	1 34.57	1 34.39	1 34.27	1 35.07	1 36.11	1 36.57	1 36.06	1 36.21	1 34.95
Correc.	+0.89	+0.73	+0.57	+0.41	+0.24	+0.08	−0.08	−0.24	−0.41	−0.57	−0.73	−0.89	
1856-64	2 08.53	2 08.73	2 09.25	2 09.26	2 09.09	2 09.61	2 10.14	2 10.51	2 11.09	2 11.21	2 11.53	2 11.52	2 10.04
Correc.	+1.43	+1.17	+0.91	+0.65	+0.39	+0.13	−0.13	−0.39	−0.65	−0.91	−1.17	−1.43	
1865-71	2 32.94	2 33.41	2 33.26	2 34.05	2 33.90	2 33.77	2 34.39	2 35.21	2 35.50	2 36.21	2 36.42	2 36.24	2 34.62
Correc.	+1.72	+1.41	+1.09	+0.78	+0.47	+0.16	−0.16	−0.47	−0.78	−1.09	−1.41	−1.72	

TABLE III.

MONTHLY MEAN DECLINATION FOR EACH GROUP, CORRECTED FOR SECULAR CHANGE, TOGETHER WITH THE MEANS OF THE THREE CORRECTED GROUPS.

Years.	Jan.	Feb.	March	April	May.	June.	July.	Aug.	Sept.	Oct.	Nov.	Dec.	Year.
	° ′	° ′	° ′	° ′	° ′	° ′	° ′	° ′	° ′	° ′	° ′	° ′	° ′
1845-51	1 34.98	1 34.44	1 34.73	1 34.98	1 34.81	1 34.47	1 34.19	1 34.83	1 35.70	1 36.00	1 35.33	1 35.32	1 34.95
1856-64	2 09.96	2 09.90	2 10.16	2 09.91	2 09.48	2 09.74	2 10.01	2 10.12	2 10.44	2 10.30	2 10.3	2 10.09	2 10.04
1865-71	2 34.66	2 34.82	2 34.35	2 34.83	2 34.46	2 33.93	2 34.23	2 34.74	2 34.72	2 35.11	2 35.01	2 34.52	2 34.62
Mean	2 06.53	2 06.39	2 06.41	2 06.57	2 06 25	2 06.05	2 06 14	2 06.56	2 06.95	2 07.14	2 06.90	2 06.64	2 06.54

TABLE IV.

ANNUAL VARIATIONS OF DECLINATION.

Years.	Jan.	Feb.	March	April	May.	June.	July.	Aug.	Sept.	Oct.	Nov.	Dec.
	′	′	′	′	′	′	′	′	′	′	′	′
1845-51	0.00	−0.54	−0.25	0.00	−0.17	−0.51	−0.79	−0.15	+0.72	+1.02	+0.35	+0.34
1856-64	−0.08	−0.14	+0.12	−0.13	−0.56	−0.30	−0.03	+0.08	+0.40	+0.26	+0.32	+0.05
1865-71	+0.04	+0.20	−0.27	+0.21	−0.16	−0.69	−0.39	+0.12	+0.10	+0.49	+0.39	−0.10
Mean	−0.01	−0.15	−0.13	+0.03	−0.29	−0.49	−0.40	+0.02	+0.41	+0.60	+0.36	+0.10

TABLE V.
MONTHLY AND YEARLY MEANS OF ABSOLUTE INCLINATION.

Years.	Jan.	Feb.	Mar.	Apr.	May.	June	July.	Aug.	Sept.	Oct	Nov.	Dec.	Year.
	75°	75°	75°	75°	75°	75°	75°	75°	75°	75°	75°	75°	75°
	′	′	′	′	′	′	′	′	′	′	′	′	′
1841	16.2	13.6	16.7	16.1	16.5	16.8	14.3	13.9	18.8	18.9	17.9	17.9	16.6
1842	17.9	16.1	18.0	19.0	17.0	11.7	16.1	16.3	14.9	16.1	17.3	16.2	16.4
1843	14.5	15.2	14.1	13.3	14.4	13.4	14.5	14.8	15.3	14.5	16.8	15.7	14.7
1844	15.4	15.7	14.5	13.2	12.5	11.6	10.1	9.8	17.7	17.9	20.3	19.0	14.8
1845	18.4	19.5	14.5	11.5	15.4	15.2	14.2	14.4	16.6	14.3	16.8	15.2	15.5
1846	16.1	16.4	16.0	14.3	14.4	14.8	14.0	14.4	15.7	15.4	15.0	15.1	15.1
1847	15.0	15.2	16.3	15.9	16.1	13.0	11.6	12.6	15.4	17.6	17.9	16.8	15.3
1848	20.3	18.7	17.2	18.0	17.2	16.8	16.4	19.0	17.3	19.0	19.4	20.6	18.3
1849	19.5	18.1	16.7	18.4	18.4	18.5	18.0	19.3	21.6	20.6	20.1	18.1	18.8
1850	19.9	18.7	18.0	19.7	19.5	19.1	19.9	18.4	21.0	21.8	21.3	22.5	20.0
1851	21.6	20.0	21.5	21.9	20.0	20.7	19.0	19.8	20.8	20.0	20.4	19.4	20.4
1852	19.3	19.4	19.6	20.0	20.8	20.5	19.9	20.0	21.6	22.2	21.3	21.2	20.5
1853	22.1	22.6	...	22.6	...	22.5	21.5	20.3	21.7	22.4	23.0	22.3	22.2
1854	21.4	23.3	23.1	23.0	23.0	22.9	24.3	23.2	23.4	21.9	22.2	23.9	23.0
1855	24.1	23.8	23.8	23.0	23.6	22.9	23.1	23.9	24.5	23.5	23.2	23.3	23.5
1856	23.7	24.3	24.0	23.5	22.7	23.6	24.2	23.8	24.8	24.9	24.6	24.6	24.1
1857	24.3	23.8	24.5	25.0	23.9	23.9	23.9	23.9	25.1	25.0	24.4	24.1	24.3
1858	24.6	25.6	26.2	23.7	23.9	22.9	23.2	23.7	25.1	24.5	24.5	24.4	24.4
1859	24.5	24.9	25.0	25.5	24.4	24.6	24.1	25.1	25.0	26.4	26.0	24.3	25.0
1860	24.4	23.5	24.6	25.1	24.3	23.4	24.2	25.1	26.4	26.0	23.8	23.9	24.6
1861	23.8	23.5	24.3	25.3	24.3	23.4	23.0	23.7	23.3	23.8	23.4	23.3	23.8
1862	23.1	23.4	23.6	22.7	23.3	22.8	22.9	23.8	23.6	23.9	22.8	22.4	23.2
1863	21.7	21.7	21.8	21.8	21.9	20.9	20.9	21.8	22.1	21.0	20.9	21.1	21.5
1864	21.5	21.9	21.4	21.3	21.3	21.2	20.2	19.6	20.7	20.5	20.6	20.8	20.9
1865	20.8	20.8	21.8	21.5	22.0	21.7	20.2	20.5	21.0	21.4	20.7	20.2	21.0
1866	20.0	20.0	20.0	20.1	20.3	19.8	19.3	18.3	17.7	17.8	18.3	18.2	19.2
1867	18.1	18.8	19.0	19.1	18.6	18.9	18.7	18.8	18.3	18.7	18.9	19.8	18.8
1868	20.4	19.4	19.3	20.9	20.9	20.2	19.6	20.2	20.2	20.8	19.4	19.6	20.1
1869	17.1	15.8	15.7	16.1	16.9	16.6	17.1	17.1	17.0	17.1	17.4	16.8	16.7
1870	16.5	16.4	17.6	17.8	15.8	15.3	15.5	15.9	15.2	16.2	17.1	16.7	16.3
1871	17.3	18.1	18.6	16.9	19.5	15.8	14.1	14.3	15.1	15.7	16.5	19.0	16.8

TORONTO MAGNETICAL OBSERVATIONS.

TABLE VI.

Monthly Annual Means of the Absolute Horizontal Force.

Years.	Jan.	Feb.	Mar.	April.	May.	June.	July.	Aug.	Sept.	Oct.	Nov.	Dec.	Year.
1845	3.5472	3.5471	3.5471	3.5446	3.5481	3.5514	3.5508	3.5473	3.5466	3.5466	3.5471	3.5479	3.5476
1846	.5475	.5413	.5441	.5414	.5434	.5458	.5446	.5397	.5390	.5386	.5360	.5433	.5419
1847	.5435	.5426	.5386	.5348	.5386	.5393	.5396	.5424	.5338	.5345	.5366	.5347	.5381
1848	.5320	.5352	.5372	.5331	.5386	.5346	.5376	.5360	.5332	.5293	.5240	.5318	.5333
1849	.5319	.5312	.5333	.5378	.5413	.5389	.5128	.5334	.5382	.5343	.5366	.5351	.5368
1850	.5344	.5354	.5397	.5373	.5368	.5380	.5384	.5190	.5217	.5320	.5361	.5283	.5322
1851	.5249	.5243	.5321	.5311	.5328	.5311	.5317	.5318	.5299	.5311	.5301	.5286	.5299
1852	.5305	.5231	.5237	.5054	.5142	.5083	.5134	.5138	.5119	.5110	.5140	.5149	.5154
1853	...	...	...	...	...	...	...	...	...	...	...	...	...
1854	...	...	...	...	...	...	...	...	...	...	...	...	...
1855	...	...	...	...	...	...	...	...	.5294	.5124	.5097	.5100	...
1856	.5018	.5064	.5052	.5064	.5057	.5101	.5108	.5070	.5077	.5033	.5046	.4950	.5049
1857	.4898	.4728	.5113	.4761	.4901	.5023	.5002	.5032	.4828	.4823	.4762	.4785	.4884
1858	.4779	.4748	.4725	.4870	.5010	.4990	.5014	.5005	.4951	.4941	.4865	.4907	.4900
1859	.4724	.4771	.4752	.4705	.4771	.4793	.4828	.5015	.4700	.4842	.4846	.4825	.4811
1860	.4771	.4842	.4760	.4767	.4832	.4822	.4805	.4778	.4739	.4774	.4769	.4764	.4792
1861	.4843	.4826	.4820	.4787	.4988	.4836	.4872	.4847	.4796	.4817	.4822	.4803	.4830
1862	.4830	.4834	.4846	.4322	.4897	.4882	.4830	.4830	.4840	.4793	.4819	.4885	.4853
1863	.4882	.4885	.4875	.4912	.4875	.4897	.4931	.4913	.4889	.4889	.4884	.4884	.4891
1864	.4941	.4932	.4903	.4935	.4923	.4946	.4913	.4914	.5069	.4890	.4915	.4910	.4932
1865	.4934	.4929	.4957	.4920	.4951	.4923	.4943	.4909	.4874	.4854	.4932	.4919	.4925
1866	.4905	.4910	.4911	.4919	.4923	.4975	.4950	.4932	.4918	.4930	.4927	.4942	.4931
1867	.4970	.4926	.4975	.4959	.5034	.4976	.4980	.4979	.4943	.4935	.4993	.5000	.4976
1868	.4950	.5013	.4947	.4960	.4958	.4934	.5032	.4969	.4958	.4960	.4974	.5010	.4980
1869	.5022	.4948	.4903	.4951	.4988	.5026	.5072	.5012	.4979	.4916	.4971	.4900	.4980
1870	.4975	.4971	.5060	.4957	.5018	.5023	.4993	.4978	.4970	.4953	.4948	.4931	.4984
1871	.4990	.5001	.4964	.4913	.5036	.5035	.5030	.4958	.4993	.5008	.5034	.5921	.5000

TORONTO MAGNETICAL OBSERVATIONS.

TABLE VII.
MONTHLY AND ANNUAL MEANS OF TOTAL FORCE.

Years	Jan.	Feb.	Mar.	Apr.	May.	June.	July.	Aug.	Sept.	Oct.	Nov.	Dec.	Year.
1845	13.9849	14.0015	13.9242	13.8685	13.9420	13.9519	13.9342	13.9235	13.9546	13.9192	13.9597	13.9581	13.9419
1846	.9504	13.9307	.9355	.8988	.9003	.9237	.9068	.6936	.9169	.9047	.8882	.9185	.9135
1847	.9178	.9173	.9185	.8974	.9154	.8730	.8287	.8767	.8858	.9225	.9354	.9109	.9008
1848	.9379	.0422	.9269	.9349	.9324	.9184	.9163	.9500	.9127	.9117	.9124	.9582	.9312
1849	.9415	.9172	.9062	.9478	.9616	.9537	.9613	.9081	.9991	.9681	.9604	.9326	.9522
1850	.9576	.9430	.9152	.9660	.9001	.9594	.9339	.8772	.9245	.9777	.9801	.9739	.9504
1851	.9465	.9193	.9734	.9757	.9529	.9570	.9330	.9458	.9487	.9462	.9496	.9270	.9479
1852	.9330	.9053	.9108	.8447	.8918	.8685	.8767	.8775	.8950	.9008	.8987	.9007	.8920
1853	...	...	...	...	...	...	...	...	...	...	...	...	
1854	...	...	...	...	...	...	...	...	...	...	...	...	
1855	...	...	...	...	...	...	...	...	14.0001	13.9258	.9124	.9135	...
1856	.8815	.9157	.9053	.8989	.8878	.9193	.9303	.9099	13.9123	.9141	.9123	.8775	.9054
1857	.8367	.7745	.9373	.8053	.8450	.8935	.8847	.8850	.8334	.8305	.7974	.8005	.8436
1858	.8068	.8252	.8101	.8290	.8570	.8632	.8792	.8829	.8524	.8096	.8386	.8548	.8524
1859	.7829	.8085	.8016	.8272	.7997	.8120	.8177	.9077	.8208	.8002	.8435	.8199	.8251
1860	.8000	.8141	.7987	.8097	.8345	.8048	.8109	.8135	.8389	.8203	.7908	.7888	.8109
1861	.8195	.8088	.8217	.8208	.8850	.8107	.8185	.8195	.7925	.8096	.8048	.7957	.8173
1862	.8073	.8093	.8180	.8344	.8222	.8194	.8163	.8180	.8147	.8004	.7952	.8108	.8143
1863	.8026	.8014	.8009	.8127	.8049	.7968	.8105	.8120	.8121	.7945	.7916	.7928	.8028
1864	.8287	.8255	.8074	.8056	.8135	.8207	.8054	.7835	.8582	.7879	.7993	.7906	.8109
1865	.8098	.8066	.8345	.8188	.8382	.8227	.8037	.7950	.7891	.7866	.8191	.7942	.8099
1866	.7855	.7872	.7888	.8048	.7977	.8098	.7920	.7583	.7668	.7618	.7679	.7734	.7828
1867	.7853	.7755	.7900	.7934	.8159	.7969	.7996	.7970	.7749	.7890	.8034	.8202	.7958
1868	.8165	.8196	.7911	.8253	.8249	.8246	.8298	.8147	.8100	.8202	.8033	.8197	.8166
1869	.7878	.7390	.7566	.7439	.7714	.7810	.8078	.7832	.7690	.7462	.7720	.7702	.7690
1870	.7597	.7561	.8101	.7730	.7603	.7617	.7525	.7524	.7379	.7469	.7578	.7579	.7612
1871	.7923	.7951	.7872	.7842	.8302	.7728	.7480	.7195	.7463	.7616	.7839	.8031	.7762

TORONTO MAGNETICAL OBSERVATIONS.

TABLE VIII.

AGGREGATE AMOUNT OF THE DISTURBANCES OF DECLINATION, HORIZONTAL FORCE, AND VERTICAL FORCE, IN DIFFERENT YEARS ENDING JUNE 30, WITH THE RATIOS EXPRESSING THEIR RELATIVE AMOUNT IN EACH YEAR, AS COMPARED WITH THE MEAN OF ALL YEARS.

YEARS.	DECLINATION.							HORIZONTAL FORCE.			VERTICAL FORCE.		
	E. & W. sums.	East sums.	West sums.	E. & W. ratios.	East ratios.	West ratios.	+ & − ratios.	Increasing ratios.	Decreasing ratios.	+ & − ratios.	Increasing ratios.	Decreasing ratios.
	(1)	(2)	(3)	(4)	(5)	(6)	(7)	(8)	(9)	(10)	(11)	(12)
1844	2053.2	1235.8	817.4	0.52	0.56	0.47	0.49	0.81	0.43	0.66	0.71	0.62
1845	2521.8	1325.4	1196.4	0.64	0.60	0.69	0.45	0.47	0.45	0.58	0.46	0.67
1846	3246.6	1973.3	1273.3	0.82	0.89	0.84	0.53	0.65	0.52	0.74	0.75	0.72
1847	5478.7	2958.9	2519.8	1.39	1.34	1.46	1.11	0.99	1.13	1.23	0.98	1.40
1848	6422.0	3573.5	2848.5	1.63	1.61	1.65	2.42	2.08	2.47	1.80	2.09	1.59
Mean.	3944.5	2213.4	1731.1	1.00	1.00	1.00	1.00	1.00	1.00	1.00	1.00	1.00

TABLE IX.

CONTAINING FOR THE TOTAL FORCE AND INCLINATION, NUMBERS ANALOGOUS TO THOSE OF TABLE VIII, TOGETHER WITH CERTAIN OTHER RATIOS IN COLUMNS 7 AND 14.

YEARS.	TOTAL FOR r.								INCLINATION.						
	General sums.	Sums increasing.	Sums decreasing.	Ratios + & −	Ratios +	Ratios −	Ratios − to +	General sums.	Sums (+)	Sums (−)	Ratios General	Ratios +	Ratios −	Ratios − to +
	(1)	(2)	(3)	(4)	(5)	(6)	(7)	(8)	(9)	(10)	(11)	(12)	(13)	(14)
1844	.4491	.2011	.2480	0.77	1.02	0.65	1.23	684.3	498.8	185.5	0.52	0.45	0.93	2.7
1845	.2775	.0616	.2159	0.48	0.31	0.56	3.51	613.9	510.5	103.4	0.47	0.46	0.52	5.0
1846	.3509	.1363	.2146	0.65	0.69	0.61	1.79	753.7	612.7	141.0	0.57	0.55	0.71	4.3
1847	.7293	.1839	.5454	1.25	0.93	1.42	2.96	1399.0	1165.8	233.2	1.06	1.04	1.17	5.0
1848	1.0747	.4067	.6680	1.85	2.06	1.74	1.64	3139.8	2809.8	330.1	2.38	2.51	1.66	8.5
Mean.	.5823	.1979	.3844	...	...	...	...	1318.1	1119.5	198.6	...	...	...	...

TORONTO MAGNETICAL OBSERVATIONS.

TABLE X.

AGGREGATE VALUES OF THE DISTURBANCES OF DECLINATION IN THE SEVERAL MONTHS, WITH THE RATIOS OF THE AGGREGATE VALUES OF THE DISTURBANCES OF THE SEVERAL ELEMENTS TO THEIR RESPECTIVE MEAN ANNUAL VALUES.

Months and Year.	Declination.						Horizontal Force.	Vertical Force.				Total Force.			Inclination.
	Sums E. & W.	Sums E.	Sums W.	Ratios E. & W.	Ratios E.	Ratios W.		Ratios + & −	Ratios +	Ratios −		Ratios + & −	Ratios +	Ratios −	Ratios + & −
	(1.)	(2.)	(3.)	(4.)	(5.)	(6.)	(7.)	(8.)	(9.)	(10.)	(11.)	(12.)	(13.)	(14.)	(15.)
January	936.0	527.0	409.0	0.57	0.57	0.57	0.58	0.56	0.71	0.45	0.86	0.58	0.72	0.43	0.65
February	1383.8	772.9	610.9	0.84	0.84	0.85	0.94	0.74	0.77	0.72	1.2	0.74	0.70	0.70	0.94
March	1824.7	1062.9	761.8	1.11	1.15	1.06	.93	1.08	1.21	0.98	1.18	1.05	1.17	0.99	0.97
April	2329.0	1187.5	1141.5	1.42	1.29	1.58	1.50	1.49	1.46	1.51	1.43	1.55	1.51	1.50	1.41
May	1603.8	904.3	699.5	0.98	0.98	0.97	1.90	1.12	0.99	1.22	1.72	1.08	1.03	1.08	0.85
June	872.4	691.1	181.3	0.53	0.75	0.25	.36	0.50	0.51	0.50	1.37	0.39	0.45	0.30	0.39
July	1542.6	903.2	639.4	0.94	0.98	0.88	0.61	1.79	0.56	0.95	2.83	0.76	0.59	0.88	0.56
August	1895.0	1255.2	639.8	1.15	1.36	0.89	0.70	1.08	0.76	1.31	2.41	1.06	0.65	1.27	0.74
September	2663.5	1504.8	1158.7	1.62	1.63	1.61	1.71	1.60	1.49	1.67	1.50	1.64	1.46	1.73	1.67
October	2144.7	1174.0	970.7	1.30	1.27	1.35	1.48	1.30	1.24	1.34	1.44	1.36	1.11	1.49	1.45
November	1282.0	556.6	725.4	0.78	0.60	1.00	0.98	0.75	0.82	0.70	1.18	0.77	0.89	0.70	1.02
December	1244.8	527.4	717.4	0.76	0.57	0.99	1.27	0.99	1.49	0.65	0.61	1.06	1.67	0.74	1.36
Mean	1643.5	922.2	721.3	1.00	1.00	1.00	1.00	1.00	1.00	1.00	...	1.00	1.00	1.00	1.00

TORONTO MAGNETICAL OBSERVATIONS.

TABLE XI.

CONTAINING FOR EACH MAGNETIC ELEMENT THE RATIOS OF THE AMOUNT OF DISTURBANCE IN EACH OF THE 24 HOURS, TO THE MEAN AMOUNT OF THE DISTURBANCES AT ALL HOURS, DISTURBANCES OF AN OPPOSITE SIGN BEING TAKEN JOINTLY AS WELL AS SEPARATELY.

TORONTO ASTRONOMICAL TIME.	DECLINATION.			HORIZONTAL FORCE.			VERTICAL FORCE.			TOTAL FORCE.			INCLINATION.		
	East and West.	Easterly.	Westerly.	+ and −	+	−	+ and −	+	−	+ and −	+	−	+ and −	+	−
(1)	(2)	(3)	(4)	(5)	(6)	(7)	(8)	(9)	(10)	(11)	(12)	(13)	(14)	(15)	
0	0.49	0.24	0.80	0.89	1.83	0.74	0.46	0.86	0.18	0.25	0.65	0.04	1.05	0.93	1.76
1	0.30	0.21	0.41	0.76	1.57	0.63	0.63	1.23	0.20	0.48	1.21	0.10	0.99	0.8	1.68
2	0.40	0.20	0.65	0.67	2.30	0.41	0.77	1.61	0.16	0.64	1.73	0.08	0.84	0.65	1.93
3	0.40	0.22	0.62	0.66	1.99	0.46	0.88	1.93	0.12	0.77	2.14	0.06	0.82	0.72	1.38
4	0.55	0.31	0.89	0.61	2.50	0.31	1.05	2.31	0.14	0.96	2.69	0.07	0.74	0.61	1.45
5	0.55	0.46	0.70	0.66	2.21	0.45	1.08	2.36	0.18	1.02	2.87	0.07	0.87	0.79	1.32
6	0.84	1.04	0.57	0.59	0.87	0.54	1.01	2.23	0.12	0.84	2.32	0.08	0.99	1.03	0.72
7	0.98	1.44	0.39	0.76	1.55	0.63	1.05	2.30	0.16	0.91	2.49	0.10	1.12	1.14	1.02
8	1.22	1.95	0.28	0.75	1.07	0.70	0.89	1.92	0.18	0.72	1.93	0.10	1.03	1.13	0.54
9	1.82	3.07	0.22	0.90	0.63	0.94	0.75	1.33	0.31	0.62	1.20	0.32	1.09	1.18	0.57
10	1.54	2.40	0.45	1.03	0.68	1.09	0.85	0.92	0.81	0.82	0.79	0.84	1.16	1.18	1.03
11	1.25	2.01	0.27	1.14	0.40	1.25	0.93	0.59	1.17	0.97	0.51	1.20	1.14	1.23	0.84
12	1.35	1.75	0.82	1.27	0.43	1.40	1.39	0.51	2.03	1.57	0.46	2.13	1.07	1.10	0.91
13	1.52	1.79	1.18	1.53	0.23	1.74	1.58	0.35	2.47	1.70	0.27	2.57	1.23	1.33	0.69
14	1.21	1.36	1.00	1.61	0.03	1.85	1.61	0.35	2.51	1.85	0.24	2.69	1.18	1.32	0.37
15	1.13	1.28	0.93	1.57	0.16	1.56	1.73	0.33	2.74	1.97	0.30	2.83	0.96	1.04	0.47
16	1.33	1.44	1.20	1.14	0.06	1.31	1.51	0.28	2.39	1.70	0.18	2.48	0.84	0.90	0.51
17	1.04	0.90	1.22	1.02	0.22	1.14	1.41	0.32	2.19	1.59	0.29	2.25	0.74	0.76	0.60
18	1.05	0.45	1.82	1.05	0.38	1.15	1.22	0.28	1.91	1.35	0.27	1.91	0.82	0.81	0.83
19	1.17	0.35	2.22	1.39	0.23	1.57	1.16	0.32	1.76	1.34	0.25	1.90	1.17	1.29	0.51
20	1.27	0.26	2.56	1.17	0.34	1.30	0.80	0.42	1.08	0.86	0.36	1.11	1.06	1.14	0.62
21	1.11	0.22	2.25	1.09	0.94	1.12	0.54	0.28	0.72	0.55	0.21	0.73	1.05	1.05	.103
22	0.87	0.28	1.62	1.00	1.46	0.93	0.37	0.40	0.34	0.26	0.24	0.27	1.04	0.96	1.46
23	0.65	0.39	1.01	0.93	1.91	0.78	0.34	0.53	0.21	0.18	0.38	0.07	1.02	0.88	1.79

TORONTO MAGNETICAL OBSERVATIONS.

TABLE XII.

SHOWING THE AGGREGATE EFFECT OF THE DISTURBANCES OF DECLINATION, TOTAL FORCE AND INCLINATION ON THE SOLAR DIURNAL VARIATIONS OF THE ELEMENTS, TOGETHER WITH THEIR AVERAGE EFFECT IN ONE DAY.

Toronto Astronomical Time.	Declination.				Total Force.				Inclination.				Toronto Civil Time.
	E.	W.	Effect in five years.	Mean daily effect.	Increasing.	Decreasing.	Effect in five years.	Mean daily effect.	Increasing.	Decreasing.	Effect in five years.	Mean daily effect.	
	(1)	(2)	(3)	(4)	(5)	(6)	(7)	(8)	(9)	(10)	(11)	(12)	
0	111.8	289.6	177.8	0.11 w	.0269	.0032	+.0237	+.000015	216.6	72.8	+143.8	+0.09	Noon.
1	97.7	146.9	49.2	0.03 w	.0500	.0083	+.0417	+.000027	201.4	69.6	+131.8	+0.09	1 p. m.
2	93.2	233.8	140.6	0.09 w	.0715	.0061	+.0654	+.000042	150.8	79.8	+ 71.0	+0.05	2 "
3	102.6	223.4	120.8	0.08 w	.0883	.0046	+.0837	+.000054	168.2	57.0	+111.2	+0.07	3 "
4	145.1	286.7	141.6	0.09 w	.1107	.0055	+.1052	+.000068	142.2	59.8	+ 82.4	+0.05	4 "
5	200.1	254.2	54.1	0.04 w	.1184	.0059	+.1125	+.000073	183.1	54.5	+128.4	+0.08	5 "
6	481.5	205.0	276.5	0.18 E	.0958	.0061	+.0897	+.000058	241.3	29.6	+211.7	+0.14	6 "
7	664.9	139.2	525.7	0.34 E	.1025	.0079	+.0946	+.000062	265.8	42.0	+223.8	+0.14	7 "
8	899.6	101.8	797.8	0.52 E	.0796	.0083	+.0713	+.000047	260.2	22.4	+237.8	+0.16	8 "
9	1417.1	77.6	1339.5	0.87 E	.0493	.0255	+.0238	+.000016	275.1	23.7	+251.4	+0.16	9 "
10	1104.7	162.2	942.5	0.61 E	.0326	.0669	—.0343	—.000022	275.2	42.5	+232.7	+0.15	10 "
11	925.4	98.7	826.7	0.53 E	.0211	.0961	—.0750	—.000047	279.3	34.6	+244.7	+0.16	11 "
12	808.9	297.4	511.5	0.33 E	.0192	.1709	—.1517	—.000098	256.6	37.5	+219.1	+0.14	Midn.
13	824.5	426.1	398.4	0.26 E	.0113	.2056	—.1943	—.000125	309.4	28.5	+280.9	+0.18	1 a. m.
14	627.6	360.8	266.8	0.17 E	.0099	.2151	—.2052	—.000132	308.2	15.2	+293.0	+0.19	2 "
15	589.5	336.5	253.0	0.16 E	.0122	.2264	—.2142	—.000138	243.3	19.6	+223.7	+0.14	3 "
16	662.5	434.0	228.5	0.15 E	.0073	.1986	—.1913	—.000123	209.4	21.1	+188.3	+0.12	4 "
17	417.0	441.0	24.0	0.02 w	.0120	.1806	—.1686	—.000109	177.9	24.7	+153.2	+0.10	5 "
18	207.8	655.9	448.1	0.29 w	.0113	.1529	—.1416	—.000092	189.7	34.2	+155.5	+0.10	6 "
19	160.2	801.7	641.5	0.41 w	.0105	.1524	—.1419	—.000092	301.7	20.9	+280.8	+0.18	7 "
20	118.1	928.6	810.5	0.52 w	.0147	.0892	—.0745	—.000047	266.8	25.5	+241.3	+0.16	8 "
21	99.2	811.8	712.6	0.46 w	.0088	.0581	—.0493	—.000032	245.1	42.5	+201.6	+0.13	9 "
22	128.0	584.2	456.2	0.30 w	.0100	.0220	—.0120	—.000008	224.4	60.4	+164.0	+0.10	10 "
23	179.9	358.3	178.4	0.11 w	.0157	.0057	+.0100	+.000007	205.8	73.8	+132.0	+0.09	11 "

3   41

TORONTO MAGNETICAL OBSERVATIONS.

TABLE XIII.

SOLAR DIURNAL VARIATIONS OF DECLINATION FOR EACH MONTH FOR THE TWO HALF YEARS, AND FOR THE YEAR, DERIVED FROM THE FIVE YEARS ENDING JUNE 30, 1848, AFTER THE SEPARATION AND OMISSION OF THE LARGER DISTURBANCES.

Hours.	Jan.	Feb.	Mar.	April.	May.	June.	July.	Aug.	Sept.	Oct.	Nov.	Dec.	SEMI-ANNUAL MEANS. Ap. to Sept.	Oct. to Mar.	Annual Means.
0	—2.50	—2.42	—3.72	—4.54	—5.24	—4.72	—4.24	—6.00	—6.26	—3.72	—3.00	—1.94	—5.17	—2.88	—4.02
1	—3.34	—3.30	—5.22	—5.08	—6.28	—6.20	—5.86	—7.22	—6.38	—4.20	—3.80	—3.02	—6.32	—3.81	—5.07
2	—3.14	—3.26	—5.36	—5.84	—6.10	—6.26	—5.96	—6.52	—5.40	—3.94	—3.30	—3.30	—6.01	—3.73	—4.87
3	—2.44	—2.54	—4.76	—4.98	—4.84	—5.26	—5.12	—5.04	—3.36	—2.66	—2.52	—2.38	—4.77	—2.80	—3.83
4	—1.64	—1.66	—3.42	—3.30	—3.12	—3.76	—3.68	—2.74	—1.16	—1.80	—1.76	—1.70	—2.96	—2.00	—2.48
5	—0.92	—1.36	—2.18	—1.66	—1.26	—1.68	—1.86	—1.02	—0.42	—1.24	—1.10	—0.80	—1.32	—1.27	—1.29
6	—0.32	—0.84	—1.12	—0.80	—0.44	—0.62	—0.70	—0.18	+0.12	—0.70	—0.12	0.00	—0.44	—0.52	—0.48
7	+0.06	—0.35	—0.56	—0.32	—0.22	—0.28	—0.36	—0.12	—0.06	—0.22	+0.04	+0.30	—0.23	—0.02	—0.12
8	+0.76	+0.32	—0.30	+0.44	—0.18	—0.32	—0.66	—0.10	+0.24	+0.24	+0.84	+0.88	—0.10	+0.46	+0.18
9	+1.02	+0.92	+0.22	+0.44	+0.16	—0.22	—0.16	+0.48	+0.64	+0.58	+0.96	+1.24	+0.22	+0.82	+0.52
10	+1.08	+0.88	+0.90	+0.82	+0.36	+0.04	+0.30	+0.16	+0.78	+0.48	+1.16	+1.10	+0.47	+0.93	+0.70
11	+0.66	+0.60	+1.02	+1.12	+0.50	+0.66	+0.58	+0.52	+0.06	+0.62	+1.16	+1.02	+0.57	+0.85	+0.71
12	+0.44	+0.44	+1.12	+0.88	+0.36	+0.42	+0.76	+0.54	+0.76	+0.56	+0.56	+0.68	+0.62	+0.63	+0.63
13	+0.12	+0.34	+0.96	+1.14	+0.82	+0.20	+0.70	+0.82	+0.74	+0.58	+0.12	+0.16	+0.74	+0.34	+0.54
14	+0.30	+0.14	+1.12	+1.08	+0.62	+0.02	+0.48	+0.52	+1.06	+0.92	0.00	—0.04	+0.63	+0.41	+0.52
15	+0.42	+0.02	+1.28	+1.48	+0.68	+0.02	+0.12	+0.72	+1.40	+0.92	+0.62	+0.30	+0.74	+0.69	+0.71
16	+0.86	+0.76	+1.50	+1.55	+1.40	+1.40	+0.92	+0.94	+1.96	+1.20	+0.52	+0.46	+1.37	+0.88	+1.12
17	+0.50	+1.34	+1.56	+2.30	+3.18	+3.04	+2.78	+2.52	+2.64	+1.70	+0.92	+0.58	+2.75	+1.10	+1.93
18	+0.74	+1.64	+2.26	+3.40	+5.10	+5.28	+4.52	+5.22	+3.90	+1.84	+1.28	+0.68	+4.58	+1.39	+2.98
19	+1.28	+2.00	+3.52	+4.64	+6.04	+6.36	+6.50	+6.04	+5.22	+2.74	+1.78	+0.92	+5.95	+2.04	+3.99
20	+2.66	+2.92	+4.72	+4.96	+5.82	+6.20	+6.26	+6.00	+4.80	+3.66	+2.00	+1.46	+5.82	+3.05	+4.44
21	+2.00	+2.78	+4.54	+3.06	+4.15	+4.72	+4.86	+4.76	+3.00	+3.04	+2.76	+2.04	+4.25	+3.01	+3.63
22	+1.48	+1.46	+2.52	+1.30	+0.64	+1.73	+1.78	+0.54	+0.56	+1.10	+1.26	+1.62	+0.90	+1.57	+1.24
23	—0.38	—0.50	—0.74	—2.02	—3.06	—2.00	—1.76	—3.12	—3.70	—1.06	—1.12	—0.26	—2.61	—0.78	—1.69

42

TORONTO MAGNETICAL OBSERVATIONS.

TABLE XIV.

SOLAR DIURNAL VARIATIONS OF HORIZONTAL FORCE FOR EACH MONTH, FOR THE TWO HALF YEARS, AND FOR THE YEAR, DERIVED FROM THE FIVE YEARS ENDING JUNE 30, 1848, AFTER THE SEPARATION AND OMISSION OF THE LARGER DISTURBANCES.

Hours.	Jan.	Feb.	Mar.	Apr	May.	June	July.	Aug.	Sept.	Oct.	Nov.	Dec.	SEMI-ANNUAL MEANS. Apr. to Sept.	Oct. to March.	Annual Means.
	.00	.00	.00	.00	.00	.00	.00	.00	.00	.00	.00	.00	.00	.00	.00
0	—099	—065	—108	—086	—052	—042	—032	—052	—007	—071	—091	—073	—056	—085	—070
1	—060	—043	—070	—042	+010	+004	+007	+003	—009	—038	—060	—052	—004	—054	—029
2	—030	—010	—030	+005	+054	+058	+049	+057	+045	—001	—017	—027	+045	—019	+013
3	+021	+017	+017	+056	+081	+085	+081	+090	+072	+024	+016	+005	+078	+016	+047
4	+048	+028	+041	+074	+085	+095	+092	+091	+076	+040	+028	+031	+085	+037	+061
5	+045	+033	+051	+074	+081	+089	+078	+080	+061	+043	+033	+031	+077	+039	+058
6	+033	+027	+040	+056	+059	+067	+055	+048	+053	+034	+032	+027	+056	+032	+044
7	+020	+028	+035	+030	+030	+039	+037	+023	+036	+031	+031	+021	+032	+028	+030
8	+018	+019	+030	+012	+013	+015	+013	+015	+021	+017	+025	+013	+015	+020	+017
9	+012	+020	+021	+011	+005	000	+009	+015	+023	+015	+019	+010	+010	+016	+013
10	+014	+012	+017	+008	+004	—004	—004	+008	+022	+016	+020	+007	+006	+013	+010
11	+003	+008	+014	+005	+001	—015	+005	+011	+018	+008	+007	+002	+004	+008	+006
12	000	+006	+014	+007	—005	—018	—013	+007	+013	+006	+000	—007	—002	+004	+001
13	+006	—001	+007	+008	—012	—019	—008	+003	+008	+013	+011	—002	—003	+005	+001
14	+005	+003	+011	+003	—006	—014	—013	+009	+011	+015	+016	+007	—002	+010	+004
15	+012	—007	+011	+013	—012	—023	—014	+001	+003	+020	+019	+005	—006	+010	+002
16	+022	+012	+019	+021	—009	—019	—018	—007	+021	+032	+028	+015	—002	+022	+010
17	+020	+017	+023	+024	—005	—012	—017	—003	+024	+033	+039	+022	+002	+026	+014
18	+031	+021	+035	+014	+001	000	—003	+001	+015	+032	+043	+034	+005	+033	+019
19	+031	+010	+013	+011	—007	—007	—011	—017	—009	+014	+034	+030	—006	+022	+008
20	+024	—011	—016	—023	—036	—033	—035	—062	—054	—027	—008	+021	—041	—003	—022
21	—008	—030	—050	—070	—085	—064	—067	—105	—103	—068	—048	—004	—082	—034	—058
22	—051	—016	—085	—102	—105	—098	—008	—118	—130	—094	—083	—040	—109	—065	—087
23	—101	—063	—111	—112	—089	—082	—081	—090	—115	—096	—103	—072	—097	—092	—094

TORONTO MAGNETICAL OBSERVATIONS.

TABLE XV.

SOLAR DIURNAL VARIATIONS OF VERTICAL FORCE FOR EACH MONTH, FOR THE TWO HALF YEARS, AND FOR THE YEAR, DERIVED FROM THE FIVE YEARS ENDING JUNE 30, 1848, AFTER THE SEPARATION AND OMISSION OF THE LARGER DISTURBANCES.

Hours.	Jan.	Feb.	Mar.	Apr.	May.	June	July.	Aug.	Sept.	Oct.	Nov.	Dec.	SEMI-ANNUAL MEANS. Apr. to Sept.	Oct. to March.	Annual Means.
	.000	.000	.000	.000	.000	.000	.000	.000	.000	.000	.000	.000	.000	.000	.000
0	—013	—068	—081	—077	—095	—075	—077	—047	—023	—055	—024	—028	—066	—045	—055
1	+014	—024	—046	—033	—041	—067	—047	+003	+046	+005	+020	+013	—023	—003	—013
2	+042	+042	—001	+031	+029	—005	+004	+070	+090	+046	+074	+054	+036	+043	+040
3	+058	+087	+042	+068	+067	+077	+081	+007	+109	+077	+070	+072	+085	+068	+076
4	+047	+084	+056	+082	+110	+116	+141	+143	+110	+074	+073	+060	+117	+066	+091
5	+056	+086	+070	+077	+133	+131	+184	+159	+110	+073	+072	+054	+132	+068	+100
6	+070	+081	+067	+063	+137	+106	+174	+133	+095	+075	+065	+043	+118	+067	+092
7	+070	+074	+061	+090	+093	+111	+145	+097	+065	+086	+068	+055	+100	+069	+084
8	+064	+055	+055	+068	+069	+074	+081	+081	+061	+073	+065	+054	+072	+061	+067
9	+050	+055	+050	+027	+043	+055	+064	+014	+045	+061	+056	+056	+041	+055	+048
10	+033	+033	+041	+004	+035	+017	+010	+005	+020	+041	+042	+042	+017	+039	+028
11	+022	+027	+036	—013	—018	000	—003	—033	—011	+013	+022	+022	—013	+024	+005
12	—004	+003	+003	+036	—045	—036	—029	—056	—050	—017	—009	—019	—030	—007	—019
13	—022	—033	—023	—041	—063	—043	—074	—069	—050	—051	—033	—027	—057	—031	—044
14	—028	—015	—036	—038	—056	—050	—119	—100	—059	—041	—046	—027	—070	—037	—054
15	—041	—036	—020	—029	—043	—065	—116	—091	—054	—026	—050	—028	—066	—033	—050
16	—047	—038	—063	—031	—026	—009	—093	—091	—080	—051	—050	—056	—056	—041	—048
17	—045	—026	—020	+004	—003	+020	—052	—005	—067	—063	—049	—050	—017	—042	—030
18	—027	—022	—011	+027	+019	+004	+004	+001	—019	—040	—061	—022	+000	—030	—012
19	—027	—010	+017	+015	+001	—022	—005	—023	—028	—019	—033	—037	—010	—018	—014
20	—036	—011	+018	—004	—027	—054	—028	—015	—013	—027	—046	—040	—033	—021	—029
21	—068	—082	—038	—042	—074	—079	—050	—074	—095	—056	—077	—016	—069	—060	—065
22	—072	—119	—101	—088	—125	—099	—078	—078	—095	—081	—090	—068	—094	—089	—091
23	—064	—124	—128	—105	—124	—095	—087	—054	—019	—001	—070	—059	—086	—089	—087

44

TABLE XVI.

SEMI-ANNUAL AND ANNUAL MEANS OF THE SOLAR DIURNAL VARIATIONS OF TOTAL FORCE AND INCLINATION, DERIVED FROM THOSE OF THE HORIZONTAL AND VERTICAL FORCES.

Toronto Astronomical Hours.	TOTAL FORCE.			INCLINATION.			Toronto Astronomical Hours.
	SEMI-ANNUAL MEANS.		Annual Means.	SEMI-ANNUAL MEANS.		Annual Means.	
	April to September.	October to March.		April to September.	October to March.		
Hours.	Parts of Force.	Parts of Force.	Parts of Force.	″	″	″	Hours.
0	−.000097	−.000098	−.000097	+25.1	+40.8	+32.8	0
1	− 024	− 039	− 031	+ 0.9	+27.2	+14.0	1
2	+ 064	+ 028	+ 046	−21.0	+11.8	− 4.7	2
3	+ 130	+ 075	+ 102	−35.3	− 4.7	−20.0	3
4	+ 165	+ 086	+ 125	−37.2	−15.3	−26.2	4
5	+ 173	+ 089	+ 131	−32.4	−16.3	−24.4	5
6	+ 146	+ 085	+ 115	−22.4	−12.9	−17.7	6
7	+ 113	+ 083	+ 098	−11.2	−10.7	−10.9	7
8	+ 078	+ 071	+ 074	− 3.9	− 6.9	− 5.4	8
9	+ 044	+ 062	+ 053	− 3.1	− 5.6	− 4.3	9
10	+ 020	+ 045	+ 032	− 2.2	− 4.6	− 3.5	10
11	− 009	+ 028	+ 009	− 2.8	− 2.8	− 2.8	11
12	− 029	− 003	− 017	− 0.5	− 2.5	− 1.5	12
13	− 055	− 025	− 040	− 1.4	− 4.1	− 2.8	13
14	− 067	− 029	− 048	− 2.8	− 7.0	− 4.8	14
15	− 066	− 026	− 046	− 0.3	− 6.7	− 3.5	15
16	− 053	− 024	− 039	− 1.9	−13.3	− 7.5	16
17	− 015	− 022	− 019	− 2.1	−15.3	− 8.7	17
18	+ 009	− 006	+ 001	− 2.3	−18.2	−10.3	18
19	− 013	− 002	− 008	+ 2.8	−12.1	− 4.8	19
20	− 058	− 024	− 041	+19.1	+ 0.3	+ 9.7	20
21	− 119	− 078	− 098	+38.2	+14.2	+26.2	21
22	− 160	− 127	− 142	+50.5	+28.4	+39.5	22
23	− 144	− 143	− 143	+44.8	+42.2	+43.4	23

TORONTO MAGNETICAL OBSERVATIONS.

TABLE XVII.

SEMI-ANNUAL INEQUALITIES OF THE DIURNAL VARIATIONS OF THE MAGNETIC ELEMENTS FOR EACH HOUR WITH THE SIGNS PROPER TO THE HALF-YEAR, APRIL TO SEPTEMBER INCLUSIVE, DERIVED FROM THE FIVE YEARS ENDING 30TH JUNE, 1848.

Astronomical Time.	Declination.	Horizontal Force.	Vertical Force.	Total Force.	Inclination.	Astronomical Time.
0	−1.15	+.00014	−.000011	.000000	− 7.7	0
1	−1.25	+ 25	− 10	+ 07	−13.1	1
2	−1.14	+ 32	− 04	+ 18	−16.3	2
3	−0.94	+ 31	+ 00	+ 28	−15.3	3
4	−0.48	+ 24	+ 20	+ 40	−11.0	4
5	−0.03	+ 19	+ 32	+ 42	− 8.0	5
6	+0.04	+ 12	+ 20	+ 31	− 4.7	6
7	−0.11	+ 02	+ 16	+ 15	− 0.3	7
8	−0.28	− 02	+ 05	+ 04	+ 1.5	8
9	−0.30	− 03	− 07	− 09	+ 1.2	9
10	−0.23	− 04	− 11	− 12	+ 1.3	10
11	−0.14	− 02	− 18	− 18	0.0	11
12	−0.01	− 03	− 11	− 12	+ 1.0	12
13	+0.20	− 04	− 13	− 15	+ 1.4	13
14	+0.11	− 06	− 16	− 19	+ 2.0	14
15	+0.03	− 08	− 10	− 20	+ 3.2	15
16	+0.25	− 12	− 08	− 14	+ 5.6	16
17	+0.52	− 12	+ 13	+ 04	+ 6.6	17
18	+1.60	− 14	+ 18	+ 08	+ 8.1	18
19	+1.96	− 14	+ 04	− 05	+ 7.0	19
20	+1.38	− 19	− 04	− 17	+ 9.4	20
21	+0.62	− 21	− 04	− 21	+12.0	21
22	−0.34	− 22	− 03	− 18	+11.0	22
23	−0.92	− 03	+ 01	− 01	+ 1.4	23

TORONTO MAGNETICAL OBSERVATIONS.

TABLE XVIII.

AGGREGATE VALUES OF THE DISTURBANCES IN DIFFERENT YEARS, EACH ENDING JUNE 30, DERIVED FROM SIX OBSERVATIONS EACH DAY.

Years.	Declination.			Horizontal Force. In parts of the Horizontal Force.			Vertical Force. In parts of the Vertical Force.			Total Force. In parts of the Total Force.			Inclination.		
	Total.	Easterly.	Westerly.	Total.	Increasing.	Decreasing.	Total.	Increasing.	Decreasing.	Total.	Increasing.	Decreasing.	Total.	Increasing.	Decreasing.
1844	614	.....	.....	.1779	.0458	.1321	.1134	.0473	.0661	.1143	.0480	.0663	154.8	.....	.....
1845	702	.....	.....	.1523	.0236	.1287	.0994	.0325	.0669	.0999	.0155	.0840	139.0	.....	.....
1840	771	.....	.....	.2015	.0447	.1568	.1333	.0588	.0745	.1009	.0420	.3592	175.0	.....	.....
1847	1373	.....	.....	.3036	.0597	.3389	.2226	.0646	.1580	.1940	.0422	.1518	303.4	.....	.....
1848	1582	.....	.....	.9342	.1161	.8181	.3099	.1624	.1475	.2725	.1123	.1602	789.4	.....	.....
1849–53	Not publish ed.														
1854	1494	846	648	.5297	.1051	.4246	.3320	.1444	.1876	.2356	.0992	.1464	464.2	354.4	109.8
1856	Obs ervations	suspend ed.													
1856	366	154	212	.2974	.0912	.2062	.1077	.0412	.0665	.0525	.0144	.0381	259.5	168.9	90.6
1857	423	293	130	.2578	.0470	.2108	.1191	.0533	.0658	.0677	.0236	.0441	218.1	174.7	43.4
1858	961	612	349	.8531	.1811	.6720	.2326	.1161	.1165	.1726	.0713	.1013	725.7	571.5	154.2
1859	1200	792	408	.7490	.1671	.5819	.2129	.1220	.0909	.1523	.0732	.0791	641.1	502.8	139.3
1860	1698	882	816	1.3136	.2886	1.0250	.3669	.1668	.2001	.2845	.1062	.1783	1123.4	875.3	248.1
1861	1465	758	707	.9377	.2134	.7243	.2808	.1415	.1393	.2253	.1027	.1226	772.9	606.4	166.5
1862	1118	570	548	.5740	.1178	.4562	.2920	.1025	.0995	.1401	.0627	.0774	513.9	403.4	110.5

TORONTO MAGNETICAL OBSERVATIONS.

TABLE XIX.

SOLAR DIURNAL VARIATIONS OF DECLINATION FOR EACH MONTH AT THE ORDINARY SIX OBSERVATION HOURS, AFTER THE SEPARATION AND OMISSION OF THE LARGER DISTURBANCES, AND DERIVED FROM DIFFERENT GROUPS OF YEARS.

JANUARY. FEBRUARY.

Toronto Astronomical Time.	2	4	10	12	18	20	2	4	10	12	18	20
1844–48	−3.14	−1.64	+1.08	+0.44	+0.74	+2.66	−3.26	−1.66	+0.88	+0.44	+1.64	+2.92
1856–62	−3.53	−1.94	+1.16	+0.57	+0.96	+2.91	−3.70	−2.69	+1.26	+0.05	+1.57	+3.57
1863–71	−3.69	−1.96	+1.50	+0.85	+0.50	+2.85	−3.91	−2.71	+1.28	+1.14	+1.66	+3.49

MARCH. APRIL.

1844–48	−5.36	−3.42	+0.90	+1.12	+2.26	+4.72	−5.84	−3.30	+0.82	+0.88	+3.40	+4.96
1856–62	−5.70	−3.28	+0.84	+0.97	+2.30	+5.08	−6.70	−3.80	+0.30	+1.18	+3.76	+6.24
1863–71	−5.86	−3.71	+0.95	+1.11	+2.45	+5.27	−6.75	−4.48	+0.64	+1.30	+4.35	+5.85

MAY. JUNE.

1844–48	−6.10	−3.12	+0.38	+0.36	+5.16	+5.82	−6.26	−3.76	+0.04	+0.42	+5.28	+6.20
1856–62	−6.19	−3.27	+0.07	+0.58	+5.27	+6.05	−6.51	−3.89	−0.31	+0.19	+5.80	+6.65
1863–71	−6.31	−3.71	+0.51	+0.72	+5.17	+6.15	−6.58	−4.22	+0.03	+0.24	+5.62	+6.82

JULY. AUGUST.

1844–48	−5.96	−3.68	+0.36	+0.76	+4.52	+6.26	−6.52	−2.74	+0.46	+0.54	+5.22	+6.90
1856–62	−6.73	−4.07	−0.26	+0.58	+5.69	+7.04	−7.43	−3.33	+0.06	+0.48	+5.99	+8.10
1863–71	−6.67	−4.28	+0.14	+0.29	+5.65	+7.11	−7.19	−3.30	+0.37	+0.27	+5.78	+7.71

SEPTEMBER. OCTOBER.

1844–48	−5.40	−1.16	+0.78	+0.76	+3.90	+4.80	−3.94	−1.80	+0.48	+0.56	+1.84	+3.66
1856–62	−5.60	−2.07	−0.04	+0.26	+4.84	+6.36	−4.85	−2.50	+0.50	+0.52	+1.82	+4.78
1863–71	−5.82	−1.90	+0.67	+0.57	+4.61	+5.54	−4.55	−2.17	+0.82	+0.86	+1.92	+3.91

NOVEMBER. DECEMBER.

1844–48	−3.30	−1.78	+1.10	+0.56	+1.28	+2.90	−3.36	−1.70	+1.10	+0.68	+0.56	+1.46
1856–62	−3.91	−2.13	+1.08	+0.90	+1.85	+3.04	−3.48	−2.13	+1.04	+0.00	+0.73	+2.01
1863–71	−3.95	−1.04	+1.11	+0.80	+1.72	+2.98	−3.16	−1.94	+1.25	+0.64	+0.65	+1.82

TORONTO MAGNETICAL OBSERVATIONS.

TABLE XX.

SOLAR DIURNAL OBSERVATIONS OF HORIZONTAL FORCE FOR EACH MONTH AT THE ORDINARY SIX OBSERVATION HOURS, AFTER THE SEPARATION AND OMISSION OF THE LARGER DISTURBANCES, AND DERIVED FROM DIFFERENT GROUPS OF YEARS.

Toronto Astronomical Time.	JANUARY.						FEBRUARY.					
	2	4	10	12	18	20	2	4	10	12	18	20
	.000	.000	.000	.000	.000	.000	.000	.000	.000	.000	.000	.000
1844–48	−300	+460	+140	.000	+310	+240	−100	+280	+120	+060	+210	−110
1856–62	−558	+177	+159	+161	+507	+410	−715	−039	+120	+102	+554	+369
1863–71	−498	+290	+100	+075	+393	+497	−502	+001	+020	+040	+445	+460

	MARCH.						APRIL.					
	.000	.000	.000	.000	.000	.000	.000	.000	.000	.000	.000	.000
1844–48	−300	+410	+170	+140	+350	−160	+050	+740	+080	+070	+140	−230
1856–62	−628	+324	+177	+182	+572	+013	−277	+612	+172	+241	+399	−272
1863–71	−419	+280	+077	+133	+407	+143	−025	+777	+007	+079	+250	−226

	MAY.						JUNE.					
	.000	.000	.000	.000	.000	.000	.000	.000	.000	.000	.000	.000
1844–48	+540	+850	+040	−050	+010	−360	+580	+950	−040	−180	.000	−330
1856–62	+308	+582	+086	+190	+315	−449	+218	+727	+162	+077	+297	−507
1863–71	+316	+733	+050	+103	+162	−311	+569	+773	−106	−019	+049	−275

	JULY.						AUGUST.					
	.000	.000	.000	.000	.000	.000	.000	.000	.000	.000	.000	.000
1844–48	+490	+020	−040	−130	−030	−350	+570	+910	+080	+070	+010	−620
1856–62	+262	+906	+045	+080	+201	−623	+233	+682	+203	+307	+355	−763
1863–71	+366	+839	−051	+016	+103	−425	+297	+854	+009	+154	+205	−577

	SEPTEMBER.						OCTOBER.					
	.000	.000	.000	.000	.000	.000	.000	.000	.000	.000	.000	.000
1844–48	+450	+760	+220	+130	+150	−540	−010	+400	+160	+060	+320	+270
1856–62	−098	+548	+541	+447	+527	−704	−431	+232	+225	+203	+631	+274
1863–71	+133	+557	+232	+235	+438	−416	−326	+156	+191	+184	+476	+093

	NOVEMBER.						DECEMBER.					
	.000	.000	.000	.000	.000	.000	.000	.000	.000	.000	.000	.000
1844–48	−170	+280	+200	+060	+430	−080	−270	+310	+070	−070	+340	+210
1856–62	−316	+072	+225	+209	+595	+055	−560	+097	+136	+090	+474	+279
1863–71	−315	+247	+133	+114	+467	+143	−324	+153	−005	+029	+371	+364

TORONTO MAGNETICAL OBSERVATIONS.

TABLE XXI.

SOLAR DIURNAL VARIATIONS OF VERTICAL FORCE FOR EACH MONTH AT THE ORDINARY SIX OBSERVATION HOURS, AFTER THE SEPARATION AND OMISSION OF THE LARGER DISTURBANCES, AND DERIVED FROM DIFFERENT GROUPS OF YEARS.

JANUARY. FEBRUARY.

Toronto Astronomical Time.	2	4	10	12	18	20	2	4	10	12	18	20
	.000	.000	.000	.000	.000	.000	.000	.000	.000	.000	.000	.000
1844-48	+042	+047	+033	−004	−027	−036	+042	+084	+033	+003	−022	−011
1856-62	+067	+089	+029	−002	−091	−032	+031	+139	+066	+015	−094	−020
1863-71	+049	+080	+065	+026	−104	−064	+078	+119	+056	+004	−096	−030

MARCH. APRIL.

	.000	.000	.000	.000	.000	.000	.000	.000	.000	.000	.000	.000
1844-48	−001	+056	+041	+003	−011	+018	+031	+082	+004	+036	+027	+004
1856-62	+089	+161	+044	−013	−098	−071	+043	+154	+055	−013	−027	−034
1863-71	+06	+115	+032	−005	−071	−021	+093	+154	+033	−043	−036	−031

MAY. JUNE.

	.000	.000	.000	.000	.000	.000	.000	.000	.000	.000	.000	.000
1844-48	+029	+110	+035	−045	+019	+027	−005	+116	+017	−036	+004	−054
1856-62	+029	+140	+052	−039	−017	−044	−015	+115	+051	−031	−019	−061
1863-71	+057	+116	+098	−022	−053	−075	+125	+154	−019	−059	−076	−051

JULY. AUGUST.

	.000	.000	.000	.000	.000	.000	.000	.000	.000	.000	.000	.000
1844-48	+004	+141	+010	−029	+004	−028	+070	+143	+008	−056	+001	−045
1856-62	+008	+141	+055	−011	−005	−082	+040	+147	+004	−057	+031	−044
1863-71	+024	+148	+012	−022	−042	−016	+100	+178	+013	−082	−030	−056

SEPTEMBER. OCTOBER.

	.000	.000	.000	.000	.000	.000	.000	.000	.000	.000	.000	.000
1844-48	+030	+116	+029	−050	−019	−043	+016	+074	+041	−017	−040	−027
1856-62	+085	+141	+029	−082	+005	−062	+048	+110	+055	−032	−086	−017
1863-71	+166	+203	+006	−058	−072	−148	+077	+122	+039	−030	−070	−058

NOVEMBER. DECEMBER.

	.000	.000	.000	.000	.000	.000	.000	.000	.000	.000	.000	.000
1844-48	+071	+073	+042	−009	−061	−010	+054	+060	+012	−019	−022	−040
1856-62	+083	+107	+036	−047	−071	−033	+091	+117	+059	+003	−113	−074
1863-71	+07	+090	+047	−004	−092	−055	+051	+063	+030	+003	−013	−029

TABLE XXII.

SOLAR DIURNAL VARIATIONS OF TOTAL FORCE FOR EACH MONTH AT THE ORDINARY SIX OBSERVATION HOURS, AFTER THE SEPARATION AND OMISSION OF THE LARGER DISTURBANCES, AND DERIVED FROM DIFFERENT GROUPS OF YEARS.

JANUARY. | FEBRUARY.

Toronto Astronomical Time.	2	4	10	12	18	20	2	4	10	12	18	20
	.000	.000	.000	.000	.000	.000	.000	.000	.000	.000	.000	.000
1856-62	+027	+095	+038	+008	—053	—004	—016	+125	+069	+020	—053	—004
1863-71	+014	+093	+067	+030	—072	—029	+041	+111	+054	+000	—061	+001

MARCH. | APRIL.

	.000	.000	.000	.000	.000	.000	.000	.000	.000	.000	.000	.000
1856-62	+044	+171	+052	000	—066	—067	+023	+183	+062	+003	000	—049
1863-71	+029	+125	+063	+004	—038	—015	+085	+193	+037	—035	—017	—044

MAY. | JUNE.

	.000	.000	.000	.000	.000	.000	.000	.000	.000	.000	.000	.000
1856-62	+047	+168	+055	—025	+005	—070	000	+154	+058	—025	+001	—090
1863-71	+074	+156	+095	—014	—039	—090	+122	+194	—024	—056	—068	—065

JULY. | AUGUST.

	.000	.000	.000	.000	.000	.000	.000	.000	.000	.000	.000	.000
1856-62	+027	+189	+054	—005	+005	—117	+053	+181	+017	—034	+052	—090
1863-71	+050	+192	—004	—020	—033	—041	+112	+221	+019	—071	—015	—090

SEPTEMBER. | OCTOBER.

	.000	.000	.000	.000	.000	.000	.000	.000	.000	.000	.000	.000
1856-62	+073	+166	+061	—048	+038	—109	+018	+118	+066	—017	—040	—033
1863-71	+164	+225	+020	—039	—040	—165	+050	+124	+040	—017	—035	—061

NOVEMBER. | DECEMBER.

	.000	.000	.000	.000	.000	.000	.000	.000	.000	.000	.000	.000
1856-62	+049	+105	+053	—030	—028	—029	+052	+115	+064	+008	—075	—052
1863-71	+053	+111	+052	—003	—056	—042	+025	+060	+027	+004	—016	—003

TORONTO MAGNETICAL OBSERVATIONS.

TABLE XXIII.

SOLAR DIURNAL VARIATIONS OF INCLINATION FOR EACH MONTH AT THE ORDINARY SIX OBSERVATION HOURS, AFTER THE SEPARATION AND OMISSION OF THE LARGER DISTURBANCES, AND DERIVED FROM DIFFERENT GROUPS OF YEARS.

Toronto Astronomical Time.	JANUARY.						FEBRUARY.					
	2	4	10	12	18	20	2	4	10	12	18	20
1856-62	+31.5	− 4.4	− 6.6	− 8.2	−30.2	−22.2	+37.6	+ 9.0	− 2.7	− 8.9	−32.7	−20.0
1863-71	+27.6	−10.6	− 1.8	− 3.4	−25.0	−28.3	+29.3	− 5.9	+ 1.8	− 1.8	−27.3	−24.8

	MARCH.						APRIL.					
1856-62	+36.1	− 8.2	− 6.7	−10.3	−33.8	− 2.9	+16.1	−23.1	− 5.9	−12.8	−21.4	+12.0
1863-71	+24.1	− 8.3	− 2.2	− 7.0	−24.0	− 8.4	+ 6.0	−31.4	+ 1.6	− 6.2	−14.4	+ 9.8

	MAY.						JUNE.					
1856-62	−14.1	−23.3	− 1.7	−11.6	−16.7	+20.4	−11.7	−30.8	− 5.6	− 5.5	−15.9	+22.4
1863-71	−13.1	−31.1	+ 2.4	− 8.2	−10.8	+11.9	−24.1	−31.2	+ 4.4	− 1.0	− 6.3	+11.3

	JULY.						AUGUST.					
1856-62	−12.8	−38.5	+ 0.5	− 4.6	−10.6	+27.3	− 9.7	−27.0	−10.0	−18.3	−16.3	+36.2
1863-71	−17.2	−34.0	+ 3.3	− 2.0	− 7.3	+20.7	− 9.9	−34.1	− 4.3	−11.9	−11.9	+26.3

	SEPTEMBER.						OCTOBER.					
1856-62	+ 0.2	−20.5	−25.8	−26.6	−26.3	+36.9	+24.1	− 6.2	− 8.6	−11.8	−36.1	+12.9
1863-71	+ 1.3	−17.0	−11.4	−14.8	−25.7	+13.5	+21.0	− 1.7	− 7.7	−10.8	−27.5	+ 1.8

	NOVEMBER.						DECEMBER.					
1856-62	+20.3	+ 1.8	− 9.6	−12.9	−33.5	− 4.5	+32.9	+ 1.0	− 3.9	− 4.4	−20.5	−17.8
1863-71	+10.9	− 7.9	− 4.3	− 6.0	−28.2	−10.0	+18.9	− 4.5	+ 1.7	− 1.4	−20.9	−19.8

TORONTO MAGNETICAL OBSERVATIONS.

TABLE XXIV.

COMPARATIVE VIEW OF THE SEMI-ANNUAL AND ANNUAL MEANS, AND SEMI-ANNUAL INEQUALITY OF THE SOLAR DIURNAL VARIATIONS OF THE MAGNETIC ELEMENTS AT THE SIX OBSERVATION HOURS, AS DERIVED FROM DIFFERENT GROUPS OF YEARS.

TORONTO ASTRONOMICAL TIME.		WINTER—OCTOBER TO MARCH.						SUMMER—APRIL TO SEPTEMBER.					
		2	4	10	12	18	20	2	4	10	12	18	20
Declination	1844-48	−3.73	−2.00	+0.93	+0.63	+1.39	+3.05	−6.01	−2.96	+0.47	+0.62	+4.58	+5.82
	1856-62	−4.10	−2.45	+0.96	+0.75	+1.54	+3.54	−6.55	−3.40	+0.07	+0.58	+5.22	+6.74
	1863-71	−4.19	−2.40	+1.17	+0.92	+1.48	+3.39	−6.55	−3.66	+0.39	+0.56	+5.20	+6.53
Horizontal Force	1844-48	−.000190	+.000370	+.000130	+.000040	+.000330	+.000030	+.000450	+.000850	+.000060	−.000020	+.000050	−.000410
	1856-62	−.000535	+.000133	+.000174	+.000175	+.000556	+.000137	+.000107	+.000676	+.000021	+.000224	+.000519	−.000521
	1863-71	−.000398	+.000189	+.000086	+.000096	+.000427	+.000252	+.000277	+.000756	+.000068	+.000095	+.000201	−.000372
Vertical Force	1844-48	+.000043	+.000066	+.000039	+.000007	+.000030	+.000024	+.000036	+.000117	+.000017	+.000030	+.000006	−.000033
	1856-62	+.000069	+.000121	+.000048	+.000013	+.000092	+.000016	+.000032	+.000140	+.000040	−.000035	−.000006	−.000055
	1863-71	+.000066	+.000098	+.000045	+.000001	+.000079	+.000044	+.000094	+.000159	+.000065	−.000048	−.000051	−.000063
Total Force	1844-48	+.000028	+.000086	+.000045	+.000003	+.000006	+.000024	+.000064	+.000165	+.000030	−.000029	+.000009	−.000058
	1850-62	+.000028	+.000122	+.000057	+.000001	+.000049	+.000031	+.000037	+.000174	+.000025	−.000022	+.000017	−.000057
	1863-71	+.000036	+.000105	+.000047	+.000004	+.000045	+.000025	+.000100	+.000197	+.000024	−.000039	−.000035	−.000063
Inclination	1844-48	+11.8	−15.3	−4.6	−2.5	−19.2	−0.3	−21.0	−37.2	−2.2	−0.5	−2.2	+19.1
	1856-62	+31.4	−1.2	−6.3	−9.4	−32.6	−7.7	−3.8	−27.0	−8.1	−13.2	−17.9	+25.3
	1863-71	+23.5	−6.5	−2.1	−5.1	−25.5	−14.9	−9.5	−39.1	−0.3	−7.3	−12.7	+15.6

TORONTO MAGNETICAL OBSERVATIONS.

TABLE XXIV.—(Continued.)

COMPARATIVE VIEW OF THE SEMI-ANNUAL AND ANNUAL MEANS, &C.

TORONTO ASTRONOMICAL TIME.		Year.						Semi-Annual Inequality. The signs are those proper to the half year, from April to Sept. inclusive					
		2	4	10	12	18	20	2	4	10	12	18	20
Declination	1844-45	−4.67	−2.48	+0.70	+0.63	+2.98	+1.44	−1.14	−0.48	−0.23	−0.01	+1.60	+1.38
	1856-62	−5.38	−2.93	+0.52	+0.67	+3.35	+5.15	−1.17	−0.47	−0.45	−0.09	+1.84	+1.59
	1863-71	−5.37	−3.03	+0.76	+0.74	+3.34	+4.96	−1.18	−0.63	−0.39	−0.19	+1.86	+1.57
Horizontal Force	1844-45	+.000130	+.000610	+.000100	+.000010	+.000190	−.000239	+.000320	+.000240	−.000040	−.000050	−.000140	−.000190
	1856-62	−.000214	+.000405	+.000188	+.000195	+.000452	−.000192	+.000321	+.000271	+.000013	+.000026	−.000103	−.000329
	1863-71	−.000060	+.000473	+.000052	+.000095	+.000314	−.000060	+.000337	−.000283	+.000024	+.000000	−.000113	−.000312
Vertical Force	1844-45	+.000040	+.000091	+.000025	+.000019	−.000012	−.000025	+.000004	+.000026	−.000011	−.000011	+.000016	−.000004
	1856-62	+.000050	+.000130	+.000044	+.000025	−.000049	−.000049	+.000016	+.000016	−.000004	−.000013	+.000043	−.000006
	1863-71	+.000050	+.000125	+.000035	+.000024	−.000063	−.000053	+.000014	−.000031	+.000010	−.000024	+.000014	−.000010
Total Force	1844-45	+.000046	+.000125	+.000032	+.000017	+.000001	−.000041	+.000015	+.000040	−.000012	−.000012	+.000008	−.000017
	1856-62	+.000033	+.000149	+.000053	+.000012	+.000016	−.000059	+.000004	+.000026	−.000001	−.000010	+.000033	−.000029
	1863-71	+.000065	+.000151	+.000036	+.000018	−.000012	−.000054	+.000032	+.000046	−.000012	−.000021	+.000007	−.000029
Inclination	1844-45	− 4.7	−26.2	− 3.5	− 1.5	−10.3	+ 9.7	−16.3	−11.0	+ 1.3	+ 1.0	+ 8.1	+ 9.4
	1856-62	+13.6	−14.1	− 7.2	−11.3	−25.3	+ 8.8	−17.6	−12.9	− 0.9	− 1.9	+ 7.4	+16.5
	1863-71	+ 7.0	−18.3	− 1.4	− 6.2	−19.1	+ 0.3	−16.5	−11.8	+ 0.7	− 1.2	+ 6.4	+15.3

TORONTO MAGNETICAL OBSERVATIONS.

TABLE XXV.

DATES (ASTRONOMICAL TIME) AT WHICH UNUSUALLY LARGE DISTURBANCES OF DECLINATION OCCURRED AT THE ORDINARY OBSERVATION HOURS, WITH THE AMOUNT OF ABNORMAL VARIATION OF EACH SUCH DISTURBANCE.

Declination, Abnormal Variation not less than 15'. The (+) sign indicates an Easterly Disturbance, and (—) a Westerly Disturbance.

Date.	Amount.	Date.	Amount.	Date.	Amount.	Date.	Amount.	Date.	Amount.	Date.	Amount.
1863.		1864.		1866.		1867.		1868.		1870.	
d h	′	d h	′	d h	′	d h	′	d h	′	d h	′
Jan. 12 18	—25.8	Nov. 15 10	+23.8	Jan. 10 10	+20.4	June 1 10	+18.8	Oct. 23 18	—33.2	Apr. 4 18	—16.7
" 24 12	+36.1	Dec. 7 10	+16.1	" 27 10	+15.9	Aug. 31 10	+16.0	" 25 18	—16.8	June14 10	+17.3
" 25 20	—24.3	" 11 20	—16.7	Feb. 7 10	+29.2	Sept.17 10	+17.0	" 25 20	—16.8	Aug. 2 18	—23.5
Feb. 6 20	—20 7	1865.		" 20 12	—54.7	" 21 12	—15.7	Nov. 19 10	+24.4	" 19 10	+36.5
" 25 18	—24.8	Mar. 20 12	—17.2	Mar. 7 10	+15.4	" 25 12	+16.1	1869.		Sept.23.18	—20.3
Apr. 8 10	+16.5	Apr. 15 10	+22.7	" 18 18	—20.2	Oct. 2 12	+15.0	Jan. 19 20	—15.2	Oct. 23 18	+15.5
May 5 10	+27 1	June 5 12	+17.9	Apr. 3 18	—15.0	" 23 18	—15.0	Feb. 3 10	+20.7	" 24 12	—22.8
July 6 10	+19.1	" 9 20	+24.0	" 17 10	+17.4	1868.		" 23 10	+33.0	" 24 20	—21.6
" 15 10	+27.4	" 15 10	—21.8	May 12 12	+17.4	April 1 12	+37.4	Apr. 5 12	—22.8	Nov. 8 10	+23.0
Sept. 9 20	—33.8	July 18 4	+15.9	June15 18	—15.4	" 1 20	—21 4	" 6 4	+21 8	" 8 18	—16.2
" 10 12	—20.0	Aug. 2 2	+22.0	Aug. 9 10	+15.5	" 18 12	+16.8	" 15 2	+20.1	" 18 20	—22.7
Oct. 8 10	+33.4	" 2 18	+28.9	" 23 10	+15.5	May 20 10	+15.8	May 7 10	+18.8	Dec. 15 20	—17.5
Nov. 5 12	+15.9	" 2 20	—63.4	" 29 18	—20.2	" 23 12	+22.7	" 8 12	+16.3	" 16 20	—17.6
" 14 10	+28.4	" 3 2	+33.2	Sept.17 18	—27.5	June10 10	+131.2	" 13 2	+31.3	1871.	
Dec. 11 20	—18.0	" 4 18	—38.8	Oct. 3 10	+25.7	" 29 12	+19.8	" 13 4	+24 1	Feb. 11 12	+16.7
1864.		" 11 18	—21.5	" 5 18	—15.9	July 10 10	+17.4	June15 18	—16.3	Mar. 26 20	—15.7
Mar. 31 12	+20.8	Sept. 20 12	—16.2	" 7 18	—18.9	" 10 12	—37.0	" 24 4	—23.0	Apr. 4 10	+16.9
Apr. 29 10	+23.8	Oct. 12 20	—17.5	" 9 12	+22.7	Aug. 4 10	+20.4	Ang. 6 10	+19.9	" 17 10	—15.5
May 5 12	+15.9	" 13 18	—26.6	" 10 18	—33.0	Sept.15 12	—20.9	" 15 18	—22.4	" 23 18	—24.9
June 7 12	+34.2	" 13 20	—31.9	" 11 18	—20 2	" 15 18	—41.7	" 24 16	+33.5	" 27 20	—20.2
" 8 18	—23.6	" 18 20	—15.5	" 13 16	+23.2	" 15 20	—17.7	Sept.27 18	—16.3	" 28 20	—18.5
July 19 10	—35.9	" 30 18	—22.2	" 18 10	+27.0	" 26 10	+44.4	Dec. 13 20	—18.7	May 24 12	+15.8
Aug.24 10	—26.9	" 30 20	—22.0	" 30 12	+16.2	" 26 12	+21.9	1870.		" 26 10	+19.0
Sept.23 4	+16.8	" 31 12	+15.4	Nov. 1 10	+37.4	" 30 12	—69.9	Jan. 8 10	+15.8	June17 12	—16.7
Oct. 12 20	—22.1	" 31 18	—42.8	" 25 20	—18.2	" 30 18	—28.2	" 26 12	+21.8	July 3 12	+15.0
" 14 12	—23.8	" 31 20	—29.5			Oct. 22 12	+42.8	Feb. 1 12	+20.2	" 21 12	+15.7
" 14 20	—15.6					" 22 18	—40.1	Mar. 30 10	+17.6	Aug.12 10	+23.1

TORONTO MAGNETICAL OBSERVATIONS.

TABLE XXVI.

A SELECTION OF DATES (ASTRONOMICAL TIME) AT WHICH EXTRA READINGS OF THE MAGNETICAL INSTRUMENTS WERE TAKEN, IN CONSEQUENCE OF PREVAILING LARGE DISTURBANCES, WITH THE AMOUNT OF ABNORMAL DEVIATIONS ($\Delta\psi$) OF DECLINATION, ($\Delta\theta$) OF INCLINATION, AND $\dfrac{\Delta\phi}{\phi}$ OF TOTAL FORCE.

Date.	$\Delta\psi$	$\Delta\theta$	$\dfrac{\Delta\phi}{\phi}$	Date.	$\Delta\psi$	$\Delta\theta$	$\dfrac{\Delta\phi}{\phi}$
1863.				1865.			
d h m	′	′		d h m	′	′	
Sept. 9 8 35	+38.9	+ 0.4	−.00124	Aug. 2 18 45	+16.6	+ 3.0	−.00259
" 8 45	+10.9	+ 1.0	— 122	" 19 0	+ 3.6	+ 7.0	— 342
" 8 55	+15.5	+ 2.6	— 131	" 19 15	+10.1	+16.4	— 487
" 9 5	+15.2	+ 1.0	— 121	" 19 30	—14.4	+14.0	— 320
" 23 9 0	+52.6	+ 3.6	— 125	" 19 45	—41.8	+18.9	— 565
" 9 5	+54.1	+ 1.8	— 048	" 20 0	—63.4	+20.4	— 711
" 9 10	+33.9	+ 1.4	— 045	" 20 15	—68.4	+17.1	— 610
" 9 15	+19.5	+ 2.8	— 035	" 20 30	—51.8	+19.1	— 527
" 9 20	+10.9	+ 4.0	— 065	" 20 45	—36.0	+19.1	— 353
" 9 25	+ 7.3	+ 4.0	— 057	" 21 0	—46.1	+19.7	— 425
" 9 30	+ 8.0	+ 3.7	— 057	" 21 30	—34.6	+12.8	— 159
1865.				" 21 45	—12.3	+14.2	— 149
Feb. 17 22 0	—16.9	+ 3.8	— 160	" 22 0	− 8.7	+17.4	— 137
" 22 30	—17.6	+ 5.3	— 145	" 22 15	− 3.0	+14.4	— 045
" 22 45	—13.0	+ 3.7	— 093	" 22 30	− 5.8	+17.0	+ 085
" 23 0	—10.1	+ 4.2	— 088	" 22 45	+23.9	+ 5.5	+ 316
" 23 15	—18.1	+ 4.2	— 073	" 23 0	+23.8	+ 1.3	+ 315
" 23 30	—21.0	+ 4.3	— 067	" 3 1 0	+67.0	—16.9	+ 843
" 23 45	—15.2	+ 3.7	— 042	" 1 30	+40.7	− 4.8	+ 528
" 18 0 0	—13.0	+ 3.0	— 022	" 2 0	+33.2	− 5.7	+ 433
" 0 15	—10.9	+ 3.2	— 017	" 2 15	+20.6	—16.6	+ 873
" 0 30	− 8.7	+ 2.6	— 002	" 2 30	+58.7	—30.0	+ 927
" 0 45	—10.2	+ 2.6	— 007	" 2 45	+30.7	—11.8	+ 464
" 1 0	− 8.0	+ 2.4	— 005	" 3 0	− 3.9	− 1.5	+ 227
Aug. 2 18 0	+28.9	+ 2.4	— 331	" 4 10 0	+ 5.9	+15.0	— 659
" 18 30	+18.8	+ 6.6	— 448	" 10 15	+ 6.3	+ 8.8	— 481

TORONTO MAGNETICAL OBSERVATIONS.

TABLE XXVI.—(Continued.)

DATES OF LARGE DISTURBANCES, WITH THE AMOUNT OF ABNORMAL VARIATION.

Date.	$\Delta \psi$	$\Delta \theta$	$\dfrac{\Delta \phi}{\phi}$	Date.	$\Delta \psi$	$\Delta \theta$	$\dfrac{\Delta \phi}{\phi}$
1865				1865.			
d h m				d h m			
Aug. 4 10 30	−38.7	+ 9.4	−.00591	Aug. 4 20 15	− 7.9	+ 4.4	−.00160
" 10 45	+ 6.5	+ 5.7	− 0278	" 20 45	−24.1	+ 9.3	− 206
" 11 00	+46.2	+ 2.3	− 0277	1866.			
" 11 15	+33.8	+ 8.6	− 0408	Feb. 20 18 0	− 1.6	+ 5.9	+ 042
" 11 30	+25.5	+21.1	− 0174	" 20 0	+ 4.0	+ 3.7	+ 062
" 11 45	−14.5	+ 1.1	− 0625	" 22 0	+ 8.3	+13.7	− 073
" 12 00	+ 2.1	+24.4	− 1724	" 22 15	+ 6.1	+12.7	− 041
" 12 15	−37.5	+16.1	− 1167	" 22 30	−10.2	+15.2	− 080
" 12 30	+30.9	+15.8	− 1223	" 22 45	−14.1	+13.0	− 020
" 12 45	+ 4.2	+16.1	− 1282	" 23 0	− 3.7	+12.2	− 049
" 13 00	−29.2	+22.0	− 1316	" 23 15	+ 5.7	+ 9.0	+ 096
" 13 15	+23.7	+24.2	− 0833	" 23 30	+ 0.6	+ 6.6	+ 100
" 13 30	−10.9	+34.9	− 1575	" 24 0 0	−11.6	+ 2.5	+ 082
" 13 45	− 0.1	+29.8	− 0866	" 0 30	− 2.8	+ 2.1	+ 052
" 14 00	+12.9	+20.1	− 0692	" 1 0	+ 5.5	+ 1.2	+ 086
" 16 30	−57.2	+35.1	− 0538	1869.			
" 17 00	−14.8	+ 9.4	− 0332	Apr. 15 3 0	+96.7	−64.2	− 215
" 17 30	−38.8	+12.2	− 0618	" 3 15	+45.6	−36.7	+ 386
" 17 45	−42.8	+ 9.1	− 0367	" 3 30	− 1.2	−29.6	+ 435
" 18 00	−38.3	+ 4.2	− 0267	" 3 45	+12.5	−20.7	+ 373
" 18 15	−31.6	+ 5.7	− 0263	" 4 0	− 5.5	−31.3	+ 374
" 18 30	− 6.4	+ 6.8	− 0261	" 4 15	+11.0	−14.4	+ 139
" 18 45	−15.8	+ 6.6	− 0247	" 4 30	− 4.8	− 8.4	+ 187
" 19 00	−21.5	+ 7.9	− 0293	" 4 45	− 7.7	− 7.9	+ 241
" 19 15	−24.5	+13.4	− 0342	" 5 0	+ 6.7	−18.2	+ 410
" 19 30	−30.2	+ 9.1	− 0302	" 5 15	+11.7	−15.0	+ 455
" 19 45	− 6.5	+ 3.9	− 0156	" 5 30	−27.1	−36.4	+ 448
" 20 00	− 5.4	+ 4.6	− 0125	" 5 45	−14.9	−33.1	+ 285

TORONTO MAGNETICAL OBSERVATIONS.

TABLE XXVI.—(Continued.)
DATES OF LARGE DISTURBANCES, WITH THE AMOUNT OF ABNORMAL VARIATION.

Date.	Δψ	Δθ	$\frac{\Delta\phi}{\phi}$	Date.	Δψ	Δθ	$\frac{\Delta\phi}{\phi}$
1869.				1869.			
d h m				d h m			
Apr. 15 6 00	+ 6.0	—24.8	+.00232	Apr. 15 13 00	+10.3	— 2.5	+.00132
" 6 15	+19.5	—24.3	+ 054	" 13 15	+ 3.1	— 1.2	+ 122
" 6 30	+15.2	—23.2	— 238	" 13 30	+13.9	+ 2.3	+ 175
" 6 45	+ 4.4	—18.3	— 406	" 14 00	— 1.9	+ 6.2	+ 050
" 7 00	—12.9	—11.1	— 422	" 14 30	+ 1.7	+ 5.3	+ 014
" 7 15	—54.2	+14.6	— 296	" 15 00	— 4.1	+ 6.4	— 108
" 7 30	—66.9	+15.5	— 552	" 15 30	— 6.3	+ 7.3	+ 052
" 7 45	— 7.8	+ 1.0	— 414	" 16 00	— 2.4	+ 5.9	— 122
" 8 00	— 5.1	+ 6.4	— 914	" 16 30	+ 1.6	+ 5.0	— 111
" 8 15	+17.2	+10.0	— 598	" 17 00	+ 5.9	+ 3.5	+ 077
" 8 30	+25.9	+14.4	— 813	" 18 00	+ 3.2	+ 2.6	— 076
" 8 45	+34.5	+20.7	— 450	" 18 30	+ 7.2	+ 2.9	— 085
" 9 00	+ 5.7	+19.8	— 223	" 19 00	+ 8.4	+ 3.1	— 086
" 9 15	—10.9	+10.4	— 031	" 16 9 00	+11.7	+ 4.0	+ 012
" 9 30	—26.0	+ 2.0	+ 105	" 9 30	+19.4	+ 3.1	— 068
" 9 45	—19.5	— 2.8	+ 011	" 10 00	+ 8.7	+ 4.3	+ 011
" 10 00	+ 4.3	+ 1.1	— 036	" 10 30	+ 3.0	— 0.3	— 353
" 10 15	—21.0	+23.9	— 001	" 11 00	+ 6.3	+ 7.4	— 245
" 10 30	—38.2	+34.6	+ 027	" 11 30	— 3.2	+ 0.7	— 097
" 10 45	+23.7	+14.0	— 651	" 12 00	+ 2.4	+ 1.3	— 077
" 11 00	—74.7	+21.0	+ 196	May 13 2 00	+131.3	—47.9	+ 032
" 11 15	—22.1	+21.2	— 522	" 2 15	+110.4	—31.9	— 1171
" 11 30	+29.0	+25.4	— 325	" 2 30	+19.2	—16.2	— 935
" 11 45	+24.3	+15.2	— 211	" 2 45	+12.0	—13.5	— 1310
" 12 00	+ 7.4	+21.6	— 307	" 3 00	+21.2	—31.4	— 1152
" 12 15	— 0.5	+20.8	— 067	" 3 15	+13.3	—31.3	— 126
" 12 30	+ 4.5	+ 9.2	+ 040	" 3 30	—13.1	—33.0	— 125
" 12 45	+16.6	+ 2.9	+ 015	" 3 45	+13.3	—10.6	+ 009

TABLE XXVI.—*(Continued.)*

DATES OF LARGE DISTURBANCES, WITH THE AMOUNT OF ABNORMAL VARIATION.

Date.	$\Delta \psi$	$\Delta \theta$	$\dfrac{\Delta \phi}{\phi}$	Date.	$\Delta \psi$	$\Delta \theta$	$\dfrac{\Delta \phi}{\phi}$
1869.				1869.			
d h m				d h m			
May 13 4 00	+24.1	−47.5	−.00165	May 13 11 30	−11.9	+ 5.0	+.00010
" 4 15	+31.7	−43.9	+ 001	" 12 00	−10.3	+ 4.5	+ 017
" 4 30	+16.6	−27.4	− 011	1870.			
" 4 45	− 1.8	−18.9	+ 168	Apr. 4 18 00	−16.7	+ 0.5	− 473
" 5 00	+ 2.5	−11.8	+ 199	" 18 30	−24.1	+ 7.2	− 561
" 5 15	− 1.4	−11.9	+ 144	" 19 00	+ 3.9	+ 2.7	− 499
" 5 30	− 5.4	−19.4	− 082	" 19 30	− 0.4	+ 2.0	− 371
" 5 45	− 5.4	−24.1	− 012	" 20 00	+ 1.7	+ 8.3	− 295
" 6 00	−13.2	−16.3	+ 016	" 22 00	+ 8.6	+16.4	− 252
" 6 15	−16.1	− 8.2	+ 264	" 22 10	− 1.6	+12.9	− 251
" 6 30	−13.2	− 1.7	+ 246	" 22 20	− 3.0	+13.0	− 159
" 6 45	−13.7	− 1.7	+ 261	" 22 30	−13.1	+ 9.3	− 131
" 7 00	−11.4	− 1.0	+ 195	" 22 40	−11.7	+ 9.1	− 125
" 7 15	− 8.9	− 0.3	+ 280	" 22 50	− 7.6	+ 8.6	− 102
" 7 30	− 4.5	− 0.5	+ 214	" 23 00	−10.8	+ 8.0	− 118
" 7 45	− 1.3	− 0.7	+ 295	" 23 10	−26.2	− 5.7	− 073
" 8 00	+ 1.4	− 3.0	+ 225	" 23 20	−30.9	− 5.1	− 054
" 8 15	− 2.2	+ 2.3	+ 181	" 23 30	−26.6	+ 3.9	− 042
" 8 30	− 0.8	+ 2.9	+ 216	" 23 40	−20.9	+ 3.2	− 034
" 8 45	+ 1.4	+ 4.7	+ 140	" 23 50	−13.7	+ 4.1	+ 003
" 9 00	− 6.5	+ 5.1	+ 120	" 5 0 00	−16.4	+ 2.6	+ 019
" 9 15	−16.3	+ 5.4	+ 151	" 0 10	− 5.8	+ 1.5	+ 020
" 9 30	− 7.3	+ 4.9	+ 094	" 0 20	−12.2	+ 3.2	− 033
" 9 45	− 8.4	+ 4.7	+ 072	" 0 30	− 1.1	+ 4.5	− 083
" 10 00	− 8.7	+ 4.6	+ 062	" 0 40	− 2.5	+ 4.8	− 013
" 10 30	−12.5	+ 4.9	+ 034	" 0 50	+ 2.9	+ 2.2	+ 008
" 11 00	− 8.7	+ 3.9	+ 044	" 1 00	+ 7.2	+ 2.1	+ 081

ABSTRACTS AND RESULTS

OF

METEOROLOGICAL OBSERVATIONS.

AT THE

MAGNETIC OBSERVATORY,

TORONTO,

FROM 1841 TO 1871 INCLUSIVE,

With Tables of Daily Means from 1863 to 1871.

CONTENTS.

TABLE.		PAGE
XIV.	Monthly and yearly means of the Diurnal Change of Temperature (exclusive of that due to annual variation), from 6 a.m. to 6 a.m., for the periods 1854-59 inclusive, and 1860-62 inclusive, arranged according to the daily resultant direction of the wind	20
XV.	Monthly and annual means of the Barometric Pressure for each of the twenty-four hours of Toronto Astronomical time, and for the twenty-four hours collectively, from hourly observations in the six years from 1st July, 1842, to 30th June, 1848. (Barometer at 32° = 29 inches + the numbers in the Table)	21
XVI.	Monthly and annual means of the Barometric Pressure in each of the thirty-one years from 1841 to 1871, with the monthly and annual means for the whole period, and for three groups of twelve, nine, and ten years respectively; also the probable variability of the monthly and annual means in a single year. (Barometer at 32° = 27 inches + the numbers in the Table)	22
XVII.	Highest readings of the Barometer observed in each month, and in the year, from 1841 to 1871, together with the averages derived from thirty-one years, and from groups of twelve, nine, and ten years. The month in which the highest reading of each year occurs is indicated by an asterisk. (Barometer at 32° = 27 inches + the numbers in the Table)	23
XVIII.	Lowest readings of the Barometer observed in each month and in the year, from 1841 to 1871, together with the averages derived from thirty-one years, and from groups of twelve, nine and ten years. (The month in which the lowest reading of each year occurs is indicated by an asterisk. Barometer at 32° = 27 inches + the numbers in the Table)	24
XIX.	Range of the Barometer, expressed in inches, in each month and in the year, from 1841 to 1871, together with the averages derived from the thirty-one years, and from groups of twelve, nine, and ten years	25
XX.	Normal daily means of the Barometric Pressure and the Pressure of Vapour, on every 5th or 6th day in the year, from observations in the years 1859-68 inclusive	26
XXI.	Changes in Barometric Pressure, Pressure of Dry Air, and Pressure of Vapor, which take place in two hours, during winds from each of the thirty-two points of the compass	27
XXII.	Monthly and annual means of the Pressure of Dry Air, for each of the twenty-four hours of Toronto Astronomical time, and for the twenty-four hours collectively, from hourly observations in the six years, 1st July, 1842, to 30th June, 1848	28
XXIII.	Monthly and annual means of the Pressure of Dry Air from 1841 to 1871 (omitting 1847), with the monthly and annual means for the whole period, and for three groups of eleven, nine, and ten years...	29
XXIV.	Monthly means of Temperature, Barometric Pressure, and Pressure of Dry Air, at the hours 2, 4, 10, 12, 18, 20, Toronto mean time, from the years 1841 to 1871 inclusive	30
XXV.	Monthly and annual means of the Pressure of Vapor for each of the twenty-four hours Toronto Astronomical time, and for the twenty-four hours collectively, from hourly observations in the six years, 1st July, 1842, to 30th June, 1848	31
XXVI.	Monthly and annual means of the Pressure of Vapor from 1841 to 1871, with the monthly and annual means for the whole period, and for three groups of eleven, nine, and ten years, 1847 being omitted from the combinations	32
XXVII.	Monthly and annual means of the Relative Humidity for each of the twenty-four hours, Toronto Astronomical time, and for the twenty-four hours collectively, from hourly observations in the six years, 1st July, 1842, to 30th June, 1848	33

CONTENTS.

Table.		Page.
XXVIII.	Monthly and annual means of the Relative Humidity from 1841 to 1871, both inclusive, with the averages derived from the whole series, omitting the year 1847	34
XXIX.	Monthly means of the extent of Sky Clouded, derived from six daily observations in each of the years from 1853 to 1871 inclusive, the hemisphere being expressed by 100	35
XXX.	Monthly means of the extent of Sky Clouded at each of the six ordinary observation hours, derived from the nineteen years, 1853 to 1871 inclusive	36
XXXI.	Depth of Rain in inches in each month and in the year, from 1840 to 1871 inclusive, months belonging to incomplete years being excluded from the general means	36
XXXII.	Depth of Snow in inches in each month and in the year, from 1843 to 1871 inclusive	37
XXXIII.	Aggregate of Rain and Melted Snow in inches, for each month and for the year, from 1843 to 1871 inclusive. (The months belonging to incomplete years are not included in general means)	38
XXXIV.	Number of days on which Rain fell in each month and in the year, from 1840 to 1871 inclusive	39
XXXV.	Number of days on which Snow fell in each month and in the year, from 1840 to 1871 inclusive	40
XXXVI.	The greatest depth of Rain which fell on a single day, in each month from 1840 to 1871. (The month which includes the day of heaviest rain is marked with an asterisk)	41
XXXVII.	Comparative duration of the several Winds on days in any part of which Rain or Snow fell, from observations in the two periods, 1853-57 and 1858-62. Rain and Snow are considered separately, and are grouped in classes, distinguished as Light, Moderate, and Heavy	42
XXXVIII.	Resultant direction of the Wind for each month and year, from 1848 to 1871, and also the monthly and annual resultants for the whole period. (The direction in every case is measured from the North)	43
XXXIX.	Resultant velocity of the Wind for each month and year, from 1848 to 1871, and also the monthly and annual resultants for the whole period	44
XL.	Mean velocity of the Wind for each month and year, from 1848 to 1871, and also the monthly and annual mean velocities for the whole period	45
XLI.	Resultant direction of the Wind in each hour, Astronomical time, for each month and for the year, from observations in the six years, 1854 to 1859 inclusive. (The direction in every case is measured from the North)	46
XLII.	Resultant velocity of the Wind in each hour, for each month and for the year, from observations in the six years, 1854 to 1859 inclusive. (Velocities in miles per hour)	47
XLIII.	Mean velocity of the Wind in each of the twenty-four hours, Astronomical time, for the four quarters and for the year, derived from two groups of years, including the six years, 1848-53, and the seventeen years, 1855-71	48
XLIV.	Mean velocity of the Wind in each of the twenty-four hours, for the four quarters and for the year, expressed in terms of the mean velocity of the twenty-four hours for the corresponding quarter; being the quotients obtained by dividing the numbers in the preceding Table by the respective averages for twenty-four hours	49

CONTENTS.

TABLE.		PAGE.
XLV.	—Relative duration of different Winds in each month, from hourly observations in the years 1853-62, being the duration of the different Winds expressed in terms of the average duration of all Winds in the month ; also the relative duration of the different Winds in each quarter, and in the year, for 1845-57, and 1858-62..................	50
XLVI.	—Number of Auroras observed in each month, from 1841 to 1871, both inclusive..	51
XLVII.	—Number of days on which Thunder, Lightning, Hail, Fog, Dew, or Aurora was recorded, and the number of days in which it was possible to see Aurora in each year, from 1853 to 1871, both inclusive ; and the ratio of the number of Auroras observed to the possibility of their being seen, with the ratios showing the relative frequency of the several years...	52
XLVIII.	—Number of days on which Thunder, Lightning, Hail, Fog, Dew, and Aurora were recorded for each month, for the period extending from 1853 to 1871, both inclusive, with the ratios showing the relative frequency in the several months.............................	52
XLIX.	—Dates of certain Periodic Events............................	53
L.	—Normal Temperatures on every fifth or sixth day in the year, at each of the hours 2, 4, 10, 12, 18, 20. Toronto mean time, from observations in the years 1859 to 1868, both inclusive.......	54-55
LI.	—Mean abnormal variations of Temperature, with their proper signs, arranged according to the direction of the wind at the time of observation, in each month, in each quarter, and in the year, from the eight years 1860-67, derived from Table XIII, by the application of certain corrections..	56

General Tables of Daily Means, etc., etc., for every month from 1863 to 1871 inclusive.

INTRODUCTION TO ABSTRACTS

OF

METEOROLOGICAL OBSERVATIONS.

The Tables collected in this volume are of the following classes:—
(1.) Tables of daily means, &c., from 1863 to 1871 inclusive.
(2.) Tables of sundry data as far back as they could be procured, and continued to the end of 1871.
(3.) Tables exhibiting various meteorological relations based on combinations of several years, including several which have been taken or abridged from volumes or articles already published.

The discussion of the temperature observations for 1841-52, as far as concerns the computation of the Tables of diurnal variation, the normal daily means, 1841-52, and the probable variability of the actual daily means in the same years, is extracted or abridged from a paper of Sir E. Sabine, as stated further on. All other deductions that have appeared before are from the Toronto volumes, 1854-59, 1860-62, and from articles in the *Canadian Journal*.

TEMPERATURE OF THE AIR.

The thermometers, throughout the series, were exposed on the north wall of the Observatory, in a shed formed of Venetian slats which extended to a distance from the ground of three to four feet.

From January, 1845, to December, 1852, the shed had a second roof, and a second enclosure of Venetian slats eighteen inches exterior to the first.

In no case was any screen interposed between the thermometers and the ground, or between the thermometers and the wall of the Observatory; this mode of exposure, though to some extent faulty, being retained to avoid a breach of continuity in the series.

The thermometers were attached to two slips of wood extending east and west from end to end of the shed, at such a height as to allow the bulbs to be $4\frac{1}{2}$ feet from the soil.

Reduction of the Temperature Observations.

In effecting the reduction of these observations, the first process was to determine the corrections for diurnal variation.

The details are given by General Sir E. Sabine, in a paper read before the Royal Society, February 10, 1853, "On the periodic and non-periodic variations of the temperature at Toronto, from 1841-52 inclusive." The following were the chief steps in the investigation :—

(1.) From hourly observations, July 1, 1842, to June 30, 1848, a Table was formed, giving the six-year averages of the monthly and annual means of temperature.

(2.) From the twelve monthly and annual means was constructed separately for each hour an interpolating formula, which may be thus written :—

$$t_n = a_0 + t_1 \sin(n \times 30° + C_1) + t_2 \sin(2n \times 30° + C_2) + \&c.,$$
$$+ t_5 \sin(5n \times 30° + C_5) \times t_6 \sin(6n \times 30° + C_6).$$

where t_n is the *provisional* normal temperature at the time (n), measured from January 15, the unit of time being the twelfth part of a year.

(3.) From the twenty-four formulæ corresponding to each of the separate hours were computed provisional normals for every hour, and for every fifth day in the year.

(4.) The corrections for diurnal variation for every fifth day were then obtained by subtracting the normals at every hour from the corresponding daily mean normals.

The results are given in Table I of this volume.

From January, 1841, to June, 1842, and from September, 1850, to April, 1851, the observations were at every second hour; and from January to April, 1850, and from July to August, 1850, at every hour.

In these cases, as well as in the six years of continuous hourly observations, the means of the observations without correction were taken as the means of the day; but in all other parts of the twelve years which extend from January, 1841, to December, 1852, corrections for diurnal variation were applied individually to the several observations; and the mean temperatures of the several days were then computed from the means of the observations so corrected.

The mean daily temperatures during the broken periods, including in all six complete years, were then grouped into monthly means, which were again combined with the monthly means from the six years, July, 1842, to June, 1848, yielding the following monthly means from the observations of twelve years :—

January...24.97	April...41.14	July......66.41	October....44.93
February..23.40	May ...51.18	August.....66.16	November..35.51
March 30.23	June...61.05	September..58.02	December..26.75
		Year....44.23	

From an interpolating formula derived from the foregoing twelve monthly means, the normal daily means of temperature were computed for every day in the year. They are given in Table IV of Sir E. Sabine's paper, and in Table II of this volume.

Finally, by applying to the normal daily means in Table II the corrections from Table I, with their signs changed, the normal temperatures may be found for every hour and for every day in the year.

Normals thus computed were employed as standards of reference in the Toronto Tables published in the *Canadian Journal* to the end of 1868.

During and prior to the time when the observations were made, on which General Sabine based his conclusions (1841-52), the mean temperature of January exceeded very decidedly the mean of February in other parts of North America, as well as at Toronto. Testimony to this effect is given by Dove, who describes the isothermal lines as moving southwards from January to February. Observations of subsequent years, however, at other places, even more than at Toronto, show a preponderance in the temperature of February, thus :—

At Isle Jesus (near Montreal).. 1853-62, February was warmer than January by 3°.4
Quebec...................... 1860-67,   "   "   "   3.6
St. John, New Brunswick..... 1861-68,   "   "   "   3.6
Halifax 1867-69,   "   "   "   2.3
Stratford, Ontario 1861-69,   "   "   "   1.9
Toronto 1859-68,   "   "   "   1.8

That the change in the time when the greatest cold occurs in Toronto has been a progressive change, is shown by comparing the means of January and February in groups of five years :

1841-45, Jan. warmer than Feb. by 2°.6 | 1856-60, Jan. colder than Feb. by 0°.3
1846-50,   "   "   "   2.6 | 1861-65,   "   "   "   1.5
1851-55,   "   "   "   0.9 | 1866-69,   "   "   "   2.1

As it is manifest from the foregoing facts that the old normals were not suitable as standards wherewith to compare the observations of more recent years, new normals were computed from the ten years 1859 to 1868, for each day in the year, and for each of the six ordinary hours of observation, namely :—

6 a.m., 8 a.m.
2 p.m., 4 p.m., 10 p.m., and midnight.

Taking each hour separately, and adopting in the first instance the erroneous hypothesis that monthly means represent the temperatures proper to the middle days of the respective months, six interpolating formulæ were constructed of the annexed form :—

$$t_n = t_0 + t_1 \sin(n \times 30° + C_1) + t_2 \sin(2n \times 30° + C_2) + \&c.$$

The coefficients t_1, t_2, &c., were then modified by multiplying them respectively by

$$\frac{\frac{\text{II}}{12}}{\sin\frac{\text{II}}{12}} \quad ; \quad \frac{\frac{2\text{II}}{12}}{\sin\frac{2\text{II}}{12}} \quad ; \quad \frac{\frac{3\text{II}}{12}}{\sin\frac{3\text{II}}{12}} \quad \&c.$$

The normal daily means of temperature from six daily observations in the ten years 1859-68, or the means of the six normals proper to each day, are given in Table III.

The normals computed separately for each of the six observation hours are given in Table L, for every fifth or sixth day through the year.

The following are the formulæ for the different hours employed in the computation of Table L:—

2h.

$T_2 = 48°.99 + 24°.98 \sin (x + 261° 57') + 0°.50 \sin (2x + 27° 18')$
$\qquad + 0°.73 \sin (3x + 262° 17') + 0°.75 \sin (4x + 10° 10')$
$\qquad + 0°.69 \sin (5x + 36°) + 0°.22 \sin (6x + 90°).$

4h.

$T_4 = 48°.57 + 25°.04 \sin (x + 262° 54') + 0°.72 \sin (2x + 27° 19')$
$\qquad + 0°.71 \sin (3x + 265° 59') + 0°.79 \sin (4x + 11° 36')$
$\qquad + 0°.66 \sin (5x + 31° 40') + 0°.22 \sin (6x + 90°).$

10h.

$T_{10} = 42°.63 + 21°.68 \sin (x + 261° 7') + 0°.35 \sin (2x + 35° 33')$
$\qquad + 0°.89 \sin (3x + 267° 59') + 0°.80 \sin (4x + 359° 8')$
$\qquad + 0°.70 \sin (5x + 26° 13') + 0°.29 \sin (6x + 90°).$

Midnight.

$T_{12} = 41°.55 + 21°.19 \sin (x + 260° 40') + 0°.31 \sin (2x + 38° 39')$
$\qquad + 0°.97 \sin (3x + 269° 28') + 0°.89 \sin (4x + 5° 25')$
$\qquad + 0°.79 \sin (5x + 21° 9') + 0°.26 \sin (6x + 90°).$

18h.

$T_{18} = 40°.34 + 21°.61 \sin (x + 260° 38') + 0°.93 \sin (2x + 128° 31')$
$\qquad + 0°.94 \sin (3x + 276° 35') + 0°.81 \sin (4x + 359° 9')$
$\qquad + 0°.76 \sin (5x + 22° 56') + 0°.27 \sin (6x + 90°).$

20h.

$T_{20} = 43°.08 + 24°.31 \sin (x + 262° 4') + 0°.50 \sin (2x + 104° 11')$
$\qquad + 0°.71 \sin (3x + 260° 16') + 0°.80 \sin (4x + 0°)$
$\qquad + 0°.79 \sin (5x + 26° 34') + 0°.28 \sin (6x \times 90°).$

The days when the temperature attains its extreme and mean values for each hour, and the values of the maxima and minima are shown in the following Table:—

TORONTO METEOROLOGICAL OBSERVATIONS. 5

1859-68.	MINIMA.		SPRING MEAN.	MAXIMA.		AUTUMN MEAN.
	Day.	Temp.	Day.	Day.	Temp.	Day.
2 P. M.	January 7	24.3°	April 23	July 25	75.0°	October 23
4 P. M.	" 5	23.7	" 22	" 24	74.8	" 22
10 P. M.	" 6	20.8	" 24	" 23	65.4	" 25
Midnight	" 5	20.1	" 24	" 22	63.9	" 26
6 A. M.	" 8	19.2	" 26	" 18	63.3	" 25
8 A. M.	" 7	19.2	" 23	" 21	68.4	" 22
Six hours	" 6	21.2	" 24	" 22	68.5	" 23

To exhibit in a more distinct manner the changes which the positions of the epochs of maximum and minimum temperatures in the annual period have undergone, from the series 1841-52 to 1859-68, the dates and temperatures are placed below in juxtaposition, together with the corresponding numbers in the years 1861-69, forwarded by Mr. C. J. Macgregor, M.A., meteorological observer at Stratford, Ontario.

	MINIMA.		SPRING MEAN.	MAXIMA.		AUTUMN MEAN.
	Day.	Temp.	Day.	Day.	Temp.	Day.
Toronto, 1841-52	February 12	23.4°	April 25	July 28	68.9°	October 17
" 1859-68	January 6	21.2	" 24	" 22	68.5	" 23
Stratford, 1861-69	" 15	19.9	" 19	" 15	67.1	" 20

On the probable variability of Daily Means of Temperature at different seasons.

(1.) Taking the difference between the normal daily means of temperature derived from the period of twelve years, and the means of the corresponding day in each of the twelve years, the non-periodic variations of each day are obtained.

(2.) Grouping together the non-periodic variation in periods of five days, and taking the difference (Δ) between the mean of each group, and its several members, the *probable daily non-periodic variation* is then computed from the formula :—

$$\text{Variability} = .6745 \sqrt{\frac{\Sigma \Delta^2}{(n-1)}}$$

(3.) Finally, collecting the latter into monthly and seasonal averages, there is found for the twelve years, what has been termed the probable variability of the *daily* temperature in the several months and seasons, as shown below :—

1841-52.

Winter.	Spring.	Summer.	Autumn.
December..5̊.6	March. ...5̊.0	June......4̊ 0	September..4̊.1
January ...6.6	April.....4.3	July 3.5	October 4.0
February ..6.5	May......4.2	August....3 0	November..4.0
Means..6.2	4.5	3 5	4.2

From the above it is inferred that in the winter the temperature of a day is as likely to differ from its normal state, 6°.2 or *more*, as it is to differ *less* than that amount.

By a process precisely similar to that employed by General Sir E. Sabine, in the production of the preceding Table, the following numbers are found for the years 1859-68 :—

Winter.	Spring.	Summer.	Autumn.
December..6̊.8	March....5̊.1	June......4̊.0	September .4̊ 2
January... 6.5	April.....4.1	July 3 8	October 4 6
February ..6.4	May......4.0	August....3.4	November..4.3
Means..6.6	4.4	3 4	4.4

Monthly and Annual Means of the Temperature of the Air at Toronto, from 1841 to 1871—Table IV.

To this Table have been added approximate monthly means obtained from observations by Rev. C. Dade, prior to the establishment of the Observatory, during portions of the years extending from January, 1831, to April, 1841.

In consequence of the absence of Mr. Dade, observations were suspended in August and September, 1831 and 1833 ; also for a few days in August, 1835, and again from October, 1838, to June, 1839, both inclusive. Excepting in the breaks above named, and occasionally in the early part of 1831, when the readings were at 7 a.m., the thermometer was read daily, Sunday included, at 8 a.m. on every day *but one*. Readings were also made at noon and at 5 p.m., but with large and numerous breaks, sometimes one hour and sometimes both having been omitted. To combine these materials so as to form monthly means, the method adopted was to reduce each reading to the mean of the day, by applying to it the corrections given in Table I of this volume, and, dividing the sum of all the corrected readings in like months of different years by the number of the readings, to regard the quotients thus found as the approximate monthly means.

Formulæ for computing Normal Daily Means from the Monthly Means at the foot of Table IV.

If, in the first instance, the erroneous assumption be admitted that the mean temperatures of the several months are the means proper to their middle days, the mean temperature t_n at a time (n), reckoned from January 15 (the unit being the twelfth part of a year), will be given by an expression of the following form, from which, by making $n = 0$, $n = 1$, &c., $n = 11$, the means of the several months would be reproduced.

$$t_n = T_0 + t_1 \sin(n \times 30° + C_1) + t_2 \sin(2n \times 30° + C_2) + \text{&c.,} + t_r \sin(rn \times 30° + C_r) + \text{&c.}$$

The error introduced by the assumption stated above is removed by multiplying the several coefficients respectively by the factors :—

$$\frac{\frac{\Pi}{12}}{\sin \frac{\Pi}{12}} \; ; \; \frac{2\frac{\Pi}{12}}{\sin 2\frac{\Pi}{12}} \; \text{&c.} \; ; \; \frac{r\frac{\Pi}{12}}{\sin r\frac{\Pi}{12}} \; ;$$

whence a more correct formula is obtained, as follows :

$$T_n = T_0 + T_1 \sin(n \times 30° + C_1) + T_2 \sin(2n \times 30° + C_2)$$
$$+ T_3 \sin(3n \times 30° + C_3) + T_4 \sin(4n \times 30° + C_4)$$
$$+ T_5 \sin(5n \times 30° + C_5) + T_6 \sin(6n \times 30° + C_6).$$

Corresponding to the five groups of means at the foot of Table IV, the values of the constants are as follows :—

	T_0	T_1	C_1	T_2	C_2	T_3	C_3	T_4	C_4	T_5	C_5	T_6	C_6
1831-41	41.26	22.71	264 7	1.22	118 30	0.73	210 52	0.90	111 11	1.38	89 9	0.89	90
1841-52	44.23	22.06	261 29	1.11	71 32	0.88	167 41	0.26	37 25	1.19	50 33	0.51	90
1853-61	44.06	23.21	260 51	0.36	82 2	0.57	232 58	0.25	18 10	0.93	49 9	0.47	90
1862-71	44.21	23.55	261 43	0.53	78 11	0.21	207 31	0.78	41 16	0.81	5 5	0.10	90
1841-71	44.17	22.89	261 22	0.70	74 27	0.50	190 11	0.42	41 52	0.94	38 44	0.36	90

From the final column of Table IV, showing the differences between the mean temperature of each year and the general annual mean from 31 years, it is found that the average deviation without regard to sign is only 0.66. The warmest year in the series was 1846, with a difference from the average of $+ 2°.19$, and the coldest, 1856—difference ($- 1°.99$), giving a total range of $4°.18$.

Probable Variability of the several Monthly Means of Temperature.

For the years 1841 to 1852, the numbers expressing the probable variability for the several months, computed by General Sabine, were as follows :

January.. ±2°.7 April.... ±1°.9 July....... ±1°.1 October.... ±1°.4
February. ±2.6   May .... ±1.8   August..... ±1.2   November.. ±2.1
March ... ±2.8   June .... ±2.0 September.. ±1.8   December.. ±2.5
And for the year, ±0°.63.

The following are the analagous numbers for the period 1841-71, from the formula, variability $= .6715 \sqrt{\frac{\Sigma \Delta^2}{n-1}}$, where Δ is the difference between the mean of a month in a single year and the general mean from similar months in the whole series of (n) years :—

January.. $\pm \overset{\circ}{3}.0$	April.... $\pm \overset{\circ}{1}.6$	July .... $\pm \overset{\circ}{1}.7$	October.... $\pm \overset{\circ}{1}.7$
February. ± 2.6	May .... ± 1.9	August..... $\pm 1\ 3$	November . ± 1.8
March ... ± 2.6	June .... ± 1.9	September.. ± 1.8	December.. ± 2.5

And for the year, $\pm 0^{\circ}.60$.

or the mean temperature of a single year is as likely to differ from the average of 31 years by $0^{\circ}.6$ or *more*, as it is to differ *less* than that amount.

In Tables V, VI, VII, are given the *monthly means* of the daily maxima, daily minima, and daily ranges of temperature in each year, with combinations of like monthly means in averages of several years; and in Table VIII are the greatest daily ranges in each month, with analagous combinations. To compare the different groups, the averages for each month have been collected into averages for the year, as follows :—

	Maximum.	Minimum.	Daily Range.	Greatest Daily Range.
1841-48.....	$5\overset{\circ}{2}.62$	$3\overset{\circ}{6}.14$	$1\overset{\circ}{6}.48$	1841-52.... $2\overset{\circ}{6}.88$
1853-61.....	51.69	35.50	16.19	1853-61.... 27.34
1862-71.....	52.12	36.95	15.17	1862-71.... 26.22
The whole..	52.12	36.22	15.90	1841-71.... 26.80

Tables IX, X, XI, show the absolutely highest temperatures in each month, the absolutely lowest, and the monthly ranges, with combinations of like monthly means in averages of several years. The following are the averages for the year, found from the monthly averages in the several groups :—

	Highest Maximum.	Lowest Minimum.	Monthly Ranges.
1841-52	$6\overset{\circ}{6}.21$	$1\overset{\circ}{9}.82$	$4\overset{\circ}{6}.39$
1853-61	66.78	19.13	• 46.65
1862-71	66.86	20.52	46.34
1841-71	66.58	19.84	46.74

Connection of Temperature with the Direction of the Wind.

In order to judge whether the observed value of any element is abnormally high or low, it has been the practice, as soon as the entry has been made in the daily register, to enter in a column adjacent to that in which the element is recorded, the difference between the observed value and the normal (or what is taken as such) for the day and hour; the difference being marked + or −, according as the observed is greater or less than the standard value.

Normals obviously cannot be derived from a series in which the current observations are included; yet, provided that they have been computed from a series of sufficient length, the differences recorded from day to day, will serve to indicate in a general way the relative values of the element : if, however, it be desired to obtain accurate measures of the mean abnormal variations during any period of years, or of their connection with the direction of the wind, or any coexistent phenomena whatever, the standards ought to be derived from the observations of *all* the years in that period, and from those years *alone ;* and hence, the differences recorded, as above stated, in the daily register are not, in strictness, suitable materials for such enquiries. Nevertheless, as the results of certain computations based on the abnormal differences between current observations and normals obtained from older series, although not strictly accurate, are not without some value, it has been thought best, either to print the results after the application of approximate corrections, or to print them as they stand, explaining in each case the method of correction applied.

Table X of the volume of Toronto Meteorological Abstracts for 1854-59, contains the mean abnormal variations of temperature, with their proper signs, arranged according to the direction of the wind to the nearest of the sixteen points, with the number of times which the wind blew from each point, and the partial results of each year, as well as the general results.

The normals to which the observed temperatures are referred in this Table, having been computed from the twelve years, 1841-52, and being therefore not necessarily applicable to 1853-59, some modifications in the results will be required. This has been effected by applying to the general means of the variations corresponding to different winds in the seven years, as an approximate correction, a constant $+0°.26$, that being the difference by which the mean temperature of 1841-52 exceeded that of 1853-59. The general results thus modified are given below :—

N. -2.54	E. $+1.99$	S. $+3.15$	W. -1.92
N.N.E. -2.02	E.S.E. $+1.44$	S.S.W. $+3.87$	W.N.W. -2.91
N.E. -1.55	S.E. $+2.05$	S.W. $+3.71$	N.W. -3.28
E.N.E. $+1.63$	S.S.E. $+2.54$	W.S.W. -0.47	N.N.W. -3.32
	Calms $+1.59$		

From this Table it appears that the temperature was above or below the normal, according as the wind blew from a point lying to the south or north of a line stretching from about N.E.^{b}E. to S.W.^{b}W.; the greatest depression, $-3°.32$, being with a wind from N.N.W., and the greatest elevation, $+3°.87$, with a wind from S.S.W.

Although modified by the application of the constant, $+0°.26$, these numbers are liable to other errors, namely, those which may arise from massing together abnormal variations for all parts of the year, whereby opposite effects, that may be proper to different seasons, may in some degree neutralize each other.

Table XIII was formed from the observations of the eight following years, 1860-67, by a process similar to that employed for 1853-59, excepting that the months were dealt with separately, the aggregate algebraical sum of the abnormal deviation for the eight years for each month and wind, being divided by the number of times when the wind under consideration, was blowing in the month of the same name at the time of observation.

The means for the quarter and year are deduced from the aggregate sums and numbers for the quarters and year.

This Table, as well as that for 1853-59, is affected by the circumstance that the normals to which the observed temperatures were referred, (the normals deduced from 1841-52) were not strictly applicable to the years 1860-67.

The anomalies that may be noticed in Table XIII, are due in some degree to the cause just stated, as well as to the insufficient number of times when the wind, in certain months, blew from some of the points. Thus, while the number of times for each month and wind is about 146 in the eight years, on the average of all months and winds; the average number of times when the wind from the S.E. occurred was only about 58 on the average of the twelve months.

The errors in Table XIII, occasioned by referring the temperature observed in 1860-67 to normals deduced from 1841-52, may be lessened, although not entirely removed, by applying to the results of each month, as an approximate correction, the differences between the mean temperatures of the several months deduced from the two series, 1841-52 and 1860-67, the corrections being + or −, according as the mean from the older series is greater or less than that from 1860-67.

The following are the corrections for the months, quarters, and year.

Jan.	Feb.	Mar.	April.	May.	June.	July.	Aug.	Sept.	Oct.	Nov.	Dec.
$+3.48$	-0.59	$+1.12$	-0.17	-0.25	-1.09	-0.71	$+0.31$	$+0.04$	-2.49	-1.05	$+0.50$

Winter.	Spring.	Summer.	Autumn.	Year.
$+1.13$	$+0.23$	-0.50	-1.16	-0.07

The results obtained by applying the above corrections to the several numbers in Table XIII, are shewn in Table LI.

The preceding enquiries relate to the comparison of the temperatures that accompany different winds at the instant of observation. The effects on the temperature produced by a given wind will be found from the *change* which has occurred in a given time, while that wind has been blowing. To ascertain the effects completely, would require simultaneous and continuous records of wind and temperature: but in the absence of these, an approximate knowledge of the effect may be obtained from the changes in twenty-four hours, which accompany different resultant winds, computed for the same twenty-four hours.

The changes corresponding to resultants to the nearest of the eight points, are shown in Table XIV, for the two groups of years, 1854-59 and 1860-62.

In examining Table XIV it will be seen that, for 1854-59, in every month, with a resultant wind from N.: N.W., and W., the temperature was lowered; in every month, with a resultant wind from S.W., S., S.E., and E., the temperature was raised; and that with a resultant from N.E., the temperature was raised in some months and lowered in others, the total effect in the whole year being a rise with a N.E. resultant.

These remarks are also applicable for the most part to 1860-62, but there are exceptions in the latter group, in consequence of the small number of resultants from some points of the compass; thus, while the average divisor for all the months and winds is 11 nearly, a resultant from the S.E. does not occur at all in January, only twice in February, once in March, and once in April.

BAROMETRIC TABLES.

The barometer in use throughout the series is one by Newman, with a tube of internal diameter of .506 of an inch. The correction for capillarity has not been applied. The readings of the barometer have been corrected for temperature, but not for gravitation; nor have they been reduced to sea level.

In Table XV are given the monthly and annual means for each of the twenty-four hours, derived from hourly observations in the six years—1st July, 1842, to 30th June, 1848. The monthly means in this Table, which correspond to the six ordinary hours of observations, were employed to the close of 1859, as normals or standards with which to compare the actual readings; after which, until the close of 1868, the means at the same hours from eighteen years ending December, 1859, were similarly employed, the same standard for any given hour being used throughout the month.

The standards employed, subsequently to 1868, were derived from the observations of the ten years, 1859 to 1868, in the following manner: The corrected readings of the barometer at the six observation hours during the ten years, being first combined in monthly means, for each of the six hours separately, and for the six hours collectively, the latter, or general means for each month, were subtracted from the six means of the same month proper to the separate hours. The mean diurnal variations or inequalities thus obtained are shown below :—

	Jan.	Feb.	Mar.	April.	May.	June.	July.	Aug.	Sept.	Oct.	Nov.	Dec.
2 P.M.........	−.021	−.015	−.018	−.015	−.007	−.006	−.008	−.011	−.013	−.017	−.020	−.020
4 "	−.012	−.017	−.019	−.024	−.020	−.020	−.021	−.023	−.022	−.018	−.013	−.009
10 "	+.009	−.003	+.003	+.005	−.001	−.001	−.003	−.001	+.004	+.006	+.002	+.011
Midnight.....	+.005	−.009	+.001	+.004	−.003	−.002	−.003	.0	+.002	+.003	−.003	+.009
6 A.M.........	+.004	+.016	+.009	+.016	+.009	+.008	+.012	+.013	+.010	+.006	+.009	−.002
8 "	+.017	+.029	+.021	+.019	+.022	+.021	+.022	+.022	+.020	+.021	+.024	+.011

The mean pressures in each month, from observations at the six hours combined, are shown in the following Table, where pressure = 29 inches + number in the Table.

Jan.	Feb.	Mar.	April.	May.	June.	July.	Aug.	Sept.	Oct.	Nov.	Dec.	Year.
.6105	.6511	.5796	.5986	.5517	.5888	.5942	.6117	.6087	.6487	.6006	.6606	.6102

Assuming that the means of each month are the pressures proper to their middle days, the mean pressure (b_x) proper to any day in the year will be given by the formula :—

$$b_x = .6162 + .0371 \sin(x + 146° 36') + .0174 \sin(2x + 24° 32')$$
$$+ .0147 \sin(3x + 78° 27') + .0127 \sin(4x + 160° 18')$$
$$+ .0147 \sin(5x + 307° 13') + .0135 \sin(6x + 270°)$$

where x is proportional to the time reckoned from 15th January, the whole year being expressed by $360°$.

The normal mean pressures computed from this formula are given in Table XX, at intervals of five or six days through the year.

For finding the daily normal pressures for each of the six observation hours, the approximate method was adopted of applying to the normal daily means the monthly means of the diurnal inequalities given above.

The application of the same diurnal inequalities to the normal daily means throughout the month, occasions a slight breach of continuity in the series of normals for the separate hours in passing from month to month; but the transitions are much less abrupt than where the monthly means of the several hours were adopted for normals, as was the practice prior to 1869.

The normals obtained in the manner above stated, are useful for standards in comparing current observations, and in any investigations relating to the whole of the series, 1859-68. No deductions from them are contained in this volume.

In Table XVI are shewn the monthly means of barometric pressure in each of the thirty-one years, 1841-71, with the monthly means for the three groups of years, and for the whole period.

For computing the daily mean pressures, formulæ were constructed for each of the groups of monthly means, at the foot of Table XVI. The general form is as follows:—

$$b_x = m_0 + m_1 \sin(x + C_1) + m_2 \sin(2x + C_2)$$
$$+ \&c., \&c., + m_6 \sin(6x + C_6)$$

where b_x expresses the mean pressure of any day corresponding to (x), x being proportional to the time reckoned from 15th January. The values of the constants for the different groups of years are shewn below:—

	m_0	m_1	C_1	m_2	C_2	m_3	C_3	m_4	C_4	m_5	C_5	m_6	C_6
1841-52	0.6206	0.0246	152 28	0.0166	317 42	0.0108	163 14	0.0081	193 57	0.0056	160 23	0.0014	270
1853-61	0.6128	0.0484	150 26	0.0137	71 22	0.0250	97 32	0.0122	97 47	0.0177	259 42	0.0005	90
1862-71	0.6154	0.0375	148 32	0.0277	0	0.0144	241 58	0.0107	185 40	0.0120	348 38	0.0018	270
1841-71	0.6166	0.0356	150 23	0.0167	8 31	0.0138	102 11	0.0101	167 14	0.0052	279 9	0.0011	270

These constants, as well as those for the formulæ which relate to barometer reduced to sea level, and to other elements, are given in full, that the reader may judge as to the degree of significance of the higher terms.

Normal Mean Daily Pressures at Sea Level.

As elsewhere stated, the separate barometric readings of the ordinary observations have not been reduced to sea level; hence, to obtain the general form of the annual curve of barometric pressure at sea level, the monthly means at the foot of Table XVI, were reduced to sea level by an approximate method, in which the following formula was employed:—

$$\text{reduction} = \frac{342}{890.6} \left\{ 1 - .002t \right\} = .3840 - .00077t$$

where 342 is the height of the cistern of barometer above sea level,
" 890.6 the height of a column of air at temperature of 40°, whose weight is equal to that of a column of mercury of the same transverse section, and one inch in height,

t the excess above 40° of the mean temperature of the air, for the same month, and same group of years, as given at the foot of Table IV.

The mean pressures, reduced, are shown in the following Table, where barometer at 32° reduced to sea level = 29 + numbers given.

	Jan.	Feb.	Mar.	April.	May.	June.	July.	Aug.	Sept.	Oct.	Nov.	Dec.	Year.
1841-52	1.0296	1.0095	1.0233	0.9991	0.9581	0.9196	0.9609	1.0079	1.0234	1.0207	1.0054	1.0403	1.0011
1853-61	1.0703	1.0225	0.9396	0.9533	0.9617	0.9154	0.9671	0.9696	1.0341	1.0319	0.9968	1.0076	0.9936
1862-71	1.0395	1.0330	1.0063	0.9710	0.9115	0.9559	0.9441	0.9735	1.007	1.0211	0.9943	1.0291	0 9962
1841-71	1.0430	1.0225	0.9935	0.9733	0.9453	0.9418	0.9573	0.9857	1.0408	1.0241	0.9976	1.0466	0.9974

The same notation being adopted as in the case of the unreduced barometric readings, the constants in the interpolating formulæ for expressing, for any day, the mean pressure reduced to sea level, are as follows:—

	m_0	m_1	C_1	m_2	C_2	m_3	C_3	m_4	C_4	m_5	C_5	m_6	C_6
1841-52	1.0014	0.0340	134 56	0.0105	344 56	0.0192	168 4	0.0083	191 50	0.0059	166 53	0.0016	270
1853-61	0.9936	0.0570	133 29	0.0135	71 6	0.0284	96 59	0.0122	98 16	0.0182	258 47	0.0002	90
1862-71	0.9902	0.0475	128 15	0.0276	359 23	0.0145	61 40	0.0201	186 34	0.0116	348 1	0.0019	270
1841-71	0.9974	0.0452	129 3	0.0162	7 27	0.0135	102 3	0.0105	108 57	0.0057	272 24	0.0016	270

In Tables XVII, XVIII, and XIX, are shewn the highest and lowest barometric readings, and the difference between them, or range of the barometer, in each month from 1841-71 inclusive, with the averages derived from thirty-one years, and groups of twelve, nine, and ten years.

The quarterly averages of the several groups are as follows:—

MAXIMA.

Years.	Winter.	Spring.	Summer.	Autumn.
1841-52	30.2311	30.0783	29 9251	30.0954
1853-61	30.2249	30.0585	29.8795	30.0613
1862-71	30.2329	30.0123	29.9107	30.1006
1841-71	30.2331	30.0513	29.9073	30.0959

MINIMA.

Years.	Winter.	Spring.	Summer.	Autumn.
1841-52	28.9175	29.0143	29.2329	29.0831
1853-61	28.9351	28.9891	29.2113	29.0262
1862-71	28.9189	29.0284	29.2093	29.1102
1841-71	28.9231	29.0115	29.2191	29.0753

RANGES.

Years.	Winter.	Spring.	Summer.	Autumn.
1841-52	1.3136	1.0640	0.6922	1.0123
1853-61	1.2898	1.0694	0.6682	1.0551
1862-71	1.3140	0.9839	0.7014	0.9994
1841-71	1.3100	1.0398	0.6882	1.0206

In Table XXIII are given the monthly means of the pressure of dry air in each of the years, 1841-71 (omitting 1847), with the monthly and annual means for the whole period, and for three groups of eleven, nine, and ten years.

For computing daily mean pressures, formulæ of the usual form—

$$D_x = m_0 + m_1 \sin(x + C_1) + m_2 \sin(2x + C_2) + \&c.$$

were constructed for each of the groups of means at the foot of Table XXIII.

The values of the constants for the different groups are as follows:—

Years.	m_0	m_1	C_1	m_2	C_2	m_3	C_3	m_4	C_4	m_5	C_5	m_6	C_6
1841-52	0.3510	0.1966	84° 17′	0.0442	263° 15′	0.0105	123° 41′	0.0103	158° 24′	0.0104	296° 49′	0.0007	270° 00′
1853-61	0.3523	0.2054	91 00	0.0274	248 24	0.0347	95 38	0.0128	87 46	0.0231	250 33	0.0002	270 00
1862-71	0.3561	0.2032	87 11	0.0380	284 00	0.0193	65 33	0.0186	192 24	0.0080	349 5	0.0035	270 00
1841-71	0.3531	0.2016	87 18	0.0361	266 59	0.0193	91 29	0.0103	157 41	0.0092	250 23	0.0014	270 00

The following are the mean differences, without regard to sign, between the pressures of dry air at 6 a.m. on consecutive days in each month, derived from 1860-62:—

Jan.	Feb.	Mar.	April.	May.	June.	July.	Aug.	Sept.	Oct.	Nov.	Dec.	Year.
.310	.321	.258	.224	.201	.219	.209	.194	.234	.237	.240	.275	.243

Table XXIV contains the means of temperature, barometric pressure, and pressure of dry air, at each of the six observation hours, from 1841 to 1871, certain broken months being omitted. The discrepancy between the means from the six hours in this Table, and the general means at the foot of Tables IV, XVI, and XXIII, are due, partly to the fact that six hours only are included in Table XXIV, and more so, to the omissions as stated above, which were rendered necessary by the absence of observations at one or more of the six hours in these months. The months omitted from the above cause, were January to April, in 1849, May and June, in 1849 and 1850, and July to December, in 1848 and 1849.

PRESSURE OF VAPOUR.

The normal daily means of the pressure of vapour given in Table XX, are computed from the following Table of monthly means, from observations in the ten years, 1859-68.

Jan.	Feb.	Mar.	April	May.	June.	July.	Aug.	Sept.	Oct.	Nov.	Dec.	Year.
.1056	.1126	.1365	.1846	.2775	.3900	.4860	.4715	.3745	.2586	.1840	.1210	.2586

The following is the formula for computation :—

$$V_x = .2585 + .1864 \sin(x + 257° 25') + .0392 \sin(2x + 63° 18')$$
$$+ .0085 \sin(3x + 252° 48') + .0033 \sin(4x + 3° 38')$$
$$+ .0011 \sin(5x + 348° 18') + .0020 \sin(6x + 90°).$$

The normals used as standards of reference for the different hours of observation, since 1st January, 1869, were obtained from the daily normals by applying to them the mean diurnal inequalities for the month, in the manner already explained in the case of the barometric pressures.

In Table XXVI are shewn the monthly and annual means of the pressure of vapour in each of the years 1841-71, omitting 1847, and for four combinations of years. The constants in the formulæ for computing the daily mean pressure of vapour, V_x, corresponding to the different groups of years, are as follows :—

Years.	m_0	m_1	C_1	m_2	C_2	m_3	C_3	m_4	C_4	m_5	C_5	m_6	C_6
1841-52	0.2684	0.1906	257 31	0.0455	62 15	0.0069	195 25	0.0050	271 9	0.0094	68 31	0.0007	270 00
1853-61	0.2601	0.1888	258 14	0.0404	68 12	0.0059	261 11	0.0034	202 45	0.0071	28 41	0.0010	90 00
1862-71	0.2587	0.1904	257 33	0.0411	63 45	0.0054	218 12	0.0024	123 2	0.0043	345 19	0.0014	00 00
1841-71	0.2627	0.1890	257 45	0.0426	64 13	0.0053	234 13	0.0019	235 29	0.0063	35 58	0.0006	00 00

The following are the mean differences, without regard to sign, between the pressure of vapour at 6 a.m. on consecutive days in each month, from the three years, 1860-62:—

Jan.	Feb.	Mar.	April.	May.	June.	July.	Aug.	Sept.	Oct.	Nov.	Dec.	Year.
.038	.043	.039	.041	.051	.091	.144	.088	.093	.065	.044	.044	.060

Connection between the Direction of the Wind and the Barometric Pressure, the Pressure of Dry Air, and the Pressure of Vapour.

The annual means of the changes in twenty-four hours, which accompany different resultant winds from 6 a.m. to 6 a.m., are shewn in the following Table, where the changes for the barometer have been deduced from the six years, 1854-59, and from the three years, 1860-62, and the changes for dry air and vapour from the three years, 1860-62:—

	N.	N.E.	E.	S.E.	S.	S.W.	W.	N.W.
Barometer........1854-59	+.097	−.102	−.179	−.197	−.009	−.036	+.144	+.170
Barometer........1860-62	+.076	−.137	−.196	−.178	−.130	−.089	+.142	+.183
Dry Air 1860-62	+.096	−.152	−.240	−.264	−.189	−.109	+.150	+.227
Vapour..........1860-62	−.020	+.015	+.043	+.085	−.057	+.021	−.036	−.044

In the earlier series for the barometer, the signs continue the same through the year, excepting that in April, May, August, and December, the barometer rises with a S.W. resultant.

In 1860-62, owing to the small number of resultants from some of the directions, the exceptions to uniformity of sign through the year are more numerous.

In the following investigation, the changes are those which accompany the different *actual*, as distinct from the *resultant*, winds:—

On the Changes of Barometric Pressures, Pressures of Dry Air, and Vapour, that accompany different Winds, from observations in the Seven Years, 1860-66.

The changes considered are limited to those in which the wind did not vary, between two consecutive observations, by more than $22\frac{1}{2}°$ on each side of one of the principal eight points; and as this constancy of direction more frequently occurs when the interval is short, those differences only have been considered which took place from 6 a.m. to 8 a.m., from 2 p.m. to 4 p.m., and from 10 p.m. to midnight.

The changes between two consecutive observations being first diminished by that due to diurnal variation, the residual changes were classed according to the direction of the wind in the interval, and their averages in each class were then taken, for the year as well as for the two half years.

The average changes of barometric pressure which take place in two hours, and found in the manner just described, are given below for each of the principal eight points of the wind's direction :—

APRIL TO SEPTEMBER.

N.	N.E.	E.	S.E.	S.	S.W.	W.	N.W.
+.0085	—.0043	—.0113	—.0057	—.0084	—.0041	+.0132	+.0150

OCTOBER TO MARCH.

N.	N.E.	E.	S.E.	S.	S.W.	W.	N.W.
+.0087	—.0160	—.0334	—.0313	—.0222	—.0037	+.0168	+.0209

THE YEAR.

N.	N.E.	E.	S.E.	S.	S.W.	W.	N.W
+.0086	—.0103	—.0215	—.0164	—.0129	—.0039	+.0156	+.0180

The most probable values of the changes corresponding to intermediate directions of the wind, are given by the following formulæ, where Ψ_1, Ψ_2, Ψ_3, represent the changes for the two half years and year, and θ the angular distance of the point from which the wind blew, measured from north to east, and expressed in degrees :—

APRIL TO SEPTEMBER.

$$\Psi_1 = +.0004 + .0125 \sin(\theta + 141° 29') + .0044 \sin(2\theta + 186° 29')$$
$$+ .0025 \sin(3\theta + 14° 2')$$

OCTOBER TO MARCH.

$$\Psi_2 = -.0075 + .0281 \sin(\theta + 148° 14') + .0024 \sin(2\theta + 160° 49')$$
$$+ .0014 \sin(3\theta + 30° 15')$$

THE YEAR.

$$\Psi_3 = -.0028 + .0195 \sin(\theta + 148° 2') + .0040 \sin(2\theta + 174° 17')$$
$$+ .0021 \sin(3\theta + 10° 47')$$

Pressure of Dry Air.

The average changes in the pressure of dry air in two hours with different winds, and the corresponding formulæ of interpolation, are as follows :—

APRIL TO SEPTEMBER.

N.	N.E.	E.	S.E.	S.	S.W.	W.	N.W.
+.0146	—.0009	—.0128	—.0088	—.0122	—.0046	+.0195	+.0219

OCTOBER TO MARCH.

N.	N.E.	E.	S.E.	S.	S.W.	W.	N.W.
+.0110	—.0182	—.0371	—.0312	—.0240	—.0026	+.0195	+.0240

THE YEAR.

N.	N.E.	E.	S.E.	S.	S.W.	W.	N.W.
+.0128	—.0091	—.0243	—.0194	—.0160	—.0034	+.0195	+.0229

TORONTO METEOROLOGICAL OBSERVATIONS.   19

April to September.

$\Psi_1 = +.0021 + .0182 \sin(\theta + 135°\,13') + .0048 \sin(2\theta + 193°\,10')$
$\quad + .0034 \sin(3\theta + 10°\,18')$

October to March.

$\Psi_2 = -.0077 + .0317 \sin(\theta + 149°\,4') + .0030 \sin(2\theta + 156°\,2')$
$\quad + .0016 \sin(3\theta + 47°\,29')$

The Year.

$\Psi_3 = -.0021 + .0237 \sin(\theta + 144°\,46') + .0040 \sin(2\theta + 174°\,17')$
$\quad + .0026 \sin(3\theta + 15°\,39')$

Pressure of Vapour.

The average changes in the pressure of vapour in two hours, that accompany winds from the eight principal points, and the formulæ for finding the most probable change, with the wind blowing from any intermediate point, are given below :—

April to September.

N.	N.E.	E.	S.E.	S.	S.W.	W.	N.W.
—.0057	—.0034	+.0020	+.0035	+.0042	+.0001	—.0073	—.0069

October to March.

N.	N.E.	E.	S.E.	S.	S.W.	W.	N.W.
—.0025	+.0009	+.0037	+.0031	+.0017	—.0013	—.0032	—.0039

The Year.

N.	N.E.	E.	S.E.	S.	S.W.	W.	N.W.
—.0041	—.0012	+.0025	+.0034	+.0034	—.0007	—.0046	—.0054

April to September.

$\Psi_1 = -.00169 + .00607 \sin(\theta + 305°\,49') + .00096 \sin(2\theta + 88°\,48')$
$\quad + .00110 \sin(3\theta + 181°\,2')$

October to March.

$\Psi_2 = -.00018 + .00385 \sin(\theta + 330°\,26') + .00034 \sin(2\theta + 287°\,6')$
$\quad + .00022 \sin(3\theta + 243°\,26')$

The Year.

$\Psi_3 = -.00084 + .00479 \sin(\theta + 312°\,43') + .00035 \sin(2\theta + 86°\,44')$
$\quad + .00037 \sin(3\theta + 216°\,15')$

If, in the nine foregoing formulæ, the variable angle, θ, be made equal in succession to $0°$, $11°\,15'$ ($11°\,15'$) × 2, ($11°\,15'$) × 3, &c. .... ($11°\,15'$) × 31, the changes of pressure will be found which would most probably occur if the wind were to blow steadily for two hours from each of the thirty-two points of the compass.

The results are given in Table XXI. By examining this Table, it will be seen that on the average of the year, the barometer rises with a wind from any point between S.W.^{b}W. (measured from left to right) to N.^{b}E., and that it falls with winds from N.N.E. to S.W. The same rule also holds (within a point) in summer and winter separately, and is true also with respect to the changes in the pressure of dry air. The pressure of vapour increases with a wind between E.N.E. to S.W.ᵇS., and diminishes with a wind between S.W. and N.E.

On the average of the year, and during the winter half year, both the rise and fall have an uninterrupted progression; and the same is true in every case where the change is an increase; but in the summer half year, besides the maximum rate of barometric fall which occurs with a wind from E., there is a second inferior maximum fall when the wind is from S.ᵇW. There are also two minima in the rate with which the pressure of dry air diminishes during the summer. They are of equal magnitude, —.0131, and also occur with winds from E. and S.ᵇW.

The most rapid changes, together with the winds that accompany them, are shewn in the following Table:—

Barometric Pressure.

	SUMMER.		WINTER.		YEAR.	
	Change in 2 hours.	Wind.	Change in 2 hours.	Wind.	Change in 2 hours.	Wind.
Most rapid rise ..	+.0162	W.N.W.	+.0214	N.W.ᵇW.	+.0194	N.W.ᵇW.¼W.
Most rapid fall.	−.0113 −.0093	E. S.ᵇW.	−.0343	E.ᵇS.	−.0218	E.

Pressure of Dry Air.

	SUMMER.		WINTER.		YEAR.	
	Change in 2 hours.	Wind.	Change in 2 hours.	Wind.	Change in 2 hours.	Wind.
Most rapid rise ..	+.0237	W.N.W.	+.0247	N.W.ᵇW.	+.0239	N.W.ᵇW.¼W.
Most rapid fall.	−.0131 −.0131	E. S.ᵇW.	−.0379	E.ᵇS.	−.0244	E.

Pressure of Vapour.

	SUMMER.		WINTER.		YEAR.	
	Change in 2 hours.	Wind.	Change in 2 hours.	Wind.	Change in 2 hours.	Wind.
Most rapid rise..	+.0042	S.	+.0037	E.ᵇS.¼S.	+.0037	S.E.ᵇS.¼.S.
Most rapid fall ..	−.0079	W.ᵇN.¼W.	−.0038	N.W.½W.	−.0054	N.W.ᵇW.½W.

EXTENT OF SKY CLOUDED.

From the final column in Table XXIX, shewing the mean extent of sky clouded in the different months and years, from 1853-71, it appears that the mean of the year on the average of nineteen years is 61 (the whole sky clouded being expressed by 100), and that in the different years it varied from 66 to 57. The monthly means shew an uninterrupted progression from a maximum 75, in December, to a minimum 48, in August.

For the different seasons the means are as follows:—

WINTER.	SPRING.	SUMMER.	AUTUMN.
December-February.	March-May.	June-August.	September-November.
73	60	50	62.

From the final column of Table XXX, which shews for every month and for the year the extent of sky clouded at each of the six hours of observation, it appears that of these hours, 2 p.m., on the average of the year, is the most, and 10 p.m. the least, cloudy hour.

From the following Table, shewing for the four seasons the extent of cloud at the several observation hours, it appears that the maximum is at 2 p.m. in every season but the winter, when it is transferred to 8 a.m. In autumn, the minimum lies between 10 p.m. and midnight :—

Hours.	Winter.	Spring.	Summer.	Autumn.
2	76.7	65.3	58.0	66.0
4	75.3	64.3	55.3	63.7
10	67.7	50.7	43.3	57.0
12	68.7	51.7	44.7	57.0
18	74.7	61.3	51.7	62.3
20	77.7	62.0	53.0	63.7

Connection between the Direction of the Wind and the Extent of Sky Clouded.

In the following Table is shewn the amount of cloud that accompanies winds from each of the sixteen points, in the years 1853-59, both inclusive, the hemisphere being expressed by 100, with the amount Δ, by which the several numbers differ from 59, the general average for the seven years :—

Cloud.	Δ	Cloud.	Δ	Cloud.	Δ	Cloud.	Δ
50 N	− 9	70 E	+11	48 S	−11	57 W	− 2
65 N.N.E.	+ 6	64 E.S.E.	+ 5	58 S.S.W.	− 1	53 W.N.W.	− 6
74 N.E.	+15	57 S.E.	− 2	67 S.W.	+ 8	53 N.W.	− 6
80 E.N.E.	+21	49 S.S.E.	−10	64 W.S.W.	+ 5	48 N.N.W.	−11

Cloud.	Δ
Calms	55 − 4

The corresponding numbers to the nearest eight points, from 1860-62, are as follows. General mean for the three years, 62 :—

Cloud.	Δ	Cloud.	Δ	Cloud.	Δ	Cloud.	Δ
54 N	− 8	77 E	+15	56 S	− 6	63 W	+ 1
76 N.E.	+14	63 S.E.	+ 1	68 S.W.	+ 6	49 N.W.	−13

Cloud.	Δ
Calms	55 − 7

RAIN AND SNOW.

On examining the yearly totals in Tables XXXI, XXXII, and XXXIII, very considerable irregularities may be noticed in the amount of rain and snow that fell in different years.

If the years prior to 1845 be left out of consideration, it will be found that the average difference between the rain in different years, and the mean of the twenty-six years, is 3.55 nearly ; that in 1866 there was a maximum, with an excess of 6.11 inches nearly ; and that in 1867 there was a minimum, the difference in defect being 9.05 inches nearly. Taking the same years, 1846-71, the average deviation from the mean, in the amount of snow in different years, was 17.9; there was a maximum excess of 53 inches in 1870, and a minimum in 1851, with a deficiency of 31 inches.

In Table XXXIII are given the total amounts of precipitation of rain, and the water equivalent of snow, on the supposition that one inch of snow is equivalent to one-tenth of an inch of water.

Taking the same twenty-six years, it is found that the actual precipitation in different years differs from the average by quantities whose average value, without regard to sign, is 3.98 inches nearly.

The maximum of precipitation occurred in 1870, with an excess of 11.13 inches; and the minimum in 1848, with a deficiency of 8.25 inches nearly.

If the mean annual fall of rain and snow in two equal groups, 1846-58 and 1859-71, be compared, it is seen that while there has been a diminution in the rain, the snow has increased, and also that the precipitation on the whole has increased:—

Years.	Rain.	Snow.	Total.
1846-58	28.552	60.82	34.634
1859-71	27.639	78.46	35.485
Change.... Decrease..	0.913 Increase..	17.64 Increase..	0.851

Again, on comparing the *number of days* in the two groups, from Tables XXXIV and XXXV, a decided increase is found in the days both of rain and snow:—

Years.	Rain.	Snow.
1846-58	106.4 days.	53.6 days.
1859-71	120.3 days.	76.0 days.
Change..... Increase..	13.9 days. Increase..	22.4 days.

From Table XXXVI, where the heaviest falls in a single day in each month are recorded, it appears that the average of the heaviest falls in the year

in 1846-58 was 2.106 inches,
and in 1859-71 was 1.966 inches,

shewing, according to the testimony of these twenty-six years, that the heaviest rain in a single day, as well as the aggregate of rain in the year, had undergone a diminution. From comparing the monthly means at the foot of Table XXXVI, it appears that the heaviest falls in a *single day* in September considerably exceed those of any other month; that the heaviest falls of the year occurred nine times in September (the month of the largest average rain fall in the year); and that the heaviest fall on record on one day (3.455 inches) was in September, 1843.

The following Table gives the heaviest fall of snow in the year, on a single day, from 1853-71:—

Years.	Inches.	Year.	Inches.	Year.	Inches.	Year.	Inches.
1853	6.5	1858	6.0	1863	16.0	1868	12.0
1854	5.5	1859	6.0	1864	10.0	1869	9.0
1855	15.0	1860	9.0	1865	7.0	1870	16.0
1856	5.8	1861	8.0	1866	6.0	1871	12.0
1857	5.5	1862	9.0	1867	15.0		

The average of the nineteen years, from the above Table, is 8.91 inches, and for the last thirteen years, 10.38 inches, shewing an increase in the average amount of the heaviest fall of snow in the year, as well as in the total annual amount.

On the whole, then, it appears that while there has been a diminution in the average annual amount of *rain*, and in the average amount of the heaviest fall of rain in the year, the snow has increased in both these respects; the total annual precipitation of rain and melted snow has also increased, as well as the number of days of rain and the number of days of snow.

On the Relative Frequency of the different Winds during Days of Rain or Snow, from the Hourly Records of Ten Years. (Table XXXVII.)

The object of this Table is to compare the different winds with reference to the number of hours that they blow during days in any part of which a fall of rain or snow takes place. If all winds continued for an equal number of hours through the year, or through the particular season under consideration, it would be sufficient to compare the *absolute* durations of the several winds on days of precipitation; but as there is a very great inequality in the frequency of winds from different points of the compass, (winds from N.W., for example, being more than three times as numerous as those from S.E.) an undue prominence would be given to the winds of greater general frequency, if the comparisons were to be made between the absolute durations. Hence it becomes requisite that the absolute durations of each wind, during the days of rain, included within a given period of time, should be divided by the whole duration of the same wind within the same period. The quotients form what may be termed the *relative* durations of the several winds, and constitute the proper quantities for intercomparison.

As winds of comparative rare occurrence on days of heavy rain, were found to blow very frequently on days of light rain, the adoption of some classification of the rainy days became necessary. In this Table the days of rain have been arranged in three classes, as well as collectively in one group. Class I includes days of light rain, in which the whole amount in the day did not exceed one-tenth of an inch. Class II includes days of moderate rain, or over one-tenth and less than half an inch; while Class III comprises days of heavy rain, wherein the fall in the day amounted to half an inch and upwards. The days in which snow fell are classified in a similar manner, and with the same limits, one inch of snow being regarded as equivalent to one-tenth of an inch of rain. With a view of learning whether the relative duration or frequency of a wind, during rain, is affected by the season, the computations have been made separately for the winter half year (October to March), for the summer half year (April to September), and for the year as a whole. As the falls of snow after March are not sufficiently numerous to furnish materials for a separate discussion, no separation of the seasons has been made in the case of snow.

Again, for the purpose of comparing the corresponding results in different years, the observations of the ten years, 1853-62, have been discussed in two separate equal groups.

For every Class, the numbers in the Table are the relative durations, expressed in terms of the average relative duration for all winds in that Class.

TABLES RELATIVE TO THE WIND.

Resultant Direction of the Wind in different Months. (Table XXXVIII.)

A comparison of the monthly resultants from the period 1848-71, given in this Table, shews that the general direction of the atmospheric current is considerably more from the westward in the winter than in the summer months, the monthly resultants oscillating about N. 48° W., from April to September inclusive, and about N. 69° W. during the remaining six months. It is also evident that there is a greater uniformity of direction in the different years for some months than for others, and that in the cold months the resultant direction of the wind is more steady than in the warm.

The resultants for the year in different years are deflected from the general resultant for twenty-four years (N. 61° W.), through an angle whose mean value is 9° 30′ nearly, the greatest deflection from the general direction to the north being 23′ in 1849 and 1853, and the greatest deflection to the west 15° in 1864.

Resultant Velocities and Mean Velocities in different Months and Years. (Tables XXXIX and XL.)

The inferiority of the velocities recorded from 1848-54, was due to the less advantageous exposure of the anemometer. Prior to 26th June, 1854, the cups had an elevation of only 20 feet above the floor of the Observatory. On that day it was moved to the top of a conical tower, where the cups had an elevation of 30 feet nearly; and on 11th June, 1855, it was mounted in the position which it has since occupied, on the tower of the Observatory (then rebuilt), where the cups revolve in a plane 4½ feet above the balustrade, and at a height above the ground of 45 feet nearly. The resultant velocity and mean velocity both have a maximum in December and March, and a well marked minimum in July.

Resultant Direction of the Wind in the different Hours. (Table XLI.)

From the column of annual resultants it is found that on the mean of the year the direction of the wind attains its extreme westerly deflection (N. 103° W.) during the hour commencing noon. From this point, at which it continues nearly steady for three hours, it draws towards north continuously till 5 a.m., when it makes its nearest approach to the north (N. 39° W). About this point it varies little from midnight to 7 a.m., after which it recedes again rapidly to the westward.

Mean Velocity of the Wind in each of the Twenty-four Hours. (Tables XLIII and XLIV.)

The first of these Tables contains the velocity in miles for two series of years included in 1848-71. The whole period is divided into two groups, 1848-53 and 1855-71, in consequence of the changes in the position of the anemometer in June, 1854, and June, 1855. As part only of 1854 is comparable with 1853, and none of it with the year following, 1855, it has been omitted from both sets of means.

In Table XLIV, the velocity in each hour is expressed in terms of the average velocity in the same group for the twenty-four hours. A comparison of the two series will show a very fair similarity, column with column; but in the early series, when the instrument occupied a lower position, the diurnal ranges are greater than in the later series, as shewn by the following numbers:—

Years.	Winter.	Spring.	Summer.	Autumn.	Year.
1848-53	0.36	0.71	1.15	0.76	0.69
1855-71	0.32	0.55	0.92	0.66	0.57

In both series the maximum velocity occurs in one of the three hours commencing 1 p.m., and the minimum near to 4 a.m

Velocity of the Wind in different Directions.

The following Table gives the mean velocity, on the average of the year for each of the sixteen points, from the seven years, 1853-59.

N	7.31	E	8.40	S	6.53	W	10.72
N.N.E	6.03	E.S.E	6.05	S.S.W	7.46	W.N.W	10.89
N.E	6.92	S.E	5.22	S.W	6.05	N.W	10.90
E.N.E	8.77	S.S.E	5.73	W.S.W	9.85	N.N.W	9.63

AURORAS.

In Table XLVI are given, as far as they could be procured, the number of Auroras recorded in every month from 1841-71.

By aid of the sums on the right and at the foot of the Table, the absolute numbers in the different years and in the different months may be compared. In Tables XLVII and XLVIII, the *relative* frequency are given in each year from 1853-71, and for each month, derived from the same years, or the ratios of the numbers of nights when Auroras were observed, to the number of nights when the sky was sufficiently clear to insure the visibility of Aurora if it were present.

The *absolute* monthly numbers in Table XLVI, and the relative numbers in Table XLVII—

both show a principal maximum in September,

a principal minimum in January or December,

a second maximum in March or April,

a second minimum in June.

Table XLIX contains the dates of certain periodic events, as far as they could be obtained. In the column, " Navigation closed," it must be understood that the year given refers to the winter commencing with December of that year, and that if the date of closing be in January, it refers to January of the next year.

The following are the dates of opening and closing of navigation for a few years prior to 1840.

	Navigation opened.	Navigation closed.
1833	April 4.	
1834	March 14.	
1835	March 30.	December 1.
1836	April 25.	December 1.
1837	April 16.	December 14.
1838	April 2.	December 14.
1839	April 2.	December 14.

TABLE I.

CORRECTIONS FOR EVERY FIFTH DAY IN THE YEAR, TO BE APPLIED TO THE TEMPERATURE OBSERVED AT TORONTO AT ANY OF THE HOURS OF MEAN ASTRONOMICAL TIME, IN ORDER TO OBTAIN THE MEAN TEMPERATURE OF THE DAY.

Mean Astronomical Time.	JANUARY.						FEBRUARY.					MARCH.					
	5	10	15	20	25	30	4	9	14	19	24	1	6	11	16	21	26	31
h 0	2.3	2.4	2.5	2.6	2.8	3.0	3.3	3.5	3.8	3.9	4.1	4.2	4.2	4.2	4.2	4.2	4.2	4.3
1	2.8	2.9	3.0	3.1	3.4	3.7	4.1	4.3	4.7	4.8	5.0	4.9	5.0	4.9	4.8	4.8	4.9	5.1
2	3.1	3.1	3.3	3.4	3.7	4.0	4.4	4.7	5.1	5.3	5.5	5.5	5.5	5.5	5.4	5.4	5.4	5.5
3 (Subtractive)	3.0	3.1	3.2	3.4	3.6	4.1	4.5	4.8	5.0	5.2	5.4	5.3	5.3	5.2	5.2	5.2	5.3	5.4
4	2.4	2.5	2.7	2.9	3.3	3.6	3.9	4.2	4.5	4.7	4.8	4.8	4.8	4.8	4.7	4.8	4.9	5.0
5	1.5	1.6	1.7	1.9	2.1	2.4	2.7	3.0	3.3	3.5	3.8	3.9	3.9	3.9	4.0	4.0	4.1	4.3
6	0.7	0.8	0.9	0.9	1.2	1.3	1.5	1.6	1.8	2.0	2.1	2.2	2.3	2.3	2.3	2.1	2.3	2.4
7	0.4	0.2	0.4	0.4	0.4	0.5	0.6	0.7	0.9	0.9	1.1	1.0	1.0	0.9	0.8	0.7	0.7	0.6
8	0.0	0.0	0.1	0.0	0.0	0.0	0.0	0.0	0.0	0.0	0.1	0.1	0.0	0.0	0.1	0.2	0.3	0.5
9	0.1	0.1	0.1	0.2	0.2	0.4	0.5	0.6	0.6	0.7	0.8	0.9	0.9	1.1	1.1	1.2	1.3	1.4
10	0.5	0.5	0.5	0.6	0.7	0.8	0.9	1.1	1.2	1.3	1.4	1.5	1.6	1.7	1.8	1.9	2.0	2.1
11	0.7	0.8	0.8	1.0	1.1	1.2	1.4	1.6	1.7	1.9	2.0	2.1	2.2	2.4	2.4	2.5	2.6	2.7
12	1.4	1.4	1.5	1.6	1.6	1.7	1.6	1.8	1.8	1.9	2.0	2.1	2.3	2.4	2.5	2.5	2.6	2.7
13	1.9	2.0	2.0	2.0	2.0	2.0	2.0	2.1	2.2	2.3	2.4	2.6	2.7	2.9	2.9	3.0	3.0	3.3
14 (Additive)	2.1	2.1	2.1	2.1	2.1	2.2	2.3	2.5	2.5	2.7	2.8	2.9	3.1	3.2	3.3	3.4	3.6	3.8
15	2.1	2.2	2.2	2.3	2.4	2.5	2.6	2.7	3.0	3.1	3.3	3.5	3.5	3.6	3.6	3.6	3.8	3.9
16	2.2	2.3	2.3	2.4	2.6	2.7	3.0	3.1	3.3	3.5	3.6	3.8	3.8	3.9	4.0	4.0	4.1	4.3
17	2.3	2.4	2.5	2.7	2.8	3.0	3.2	3.4	3.7	3.8	4.0	4.2	4.3	4.4	4.5	4.6	4.7	4.8
18	1.8	1.7	1.8	2.0	2.3	2.8	3.3	3.8	4.2	4.5	4.7	4.8	4.8	4.8	4.8	4.8	4.9	5.0
19	1.9	1.8	1.9	2.1	2.5	3.0	3.5	4.0	4.3	4.6	4.6	4.5	4.4	4.2	3.9	3.6	3.6	3.5
20	1.6	1.6	1.6	1.8	2.1	2.5	2.8	3.2	3.3	3.4	3.2	3.0	2.7	2.3	1.9	1.7	1.4	1.2
21	0.7	0.7	0.7	0.7	0.8	0.9	1.0	1.0	1.0	0.9	0.6	0.4	0.2	0.0	0.2	0.4	0.5	0.6
22 (Subtractive)	0.5	0.5	0.6	0.6	0.6	0.6	0.7	0.8	1.0	1.2	1.4	1.6	1.7	1.8	1.9	2.0	2.0	2.1
23	1.6	1.7	1.7	1.8	1.9	2.0	2.2	2.4	2.6	2.7	2.9	3.0	3.1	3.1	3.2	3.2	3.3	3.3

TABLE I.—(Continued.)

CORRECTIONS FOR EVERY FIFTH DAY IN THE YEAR, TO BE APPLIED TO THE TEMPERATURE OBSERVED AT TORONTO AT ANY OF THE HOURS OF MEAN ASTRONOMICAL TIME, IN ORDER TO OBTAIN THE MEAN TEMPERATURE OF THE DAY.

Mean Astronomical Time.		APRIL.						MAY.						JUNE.					
		5	10	15	20	25	30	5	10	15	20	25	30	5	10	15	20	25	30
h 0		4.5	4.6	4.9	5.1	5.4	5.6	5.7	5.9	5.9	5.9	5.9	5.8	5.8	5.8	5.9	6.0	6.1	6.3
1		5.3	5.5	5.8	6.1	6.4	6.6	6.7	6.8	6.8	6.8	6.7	6.6	6.6	6.6	6.6	6.7	6.9	7.2
2		5.7	5.9	6.2	6.5	6.8	7.0	7.1	7.2	7.2	7.1	7.0	6.9	6.9	6.9	7.0	7.2	7.5	7.8
3	Subtractive.	5.7	6.0	6.3	6.6	6.8	7.1	7.2	7.3	7.2	7.2	7.2	7.2	7.2	7.3	7.4	7.6	7.8	8.1
4		5.3	5.6	5.9	6.2	6.5	6.8	7.0	7.1	7.2	7.3	7.3	7.3	7.4	7.5	7.6	7.9	8.0	8.3
5		4.5	4.8	5.2	5.6	5.9	6.2	6.5	6.7	6.8	6.9	6.9	6.8	6.9	7.0	7.0	7.2	7.3	7.7
6		2.7	3.0	3.4	3.7	4.0	4.4	4.6	4.9	5.0	5.4	5.5	5.5	5.6	5.7	5.7	5.9	6.2	6.4
7		0.6	0.7	0.8	1.0	1.3	1.5	1.7	2.0	2.2	2.4	2.5	2.6	2.7	2.9	3.0	3.1	3.3	3.4
8		0.6	0.7	0.7	0.8	0.8	0.8	0.7	0.6	0.5	0.4	0.4	0.3	0.3	0.2	0.3	0.3	0.4	0.4
9		1.6	1.7	1.8	2.0	2.1	2.1	2.2	2.2	2.3	2.3	2.3	2.3	2.3	2.3	2.5	2.5	2.7	2.8
10		2.3	2.5	2.6	2.7	2.9	3.0	3.1	3.1	3.3	3.3	3.4	3.5	3.6	3.6	3.8	3.9	4.0	4.1
11		2.8	3.0	3.1	3.3	3.5	3.7	3.9	4.0	4.2	4.3	4.4	4.4	4.5	4.6	4.8	4.9	5.1	5.2
12		2.6	3.0	3.3	3.5	3.9	4.2	4.6	4.8	5.0	5.1	5.2	5.2	5.2	5.2	5.3	5.5	5.7	5.9
13		3.5	3.7	4.0	4.4	4.8	5.1	5.5	5.7	5.9	5.9	6.0	5.9	5.9	5.9	6.0	6.2	6.4	6.7
14	Additive.	4.0	4.3	4.7	5.1	5.5	5.9	6.3	6.5	6.7	6.7	6.8	6.7	6.6	6.6	6.7	6.8	7.0	7.3
15		4.1	4.5	4.9	5.1	5.9	6.4	6.9	7.2	7.4	7.5	7.5	7.5	7.5	7.4	7.5	7.7	7.8	8.0
16		4.5	4.9	5.3	5.8	6.4	6.9	7.3	7.6	7.9	8.0	8.0	8.0	8.0	7.9	8.0	8.2	8.4	8.7
17		5.0	5.3	5.7	6.1	6.6	6.8	7.4	7.7	7.8	7.9	7.9	7.8	7.8	7.9	7.9	8.1	8.3	8.6
18		5.2	5.4	5.5	5.7	5.7	5.7	5.7	5.5	5.4	5.2	6.1	5.1	5.1	5.1	5.2	5.3	5.5	5.6
19		3.4	3.4	3.3	3.1	3.0	2.9	2.7	2.5	2.4	2.3	2.3	2.3	2.4	2.4	2.4	2.4	2.3	2.3
20		1.2	1.1	1.0	0.9	0.8	0.7	0.5	0.3	0.2	0.1	0.1	0.1	0.1	0.0	0.1	0.1	0.0	0.0
21	Subtractive.	0.7	0.8	1.0	1.1	1.3	1.6	1.8	2.0	2.1	2.0	2.2	2.1	2.0	1.9	1.8	1.8	1.8	1.9
22		2.2	2.3	2.5	2.7	3.0	3.2	3.5	3.7	3.8	3.0	3.9	3.8	3.7	3.6	3.5	3.5	3.5	3.6
23		3.5	3.6	3.9	4.1	4.3	4.6	4.7	4.9	4.9	5.0	5.0	4.9	4.8	4.8	4.8	4.8	4.9	5.0

TORONTO METEOROLOGICAL OBSERVATIONS.

TABLE I.—(Continued.)

CORRECTIONS FOR EVERY FIFTH DAY IN THE YEAR, TO BE APPLIED TO THE TEMPERATURE OBSERVED AT TORONTO AT ANY OF THE HOURS OF MEAN ASTRONOMICAL TIME, IN ORDER TO OBTAIN THE MEAN TEMPERATURE OF THE DAY.

Mean Astronomical Time.		JULY.						AUGUST.						SEPTEMBER.					
		5	10	15	20	25	30	5	10	15	20	25	30	5	10	15	20	25	30
h 0		8.5	8.7	8.9	7.0	7.0	7.0	6.9	6.6	6.5	6.3	6.2	6.1	6.0	5.9	5.9	5.9	5.9	5.8
1		7.4	7.6	7.8	7.8	7.9	7.9	7.7	7.4	7.3	7.0	6.8	6.7	6.6	6.5	6.5	6.5	6.5	6.4
2		8.1	8.4	8.6	8.7	8.8	8.7	8.5	8.1	7.9	7.6	7.3	7.1	7.0	6.9	6.9	6.9	6.9	6.8
3	Subtractive.	8.4	8.6	8.8	8.9	8.9	8.9	8.8	8.4	8.2	7.9	7.6	7.4	7.2	7.0	7.0	6.9	6.7	6.6
4		8.5	8.7	8.8	8.9	8.9	8.8	8.6	8.3	8.1	7.8	7.5	7.2	7.0	6.9	6.7	6.5	6.4	6.2
5		8.0	8.2	8.4	8.4	8.4	8.3	8.1	7.8	7.5	7.2	7.0	6.6	6.3	6.1	5.8	5.5	5.1	4.7
6		6.7	6.8	6.9	6.8	6.7	6.5	6.3	5.9	5.6	5.2	4.7	4.3	3.9	3.4	3.1	3.0	2.6	2.3
7		3.5	3.5	3.5	3.3	3.1	2.8	2.4	2.0	1.7	1.3	1.0	0.7	0.6	0.4	0.4	0.3	0.4	0.3
8		0.5	0.6	0.7	0.9	1.0	1.1	1.2	1.3	1.3	1.3	1.2	1.2	1.0	1.0	0.9	0.8	0.7	0.6
9		2.9	3.0	3.1	3.2	3.2	3.1	3.1	3.1	2.8	2.7	2.5	2.3	2.1	2.0	1.9	1.8	1.7	1.6
10		4.2	4.3	4.3	4.3	4.3	4.2	4.2	4.0	3.9	3.7	3.5	3.4	3.2	3.1	3.0	2.9	2.7	2.6
11		5.3	5.5	5.5	5.5	5.4	5.3	5.1	5.0	4.7	4.4	4.2	4.0	3.9	3.7	3.6	3.5	3.4	3.3
12		6.2	6.4	6.5	6.6	6.6	6.4	6.1	5.9	5.5	5.1	4.8	4.5	4.3	4.1	4.0	3.9	3.8	3.7
13	Additive.	6.9	7.2	7.4	7.5	7.4	7.2	6.9	6.6	6.1	5.7	5.4	5.1	4.8	4.7	4.6	4.5	4.4	4.3
14		7.6	7.8	8.0	8.0	8.0	7.8	7.5	7.3	6.8	6.4	6.1	5.8	5.5	5.3	5.2	5.0	4.9	4.8
15		8.3	8.5	8.7	8.8	8.7	8.5	8.2	7.9	7.5	7.1	6.7	6.4	6.1	5.8	5.6	5.4	5.3	5.0
16		8.9	9.2	9.3	9.3	9.2	9.0	8.6	8.3	7.6	7.5	7.1	6.8	6.6	6.4	6.2	6.0	5.8	5.5
17		9.0	9.2	9.4	9.4	9.3	9.0	8.7	8.4	8.0	7.8	7.5	7.3	6.7	7.0	6.8	6.7	6.4	6.1
18		5.8	6.0	6.2	6.4	6.4	6.5	6.6	6.7	6.6	6.5	6.5	6.4	6.3	6.2	6.2	6.1	6.0	5.7
19		2.3	2.4	2.5	2.7	2.9	3.1	3.3	3.6	3.6	3.7	3.6	3.6	3.6	3.6	3.6	3.7	3.8	3.9
20		0.1	0.1	0.1	0.1	0.0	0.1	0.2	0.3	0.3	0.4	0.4	0.5	0.6	0.7	0.9	1.0	1.2	1.4
21	Subtractive.	2.0	2.2	2.3	2.4	2.4	2.4	2.4	2.2	2.2	2.0	1.9	1.8	1.7	1.6	1.6	1.4	1.4	1.3
22		3.7	3.9	4.0	4.1	4.3	4.3	4.3	4.2	4.1	4.0	3.9	3.8	3.6	3.6	3.5	3.4	3.4	3.3
23		5.2	5.4	5.6	5.7	5.8	5.8	5.8	5.6	5.6	5.4	5.3	5.2	5.1	5.0	5.0	4.9	4.9	4.8

TORONTO METEOROLOGICAL OBSERVATIONS.

TABLE I.—*(Continued.)*

CORRECTIONS FOR EVERY FIFTH DAY IN THE YEAR, TO BE APPLIED TO THE TEMPERATURE OBSERVED AT TORONTO AT ANY OF THE HOURS OF MEAN ASTRONOMICAL TIME, IN ORDER TO OBTAIN THE MEAN TEMPERATURE OF THE DAY.

Mean Astronomical Time.		OCTOBER.						NOVEMBER.						DECEMBER.					
		5	10	15	20	25	30	5	10	15	20	25	30	5	10	15	20	25	30
h 0		°5.7	°5.6	°5.3	°5.0	°4.7	°4.3	°3.9	°3.6	°3.3	°3.1	°2.9	°2.8	°2.7	°2.5	°2.5	°2.4	°2.4	°2.3
1		6.2	6.0	5.7	5.4	5.0	4.6	4.3	3.9	3.7	3.5	3.4	3.4	3.3	3.2	3.2	3.1	3.0	2.9
2	Subtractive.	6.6	6.4	6.1	5.7	5.3	4.8	4.4	4.1	3.8	3.6	3.5	3.5	3.4	3.4	3.4	3.3	3.2	3.1
3		6.4	6.2	5.8	5.5	5.1	4.6	4.2	3.9	3.6	3.4	3.3	3.2	3.2	3.1	3.1	3.0	3.0	3.0
4		5.9	5.6	5.1	4.7	4.2	3.7	3.3	3.0	2.7	2.6	2.5	2.5	2.5	2.4	2.5	2.4	2.4	2.2
5		4.3	3.9	3.4	2.9	2.5	2.1	1.9	1.6	1.5	1.5	1.4	1.5	1.5	1.5	1.5	1.5	1.6	1.5
6		1.9	1.7	1.3	1.1	1.0	0.8	0.6	0.7	0.7	0.5	0.5	0.6	0.7	0.7	0.8	0.8	0.8	0.8
7		0.3	0.3	0.2	0.2	0.1	0.1	0.1	0.1	0.1	0.2	0.2	0.3	0.4	0.4	0.5	0.5	0.4	0.4
8		0.6	0.5	0.5	0.5	0.4	0.4	0.3	0.3	0.2	0.1	0.1	0.0	0.0	0.0	0.1	0.1	0.1	0.1
9		1.5	1.4	1.3	1.1	1.0	0.9	0.7	0.6	0.5	0.4	0.3	0.2	0.2	0.2	0.2	0.1	0.1	0.1
10		2.4	2.2	2.0	1.8	1.6	1.4	1.2	1.0	0.8	0.7	0.6	0.5	0.5	0.5	0.5	0.4	0.4	0.5
11		3.2	2.9	2.7	2.4	2.2	1.9	1.6	1.4	1.2	1.0	0.8	0.7	0.6	0.6	0.6	0.6	0.6	0.7
12		3.6	3.4	3.2	3.1	2.9	2.7	2.4	2.1	1.8	1.6	1.3	1.1	1.0	0.9	0.9	1.0	1.1	1.2
13	Additive.	4.2	4.0	3.8	3.6	3.3	3.0	2.7	2.4	2.1	1.9	1.6	1.5	1.4	1.5	1.5	1.6	1.7	1.8
14		4.6	4.4	4.2	3.9	3.6	3.3	2.9	2.7	2.4	2.2	2.0	1.9	1.8	1.9	1.9	1.9	1.9	2.0
15		4.8	4.6	4.3	4.0	3.7	3.5	3.2	3.0	2.7	2.5	2.3	2.2	2.1	2.1	2.0	2.1	2.0	2.0
16		5.3	4.9	4.6	4.4	4.0	3.7	3.4	3.1	2.9	2.6	2.5	2.3	2.1	2.1	2.0	2.0	2.0	2.1
17		5.7	5.2	4.8	4.4	4.0	3.6	3.3	3.0	2.8	2.4	2.4	2.2	2.1	1.9	2.0	2.0	2.1	2.1
18		5.4	5.0	4.6	4.1	3.6	3.2	2.9	2.6	2.5	2.5	2.5	2.5	2.5	2.5	2.5	2.3	2.2	1.9
19		4.0	3.9	3.8	3.6	3.3	3.1	2.8	2.6	2.5	2.5	2.5	2.6	2.7	2.7	2.6	2.5	2.2	2.0
20		1.5	1.5	1.6	1.5	1.4	1.4	1.3	1.4	1.4	1.6	1.8	2.0	2.1	2.2	2.2	2.1	1.9	1.8
21	Subtractive.	1.2	1.2	1.1	1.0	0.9	0.7	0.6	0.3	0.1	0.2	0.5	0.7	0.9	1.0	1.0	1.0	0.9	0.8
22		3.2	3.2	3.0	2.9	2.6	2.4	2.1	1.8	1.6	1.2	1.0	0.8	0.6	0.5	0.4	0.4	0.4	0.5
23		4.7	4.6	4.4	4.1	3.9	3.5	3.2	2.8	2.5	2.3	2.0	1.9	1.8	1.8	1.7	1.6	1.6	1.0

TORONTO METEOROLOGICAL OBSERVATIONS.

TABLE II.

NORMAL DAILY MEANS OF TEMPERATURE DERIVED FROM THE MONTHLY MEANS OF THE TWELVE YEARS, 1841 TO 1852.

Day.	Jan.	Feb.	Mar.	April.	May.	June.	July.	Aug.	Sept.	Oct.	Nov.	Dec.	Day.
1	25.2°	23.9°	25.4°	36.3°	46.4°	56.9°	64.7°	66.9°	63.1°	50.5°	40.5°	30.8°	1
2	25.2	23.9	25.6	36.7	46.7	57.2	64.9	66.8	62.8	50.0	40.3	30.5	2
3	25.1	23.8	25.9	37.1	47.0	57.5	65.1	66.8	62.5	49.6	40.0	30.1	3
4	25.1	23.7	26.2	37.4	47.4	57.8	65.2	66.8	62.2	49.1	39.8	29.8	4
5	25.1	23.6	26.4	37.8	47.7	58.1	65.3	66.8	61.9	48.7	39.5	29.4	5
6	25.1	23.6	26.7	38.1	48.0	58.4	65.5	66.8	61.5	48.3	39.2	29.1	6
7	25.1	23.5	27.0	38.5	48.4	58.7	65.6	66.7	61.2	47.9	39.0	28.7	7
8	25.1	23.5	27.4	38.8	48.7	59.0	65.7	66.7	60.8	47.5	38.7	28.6	8
9	25.1	23.4	27.7	39.1	49.1	59.4	65.9	66.6	60.4	47.1	38.4	28.2	9
10	25.1	23.4	28.0	39.5	49.4	59.7	66.0	66.6	60.1	46.7	38.1	27.9	10
11	25.0	23.4	28.4	39.8	49.8	59.9	66.1	66.5	59.7	46.3	37.8	27.7	11
12	25.0	23.4	28.7	40.2	50.1	60.2	66.2	66.4	59.3	46.0	37.5	27.4	12
13	25.0	23.4	29.1	40.5	50.5	60.5	66.3	66.3	58.9	45.6	37.2	27.2	13
14	25.0	23.4	29.5	40.8	50.8	60.8	66.3	66.3	58.4	45.3	36.9	27.0	14
15	25.0	23.4	29.9	41.1	51.2	61.1	66.4	66.2	58.0	44.9	36.5	26.8	15
16	24.9	23.5	30.2	41.5	51.5	61.3	66.5	66.1	57.6	44.6	36.2	26.6	16
17	24.9	23.5	30.6	41.8	51.9	61.6	66.6	66.0	57.1	44.3	35.8	26.4	17
18	24.9	23.6	31.0	42.1	52.2	61.9	66.6	65.9	56.7	44.1	35.5	26.2	18
19	24.8	23.7	31.4	42.4	52.5	62.1	66.7	65.8	56.2	43.8	35.1	26.1	19
20	24.8	23.8	31.8	42.8	52.9	62.4	66.7	65.6	55.7	43.6	34.8	25.9	20
21	24.7	23.9	32.2	43.1	53.2	62.6	66.7	65.5	55.2	43.3	34.4	25.8	21
22	24.7	24.0	32.6	43.4	53.6	62.9	66.8	65.4	54.7	43.0	34.1	25.7	22
23	24.6	24.1	32.9	43.7	53.9	63.1	66.8	65.2	54.3	42.8	33.7	25.6	23
24	24.5	24.3	33.3	44.0	54.2	63.3	66.8	65.0	53.8	42.5	33.3	25.5	24
25	24.5	24.5	33.7	44.4	54.6	63.5	66.9	64.8	53.3	42.3	33.0	25.4	25
26	24.4	24.7	34.1	44.7	54.9	63.8	66.9	64.6	52.8	42.0	32.6	25.3	26
27	24.3	24.9	34.5	45.0	55.2	64.0	66.9	64.4	52.3	41.8	32.2	25.3	27
28	24.3	25.1	34.8	45.4	55.6	64.2	66.9	64.2	51.9	41.5	31.9	25.2	28
29	24.2	...	35.2	45.7	55.9	64.4	66.9	63.9	51.4	41.3	31.5	25.2	29
30	24.1	...	35.6	46.0	56.2	64.5	66.9	63.7	50.9	41.0	31.1	25.2	30
31	24.0	...	36.0	...	56.5	...	66.9	63.4	...	40.8	...	25.2	31

TORONTO METEOROLOGICAL OBSERVATIONS.

TABLE III.

NORMAL DAILY MEANS OF TEMPERATURE AT TORONTO, FROM SIX DAILY OBSERVATIONS IN THE TEN YEARS, 1859 TO 1868, INCLUSIVE.

Day.	Jan.	Feb.	Mar.	April.	May.	June.	July.	Aug	Sept.	Oct.	Nov.	Dec.	Day.
1	21.3	22.6	25.6	35.6	46.8	57.5	66.3	68.1	62.5	51.0	42.2	30.5	1
2	21.3	22.6	25.8	36.0	47.2	57.8	66.5	68.0	62.2	50.6	41.9	30.0	2
3	21.3	22.7	26.0	36.4	47.6	58.1	66.7	67.9	62.0	50.2	41.7	29.6	3
4	21.2	22.7	26.3	36.7	47.9	58.4	66.9	67.9	61.7	49.9	41.4	29.1	4
5	21.2	22.8	26.5	37.1	48.3	58.8	67.1	67.8	61.4	49.5	41.2	28.6	5
6	21.2	22.8	26.8	37.5	48.6	59.1	67.2	67.7	61.1	49.2	40.9	28.2	6
7	21.2	22.9	27.0	37.9	49.0	59.4	67.4	67.6	60.7	48.8	40.6	27.7	7
8	21.2	23.0	27.3	38.3	49.3	59.7	67.5	67.4	60.4	48.5	40.3	27.3	8
9	21.2	23.0	27.6	38.7	49.7	60.0	67.7	67.3	60.0	48.1	40.0	26.9	9
10	21.3	23.1	27.9	39.0	50.0	60.4	67.8	67.2	59.6	47.8	39.7	26.4	10
11	21.3	23.2	28.2	39.4	50.4	60.7	67.9	67.0	59.2	47.5	39.3	26.0	11
12	21.4	23.2	28.5	39.8	50.7	61.0	68.0	66.9	58.8	47.2	39.0	25.6	12
13	21.4	23.3	28.8	40.2	51.1	61.3	68.1	66.7	58.4	46.9	38.6	25.3	13
14	21.4	23.4	29.1	40.6	51.4	61.7	68.2	66.6	58.0	46.6	38.2	24.9	14
15	21.5	23.5	29.4	40.9	51.8	62.0	68.2	66.4	57.6	46.3	37.8	24.6	15
16	21.6	23.6	29.7	41.3	52.1	62.3	68.3	66.3	57.2	46.1	37.4	24.2	16
17	21.6	23.7	30.1	41.7	52.5	62.6	68.3	66.1	56.8	45.8	37.0	23.9	17
18	21.7	23.8	30.4	42.1	52.8	62.9	68.4	65.9	56.4	45.5	36.6	23.6	18
19	21.7	23.9	30.8	42.4	53.2	63.2	68.4	65.7	56.0	45.3	36.2	23.3	19
20	21.8	24.0	31.1	42.8	53.5	63.5	68.4	65.5	55.5	45.0	35.7	23.1	20
21	21.9	24.2	31.5	43.2	53.9	63.8	68.4	65.3	55.1	44.8	35.3	22.8	21
22	21.9	24.3	31.8	43.6	54.2	64.1	68.5	65.1	54.7	44.5	34.8	22.6	22
23	22.0	24.5	32.2	43.9	54.6	64.4	68.4	64.8	54.3	44.3	34.4	22.4	23
24	22.1	24.6	32.6	44.3	54.9	64.6	68.4	64.6	53.8	44.0	33.9	22.2	24
25	22.1	24.8	32.9	44.7	55.2	64.9	68.4	64.4	53.4	43.8	33.4	22.0	25
26	22.2	25.0	33.3	45.0	55.6	65.2	68.4	64.1	53.0	43.6	32.9	21.9	26
27	22.2	25.2	33.7	45.4	55.9	65.4	68.3	63.8	52.6	43.3	32.5	21.7	27
28	22.3	25.4	34.1	45.7	56.2	65.6	68.3	63.6	52.2	43.1	32.0	21.6	28
29	22.4	...	34.4	46.1	56.5	65.9	68.2	63.3	51.8	42.9	31.5	21.5	29
30	22.4	...	34.8	46.5	56.9	66.1	68.2	63.1	51.4	42.6	31.0	21.4	30
31	22.5	...	35.2	...	57.2	...	68.1	62.8	...	42.4	...	21.4	31

TORONTO METEOROLOGICAL OBSERVATIONS.

TABLE IV.

MONTHLY AND ANNUAL MEANS OF THE TEMPERATURE OF THE AIR IN EACH OF THE THIRTY-ONE YEARS FROM 1841 TO 1871, WITH THE MONTHLY AND ANNUAL MEANS FOR THE WHOLE PERIOD, AND FOR THREE GROUPS OF TWELVE, NINE AND TEN YEARS RESPECTIVELY. ALSO, THE CORRESPONDING APPROXIMATE MEANS, FROM OBSERVATIONS BY THE LATE REV. CHARLES DADE, PRIOR TO THE ESTABLISHMENT OF THE OBSERVATORY, AND EMBRACING THE GREATER PORTION OF THE YEARS 1831 TO 1841.

Years.	Jan.	Feb.	Mar.	April	May.	June.	July.	Aug.	Sept.	Oct.	Nov.	Dec.	Mean Annual Temp.	Differ. from Average.
1841	25.6	22.4	27.7	39.2	50.5	65.6	65.0	64.4	61.3	41.6	35.0	28.7	43.92	—0.25
1842	27.9	26.9	35.8	43.1	49.1	55.6	64.7	65.7	55.7	45.1	33.3	24.7	43.96	—0.21
1843	28.7	14.5	21.3	40.9	49.1	58.4	64.5	66.4	59.1	41.8	33.5	30.0	42.35	—1.82
1844	20.2	26.0	31.3	47.5	53.6	59.9	66.0	64.3	58.6	43.3	34.9	28.2	44.48	+0.31
1845	26.5	26.0	35.4	42.1	49.6	61.0	66.2	67.9	56.0	46.4	36.8	21.1	44.58	+0.41
1846	26.7	20.4	33.1	44.0	55.5	63.3	65.0	68.4	63.6	44.6	41.3	27.5	46.36	+2.19
1847	23.3	21.5	26.2	39.2	54.4	58.4	68.0	65.1	55.6	44.0	38.6	30.1	43.70	—0.47
1848	28.7	26.6	28.6	41.3	54.1	62.9	65.5	69.2	54.2	46.3	34.5	29.1	45.08	+0.91
1849	18.5	19.5	33.5	39.0	48.0	63.2	68.4	66.3	58.2	45.3	42.6	26.5	44.09	—0.08
1850	29.7	26.0	29.8	37.9	47.6	64.3	68.9	66.8	56.5	45.4	38.8	21.7	44.45	+0.28
1851	25.5	27.6	32.4	41.3	51.3	59.2	65.0	63.6	60.0	47.4	32.9	21.5	43.98	—0.19
1852	18.4	23.4	27.7	38.2	51.4	60.8	66.8	65.9	57.5	48.0	36.0	31.9	43.84	—0.33
1853	22.9	24.2	30.8	41.9	50.8	65.4	65.5	68.7	58.9	44.5	38.7	25.4	44.80	+0.63
1854	23.5	21.2	30.8	41.1	52.1	64.1	72.4	68.1	61.1	49.5	36.9	21.9	45.23	+1.06
1855	25.9	15.6	23.6	42.5	53.0	59.9	67.9	64.1	59.6	45.4	38.6	26.9	43.98	—0.19
1856	16.0	15.8	23.2	42.3	50.4	62.1	69.8	63.6	57.2	45.4	37.4	22.9	42.18	—1.99
1857	12.7	23.7	28.0	35.4	48.8	56.9	67.7	65.4	58.7	45.5	33.6	31.9	42.75	—1.42
1858	30.0	17.1	28.6	41.5	48.8	66.1	67.8	67.7	59.2	48.8	34.2	27.4	44.76	+0.59
1859	26.4	26.2	36.5	39.6	55.1	58.2	66.8	66.7	55.2	43.0	38.9	17.9	44.21	+0.04
1860	23.3	23.0	34.6	39.6	55.5	63.1	63.8	64.5	55.4	47.3	38.0	24.0	44.34	+0.17
1861	19.8	26.2	27.1	42.1	47.4	61.2	65.3	65.5	59.1	48.8	37.2	31.2	44.24	+0.07
1862	21.7	22.6	28.9	39.6	52.1	60.5	66.6	67.7	59.7	48.7	35.6	28.8	44.37	+0.20
1863	28.0	22.6	26.0	42.1	54.2	60.1	67.5	66.6	55.9	46.0	39.1	27.0	44.59	+0.42
1864	22.8	24.3	29.1	40.9	54.8	63.0	69.7	68.6	56.4	45.2	36.9	24.7	44.70	+0.53
1865	17.7	22.4	33.5	43.1	52.3	64.5	65.0	65.2	64.5	44.5	38.6	27.7	44.92	+0.75
1866	20.7	22.5	27.6	43.9	48.3	60.2	70.4	60.8	55.2	49.1	38.4	25.1	43.51	—0.66
1867	17.6	28.9	26.6	39.5	46.5	64.3	68.2	68.1	57.0	49.9	36.0	21.6	43.84	—0.33
1868	19.0	17.2	31.3	38.0	51.8	62.0	75.8	67.2	56.6	42.4	36.1	22.5	43.33	—0.84
1869	27.7	25.0	23.1	40 0	50.8	58.4	64.5	63.6	60.7	42.3	32.7	28.7	43.13	—1.04
1870	24.4	21.5	26.3	44.6	56.3	67.3	68.8	67.1	61.8	50.0	36.5	26.5	45.93	+1.76
1871	21.3	24.3	34.6	42.9	54.1	61.4	66.0	67.4	54.8	48.3	30.6	19.9	43.81	—0.36
Means. 1831–41	24.00	21.22	31.40	41.65	52.54	63.08	68.20	65.07	56.05	45.08	35.90	26.07	44.26	By Rev. Mr.Dade
Means. 1841–52	24.97	23.40	30.23	41.14	51.18	61.05	66.41	66.16	58.02	44.93	36.51	26.75	44.23	...
Means. 1853–61	22.27	22.00	29.80	40.67	51.32	61.89	67.44	66.03	58.27	46.47	37.06	25.50	44.06	...
Means. 1862–71	22.09	23.13	28.69	41.46	52.12	62.17	68.25	66.23	58.35	46.64	36.14	25.25	44.21	...
Means. 1841–71	23.26	22.91	29.61	41.11	51.52	61.65	67.30	66.15	58.20	45.93	36.55	25.90	44.17	...

TORONTO METEOROLOGICAL OBSERVATIONS.

TABLE V.

Monthly Means of the Daily Maxima of Temperature from 1841 to 1871, excluding 1849 to 1852, together with the Averages derived from the Twenty-seven Years, and also from groups of Eight, Nine and Ten Years.

Years.	Jan.	Feb.	Mar.	April.	May.	June.	July.	Aug.	Sept.	Oct.	Nov.	Dec.
1841	30.9	29.8	35.9	47.8	61.8	77.4	78.4	78.5	68.9	50.1	40.4	33.8
1842	35.5	35.2	44.7	53.1	61.0	68.7	77.7	76.9	65.8	54.6	40.3	31.9
1843	34.4	24.0	30.1	49.2	61.4	68.5	77.8	77.7	70.3	50.6	38.9	35.5
1844	27.4	33.3	40.9	59.0	66.1	71.2	78.4	74.8	69.8	52.1	45.5	35.3
1845	33.2	32.7	43.0	51.1	61.5	71.1	77.7	77.5	65.0	54.6	43.0	27.5
1846	32.1	28.1	39.0	51.7	64.5	72.3	78.9	76.7	71.1	52.3	45.8	32.2
1847	28.3	28.1	32.7	44.9	61.1	65.8	77.1	72.8	62.5	51.0	42.9	33.0
1848	33.0	33.0	34.2	49.3	63.0	71.4	72.9	76.3	62.9	51.8	38.1	34.7
1849	...	...	...	...	...	...	...	...	...	...	...	...
1850	...	...	...	...	...	...	...	...	...	...	...	...
1851	...	...	...	...	...	...	...	...	...	...	...	...
1852	...	...	...	...	...	...	...	...	...	...	...	...
1853	29.0	29.8	36.8	47.7	56.7	74.0	77.0	78.5	67.9	53.3	44.1	31.3
1854	29.3	20.6	36.4	47.8	61.8	74.5	84.8	80.7	72.6	59.0	42.1	20.5
1855	32.8	23.2	36.5	52.9	65.4	68.9	76.7	74.6	68.4	52.6	45.5	32.9
1856	22.7	24.2	30.5	50.5	59.6	71.6	80.4	73.7	66.7	54.0	43.0	28.7
1857	19.5	35.7	35.2	43.4	57.2	65.5	76.8	74.4	67.5	51.9	39.9	35.8
1858	35.3	24.1	37.0	48.3	55.7	73.9	75.4	75.4	67.5	55.8	37.9	33.2
1859	30.5	31.8	42.1	46.5	63.4	66.9	74.7	75.0	62.7	50.4	41.0	25.3
1860	29.8	29.4	41.9	47.0	64.0	72.6	73.0	73.7	63.1	53.6	43.2	28.8
1861	25.1	32.4	33.5	49.7	55.7	70.4	74.7	74.3	66.4	55.3	42.4	37.0
1862	27.6	28.3	34.6	46.3	61.4	69.1	76.4	76.1	68.4	54.8	40.6	34.1
1863	33.3	30.1	32.8	50.0	63.4	69.2	74.9	75.7	64.5	62.8	44.8	34.0
1864	29.6	31.5	35.6	47.5	62.9	73.1	80.0	77.2	63.9	52.0	42.8	32.2
1865	24.6	28.6	39.3	50.7	61.2	74.2	74.1	74.9	74.1	52.3	44.9	34.7
1866	26.3	33.6	33.0	52.9	57.5	69.5	79.0	69.6	64.0	57.6	43.8	31.2
1867	23.2	34.3	33.9	47.7	54.8	73.4	77.6	78.7	68.8	48.9	45.4	29.4
1868	24.1	26.6	39.1	46.1	59.7	70.6	85.4	76.9	64.3	49.8	41.4	29.1
1869	34.6	35.3	31.2	48.0	58.8	67.4	73.1	72.1	69.4	50.1	38.3	34.1
1870	32.2	28.0	33.0	53.5	66.5	76.4	77.7	76.9	69.2	53.4	44.1	32.0
1871	29.4	30.4	41.1	52.8	63.7	71.5	76.1	77.4	64.5	58.3	37.0	29.5
Means. 1841–48	31.85	30.53	37.56	50.76	62.55	70.80	77.36	76.02	67.04	52.14	41.86	32.99
Means. 1853–61	28.22	28.91	36.66	48.20	59.04	70.92	77.06	75.59	66.08	53.09	42.46	31.39
Means. 1862–71	28.39	30.67	35.36	49.55	60.99	71.44	77.49	75.55	67.11	54.60	42.31	32.03
Means. 1841–71	29.36	30.04	36.46	49.46	61.10	71.08	77.31	75.70	67.03	53.63	42.23	32.10

TORONTO METEOROLOGICAL OBSERVATIONS.

TABLE VI.

MONTHLY MEANS OF THE DAILY MINIMA OF TEMPERATURE FROM 1841 TO 1871, EXCLUDING 1849 TO 1852, TOGETHER WITH THE AVERAGES DERIVED FROM THE TWENTY-SEVEN YEARS, AND ALSO FROM GROUPS OF EIGHT, NINE, AND TEN YEARS.

Year.	Jan.	Feb.	Mar.	April.	May.	June.	July.	Aug.	Sept.	Oct.	Nov.	Dec.
1841	17.0	14.5	19.8	31.7	41.4	50.0	54.7	55.4	53.0	34.4	28.0	22.6
1842	18.3	21.0	29.0	36.0	39.6	47.4	53.2	57.1	47.6	37.1	27.2	18.4
1843	21.9	9.1	13.0	33.1	41.1	48.3	54.2	55.8	52.4	36.1	27.4	25.9
1844	13.3	17.6	25.8	38.2	45.1	50.5	55.5	55.2	49.1	35.5	31.8	21.1
1845	19.2	18.5	26.6	33.3	39.3	40.8	55.3	56.0	44.6	36.3	30.4	13.7
1846	18.1	9.1	24.2	35.3	40.6	53.9	58.1	59.0	54.9	37.7	36.3	21.5
1847	16.6	15.7	19.5	30.9	43.9	50.0	58.4	54.8	48.3	37.6	53.3	23.9
1848	20.6	20.3	21.9	32.1	44.4	51.4	55.6	58.1	45.2	39.2	28.9	23.6
1849	...	...	...	...	...	...	...	...	...	...	...	...
1850	...	...	...	...	...	...	...	...	...	...	...	...
1851	...	...	...	...	...	...	...	...	...	...	...	...
1852	...	...	...	...	...	...	...	...	...	...	...	...
1853	14.9	15.3	21.9	33.6	42.6	54.3	53.2	57.1	49.4	32.8	31.0	17.2
1854	13.5	9.2	22.9	39.7	37.9	49.8	58.5	55.3	49.1	41.3	28.1	14.4
1855	17.5	4.8	19.6	32.1	41.4	50.7	60.0	54.1	49.9	34.6	28.7	18.7
1856	6.0	3.6	12.9	33.4	40.6	52.4	59.0	53.0	45.7	35.2	28.7	15.6
1857	9.8	20.4	17.8	27.2	40.2	49.0	59.3	55.0	48.1	37.5	20.6	24.2
1858	23.7	10.8	21.9	34.1	41.7	56.4	60.0	59.2	50.8	43.4	30.0	21.4
1859	18.5	19.7	30.5	32.9	47.1	49.8	59.2	59.4	49.3	37.0	32.8	12.9
1860	17.6	15.3	27.3	32.2	47.8	55.3	55.8	56.3	47.3	41.6	33.5	19.2
1861	13.9	18.5	20.7	35.4	40.0	51.3	56.2	58.1	51.8	41.6	32.0	24.2
1862	15.0	15.4	23.1	33.4	42.0	51.0	58.1	58.2	52.8	41.4	30.5	23.6
1863	22.9	15.5	19.4	33.4	46.3	52.0	59.7	58.0	47.0	40.5	33.3	20.7
1864	17.5	18.9	22.4	34.6	46.2	52.9	59.8	61.4	49.0	39.7	31.3	19.7
1865	10.1	15.5	25.1	34.9	43.7	56.7	55.6	55.4	57.1	38.1	32.9	23.3
1866	12.7	18.1	21.6	36.0	39.8	51.4	60.6	52.7	48.7	43.8	33.2	20.0
1867	11.6	21.6	21.1	33.8	39.7	55.6	58.5	58.8	49.4	42.5	32.4	15.3
1868	11.8	8.2	23.0	29.7	44.5	52.3	66.2	58.2	50.1	36.2	31.7	17.1
1869	22.0	20.3	15.7	32.3	42.7	50.0	57.6	55.6	53.9	35.7	26.9	24.3
1870	17.6	14.7	20.5	36.5	47.4	57.4	60.0	57.1	54.3	43.2	30.2	20.5
1871	13.4	17.0	28.9	35.6	43.9	52.2	55.7	57.9	46.9	40.8	26.1	14.9
Means. 1841–48	18.13	15.72	22.48	33.82	42.67	50.91	55.62	56.43	49.39	36.74	30.41	21.36
Means. 1853–61	14.04	13.07	21.72	32.40	42.14	52.11	57.91	56.39	49.04	38.33	30.16	18.64
Means. 1862–71	15.46	16.52	22.17	34.02	43.62	53.15	59.18	57.33	50.92	40.19	30.85	19.94
Means. 1841–71	15.78	15.13	22.11	33.42	42.85	52.14	57.70	56.75	49.84	38.55	30.49	19.93

TORONTO METEOROLOGICAL OBSERVATIONS.

TABLE VII.

MONTHLY MEANS OF THE DAILY RANGES OF TEMPERATURE FROM 1841 TO 1871, TOGETHER WITH THE AVERAGES DERIVED FROM THE TWENTY-SEVEN YEARS, AND ALSO FROM GROUPS OF EIGHT, NINE, AND TEN YEARS.

The Years 1849 to 1852 are excluded from the General Averages for the sake of uniformity with the two previous Tables.)

Year.	Jan.	Feb.	Mar.	April.	May.	June.	July.	Aug.	Sept.	Oct.	Nov.	Dec.
1841	13.9	13.3	16.1	16.1	20.4	21.4	23.7	20.1	18.9	13.7	12.4	11.0
1842	17.2	14.2	15.7	17.1	21.4	21.3	24.5	19.8	18.2	17.5	13.1	13.5
1843	12.5	14.9	17.1	16.1	20.3	20.2	23.6	21.9	17.9	14.5	11.5	9.6
1844	14.1	15.7	15.1	20.8	21.0	20.7	22.9	19.6	20.7	16.6	12.7	14.2
1845	14.0	14.2	16.4	17.8	22.2	21.3	22.4	21.5	20.4	18.3	12.6	13.8
1846	14.0	19.0	14.8	16.4	17.0	18.4	20.8	17.7	16.2	14.6	9.5	10.7
1847	11.7	12.4	13.2	14.0	17.2	15.8	18.7	18.0	14.2	13.4	9.6	9.1
1848	12.4	12.7	12.3	17.2	18.6	20.0	17.3	18.2	17.7	12.6	9.2	11.1
1849	11.4	11.0	11.3	14.0	13.6	16.6	19.8	18.2	16.0	13.2	9.2	9.6
1850	11.6	15.4	14.4	15.9	19.9	22.0	18.2	17.3	20.1	17.8	15.5	11.8
1851	13.9	10.3	13.0	12.9	16.1	16.3	14.7	17.1	17.0	13.0	9.6	12.0
1852	10.9	13.2	14.0	10.8	17.0	18.1	18.3	15.8	17.8	15.7	9.6	10.0
1853	14.1	14.5	14.9	14.1	14.1	19.7	23.8	21.4	18.5	20.5	13.1	14.1
1854	15.8	20.4	13.5	17.1	23.9	24.7	26.3	25.4	23.5	17.7	13.9	15.1
1855	15.3	18.4	16.9	20.8	24.0	18.2	16.7	20.5	18.5	19.0	16.8	14.2
1856	16.7	20.6	17.6	17.1	19.0	19.2	21.4	20.7	21.0	18.8	14.3	13.1
1857	18.7	15.3	17.4	16.2	17.0	16.5	17.5	19.4	19.4	14.4	13.3	11.6
1858	11.6	13.3	15.1	14.2	14.0	17.5	15.4	16.2	16.7	12.4	7.9	11.8
1859	12.0	12.1	11.6	13.6	16.3	17.1	15.5	15.6	13.4	13.4	11.2	12.4
1860	12.2	14.1	14.6	14.8	16.2	17.3	17.2	17.4	15.8	12.0	9.7	9.6
1861	11.2	13.9	12.8	14.3	15.7	19.1	18.5	16.2	14.6	13.7	10.4	12.8
1862	12.6	12.9	11.5	12.9	19.4	18.1	18.3	17.9	15.6	13.4	10.1	10.5
1863	10.4	14.6	13.3	16.6	17.1	17.2	15.2	17.7	17.5	12.3	11.5	13.3
1864	12.1	12.6	13.2	12.9	16.7	20.2	20.2	15.8	14.9	12.3	11.5	12.5
1865	14.5	13.1	14.2	15.8	17.5	17.5	18.5	19.5	17.0	14.2	12.0	11.4
1866	13.6	15.5	11.4	16.9	17.7	18.1	19.0	16.9	15.3	13.8	10.6	11.2
1867	11.6	12.7	12.8	13.9	15.1	17.8	19.1	19.9	19.4	16.4	13.0	14.1
1868	12.3	18.4	15.2	16.4	15.2	18.3	19.2	18.7	14.2	13.6	9.7	12.0
1869	12.6	15.0	15.5	15.7	16.1	17.4	15.5	16.5	15.5	14.4	11.4	0.8
1870	14.6	13.3	12.5	17.0	19.1	19.0	17.7	19.8	14.9	15.2	13.9	11.5
1871	15.0	13.4	12.2	17.2	19.8	19.3	20.4	19.5	17.6	17.5	10.9	14.6
Means. 1841-48	13.72	14.80	15.09	16.94	19.88	19.89	21.74	19.60	17.65	15.40	11.45	11.63
Means. 1853-61	14.18	15.84	14.93	15.80	17.80	18.81	19.15	19.20	17.93	15.06	12.30	12.75
Means. 1862-71	12.93	14.15	13.18	15.53	17.37	18.29	18.31	18.22	16.19	14.31	11.46	12.09
Means. 1841-71	13.58	14.91	14.33	16.04	18.25	18.91	19.61	18.95	17.20	15.08	11.74	12.17

TORONTO METEOROLOGICAL OBSERVATIONS.

TABLE VIII.

Greatest Daily Range of Temperature in each Month from 1841 to 1871, together with the Averages derived from the Thirty-one Years, and also from Groups of Twelve, Nine and Ten Years.

[NOTE.—*The highest Daily Range in each year is indicated by an asterisk.*]

Year.	Jan.	Feb.	Mar.	April.	May.	June.	July.	Aug.	Sept.	Oct.	Nov.	Dec.
1841	36.8*	32.0	29.9	30.7	30.3	32.5	35.4	27.2	27.0	24.0	22.3	24.1
1842	36.1	27.7	32.7	52.1*	35.5	33.3	34.9	29.7	30.1	26.9	23.6	32.1
1843	27.1	24.6	29.2	33.4	33.8	30.9	33.1	28.9	39.9*	22.2	20.0	24.2
1844	32.9	24.8	25.9	35.9	32.8	40.6	33.0	31.7	44.6*	29.9	27.5	32.8
1845	25.4	39.8*	29.3	29.7	34.5	31.7	31.5	31.7	34.5	28.8	25.8	28.7
1846	26.8	34.5	24.3	39.6*	22.2	26.9	33.1	25.4	27.5	34.0	23.7	21.9
1847	32.3*	24.2	23.1	25.8	28.3	25.7	30.6	24.9	24.8	25.3	21.4	21.5
1848	31.4	21.0	28.3	31.5*	31.5	28.9	26.5	26.8	29.6	30.1	17.1	26.7
1849	31.2	24.1	31.6	35.3*	28.7	31.9	29.7	27.5	27.9	24.4	22.2	25.8
1850	22.0	29.2	23.8	26.7	39.7	40.8*	27.0	31.2	32.1	35.4	26.0	32.1
1851	32.8*	30.0	25.7	21.6	26.3	29.8	24.2	30.4	30.0	22.7	22.8	27.2
1852	21.2	27.2	34.1*	19.5	30.8	29.1	29.3	24.9	28.4	26.5	20.4	22.2
1853	40.9*	35.4	26.0	28.8	28.4	32.8	30.7	29.1	32.2	31.5	27.6	24.9
1854	39.6	37.1	27.1	35.4	32.2	41.8	44.5*	28.4	35.9	27.4	29.1	31.2
1855	25.0	34.2	37.3	37.2	35.4*	30.8	33.0	34.2	28.8	33.2	26.5	25.6
1856	34.6	28.7	32.4	29.4	44.2*	29.8	28.7	31.5	29.5	28.5	32.4	25.5
1857	35.0	32.0	37.0*	32.5	26.8	24.4	24.8	28.0	28.5	26.2	27.0	29.8
1858	25.5	25.6	25.4	24.8	25.0	26.4	24.6	31.2	29.0	24.0	17.3	27.3
1859	39.8*	21.9	29.9	27.2	25.4	27.8	24.3	24.7	22.8	26.0	25.4	26.7
1860	39.5	26.5	30.1	25.8	24.6	29.9	30.7*	24.4	26.2	23.2	25.0	23.5
1861	25.2	32.4	33.3	28.8	28.4	29.5	29.1	25.0	24.0	31.9	20.4	26.4
1862	25.8	30.0	23.6	23.5	37.0*	31.8	31.9	28.8	25.8	28.2	19.2	23.8
1863	24.6	35.6	39.6*	39.5	34.6	27.2	23.5	35.5	27.1	23.8	23.0	28.5
1864	26.9	37.4*	28.4	24.4	26.2	31.7	31.2	29.2	27.0	26.0	24.2	31.4
1865	31.4	26.0	26.8	30.0	27.0	36.9	29.0	30.8	24.9	24.8	24.2	30.6
1866	40.8*	38.1	21.6	36.2	31.6	28.0	35.0	27.1	24.5	24.8	24.2	33.8
1867	31.6	27.6	27.6	27.2	26.3	28.0	29.2	31.7	29.7	31.8	23.7	30.0
1868	30.0	38.7*	34.6	31.1	25.4	27.2	27.4	33.7	26.4	22.2	23.2	32.7
1869	33.6*	23.0	27.6	32.4	30.4	25.6	24.1	24.0	24.2	23.0	24.6	23.5
1870	36.2*	33.2	26.4	29.6	30.8	31.8	24.0	30.8	24.0	29.4	22.7	36.0
1871	34.6*	27.0	21.5	31.3	32.2	29.6	28.6	28.5	27.6	30.8	20.8	34.3
Means. 1841-52	29.67	28.26	28.67	32.07	31.28	31.84	30.69	28.36	31.42	27.52	22.74	26.61
Means. 1853-61	34.01	30.42	29.93	29.97	30.49	30.13	30.04	30.72	29.77	27.99	25.63	26.77
Means. 1862-71	31.55	31.66	27.77	29.62	30.17	30.08	28.39	29.81	26.12	26.48	22.98	30.46
Means. 1841-71	31.54	29.98	28.75	30.67	30.69	30.78	29.76	29.51	28.94	27.32	23.66	27.90

TORONTO METEOROLOGICAL OBSERVATIONS.

TABLE IX.

TABLE CONTAINING THE ABSOLUTELY HIGHEST TEMPERATURE IN EACH MONTH AND YEAR FROM 1841 TO 1871, TOGETHER WITH THE AVERAGES DERIVED FROM THIRTY-ONE YEARS, AND ALSO FROM GROUPS OF TWELVE, NINE, AND TEN YEARS.

Years.	Jan.	Feb.	Mar.	April.	May.	June.	July.	Aug.	Sept.	Oct.	Nov.	Dec.	Year.
1841	42.3	43.1	54.6	64.8	78.0	93.1	89.0	84.8	80.2	59.7	63.8	46.1	93.1
1842	49.4	50.2	70.3	89.8	74.8	80.2	91.0	81.8	83.8	68.6	56.6	40.5	91.0
1843	55.4	38.5	39.9	71.6	79.8	83.3	86.8	83.1	89.0	68.0	52.6	48.5	89.0
1844	45.3	47.9	50.8	74.6	78.4	83.3	86.6	86.8	81.8	71.6	56.0	48.5	86.8
1845	45.7	49.1	62.7	66.7	77.8	84.6	95.0	84.8	79.6	64.0	59.5	39.7	95.0
1846	44.0	41.9	49.6	81.8	79.7	84.2	91.6	96.4	84.3	70.1	55.6	49.2	94.6
1847	42.4	40.9	43.9	65.1	72.1	77.2	87.0	92.6	74.5	64.6	57.9	49.6	87.0
1848	51.1	46.6	58.6	65.1	78.0	92.0	82.2	87.0	80.4	61.8	49.0	48.8	92.0
1849	39.5	40.6	53.0	72.0	72.2	84.4	88.6	79.0	80.1	58.9	56.4	40.8	88.6
1850	46.4	49.6	46.5	65.7	77.8	85.6	86.2	85.0	76.0	66.7	62.8	48.8	86.2
1851	43.4	50.2	59.3	59.3	73.3	79.2	82.7	79.8	86.3	66.2	50.2	44.0	86.3
1852	37.3	41.2	44.8	53.8	73.3	86.1	90.1	81.2	81.8	70.7	50.4	51.0	90.1
1853	40.9	43.4	56.3	65.7	78.4	89.5	91.3	94.9	85.5	64.7	55.6	46.4	94.9
1854	46.4	42.8	55.1	64.5	71.4	92.5	98.0	99.2	93.6	75.4	55.4	44.6	99.2
1855	49.0	39.0	49.4	69.4	77.5	91.5	92.8	83.5	82.6	68.0	50.2	47.0	92.8
1856	34.4	37.8	41.4	72.2	82.2	89.2	96.6	82.7	78.4	71.4	56.4	42.2	96.6
1857	37.2	52.4	57.0	52.0	74.8	76.0	86.6	88.2	82.0	64.0	58.2	46.0	88.2
1858	47.4	42.4	55.4	65.2	69.8	90.2	85.0	84.0	81.4	76.3	53.0	45.4	90.2
1859	43.2	40.2	51.2	64.8	70.6	86.4	88.0	83.2	75.4	69.8	62.6	54.8	88.0
1860	46.4	50.2	67.0	61.8	74.5	81.6	88.0	87.0	75.8	68.0	64.5	39.0	86.0
1861	37.0	46.0	47.4	67.0	73.0	87.8	84.5	85.2	76.8	71.0	52.4	55.2	87.8
1862	44.5	37.8	43.2	68.0	78.5	85.4	95.5	89.5	79.4	76.6	58.0	50.1	95.5
1863	47.0	41.5	42.2	69.0	79.0	84.8	83.5	88.0	80.0	66.4	67.0	53.4	88.0
1864	41.2	45.0	50.2	59.4	79.0	93.4	90.2	94.0	73.0	67.0	60.2	50.4	94.0
1865	37.2	42.2	55.6	62.5	79.0	90.2	83.0	87.8	90.5	71.4	63.2	54.2	90.5
1866	41.0	45.0	45.8	71.0	73.4	90.5	94.0	77.0	80.0	71.0	54.2	51.0	94.0
1867	43.8	41.0	46.8	65.5	65.0	89.6	94.0	95.2	87.0	75.4	60.4	49.5	95.2
1868	39.0	45.0	59.0	64.0	73.0	84.2	93.4	84.4	75.0	67.6	50.5	41.2	93.4
1869	45.0	46.0	46.8	72.2	74.2	81.4	84.9	89.0	81.0	69.8	58.0	45.0	89.0
1870	45.0	40.6	41.0	67.0	81.2	88.4	87.4	84.0	78.0	68.5	57.2	45.2	88.4
1871	46.4	48.0	58.5	72.8	85.0	83.0	88.4	89.5	81.8	72.2	47.1	48.2	89.5
Means 1841-52	45.18	45.07	52.83	69.10	76.27	84.48	88.32	83.52	81.48	65.91	55.02	46.20	89.97
Means 1853-61	42.43	44.47	53.76	64.73	75.09	87.19	90.09	87.43	81.50	69.84	57.48	46.76	91.74
Means 1862-71	43.01	43.51	49.21	67.14	76.73	86.09	89.43	87.84	80.57	70.59	57.68	49.12	91.75
Means 1841-71	43.88	44.39	51.93	67.24	76.25	86.08	89.19	86.05	81.19	68.50	56.91	47.34	91.06

12

TORONTO METEOROLOGICAL OBSERVATIONS.

TABLE X.

TABLE CONTAINING THE ABSOLUTELY LOWEST TEMPERATURE IN EACH MONTH AND YEAR FROM 1841 TO 1871, TOGETHER WITH THE AVERAGES DERIVED FROM THIRTY-ONE YEARS, AND ALSO FROM GROUPS OF TWELVE, NINE, AND TEN YEARS.

Year.	Jan.	Feb.	Mar.	April.	May.	June.	July.	Aug.	Sept.	Oct.	Nov.	Dec.	Year.
1841	-6.4	-1.3	-6.7	19.9	26.5	45.3	39.9	45.7	34.2	20.6	8.5	3.1	-6.7
1842	1.9	2.9	15.1	20.1	27.3	28.1	42.5	45.9	27.9	27.5	8.1	3.2	1.9
1843	-1.8	-9.4	-2.5	14.7	29.2	28.2	38.7	44.0	32.2	24.2	14.1	3.1	-9.4
1844	-7.2	0.6	9.6	14.9	28.7	30.2	40.1	43.5	28.2	15.9	12.1	1.6	-7.2
1845	-0.2	-4.2	6.6	15.5	27.8	39.5	45.7	41.5	34.0	19.7	8.1	-2.4	-4.2
1846	-1.3	-16.7	8.3	24.2	33.1	39.1	44.5	49.5	37.3	29.7	18.0	3.9	-16.7
1847	2.7	0.0	5.6	9.3	26.7	36.7	43.2	44.6	35.0	20.4	8.7	0.3	0.0
1848	-11.4	0.0	0.0	22.7	31.3	37.4	44.1	48.7	28.1	24.5	15.9	1.1	-11.4
1849	-14.2	-9.8	15.1	15.5	27.9	35.2	45.2	49.6	32.7	24.2	26.5	-6.5	-14.2
1850	9.9	2.2	7.2	18.0	27.5	34.2	51.6	41.0	29.5	22.4	11.0	-9.0	-9.0
1851	-12.8	2.0	12.0	25.8	28.0	37.0	46.5	42.0	32.0	25.2	13.8	-14.8	-14.8
1852	-10.6	-6.2	-7.4	20.0	32.0	37.2	48.5	45.8	35.8	23.8	18.2	13.2	-10.6
1853	-9.7	-1.4	0.0	25.0	32.2	39.2	41.6	42.5	33.9	23.4	12.8	-8.4	-9.7
1854	-5.4	-10.8	7.4	20.2	25.2	35.2	42.5	45.6	35.8	26.4	13.8	-7.0	-10.8
1855	-5.4	-25.4	-2.9	10.7	33.0	36.2	40.2	40.0	33.0	22.6	15.5	-5.2	-25.4
1856	-12.0	-18.7	-14.0	14.2	31.2	42.0	49.5	41.5	35.0	23.0	18.8	-9.1	-18.7
1857	-20.1	-5.9	-5.5	5.9	26.0	35.0	47.0	46.0	34.1	26.5	-3.5	4.7	-20.1
1858	6.5	-7.3	-5.5	21.8	31.0	42.5	52.0	44.0	25.6	31.5	15.3	4.2	-7.3
1859	-26.5	2.1	9.8	22.6	39.5	32.2	44.7	45.8	35.7	22.3	21.8	-6.0	-26.5
1860	-6.8	-8.5	12.8	19.5	32.5	49.2	43.8	46.8	28.7	26.4	13.2	-7.0	-8.5
1861	-11.2	-20.8	-5.2	23.8	28.0	41.6	47.0	47.0	37.1	29.0	23.0	5.5	-20.8
1862	-2.6	-5.2	8.0	14.5	32.4	39.4	48.2	42.8	30.0	26.2	16.2	-3.4	-5.2
1863	-14.0	-19.8	-4.0	8.6	30.4	27.4	48.0	42.4	31.4	30.5	17.8	-1.5	-19.8
1864	-9.0	-15.0	3.0	28.1	32.2	34.8	49.0	47.0	37.8	28.0	21.0	-10.4	-15.0
1865	-9.0	-10.0	-3.5	23.0	30.0	43.0	45.8	44.4	42.0	21.9	23.6	5.7	-10.0
1866	-14.0	-8.0	7.5	26.5	33.4	40.0	47.8	42.4	31.4	31.8	21.8	-5.0	-14.0
1867	-4.8	0.2	3.0	25.4	24.6	44.0	48.2	42.2	31.8	31.0	9.6	-12.8	-12.8
1868	-7.0	-11.5	-15.6	9.2	33.2	38.0	59.0	46.8	36.0	24.0	20.1	-3.2	-15.6
1869	-1.0	-1.0	-5.4	16.6	31.4	36.4	49.8	43.5	34.4	18.7	13.0	6.0	-5.4
1870	-3.2	-6.6	5.2	29.6	38.8	50.0	48.0	40.0	45.8	30.2	20.8	-5.8	-6.6
1871	-13.2	-15.8	17.6	26.4	32.4	41.2	47.8	46.0	31.0	28.6	0.0	-21.0	-21.0
Means. 1841–52	-4.26	-3.33	5.24	18.38	28.83	35.84	44.21	44.93	32.24	22.48	13.55	-0.27	-8.52
Means. 1853–61	-10.07	-10.74	-0.34	18.19	30.96	39.23	46.37	41.36	34.32	25.90	14.52	-3.14	-16.42
Means. 1862–71	-7.78	-9.27	1.52	20.99	32.48	40.42	49.16	43.75	36.06	27.06	16.39	-5.14	-12.54
Means. 1841–71	-7.09	-7.40	2.42	19.17	30.63	38.30	46.43	44.36	34.27	24.93	14.76	-2.67	-12.11

13

TORONTO METEOROLOGICAL OBSERVATIONS.

TABLE XI.

MONTHLY AND YEARLY RANGES OF TEMPERATURE FROM 1841 TO 1871, OR THE DIFFERENCES BETWEEN THE HIGHEST AND LOWEST TEMPERATURES IN EACH MONTH, AND THE DIFFERENCES BETWEEN THE HIGHEST AND LOWEST TEMPERATURES IN EACH YEAR; ALSO, AVERAGES DERIVED FROM THIRTY-ONE YEARS, AND FROM GROUPS OF TWELVE, NINE, AND TEN YEARS.

Year.	Jan.	Feb.	Mar.	April	May.	June.	July.	Aug.	Sept.	Oct.	Nov.	Dec.	Year.
1841	48.7	45.4	61.3	43.9	51.5	47.8	49.1	39.1	46.0	39.1	55.3	43.0	99.8
1842	47.5	47.3	55.2	69.7	47.5	52.1	48.5	31.9	55.9	41.1	48.7	37.3	89.1
1843	57.2	47.9	42.4	56.9	50.6	55.1	48.1	39.1	56.8	43.8	38.5	45.4	98.4
1844	52.5	47.3	41.2	59.7	49.7	50.1	46.5	43.3	53.0	55.7	43.0	46.0	94.0
1845	45.9	53.3	56.1	51.2	50.0	46.1	40.3	43.3	45.0	44.3	51.4	42.1	99.2
1846	45.3	58.0	41.3	57.6	46.0	45.1	50.1	36.9	47.0	49.4	37.6	45.3	111.3
1847	39.7	49.9	38.3	55.8	45.4	41.1	43.8	38.0	39.5	44.2	49.2	49.3	87.0
1848	62.5	46.6	58.6	42.4	46.7	54.6	38.1	38.3	52.3	37.3	53.1	47.7	103.4
1849	53.7	50.4	37.9	50.5	44.3	49.2	43.4	30.0	47.4	34.7	29.0	47.3	102.8
1850	36.5	47.4	39.3	47.7	50.3	51.4	34.6	44.0	46.5	44.8	51.8	57.8	95.2
1851	56.2	48.2	47.3	33.5	45.3	42.2	36.2	37.8	54.3	41.0	36.4	58.6	101.1
1852	47.9	47.4	52.2	33.8	41.3	48.9	41.6	35.4	46.0	46.9	32.2	37.8	100.7
1853	50.6	44.8	56.3	49.7	46.2	50.3	49.7	52.4	51.6	41.3	42.8	54.8	104.6
1854	51.8	53.6	47.7	44.3	46.2	67.3	55.5	53.6	57.8	49.0	41.6	51.8	110.0
1855	54.4	64.4	52.3	58.7	41.5	55.3	43.6	43.5	49.6	45.4	43.7	32.2	118.2
1856	46.4	56.5	55.4	58.0	51.0	47.2	47.1	41.2	43.4	48.4	37.6	51.3	115.3
1857	57.3	58.3	63.1	46.1	48.8	41.0	39.6	42.2	47.0	37.5	61.7	41.3	108.3
1858	40.9	49.7	60.9	43.4	38.8	47.7	33.0	40.0	45.8	41.8	37.7	41.2	97.5
1859	69.7	44.1	44.4	42.2	40.1	54.2	43.3	36.4	39.7	47.5	40.8	60.8	114.5
1860	53.2	58.7	51.2	42.3	42.0	32.4	44.2	40.2	47.1	39.6	51.3	46.0	96.5
1861	48.2	66.6	52.6	43.2	45.0	46.2	37.5	38.2	41.7	42.0	29.4	49.7	108.0
1862	47.1	43.0	35.2	53.5	46.1	46.0	47.3	46.7	40.4	50.4	41.8	53.5	100.7
1863	61.0	61.3	46.2	60.4	42.6	47.4	35.5	45.6	48.6	35.9	49.2	54.9	107.8
1864	53.2	60.0	47.2	31.3	46.8	58.6	41.2	47.0	35.2	39.0	39.2	60.8	109.0
1865	46.2	52.2	59.1	39.5	49.0	47.2	57.2	43.4	48.5	40.8	39.6	48.5	100.5
1866	58.0	53.0	38.3	42.5	40.0	50.5	46.2	34.6	45.6	39.2	32.4	56.0	108.0
1867	48.6	43.8	43.8	40.1	40.4	44.6	43.8	53.0	55.2	44.4	50.8	62.3	108.0
1868	46.0	56.5	74.0	54.8	39.8	46.2	34.4	37.6	39.0	43.6	30.4	47.4	109.0
1869	46.0	47.0	52.2	55.6	42.8	45.0	35.1	45.5	46.0	51.1	45.0	39.0	94.4
1870	48.2	47.2	38.8	37.4	42.4	38.4	39.4	44.0	32.2	38.5	36.4	51.0	95.0
1871	59.6	63.8	41.5	46.4	52.6	41.8	40.6	43.5	47.8	43.6	47.1	69.2	110.5
Means 1841-52	49.47	49.39	47.50	50.81	47.43	48.01	44.11	38.19	49.24	43.48	42.33	46.50	98.60
Means 1853-61	52.50	55.21	54.10	46.54	44.73	47.94	43.72	43.08	47.18	43.01	42.96	49.90	108.10
Means 1862-71	51.39	52.78	47.69	46.15	44.25	44.57	40.27	44.09	43.55	41.19	51.20	104.29
Means 1841-71	50.98	51.79	49.51	49.07	45.62	47.77	42.70	41.67	46.92	43.61	42.15	50.01	103.17

14

TORONTO METEOROLOGICAL OBSERVATIONS.

TABLE XII.

AVERAGES OF THE DAILY MEAN TEMPERATURES IN EVERY DAY OF THE YEAR, DERIVED FROM GROUPS OF TWELVE AND NINETEEN YEARS, WITH THE NUMBER OF DAYS INCLUDED IN EACH AVERAGE.

Days.	JANUARY.				FEBRUARY.				MARCH.				Days.
	1841 to 1852.		1853 to 1871.		1841 to 1852.		1853 to 1871.		1841 to 1852.		1853 to 1871.		
	Average	Nos.	Average	Nos.	Average	Nos.	Average	Nos.	Average	Nos.	Average	Nos.	
1	27.9	11	25.2	15	21.0	10	24.7	17	26.9	11	27.3	16	1
2	24.7	10	22.4	16	28.1	10	20.4	17	22.8	10	25.4	17	2
3	23.4	10	23.9	16	26.7	11	18.0	16	23.7	10	25.7	17	3
4	21.9	10	22.2	17	26.0	10	19.4	17	25.2	11	22.7	16	4
5	23.8	10	24.5	17	23.9	11	18.8	16	29.7	10	24.1	16	5
6	26.7	11	22.6	16	22.1	10	20.3	16	26.8	11	24.3	15	6
7	26.2	10	18.3	18	21.8	10	19.7	16	30.5	9	27.7	17	7
8	24.1	11	17.5	15	20.2	10	21.7	17	31.4	11	27.5	16	8
9	25.8	10	21.5	16	22.9	10	22.1	17	30.2	10	28.6	17	9
10	21.9	10	22.0	16	23.0	11	17.2	16	29.5	10	25.5	17	10
11	23.4	10	22.7	17	21.1	10	20.8	17	28.5	11	27.3	16	11
12	24.5	10	24.3	17	18.9	11	22.6	15	30.6	10	26.1	16	12
13	25.8	11	23.9	16	20.8	10	23.7	16	32.0	11	27.6	15	13
14	28.7	10	23.1	17	21.4	10	22.5	16	29.1	9	29.6	17	14
15	30.2	11	23.0	15	21.9	10	24.3	17	26.8	11	30.1	16	15
16	27.0	10	21.0	16	19.6	10	24.1	17	28.3	10	30.9	17	16
17	22.3	10	18.5	16	19.4	11	23.2	16	29.7	10	33.1	17	17
18	20.8	10	21.2	17	23.5	10	21.8	17	28.4	11	28.5	16	18
19	18.3	10	22.4	17	23.5	11	22.6	15	31.2	10	26.8	16	19
20	24.0	11	27.0	16	27.0	10	24.3	16	31.0	11	29.1	15	20
21	26.3	10	22.9	17	30.0	10	21.4	16	30.9	8	29.9	16	21
22	20.6	11	18.7	15	27.4	10	25.4	17	31.4	11	30.3	16	22
23	28.2	10	20.6	16	21.6	10	22.0	17	32.0	10	32.7	17	23
24	28.6	10	21.6	16	25.5	11	23.6	16	34.0	10	30.4	17	24
25	26.5	10	20.2	17	26.2	10	24.1	17	33.4	10	31.5	15	25
26	25.1	10	21.3	17	28.3	11	24.6	15	36.6	2	30.3	15	26
27	23.9	11	20.9	16	27.5	10	25.1	16	34.5	11	30.9	15	27
28	30.0	10	20.8	17	28.4	10	26.6	16	36.5	9	31.4	17	28
29	26.2	11	25.0	15	...	...	24.4	4	36.3	10	32.0	16	29
30	19.9	10	21.7	17	...	...	...	...	31.8	10	38.1	16	30
31	20.1	10	24.3	16	...	...	...	...	35.2	10	37.1	17	31

TORONTO METEOROLOGICAL OBSERVATIONS.

TABLE XII.—*(Continued.)*

AVERAGES OF THE DAILY MEAN TEMPERATURES IN EVERY DAY OF THE YEAR, DERIVED FROM GROUPS OF TWELVE AND NINETEEN YEARS, WITH THE NUMBER OF DAYS INCLUDED IN EACH AVERAGE.

	APRIL.				MAY.				JUNE.				
Days.	1841 to 1852.		1853 to 1871.		1841 to 1852.		1853 to 1871.		1841 to 1852.		1853 to 1871.		Days.
	Average	Nos.	Average	Nos.	Average	Nos.	Average	Nos.	Average	Nos.	Average	Nos.	
1	34.1	11	37.8	16	45.8	10	43.7	15	54.6	10	58.3	17	1
2	39.3	9	33.6	15	46.0	9	44.6	17	58.5	10	59.0	17	2
3	39.0	11	36.1	14	45.8	10	45.8	16	57.5	11	60.0	16	3
4	39.7	0	37.2	17	46.4	10	49.1	17	58.7	10	56.0	15	4
5	35.3	10	38.6	16	46.6	10	49.2	17	55.9	11	58.1	15	5
6	38.9	9	37.3	15	48.9	11	48.5	16	54.2	9	59.0	17	6
7	39.1	10	32.9	17	48.3	10	49.0	16	57.9	11	59.8	16	7
8	38.1	11	38.0	16	50.8	11	49.5	15	57.5	10	58.4	17	8
9	33.6	9	39.6	16	49.3	9	50.4	17	61.1	10	57.4	17	9
10	40.1	10	38.3	13	49.4	11	49.4	16	56.9	11	59.2	16	10
11	40.0	9	40.1	17	49.7	10	48.5	17	56.0	10	57.9	16	11
12	40.3	11	41.9	16	53.2	10	51.4	17	57.1	11	60.5	15	12
13	38.8	10	38.3	17	52.9	11	50.5	16	58.3	9	61.4	17	13
14	37.0	9	40.4	15	51.4	10	52.2	16	59.5	11	61.7	16	14
15	40.7	11	41.3	15	51.8	11	52.1	15	62.4	10	63.1	17	15
16	39.4	10	43.5	16	52.6	9	53.8	17	61.0	10	60.9	17	16
17	40.3	11	42.8	16	52.0	11	52.5	16	61.2	11	62.9	10	17
18	38.5	8	43.0	16	52.3	10	51.2	17	64.1	10	63.1	16	18
19	40.2	11	44.8	15	51.9	10	52.8	17	64.8	11	63.0	15	19
20	42.1	2	44.4	17	50.4	11	53.4	16	64.2	9	63.2	17	20
21	46.7	9	45.5	17	50.8	10	53.0	16	64.2	11	63.6	16	21
22	47.2	11	41.1	15	52.5	11	53.5	15	63.9	10	64.3	17	22
23	44.6	10	40.9	15	52.7	9	53.3	17	64.6	10	64.0	17	23
24	46.2	11	42.9	16	54.3	11	54.1	13	64.0	11	64.5	16	24
25	45.6	9	42.7	17	56.7	10	57.8	17	63.6	10	66.8	16	25
26	45.0	11	41.7	16	55.6	10	56.9	17	66.6	11	68.5	15	26
27	42.8	10	43.0	17	55.0	11	56.1	16	65.4	9	66.9	17	27
28	45.8	10	45.9	17	58.5	10	54.2	16	64.4	11	67.3	16	28
29	44.2	11	45.0	16	55.7	11	55.5	15	66.5	10	66.8	17	29
30	47.6	10	47.5	15	51.6	9	57.0	17	66.6	10	66.6	17	30
31	...	...	...	...	51.6	11	57.1	16	...	...	...	...	31

TORONTO METEOROLOGICAL OBSERVATIONS.

TABLE XII.—(Continued.)

AVERAGES OF THE DAILY MEAN TEMPERATURES IN EVERY DAY OF THE YEAR, DERIVED FROM GROUPS OF TWELVE AND NINETEEN YEARS, WITH THE NUMBER OF DAYS INCLUDED IN EACH AVERAGE.

Days.	JULY.				AUGUST.				SEPTEMBER.				Days.
	1841 to 1852.		1853 to 1871.		1841 to 1852.		1853 to 1871.		1841 to 1852.		1853 to 1871.		
	Average	Nos	Average	Nos.	Average	Nos.	Average	Nos.	Average	Nos.	Average	Nos.	
1	64.1	11	64.1	15	62.9	9	69.8	17	67.3	10	61.9	17	1
2	62.4	10	65.2	16	63.2	11	68.8	16	66.7	11	62.4	16	2
3	61.4	11	69.9	15	65.5	10	68.8	17	63.8	10	61.4	16	3
4	62.6	9	68.2	17	66.4	10	68.0	17	65.0	11	64.0	15	4
5	64.0	11	66.1	16	67.5	11	69.6	16	63.3	9	64.8	17	5
6	65.3	10	67.3	17	66.7	10	68.4	16	61.8	11	64.9	16	6
7	66.1	10	67.8	17	67.9	11	67.5	15	63.3	10	60.9	17	7
8	66.1	11	69.6	16	67.2	9	70.3	17	61.4	10	61.3	17	8
9	67.3	10	67.5	16	68.2	11	69.5	16	60.0	11	62.3	16	9
10	68.2	11	67.3	15	65.8	10	69.6	17	61.8	10	60.9	16	10
11	67.6	9	68.0	17	65.3	10	68.1	17	59.8	11	62.8	15	11
12	69.5	11	66.5	16	67.5	11	66.8	16	58.7	9	61.1	17	12
13	68.5	10	67.6	17	66.5	10	66.8	16	54.9	11	58.2	16	13
14	67.3	10	69.2	17	66.5	11	65.8	15	56.9	10	58.0	17	14
15	66.3	11	68.7	16	65.6	9	66.1	17	55.3	10	59.3	17	15
16	67.5	10	69.7	16	66.6	11	65.9	16	55.5	11	58.5	16	16
17	68.1	11	69.0	15	65.5	10	65.2	17	58.2	10	60.3	16	17
18	68.0	9	69.6	17	64.9	10	64.1	17	57.7	11	56.8	15	18
19	67.5	10	68.3	16	64.4	11	65.0	16	57.2	9	56.2	17	19
20	67.8	10	67.8	17	64.4	10	65.4	16	57.3	11	55.7	16	20
21	68.6	10	65.9	17	65.7	11	65.8	15	56.0	10	53.0	17	21
22	68.7	11	67.5	16	65.4	9	65.3	17	52.0	10	53.8	17	22
23	68.4	10	67.3	16	65.9	11	63.6	16	56.2	11	56.9	16	23
24	66.9	11	68.6	15	64.3	10	65.4	17	53.0	10	55.8	16	24
25	65.6	9	69.2	17	66.7	10	63.4	17	52.4	11	55.5	15	25
26	65.5	11	68.9	16	65.0	11	64.8	16	48.2	9	53.5	17	26
27	63.6	10	68.8	17	61.9	10	62.7	16	48.7	11	53.1	16	27
28	64.6	10	68.0	17	63.3	11	64.3	15	49.6	10	52.2	17	28
29	66.8	11	67.1	16	65.6	9	61.7	16	52.8	10	52.2	17	29
30	64.6	10	68.3	16	66.2	11	60.8	16	50.7	11	51.2	16	30
31	63.2	11	67.5	15	66.0	10	61.1	17	...	...	...	...	31

TORONTO METEOROLOGICAL OBSERVATIONS.

TABLE XII.—*(Continued.)*

AVERAGES OF THE DAILY MEAN TEMPERATURES IN EVERY DAY OF THE YEAR, DERIVED FROM GROUPS OF TWELVE AND NINETEEN YEARS, WITH THE NUMBER OF DAYS INCLUDED IN EACH AVERAGE.

Days.	OCTOBER.				NOVEMBER.				DECEMBER.				Days.
	1841 to 1852.		1853 to 1871.		1841 to 1852.		1853 to 1871.		1841 to 1852.		1853 to 1871.		
	Average	Nos.	Average	Nos.	Average	Nos.	Average	Nos.	Average	Nos.	Average	Nos.	
1	48.9	10	51.7	16	43.8	11	45.0	16	27.8	10	30.8	17	1
2	49.8	11	53.1	15	42.9	10	42.1	17	30.6	11	28.7	16	2
3	49.8	9	52.0	17	41.1	10	39.7	17	32.5	10	28.4	16	3
4	50.0	11	52.5	16	30.5	11	40.2	16	33.1	11	29.4	15	4
5	50.1	10	51.2	17	41.2	10	39.9	16	28.1	9	30.1	16	5
6	50.5	10	52.3	16	38.3	11	37.6	15	29.4	11	29.0	16	6
7	50.8	11	53.8	15	39.8	9	37.9	17	32.5	10	29.6	17	7
8	52.5	10	49.0	16	37.7	11	38.9	16	33.9	10	25.3	17	8
9	51.7	11	52.9	15	37.8	10	40.2	17	31.9	11	25.9	16	9
10	48.8	9	50.5	17	38.0	10	36.2	17	28.2	10	26.9	16	10
11	49.3	11	49.3	16	37.4	11	36.3	16	27.1	11	26.9	15	11
12	45.9	10	46.1	17	39.2	10	39.0	16	23.3	9	25.1	17	12
13	44.2	10	46.1	18	37.1	11	37.8	15	26.5	11	26.0	16	13
14	43.6	11	46.7	16	37.1	9	37.3	17	30.3	10	24.8	17	14
15	42.7	10	45.5	16	35.8	11	34.3	16	27.4	10	26.1	17	15
16	45.0	11	45.9	15	37.9	10	35.5	17	24.8	11	27.6	16	16
17	42.6	9	47.3	16	38.6	10	37.3	17	21.2	10	26.8	16	17
18	44.5	11	46.8	16	35.5	11	35.3	16	24.4	11	22.3	15	18
19	40.8	10	46.5	17	34.7	10	36.2	16	25.0	9	23.4	17	19
20	42.3	10	44.3	17	36.4	11	32.4	16	22.0	11	21.9	16	20
21	40.9	11	44.3	16	35.3	9	34.4	17	23.4	10	22.6	17	21
22	40.9	10	45.0	16	35.7	11	34.0	16	19.0	10	21.5	17	22
23	40.2	11	43.2	15	36.5	10	33.8	17	22.1	11	20.4	16	23
24	43.7	9	40.9	17	34.5	10	30.8	17	24.1	10	19.2	16	24
25	41.1	11	41.4	16	30.8	11	33.7	16	...	...	...	...	25
26	39.7	10	40.9	17	29.7	10	34.2	16	23.3	9	26.6	13	26
27	38.9	10	41.0	17	28.7	11	33.4	15	26.6	11	26.2	16	27
28	40.5	11	41.0	16	29.7	9	32.8	17	27.3	10	28.4	17	28
29	42.9	10	42.5	16	28.1	11	34.2	16	30.7	10	20.6	17	29
30	42.2	11	44.7	15	30.1	10	31.0	17	28.8	11	24.4	16	30
31	38.9	9	43.4	17	...	...	...	...	26.1	10	23.4	16	31

TORONTO METEOROLOGICAL OBSERVATIONS.

TABLE XIII.

Mean Abnormal Variations of Temperature, with their proper Signs arranged according to the direction of the Wind at the time of observation, in each Month, in each Quarter, and in the Year, for the Eight Years, 1860–67.

	N.	N. E.	E.	S. E.	S.	S. W.	W.	N. W.	Calms.
January............	−11.42	−3.39	+4.07	+7.04	+4.94	+0.26	−4.13	−8.34	−4.68
February	−5.98	+0.75	+3.97	+2.94	+7.43	+5.28	−0.41	−5.68	+0.01
March...............	−3.27	−0.83	+0.91	−0.25	+1.41	+2.59	−2.42	−4.05	−1.67
April	−1.54	+0.07	+1.16	+1.37	+0.17	+1.85	−0.91	−2.34	+0.75
May..................	+1.06	+1.26	−1.61	−0.08	+0.19	+2.20	−0.99	−1.40	+0.70
June	+1.21	+1.18	−0.16	+0.15	+0.23	+3.13	+2.84	+0.75	+1.27
July	+0.43	−0.28	−1.26	+0.68	−0.20	+3.78	+2.31	−0.47	+2.75
August	−0.06	−1.19	+0.12	−0.06	+0.20	+2.45	−0.30	−1.34	+0.61
September........	−2.46	−1.15	+0.71	−0.14	+2.64	+5.27	+0.60	−2.52	+1.89
October	−0.02	+2.73	+4.43	+3.99	+5.07	+7.31	+0.99	−1.39	+2.13
November	−2.56	−0.22	+3.72	−6.09	+6.32	+4.20	−0.21	−1.34	+0.70
December	−10.50	−4.35	+5.74	+3.01	+4.94	+5.51	−1.81	−4.44	−1.36
Spring. Mar. to May ...	−1.08	+0.18	+0.32	+0.40	+0.45	+2.25	−1.69	−2.56	+0.12
Summer. June to Aug...	+0.45	+0.01	−0.41	+0.22	+0.05	+3.15	+1.53	−0.44	+1.47
Autumn. Sept. to Nov....	−1.51	+0.68	+2.95	+3.11	+4.43	+5.41	+0.33	−1.71	+1.63
Winter. Dec. to Feb......	−9.52	−2.15	+4.56	+3.91	+5.74	+3.39	−2.14	−6.19	−2.37
Year	−2.85	−0.30	+1.58	+1.76	+1.95	+3.64	−0.83	−2.61	+0.49

TORONTO METEOROLOGICAL OBSERVATIONS.

TABLE XIV.

MONTHLY AND YEARLY MEANS OF THE DIURNAL CHANGE OF TEMPERATURE (EXCLUSIVE OF THAT DUE TO ANNUAL VARIATION), FROM 6 A.M. TO 6 A.M., FOR THE PERIODS 1854-59 INCLUSIVE, AND 1860-62 INCLUSIVE, ARRANGED ACCORDING TO THE DAILY RESULTANT DIRECTION OF THE WIND.

	N.		N. E.		E.		S. E.	
	1854-59.	1860-62.	1854-59.	1860-62.	1854-59.	1860-62.	1854-59.	1860-62.
January	−5.1	−3.c	+3.3	+6.8	+10.5	+10.6	+6.0	*
February	−4.6	−2.2	+1.4	+4.1	+9.0	+12.0	−17.8	+5.1
March	−0.8	−3.4	0.0	+2.7	+5.6	+5.1	+7.0	−4.8
April	−2.7	−2.3	+2.2	+3.0	+2.9	+2.2	+4.8	+5.5
May	−2.0	−0.1	+0.6	+0.4	+1.8	+1.1	+2.5	+3.0
June	−2.3	−2.0	+0.7	+0.3	+0.3	−0.3	+2.8	+6.8
July	−1.6	−2.3	−0.5	+0.6	+1.5	+1.9	+2.1	+2.2
August	−4.0	−2.0	+3.2	−1.2	+1.7	+1.7	+3.7	+8.1
September	−3.7	−3.7	+0.2	+0.7	+3.8	+7.3	+5.3	+9.9
October	−6.2	−2.0	+1.2	+1.3	+3.4	+4.8	+5.4	+3.2
November	−3.8	−0.8	−1.7	+2.3	+4.1	+1.4	+4.3	+11.6
December	−1.7	+1.4	+4.3	+4.8	+4.8	+8.1	+10.2	+10.9
Year	−3.3	−1.9	+1.5	+2.4	+3.5	+4.0	+4.6	+6.3

	S.		S. W.		W.		N. W.	
	1854-59.	1860-62	1854-59.	1860-62.	1854-59.	1860-62.	1854-59.	1860-62.
January	+11.7	−3.8	+3.1	+5.3	−4.1	−3.5	−9.0	−12.4
February	+1.6	+7.8	+7.4	+3.4	−1.8	−2.7	−7.1	−7.4
March	+3.2	+8.4	+4.4	+5.7	−3.8	−2.2	−3.6	−4.5
April	+2.1	+5.8	+0.4	+2.5	−2.4	−4.4	−3.4	−4.2
May	+0.6	+1.4	+0.8	+3.5	−1.7	−2.6	−3.6	−2.6
June	+1.6	+4.7	+1.5	+4.0	−0.4	−2.2	−3.6	−2.1
July	+2.5	+2.7	+0.8	+2.5	−3.4	−3.2	−4.2	−2.3
August	+1.8	+1.1	+2.6	+1.8	−2.0	−2.3	−3.4	−4.3
September	+5.1	+6.1	+1.6	−0.2	−4.4	−3.5	−6.4	−6.6
October	+3.7	+14.1	+3.0	+1.3	−3.0	−3.7	−2.4	−5.1
November	+9.9	+6.0	+0.7	−0.3	−2.9	−2.5	−4.2	−3.5
December	+18.0	+0.6	+0.1	+5.2	−3.4	−5.0	−4.5	−4.3
Year	+3.0	+3.9	+2.2	+2.7	−2.9	−3.2	−4.5	−4.5

* No case of a S. E. Resultant in January, 1860-62.

TORONTO METEOROLOGICAL OBSERVATIONS.

TABLE XV.

MONTHLY AND ANNUAL MEANS OF THE BAROMETRIC PRESSURE FOR EACH OF THE TWENTY-FOUR HOURS OF TORONTO ASTRONOMICAL TIME, AND FOR THE TWENTY-FOUR HOURS COLLECTIVELY, FROM HOURLY OBSERVATIONS IN THE SIX YEARS FROM 1ST JULY, 1842, TO 30TH JUNE, 1848.

Barometer at $32° = 29$ inches + the numbers in the Table.

Toronto Astronomical Time.	Jan.	Feb	Mar.	April.	May.	June.	July.	Aug.	Sept.	Oct.	Nov.	Dec.	Annual Means.
	in.	in.	in.	in.	in.	in.	in.	in.	in.	in.	in.	in.	in.
0	0.610	0.623	0.630	0.074	0.573	0.590	0.602	0.654	0.659	0.666	0.626	0.040	0.629
1	.596	.606	.616	.660	.563	.580	.593	.646	.649	.653	.615	.628	.018
2	.593	.596	.604	.654	.555	.572	.584	.635	.636	.645	.608	.621	.608
3	.599	.596	.600	.644	.546	.565	.576	.624	.628	.643	.610	.625	.605
4	.604	.596	.600	.640	.540	.558	.570	.620	.625	.643	.612	.632	.603
5	.610	.600	.605	.642	.538	.553	.564	617	.625	.647	.616	.634	.604
6	.618	.607	.609	.642	.540	.553	.567	.618	.626	.652	.621	.640	.608
7	.622	.614	.615	.643	.544	.556	.569	.619	.632	.656	.622	.644	.611
8	.623	.616	.622	.652	.553	.560	.574	.628	.641	.660	.662	.643	.616
9	.623	.618	.627	.653	.562	.571	.580	.633	.642	.663	.662	.641	.620
10	.621	.617	.622	.650	.565	.573	.588	.633	.643	665	.621	.641	.620
11	.619	.614	.626	.648	.566	.575	.590	.635	.642	.663	.618	.638	.620
12	.618	.602	.619	.644	.562	.568	.586	.633	.637	.663	.626	.637	.616
13	.620	.602	.619	.637	.560	.566	.584	.629	.636	.666	.626	.635	.615
14	.625	.604	.618	.636	.558	.565	.583	.626	.636	.664	.629	.641	.615
15	.623	.604	.613	.637	.560	.566	.583	.626	.636	.662	.628	.641	.615
16	.617	.605	.613	.638	.562	.572	.587	.629	.640	.664	.628	.635	.616
17	.613	.607	.620	.646	.574	.585	.598	.635	.648	.608	.626	.634	.621
18	.617	.614	.626	.673	.582	.595	.603	.651	.665	.664	.630	.649	.631
19	.622	.625	.637	.685	.589	.602	.610	.659	.672	.677	.638	.654	.639
20	.634	.638	.643	.692	.592	.605	614	.663	.674	.684	.647	.665	.646
21	.641	.644	.645	.693	.590	.604	.614	.666	.678	.686	.648	.669	.648
22	.643	.643	.644	.692	.590	.603	.613	.667	.676	.684	.651	.673	.648
23	.631	.639	.638	.685	.583	.598	.609	.662	.669	.679	.642	.659	.641
	.618	.614	.622	.657	.565	.577	.589	.638	.647	.663	.626	.643	.621

21

TORONTO METEOROLOGICAL OBSERVATIONS.

TABLE XVI.

MONTHLY AND ANNUAL MEANS OF THE BAROMETRIC PRESSURE IN EACH OF THE THIRTY-ONE YEARS FROM 1841 TO 1871, WITH THE MONTHLY AND ANNUAL MEANS FOR THE WHOLE PERIOD, AND FOR THREE GROUPS OF TWELVE, NINE, AND TEN YEARS RESPECTIVELY; ALSO, THE PROBABLE VARIABILITY OF THE MONTHLY AND ANNUAL MEANS IN A SINGLE YEAR.

Barometer at 32° = 27 inches + the numbers in the Table.

Years.	Jan.	Feb.	Mar.	April.	May.	June.	July.	Aug.	Sept.	Oct.	Nov.	Dec.	Yearly Means.
1841	2.666	2.491	2.654	2.623	2.543	2.544	2.617	2.701	2.604	2.644	2.568	2.598	2.604
1842	.509	.547	.634	.555	.585	.586	.657	.710	.659	.640	.609	.650	.612
1843	.596	.557	.558	.598	.615	.552	.620	.680	.691	.543	.668	.666	.612
1844	.612	.660	.653	.737	.550	.609	.537	.529	.731	.636	.611	.549	.618
1845	.624	.575	.592	.599	.636	.598	.508	.632	.561	.794	.508	.692	.610
1846	.617	.662	.603	.702	.607	.594	.585	.638	.625	.696	.671	.642	.628
1847	.595	.620	.676	.573	.584	.562	.631	636	.610	.675	.685	.657	.625
1848	.666	.608	.648	.731	.496	.544	.575	.644	.590	.601	.654	.678	.620
1849	.803	.754	.714	.586	.673	.626	.684	.622	.684	.602	.587	.680	.668
1850	.687	.594	.600	.565	.558	.644	.588	.601	.624	.597	.657	.676	.616
1851	.610	.756	.657	.599	.630	.602	.555	.670	.759	.597	.632	.665	.645
1852	.575	.528	.592	.415	.619	.521	.610	.666	.702	.661	.575	.600	.589
1853	.716	.585	.555	.567	.597	.616	.653	.590	.642	.651	.794	.601	.631
1854	.610	.698	.527	.636	.565	.550	.639	.646	.701	.698	.441	.589	.608
1855	.643	.628	.515	.652	.650	.512	.609	.652	.721	.554	.666	.704	.626
1856	.673	.491	.561	.577	.581	.546	.589	.520	.600	.709	.644	.713	.600
1857	.740	.739	.598	.528	.534	.425	.587	.593	.712	.669	.526	.621	.606
1858	.679	.663	.622	497	.583	.604	.603	.618	.650	.684	.629	.696	.627
1859	.681	.635	.415	.533	.659	.618	.647	.598	.669	.617	.677	.711	.622
1860	.646	.635	.513	.576	.565	.496	.562	.581	.674	.673	.525	.609	.593
1861	.665	.547	.623	.562	.544	.568	.549	.652	.609	.621	.539	.748	.602
1862	.731	.611	.506	.724	.588	.563	.546	.615	.683	.621	.638	.680	.625
1863	.650	.795	.665	.644	.617	.551	.595	.644	.733	.700	.558	.700	.654
1864	.592	.494	.510	.595	.471	.653	.637	.544	.610	.523	.581	.522	.560
1865	.592	.705	.530	.615	.584	.631	.593	.679	.718	.621	.657	.678	.634
1866	.722	.710	.669	.608	.483	.519	.604	.560	.621	.708	.614	.649	.622
1867	.571	.661	.715	.526	.476	.616	.604	.591	.715	.667	.586	.649	.615
1868	.599	.747	.671	.585	.519	.658	.599	.643	.660	.759	.651	.622	.643
1869	.570	.519	.652	.520	.481	.585	.566	.603	.764	.573	.552	.726	.598
1870	.628	.534	.646	.607	.562	.572	.531	.581	.752	.615	.594	.535	.596
1871	.762	.634	.572	.457	.617	.542	.553	.577	.720	.635	.642	.576	.607
Means. 1841–52	2.6300	2.6127	2.6317	2.6069	2.5830	2.5818	2.5972	2.6441	2.6533	2.6405	2.6187	2.6461	2.6206
Means. 1853–61	2.6726	2.6246	2.5477	2.5698	2.5864	2.5483	2.6042	2.6056	2.6642	2.6529	2.6046	2.6724	2.6128
Means. 1862–71	2.6417	2.6410	2.6136	2.5881	2.5398	2.5890	2.5818	2.6097	2.6976	2.6422	2.6073	2.6337	2.6154
Means. 1841–71	2.6461	2.6253	2.6015	2.5901	2.5701	2.5744	2.5943	2.6218	2.6708	2.6446	2.6109	2.6497	2.6166
Variability.	.0434	.0577	.0472	.0493	.0557	.0342	.0273	.0324	.0373	.0403	.0453	.0381	.0140

TORONTO METEOROLOGICAL OBSERVATIONS.

TABLE XVII.

HIGHEST READINGS OF THE BAROMETER OBSERVED IN EACH MONTH AND IN THE YEAR, FROM 1841 TO 1871, TOGETHER WITH THE AVERAGES DERIVED FROM THIRTY-ONE YEARS, AND FROM GROUPS OF TWELVE, NINE, AND TEN YEARS.

The month in which the Highest Reading of each year occurs is indicated by an asterisk.

Barometer at 32° = 27 inches + the numbers in the Table.

Years.	Jan.	Feb.	Mar.	April.	May.	June.	July.	Aug.	Sept.	Oct.	Nov.	Dec.	Year.
1841	3.355	3.016	3.239	3.165	2.813	2.761	2.933	3.021	2.964	3.091	3.078	3.417*	3.417
1842	3.258*	3.032	3.177	3.074	3.035	3.016	3.001	2.993	2.991	2.994	3.182	3.222	3.258
1843	3.211	3.078	3.087	2.958	3.102	2.890	2.941	2.961	3.016	3.067	3.088	3.263*	3.263
1844	3.188	3.100	3.191	3.265*	3.048	3.046	2.864	2.922	3.123	3.090	2.973	3.140	3.265
1845	3.206	3.164	2.984	2.922	3.012	2.875	2.798	2.017	3.025	3.242*	3.129	3.215	3.242
1846	3.335*	3.255	3.117	3.194	2.862	3.045	3.027	2.844	2.955	3.201	3.206	3.235	3.335
1847	3.272	3.100	3.064	3.038	2.970	2.883	2.886	2.953	3.007	3.396*	3.256	3.125	3.396
1848	3.298*	3.160	3.026	3.089	2.861	2.917	2.800	2.865	2.974	3.047	3.104	3.147	3.298
1849	3.502*	3.332	3.174	3.032	3.214	2.939	3.052	2.821	3.124	3.016	2.995	3.276	3.502
1850	3.240	3.502*	3.266	3.088	2.999	2.942	2.832	2.907	3.018	2.999	3.102	3.260	3.502
1851	3.428*	3.325	3.078	3.307	3.074	3.034	2.811	2.995	3.231	3.005	3.410	3.232	3.428
1852	3.037	3.371*	3.332	2.822	3.128	2.935	2.918	2.955	3.006	3.140	3.184	3.210	3.371
1853	3.315*	2.937	3.168	2.974	3.074	2.982	2.906	2.850	2.999	3.066	3.270	3.084	3.315
1854	3.219	3.172	3.098	3.233	2.986	2.955	2.885	2.845	3.142	3.121	3.196	3.245*	3.245
1855	3.552*	3.088	3.078	2.998	2.902	2.811	2.833	3.019	3.092	2.923	3.131	3.201	3.552
1856	3.280	3.086	3.082	3.099	2.969	2.798	2.844	2.797	3.013	3.200	3.048	3.480*	3.480
1857	3.168	3.361*	3.006	3.006	2.896	2.707	2.848	2.860	3.076	2.994	3.281	3.258	3.361
1858	3.408*	3.060	3.159	3.006	3.198	2.891	2.915	2.939	3.098	3.042	2.970	3.351	3.408
1859	3.311	3.002	3.255	3.046	2.986	2.966	3.141	2.811	3.049	2.962	3.252	3.392*	3.392
1860	3.142	3.136	2.934	3.265	2.886	2.859	2.839	2.003	3.170	2.982	2.959	3.267*	3.267
1861	3.330*	3.144	3.200	3.120	2.935	2.810	2.830	2.902	3.104	3.054	3.000	3.182	3.330
1862	3.300	3.138	2.828	3.117	2.942	3.109	2.957	2.977	3.031	3.039	3.469*	3.453	3.469
1863	3.378	3.502*	3.180	3.076	2.901	2.844	2.912	2.989	3.140	3.218	3.181	3.313	3.502
1864	3.102	3.124	3.067	2.964	2.788	2.961	2.831	2.863	2.975	2.890	3.126	3.327*	3.327
1865	3.191	3.232	3.058	3.156	3.003	2.877	2.976	2.959	3.021	3.045	3.354*	3.151	3.354
1866	3.940*	3.364	3.089	2.972	2.666	2.907	2.915	2.977	2.936	3.210	3.372	3.313	3.940
1867	3.046	3.332*	3.127	2.958	3.093	2.870	2.935	2.839	3.117	3.184	2.939	3.228	3.332
1868	3.145	3.445*	3.274	3.097	2.907	2.921	2.782	2.915	2.998	3.158	3.068	3.027	3.445
1869	2.032	3.068	3.194	2.912	2.803	2.982	2.950	2.960	3.045	2.986	3.104	3.223*	3.223
1870	3.212*	3.175	3.174	2.956	2.918	2.878	2.773	2.977	3.001	3.162	3.071	3.066	3.212
1871	3.388*	3.119	2.969	3.116	2.952	2.795	2.842	2.847	3.090	3.042	3.315	3.027	3.388
1841-52	3.2783	3.1863	3.1438	3.0812	3.0098	2.9405	2.9053	2.9295	3.0362	3.1073	3.1428	3.2288	3.3398
1853-61	3.3028	3.1096	3.1089	3.0530	2.9836	2.8643	2.8934	2.8807	3.0826	3.0082	3.1230	3.2622	3.3722
1862-71	3.2634	3.2519	3.0870	3.0326	2.9173	2.9144	2.8873	2.9303	3.0354	3.0936	3.1999	3.2128	3.4192
1841-71	3.2806	3.1852	3.1154	3.0690	2.9724	2.9100	2.8960	2.9156	3.0404	3.0828	3.1555	3.2334	3.3748

TORONTO METEOROLOGICAL OBSERVATIONS.

TABLE XVIII.

LOWEST READINGS OF THE BAROMETER OBSERVED IN EACH MONTH AND IN THE YEAR, FROM 1841 TO 1871, TOGETHER WITH THE AVERAGES DERIVED FROM THIRTY-ONE YEARS, AND FROM GROUPS OF TWELVE, NINE, AND TEN YEARS.

The month in which the Lowest Reading of each year occurs is indicated by an asterisk.
Barometer at $32^\circ = 27$ inches + the numbers in the Table.

Years.	Jan.	Feb.	Mar.	April.	May.	June	July.	Aug	Sept.	Oct.	Nov.	Dec.	Year.
1841	1.981	1.727	1.985	1.873	2.070	2.336	2.263	2.361	2.259	2.102	2.027	1.672*	1.672
1842	1.962	1.879	1.872	2.005	2.086	2.191	2.267	2.335	2.140	2.113	1.781*	1.964	1.781
1843	1.579*	1.879	1.635	2.009	2.114	2.166	2.307	2.255	2.152	2.050	2.021	2.202	1.579
1844	1.614*	2.262	2.166	2.371	1.966	2.273	2.157	2.125	2.202	1.864	2.04	1.970	1.614
1845	2.111	2.070	1.939*	2.154	2.006	2.182	2.101	2.289	2.151	2.302	2.053	2.217	1.939
1846	1.829*	1.917	1.927	2.085	2.177	2.241	2.258	2.320	2.246	1.998	2.005	2.020	1.829
1847	1.840	1.721*	2.109	2.073	2.099	2.010	2.308	2.263	2.182	2.011	2.222	1.954	1.721
1848	2.021	1.807	2.108	2.291	2.140	2.168	2.115	2.112	1.863*	2.025	1.864	1.937	1.863
1849	2.046	2.102	1.902*	2.027	1.980	2.336	2.309	2.140	1.999	2.064	2.158	2.175	1.902
1850	1.910	1.535*	1.594	1.856	1.890	2.363	2.273	2.238	2.244	2.176	2.264	1.840	1.535
1851	1.793*	2.004	2.279	2.080	2.108	2.262	2.281	2.365	2.186	2.171	1.905	1.857	1.793
1852	1.907	1.669	1.603*	1.778	2.198	1.973	2.135	2.310	1.910	2.138	1.943	1.966	1.603
1853	1.653*	2.074	1.892	1.985	2.213	2.265	2.274	2.309	1.946	1.985	2.159	1.952	1.653
1854	1.693	2.002	1.788	2.045	2.066	2.287	2.308	2.384	2.302	1.731	1.685*	1.917	1.685
1855	1.717	2.172	1.792	2.233	2.283	1.942	2.337	2.130	2.247	1.945	1.985	1.450*	1.450
1856	2.186	1.778	1.828	2.081	2.125	2.207	2.241	2.174	2.149	2.217	1.902	1.459*	1.459
1857	2.181	2.152	2.115	1.808	2.199	1.952	2.255	2.155	2.248	2.289	1.452*	1.852	1.452
1858	1.973	1.040	1.840*	2.011	2.032	2.147	2.290	2.231	2.167	2.000	2.190	2.008	1.840
1859	1.934	1.877	1.286*	1.993	2.224	2.260	2.159	2.306	2.038	2.018	1.881	2.201	1.286
1860	2.155	1.920	2.044	1.896	2.058	1.909	2.157	2.211	2.233	2.019	1.844	1.838*	1.838
1861	2.006	1.979	2.034	2.055	1.644*	2.176	2.269	2.382	2.076	1.998	2.005	2.171	1.644
1862	1.965	2.011	1.805*	2.076	2.238	2.163	2.196	2.326	2.107	2.047	2.132	2.105	1.805
1863	1.846	2.037	2.129	1.704*	2.011	1.982	2.390	2.321	2.259	2.272	2.096	1.769	1.704
1864	1.910	2.009	1.820	2.301	2.166	2.007	2.319	2.099	2.250	2.026	1.671*	1.854	1.671
1865	2.114	2.082	1.707*	1.980	2.179	2.232	2.247	2.308	2.443	1.770	1.949	1.926	1.707
1866	2.110	2.120	2.043	1.927	1.919	1.967	2.305	2.258*	2.142	2.082	1.855	1.807	1.807
1867	1.920	1.799	1.912	1.930	2.044	2.143	2.292	2.297	2.354	2.051	1.843	1.768*	1.768
1868	1.975	2.129	2.049	1.962	2.190	2.274	2.340	2.229	2.334	2.152	2.165	1.824*	1.824
1869	2.074	1.845	2.178	1.896	2.054	2.074	2.193	2.338	2.369	2.144	1.793*	1.992	1.793
1870	1.166*	1.900	1.881	2.273	2.116	2.184	2.185	2.221	2.413	2.046	2.076	1.807	1.166
1871	2.048	1.673*	2.074	2.014	2.205	2.039	2.225	2.141	2.300	2.163	2.012	1.976	1.673
1841–52	1.8828	1.8855	1.9266	2.0494	2.0070	2.2079	2.2314	2.2594	2.1355	2.0848	2.0291	1.9812	1.7350
1853–61	1.9412	1.9842	1.8476	2.0219	2.0971	2.1272	2.2544	2.2522	2.1562	2.0224	1.9901	1.8730	1.5916
1862–71	1.0128	1.9611	1.9607	2.0003	2.1182	2.1065	2.2692	2.2522	2.2951	2.0762	1.9592	1.8828	1.6918
1841–71	1.9103	1.9409	1.9146	2.0275	2.0923	2.1518	2.2503	2.2551	2.1929	2.0639	1.9901	1.9180	1.6708

24

TORONTO METEOROLOGICAL OBSERVATIONS.

TABLE XIX.

RANGE OF THE BAROMETER, EXPRESSED IN INCHES, IN EACH MONTH AND IN THE YEAR, FROM 1841 TO 1871, TOGETHER WITH THE AVERAGES DERIVED FROM THE THIRTY-ONE YEARS, AND FROM GROUPS OF TWELVE, NINE, AND TEN YEARS.

Years.	Jan.	Feb.	Mar.	April	May.	June.	July.	Aug.	Sept.	Oct.	Nov.	Dec.	Year.
1841	1.374	1.289	1.245	1.312	0.743	0.425	0.670	0.609	0.705	0.989	1.051	1.745	1.745
1842	1.296	1.153	1.305	1.069	0.949	0.825	0.734	0.658	0.851	0.881	1.401	1.259	1.477
1843	1.632	1.199	1.452	0.958	0.988	0.724	0.634	0.706	0.864	1.017	1.067	1.061	1.684
1844	1.574	0.838	1.025	0.894	1.082	0.773	0.707	0.797	0.831	1.226	0.927	1.170	1.651
1845	1.095	1.094	1.045	0.768	1.006	0.693	0.697	0.628	0.874	0.940	1.076	0.998	1.303
1846	1.506	1.338	1.190	1.109	0.685	0.804	0.769	0.524	0.709	1.203	1.201	1.218	1.506
1847	1.432	1.379	0.955	0.965	0.871	0.873	0.578	0.690	0.825	1.382	1.034	1.171	1.675
1848	1.277	1.263	0.918	0.798	0.721	0.749	0.685	0.753	1.111	1.022	1.240	1.210	1.435
1849	1.456	1.230	1.272	1.005	1.234	0.609	0.743	0.681	1.125	0.952	0.837	1.101	1.600
1850	1.339	1.767	1.672	1.232	1.109	0.579	0.559	0.669	0.774	0.823	0.835	1.420	1.767
1851	1.035	1.321	0.799	1.227	0.966	0.772	0.527	0.630	1.045	0.834	1.451	1.375	1.635
1852	1.130	1.702	1.729	1.044	0.900	0.965	0.783	0.645	1.006	1.002	1.241	1.244	1.768
1853	1.062	0.863	1.276	0.989	0.861	0.717	0.632	0.550	1.053	1.081	1.111	1.032	1.662
1854	1.526	1.170	1.310	1.188	0.920	0.668	0.577	0.461	0.840	1.390	1.511	1.328	1.560
1855	1.835	0.916	1.287	0.765	0.619	0.809	0.496	0.889	0.845	0.978	1.148	1.742	2.093
1856	1.094	1.308	1.254	1.018	0.844	0.691	0.603	0.623	0.864	0.983	1.146	2.021	2.021
1857	0.987	1.209	0.891	1.108	0.697	0.755	0.593	0.705	0.828	0.705	1.829	1.406	1.909
1858	1.435	1.120	1.310	0.995	1.166	0.744	0.625	0.708	0.931	1.042	0.780	1.343	1.559
1859	1.377	1.125	1.969	1.053	0.762	0.706	0.982	0.505	1.011	0.944	1.371	1.191	2.106
1860	0.987	1.216	0.890	1.309	0.798	0.950	0.682	0.692	0.937	0.965	1.115	1.429	1.429
1861	1.324	1.165	1.166	1.065	1.311	0.634	0.561	0.520	1.028	1.056	0.995	1.011	1.656
1862	1.335	1.127	1.023	1.041	0.704	0.946	0.761	0.651	0.924	0.992	1.337	1.348	1.664
1863	1.532	1.465	1.051	1.374	0.590	0.862	9.522	0.668	0.881	0.946	1.085	1.544	1.798
1864	1.192	1.115	1.238	0.663	0.622	0.954	0.512	0.764	0.745	0.864	1.455	1.473	1.656
1865	1.077	1.150	1.351	1.176	0.824	0.645	0.729	0.651	0.578	1.266	1.405	1.225	1.647
1866	1.830	1.238	1.646	1.045	0.947	0.940	0.610	0.719	0.794	1.128	1.517	1.506	2.133
1867	1.126	1.533	1.215	1.028	1.040	0.727	0.643	0.532	0.763	1.133	1.096	1.460	1.564
1868	1.170	1.316	1.225	1.135	0.717	0.647	0.442	0.695	0.664	1.000	0.903	1.203	1.621
1869	0.858	1.243	0.926	1.016	0.749	0.508	0.757	0.622	0.676	0.844	1.311	1.231	1.430
1870	2.046	1.275	1.293	0.683	0.802	0.694	0.598	0.753	0.598	1.116	0.995	1.259	2.046
1871	1.340	1.446	0.895	1.102	0.687	0.756	0.617	0.706	0.790	0.879	1.303	1.051	1.715
1841-52	1.3955	1.2977	1.2173	1.0318	0.9429	0.7326	0.6738	0.6701	0.9008	1.0226	1.1137	1.2477	1.6038
1853-61	1.3586	1.1213	1.2614	1.0611	0.8864	0.7371	0.6399	0.6281	0.9263	1.0158	1.2228	1.3892	1.7806
1862-71	1.3506	1.2908	1.1263	1.0263	0.7991	0.8079	0.6161	0.6781	0.7403	1.0174	1.2407	1.3300	1.7274
1841-71	1.3703	1.2443	1.2007	1.0355	0.8801	0.7582	0.6457	0.6605	0.8565	1.0189	1.1864	1.3153	1.6950

TABLE XX.

NORMAL DAILY MEANS OF THE BAROMETRIC PRESSURE, AND THE PRESSURE OF VAPOUR, ON EVERY FIFTH OR SIXTH DAY IN THE YEAR, FROM OBSERVATIONS IN THE TEN YEARS, 1859-68, INCLUSIVE.

Date.	Barometric Pressure.	Pressure of Vapour.	Date.	Barometric Pressure.	Pressure of Vapour.	Date.	Barometric Pressure.	Pressure of Vapour.
Jan.			May.			Sept.		
5	29.646	0.106	5	29.569	0.243	5	29.651	0.413
10	.642	.105	10	.559	.260	10	.661	.394
15	.641	.105	15	.552	.277	15	.669	.374
20	.643	.106	20	.549	.295	20	.675	.354
25	.647	.107	25	.551	.313	25	.677	.333
30	.652	.108	30	.558	.332	30	.676	.313
Feb.			June.			Oct.		
4	.655	.109	5	.567	.351	5	.671	.293
9	.655	.111	10	.578	.371	10	.661	.275
14	.651	.112	15	.589	.391	15	.649	.259
19	.642	.115	20	.597	.411	20	.634	.244
24	.629	.118	25	.602	.430	25	.620	.230
			30	.603	.448	30	.607	.218
Mar.			July.			Nov.		
1	.614	.122	5	.601	.463	5	.600	.206
6	.599	.126	10	.598	.476	10	.597	.195
11	.587	.131	15	.594	.486	15	.601	.184
16	.580	.136	20	.592	.492	20	.609	.172
21	.577	.142	25	.591	.494	25	.621	.161
26	.579	.148	30	.593	.493	30	.635	.149
31	.584	.156						
April.			Aug.			Dec.		
5	.591	.164	5	.597	.480	5	.647	.138
10	.596	.173	10	.604	.481	10	.656	.129
15	.599	.185	15	.612	.472	15	.661	.121
20	.596	.197	20	.621	.460	20	.661	.114
25	.590	.211	25	.631	.446	25	.657	.110
30	.580	.227	30	.641	.430	30	.651	.107

TORONTO METEOROLOGICAL OBSERVATIONS.

TABLE XXI.

CHANGE IN BAROMETRIC PRESSURE, PRESSURE OF DRY AIR, AND PRESSURE OF VAPOUR, WHICH TAKES PLACE IN TWO HOURS, DURING WINDS FROM EACH OF THE THIRTY-TWO POINTS OF THE COMPASS.

Wind from	Barometric Pressure.			Pressure of Dry Air.			Pressure of Vapour.		
	April to Sept.	Oct. to March.	Year.	April to Sept.	Oct. to March.	Year.	April to Sept.	Oct. to March.	Year.
N.	+.0083	+.0088	+.0083	+.0144	+.0110	+.0127	−.0057	−.0026	−.0042
N. b E.	+.0058	+.0035	+.0044	+.0117	+.0046	+.0083	−.0056	−.0019	−.0037
N. N E.	+.0029	−.0026	−.0001	+.0082	−.0027	+.0032	−.0052	−.0010	−.0030
N. E. b N.	−.0005	−.0092	−.0050	+.0040	−.0105	−.0027	−.0045	.0000	−.0021
N. E.	−.0041	−.0158	−.0100	−.0007	−.0182	−.0098	−.0034	+.0010	−.0011
N E. b E.	−.0074	−.0220	−.0146	−.0054	−.0252	−.0146	−.0020	+.0010	.0000
E. N. E.	−.0099	−.0272	−.0184	−.0093	−.0309	−.0195	−.0005	+.0027	+.0009
E. b N.	−.0112	−.0310	−.0208	−.0120	−.0349	−.0228	+.0009	+.0033	+.0017
E.	−.0113	−.0334	−.0218	−.0131	−.0372	−.0244	+.0020	+.0036	+.0024
E. b S.	−.0103	−.0343	−.0214	−.0127	−.0379	−.0243	+.0028	+.0037	+.0025
E. S. E.	−.0086	−.0340	−.0190	−.0114	−.0373	−.0230	+.0032	+.0037	+.0032
S. E. b E.	−.0068	−.0320	−.0180	−.0098	−.0359	−.0211	+.0034	+.0035	+.0034
S. E.	−.0055	−.0312	−.0160	−.0086	−.0341	−.0192	+.0035	+.0032	+.0036
S. E. b S	−.0052	−.0293	−.0147	−.0084	−.0321	−.0178	+.0036	+.0029	+.0037
S. S. E.	−.0058	−.0273	−.0132	−.0093	−.0298	−.0170	+.0039	+.0025	+.0037
S. b E.	−.0071	−.0250	−.0134	−.0109	−.0272	−.0166	+.0041	+.0021	+.0036
S.	−.0085	−.0222	−.0131	−.0124	−.0239	−.0161	+.0042	+.0010	+.0033
S. b W.	−.0093	−.0187	−.0123	−.0131	−.0199	−.0149	+.0040	+.0010	+.0027
S. S. W.	−.0090	−.0145	−.0106	−.0122	−.0149	−.0124	+.0032	+.0003	+.0018
S. W. b S.	−.0071	−.0094	−.0077	−.0093	−.0090	−.0086	+.0019	−.0004	+.0007
S. W.	−.0038	−.0037	−.0036	−.0044	−.0027	−.0033	+.0001	−.0012	−.0006
S. W. b W	+.0005	+.0022	+.0014	+.0018	+.0038	+.0028	−.0021	−.0019	−.0019
W. S W.	+.0052	+.0079	+.0066	+.0084	+.0099	+.0091	−.0042	−.0025	−.0030
W. b S.	+.0096	+.0129	+.0115	+.0146	+.0152	+.0148	−.0060	−.0029	−.0040
W.	+.0131	+.0168	+.0154	+.0195	+.0194	+.0194	−.0073	−.0033	−.0047
W. b N.	+.0153	+.0196	+.0181	+.0225	+.0223	+.0224	−.0079	−.0035	−.0052
W. N. W.	+.0162	+.0211	+.0194	+.0237	+.0241	+.0239	−.0079	−.0037	−.0054
N. W. b W.	+.0160	+.0214	+.0194	+.0234	+.0247	+.0239	−.0075	−.0038	−.0054
N. W.	+.0151	+.0208	+.0184	+.0222	+.0242	+.0230	−.0069	−.0038	−.0053
N. W. b N.	+.0137	+.0191	+.0167	+.0204	+.0227	+.0213	−.0063	−.0037	−.0051
N. N. W.	+.0121	+.0166	+.0144	+.0186	+.0200	+.0190	−.0059	−.0035	−.0049
N. b W.	+.0103	+.0132	+.0116	+.0166	+.0161	+.0162	−.0057	−.0031	−.0046

TORONTO METEOROLOGICAL OBSERVATIONS.

TABLE XXII.

MONTHLY AND ANNUAL MEANS OF THE PRESSURE OF DRY AIR FOR EACH OF THE TWENTY-FOUR HOURS OF TORONTO ASTRONOMICAL TIME, AND FOR THE TWENTY-FOUR HOURS COLLECTIVELY, FROM HOURLY OBSERVATIONS IN THE SIX YEARS FROM 1ST JULY, 1842 TO 30TH JUNE, 1848.

Pressure of Dry Air = 29 inches + the numbers in the Table.

Toronto Astronomical Time.	Jan.	Feb.	Mar.	April.	May.	June.	July.	Aug	Sept.	Oct.	Nov.	Dec.	Annual Means.
	in.	in.	in.	in.	in.	in.	in	in.	in.	in.	in.	in.	in.
0	0.484	0.509	0.494	0.455	0.237	0.144	0.091	0.108	0.240	0.405	0.433	0.507	0.342
1	.469	.491	.474	.446	.232	.134	.077	.094	.233	.394	.419	.492	.330
2	.464	.479	.461	.433	.227	.129	.072	.084	.219	.389	.412	.484	.321
3	.471	.479	.457	.424	.225	.121	.067	.077	.213	.387	.416	.487	.319
4	.479	.479	.460	.421	.219	.117	.061	.078	.214	.390	.420	.497	.320
5	.487	.486	.464	.422	.217	.117	.061	.079	.214	.398	.427	.500	.323
6	.497	.498	.473	.430	.230	.129	.067	.088	.226	.408	.434	.509	.332
7	.504	.507	.484	.436	.246	.146	.085	.118	.246	.415	.437	.515	.345
8	.505	.512	.493	.449	.266	.167	.113	.143	.266	.422	.439	.516	.358
9	.506	.515	.498	.452	.280	.191	.138	.164	.269	.429	.440	.515	.366
10	.505	.515	.500	.454	.289	.200	.152	.174	.282	.434	.441	.517	.372
11	.504	.513	.502	.453	.295	.200	.164	.185	.268	.411	.441	.514	376
12	.505	.501	.491	.452	.297	.201	.167	.186	.283	.435	.451	.512	.373
13	.509	.592	.494	.446	.299	.207	.169	.190	.289	.445	.453	.514	.376
14	.513	.504	.495	.448	.299	.213	.173	.193	.295	.445	.456	.523	.380
15	.513	.507	.492	.451	.303	.219	.181	.199	.300	.444	.458	.521	.382
16	.508	.510	.492	.452	.307	.231	.189	.204	.308	.446	.457	.515	.385
17	.505	.510	.499	.465	.317	.241	.201	.215	.318	.452	.455	.514	.391
18	.503	.522	.510	.494	.312	.228	.167	.215	.328	.446	.456	.530	.393
19	.500	.533	.520	.497	.306	.216	.149	.188	.309	.453	.463	.537	.390
20	.521	.542	.517	.498	.298	.202	.135	.166	.294	.446	.469	.545	.386
21	.523	.542	.519	.488	.282	.186	.124	.144	.284	.440	.465	.545	.379
22	.523	.538	.511	.481	.273	.171	.111	.138	.267	.433	.462	.545	.371
23	.508	.532	.502	.469	.257	.154	.105	.121	.255	.424	.449	.528	.359
	.500	.510	.492	.454	.272	.179	.126	.148	.269	.425	.444	.516	.361

TORONTO METEOROLOGICAL OBSERVATIONS.

TABLE XXIII.

MONTHLY AND ANNUAL MEANS OF THE PRESSURE OF DRY AIR FROM 1841 TO 1871, OMITTING 1847, WITH THE MONTHLY AND ANNUAL MEANS FOR THE WHOLE PERIOD, AND FOR THREE GROUPS OF ELEVEN, NINE, AND TEN YEARS.

Pressure = 27 inches + the numbers in the Table.

Years.	Jan.	Feb.	Mar.	April.	May.	June	July.	Aug.	Sept.	Oct.	Nov.	Dec.	Year.
1841	2.529	2.382	2.527	2.447	2.287	2.090	2.170	2.215	2.152	2.423	2.396	2.444	2.339
1842	2.378	2.410	2.475	2.349	2.362	2.237	2.217	2.221	2.311	2.384	2.443	2.544	2.361
1843	2.460	2.501	2.467	2.409	2.375	2.157	2.177	2.172	2.291	2.324	2.567	2.519	2.363
1844	2.515	2.532	2.505	2.491	2.237	2.216	2.058	2.056	2.352	2.404	2.439	2.413	2.351
1845	2.500	2.448	2.432	2.396	2.362	2.175	2.041	2.108	2.190	2.522	4.325	2.559	2.341
1846	2.482	2.479	2.443	2.486	2.154	2.158	2.070	2.110	2.137	2.435	2.444	2.508	2.325
1847	2.487	2.512	2.562	...	2.265	2.186	2.115	2.166	2.251	2.434	2.479	2.503	...
1848	2.527	2.494	2.515	2.560	2.185	2.131	2.107	2.122	2.272	2.339	2.493	2.539	2.357
1849	2.714	2.635	2.557	2.404	2.403	2.167	2.160	2.126	2.299	2.351	2.349	2.552	2.393
1850	2.545	2.466	2.472	2.386	2.315	2.182	2.027	2.063	2.238	2.337	2.450	2.503	2.337
1851	2.482	2.613	2.500	2.402	2.322	2.193	2.041	2.157	2.310	2.307	2.469	2.556	2.365
1852	2.476	2.409	2.455	2.249	2.353	2.127	2.150	2.186	2.336	2.377	2.398	2.429	2.329
1853	2.601	2.465	2.408	2.357	2.300	2.126	2.230	2.078	2.243	2.425	2.591	2.476	2.358
1854	2.485	2.594	2.369	2.430	2.278	2.117	2.090	2.168	2.271	2.405	2.259	2.479	2.328
1855	2.514	2.537	2.381	2.446	2.393	2.108	2.081	2.209	2.378	2.304	2.475	2.579	2.367
1856	2.589	2.409	2.460	2.376	2.324	2.117	2.102	2.102	2.249	2.475	2.403	2.601	2.356
1857	2.653	2.589	2.472	2.374	2.283	2.074	2.068	2.126	2.319	2.423	2.367	2.470	2.352
1858	2.541	2.550	2.501	2.323	2.345	2.141	2.125	2.142	2.266	2.426	2.466	2.567	2.369
1859	2.551	2.515	2.245	2.391	2.361	2.265	2.177	2.136	2.331	2.400	2.484	2.610	2.371
1860	2.533	2.520	2.362	2.393	2.228	2.084	2.136	2.119	2.332	2.400	2.327	2.551	2.332
1861	2.549	2.414	2.493	2.365	2.314	2.192	2.084	2.158	2.209	2.327	2.359	2.594	2.338
1862	2.624	2.501	2.372	2.542	2.337	2.219	2.075	2.106	2.265	2.318	2.465	2.536	2.363
1863	2.506	2.682	2.549	2.404	2.318	2.179	2.062	2.139	2.382	2.437	2.358	2.569	2.357
1864	2.479	2.372	2.373	2.403	2.139	2.274	2.156	2.029	2.262	2.273	2.367	2.399	2.296
1865	2.502	2.597	2.369	2.414	2.307	2.201	2.192	2.246	2.260	2.379	2.470	2.547	2.374
1866	2.617	2.598	2.543	2.414	2.273	2.140	2.071	2.171	2.272	2.434	2.421	2.529	2.374
1867	2.482	2.526	2.506	2.347	2.244	2.188	2.148	2.118	2.345	2.393	2.411	2.546	2.362
1868	2.504	2.658	2.529	2.417	2.222	2.237	1.981	2.181	2.285	2.541	2.474	2.514	2.379
1869	2.439	2.402	2.544	2.349	2.224	2.220	2.098	2.205	2.334	2.350	2.301	2.586	2.345
1870	2.509	2.433	2.528	2.410	2.281	2.058	2.010	2.094	2.310	2.318	2.417	2.403	2.317
1871	2.649	2.522	2.415	2.264	2.335	2.162	2.133	2.120	2.403	2.382	2.503	2.479	2.364
Means. 1841–52	2.5099	2.4881	2.4862	2.4155	2.3050	2.1666	2.1107	2.1424	2.2625	2.3831	2.4295	2.5149	2.3510
Means. 1853–61	2.5573	2.5126	2.4101	2.3928	2.3140	2.1360	2.1214	2.1376	2.2886	2.3987	2.4212	2.5474	2.3523
Means. 1862–71	2.5311	2.5291	2.4818	2.4024	2.2680	2.1908	2.0926	2.1412	2.3118	2.3925	2.4307	2.5108	2.3561
Means. 1841–71	2.5312	2.5091	2.4619	2.4013	2.2954	2.1655	2.1079	2.1405	2.2868	2.3876	2.4270	2.5232	2.3531

TORONTO METEOROLOGICAL OBSERVATIONS.

TABLE XXIV.

MONTHLY MEANS OF TEMPERATURE, BAROMETER, AND PRESSURE OF DRY AIR, AT THE HOURS 2, 4, 10, 12, 18 AND 20, TORONTO MEAN TIME, FROM THE YEARS 1841-71 INCLUSIVE, OMITTING BROKEN YEARS. *(See Introduction.)*

TEMPERATURE.

Toronto Mean Time.	Jan.	Feb.	March.	April.	May.	June.	July.	Aug.	Sept.	Oct.	Nov.	Dec.
2	26.6	26.9	34.2	46.8	57.9	68.2	74.5	73.2	64.9	51.8	40.0	29.0
4	26.1	26.6	34.0	46.6	57.8	68.1	74.3	72.9	64.4	50.8	39.0	28.2
10	22.9	22.4	28.6	39.2	49.0	58.2	63.9	62.8	55.8	44.2	35.5	25.4
12	22.2	21.7	27.6	38.2	47.5	56.7	62.2	61.2	54.5	43.1	34.8	25.0
18	21.2	19.7	25.2	36.2	47.1	57.0	62.1	59.6	52.4	41.4	34.0	24.1
20	21.3	20.2	27.4	40.1	51.7	61.7	67.6	65.8	57.5	44.4	34.7	24.3
Means.	23.4	22.9	29.5	41.2	51.8	61.6	67.4	65.9	58.2	46.0	36.4	26.0

BAROMETRIC PRESSURE.
Pressure = 29 inches + numbers in the Table.

	Jan.	Feb.	March.	April.	May.	June.	July.	Aug.	Sept.	Oct.	Nov.	Dec.
2	.614	.602	.578	.580	.558	.564	.586	.613	.661	.628	.591	.626
4	.624	.603	.575	.569	.546	.551	.572	.600	.650	.627	.597	.626
10	.647	.622	.603	.594	.568	.570	.559	.619	.671	.650	.612	.653
12	.644	.613	.599	.592	.565	.568	.589	.620	.668	.648	.609	.650
18	.640	.626	.602	.603	.581	.584	.607	.636	.689	.652	.613	.648
20	.653	.643	.616	.613	.591	.594	.618	.645	.698	.668	.628	.661
Means.	.637	.618	.596	.592	.568	.572	.593	.622	.673	.645	.608	.646

PRESSURE OF DRY AIR.
Pressure = 29 inches + numbers in the Table.

	Jan.	Feb.	March.	April.	May.	June.	July.	Aug.	Sept.	Oct.	Nov.	Dec.
2	.492	.481	.435	.377	.257	.121	.064	.092	.239	.355	.404	.497
4	.505	.482	.434	.370	.252	.116	.058	.089	.238	.360	.413	.508
10	.533	.507	.469	.405	.300	.185	.121	.157	.290	.401	.433	.527
12	.531	.500	.467	.406	.302	.192	.133	.171	.298	.403	.431	.528
18	.529	.519	.477	.427	.320	.201	.144	.195	.334	.416	.437	.525
20	.543	.536	.486	.427	.311	.181	.119	.156	.303	.416	.452	.530
Means.	.522	.504	.461	.402	.290	.166	.106	.143	.284	.392	.428	.520

TABLE XXV.

MONTHLY AND ANNUAL MEANS OF THE PRESSURE OF VAPOUR FOR EACH OF THE TWENTY-FOUR HOURS OF TORONTO ASTRONOMICAL TIME, AND FOR THE TWENTY-FOUR HOURS COLLECTIVELY, FROM HOURLY OBSERVATIONS IN THE SIX YEARS, JULY 1, 1842, TO JUNE 30, 1848.

Toronto Astronomical Time.	Jan.	Feb.	Mar.	April.	May.	June	July.	Aug.	Sept.	Oct.	Nov.	Dec.	Annual Means.
0	0.126	0.114	0.136	0.219	0.336	0.446	0.511	0.546	0.419	0.261	0.193	0.133	0.287
1	.127	.115	.142	.220	.331	.446	.516	.552	.416	.259	.196	.136	.288
2	.129	.117	.143	.221	.328	.443	.512	.551	.417	.256	.196	.137	.288
3	.128	.117	.143	.220	.321	.444	.509	.547	.415	.256	.194	.136	.286
4	.125	.117	.140	.219	.321	.441	.509	.542	.411	.253	.192	.135	.284
5	.123	.114	.141	.220	.321	.436	.503	.538	.411	.249	.189	.134	.282
6	.121	.109	.136	.212	.310	.424	.500	.530	.400	.244	.187	.131	.275
7	.118	.107	.131	.207	.293	.410	.494	.501	.386	.241	.185	.129	.263
8	.118	.104	.129	.203	.287	.393	.461	.485	.375	.238	.183	.127	.259
9	.117	.103	.129	.201	.282	.380	.448	.469	.373	.234	.182	.126	.254
10	.116	.102	.126	.196	.276	.373	.436	.459	.361	.231	.180	.124	.248
11	.115	.101	.124	.195	.271	.366	.426	.450	.354	.222	.177	.124	.244
12	.113	.101	.128	.192	.265	.367	.419	.447	.354	.228	.175	.125	.243
13	.111	.100	.125	.191	.261	.359	.415	.439	.347	.221	.173	.123	.239
14	.112	.100	.123	.188	.259	.352	.410	.433	.341	.219	.173	.118	.236
15	.110	.097	.121	.186	.257	.347	.402	.427	.336	.218	.170	.120	.233
16	.109	.095	.121	.186	.255	.341	.398	.425	.332	.218	.171	.120	.231
17	.108	.097	.121	.181	.257	.344	.397	.420	.330	.216	.171	.120	.230
18	.114	.092	.116	.179	.270	.367	.436	.436	.337	.218	.174	.119	.238
19	.113	.092	.117	.188	.283	.386	.461	.471	.363	.224	.175	.117	.249
20	.113	.096	.126	.194	.294	.403	.479	.497	.380	.238	.178	.120	.260
21	.118	.102	.126	.205	.308	.418	.490	.522	.394	.246	.183	.124	.270
22	.120	.105	.133	.211	.317	.432	.502	.529	.409	.251	.189	.128	.277
23	.123	.107	.136	.216	.326	.444	.504	.541	.414	.255	.193	.131	.283
Monthly Means	0.118	0.104	0.130	0.203	0.293	0.398	0.464	0.490	0.378	0.238	0.182	0.127	0.260

TORONTO METEOROLOGICAL OBSERVATIONS.

TABLE XXVI.

MONTHLY AND ANNUAL MEANS OF THE PRESSURE OF VAPOUR FROM 1841 TO 1871 WITH THE MONTHLY AND ANNUAL MEANS FOR THE WHOLE PERIOD, AND FOR THREE GROUPS OF ELEVEN, NINE, AND TEN YEARS RESPECTIVELY, 1847 BEING OMITTED FROM THE COMBINATIONS.

Years.	Jan.	Feb.	Mar.	April	May.	June.	July.	Aug.	Sept.	Oct.	Nov.	Dec.	Year.
1841	.135	.107	.131	.173	.258	.453	.450	.483	.453	.210	.173	.153	.265
1842	.130	.138	.162	.199	.227	.347	.438	.491	.350	.251	.173	.111	.251
1843	.136	.056	.091	.193	.240	.305	.443	.507	.400	.219	.161	.147	.249
1844	.096	.128	.146	.247	.313	.399	.478	.477	.379	.231	.172	.135	.266
1845	.121	.127	.160	.203	.273	.424	.467	.524	.371	.271	.184	.102	.269
1846	.123	.113	.159	.216	.353	.436	.514	.528	.480	.260	.227	.134	.297
1847	.109	.108	.114	...	.310	.376	.517	.470	.350	.242	.206	.154	...
1848	.139	.120	.132	.170	.311	.413	.469	.524	.320	.262	.161	.140	.263
1849	.089	.112	.157	.182	.270	.456	.523	.496	.385	.251	.238	.127	.274
1850	.142	.128	.129	.179	.246	.403	.561	.538	.386	.260	.207	.111	.279
1851	.129	.143	.157	.197	.308	.410	.515	.484	.440	.291	.163	.169	.270
1852	.096	.119	.135	.177	.267	.396	.461	.481	.366	.282	.176	.159	.260
1853	.110	.117	.145	.212	.297	.491	.425	.513	.399	.223	.201	.122	.271
1854	.122	.110	.156	.207	.288	.431	.550	.478	.410	.287	.180	.109	.279
1855	.125	.088	.132	.208	.255	.406	.539	.444	.406	.247	.190	.123	.263
1856	.080	.030	.099	.203	.259	.432	.480	.419	.351	.231	.179	.110	.244
1857	.083	.117	.124	.156	.254	.358	.520	.467	.393	.243	.157	.149	.254
1858	.134	.080	.119	.176	.239	.405	.481	.478	.384	.256	.162	.123	.259
1859	.126	.117	.108	.154	.298	.355	.471	.463	.337	.214	.100	.099	.240
1860	.110	.112	.148	.185	.338	.411	.427	.463	.342	.272	.195	.115	.260
1861	.102	.130	.127	.199	.232	.377	.467	.495	.400	.292	.178	.151	.262
1862	.103	.107	.132	.184	.253	.346	.473	.510	.418	.300	.171	.142	.262
1863	.110	.110	.116	.181	.291	.373	.535	.506	.350	.260	.198	.129	.266
1864	.110	.119	.135	.191	.333	.380	.473	.516	.347	.248	.182	.121	.263
1865	.086	.105	.159	.203	.278	.432	.402	.434	.458	.210	.186	.129	.259
1866	.101	.108	.124	.195	.212	.381	.535	.390	.349	.272	.192	.118	.248
1867	.086	.132	.116	.181	.233	.429	.458	.475	.369	.272	.173	.101	.252
1868	.092	.086	.140	.170	.299	.422	.619	.463	.375	.216	.175	.105	.264
1869	.127	.114	.105	.173	.258	.367	.470	.458	.430	.221	.100	.138	.252
1870	.115	.099	.116	.198	.282	.485	.527	.488	.442	.295	.175	.129	.279
1871	.110	.109	.154	.194	.283	.382	.422	.458	.317	.250	.136	.094	.242
Means, 1841–51 omitting 1847	.1226	.1174	.1417	.1939	.2787	.4169	.4835	.5030	.3950	.2535	.1850	.1298	.2684
Means, 1852–61	.1102	.1090	.1353	.1888	.2737	.4111	.4944	.4680	.3824	.2517	.1813	.1223	.2601
Means, 1862–71	.1070	.1089	.1297	.1873	.2730	.3997	.4910	.4698	.3855	.2571	.1748	.1236	.2587
Means, 1841–71	.1137	.1121	.1358	.1902	.2753	.4103	.4903	.4817	.3879	.2543	.1805	.1255	.2627

TORONTO METEOROLOGICAL OBSERVATIONS.

TABLE XXVII.

MONTHLY AND ANNUAL MEANS OF THE RELATIVE HUMIDITY FOR EACH OF THE TWENTY-FOUR HOURS, TORONTO ASTRONOMICAL TIME, AND FOR THE TWENTY-FOUR HOURS COLLECTIVELY, FROM HOURLY OBSERVATIONS IN THE SIX YEARS FROM JULY 1, 1842, TO JUNE 30, 1848.

Toronto Astronomical Time.	Jan.	Feb.	Mar.	April.	May.	June.	July.	Aug.	Sept.	Oct.	Nov.	Dec.	Means.
0	80	73	68	66	68	71	65	71	73	75	79	79	72
1	80	72	70	64	65	69	63	70	71	73	79	79	71
2	81	71	69	63	64	67	62	68	70	72	79	79	70
3	80	72	69	62	63	67	61	67	70	72	79	79	70
4	80	73	69	63	63	65	61	67	70	73	81	80	70
5	81	74	72	64	64	66	61	68	72	76	83	82	72
6	83	76	73	67	65	67	64	71	77	81	85	83	74
7	83	76	75	72	69	72	69	76	81	83	86	83	77
8	83	77	77	74	73	76	76	82	83	85	86	82	79
9	84	78	79	77	77	80	80	84	85	86	87	83	82
10	84	79	80	77	78	82	81	84	86	87	87	83	82
11	84	79	80	79	79	83	83	85	86	88	87	82	83
12	86	80	83	79	80	85	84	87	87	89	88	85	84
13	85	80	82	79	81	86	86	85	87	89	88	84	85
14	86	82	82	80	84	86	86	89	87	90	89	82	85
15	86	80	82	81	85	87	87	89	88	89	89	85	86
16	85	80	83	82	86	87	88	90	89	90	89	85	86
17	85	78	84	81	86	87	88	90	90	90	89	84	86
18	86	79	82	80	83	86	86	90	90	90	89	85	86
19	86	80	81	77	78	81	81	86	88	90	90	85	84
20	86	80	79	72	74	78	76	81	84	88	88	85	81
21	88	78	74	71	73	75	73	80	80	83	85	84	79
22	83	74	73	69	70	74	71	75	77	78	83	82	76
23	81	72	70	68	69	73	67	73	75	75	82	80	74
	84	77	76	73	74	77	75	80	81	83	85	82	79

TORONTO METEOROLOGICAL OBSERVATIONS.

TABLE XXVIII.

MONTHLY MEANS OF THE RELATIVE HUMIDITY FROM 1841 TO 1871 INCLUSIVE, WITH THE AVERAGE DERIVED FROM THIRTY YEARS.

The year 1847 is not included in the general averages.

Year.	Jan.	Feb.	Mar.	April.	May.	June.	July.	Aug.	Sept.	Oct.	Nov.	Dec.	Year.
1841	67	80	79	70	67	72	74	81	83	78	81	66	78
1842	81	84	76	71	64	76	74	79	78	83	86	78	77
1843	85	58	74	74	68	81	75	80	81	83	85	85	77
1844	63	84	81	75	76	77	77	82	79	82	85	84	81
1845	83	80	75	73	73	79	73	79	84	83	81	79	78
1846	87	84	81	73	77	75	76	78	82	84	85	84	80
1847	79	83	76	...	73	78	77	80	83	81	84	80	...
1848	85	80	78	69	74	72	76	77	77	81	82	83	78
1849	75	77	81	76	79	79	78	82	82	83	88	84	79
1850	84	82	75	74	72	77	81	84	84	83	85	82	80
1851	83	85	81	75	76	80	84	83	84	85	86	81	82
1852	85	83	83	76	70	74	72	78	78	83	83	83	79
1853	82	82	81	80	80	79	70	74	79	75	81	81	79
1854	84	86	85	80	74	74	71	72	79	80	80	80	79
1855	82	80	81	75	65	78	79	74	79	76	74	77	77
1856	78	76	74	75	71	79	69	73	75	75	78	82	75
1857	69	84	77	74	74	77	78	77	78	78	77	80	79
1858	78	77	69	66	69	69	70	70	74	72	79	61	73
1859	81	79	75	63	67	69	70	70	75	72	78	87	74
1860	81	81	71	74	76	71	72	76	74	81	80	84	77
1861	88	84	80	73	69	69	73	78	79	82	79	79	78
1862	81	84	82	73	65	66	72	74	80	82	80	63	77
1863	85	83	78	68	69	71	78	76	75	80	80	83	77
1864	82	82	80	75	75	63	66	73	75	80	78	82	76
1865	81	83	79	72	60	70	65	69	75	77	77	79	75
1866	83	81	77	65	62	72	72	73	78	75	80	79	75
1867	82	81	78	73	72	71	66	68	73	73	75	77	74
1868	82	81	74	71	75	74	69	70	77	77	81	83	76
1869	80	80	78	69	67	74	77	76	79	78	84	83	77
1870	82	80	78	67	63	72	74	72	79	79	79	82	76
1871	84	77	76	69	63	69	72	68	71	72	76	80	73
	83	81	78	72	71	74	73	76	78	79	81	81	77

TORONTO METEOROLOGICAL OBSERVATIONS.

TABLE XXIX.

Monthly Means of the Extent of Sky Clouded, derived from Six Daily Observations, in each of the Years from 1853 to 1871 inclusive, the Hemisphere being expressed by 100.

Years.	Jan.	Feb.	Mar.	April	May.	June.	July.	Aug.	Sept.	Oct.	Nov.	Dec.	Year.
1853	68	74	59	46	57	43	84	47	53	49	74	75	57
1854	78	71	62	63	58	49	35	44	47	65	75	79	59
1855	79	71	67	51	46	65	59	44	45	68	69	67	60
1856	66	55	52	60	59	47	39	48	49	47	81	76	57
1857	68	72	61	54	61	69	46	47	43	62	67	73	60
1858	61	69	50	65	69	48	50	42	41	60	81	83	60
1859	72	74	65	59	41	50	46	40	64	64	81	73	61
1860	71	67	49	59	57	58	43	43	48	70	70	83	60
1861	76	83	62	61	49	45	56	54	60	61	74	62	62
1862	73	78	63	65	45	60	56	45	47	72	79	75	63
1863	83	66	63	54	48	54	64	45	42	64	71	72	61
1864	67	72	66	74	68	30	44	70	58	74	75	83	65
1865	70	71	78	64	53	62	53	38	39	58	79	73	61
1866	76	82	65	58	54	54	50	56	57	50	72	63	61
1867	73	82	72	62	69	45	48	50	29	48	75	78	61
1868	77	66	58	62	67	51	59	55	62	63	78	75	64
1869	68	75	60	61	67	67	67	53	47	60	82	83	66
1870	77	73	69	56	61	51	58	48	53	62	60	82	62
1871	80	71	70	71	48	46	47	51	56	68	77	81	64
	73	72	63	60	56	53	50	48	50	61	74	75	61

TABLE XXX.

Monthly Means of the Extent of Sky Clouded at each of the Six Ordinary Observation Hours, derived from the Nineteen Years, 1853 to 1871 inclusive.

Toronto Astronomical Time.	Jan.	Feb.	Mar.	April.	May.	June	July.	Aug.	Sept.	Oct.	Nov.	Dec.	Year.
2	76	75	66	66	64	59	58	57	55	65	78	79	66
4	75	74	65	65	63	58	54	54	52	63	76	77	65
10	67	66	53	53	46	47	42	41	43	56	72	70	55
12	67	67	57	54	46	48	44	42	43	57	71	72	56
18	74	75	65	61	58	54	52	49	52	63	72	75	62
20	78	77	64	64	58	56	52	48	53	63	75	78	64
	73	72	63	60	56	53	50	48	50	61	74	75	61

TORONTO METEOROLOGICAL OBSERVATIONS.

TABLE XXXI.

Depth of Rain in Inches in each Month and in the Year, from 1840 to 1871 inclusive.

Months of incomplete years not included in general means. The letter R denotes that Rain fell, but that the amount was inappreciable.

Years	Jan.	Feb.	Mar.	April	May	June	July	Aug.	Sept.	Oct.	Nov.	Dec.	Year
1840	1.305	1.475	1.640	3.420	4.150	4.860	5.270	2.005	1.380	1.860	1.220	0.000	29.575
1841	2.150	0.000	1.170	1.370	2.350	1.500	8.150	6.170	3.340	1.360	2.450	6.600	36.670
1842	2.170	3.625	3.150	3.740	1.275	5.755	3.050	2.500	6.160	5.175	5.310	0.880	42.790
1843	4.295	0.475	0.625	3.185	1.570	4.595	4.605	4.850	9.700	3.790	4.765	1.040	43.555
1844	3.005	0.430	2.470	1.515	5.070	3.535	2.815	...	...	...	...	...	...
1845	...	...	...	3.290	2.300	3.715	2.195	1.725	6.245	1.760	1.105	0.000	...
1846	2.335	0.000	1.065	1.300	4.375	1.920	2.895	1.770	4.595	4.180	5.805	1.215	32.355
1847	2.125	0.550	0.850	2.870	2.040	2.625	3.355	2.140	6.605	4.390	3.155	1.185	31.960
1848	2.245	0.775	1.220	1.455	2.520	1.810	1.890	0.855	3.115	1.550	2.020	2.750	22.205
1849	1.175	0.240	1.525	2.655	5.115	2.020	3.415	4.970	1.480	5.935	2.815	0.840	32.215
1850	1.250	1.235	0.745	4.720	0.545	3.345	5.270	4.355	1.735	2.085	2.955	0.190	28.430
1851	1.275	2.600	0.770	2.295	2.050	2.695	3.625	1.360	2.665	1.680	3.885	1.075	26.875
1852	0.000	0.650	3.080	1.990	1.125	3.160	4.025	2.095	3.630	5.280	1.775	3.995	31.405
1853	0.290	1.030	1.080	2.025	4.420	1.550	0.915	2.575	5.140	0.875	2.425	0.625	23.550
1854	1.270	1.400	2.425	2.685	4.630	1.460	4.805	0.455	5.375	1.495	1.115	0.590	27.705
1855	0.525	1.770	1.485	2.030	2.565	4.070	3.245	1.455	6.585	2.485	4.590	1.845	31.050
1856	0.000	0.000	0.000	2.780	4.580	3.200	1.120	1.680	4.105	0.875	1.375	1.790	21.505
1857	R.	3.050	0.335	1.755	4.145	5.060	3.475	5.265	2.040	1.040	3.235	3.205	33.205
1858	1.152	R.	0.917	1.642	6.367	2.943	3.072	3.890	0.735	1.797	3.879	1.657	28.051
1859	1.449	0.455	4.054	2.527	3.410	4.085	2.011	3.900	3.525	0.940	5.193	1.035	33.274
1860	0.740	1.330	0.882	1.282	1.815	2.136	4.336	3.405	1.959	1.618	2.569	1.362	23.434
1861	0.685	0.815	2.125	1.610	3.389	2.329	2.635	2.953	3.607	1.993	4.294	0.560	26.995
1862	0.115	0.180	2.500	2.235	1.427	1.007	5.344	3.483	2.344	2.684	2.205	1.945	25.529
1863	1.122	1.450	0.697	2.210	3.363	1.662	3.408	2.208	1.235	2.522	3.656	2.060	26.483
1864	1.165	0.397	1.620	3.633	4.070	0.570	1.332	5.060	2.508	3.321	3.765	2.045	29.486
1865	0.410	0.810	3.050	3.072	4.005	2.005	2.470	1.090	2.450	2.705	0.975	1.727	26.599
1866	0.522	0.830	1.915	1.675	2.820	2.720	5.390	4.457	5.657	2.470	2.063	2.790	34.209
1867	R.	1.328	0.617	2.147	3.220	0.885	1.965	2.410	1.226	1.970	1.835	1.408	19.041
1868	R.	0.040	2.060	0.930	7.670	2.217	0.510	1.562	4.239	1.365	5.150	0.005	26.408
1869	0.887	0.165	0.985	2.965	2.805	4.373	4.610	4.273	4.027	0.962	2.540	2.590	31.182
1870	3.412	0.520	0.755	2.145	1.150	8.090	1.896	3.422	6.794	2.690	0.594	2.430	33.898
1871	0.864	0.040	2.782	3.318	2.302	3.340	1.255	2.800	1.290	1.185	2.655	0.940	22.771
Means	1.224	0.894	1.618	2.439	3.254	2.978	3.218	3.021	3.716	2.389	2.977	1.654	29.416

TORONTO METEOROLOGICAL OBSERVATIONS.

TABLE XXXII.

DEPTH OF SNOW IN INCHES IN EACH MONTH AND IN THE YEAR, FROM 1843 TO 1871 INCLUSIVE.

The letter S denotes that Snow fell, but that the amount was inappreciable.

Years.	Jan.	Feb.	Mar.	April.	May.	June.	July.	Aug.	Sept.	Oct.	Nov.	Dec.	Year.
1843	14.2	14.4	25.7	0.1	...	...	...	...	...	2.5	1.2	8.1	66.2
1844	24.9	10.0	14.0	S.	...	...	...	...	...	12.0	8.0	4.2	73.1
1845	22.7	19.0	2.8	1.5	...	...	...	...	...	S.	5.0	4.7	55.7
1846	6.0	46.1	2.3	1.3	...	...	...	...	...	S.	0.4	6.0	62.1
1847	7.5	27.3	4.2	4.0	...	...	...	...	...	S.	S.	6.8	49.8
1848	7.1	10.8	9.7	0.5	...	...	...	...	...	0.0	1.4	16.5	46.0
1849	9.2	19.2	2.3	1.7	...	...	...	...	...	S.	1.0	9.6	43.0
1850	5.2	23.1	11.2	1.1	S.	...	...	...	...	0.0	S.	29.5	70.1
1851	7.8	2.4	8.8	1.2	0.5	...	...	...	...	0.3	6.7	10.7	38.4
1852	30.9	13.0	19.5	9.4	S.	...	...	...	...	0.0	2.0	20.1	94.9
1853	7.5	12.6	7.1	1.0	S.	...	...	...	...	S.	2.7	22.3	53.2
1854	7.5	18.0	2.8	2.7	...	...	...	...	...	S.	1.3	17.2	49.5
1855	23.3	21.8	19.1	1.6	0.9	...	...	...	...	0.8	3.0	29.5	99.0
1856	13.6	9.7	16.2	0.1	S.	...	...	...	...	0.1	9.5	16.3	65.5
1857	21.8	11.7	11.3	12.9	S.	...	...	...	...	0.2	6.9	9.0	73.8
1858	4.0	26.7	0.2	0.1	...	...	...	...	...	S.	4.0	10.4	45.4
1859	16.4	8.3	1.0	1.2	...	S.	...	...	...	S.	0.6	37.4	64.9
1860	8.7	18.8	2.4	0.3	...	...	...	...	...	S.	1.9	13.5	45.6
1861	20.6	29.7	7.1	6.9	0.5	...	...	...	...	S.	3.2	6.8	74.8
1862	27.4	23.1	18.5	0.2	...	...	...	...	...	0.5	5.3	10.4	85.5
1863	20.6	22.0	11.4	1.6	0.1	...	...	...	...	0.0	0.1	7.1	62.9
1864	26.3	9.5	3.7	3.5	...	...	...	...	...	S.	4.5	27.1	74.6
1865	14.8	16.8	18.9	2.0	...	...	...	...	...	4.5	1.1	5.2	63.3
1866	10.3	16.9	7.2	S.	...	...	...	...	...	S.	2.2	15.5	52.1
1867	42.0	13.4	33.4	7.2	S.	...	...	...	...	0.0	0.9	13.6	110.5
1868	14.6	32.6	4.2	5.3	...	...	...	...	...	2.0	4.3	15.5	78.7
1869	9.8	39.7	15.0	0.5	S.	...	...	...	...	2.3	10.2	7.1	84.6
1870	21.3	29.1	62.4	0.1	...	...	...	...	...	0.0	3.1	15.9	122.9
1871	43.6	23.0	13.0	1.3	...	...	...	...	...	0.0	4.5	14.2	99.6
Means..	16.88	19.31	12.22	2.39	0.07	...	...	...	...	0.87	3.28	14.14	69.16

TORONTO METEOROLOGICAL OBSERVATIONS.

TABLE XXXIII.

AGGREGATE OF RAIN AND MELTED SNOW IN INCHES FOR EACH MONTH AND FOR THE YEAR, FROM 1843 TO 1871 INCLUSIVE.

The months of incomplete years are not included in the general means.

Years.	Jan.	Feb.	Mar.	April.	May.	June.	July.	Aug.	Sept.	Oct.	Nov.	Dec.	Year.
1843	5.715	1.915	3.195	3.195	1.570	4.595	4.005	4.850	9.760	4.040	4.885	1.850	50.175
1844	5.495	1.430	3.870	1.515	5.870	3.535	2.815	...	...	...	...	...	...
1845	...	...	...	3.440	2.300	3.715	2.195	1.725	6.245	1.760	1.005	0.470	...
1846	2.035	4.010	2.195	1.430	4.375	1.920	2.895	1.770	4.505	4.180	5.845	1.815	38.565
1847	2.885	3.280	1.270	2.270	2.040	2.025	3.355	2.140	6.005	4.390	3.155	1.805	36.040
1848	2.955	1.855	2.190	1.500	2.520	1.810	1.890	0.855	3.115	1.550	2.160	4.400	26.805
1849	2.005	2.100	1.755	2.825	5.115	2.020	3.415	4.970	1.480	5.005	2.915	1.800	36.515
1850	1.770	3.545	1.805	4.830	0.515	3.515	5.270	4.355	1.735	2.085	2.955	3.140	35.440
1851	2.055	2.840	1.050	2.415	3.000	2.035	3.625	1.360	2.605	1.710	4.555	2.145	30.715
1852	3.090	1.950	5.030	2.930	1.125	3.160	4.025	2.695	3.630	5.280	1.975	6.005	40.895
1853	1.040	2.290	1.790	2.725	4.420	1.550	9.915	2.575	5.140	0.875	2.695	2.855	28.870
1854	2.020	3.260	2.705	2.955	4.630	1.460	4.805	0.455	5.375	1.495	1.245	2.310	32.715
1855	2.855	3.950	3.295	2.190	2.055	4.070	3.245	1.455	5.585	2.565	4.890	4.795	41.550
1856	1.300	0.970	1.620	2.790	4.580	3.200	1.120	1.080	4.105	0.885	2.325	3.420	28.055
1857	2.180	4.220	1.465	3.045	4.145	5.060	3.475	5.205	2.640	1.000	3.925	4.105	40.585
1858	1.552	2.670	0.937	1.052	6.367	2.043	3.072	3.890	0.735	1.797	4.279	2.697	32.501
1859	3.089	1.285	4.154	2.647	3.410	4.085	2.011	3.990	3.525	0.940	5.253	4.775	39.764
1860	1.610	3.210	1.122	1.312	1.815	2.130	4.336	3.405	1.959	1.018	2.759	2.712	27.094
1861	2.715	3.785	2.835	2.300	3.430	2.320	2.635	2.953	3.007	1.903	4.614	1.240	34.475
1862	2.855	2.490	4.410	2.255	1.427	1.007	5.344	3.483	2.344	2.734	2.735	2.985	34.000
1863	3.182	3.650	1.827	2.370	3.373	1.602	3.408	2.208	1.235	2.522	3.066	3.670	32.773
1864	3.795	1.347	1.990	3.958	4.079	0.570	1.332	5.000	2.508	3.321	4.215	4.755	36.946
1865	1.920	2.490	4.910	4.172	4.005	2.005	2.470	1.990	2.450	3.155	1.085	2.247	32.929
1866	1.552	2.520	2.635	1.675	2.850	2.720	5.390	4.457	5.657	2.470	3.183	4.340	39.419
1867	4.200	2.608	3.957	2.867	3.220	0.885	1.905	2.440	1.220	1.070	1.925	2.708	30.001
1868	1.460	3.320	3.080	1.520	7.670	2.217	0.510	1.562	4.239	1.505	5.580	1.555	34.278
1869	1.867	4.135	2.495	3.015	2.805	4.373	4.610	4.273	4.027	1.192	3.660	3.300	39.642
1870	5.512	2.620	6.995	2.155	1.150	8.090	1.896	3.422	6.794	2.090	0.904	4.020	40.188
1871	5.224	2.310	4.082	3.448	2.302	3.340	1.255	2.800	1.290	1.185	3.105	2.360	32.731
Means	2.721	2.788	2.795	2.648	3.281	2.810	3.092	2.970	3.633	2.410	3.348	3.109	35.619

TORONTO METEOROLOGICAL OBSERVATIONS.

TABLE XXXIV.

NUMBER OF DAYS IN WHICH RAIN FELL IN EACH MONTH AND IN THE YEAR, FROM 1840 TO 1871 INCLUSIVE.

Years.	Jan.	Feb.	Mar.	April.	May.	June.	July.	Aug.	Sept.	Oct.	Nov.	Dec.	Year.
1840	4	8	8	14	9	11	6	12	4	13	5	3	97
1841	2	1	5	3	11	9	10	9	9	6	8	7	80
1842	5	8	4	8	7	15	14	6	12	8	9	3	89
1843	6	1	2	7	5	12	8	4	10	12	10	6	83
1844	7	4	8	10	14	9	12	17	4	7	8	6	106
1845	5	5	5	11	6	11	7	9	16	11	7	2	97
1846	5	0	9	10	9	10	9	9	11	14	12	5	103
1847	7	2	5	8	12	14	8	10	15	13	14	7	115
1848	7	4	5	5	13	8	10	8	11	11	9	7	98
1849	4	2	7	10	16	7	4	10	9	13	10	5	97
1850	5	7	2	7	7	10	12	13	11	10	7	2	93
1851	4	7	3	11	12	11	12	10	9	10	5	6	100
1852	0	3	8	6	7	10	8	9	10	12	7	7	87
1853	1	4	6	10	17	9	10	11	12	10	15	4	109
1854	7	5	9	12	11	9	9	5	14	15	13	5	114
1855	5	2	5	8	6	17	13	7	12	14	8	6	103
1856	0	0	0	13	14	13	8	12	13	10	10	6	99
1857	3	11	4	10	15	21	15	13	11	10	14	7	134
1858	6	1	10	13	17	12	13	11	8	17	12	11	131
1859	6	6	15	9	11	16	12	11	15	11	12	3	127
1860	6	7	5	11	16	14	13	14	14	15	12	3	130
1861	4	4	8	12	12	13	16	15	17	15	14	6	136
1862	5	3	8	10	8	10	15	15	9	19	11	5	118
1863	10	7	4	8	14	13	15	12	8	16	13	10	130
1864	5	2	9	16	18	5	8	16	11	22	11	9	132
1865	1	5	10	17	11	7	11	8	12	17	5	7	111
1866	4	3	8	7	13	15	10	14	15	11	13	7	126
1867	1	8	6	12	18	8	12	10	9	11	8	7	110
1868	2	1	7	7	16	11	5	13	16	10	14	1	103
1869	4	2	3	9	16	22	13	11	8	8	9	10	115
1870	8	2	2	9	10	16	16	14	11	16	6	6	116
1871	8	3	8	17	7	13	11	8	8	13	10	4	110
Means..	4.50	4.00	6.24	10.00	11.85	11.91	10.66	10.81	11.06	12.50	10.03	5.72	109.37

TORONTO METEOROLOGICAL OBSERVATIONS.

TABLE XXXV.

NUMBER OF DAYS IN WHICH SNOW FELL IN EACH MONTH AND IN THE YEAR, FROM 1840 TO 1871 INCLUSIVE.

Years.	Jan.	Feb.	Mar.	April.	May.	June.	July.	Aug.	Sept.	Oct.	Nov.	Dec.	Year.
1840	11	6	8	2	...	...	...	...	...	3	8	18	56
1841	14	9	7	3	1	...	...	...	...	2	5	5	46
1842	9	9	8	2	...	...	...	...	...	0	10	17	65*
1843	12	21	18	3	...	...	...	...	...	4	7	8	73
1844	11	7	8	1	...	...	...	...	...	4	4	6	41
1845	9	0	8	4	...	...	...	...	...	1	4	12	47
1846	10	13	5	2	...	...	...	...	...	2	2	9	43
1847	5	13	6	2	...	...	...	...	...	2	3	8	39
1848	8	8	6	1	...	...	...	...	...	0	3	7	33
1849	10	13	2	2	...	...	...	...	...	1	2	12	42
1850	8	9	7	2	1	...	...	...	...	0	1	18	46
1851	10	4	9	3	1	...	...	...	...	2	6	15	50
1852	19	11	12	4	1	...	...	...	...	0	3	10	60
1853	6	15	8	1	1	...	...	...	...	2	6	13	52
1854	11	15	3	4	...	...	...	...	...	3	4	12	52
1855	13	14	11	3	2	...	...	...	...	5	6	10	64
1856	14	8	12	3	1	...	...	...	...	2	9	20	69
1857	16	11	15	11	1	...	...	...	...	2	0	14	70
1858	11	16	6	2	...	...	...	...	..1	1	13	18	67
1859	19	14	8	8	...	2	...	...	...	4	9	23	87
1860	16	13	11	5	...	...	...	...	...	1	8	21	75
1861	23	17	14	4	1	...	...	...	...	1	8	8	76
1862	19	17	11	4	...	...	...	...	...	2	11	8	72
1863	17	12	17	4	1	...	...	...	...	0	6	7	74
1864	14	14	12	3	...	...	...	...	...	1	8	18	70
1865	18	11	12	6	...	...	...	...	...	3	7	11	68
1866	10	12	18	2	...	...	...	...	...	1	4	13	69
1867	21	13	14	5	1	...	...	...	...	0	9	21	84
1868	21	16	5	10	...	...	...	...	...	2	10	18	82
1869	12	19	9	6	1	...	...	...	...	7	18	0	81
1870	18	18	18	2	...	...	...	...	...	0	5	16	77
1871	23	15	12	2	...	...	...	...	...	0	12	20	84
Means.	13.97	12.56	10.00	3.63	0.41	0.06	...	...	...	1.81	6.88	13.59	62.91

TORONTO METEOROLOGICAL OBSERVATIONS.

TABLE XXXVI.

THE GREATEST DEPTH OF RAIN WHICH FELL IN A SINGLE DAY, IN EACH MONTH FROM 1840 TO 1871.

The month which includes the day of heaviest rain in the year is marked with an asterisk.

Years.	Jan.	Feb.	Mar.	April.	May.	June.	July.	Aug.	Sept	Oct.	Nov.	Dec.	Year.
1840	...	...	0.581	0.910	1.745	1.530	1.890*	0.900	1.250	0.350	0.500	...	1.890
1841	1.900	0.000	0.500	0.840	1.240	0.500	2.000	2.340*	1.050	0.500	1.040	1.810	2.340
1842	1.250	1.570	1.550	1.420	0.370	1.280	1.300	1.650	2.930*	2.150	2.000	0.440	2.930
1843	2.500	0.475	0.375	0.800	0.740	1.220	1.000	3.250	3.455*	1.685	2.020	0.450	3.455
1844	1.420*	0.420	0.730	0.390	1.190	1.030	0.790	0.610	0.120	0.710	0.770	...	1.420
1845	...	...	0.250	1.310*	0.680	1.250	0.760	0.460	1.020	0.650	0.300	0.000	1.310
1846	0.450	0.000	0.570	0.610	1.650	0.780	1.490	0.550	1.800*	0.540	1.450	0.500	1.800
1847	1.100	0.550	0.550	1.000	0.600	0.520	0.840	0.790	2.500*	1.180	0.710	0.270	2.500
1848	0.950	0.410	0.970	0.230	0.440	0.760	0.290	0.310	1.000*	0.290	0.890	0.780	1.000
1849	0.820	0.230	1.025	0.675	1.050	0.990	1.775	1.045	0.645	3.160*	0.840	0.515	3.160
1850	0.360	0.500	0.410	2.350	0.270	1.505	2.750*	2.100	0.350	0.640	1.420	0.140	2.750
1851	0.585	0.570	0.640	0.650	0.790	1.090	1.155	0.390	0.610	0.320	2.770*	0.325	2.770
1852	0.000	0.550	0.850	1.025	0.550	0.625	1.860	1.055	1.160	1.825*	0.570	1.100	1.825
1853	0.800	0.510	0.410	0.715	1.400	0.895	0.480	1.020	1.990*	0.350	0.580	0.450	1.990
1854	0.485	0.685	0.875	0.840	0.915	0.635	1.135	0.210	1.705*	0.465	0.315	0.330	1.705
1855	0.360	1.705	0.680	0.695	0.345	0.875	1.205	0.615	2.535*	0.510	1.120	1.030	2.535
1856	0.000	0.000	0.000	0.705	2.135*	1.295	0.405	0.735	1.195	0.365	0.290	0.855	2.135
1857	R.	1.620*	0.145	0.670	1.375	1.070	1.260	1.110	1.213	0.385	1.020	1.055	1.620
1858	0.517	R.	0.305	0.630	1.590*	0.785	1.300	1.015	0.315	0.500	0.977	0.440	1.590
1859	0.655	0.290	1.615	1.145	0.945	1.575	0.879	1.655*	1.185	0.397	1.470	0.780	1.655
1860	0.340	0.385	0.585	0.410	0.935	0.750	0.935	0.890	0.610	0.325	0.818	1.265*	1.265
1861	0.475	0.430	0.865	0.615	1.845	0.598	0.875	0.760	1.855	0.625	3.132*	0.250	3.132
1862	0.060	0.125	0.745	1.555*	0.855	0.650	1.335	0.697	0.800	0.035	0.680	1.250	1.555
1863	0.445	0.630	0.315	0.835	0.925	0.625	1.665*	0.805	0.770	0.970	0.647	0.920	1.655
1864	0.920	0.365	0.480	1.280	0.620	0.395	0.440	1.325*	1.150	1.190	1.020	1.130	1.325
1865	0.440	0.435	0.660	1.600	2.220*	0.550	1.190	0.925	0.940	1.275	0.335	0.810	2.220
1866	0.317	0.600	0.625	1.080	1.290	0.950	2.345*	2.145	1.010	0.895	0.875	1.120	2.345
1867	R.	0.630	0.355	1.155*	1.090	0.520	1.110	0.950	0.355	1.070	0.795	0.553	1.155
1868	R.	0.040	0.770	0.610	2.220*	0.825	0.245	0.662	1.585	0.865	2.230	0.005	2.230
1869	0.825	0.160	0.660	1.490	0.810	0.925	1.600	1.150	2.350*	0.465	1.400	1.405	2.350
1870	1.000	0.520	0.550	0.720	0.350	2.360*	0.630	1.490	2.285	0.930	0.424	1.950	2.360
1871	0.400	0.040	1.050	1.025	1.500	0.880	0.415	1.036	0.650	0.510	2.310*	0.320	2.310
Means.	0.646	0.481	0.647	0.859	1.084	0.945	1.189	1.083	1.353	0.835	1.116	0.742	2.071

TORONTO METEOROLOGICAL OBSERVATIONS.

TABLE XXXVII.

COMPARATIVE DURATION OF THE SEVERAL WINDS ON DAYS IN ANY PART OF WHICH RAIN OR SNOW FELL, FROM OBSERVATIONS IN THE TWO PERIODS—1853-57 AND 1858-62. RAIN AND SNOW ARE CONSIDERED SEPARATELY, AND ARE GROUPED IN CLASSES DISTINGUISHED AS LIGHT, MODERATE, AND HEAVY.

LIGHT.—Rain, not exceeding one-tenth of an inch. Snow, not exceeding one inch.

		N.	N.N.E.	N.E.	E.N.E.	E.	E.S.E.	S.E.	S.S.E.	S.	S.S.W.	S.W.	W.S.W.	W.	W.N.W.	N.W.	N.N.W.	Calms.
Rain	Winter {1853-57	0.83	0.67	0.92	1.26	1.02	1.24	1.72	1.50	1.29	1.09	1.07	0.88	0.82	0.61	0.70	0.86	1.12
	1858-62	0.62	0.49	0.80	1.16	1.22	1.24	1.51	1.01	1.18	1.24	0.96	0.97	1.99	1.19	0.69	0.76	1.01
	Summer {1853-57	0.72	0.73	0.99	1.17	1.08	0.95	0.82	0.75	0.84	1.03	1.14	1.39	1.51	1.67	0.89	0.80	1.11
	1858-62	0.95	0.58	0.99	0.90	0.99	0.72	0.71	0.69	0.66	1.07	1.34	1.84	1.41	1.17	1.25	0.90	0.82
	Year {1853-57	0.80	0.73	1.00	1.26	1.14	1.12	0.97	1.02	1.04	1.13	1.11	0.98	1.03	0.83	0.82	0.86	1.16
	1858-62	0.84	0.56	0.93	1.05	1.15	0.96	1.0	0.85	0.86	1.2	1.13	1.21	1.14	1.20	1.05	0.90	0.94
Snow	Year {1853-57	1.20	1.12	1.06	0.47	0.43	0.70	0.64	0.48	0.44	0.43	1.20	1.88	1.96	1.51	1.42	1.27	0.73
	1858-62	1.29	1.10	0.67	0.54	0.40	0.49	0.52	0.69	0.45	0.55	1.02	2.03	2.01	1.87	1.35	1.24	0.70

MODERATE.—Rain, more than one-tenth and less than half an inch. Snow, more than one inch and less than five inches.

		N.	N.N.E.	N.E.	E.N.E.	E.	E.S.E.	S.E.	S.S.E.	S.	S.S.W.	S.W.	W.S.W.	W.	W.N.W.	N.W.	N.N.W.	Calms.
Rain	Winter {1853-57	0.28	0.72	0.90	2.08	2.52	1.52	1.74	1.65	1.43	0.92	0.64	0.43	0.38	0.44	0.30	0.25	0.69
	1858-62	0.54	0.64	0.80	1.90	2.00	1.84	1.55	1.64	1.33	1.23	0.88	0.61	0.28	0.16	0.34	0.34	0.92
	Summer {1853-57	0.69	1.01	1.27	1.30	1.01	1.00	1.03	0.97	1.06	1.06	1.20	1.28	0.95	0.93	0.93	0.69	0.64
	1858-62	0.87	0.70	1.07	1.53	1.16	1.26	0.83	0.87	0.70	0.90	1.37	1.26	0.90	0.82	0.78	0.70	0.83
	Year {1853-57	0.57	0.94	1.16	1.69	1.62	1.26	1.34	1.25	1.28	1.12	0.93	0.65	0.56	0.58	0.49	0.54	0.70
	1858-62	0.74	0.75	1.13	1.80	1.60	1.58	1.16	1.19	0.90	1.08	1.14	0.83	0.54	0.47	0.60	0.55	0.93
Snow	Year {1853-57	1.04	1.79	2.22	1.06	0.91	0.97	1.27	0.55	0.59	0.63	0.95	0.89	0.95	0.78	0.70	1.22	0.49
	1858-62	1.04	1.82	3.26	1.53	1.21	0.82	0.60	0.99	0.45	0.5	0.73	0.97	0.45	0.69	0.80		0.65

HEAVY.—Rain, half an inch and upwards. Snow, five inches and upwards.

		N.	N.N.E.	N.E.	E.N.E.	E.	E.S.E.	S.E.	S.S.E.	S.	S.S.W.	S.W.	W.S.W.	W.	W.N.W.	N.W.	N.N.W.	Calms.
Rain	Winter {1853-57	0.06	0.38	0.63	2.87	3.73	2.91	1.64	1.26	0.60	0.79	0.63	0.35	0.19	0.19	0.10	0.09	0.57
	1858-62	0.91	1.30	1.39	3.79	3.37	1.50	0.68	1.00	0.55	0.42	0.29	0.42	0.32	0.19	0.19	0.32	0.23
	Summer {1853-57	0.87	0.70	1.74	1.85	1.86	1.42	0.87	1.21	0.64	0.89	1.08	0.41	0.60	0.87	0.69	0.58	0.63
	1858-62	0.75	1.13	1.44	2.62	1.61	0.98	1.27	0.47	0.56	0.99	1.77	0.90	0.70	0.50	0.39	0.51	0.40
	Year {1853-57	0.66	0.62	1.40	2.22	2.49	1.91	1.13	1.38	0.73	0.95	0.84	0.20	0.35	0.54	0.45	0.43	0.62
	1858-62	0.81	1.17	1.40	3.09	2.20	1.23	1.27	0.66	0.68	0.95	1.02	0.53	0.47	0.36	0.32	0.49	0.36
Snow	Year {1853-57	1.59	2.09	2.81	2.08	2.57	1.34	0.25	0.12	0.12	0.24	0.25	0.49	0.49	0.43	0.49	0.73	0.24
	1858-62	1.17	1.76	2.78	2.49	2.49	0.59	0.44	0.44	0.00	0.29	0.88	0.73	0.59	0.20	0.73		0.59

RAIN OR SNOW IN THE YEAR, WITHOUT REFERENCE TO AMOUNT.

	N.	N.N.E.	N.E.	E.N.E.	E.	E.S.E.	S.E.	S.S.E.	S.	S.S.W.	S.W.	W.S.W.	W.	W.N.W.	N.W.	N.N.W.	Calms.
Rain 1853-62	0.75	0.75	1.08	1.57	1.47	1.20	1.11	1.05	0.97	1.12	1.06	0.87	0.61	0.79	0.76	0.71	0.89
Snow 1853-62	1.20	1.33	1.40	0.78	0.68	0.71	0.67	0.61	0.45	0.49	1.00	1.62	1.67	1.38	1.18	1.18	0.66

TABLE XXXVIII.

RESULTANT DIRECTION OF THE WIND FOR EACH MONTH AND YEAR FROM 1848 TO 1871, AND ALSO THE MONTHLY AND ANNUAL RESULTANTS FOR THE WHOLE PERIOD.

The direction in every case is measured from the North.

Years.	Jan.	Feb.	Mar.	April.	May.	June.	July.	Aug.	Sept.	Oct.	Nov.	Dec.	Year.
1848	82° w	65° w	66° w	77° w	40° w	61° w	14° w	159° e	71° w	54° w	81° w	97° w	71° w
1849	63 w	41 w	3 w	43 w	51 e	109 e	175 w	71 w	75 w	12 w	39 w	82 w	38 w
1850	37 w	80 w	52 w	39 w	64 w	120 w	81 e	15 e	115 w	66 w	42 w	44 w	57 w
1851	103 w	64 w	21 w	14 e	32 w	172 w	60 w	63 w	14 e	108 w	50 w	82 w	61 w
1852	68 w	105 w	8 w	23 e	98 w	104 w	43 w	70 e	77 w	5 e	59 w	111 w	62 w
1853	27 w	49 w	58 w	12 w	2 w	1 w	122 e	144 e	0	92 w	9 w	35 w	38 w
1854	77 w	7 e	53 w	50 e	90 e	24 e	131 w	64 w	22 w	45 w	90 w	44 w	45 w
1855	73 w	40 w	88 w	36 w	1 w	69 w	161 w	63 w	20 e	82 w	66 w	92 w	64 w
1856	75 w	81 w	71 w	29 e	4 e	159 w	79 w	50 w	101 w	76 w	95 w	93 w	71 w
1857	70 w	102 w	63 w	60 w	20 w	49 w	112 e	77 w	68 w	19 w	119 w	89 w	74 w
1858	71 w	72 w	58 w	14 w	42 e	160 e	15 e	69 w	100 w	34 w	25 w	18 w	41 w
1859	99 w	54 w	64 w	36 w	72 e	77 w	56 w	36 w	44 w	68 w	81 w	53 w	61 w
1860	89 w	61 w	64 w	37 w	26 e	44 w	60 w	70 w	71 w	9 w	119 w	62 w	60 w
1861	86 w	77 w	54 w	37 e	47 w	39 w	74 w	8 e	71 w	61 w	46 w	72 w	56 w
1862	26 w	55 w	12 w	50 e	52 w	26 w	91 w	78 w	59 w	79 w	46 w	73 w	48 w
1863	61 w	23 w	27 w	14 e	56 e	50 w	18 w	119 w	16 w	109 w	88 w	41 w	41 w
1864	107 w	96 w	53 w	41 e	7 w	55 w	61 w	70 w	39 w	60 w	108 w	98 w	76 w
1865	85 w	23 w	61 w	84 w	3 w	150 w	86 w	60 w	124 e	36 w	79 w	99 w	66 w
1866	75 w	100 w	73 w	42 w	46 w	165 w	101 w	59 w	33 w	30 w	88 w	92 w	73 w
1867	55 w	57 w	34 w	51 w	51 w	96 e	42 w	76 w	37 w	45 w	87 w	99 w	60 w
1868	97 w	69 w	21 w	63 w	38 e	16 e	93 e	122 w	74 w	89 w	35 w	71 w	57 w
1869	72 w	34 w	52 w	59 w	20 w	80 w	113 w	42 w	53 w	73 w	78 w	80 w	64 w
1870	91 w	29 w	18 e	40 e	23 e	17 e	102 w	75 w	29 e	85 w	89 w	89 w	45 w
1871	49 w	70 w	31 w	48 w	23 w	80 w	88 w	52 w	74 w	114 w	45 w	110 w	72 w
1848–71	79 w	66 w	49 w	18 w	12 w	64 w	77 w	66 w	52 w	64 w	76 w	80 w	61 w

TORONTO METEOROLOGICAL OBSERVATIONS.

TABLE XXXIX.

RESULTANT VELOCITY OF THE WIND, IN MILES, FOR EACH MONTH AND YEAR FROM 1848 TO 1871, AND ALSO THE MONTHLY AND ANNUAL RESULTANTS FOR THE WHOLE PERIOD.

Years.	Jan.	Feb.	Mar.	April.	May.	June.	July.	Aug.	Sept.	Oct.	Nov.	Dec.	Year.
1848	2.03	2.53	2.03	1.46	1.31	1.90	0.18	0.98	2.38	1.24	1.81	1.12	1.41
1849	3.05	1.48	1.48	3.14	1.97	0.49	0.75	0.60	0.60	1.27	1.55	2.56	1.20
1850	0.69	3.43	2.02	1.12	2.05	0.38	0.59	0.35	1.02	1.10	1.43	2.93	1.24
1851	3.26	1.99	1.93	2.52	1.59	1.26	0.88	0.40	1.03	1.06	1.25	4.00	1.22
1852	3.14	3.34	0.71	2.44	0.99	1.49	0.93	0.56	0.53	1.19	1.53	1.03	0.98
1853	2.52	2.51	2.60	1.95	0.83	0.10	0.24	0.30	1.06	1.74	0.55	2.39	1.18
1854	2.44	1.73	3.39	2.57	0.40	0.71	0.37	1.76	1.33	1.52	3.44	4.30	1.47
1855	1.91	4.34	4.76	3.99	2.76	1.33	0.73	1.04	1.29	4.91	3.18	5.29	2.47
1856	5.24	7.70	7.68	1.64	3.99	0.90	1.57	2.88	1.98	2.15	2.95	4.62	3.03
1857	4.96	3.69	6.63	4.15	1.14	1.15	0.81	1.51	1.61	2.93	5.45	2.51	2.54
1858	2.33	3.22	5.45	1.64	3.33	0.25	1.13	1.57	1.53	0.36	3.14	1.06	1.59
1859	3.17	2.72	1.96	2.33	1.59	1.95	1.48	1.62	1.60	5.04	3.39	4.29	2.24
1860	6.09	3.28	7.61	4.10	2.66	3.13	2.15	1.83	2.03	2.00	4.95	4.66	3.32
1861	2.92	3.86	4.33	2.31	3.60	2.29	1.43	0.46	1.39	1.06	1.04	3.50	2.11
1862	2.09	3.93	2.50	2.48	2.80	1.77	1.42	1.67	1.07	2.89	3.00	3.17	2.03
1863	1.13	2.27	2.62	3.75	0.41	2.26	0.40	1.80	0.92	0.48	3.50	1.01	1.34
1864	6.00	6.48	2.29	3.39	1.86	1.72	2.23	1.38	1.89	3.17	3.82	4.94	2.49
1865	4.80	3.95	2.16	2.11	1.65	0.60	2.28	1.55	0.47	0.58	2.98	3.07	1.98
1866	2.98	5.14	6.84	3.34	4.49	0.71	0.94	2.58	1.45	0.84	3.06	4.98	2.83
1867	3.27	1.58	2.12	2.68	3.55	0.48	1.13	1.25	1.48	1.51	4.02	4.82	2.05
1868	3.97	3.23	2.12	2.43	3.16	0.85	0.72	1.01	0.88	1.27	2.10	4.05	1.47
1869	3.40	4.18	2.86	4.03	2.38	1.77	2.01	1.98	1.16	3.72	3.09	2.31	2.55
1870	2.63	2.84	4.73	3.55	1.09	0.40	1.59	1.80	2.26	1.86	4.36	5.06	1.61
1871	2.56	4.26	2.59	1.86	2.53	2.04	1.55	1.09	1.72	3.75	4.08	6.91	2.49
1848–71	3.12	3.14	3.14	2.04	1.63	0.83	0.78	1.10	1.06	1.82	2.08	3.31	1.91

TORONTO METEOROLOGICAL OBSERVATIONS.

TABLE XL.

MEAN VELOCITY OF THE WIND, IN MILES, FOR EACH MONTH AND YEAR FROM 1848 TO 1871, AND ALSO THE MONTHLY AND ANNUAL MEAN VELOCITIES FOR THE WHOLE PERIOD.

Years.	Jan.	Feb.	Mar.	April.	May.	June.	July.	Aug.	Sept.	Oct.	Nov.	Dec.	Year.
1848	5.82	5.69	5.80	4.89	4.93	4.51	4.94	4.55	5.81	4.60	4.81	5.44	5.15
1849	6.71	6.58	5.37	7.50	5.33	3.32	3.52	3.76	4.23	4.76	4.78	6.23	5.17
1850	5.80	7.61	7.62	7.64	6.32	4.54	4.56	4.46	4.78	5.39	5.27	7.40	5.94
1851	7.69	6.94	7.65	8.07	6.34	4.42	4.13	4.63	5.45	4.39	4.70	7.37	5.98
1852	7.67	6.42	5.81	6.08	4.00	4.09	3.33	3.30	4.60	4.47	6.50	6.54	5.20
1853	6.34	7.30	5.96	5.20	5.16	3.73	3.69	4.26	4.83	4.77	5.52	4.98	5.10
1854	6.91	6.91	8.03	6.91	5.38	4.15	4.03	4.60	4.04	4.57	7.54	8.56	5.96
1855	7.26	8.17	9.95	7.57	5.93	5.70	6.47	6.97	7.61	9.88	10.81	11.38	8.14
1856	10.69	10.71	11.30	6.05	9.61	5.30	5.84	7.03	6.53	6.07	8.75	11.56	8.31
1857	10.31	9.82	10.84	10.24	8.13	7.60	4.74	6.36	5.55	6.24	9.25	6.84	7.99
1858	7.40	9.12	8.56	9.57	9.30	5.53	5.76	6.50	5.69	5.96	8.87	9.36	7.64
1859	8.76	8.50	10.39	10.79	5.70	7.19	5.81	5.96	6.36	8.12	9.65	10.77	8.17
1860	9.37	8.73	12.41	10.30	7.17	7.61	7.29	5.80	5.79	6.93	11.02	10.14	8.55
1861	9.30	10.58	10.56	8.90	9.17	6.11	4.66	4.21	4.81	5.96	7.44	7.96	7.47
1862	8.83	8.52	9.38	9.77	7.97	5.99	3.80	5.96	5.11	6.53	6.60	7.58	7.33
1863	7.23	10.13	9.27	9.20	5.89	5.24	3.80	4.80	6.46	6.16	7.86	9.40	7.13
1864	10.22	10.11	8.41	7.77	5.64	4.53	6.00	4.75	7.06	6.66	7.64	9.98	7.40
1865	9.39	8.23	8.80	8.33	5.48	4.06	5.34	5.07	4.12	7.26	7.90	7.33	6.78
1866	9.34	9.40	11.51	7.95	9.26	5.09	4.17	5.16	4.63	5.53	6.96	9.91	7.41
1867	6.96	8.85	8.52	7.89	8.40	4.13	5.45	4.52	5.43	5.73	7.76	10.32	7.00
1868	8.90	10.84	8.58	9.24	6.87	5.26	4.66	6.15	6.68	7.10	8.16	9.80	7.09
1869	9.21	10.04	8.02	8.91	6.55	5.23	5.07	5.13	4.89	6.73	8.12	8.44	7.20
1870	8.98	8.10	10.15	7.03	5.48	5.14	4.82	5.92	5.04	7.11	8.74	11.46	7.33
1871	9.84	9.67	8.51	8.85	7.70	6.57	5.67	6.86	5.50	7.84	10.35	11.52	8.24
Means 1848-71	8.29	8.63	8.80	8.13	6.74	5.21	4.99	5.28	5.44	6.20	7.71	8.76	7.02

TORONTO METEOROLOGICAL OBSERVATIONS.

TABLE XLI.

RESULTANT DIRECTION OF THE WIND IN EACH HOUR, ASTRONOMICAL TIME, FOR EACH MONTH AND FOR THE YEAR, FROM OBSERVATIONS IN THE SIX YEARS, 1854 TO 1859 INCLUSIVE.

The direction in every case is measured from the North.

Hours commencing	Jan.	Feb.	Mar.	April.	May.	June.	July	Aug.	Sept.	Oct.	Nov.	Dec.	Year.
0	84 w	83 w	83 w	111 w	107 E	158 w	180	142 w	146 w	86 w	91 w	73 w	103 w
1	86 w	82 w	84 w	110 w	108 E	164 w	175 w	139 w	142 w	87 w	90 w	79 w	103 w
2	87 w	81 w	83 w	97 w	80 E	168 w	175 w	123 w	135 w	84 w	90 w	81 w	101 w
3	82 w	79 w	80 w	75 w	49 E	154 w	176 w	105 w	120 w	77 w	88 w	82 w	90 w
4	79 w	72 w	76 w	51 w	19 E	118 w	153 w	79 w	92 w	70 w	83 w	82 w	77 w
5	82 w	70 w	74 w	45 w	0	87 w	94 w	56 w	78 w	70 w	84 w	80 w	70 w
6	82 w	64 w	72 w	47 w	3 w	52 w	55 w	49 w	61 w	66 w	83 w	80 w	64 w
7	76 w	62 w	66 w	34 w	1 w	39 w	52 w	41 w	55 w	60 w	83 w	81 w	59 w
8	79 w	61 w	68 w	25 w	6 E	24 w	36 w	38 w	44 w	59 w	78 w	81 w	56 w
9	81 w	56 w	64 w	20 w	0	16 w	32 w	32 w	35 w	51 w	77 w	76 w	51 w
10	76 w	58 w	61 w	13 w	1 E	16 w	29 w	30 w	30 w	52 w	80 w	70 w	48 w
11	73 w	62 w	58 w	9 w	3 E	18 w	28 w	29 w	21 w	51 w	79 w	68 w	46 w
12	72 w	58 w	56 w	2 w	6 E	18 w	18 w	24 w	22 w	44 w	79 w	66 w	43 w
13	71 w	55 w	54 w	2 w	6 E	17 w	14 w	22 w	20 w	51 w	81 w	62 w	40 w
14	70 w	56 w	54 w	3 w	2 E	16 w	11 w	26 w	20 w	52 w	80 w	57 w	40 w
15	74 w	59 w	53 w	2 w	10 E	21 w	9 w	25 w	17 w	43 w	79 w	54 w	39 w
16	70 w	61 w	50 w	2 w	15 E	18 w	11 w	20 w	15 w	43 w	83 w	56 w	39 w
17	73 w	62 w	53 w	2 w	15 E	24 w	15 w	18 w	14 w	39 w	84 w	56 w	38 w
18	73 w	64 w	53 w	1 w	16 E	29 w	15 w	30 w	21 w	39 w	86 w	62 w	40 w
19	71 w	66 w	52 w	10 w	27 E	42 w	14 w	38 w	36 w	45 w	82 w	56 w	42 w
20	68 w	65 w	53 w	9 w	29 E	67 w	19 w	55 w	49 w	50 w	83 w	59 w	48 w
21	69 w	68 w	62 w	12 w	30 E	126 w	140 w	74 w	78 w	58 w	87 w	59 w	63 w
22	75 w	72 w	72 w	40 w	61 E	145 w	171 E	112 w	121 w	66 w	88 w	62 w	80 w
23	82 w	76 w	78 w	89 w	84 E	157 w	173 E	138 w	145 w	79 w	92 w	67 w	96 w
Period of 24 hours.	77 w	67 w	70 w	23 w	20 E	73 w	66 w	58 w	61 w	62 w	85 w	70 w	62 w

TABLE XLII.

RESULTANT VELOCITY OF THE WIND IN EACH HOUR, FOR EACH MONTH AND FOR THE YEAR, FROM OBSERVATIONS IN THE SIX YEARS, 1854 TO 1859 INCLUSIVE.

Velocities in miles per hour.

Hours.	Jan.	Feb.	Mar.	April	May.	June.	July.	Aug.	Sept.	Oct.	Nov.	Dec.	Year.
0	4.71	4.34	5.97	1.17	1.49	2.35	2.97	2.67	2.35	3.54	4.40	4.39	2.61
1	4.69	4.17	6.14	1.50	1.17	2.45	2.90	2.92	2.10	3.29	4.75	4.46	2.71
2	4.45	3.94	6.26	1.68	0.98	2.34	2.73	2.73	2.05	3.34	4.15	4.24	2.70
3	3.92	3.98	6.26	1.92	1.03	1.70	1.97	2.29	1.75	3.21	4.07	3.94	2.56
4	3.48	3.76	6.27	1.99	1.37	1.42	1.16	1.96	1.70	3.39	3.77	3.89	2.60
5	3.02	2.94	5.99	2.45	1.89	0.96	0.75	2.50	1.43	2.85	3.10	3.75	2.49
6	3.10	3.13	5.48	2.68	2.29	0.86	0.69	2.50	1.38	2.47	2.83	3.82	2.44
7	3.05	3.29	5.10	2.47	2.27	1.14	0.69	2.21	1.47	2.47	2.59	3.92	2.38
8	3.02	3.28	4.93	2.84	2.04	1.19	0.80	2.30	1.58	2.45	2.53	4.00	2.35
9	2.55	3.12	5.15	3.38	1.95	1.50	1.05	2.37	1.60	2.34	2.44	3.98	2.38
10	2.73	2.92	4.60	3.17	2.02	1.66	1.46	2.24	1.92	2.15	2.53	3.88	2.36
11	2.88	2.80	4.39	2.79	2.28	1.58	1.64	2.03	1.92	2.00	2.38	3.80	2.28
12	2.77	2.92	4.24	3.01	2.21	1.65	1.81	2.08	1.69	1.92	2.61	3.56	2.25
13	2.73	3.42	4.29	3.07	2.39	1.73	2.05	2.25	1.80	2.04	2.52	2.94	2.32
14	2.92	3.35	3.95	3.01	2.69	1.53	2.05	2.15	1.96	2.23	2.64	2.76	2.33
15	2.81	3.23	3.92	2.84	2.43	1.40	2.01	2.31	1.90	2.21	2.75	2.67	2.25
16	2.71	3.34	3.97	2.95	2.24	1.16	1.93	2.12	1.73	2.06	2.62	2.55	2.15
17	2.74	3.23	3.75	3.10	2.47	1.31	1.79	2.10	1.61	2.16	2.43	2.44	2.11
18	2.74	3.73	3.80	3.25	3.52	1.34	1.74	2.26	1.58	2.10	2.06	2.41	2.23
19	3.02	3.57	4.21	3.09	3.54	0.97	1.54	2.09	1.72	2.43	2.58	2.27	2.22
20	3.30	3.53	4.50	2.63	3.39	0.84	0.69	2.25	1.43	3.09	2.75	2.85	2.22
21	3.77	4.00	5.09	1.92	2.56	1.12	0.57	1.95	1.24	3.14	3.52	3.11	2.24
22	3.96	3.98	5.36	1.17	1.82	1.62	1.82	1.77	1.41	3.18	4.17	3.87	2.18
23	4.45	4.30	5.71	0.92	1.49	2.08	2.48	2.49	2.01	3.33	4.43	3.93	2.37
Period of 24 hours.	3.29	3.45	4.89	2.14	1.91	0.69	0.41	1.68	1.16	2.60	3.13	3.42	2.18

TORONTO METEOROLOGICAL OBSERVATIONS.

TABLE XLIII.

MEAN VELOCITY OF THE WIND IN EACH OF THE TWENTY-FOUR HOURS, ASTRO-NOMICAL TIME, FOR THE FOUR QUARTERS, AND THE YEAR; DERIVED FROM TWO GROUPS OF YEARS, INCLUDING THE SIX YEARS, 1848-53, AND THE SEVENTEEN YEARS, 1855-71.

Hour commencing	1848-53.					1855-71.				
	Winter.	Spring.	Summer.	Autumn.	Year.	Winter.	Spring.	Summer.	Autumn.	Year.
0	8.16	8.23	6.76	7.23	7.59	10.93	11.13	8.48	10.02	10.14
1	8.07	8.40	6.86	7.47	7.70	11.17	11.38	8.67	10.16	10.34
2	8.12	8.78	7.03	7.49	7.85	10.93	11.12	8.67	9.91	10.16
3	7.92	8.40	6.87	7.16	7.61	10.48	10.92	8.44	9.42	9.82
4	7.39	8.26	6.53	6.45	7.16	9.95	10.41	8.02	8.48	9.21
5	6.71	7.56	5.85	5.52	6.41	9.32	9.49	6.82	7.14	8.19
6	6.43	6.77	5.03	4.72	5.74	9.16	8.35	5.55	6.32	7.34
7	6.41	5.67	3.78	4.23	5.02	9.06	7.74	4.45	5.98	6.81
8	6.09	5.20	2.80	4.07	4.69	8.81	7.49	4.12	5.88	6.58
9	6.00	4.96	2.51	3.88	4.34	8.58	7.26	3.96	5.69	6.37
10	6.10	5.08	2.40	3.78	4.34	8.55	6.98	4.02	5.55	6.27
11	5.95	4.86	2.34	3.86	4.25	8.57	6.86	4.03	5.59	6.27
12	5.76	4.60	2.36	3.86	4.17	8.49	6.79	3.88	5.51	6.17
13	5.77	4.50	2.37	4.01	4.18	8.48	6.78	3.82	5.54	6.16
14	5.83	4.52	2.36	3.88	4.15	8.40	6.77	3.78	5.63	6.16
15	5.85	4.37	2.28	3.78	4.07	8.30	6.84	3.70	5.66	6.14
16	5.80	4.42	2.31	3.73	4.07	8.26	6.69	3.62	5.52	6.02
17	5.88	4.50	2.37	3.85	4.15	8.35	6.84	3.64	5.61	6.11
18	5.94	4.67	2.45	3.74	4.20	8.48	7.44	4.02	5.51	6.36
19	5.83	5.11	3.04	3.75	4.43	8.44	8.42	4.77	5.91	6.89
20	5.98	6.15	3.73	4.24	5.03	8.89	9.12	5.55	6.90	7.61
21	6.70	6.84	4.72	5.31	5.89	9.73	9.86	6.59	8.17	8.59
22	7.13	7.28	5.36	5.94	6.43	10.27	10.43	7.39	9.06	9.29
23	7.63	7.79	6.24	6.80	7.11	10.74	10.92	8.10	9.69	9.86
Means	6.56	6.13	4.10	4.95	5.44	9.27	8.58	5.50	7.04	7.62

TABLE XLIV.

MEAN VELOCITY OF THE WIND IN EACH OF THE TWENTY-FOUR HOURS, FOR THE FOUR QUARTERS AND YEAR, EXPRESSED IN TERMS OF THE MEAN VELOCITY OF THE TWENTY-FOUR HOURS FOR THE CORRESPONDING QUARTER; BEING THE QUOTIENTS OBTAINED BY DIVIDING THE NUMBERS IN THE PRECEDING TABLE BY THEIR RESPECTIVE AVERAGES FOR TWENTY-FOUR HOURS.

Hour commencing	1848–53.					1855–71.				
	Winter.	Spring.	Summer.	Autumn.	Year.	Winter.	Spring.	Summer.	Autumn.	Year.
0	1.24	1.34	1.65	1.46	1.40	1.18	1.30	1.52	1.42	1.33
1	1.23	1.37	1.67	1.51	1.41	1.21	1.33	1.55	1.44	1.36
2	1.24	1.43	1.71	1.51	1.44	1.18	1.30	1.55	1.41	1.33
3	1.21	1.38	1.68	1.45	1.40	1.13	1.27	1.57	1.34	1.29
4	1.13	1.35	1.59	1.30	1.32	1.07	1.21	1.43	1.21	1.21
5	1.02	1.23	1.43	1.12	1.18	1.01	1.11	1.22	1.01	1.08
6	0.98	1.10	1.23	0.95	1.06	0.99	0.97	0.99	0.90	0.96
7	0.98	0.93	0.92	0.86	0.92	0.98	0.90	0.80	0.85	0.89
8	0.93	0.85	0.68	0.82	0.86	0.95	0.87	0.74	0.84	0.86
9	0.91	0.81	0.61	0.78	0.80	0.93	0.85	0.71	0.81	0.84
10	0.93	0.83	0.59	0.76	0.80	0.92	0.80	0.72	0.79	0.82
11	0.91	0.79	0.57	0.78	0.78	0.92	0.80	0.72	0.79	0.82
12	0.88	0.76	0.58	0.78	0.77	0.92	0.79	0.70	0.78	0.81
13	0.88	0.75	0.58	0.81	0.77	0.91	0.79	0.69	0.79	0.81
14	0.89	0.74	0.58	0.78	0.76	0.91	0.79	0.68	0.81	0.81
15	0.89	0.72	0.56	0.76	0.75	0.90	0.79	0.66	0.80	0.81
16	0.88	0.72	0.56	0.75	0.75	0.89	0.78	0.65	0.78	0.79
17	0.90	0.73	0.58	0.78	0.76	0.90	0.80	0.65	0.80	0.80
18	0.90	0.76	0.60	0.76	0.77	0.91	0.87	0.72	0.78	0.84
19	0.89	0.83	0.74	0.76	0.81	0.91	0.98	0.85	0.84	0.90
20	0.91	1.00	0.91	0.86	0.92	0.96	1.06	0.99	0.93	1.00
21	1.02	1.12	1.15	1.07	1.08	1.05	1.15	1.18	1.16	1.13
22	1.09	1.19	1.31	1.20	1.18	1.11	1.22	1.32	1.29	1.22
23	1.16	1.27	1.52	1.37	1.31	1.16	1.27	1.45	1.38	1.29
	1.00	1.00	1.00	1.00	1.00	1.00	1.00	1.00	1.00	1.00

TABLE XLV.

Relative duration of different Winds in each Month, from hourly observations in the Years 1853-62, being the duration of the different Winds, expressed in terms of the average duration of all Winds in the Month. Also, the relative duration of the different Winds in each Quarter and in the Year, for 1853-57, and 1858-62.

	N.	N.N.E.	N.E.	E.N.E.	E.	E.S.E.	S.E.	S.S.E.	S.	S.S.W.	S.W.	W.S.W.	W.	W.N.W.	N.W.	N.N.W.
January	1.17	0.83	0.97	0.67	0.80	0.39	0.21	0.23	0.25	1.72	1.55	2.60	1.83	1.16	1.19	1.40
February	1.13	0.78	0.75	0.78	1.01	0.36	0.24	0.26	0.32	0.88	1.29	1.86	2.00	1.58	1.29	1.37
March	0.66	0.37	0.52	1.09	1.20	0.42	0.39	0.24	0.42	0.78	1.25	1.21	1.81	2.11	2.19	1.34
April	1.22	0.57	0.59	1.50	2.05	0.87	0.50	0.46	0.59	0.91	0.73	0.68	0.90	1.22	1.17	1.44
May	1.17	0.63	0.85	1.70	1.90	0.94	0.50	0.55	0.93	1.30	0.63	0.44	0.62	0.96	1.18	1.70
June	0.95	0.43	0.66	1.28	1.61	0.50	0.44	0.53	1.25	1.60	1.17	0.69	0.89	0.89	1.43	1.42
July	1.01	0.69	0.53	0.98	1.29	0.88	0.66	0.99	1.48	1.64	0.86	0.58	0.62	0.96	1.24	1.60
August	1.10	0.86	0.69	0.71	1.14	0.67	0.64	0.65	1.19	1.38	0.90	0.55	0.88	1.33	1.59	1.73
September	1.32	0.88	0.75	0.97	1.13	0.60	0.63	0.67	1.04	1.59	1.02	0.71	0.99	1.11	1.23	1.43
October	1.11	0.81	0.88	1.10	1.14	0.62	0.29	0.43	0.87	1.10	1.09	0.90	1.31	1.73	1.33	1.29
November	0.88	0.68	0.73	1.09	1.22	0.50	0.37	0.38	0.40	0.83	1.43	2.14	1.66	1.36	1.18	1.15
December	1.24	1.01	0.88	0.61	0.74	0.46	0.23	0.21	0.16	0.55	1.51	2.38	1.98	1.21	1.22	1.41
Winter { 1853-57	1.29	0.95	0.86	0.64	0.77	0.46	0.23	0.22	0.27	0.64	1.40	2.45	1.96	1.25	1.13	1.45
{ 1858-62	1.08	0.78	0.57	0.86	0.93	0.35	0.23	0.25	0.21	0.78	1.53	2.14	1.97	1.36	1.33	1.34
Spring { 1853-57	1.18	0.65	0.66	1.06	1.32	0.85	0.52	0.42	0.79	1.25	1.12	0.79	1.01	1.30	1.45	1.66
{ 1858-62	0.84	0.39	0.84	1.79	2.10	0.63	0.41	0.41	0.51	0.77	0.63	0.77	1.22	1.57	1.59	1.33
Summer { 1853-57	1.08	0.76	0.73	1.01	1.38	0.77	0.68	0.83	1.27	1.58	1.02	0.57	0.84	1.04	1.10	1.34
{ 1858-62	0.96	0.60	0.53	0.97	1.31	0.79	0.48	0.62	1.33	1.50	0.93	0.58	0.75	1.09	1.73	1.83
Autumn { 1853-57	1.02	0.76	0.79	1.11	1.16	0.57	0.51	0.59	0.86	1.13	1.25	1.28	1.24	1.22	1.19	1.32
{ 1858-62	1.19	0.81	0.80	0.99	1.17	0.58	0.35	0.39	0.67	1.21	1.11	1.25	1.36	1.58	1.30	1.25
Year { 1853-57	1.14	0.79	0.76	0.95	1.16	0.66	0.48	0.52	0.80	1.14	1.20	1.27	1.26	1.20	1.22	1.44
{ 1858-62	1.01	0.69	0.76	1.16	1.38	0.69	0.37	0.42	0.68	1.06	1.05	1.18	1.32	1.40	1.49	1.44

TORONTO METEOROLOGICAL OBSERVATIONS.

TABLE XLVI.

NUMBER OF AURORAS OBSERVED IN EACH MONTH, FROM 1841 TO 1871, BOTH INCLUSIVE.

Years.	Jan.	Feb.	Mar.	April.	May.	June.	July.	Aug.	Sept.	Oct.	Nov.	Dec.	Year.
1841	3	4	2	2	0	1	5	6	3	4	2	1	33
1842	1	0	0	3	0	1	3	1	2	0	0	0	11
1843	0	0	2	0	0	1	3	1	2	0	1	1	11
1844	1	0	1	1	4	1	1	1	2	1	2	0	15
1845	1	0	2	1	0	1	3	2	5	1	1	0	17
1846	0	0	1	1	5	0	1	2	5	4	0	1	20
1847	0	3	4	4	1	1	2	2	0	4	3	3	27
1848	4	7	8	12	8	2	3	3	4	7	9	2	69
1849	3	7	8	5	5	2	8	4	6	6	6	3	63
1850	3	3	3	6	5	3	5	4	5	9	3	1	50
1851	2	3	7	2	3	4	5	7	9	7	5	9	63
1852	...	...	3	7	...	...	3	5	8	...	...	3	...
1853	2	4	8	7	8	5	6	2	7	6	2	6	63
1854	3	4	12	8	6	2	4	1	6	5	2	1	54
1855	1	4	5	9	3	4	2	6	2	4	5	1	46
1856	0	5	7	4	0	1	4	5	3	3	1	1	34
1857	0	1	2	1	3	1	5	1	6	2	2	2	26
1858	2	6	4	4	5	4	5	6	8	10	3	2	59
1859	0	3	8	7	4	3	4	4	8	5	2	5	53
1860	5	2	12	7	7	2	6	8	6	0	1	2	58
1861	0	3	6	6	5	2	1	4	5	6	1	4	43
1862	4	1	2	5	5	2	6	9	8	6	0	0	48
1863	3	4	5	5	0	4	6	5	8	3	1	0	44
1864	0	4	2	4	3	5	3	6	4	2	1	0	34
1865	3	4	2	4	5	5	7	8	7	9	1	0	55
1866	3	3	8	1	7	1	3	4	3	8	2	1	44
1867	0	0	1	2	8	5	3	4	13	5	1	1	43
1868	1	3	10	6	5	4	4	2	5	5	1	4	50
1869	2	3	5	12	4	3	1	4	9	3	1	0	47
1870	4	1	6	11	7	7	4	12	8	5	8	4	77
1871	3	4	5	6	9	5	5	4	4	3	5	2	55
	54	86	148	146	125	82	118	128	163	133	72	57	1,312

TORONTO METEOROLOGICAL OBSERVATIONS.

TABLE XLVII.

NUMBER OF DAYS IN WHICH THUNDER, LIGHTNING, HAIL, FOG, DEW, OR AURORA WAS RECORDED, AND THE NUMBER OF DAYS IN WHICH IT WAS POSSIBLE TO SEE AURORA, IN EACH YEAR FROM 1853 TO 1871; AND THE RELATIVE FREQUENCY, OR THE RATIO OF THE NUMBER OF AURORAS OBSERVED TO THE POSSIBILITY OF THEIR BEING SEEN, WITH THEIR RATIOS EXPRESSED IN TERMS OF THEIR MEAN FOR NINETEEN YEARS.

	1853.	1854.	1855.	1856.	1857.	1858.	1859.	1860.	1861.	1862.	1863.	1864.	1865.	1866.	1867.	1868.	1869.	1870.	1871.
Thunder	31	35	31	23	28	29	34	34	28	25	28	30	24	25	23	25	32	39	30
Lightning	23	44	33	30	41	40	35	41	34	38	41	33	30	28	47	35	35	42	32
Hail	3	5	5	5	9	6	6	4	1	4	6	2	3	1	1	4	3	0	4
Fog	...	...	...	...	26	19	36	23	34	35	36	41	30	34	43	36	50	40	41
Dew	...	...	...	...	46	49	31	52	57	55	69	42	44	58	56	41	79	49	39
Possible to see Aurora	219	214	207	213	189	198	193	190	180	176	182	158	201	209	202	193	182	206	209
Auroras observed	63	54	46	34	26	59	53	58	43	48	44	34	55	44	43	50	47	77	55
Relative frequency	0.29	0.25	0.22	0.16	0.14	0.30	0.27	0.31	0.24	0.27	0.24	0.22	0.27	0.21	0.21	0.26	0.26	0.37	0.26
Ratios to Mean	1.16	1.00	0.88	0.64	0.56	1.20	1.08	1.24	0.96	1.05	0.96	0.88	1.08	0.84	0.84	1.04	1.04	1.48	1.04

TABLE XLVIII.

NUMBER OF DAYS IN WHICH THUNDER, LIGHTNING, HAIL, FOG, AND DEW WERE RECORDED FOR EACH MONTH IN THE PERIOD FROM 1853 TO 1871 INCLUSIVE. ALSO, THE NUMBER OF AURORAS, WITH THEIR RELATIVE FREQUENCY OR THE RATIOS OF THE NUMBER OBSERVED TO THE NUMBER OF SUFFICIENTLY CLEAR NIGHTS; ALSO, THE RELATIVE FREQUENCY EXPRESSED IN TERMS OF THE MEAN FOR TWELVE MONTHS.

	Jan.	Feb.	Mar.	April.	May.	June.	July.	Aug.	Sept.	Oct.	Nov.	Dec.	Year.
Thunder	0	2	11	37	65	117	137	98	61	20	4	2	554
Lightning	0	5	14	36	56	115	169	153	92	33	8	1	682
Hail	4	6	8	10	11	6	2	2	4	12	3	4	72
Fog	25	35	41	42	43	39	39	34	68	76	43	39	524
Dew	0	0	0	0	106	141	139	163	172	46	0	0	767
Possible to see Aurora	218	224	298	328	365	370	395	404	385	312	217	211	3,727
Auroras observed	36	59	110	109	94	65	79	95	120	90	40	36	933
Relative frequency	0.17	0.26	0.37	0.33	0.26	0.18	0.20	0.24	0.31	0.29	0.18	0.17	0.25
Ratios to Mean	0.46	0.76	1.41	1.40	1.21	0.84	1.02	1.22	1.54	1.17	0.61	0.46	1.00

TORONTO METEOROLOGICAL OBSERVATIONS.

TABLE XLIX.

Dates of certain Periodic Events.

Years.	Latest Snow.	Earliest Snow.	Latest Hoar Frost.	Earliest Hoar Frost.	Latest Ice.	Earliest Ice.	Earliest Thunder or Lightning.	Latest Thunder or Lightning.	Indian Summer.	Navigation Opened.	Navigation Closed.
1840	April 27	Oct. 9	May.	Sept.	...	...	Mar. 19	Oct. 8	Nov. 1 to 5	Mar. 28	Dec. 6
1841	" 20	" 16	May.	Oct.	...	...	" 25	" 7	Oct. 20 to Nov. 2	April 12	" 18
1842	" 8	Nov. 10	May.	Sept.	...	...	Jan. 29	" 1	Oct. 28 to Nov. 4	Mar. 17	" 18
1843	" 16	Oct. 17	June 1	Oct.	...	...	April 25	" 20	Oct. 23 to 25	April 23	" 13
1844	" 1	" 19	May.	Sept.	...	...	" 4	Nov. 10	" 22 to 26	" 23	" 18
1845	" 8	" 15	May.	Oct.	...	...	" 18	Sept. 19	" 24 to 29	" 23	" 3
1846	Mar. 30	" 17	May.	Sept.	...	...	May 22	Oct. 16	Nov. 4 to 7	" 6	" 15
1847	April 1	" 14	May.	Sept. 29	...	...	June 15	Nov. 7	Oct. 28 to 31	" 19	" 26
1848	" 18	Nov. 7	May.	" 15	...	...	May 4	Sept. 14	Nov. 20 to 23	Mar. 31	" 25
1849	April.	Oct. 30	May.	Sept.	...	...	...	Nov. 8	" 13 to 18	" 29	" 26
1850	May 2	Nov. 16	May 10	Sept.	...	...	Feb. 28	...	" 7 to 13	April 3	" 13
1851	May.	Oct. 25	May.	Sept.	...	...	...	Nov. 1	Oct. 6 to 11	Mar. 24	" 13
1852	May 20	Nov. 11	May.	Sept. 13	...	...	...	...	Nov. 16 to 21	April 17	Jan. 5
1853	" 10	Oct. 25	May 20	" 12	May 20	Oct. 7	Mar. 26	Dec. 6	Oct. 12 to 20	Mar. 31	Dec. 10
1854	April 29	" 16	" 11	" 19	" 11	" 18	" 15	Nov. 17	" 23 to 29	April 8	" 2
1855	May 8	" 12	" 9	" 28	April 27	" 12	April 14	Oct. 29	" 18 to 20	" 16	" 18
1856	" 30	" 30	" 31	" 22	May 31	" 13	" 12	" 22	" 8 to 11	" 19	" 8
1857	" 10	" 28	June 6	" 21	" 18	" 17	Feb. 18	Nov. 6	" 6 to 10	Mar. 30	Nov. 25
1858	April 25	" 8	" 14	" 18	" 16	" 7	April 4	Oct. 19	" 17 to 20	" 27	Dec. 24
1859	June 4	" 19	" 11	" 6	June 11	Sept. 15	Feb. 20	Sept. 24	Nov. 3 to 9	Jan. 27	" 23
1860	April 25	Sept. 25	May 2	" 21	May 2	" 21	" 22	Oct. 25	Oct. 29 to Nov. 3	Mar. 15	" 14
1861	May 6	Oct. 24	" 30	" 22	" 18	" 29	Mar. 29	" 26	{Oct. 27 to 29 / Nov. 17 to 19}	" 29	Nov. 27
1862	April 23	" 25	June 20	Aug. 30	" 29	" 3	" 29	Nov. 2	Oct. 29 to Nov. 2	Feb. 28	Dec. 20
1863	May 5	Nov. 8	" 4	" 26	April 26	" 26	April 11	Oct. 15	Nov. 11 to 19	" 14	" 16
1864	April 13	Oct. 8	" 7	Sept. 17	May 11	Oct. 9	Mar. 28	Nov. 29	Not well marked.	Mar. 2	" 16
1865	" 23	" 26	" 11	" 12	" 23	" 2	" 20	Oct. 7	Nov. 13 to 17	April 1	" 17
1866	" 26	" 31	" 1	" 15	" 14	Sept. 15	" 20	" 9	{Oct. 12 to 16 / Nov. 6 to 9}	" 2	" 15
1867	May 2	Nov. 4	May 27	" 11	" 7	" 14	" 1	Nov. 3	Oct. {16 to 23 / 25 to 27}	Mar. 27	" 11
1868	April 23	Oct. 16	" 9	" 17	" 8	Oct. 1	" 15	Oct. 27	Nov. 13 to 24	April 1	" 11
1869	May 1	" 18	June 6	Aug. 31	" 3	" 11	Apr {18 / 19}	" 14	Not well marked.	" 1	" 8
1870	April 5	Nov. 10	May 13	" 27	" 13	" 19	" 13	Nov. 8	Oct. 24 to Nov. 2	" 1	" 22
1871	" 12	Oct. 17	June 16	Sept. 18	" 8	Sept. 21	Mar. 2	Dec. 23	Not well marked.	Mar. 13	Nov. 30

TORONTO METEOROLOGICAL OBSERVATIONS.

TABLE I.

NORMAL TEMPERATURES ON EVERY FIFTH OR SIXTH DAY IN THE YEAR, AT EACH OF THE HOURS, 2, 4, 10, 12, 18, 20, TORONTO MEAN TIME, FROM OBSERVATIONS IN THE YEARS 1859 TO 1868, BOTH INCLUSIVE.

	2h.	4h.	10h.	12h.	18h.	20h.		2h.	4h.	10h.	12h.	18h.	20h.		2h.	4h.	10h.	12h.	18h.	20h.
Jan. 5	21.3	21.7	20.8	20.1	19.2	19.2	Mar. 1	29.1	29.1	23.4	21.4	22.3	23.2	May. 5	53.5	53.3	46.2	44.9	43.8	47.8
10	24.3	23.8	20.9	20.2	19.2	19.2	6	30.5	30.5	26.5	25.5	23.2	24.5	10	55.3	55.2	47.9	46.5	45.6	49.7
15	24.5	24.1	21.1	20.5	19.4	19.4	11	32.0	32.0	27.8	26.7	24.4	25.9	15	57.2	57.0	49.5	48.0	47.4	51.5
20	24.5	24.5	21.4	20.9	19.6	19.7	16	33.8	33.8	29.3	28.1	25.8	27.6	20	59.1	58.9	51.1	49.5	49.2	53.4
25	25.1	24.8	21.8	21.3	19.8	20.0	21	35.7	35.6	30.9	29.8	27.4	29.5	25	60.9	60.7	52.7	51.0	50.9	55.2
30	25.4	25.2	22.1	21.7	20.0	20.2	26	37.7	37.6	32.5	31.4	29.1	31.5	30	62.8	62.5	54.3	52.6	52.7	57.0
Feb. 4	25.7	25.6	22.4	22.0	20.2	20.4	31	39.8	39.6	34.2	33.2	30.8	33.5	June 5	64.5	64.3	55.8	54.2	54.4	58.8
9	26.0	26.0	22.6	22.3	20.4	20.7	April 5	41.8	41.7	36.0	35.0	32.7	35.6	10	66.3	66.0	57.4	55.8	56.1	60.6
14	26.5	26.6	23.2	22.5	20.6	21.0	10	43.8	43.7	37.7	36.8	34.5	37.7	15	68.0	67.7	58.9	57.4	57.7	62.2
19	27.1	27.1	23.7	23.0	21.0	21.5	15	45.8	45.7	39.4	38.5	36.4	39.8	20	69.6	69.3	60.4	58.9	59.2	63.7
24	29.0	28.0	24.4	23.6	21.5	22.3	20	47.8	47.6	41.2	40.2	38.3	41.8	25	71.0	70.8	61.7	60.3	60.5	65.1
							25	49.7	49.6	42.9	41.8	40.1	43.9	30	72.3	72.1	62.9	61.6	61.6	66.3
							30	51.6	51.5	44.6	43.4	42.0	45.8							

54

TORONTO METEOROLOGICAL OBSERVATIONS.

TABLE L.—(Continued.)

NORMAL TEMPERATURES ON EVERY FIFTH OR SIXTH DAY IN THE YEAR, AT EACH OF THE HOURS, 2, 4, 10, 12, 18, 20, TORONTO MEAN TIME, FROM OBSERVATIONS IN THE YEARS 1859 TO 1868, BOTH INCLUSIVE.

	2h.	4h.	10h.	12h.	18h.	20h.		2h.	4h.	10h.	12h.	18h.	20h.		2h.	4h.	10h.	12h.	18h.	20h.
July.							Sept.							Nov.						
5	73.3	73.1	63.9	63.5	62.4	67.2	5	67.8	67.2	59.0	57.5	55.8	61.0	5	45.3	44.2	40.2	39.6	38.4	39.7
10	74.1	73.9	64.6	63.2	63.0	67.0	10	66.8	65.3	57.4	55.9	54.1	59.1	10	43.4	42.4	38.6	38.2	37.1	38.1
15	74.6	74.5	65.1	63.7	63.3	68.3	15	63.7	63.1	55.5	54.1	52.3	57.0	15	41.4	40.3	37.1	36.6	35.6	36.3
20	74.9	74.8	65.3	63.9	63.3	68.4	20	61.6	60.9	53.6	52.1	50.3	54.8	20	39.0	39.0	35.0	34.5	33.6	34.2
25	75.0	74.8	65.4	63.9	63.1	63.5	25	59.3	58.6	51.5	50.2	48.4	52.6	25	36.6	35.6	32.8	32.3	31.5	31.8
30	74.9	74.7	65.2	63.6	62.7	68.1	30	57.1	56.4	49.6	48.3	46.6	50.3	30	34.1	33.1	30.6	29.9	29.2	29.4
Aug.							Oct.							Dec.						
5	74.5	74.2	64.8	63.2	62.2	67.6	5	55.1	54.3	47.8	46.7	44.9	48.2	5	31.7	30.7	28.1	27.5	26.9	26.9
10	73.9	73.6	64.3	62.7	61.5	67.0	10	53.2	52.4	46.2	45.1	43.6	46.4	10	29.5	28.5	26.0	25.3	24.7	24.7
15	73.2	72.8	63.6	62.0	60.7	66.2	15	51.5	50.7	44.8	43.9	42.3	44.9	15	27.6	26.7	24.1	23.4	22.8	22.8
20	72.2	71.8	62.8	61.2	59.7	65.3	20	50.0	49.1	43.6	42.8	41.2	43.5	20	26.1	25.3	22.0	21.0	21.3	21.2
25	71.0	70.5	61.7	60.2	58.6	64.1	25	48.5	47.5	42.5	41.8	40.3	42.2	25	25.1	24.4	21.6	20.8	20.2	20.1
30	69.6	69.0	60.6	59.0	57.3	62.7	30	46.9	46.0	41.4	40.7	39.4	41.0	30	23.5	23.6	21.0	20.2	19.5	19.5

55

TABLE LI.

MEAN ABNORMAL VARIATIONS OF TEMPERATURE, WITH THEIR PROPER SIGNS, ARRANGED ACCORDING TO THE DIRECTION OF THE WIND AT THE TIME OF OBSERVATION, IN EACH MONTH, IN EACH QUARTER, AND IN THE YEAR, FROM THE EIGHT YEARS, 1860-67, DERIVED FROM TABLE XIII BY THE APPLICATION OF CERTAIN CORRECTIONS.

Months.	N.	N.E.	E.	S.E.	S.	S.W.	W.	N.W.	Calms.
January	-7.94	$+0.10$	$+7.55$	$+10.52$	$+8.42$	$+3.74$	-0.05	-4.86	-1.20
February	-6.57	$+0.16$	$+3.38$	$+2.35$	$+6.84$	$+4.60$	-1.00	-6.27	-0.58
March	-2.15	$+0.20$	$+2.03$	$+0.87$	$+2.53$	$+3.71$	-1.30	-2.93	-0.55
April	-1.71	-0.10	$+0.99$	$+1.20$	0.00	$+1.68$	-1.08	-2.51	$+0.58$
May	$+0.81$	$+1.01$	-1.86	-0.33	-0.06	$+1.95$	-1.24	-1.65	$+0.45$
June	$+0.12$	$+0.09$	-1.25	-0.94	-0.86	$+2.04$	$+1.75$	-0.34	$+0.18$
July	-0.28	-0.99	-1.97	-0.03	-0.91	$+3.07$	$+1.60$	-1.18	$+2.04$
August	$+0.25$	-0.88	$+0.43$	$+0.25$	$+0.51$	$+2.76$	$+0.01$	-1.03	$+0.92$
September	-2.42	-1.11	$+0.75$	-0.10	$+2.68$	$+5.31$	$+0.64$	-2.48	$+1.03$
October	-2.51	$+0.24$	$+1.04$	$+1.50$	$+2.58$	$+4.82$	-1.50	-3.88	-0.36
November	-3.61	-1.27	$+2.07$	$+5.04$	$+5.27$	$+3.15$	-1.26	-2.30	-0.35
December	-10.00	-3.85	$+6.24$	$+3.51$	$+5.44$	$+6.01$	-1.31	-3.94	-0.86
Spring. Mar. to May..	-0.85	$+0.41$	$+0.55$	$+0.63$	$+0.68$	$+2.48$	-1.46	-2.33	$+0.35$
Summer. June to Aug..	-0.05	-0.49	-0.91	-0.28	$+0.45$	$+2.65$	$+1.03$	-0.94	$+0.97$
Autumn. Sept. to Nov..	-2.67	-0.48	$+1.79$	$+1.95$	$+3.27$	$+4.25$	-0.83	-2.87	$+0.47$
Winter. Dec. to Feb....	-8.39	-1.02	$+5.69$	$+5.04$	$+6.87$	$+4.52$	-1.01	-5.06	-1.24
Year	-2.92	-0.37	$+1.51$	$+1.09$	$+1.88$	$+3.57$	-0.90	-2.68	$+0.42$

TORONTO.
GENERAL METEOROLOGICAL ABSTRACT, JANUARY, 1863.

Days.	DAILY MEANS.						WIND.			EXTREMES OF TEMPERATURE.			RAIN.		SNOW.		TOTAL FALL.	
	Temperature of Air	Pressure of Vapour.	Rel. Humid.	Barometric Pressure.	Pressure of Dry Air.	Clouded Sky.	Resultant Direction.	Resultant Velocity.	Mean Velocity.	Maximum.	Minimum.	Difference.	Depth in inches	Approximate duration	Depth in inches	Approximate duration	Depth in inches.	Approximate duration.
1	29.3	0.122	75	29.907	29.785	0.5	S 42 W	8.1	8.2	36.4	19.2	17.2	...	...	...	...	...	...
2	35.6	.169	80	.684	.515	0.8	S 36 E	1.8	2.1	41.5	25.8	15.7	...	...	...	...	...	...
3	40.6	.219	86	.537	.319	0.9	S 78 E	1.3	1.3	45.0	34.8	10.2	0.030	2.5	...	...	0.030	2.5
4	Sunday						S 55 W	7.5	11.0	47.0	38.5	8.5	R	0.4	...	...	R	0.4
5	38.7	.178	75	.264	.086	0.7	S 56 W	6.0	6.3	45.4	33.0	12.4	.015	3.0	...	...	.015	3.0
6	32.5	.146	79	.230	.063	0.9	N 59 W	16.2	16.9	37.2	35.0	2.2	R	0.3	0.1	3.2	.010	3.5
7	16.0	.003	70	.783	.720	0.6	N 33 W	5.9	6.3	20.5	11.5	9.0	...	...	0.1	2.5	.010	2.5
8	22.4	.102	8	.946	.844	1.0	N 34 E	0.3	1.7	25.8	15.5	10.3	...	...	4.0	18.0	.400	18.0
9	29.7	.141	85	.913	.771	1.0	S 20 E	6.5	6.8	33.0	21.6	11.4	...	...	0.7	5.0	.070	5.0
10	34.6	.172	85	.289	.117	1.0	S 37 W	9.5	12.6	37.5	29.2	8.3	.445	2.5	2.0	5.0	.645	7.5
11	Sunday						N 59 W	9.3	10.9	33.0	29.7	3.3	...	...	0.1	1.5	.010	1.5
12	23.3	.117	89	.775	.658	0.8	N 43 E	1.4	2.3	30.4	12.2	18.2	...	...	...	...	...	...
13	30.7	.160	93	.795	.635	1.0	S 84 E	9.9	10.2	38.5	22.7	15.8	.250	9.0	1.0	3.0	.350	12.0
14	38.1	.221	96	.306	.085	1.0	S 80 W	5.4	7.2	41.2	29.2	12.0	.255	6.0	...	...	.255	6.0
15	26.5	.122	85	.278	.155	1.0	N 10 E	9.9	10.6	30.0	27.8	2.2	...	...	6.0	15.5	.600	15.5
16	9.1	.044	85	.274	.231	0.6	N 21 W	9.7	10.1	8.9	3.1	5.8	...	...	1.5	6.0	.150	6.0
17	-0.3	.039	56	30.126	30.087	0.5	N 21 E	4.1	4.2	8.8	-14.0	22.8	...	...	0.2	3.5	.020	3.5
18	Sunday						S 33 E	2.4	4.8	22.0	2.4	19.0	...	...	3	0.5	S	0.5
19	22.4	.110	86	30.138	30.028	0.0	N 51 E	2.0	2.3	31.8	7.2	24.6	...	...	...	...	...	...
20	30.1	.153	91	29.929	29.776	1.0	N 75 E	15.5	15.3	31.8	26.2	5.6	...	...	1.5	4.7	.150	4.7
21	31.7	.161	90	.863	.702	1.0	N 74 E	7.4	7.5	34.4	27.9	6.5	R	1.0	0.4	3.2	.040	4.2
22	34.3	.186	94	.779	.593	1.0	S 31 W	3.1	4.0	36.2	31.0	5.2	.012	1.5	...	...	.012	1.5
23	35.1	.173	85	.849	.676	0.8	N 78 E	5.0	7.1	38.0	32.6	5.4	...	...	...	...	...	...
24	34.9	.180	88	.761	.581	0.8	S 42 E	2.0	9.3	39.8	29.5	10.3	...	...	3	0.2	S	0.2
25	Sunday						S 59 W	4.9	5.8	38.5	34.8	3.7	...	...	...	...	...	...
26	32.8	.174	93	.625	.451	1.0	N 23 E	3.0	3.5	38.6	29.0	9.6	.115	3.5	1.0	7.0	.215	10.5
27	30.1	.140	83	.520	.350	0.9	N 11 E	7.0	7.2	33.5	29.8	3.7	...	...	1.0	5.5	.100	5.5
28	21.4	.103	89	.584	.481	0.6	N 20 W	4.7	4.8	28.5	22.0	6.4	...	...	...	...	...	...
29	23.7	.111	85	.301	.190	0.8	S 76 W	3.3	4.1	29.2	11.7	17.5	...	...	1.0	3.8	.10₀	3.5
30	30.0	.137	83	.432	.295	0.9	S 84 W	8.4	8.9	36.5	25.2	11.3	...	...	...	...	...	...
31	30.8	.138	80	.567	.429	0.0	S 54 W	10.9	11.0	34.0	26.8	7.2	...	...	...	...	...	...
	28.1	0.140	85	29.647	29.506	0.8	N 61 W	1.1	7.2	33.8	22.9	10.4	1.122	29.7	20.6	87.8	3.182	117.5

TORONTO.
GENERAL METEOROLOGICAL ABSTRACT, FEBRUARY, 1863.

Days.	DAILY MEANS.						WIND.		EXTREMES OF TEMPERATURE.			RAIN.		SNOW.		TOTAL FALL.	
	Temperature of Air.	Pressure of Vapour.	Rel. Humid.	Barometric Pressure.	Pressure of Dry Air.	Clouded Sky.	Resultant Direction.	Resultant Velocity.	Mean Velocity.	Maximum.	Minimum.	Difference.	Depth in inches.	Approximate duration.	Depth in inches.	Approximate duration.	Depth in inches.	Approximate duration.
1	Sunday						S 51 W	13.2	17.4	37.8	27.0	10.8	0.085	1.5	0.4	3.0	0.125	4.5
2	13.5	0.062	76	29.655	29.593	0.3	N 79 W	11.3	13.0	19.0	16.1	2.9	...	...	...	...	...	...
3	-0.2	.036	80	.966	.920	0.3	N 16 W	10.7	11.2	11.0	0.5	10.5	...	...	...	...	...	...
4	-4.5	.034	84	30.412	30.378	0.6	N 71 E	10.2	12.7	15.8	-19.8	35.6	...	...	1.0	7.2	.100	7.1
5	22.7	.110	92	29.888	29.772	1.0	S 65 E	12.7	13.3	31.8	-3.0	34.8	...	...	16.0	19.8	1.600	19.5
6	24.7	.120	91	.573	.453	1.0	N 66 W	5.2	7.6	28.0	8.8	19.2	...	...	2.0	10.0	.200	10.0
7	24.4	.104	80	.867	.762	0.4	N 51 W	9.3	10.0	31.2	21.5	9.7	...	...	...	...	...	...
8	Sunday						N 3 E	5.5	7.3	32.4	16.4	16.0	...	...	0.1	0.5	.010	0.5
9	29.3	.151	89	.711	.561	1.0	N 84 E	2.6	15.8	40.0	21.8	18.2	.630	7.5	2.0	7.5	.830	15.0
10	28.0	.123	80	.860	.737	1.0	N 66 W	10.3	10.5	32.5	25.4	7.1	...	...	S	1.0	S	1.0
11	25.9	.111	80	.817	.706	0.8	N 80 E	3.5	6.0	30.0	19.7	10.9	...	...	...	...	...	...
12	23.5	.104	81	.645	.540	0.7	N 10 W	7.4	8.3	29.0	22.3	6.7	...	...	0.1	2.0	.010	2.0
13	11.7	.061	80	30.025	.964	0.2	N 7 E	3.5	4.5	21.8	1.5	20.3	...	...	...	...	...	...
14	28.7	.134	82	29.691	.557	0.4	S 29 W	7.7	14.5	41.2	9.4	31.8	.045	1.6	...	...	.045	16.0
15	Sunday						S 80 W	16.2	17.0	37.4	27.6	9.8	...	...	...	...	...	...
16	22.1	.080	74	30.051	.962	0.5	N 32 W	4.3	6.2	28.0	22.6	5.4	...	...	...	...	...	...
17	24.8	.096	73	29.894	.798	0.3	N 54 E	5.5	6.1	31.6	14.2	17.4	...	...	...	...	...	...
18	30.8	.151	85	.656	.485	0.6	N 82 E	5.2	5.9	37.0	20.4	16.6	.040	5.1	...	...	.040	5.1
19	35.4	.198	96	.247	.048	1.0	N 28 E	3.7	6.7	33.2	31.4	6.8	.590	16.6	...	...	.590	16.6
20	26.3	.117	80	.489	.372	0.8	N 38 W	18.4	19.1	36.0	27.9	8.1	...	...	S	0.5	S	0.5
21	7.5	.053	85	30.157	30.104	0.3	N 16 E	11.2	12.6	12.8	3.5	9.3	...	...	0.2	2.0	.020	2.0
22	Sunday						N 43 E	12.5	12.9	14.2	1.8	12.4	...	...	0.2	4.5	.020	4.5
23	14.5	.076	85	30.036	29.960	0.8	N 46 E	3.3	4.0	22.0	3.5	18.5	...	...	...	...	...	...
24	24.7	.112	83	29.826	.714	0.8	S 53 W	4.9	5.8	35.0	14.6	20.4	...	...	...	...	...	...
25	29.2	.130	80	.812	.682	0.3	S 18 E	1.6	5.0	36.4	21.4	15.0	R	1.0	...	...	R	1.0
26	35.2	.188	91	.372	.184	1.0	N 80 E	2.2	8.7	41.5	22.2	19.3	.060	7.8	...	...	.060	7.5
27	31.7	.157	76	.592	.455	0.7	N 76 W	11.9	13.3	38.5	33.6	4.9	...	...	S	0.5	S	0.5
28	28.2	.129	83	.790	.660	1.0	N 69 E	7.6	8.5	30.9	21.0	9.9	...	...	...	...	...	...
	22.4	0.110	83	29.792	29.682	0.7	N 23 W	2.3	10.1	80.1	15.5	14.6	1.450	40.7	22.0	58.2	3.650	98.0

TORONTO.
General Meteorological Abstract. March. 1863.

Days.	Temperature of Air.	Pressure of Vapour.	Rel. Humid.	Barometric Pressure.	Pressure of Dry Air.	Clouded Sky.	Resultant Direction.	Resultant Velocity.	Mean Velocity.	Maximum.	Minimum.	Difference.	Depth in inches.	Approximate duration.	Depth in inches.	Approximate duration.	Depth in inches.	Approximate duration.
				DAILY MEANS.			WIND.			EXTREMES OF TEMPERATURE.			RAIN.		SNOW.		TOTAL FALL.	
1	nday						N 10 W	4.0	7.1	32.5	26.8	5.7	...	...	1.5	7.0	0.150	7.0
2	32.-	0.160	88	29.474	29.314	1.0	S 63 E	0.8	5.1	38.0	24.6	13.4		...	2.0	9.5	.200	9.5
3	19.4	.089	83	.599	.510	0.7	N 22 W	9.3	10.2	25.2	20.9	4.3	...	...	1.5	9.5	.150	9.5
4	7.1	.043	84	.966	.923	0.0	N 38 W	4.6	4.8	16.4	-2.1	18.5	...	...	...	...	...	...
5	18.6	.089	78	.812	.723	0.7	S 24 W	11.2	11.4	35.6	-4.0	39.6	...	...	0.2	1.0	.020	1.0
6	32.7	.132	71	.468	.336	0.5	N 81 W	10.2	12.0	41.0	21.2	19.8	...	...	...	...	...	...
7	21.6	.102	58	.664	.562	1.0	N 48 E	9.2	9.4	25.5	20.3	5.2	...	...	1.5	6.5	.150	6.5
8	Sunday						S 50 W	1.4	5.2	25.8	16.2	12.6	...	...	0.2	4.5	.020	4.5
9	26.8	.100	68	.542	.442	0.6	S 75 W	14.6	15.0	30.0	24.0	6.0	...	...	...	...	...	...
10	27.5	.119	77	.613	.494	0.1	S 29 W	5.3	5.6	36.2	16.0	20.2	...	...	...	...	...	...
11	23.8	.096	75	.502	.406	0.0	N 31 W	8.7	8.9	33.2	25.9	7.3	...	...	...	...	...	...
12	13.9	.063	77	.737	.674	0.5	N 26 W	6.4	6.7	21.0	12.7	8.3	...	...	...	...	...	...
13	15.2	.065	74	.738	.673	0.8	N 68 W	6.0	7.2	21.8	6.0	15.8	...	...	0.2	1.0	.020	1.0
14	22.7	.087	70	.600	.513	0.7	N 55 W	4.0	10.9	30.9	14.0	16.9	...	...	...	...	...	...
15	Sunday						N 45 E	11.9	12.3	21.2	3.9	17.3	...	...	0.2	4.5	.020	4.5
16	23.6	.095	73	.765	.670	0.4	N 86 W	0.9	3.3	30.0	13.2	16.8	...	...	0.2	2.0	.020	2.0
17	33.4	.153	80	.647	.494	1.0	N 7 W	4.1	6.9	39.8	23.0	16.8	...	...	...	...	...	...
18	19.2	.066	65	.987	.921	0.0	N 2 W	8.0	8.3	28.5	14.8	13.7	...	...	...	...	...	...
19	18.6	.073	72	30.145	30.072	0.0	N 54 E	3.2	4.1	26.4	10.6	15.8	...	...	...	...	...	...
20	25.0	.090	66	30.143	30.053	0.6	S 83 E	15.6	15.7	28.0	15.2	12.8	...	...	...	...	...	...
21	30.0	.160	96	29.833	29.673	1.0	S 54 E	6.2	7.0	34.0	23.0	11.0	0.030	3.0	3.0	9.8	.330	12.8
22	Sunday						N 87 E	3.1	3.4	40.8	28.7	12.1	...	...	...	...	...	...
23	34.4	.158	79	.727	.569	1.0	N 80 E	16.1	16.1	38.0	32.0	6.0	.102	3.5	0.1	0.5	.112	4.0
24	38.2	.217	93	.371	.154	1.0	N 86 E	7.1	10.7	42.0	33.2	8.6	.315	13.5	...	...	.315	13.5
25	36.2	.199	93	.224	.023	1.0	N 65 W	6.4	8.9	40.8	35.0	5.8	.240	6.1	0.2	1.5	.260	7.6
26	31.5	.143	80	.490	.347	0.8	N 73 W	9.2	10.2	37.8	30.8	7.0	...	...	0.1	6.0	.010	6.0
27	32.1	.129	72	.729	.600	0.5	S 25 W	2.8	5.2	39.6	26.2	13.4	...	...	0.1	3.0	.010	3.0
28	30.6	.142	82	.338	.196	0.7	N 38 W	8.4	13.7	39.0	27.4	11.6	...	...	0.3	2.5	.030	2.5
29	Sunday						N 53 W	20.3	21.1	34.0	17.0	17.0	...	...	S	0.5	S	0.5
30	29.2	.120	75	.807	.687	0.1	S 5 W	3.9	5.3	38.8	20.3	18.5	...	...	...	...	...	...
31	27.9	.127	80	.364	.237	1.0	N 24 W	13.8	15.6	42.2	25.2	17.0	...	...	0.1	2.0	.010	2.0
	25.8	0.116	78	29.665	29.549	0.6	N 27 W	2.6	9.3	32.8	19.4	13.4	0.687	2.6	11.4	71.3	1.827	97.4

3

TORONTO.
GENERAL METEOROLOGICAL ABSTRACT, APRIL, 1863.

Days.	DAILY MEANS.						WIND.			EXTREMES OF TEMPERATURE.			RAIN.		SNOW.		TOTAL FALL.	
	Temperature of Air.	Pressure of Vapour.	Rel. Humid.	Barometric Pressure.	Pressure of Dry Air.	Clouded Sky.	Resultant Direction.	Resultant Velocity.	Mean Velocity.	Maximum.	Minimum.	Difference.	Depth in inches.	Approximate duration.	Depth in inches.	Approximate duration.	Depth in inches.	Approximate duration.
1	22.3	0.101	78	29.343	29.242	0.8	S 56 W	9.9	12.0	38.8	8.6	30.2	...	...	0.1	3.2	0.010	3.2
2	37.2	.159	72	28.901	28.832	0.0	N 59 W	14.0	15.4	44.0	23.0	21.0	...	...	0.1	1.0	.010	1.0
3	...	...	...	...	...	...	N 9 W	11.8	12.9	37.2	28.3	8.9	...	...	...	...	...	...
4	28.3	.163	68	29.966	29.862	0.0	N 19 E	2.7	6.3	36.4	20.7	15.7	...	...	...	...	...	...
5	Sunday						N 31 W	10.2	10.5	49.0	24.2	24.8	...	...	...	...	...	...
6	36.4	.162	77	.484	.322	1.0	N 5 E	11.9	12.3	45.0	29.0	16.0	0.060	3.5	1.2	10.0	.180	13.5
7	29.7	.136	83	.810	.673	1.0	N 1 W	9.3	9.0	33.4	26.2	7.2	...	...	0.2	4.5	.020	4.5
8	32.9	.150	81	.904	.754	0.5	N 35 W	4.0	7.0	38.4	29.8	8.6	...	...	...	...	...	...
9	37.1	.137	63	.876	.739	0.1	S 67 W	4.4	7.3	48.0	29.5	18.5	...	...	...	...	...	...
10	39.5	.192	78	.597	.405	1.0	N 82 E	2.9	3.4	46.0	28.5	17.5	.035	3.0	...	...	.035	3.0
11	50.2	.278	77	.394	.116	0.9	S 59 W	8.7	10.2	61.2	39.8	21.4	.585	4.0	...	...	.585	4.0
12	Sunday						N 29 W	14.3	14.8	44.6	37.8	7.0	...	...	...	...	...	...
13	34.3	.143	72	.847	.704	0.0	5	1.6	4.0	41.0	37.2	13.8	...	...	...	...	...	...
14	41.3	.114	47	.797	.683	0.1	N 60 E	7.6	8.2	50.4	27.1	23.3	...	...	...	...	...	...
15	44.8	.183	63	.086	.603	0.9	N 77 E	10.3	10.4	51.2	39.6	11.0	.155	9.5	...	...	.155	9.5
16	43.3	.251	89	.652	.401	1.0	N 51 E	10.7	11.3	46.8	40.0	6.8	.520	16.0	...	...	.520	16.0
17	42.8	.261	95	.634	.373	1.0	N 74 E	1.6	3.0	46.0	41.6	4.4	.020	6.5	...	...	.020	6.5
18	44.1	.243	84	.693	.450	1.0	S 72 E	2.5	4.0	51.4	39.0	12.4	...	...	...	...	...	...
19	Sunday						N 84 E	12.0	12.1	56.0	40.2	15.8	...	...	...	...	...	...
20	42.7	.231	85	.826	.595	1.0	N 85 E	10.7	11.1	50.8	39.0	11.8	.835	11.5	...	...	.835	11.5
21	45.2	.241	90	.957	.716	0.6	N 78 E	11.1	11.2	50.0	38.6	11.4	R	2.5	...	...	R	2.5
22	49.0	.172	50	.800	.628	0.0	N 77 E	11.8	11.9	57.5	39.0	18.5	...	...	...	...	...	...
23	50.9	.164	44	.561	.396	0.6	N 70 E	5.3	6.2	58.2	44.4	13.8	...	...	...	...	...	...
24	34.1	.208	72	.433	.224	0.1	N 16 W	15.0	15.7	39.0	39.6	29.4	...	...	...	...	...	...
25	40.3	.097	39	.682	.585	0.0	N 20 W	17.5	17.8	50.0	32.6	17.4	...	...	...	...	...	...
26	Sunday						N 27 W	8.2	8.4	59.8	35.0	24.8	...	...	...	...	...	...
27	49.7	.176	52	.634	.459	0.2	S 35 W	3.1	4.3	63.5	33.0	30.5	...	...	...	...	...	...
28	53.6	.245	61	.483	.238	0.7	S 87 E	3.3	5.0	62.8	37.4	25.4	...	...	...	...	...	...
29	47.9	.212	63	.483	.271	0.5	N 83 E	2.0	4.3	53.0	41.8	11.2	...	...	...	...	...	...
30	53.4	.177	42	.601	.425	0.0	S 78 E	1.8	4.9	60.0	42.0	18.0	...	...	...	...	...	...
	42.0	0.181	68	29.645	29.464	0.5	N 14 E	3.8	9.2	50.0	33.4	16.6	2.210	56.5	1.6	18.7	2.370	75.2

TORONTO.
GENERAL METEOROLOGICAL ABSTRACT, MAY, 1863.

Days.	DAILY MEANS.					WIND.		EXTREMES OF TEMPERATURE			RAIN.		SNOW.		TOTAL FALL.	
	Temperature of Air.	Pressure of Vapour.	Rel. Humid.	Barometric Pressure.	Pressure of Dry Air.	Clouded Sky.	Resultant Direction.	Resultant Velocity.	Mean Velocity.	Maximum.	Minimum.	Difference.	Depth in inches.	Approximate duration.	Depth in inches.	Approximate duration.	Depth in inches	Approximate duration.
1	52.5	0.202	52	29.553	29.352	0.0	S 29 W	6.2	6.8	66.2	36.4	29.8	...	...	...	...	...	...
2	46.0	.199	65	.636	.436	0.6	N 62 E	5.2	7.5	58.0	42.6	15.4	...	...	...	...	...	...
3	Sunday						N 73 E	8.1	8.3	47.0	37.6	9.4	R	0.5	...	...	R	0.5
4	44.7	.219	74	.581	.362	1.0	N 81 E	5.5	6.5	50.8	41.0	9.8	...	...	...	...	...	...
5	40.1	.171	69	.615	.444	1.0	N 73 E	13.6	13.8	45.0	39.6	5.4	0.170	10.5	0.1	1.0	0.180	11.5
6	40.3	.207	82	.678	.471	0.8	N 69 E	9.7	10.0	45.2	37.4	7.8	.105	5.0	...	...	.105	5.0
7	46.5	.208	66	.593	.385	0.4	N 47 E	3.2	6.9	54.0	38.8	15.2	...	...	...	...	...	...
8	51.3	.227	60	.603	.376	0.1	S 43 E	2.1	3.8	61.8	41.0	20.8	...	...	...	...	...	...
9	55.5	.260	59	.576	.316	0.4	S 41 W	1.6	2.2	66.5	42.0	24.5	...	...	...	...	...	...
10	Sunday						S 83 W	0.3	1.4	64.2	45.2	19.0	.098	4.0	...	...	.098	4.0
11	51.0	.322	87	.654	.832	0.9	N 73 E	4.6	5.3	55.4	52.0	3.4	.825	15.5	...	...	.825	15.5
12	48.9	.323	93	.661	.338	0.9	N 89 E	1.2	1.7	54.0	46.4	7.6	.150	4.0	...	...	.150	4.0
13	52.1	.295	76	.621	.326	0.6	N 16 E	1.0	5.1	61.5	45.2	16.3	.242	4.2	...	...	.242	4.2
14	48.4	.259	79	.574	.315	0.7	N 30 W	8.4	9.6	54.2	45.8	8.4	.533	8.5	...	...	.533	8.5
15	51.0	.235	62	.608	.373	0.0	S 16 W	5.1	6.7	63.0	43.0	20.0	.030	0.8	...	...	.030	0.8
16	52.5	.305	77	.356	.051	0.8	N 82 W	3.7	9.0	64.5	44.5	20.0	R	0.2	...	...	R	0.2
17	Sunday						N 79 W	6.5	9.8	59.2	40.2	19.0	.045	2.5	...	...	.045	2.5
18	50.3	.244	68	.635	.391	0.3	N 54 W	11.2	11.5	60.0	41.4	18.6	...	...	...	...	...	...
19	59.0	.270	55	.665	.395	0.3	S 56 W	8.9	9.3	74.0	39.2	34.8	...	...	...	...	...	...
20	57.5	.376	79	.684	.308	0.8	S 54 W	4.4	4.4	66.6	50.0	16.6	.030	1.0	...	...	.030	1.0
21	64.8	.378	62	.829	.451	0.1	S 45 W	6.2	6.9	75.4	50.4	25.0	...	...	...	...	...	...
22	67.8	.443	67	.820	.377	0.1	S 60 W	2.7	3.2	79.0	52.8	26.2	...	...	...	...	...	...
23	69.6	.427	59	.621	.194	0.0	N 84 W	1.7	2.7	78.5	56.2	22.3	...	...	...	...	...	...
24	Sunday						N 85 W	1.6	6.5	75.4	59.8	15.6	...	...	...	...	...	...
25	56.3	.305	66	.626	.321	0.0	N 86 E	9.4	10.0	61.8	51.0	10.8	...	...	...	...	...	...
26	57.0	.326	71	.732	.405	0.2	N 68 E	5.0	5.7	64.0	47.8	16.2	...	...	...	...	...	...
27	59.8	.357	70	.791	.434	0.2	S 17 W	0.2	0.3	70.0	52.0	18.0	...	...	...	...	...	...
28	63.2	.361	62	.703	.342	0.1	S 51 W	0.5	0.6	75.2	49.0	26.2	...	...	...	...	...	...
29	64.0	.380	64	.484	.104	0.6	N 62 E	0.4	0.5	76.2	52.6	23.6	...	...	...	...	...	...
30	61.6	.469	86	.143	28.674	0.9	S 33 W	1.4	3.1	70.4	55.8	14.6	.210	3.5	...	...	.210	3.5
31	Sunday						S 63 W	2.4	3.4	69.0	57.5	11.5	.925	7.5	...	...	.925	7.5
	54.3	0.299	69	29.617	29.318	0.8	N 56 E	0.4	5.9	83.4	46.3	17.2	3.363	67.7	0.1	1.0	3.373	68.7

TORONTO.
GENERAL METEOROLOGICAL ABSTRACT, JUNE, 1863.

Days	DAILY MEANS.						WIND.			EXTREMES OF TEMPERATURE.			RAIN.		SNOW.		TOTAL FALL.	
	Temperature of Air.	Pressure of Vapour.	Rel. Humid.	Barometric Pressure.	Pressure of Dry Air.	Clouded Sky.	Resultant Direction.	Resultant Velocity.	Mean Velocity.	Maximum.	Minimum.	Difference.	Depth in inches.	Approximate duration.	Depth in inches.	Approximate duration.	Depth in inches.	Approximate duration.
1	57.1	0.326	69	29.049	28.723	1.0	S 78 W	13.8	14.1	64.0	54.5	9.5	0.065	2.1	...	...	0.065	2.1
2	52.9	.290	72	.334	29.045	0.8	N 77 W	10.6	11.1	59.6	49.4	10.2	R	0.2	...	...	R	0.2
3	50.9	.267	72	.558	.291	0.5	N 49 W	1.0	3.5	58.2	43.6	14.6	...	...	...	...	...	...
4	53.5	.303	74	.558	.254	0.7	S 16 W	2.7	3.0	64.0	37.4	26.6	.125	1.5	...	...	.125	1.5
5	52.6	.325	82	.591	.260	0.9	N 20 W	2.3	3.3	64.0	50.5	13.3	.625	8.5	...	...	.625	8.5
6	51.4	.240	64	.768	.528	0.2	N 23 W	10.2	10.3	60.0	44.0	16.0	...	...	...	...	...	...
7	Sunday						N 30 W	12.1	12.2	61.6	44.0	17.8	R	...	...	...	R	...
8	58.5	.305	63	.664	.359	0.5	N 30 W	10.9	11.3	68.0	49.2	18.8	R	...	...	...	R	...
9	65.4	.255	42	.568	.313	0.0	N 36 W	12.6	12.7	76.0	52.8	23.2	...	...	...	...	...	...
10	64.5	.333	56	.530	.197	0.3	S 36 W	3.4	3.7	81.2	54.0	27.2	...	...	...	...	...	...
11	59.3	.393	78	.506	.114	1.0	N 47 W	0.5	1.3	67.4	52.4	15.0	.075	2.5	...	...	.075	2.5
12	62.5	.451	80	.507	.146	0.9	N 28 W	0.6	7.3	67.0	56.8	10.2	.077	5.3	...	...	.077	5.3
13	66.8	.467	71	.709	.242	0.1	S 14 W	0.8	1.7	73.0	59.0	14.0	...	...	...	...	...	...
14	Sunday						N 64 W	3.5	4.0	82.8	56.8	26.0	...	...	...	...	...	...
15	69.5	.382	55	.577	.195	0.5	S 27 W	10.9	11.5	84.8	60.0	24.8	...	...	...	...	...	...
16	56.0	.243	64	.702	.459	0.1	S 6 E	1.1	2.5	64.2	48.8	15.4	...	...	...	...	...	...
17	55.9	.320	72	.330	.010	0.7	N 78 E	1.9	2.2	63.4	50.5	12.0	...	...	...	...	...	...
18	62.0	.369	67	.321	28.952	0.5	S 22 W	0.8	1.7	73.0	48.0	25.0	...	...	...	...	...	...
19	62.1	.432	78	.365	28.933	0.6	S 58 E	1.3	1.8	71.2	51.6	19.6	...	...	...	...	...	...
20	55.6	.390	87	.443	29.044	0.8	N 79 E	1.7	2.6	65.0	52.2	12.8	.475	3.8	...	...	.475	3.8
21	Sunday						S 25 W	2.3	2.5	63.0	47.5	15.5	.030	1.3	...	...	.030	1.3
22	56.4	.382	84	.483	.101	0.6	S 60 W	3.1	4.4	63.8	49.4	14.4	.185	1.2	...	...	.185	1.2
23	57.7	.365	77	.671	.306	0.8	N 61 W	6.2	6.4	63.8	47.2	16.6	...	...	...	...	...	...
24	57.7	.370	78	.787	.417	0.2	S 14 W	0.8	1.7	68.0	49.8	18.2	...	...	...	...	...	...
25	61.5	.372	70	.783	.411	0.6	S 88 E	1.2	2.4	70.8	49.5	21.3	...	...	...	...	...	...
26	65.3	.432	70	.739	.306	0.0	S 88 E	2.9	3.1	74.8	53.0	21.8	...	...	...	...	...	...
27	65.3	.495	80	.728	.234	0.6	S 74 E	2.7	2.7	72.2	59.6	12.6	...	...	...	...	...	...
28	Sunday						S 75 E	3.9	4.1	75.5	59.2	16.3	...	...	...	...	...	...
29	70.2	.534	72	.511	28.977	0.7	S 81 E	5.4	5.9	75.6	62.2	13.4	R	...	...	...	R	...
30	71.8	.653	83	.490	28.837	0.7	S 24 E	1.8	2.4	81.0	69.8	11.2	.005	0.5	...	...	.005	0.5
	60.1	0.373	71	29.552	29.179	0.5	N 50 W	2.3	5.2	69.2	52.0	17.2	1.662	26.9	...	...	1.662	26.9

TORONTO.
GENERAL METEOROLOGICAL ABSTRACT, JULY, 1863.

Days.	DAILY MEANS.						WIND.			EXTREMES OF TEMPERATURE.			RAIN.		SNOW.		TOTAL FALL.	
	Temperature of Air.	Pressure of Vapour.	Rel. Humid.	Barometric Pressure.	Pressure of Dry Air.	Clouded Sky.	Resultant Direction.	Resultant Velocity.	Mean Velocity.	Maximum.	Minimum.	Difference.	Depth in inches.	Approximate duration.	Depth in inches.	Approximate duration.	Depth in inches.	Approximate duration.
1	75.1	0.672	77	29.576	28.904	0.6	S 19 E	0.1	2.9	83.5	65.4	18.1	0.275	1.5	...	...	0.275	1.5
2	71.3	.667	88	.622	28.955	0.7	N 80 E	2.2	2.6	79.0	66.6	12.4	.005	1.2	...	...	.005	1.2
3	71.7	.661	85	.686	29.024	0.6	S 67 E	0.9	1.4	81.0	66.0	15.0	...	...	...	...	...	...
4	72.2	.648	82	.625	28.980	0.6	S 48 W	1.5	4.2	80.2	66.0	14.2	...	...	...	...	...	...
5	Sunday						N 32 E	0.9	3.8	79.4	64.0	15.4	...	...	...	...	...	...
6	71.8	.594	76	.565	28.971	0.1	N 83 E	3.0	3.6	78.0	64.2	13.8	...	...	...	...	...	...
7	73.1	.629	77	.556	28.927	0.5	S 68 E	1.5	2.0	80.0	65.0	15.0	.290	1.2	...	...	.290	1.2
8	73.7	.637	77	.458	28.821	0.7	S 74 W	0.9	3.2	81.4	66.2	15.2	.075	1.3	...	...	.075	1.3
9	71.1	.596	79	.437	28.841	1.0	S 55 E	0.3	1.2	78.2	65.8	12.4	...	...	...	...	...	...
10	70.8	.630	84	.447	28.817	1.0	S 61 E	0.1	0.2	79.0	64.2	14.8	...	...	...	...	...	...
11	69.4	.591	82	.527	28.936	1.0	N 33 W	4.9	7.8	77.1	65.0	12.1	R	0.3	...	...	R	0.3
12	Sunday						N 37 E	3.2	4.2	67.6	55.4	12.2	...	...	...	...	...	...
13	62.1	.466	83	.622	29.164	1.0	N 43 E	2.3	2.4	66.2	57.0	9.2	.645	9.5	...	...	.645	9.5
14	66.3	.580	90	.484	28.904	0.9	S 87 W	1.1	2.8	72.5	60.1	12.4	.010	1.0	...	...	.010	1.0
15	66.7	.495	75	.585	29.090	0.6	S 79 W	2.9	6.5	77.0	60.0	17.0	.020	1.6	...	...	.020	1.6
16	56.5	.313	68	.798	.485	0.7	N 49 W	8.0	9.2	65.2	48.0	17.2	...	...	...	...	...	...
17	56.5	.320	70	.881	.561	0.5	N 89 E	1.1	2.9	67.6	48.2	19.4	...	...	...	...	...	...
18	61.1	.369	69	.865	.499	0.2	S 40 E	1.0	3.4	70.0	49.4	20.6	...	...	...	...	...	...
19	Sunday						S 48 E	1.5	1.9	71.6	49.5	22.1	...	...	...	...	...	...
20	62.8	.501	87	.530	.029	1.0	N 50 E	8.2	9.7	69.2	57.2	12.0	1.665	11.3	...	...	1.665	11.3
21	62.8	.399	70	.590	.191	0.8	N 18 W	10.2	10.4	70.5	58.8	11.7	...	...	...	...	...	...
22	64.6	.390	65	.670	.280	0.4	S 23 W	2.7	3.1	73.0	51.2	21.8	...	...	...	...	...	...
23	66.0	.478	76	.627	.149	0.3	S 73 E	1.7	2.2	73.0	56.0	17.0	.008	0.5	...	...	.008	0.5
24	71.5	.581	70	.601	.020	0.7	N 77 W	0.3	2.0	80.0	59.0	21.0	.015	0.5	...	...	.015	0.5
25	65.6	.540	86	.493	28.953	1.0	N 61 E	3.6	4.2	67.2	64.2	3.0	.345	8.0	...	...	.345	8.0
26	Sunday						S 53 W	2.4	3.2	75.0	63.8	11.2	.030	2.0	...	...	.030	2.0
27	66.5	.424	67	.491	29.067	0.3	S 88 W	6.4	6.8	75.0	58.0	17.0	...	...	...	...	...	...
28	66.7	.502	77	.640	.130	0.3	S 10 W	3.9	4.8	76.5	53.0	23.5	...	...	...	...	...	...
29	69.4	.535	75	.620	.085	0.6	S 9 E	1.8	3.0	77.8	57.0	20.5	...	...	...	...	...	...
30	67.6	.592	87	.559	28.967	1.0	S 59 E	1.7	0.9	72.0	62.8	9.2	.025	2.0	...	...	.025	2.0
31	71.0	.624	81	.541	28.917	0.9	S 33 W	4.4	4.7	77.6	63.4	14.2	R	0.1	...	...	R	0.1
	67.6	0.535	78	29.596	29.082	0.6	N 18 W	0.4	3.9	74.9	59.7	15.2	3.408	42.0	...	...	3.408	42.0

TORONTO.
GENERAL METEOROLOGICAL ABSTRACT, AUGUST, 1863.

Days.	DAILY MEANS.						WIND.			EXTREMES OF TEMPERATURE.			RAIN.		SNOW.		TOTAL FALL.	
	Temperature of Air.	Pressure of Vapour.	Rel. Humid.	Barometric Pressure.	Pressure of Dry Air.	Clouded Sky.	Resultant Direction.	Resultant Velocity.	Mean Velocity.	Maximum.	Minimum.	Difference.	Depth in inches.	Approximate duration.	Depth in inches.	Approximate duration.	Depth in inches.	Approximate duration.
1	74.6	0.716	83	29.513	28.797	0.6	S 3° W	5.1	5.2	84.0	65.0	19.0	...	...	...	...	...	...
2	Sunday						S 62 W	5.3	8.4	85.8	67.2	18.6	...	...	...	...	...	...
3	69.6	.431	59	.800	29.369	0.1	N 16 W	2.7	4.3	78.0	65.0	13.0	...	...	...	...	...	...
4	69.2	.487	67	.746	.259	0.0	S 78 E	2.2	2.4	76.8	52.5	24.3	...	...	...	...	...	...
5	74.9	.687	80	.548	28.861	0.3	S 63 W	3.7	6.6	85.8	63.0	22.8	0.075	2.0	...	...	0.075	2.0
6	71.5	.468	63	.665	29.197	0.2	N 33 W	4.9	5.2	83.2	63.4	19.8	...	...	...	...	...	...
7	68.2	.536	78	.600	.064	0.7	N 78 E	1.2	1.5	76.5	57.0	19.5	.700	5.0	...	...	.700	5.0
8	73.7	.688	83	.428	28.740	1.0	S 63 W	2.7	4.2	80.5	65.0	15.5	...	...	...	...	...	...
9	Sunday						S 31 W	1.6	1.8	80.2	65.4	14.8	.055	0.6	...	...	.055	0.6
10	74.7	.693	81	.583	28.889	0.8	S 21 E	1.1	1.5	81.0	66.8	14.5	.023	0.7	...	...	.023	0.7
11	74.4	.655	76	.470	28.815	0.4	S 51 W	7.3	9.1	84.0	70.2	13.8	...	...	...	...	...	...
12	62.8	.412	72	.788	29.376	0.0	N 86 W	2.0	3.5	73.8	54.0	19.8	...	...	...	...	...	...
13	65.9	.467	74	.760	.293	0.2	N 71 E	0.8	2.2	75.8	53.4	22.4	...	...	...	...	...	...
14	73.2	.590	74	.638	.045	0.6	S 84 W	2.2	4.4	87.2	59.8	27.4	...	...	...	...	...	...
15	67.4	.572	85	.734	.162	0.9	N 77 E	1.6	2.1	74.0	62.8	11.2	R	...	...	...	R	...
16	Sunday						N 43 E	4.1	4.9	74.0	65.5	8.5	.080	7.0	...	...	.080	7.0
17	59.5	.354	71	.895	.541	0.0	S 74 E	1.5	3.1	69.0	53.0	16.0	...	...	...	...	...	...
18	61.1	.405	75	.867	.462	0.4	S 13 W	0.9	1.4	69.8	51.0	18.8	...	...	...	...	...	...
19	71.9	.580	74	.646	.066	0.2	N 88 W	2.8	4.7	88.0	52.5	35.5	.050	0.5	...	...	.050	0.5
20	65.2	.575	92	.576	.000	1.0	N 54 E	2.0	2.2	70.0	65.5	4.5	.805	12.6	...	...	.805	12.6
21	68.7	.571	82	.562	28.991	0.4	S 24 W	2.2	2.5	75.4	62.0	13.4	...	...	...	...	...	...
22	67.9	.531	78	.471	28.940	0.9	N 63 W	5.0	7.0	78.0	64.8	13.2	.030	0.5	...	...	.030	0.5
23	Sunday						S 54 E	3.9	4.4	68.0	51.7	16.3	.005	1.5	...	...	.005	1.5
24	67.7	.563	79	.487	28.924	0.7	S 87 W	7.6	11.5	81.5	61.0	20.5	.005	3.8	...	...	.005	3.8
25	57.1	.309	67	.780	29.471	0.6	N 32 W	1.7	5.7	68.4	48.8	19.6	...	...	...	...	...	...
26	56.0	.311	67	.791	.480	0.1	S 43 W	3.2	5.4	66.8	43.2	23.6	...	...	...	...	...	...
27	62.7	.449	79	.619	.170	0.3	S 24 W	7.8	8.0	73.0	49.8	23.2	...	...	...	...	...	...
28	64.5	.402	82	.366	28.874	1.0	S 21 W	7.9	8.6	72.4	56.2	16.2	.380	7.0	...	...	.380	7.0
29	54.1	.304	72	.519	29.215	0.6	S 78 W	9.7	9.7	62.6	57.0	5.6	...	...	...	...	...	...
30	Sunday						N 87 W	3.4	5.5	60.4	42.6	17.8	...	...	...	...	...	...
31	53.8	.316	77	.925	.609	0.0	S 79 E	2.7	1.9	63.0	42.4	20.6	...	...	...	...	...	...
	66.0	0.506	76	29.645	29.130	0.5	S 61 W	1.8	4.9	75.7	58.0	17.7	2.208	41.2	...	...	2.208	41.2

TORONTO.
GENERAL METEOROLOGICAL ABSTRACT, SEPTEMBER, 1863.

Days.	DAILY MEANS.					WIND.			EXTREMES OF TEMPERATURE.			RAIN.		SNOW.		TOTAL FALL.	
	Temperature of Air.	Pressure of Vapour.	Rel. Humid.	Barometric Pressure.	Pressure of Dry Air.	Clouded Sky.	Resultant Direction.	Resultant Velocity.	Mean Velocity.	Maximum.	Minimum.	Difference.	Depth in Inches.	Approximate duration.	Depth in inches.	Approximate duration.	Depth in Inches.	Approximate duration.
1	58.4	0.370	76	29.801	29.431	0.3	S 16 E	1.3	2.4	69.8	45.0	24.8	...	...	...	...	...	...
2	60.7	.417	78	.676	.258	0.0	N 17 E	5.0	7.6	72.5	51.4	21.1	...	...	...	...	...	...
3	54.6	.252	60	.765	.512	0.3	N 1 W	11.0	11.1	62.2	51.4	10.8	...	...	...	...	...	...
4	51.6	.237	62	.790	.553	0.0	S 85 E	2.6	6.0	61.0	43.4	17.6	...	...	...	...	...	...
5	58.1	.375	76	.614	.239	0.5	N 78 E	2.9	3.7	67.0	44.0	23.0	...	...	...	...	...	...
6	Sunday						N 11 W	5.5	5.6	70.8	54.6	16.2	R	0.5	...	...	R	0.5
7	59.4	.410	81	.782	.372	0.6	N 86 E	3.4	4.0	65.2	53.6	11.6	...	...	...	...	...	...
8	62.0	.463	81	.709	.246	0.6	N 39 W	7.4	10.0	71.0	54.8	16.2	R	0.2	...	...	R	0.2
9	51.2	.238	64	.957	.719	0.0	N 57 E	3.3	6.2	59.6	45.6	14.6	...	...	...	...	...	...
10	54.9	.309	72	.909	.599	0.2	S 84 E	4.3	4.7	62.5	43.2	19.3	...	...	...	...	...	...
11	63.4	.508	87	.624	.126	1.0	S 55 W	3.3	5.0	70.8	52.8	18.0	.15	3.6	...	...	0.215	3.6
12	60.1	.406	78	.640	.234	0.8	N	6.5	7.3	67.0	59.0	8.0	R	0.5	...	...	R	0.5
13	Sunday						S 85 E	3.9	4.4	62.4	46.0	16.4	...	...	...	...	...	...
14	62.1	.433	78	.739	.306	0.2	S 24 W	5.1	5.3	72.2	50.0	22.2	...	...	...	...	...	...
15	67.6	.503	76	.733	.230	0.0	S 35 W	6.4	6.4	79.0	54.8	24.2	...	...	...	...	...	...
16	67.9	.562	83	.650	.089	0.2	S 20 E	3.4	3.7	77.0	56.5	20.5	...	...	...	...	...	...
17	70.4	.590	80	.388	28.798	0.9	S 19 W	7.0	9.0	80.0	63.7	16.3	.770	8.5	...	...	.770	8.5
18	48.7	.268	76	.363	29.095	0.7	N 41 W	12.8	13.3	56.0	49.0	7.0	.195	2.5	...	...	.195	2.5
19	43.8	.219	76	.614	.395	0.3	S 83 W	4.4	6.1	54.8	36.0	18.8	...	...	...	...	...	...
20	Sunday						S 60 W	4.8	5.0	55.0	35.8	19.2	.055	1.7	...	...	.055	1.7
21	49.9	.260	71	.730	.470	0.8	N 48 W	9.5	10.4	59.8	47.0	12.8	...	...	...	...	...	...
22	45.8	.196	64	30.097	.901	0.3	S 5 W	3.2	7.1	53.2	37.2	16.0	...	...	...	...	...	...
23	55.1	.315	73	29.908	.593	0.2	S 1 E	6.0	6.1	63.2	41.4	21.8	...	...	...	...	...	...
24	52.0	.325	81	.708	.383	1.0	N 16 W	9.4	10.2	65.0	47.8	17.2	R	1.5	...	...	R	1.5
25	42.6	.196	71	.863	.667	0.3	N 9 W	10.3	10.6	51.0	37.5	13.5	...	...	...	...	...	...
26	41.8	.173	65	.812	.640	0.0	N 55 W	0.7	5.3	52.2	33.2	19.0	...	...	...	...	...	...
27	Sunday						S 9 E	1.9	2.4	58.5	31.4	27.1	...	...	...	...	...	...
28	54.2	.344	82	.688	.344	0.8	N 75 E	3.6	4.6	65.0	41.8	23.2	...	...	...	...	...	...
29	57.6	.373	78	.747	.374	0.3	N 63 E	3.5	4.3	65.0	50.5	14.5	...	...	...	...	...	...
30	58.9	.367	74	.727	.360	0.1	N 66 E	5.9	6.2	66.0	51.8	14.2	...	...	...	...	...	...
	55.9	0.350	75	29.732	29.382	0.4	N 16 W	0.9	6.5	64.5	47.0	17.5	1.235	19.0	...	...	1.235	19.0

TORONTO.
GENERAL METEOROLOGICAL ABSTRACT, OCTOBER, 1863.

Days.	DAILY MEANS.						WIND.			EXTREMES OF TEMPERATURE.			RAIN.		SNOW.		TOTAL FALL.	
	Temperature of Air.	Pressure of Vapour.	Rel. Humid.	Barometric Pressure.	Pressure of Dry Air.	Clouded Sky.	Resultant Direct'n.	Resultant Velocity.	Mean Velocity.	Maximum.	Minimum.	Difference.	Depth in inches.	Approximate duration.	Depth in Inches.	Approximate duration.	Depth in Inches.	Approximate duration.
1	59.5	0.413	82	29.500	29.186	0.8	S 75 E	5.1	6.6	63.4	53.0	13.4	0.100	5.2	...	...	0.100	5.2
2	55.6	.382	84	.475	.094	0.7	S 66 W	3.5	5.6	62.5	56.4	6.1	.020	3.0	...	...	.020	3.0
3	50.6	.322	86	.459	.137	0.2	S 2 E	2.0	3.6	59.6	39.0	20.6	.018	1.0	...	...	.018	1.0
4	Sunday						S 40 W	11.8	11.9	54.5	46.6	7.9	.012	0.5	...	...	.012	0.5
5	47.1	.270	83	.570	.309	1.0	S 70 W	7.4	7.5	51.4	43.4	8.0	.007	3.0	...	...	.007	3.0
6	45.2	.243	81	.706	.463	1.0	S 37 W	4.0	4.1	51.0	44.0	7.0	R	0.7	...	...	R	0.7
7	45.9	.284	91	.622	.338	1.0	N 40 E	2.9	4.0	50.0	42.0	8.6	.207	12.5	...	...	.207	12.5
8	46.0	.255	82	.519	.264	0.6	N 66 W	4.7	4.8	54.0	44.0	10.0	.005	0.6	...	...	.005	0.6
9	45.3	.251	83	.653	.402	1.0	N 6 E	3.6	3.8	50.2	39.0	11.2	.043	2.0	...	...	.043	2.0
10	42.2	.198	74	.800	.602	0.5	N 7 W	7.7	7.9	54.0	38.2	15.8	...	...	...	...	...	...
11	Sunday						N 20 W	4.4	4.6	47.0	35.5	11.5	...	...	...	...	...	...
12	39.0	.174	73	.764	.590	0.1	N	2.4	4.5	49.0	30.6	18.4	...	...	...	...	...	...
13	41.8	.201	76	.751	.550	0.2	N 50 E	4.1	4.9	50.8	33.4	17.4	...	...	...	...	...	...
14	49.2	.303	87	.634	.332	0.4	N 30 E	0.1	1.1	59.4	38.8	20.6	R	0.2	...	...	R	0.2
15	53.2	.321	79	.606	.285	0.1	N 53 E	2.7	3.2	64.4	42.5	21.9	R	0.1	...	...	R	0.1
16	57.2	.431	92	.413	28.982	1.0	N 58 E	6.8	6.9	62.0	50.0	12.0	.305	8.5	...	...	.305	8.5
17	59.7	.462	93	.334	28.872	0.4	S 67 E	3.4	4.8	64.2	55.4	8.8	.180	2.5	...	...	.180	2.5
18	Sunday						S 30 W	7.5	8.1	58.0	47.0	11.0	...	...	...	...	...	...
19	46.8	.263	81	.560	29.207	0.4	S 17 W	3.2	4.8	53.2	46.0	7.2	...	...	...	...	...	...
20	51.7	.293	74	.526	.244	0.7	S 34 W	5.1	8.7	59.8	36.0	23.8	...	...	...	...	...	...
21	44.8	.183	63	.834	.651	0.3	N 81 W	8.2	8.9	53.6	40.4	13.2	...	...	...	...	...	...
22	40.1	.184	74	.995	.811	0.7	N 43 E	3.4	4.8	47.5	33.0	14.5	.205	6.5	...	...	.205	6.5
23	39.5	.222	92	.080	.458	1.0	N 40 W	3.4	5.1	44.2	36.5	7.7	.390	7.8	...	...	.390	7.8
24	35.8	.161	77	.989	.825	0.7	N 4 E	6.1	6.3	42.0	33.8	8.2	...	...	...	...	...	...
25	Sunday						N 48 E	4.2	4.9	39.2	32.4	6.8	...	...	...	...	...	...
26	36.4	.169	78	30.141	.972	0.7	N 55 E	3.1	4.4	43.5	30.5	13.0	...	...	...	...	...	...
27	38.1	.167	73	30.086	.919	1.0	N 64 E	3.6	4.8	43.8	36.3	7.5	...	...	...	...	...	...
28	37.4	.151	68	30.024	.873	0.5	S 73 E	5.8	6.5	44.8	33.2	11.6	...	...	...	...	...	...
29	42.9	.216	77	29.827	.611	0.7	S 37 E	8.0	9.9	48.0	33.0	15.0	...	...	...	...	...	...
30	48.3	.316	93	.461	.145	1.0	S 8 E	8.4	9.9	54.0	43.5	10.2	.970	11.8	...	...	.070	11.8
31	42.3	.189	69	.096	.507	0.6	S 76 W	13.7	14.1	54.0	43.0	11.0	...	...	...	...	...	...
	45.9	0.260	80	29.697	29.437	0.6	S 71 W	0.5	6.2	52.8	40.5	12.3	2.522	65.9	...	...	2.522	65.9

10

TORONTO.
General Meteorological Abstract, November, 1863.

Days.	DAILY MEANS.						WIND.			EXTREMES OF TEMPERATURE.			RAIN.		SNOW.		TOTAL FALL.	
	Temperature of Air.	Pressure of Vapour.	Rel. Humid.	Barometric Pressure.	Pressure of Dry Air.	Clouded Sky.	Resultant Direction.	Resultant Velocity.	Mean Velocity.	Maximum.	Minimum.	Difference.	Depth in Inches.	Approximate duration.	Depth in Inches.	Approximate duration.	Depth in Inches.	Approximate duration.
1	Su	nday					N 81 E	3.3	4.8	42.0	30.8	11.2	...	...	...	...	...	...
2	43.3	0.231	81	29.696	29.465	0.9	S 57 E	3.1	9.0	50.0	31.0	19.0	.647	6.8	...	...	0.647	6.8
3	41.6	.183	69	.704	.521	0.5	W	10.3	10.4	48.0	41.2	6.8	...	...	...	...	...	...
4	43.2	.204	72	.720	.516	0.0	S 19 E	3.7	6.0	51.4	30.0	21.4	.355	2.0	...	...	0.355	2.0
5	50.2	.281	77	.273	28.992	0.8	S 85 W	10.7	12.1	67.0	44.0	23.0	...	...	...	...	...	...
6	39.4	.194	79	.463	29.260	0.5	N 76 W	9.6	9.9	46.2	38.6	7.6	.180	4.5	...	...	.180	4.5
7	38.5	.220	94	.425	.205	1.0	N 9 E	2.3	4.5	44.0	33.2	10.8	.250	7.0	...	...	.250	7.0
8	Su	nday					N 24 W	7.7	7.8	37.2	32.0	5.2	...	...	S	3.0	S	3.0
9	30.6	.126	74	.833	.708	0.0	N 28 W	6.6	7.0	37.5	26.0	11.5	...	...	...	...	...	...
10	30.2	.129	77	.854	.725	0.7	S 79 W	8.0	9.9	37.4	24.0	13.4	...	...	S	0.1	S	0.1
11	42.0	.204	76	.413	.209	0.0	S 53 W	11.5	11.7	48.0	29.2	18.8	...	...	...	...	...	...
12	42.6	.230	84	.453	.223	0.8	S 40 W	1.2	1.3	52.0	35.0	17.0	...	...	...	...	...	...
13	39.4	.213	88	.521	.305	1.0	N 76 E	9.3	9.5	44.0	34.2	9.8	.095	6.5	...	...	.095	6.5
14	43.9	.265	91	.372	.107	1.0	N 74 E	4.9	6.2	49.8	36.4	13.4	.242	14.0	...	...	.242	14.0
15	Su	nday					N 15 E	5.7	6.0	49.0	42.8	6.2	.405	17.0	...	...	.405	17.0
16	43.3	.271	96	.566	.295	1.0	N 82 E	1.2	1.8	45.8	42.5	3.3	.070	9.5	...	...	.070	9.5
17	44.2	.233	81	.438	.205	1.0	N 52 W	12.9	13.4	49.0	39.0	10.0	...	...	...	...	...	...
18	43.5	.218	76	.242	.025	0.0	S 57 W	5.8	12.9	48.0	42.6	6.0	...	...	...	...	...	...
19	47.0	.267	82	.325	.058	0.1	S 45 W	8.0	6.6	53.5	37.8	15.7	R	0.5	...	...	R	0.5
20	39.2	.189	78	.520	.331	0.4	S 76 W	7.3	7.4	44.8	40.8	4.0	...	...	...	...	...	...
21	34.7	.173	85	.541	.368	0.5	S 47 W	1.9	3.7	44.2	26.8	15.2	...	...	...	...	...	...
22	Su	nday					S 82 W	6.4	6.6	41.2	32.0	9.2	...	...	...	...	...	...
23	35.4	.147	71	30.060	.912	0.0	N 74 E	5.0	5.8	40.0	28.2	11.8	.230	3.0	...	...	.230	3.0
24	39.7	.206	84	29.376	.170	0.9	S 57 W	5.3	14.7	51.2	34.0	17.2	.532	10.5	...	...	.532	10.5
25	33.4	.129	68	.558	.429	0.8	N 87 W	7.6	7.9	38.0	32.0	6.0	...	...	S	0.3	S	0.3
26	34.2	.145	74	.730	.585	0.6	S 56 W	6.0	6.1	40.4	27.0	12.8	...	...	...	...	...	...
27	38.9	.201	84	.643	.442	0.5	S 17 W	3.8	4.0	48.0	30.2	17.8	.510	5.0	...	...	.510	5.0
28	37.4	.202	87	.345	.142	1.0	N 62 W	11.3	13.4	44.0	37.0	7.0	.140	7.5	S	1.0	.140	8.5
29	Su	nday					N 41 W	4.3	5.4	27.5	23.4	4.1	...	...	0.1	5.5	.010	5.5
30	22.7	.093	76	.820	.727	0.7	S 73 W	13.5	13.7	27.2	17.8	9.4	...	...	S	1.0	S	1.0
	39.1	0.198	80	29.556	29.358	0.7	N 88 W	3.5	7.9	44.8	33.3	11.5	3.656	93.8	0.1	10.9	3.666	104.7

11

TORONTO.
GENERAL METEOROLOGICAL ABSTRACT, DECEMBER, 1863.

Days.	DAILY MEANS.						WIND.			EXTREMES OF TEMPERATURE.			RAIN.		SNOW.		TOTAL FALL.	
	Temperature of Air.	Pressure of Vapour.	Rel. Humid.	Barometric Pressure.	Pressure of Dry Air.	Clouded Sky.	Resultant Direction.	Resultant Velocity.	Mean Velocity.	Maximum.	Minimum.	Difference.	Depth in inches.	Approximate duration.	Depth in inches.	Approximate duration.	Depth in inches.	Approximate duration.
1	33.5	0.142	73	29.074	29.532	0.6	S 52 W	15.3	15.3	41.5	21.8	19.7	...	...	...	...	...	...
2	33.2	.154	78	.689	.535	1.0	N 61 W	9.1	12.2	44.0	32.7	11.3	...	...	...	...	...	...
3	32.9	.152	78	.784	.632	0.8	S	5.8	8.3	43.0	21.8	21.2	...	...	...	...	...	...
4	42.3	.199	75	.539	.340	0.3	S 81 W	7.9	9.0	53.4	33.0	20.4	...	...	...	...	...	...
5	24.8	.110	79	.922	.812	0.8	N 89 W	9.8	10.1	33.2	25.2	8.0	...	...	S	1.5	S	1.5
6	Sunday						N 71 E	1.8	2.8	27.0	12.2	14.8	...	...	...	...	...	...
7	27.5	.121	81	30.115	.994	0.0	S 36 E	1.8	1.9	37.8	18.8	19.0	...	...	...	...	...	...
8	32.0	.157	79	29.831	.674	0.6	S 55 W	2.2	2.0	41.8	23.0	18.8	...	...	...	...	...	...
9	22.5	.106	77	.933	.827	0.5	N 17 W	13.4	14.2	35.8	26.2	9.6	R	0.2	...	...	R	0.2
10	13.8	.068	79	30.153	30.085	0.7	N 84 E	8.5	9.7	27.0	-1.5	28.5	..	...	0.2	6.0	0.020	6.0
11	28.2	.139	88	29.728	29.589	1.0	S 89 E	4.4	4.7	34.8	14.0	20.8	0.040	4.8	S	2.0	.040	6.8
12	36.2	.207	90	.590	.383	1.0	N 65 E	6.8	6.9	43.0	27.8	15.2	.920	16.5	...	...	.920	16.5
13	Sunday						N 50 E	6.6	7.4	46.0	36.8	9.2	.455	20.0	...	...	.455	20.0
14	35.1	.187	88	28.964	28.777	1.0	S 84 W	15.0	21.4	44.4	36.0	8.4	.400	4.2	0.1	0.7	.470	4.9
15	24.7	.098	74	29.737	29.639	0.4	N 81 W	17.4	18.0	28.8	20.0	8.8	...	...	0.1	2.2	.010	2.2
16	19.2	.079	76	30.128	30.049	0.9	N 51 E	8.5	8.9	24.4	17.2	7.2	...	...	0.5	4.0	.050	4.0
17	28.2	.151	96	29.449	29.298	1.0	N 81 E	16.2	17.5	36.0	16.4	19.6	.130	11.0	1.5	10.0	.280	21.0
18	20.3	.123	84	.314	.191	0.0	S 73 W	13.1	13.5	31.3	27.3	4.0	...	...	S	0.5	S	0.5
19	18.4	.078	77	.544	.466	0.8	N 71 W	10.9	11.5	21.0	14.7	7.2	...	...	0.1	2.2	.010	2.2
20	Sunday						N 73 W	5.4	5.0	24.2	7.8	16.4	...	...	S	0.2	S	0.2
21	20.2	.101	92	.622	.521	1.0	N 45 E	4.8	5.0	25.0	16.6	8.4	...	...	0.3	7.5	.030	7.5
22	11.8	.004	85	.738	.674	0.8	N 20 E	3.9	4.1	16.5	14.5	2.0	...	...	S	1.0	S	1.0
23	14.3	.068	82	.893	.825	0.2	N 23 W	7.8	7.8	20.4	2.0	18.4	...	...	...	...	...	...
24	16.9	.072	77	30.010	.939	0.4	N 3 E	2.8	2.9	24.2	10.0	14.2	...	...	...	...	...	...
25	...	...	...	...	...	...	N 76 E	2.8	3.1	31.0	13.2	17.8	...	...	...	...	...	...
26	29.8	.131	83	29.915	.784	0.7	N 40 E	0.9	0.9	34.0	21.0	13.0	...	...	1.0	4.0	.100	4.0
27	Sunday						N 60 E	9.7	10.1	31.8	27.6	7.2	R	1.0	0.3	3.0	.030	4.0
28	32.7	.171	92	.264	.093	1.0	S 61 E	6.6	14.6	38.2	25.4	12.8	.515	9.3	1.5	2.5	.065	11.8
29	34.0	.166	85	.344	.178	0.9	S 59 W	14.2	14.5	37.0	2.0	5.0	R	0.2	S	1.0	S	1.2
30	28.9	.140	87	.827	.687	0.8	N 81 W	7.4	0.5	31.8	19.0	2.8	...	...	...	...	...	...
31	32.1	.109	92	.427	.257	1.0	S 82 E	14.2	18.1	41.8	19.3	22.5	.440	8.0	1.5	7.5	.590	15.5
	27.0	0.129	83	29.998	29.569	0.7	N 41 W	1.0	9.4	34.0	20.7	13.3	2.960	75.2	7.1	55.8	3.670	131.0

TORONTO.
GENERAL METEOROLOGICAL ABSTRACT, JANUARY, 1864.

Days.	DAILY MEANS.						WIND.			EXTREMES OF TEMPERATURE.			RAIN.		SNOW.		TOTAL FALL.	
	Temperature of Air.	Pressure of Vapour.	Rel. Humid.	Barometric Pressure.	Pressure of Dry Air.	Clouded Sky.	Resultant Direction.	Resultant Velocity.	Mean Velocity.	Maximum.	Minimum.	Difference.	Depth in inches.	Approximate duration.	Depth in inches.	Approximate duration.	Depth in inches.	Approximate duration.
1	0.8	0.071	70	29.280	29.209	0.6	S 66 W	28.2	28.4	34.2	8.2	26.0	...	...	0.2	3.0	0.020	3.0
2	-2.4	.032	83	.737	.705	0.2	S 67 W	24.2	24.2	3.0	-9.0	12.0	...	...	...	...	...	...
3	Sunday						S 65 W	15.5	15.6	12.8	-0.6	13.4	...	...	...	...	...	...
4	12.5	.065	86	.808	.743	0.9	N 40 W	3.1	4.7	16.2	9.8	6.4	...	...	2.0	4.0	.200	4.6
5	15.4	.075	87	.574	.499	1.0	S 88 W	7.6	10.7	20.0	10.0	10.0	...	...	3.0	6.2	.300	6.2
6	12.5	.062	81	.916	.854	0.7	S 81 W	7.1	10.0	16.0	11.8	4.2	...	...	...	...	...	...
7	9.4	.057	82	.977	.920	0.0	S 89 W	3.8	4.3	17.0	2.0	15.0	...	...	S	0.7	S	0.7
8	11.1	.060	84	.646	.586	1.0	S 69 W	10.2	10.8	14.0	5.8	8.2	...	...	S	0.7	S	0.7
9	9.9	.060	86	.549	.489	0.4	S 59 W	17.4	17.5	15.2	5.7	9.5	...	...	...	...	...	...
10	Sunday						S 60 W	13.0	13.0	19.0	6.2	12.8	...	...	...	...	...	...
11	17.0	.073	77	.453	.380	0.3	S 69 W	11.9	12.0	22.0	11.0	11.0	...	...	...	...	...	...
12	27.4	.116	77	.246	.130	0.5	S 47 W	12.9	13.1	34.0	16.4	17.6	...	...	...	...	...	...
13	29.8	.133	80	.310	.177	0.6	S 50 W	7.8	8.2	35.8	26.2	9.6	...	...	...	...	...	...
14	29.6	.141	84	.472	.332	0.8	S 83 E	3.7	4.1	36.0	19.7	16.3	...	...	2.0	4.0	.200	4.0
15	28.4	.128	79	.439	.311	0.9	S 89 W	10.0	11.7	34.8	30.0	4.8	...	...	3.0	6.5	.300	6.5
16	25.0	.105	77	.780	.675	0.7	S 45 W	6.7	6.7	31.8	16.4	15.4	...	...	...	...	...	...
17	Sunday						S 31 W	5.6	5.6	38.2	24.4	13.8	...	...	0.5	2.0	.050	2.0
18	31.2	.140	85	.645	.496	1.0	N 8 E	10.2	10.3	35.0	32.2	2.8	...	...	4.0	15.5	.400	15.5
19	25.4	.121	88	.156	.035	1.0	N 48 W	21.5	24.8	29.1	25.4	3.7	...	...	10.0	14.5	1.000	14.5
20	19.4	.086	81	.731	.645	0.0	N 36 W	4.1	4.7	27.4	16.2	11.2	...	...	...	...	...	...
21	19.0	.092	83	.968	.876	0.3	S 46 W	6.1	6.9	31.5	4.6	26.9	...	...	0.5	1.5	.050	1.5
22	27.9	.135	87	.726	.591	0.4	S 65 W	9.1	9.3	35.0	18.2	16.8	...	...	0.1	2.0	.010	2.0
23	33.4	.068	86	.479	.311	0.9	S 51 W	7.2	7.7	42.0	18.0	24.0	R	0.2	...	...	R	0.2
24	Sunday						S 44 W	5.2	5.4	44.2	35.4	8.8	...	...	...	...	...	...
25	34.9	.170	84	.235	.065	0.4	S 50 W	2.0	5.1	40.4	29.2	11.2	R	0.2	...	...	R	0.2
26	36.0	.162	76	.373	.211	0.7	N 65 W	3.4	5.4	38.0	33.8	4.2	...	...	...	...	...	...
27	36.4	.168	78	.507	.339	0.4	S 73 W	1.3	1.5	43.4	30.2	17.4	...	...	...	...	...	...
28	36.8	.174	79	.650	.476	0.3	N 11 W	3.5	4.2	44.0	26.6	8.0	...	...	...	...	...	...
29	29.9	.125	75	.920	.795	1.0	N 59 E	9.6	9.8	37.8	29.8	8.0	.020	1.0	...	...	.020	1.0
30	27.1	.133	89	.729	.596	1.0	N 60 E	8.5	8.8	31.8	22.1	9.7	.225	9.0	1.0	4.0	.325	10.0
31	Sunday						N 81 E	11.4	11.5	37.4	27.0	10.4	.920	6.0	S	0.3	.920	6.3
	22.8	0.110	82	29.550	29.479	0.7	S 73 W	6.0	10.2	29.6	17.5	12.1	1.165	16.4	26.3	65.5	3.795	81.9

13

TORONTO.
GENERAL METEOROLOGICAL ABSTRACT, FEBRUARY, 1864.

Days.	DAILY MEANS.						WIND.			EXTREMES OF TEMPERATURE.			RAIN.		SNOW.		TOTAL FALL.	
	Temperature of Air	Pressure of Vapour.	Rel. Humid.	Barometer Pressure.	Pressure of Dry Air.	Clouded Sky.	Resultant Direction.	Resultant Velocity.	Mean Velocity.	Maximum.	Minimum.	Difference.	Depth in inches	Approximate duration.	Depth in inches.	Approximate duration.	Depth in inches.	Approximate duration.
1	36.9	0.186	85	29.345	29.159	1.0	S 59 W	12.5	14.8	43.2	23.4	14.8	0.365	6.0	...	...	0.365	6.0
2	34.5	.165	82	.347	.182	0.8	S 71 W	7.0	8.4	38.2	34.0	4.2	...	...	...	...	...	...
3	30.2	.130	81	.362	.220	0.7	S 74 W	10.5	11.8	34.5	27.9	6.6	...	...	0.2	1.5	.020	1.5
4	31.2	.155	87	.106	28.951	0.9	S	7.3	8.8	36.0	25.0	11.0	...	...	1.0	8.0	.100	8.0
5	32.5	.161	87	.252	29.091	0.9	N 9 W	1.8	4.3	36.0	31.0	5.0	...	...	0.2	6.5	.020	6.5
6	28.2	.135	87	.444	.309	1.0	N 26 W	6.6	7.4	31.4	27.0	4.4	...	...	3.0	8.5	.300	8.5
7	Sunday						S 38 W	14.1	14.6	34.0	2?.1	3.9	...	...	0.5	3.7	.050	3.7
8	22.7	.104	83	.242	.138	0.7	N 89 W	13.3	13.4	28.8	25.5	3.3	...	...	0.1	0.3	.010	0.3
9	11.0	.058	81	.598	.540	0.3	N 49 W	7.5	7.9	19.1	8.4	11.0	...	...	...	...	...	...
10	4.6	.046	85	.965	.919	0.3	N 47 W	4.0	5.2	16.4	-0.6	17.0	...	...	...	...	...	...
11	27.1	.111	69	.584	.473	0.9	S 62 W	11.9	13.6	35.8	-1.6	37.4	...	...	0.1	1.8	.010	1.8
12	29.0	.131	80	.441	.310	0.0	S 77 W	11.6	12.3	35.2	23.0	12.2	...	...	...	...	...	...
13	33.4	.150	78	.253	.103	0.8	S 52 W	9.9	10.0	39.0	27.6	11.4	...	...	...	...	...	...
14	Sunday						N 38 W	13.6	15.0	33.4	21.7	11.7	...	...	...	...	...	...
15	25.0	.100	77	.295	.192	0.7	N 20 E	0.4	9.6	31.5	10.6	20.9	...	...	0.5	3.1	.050	3.1
16	12.4	.064	79	.185	.121	0.7	N 57 W	20.4	21.5	21.9	14.3	7.6	...	...	1.2	4.0	.120	4.0
17	-4.6	.034	91	.739	.705	0.7	N 70 W	10.8	11.3	1.5	-15.0	16.5	...	...	...	...	...	...
18	-0.4	.039	89	30.042	30.003	0.4	S 81 W	9.6	9.7	6.8	-7.0	13.8	...	...	...	...	...	...
19	8.5	.056	82	29.904	29.848	0.7	S 49 W	15.0	15.3	22.0	-6.8	28.8	...	...	0.1	1.0	.010	1.0
20	27.3	.116	77	.626	.510	1.0	S 28 W	9.0	9.3	31.8	12.0	19.8	...	...	0.1	0.5	.010	0.5
21	Sunday						S 14 W	4.1	4.1	36.5	27.4	9.1	...	...	...	...	...	...
22	37.6	.180	83	.322	.133	0.8	S 37 W	5.3	6.7	41.8	33.8	8.0	.032	1.5	...	...	.032	1.5
23	38.7	.182	78	.215	.033	0.8	S 42 W	6.5	5.9	45.0	32.2	12.8	...	...	...	...	...	...
24	36.2	.161	76	.278	.217	0.6	N 69 W	8.7	9.3	41.8	32.0	9.8	...	...	...	...	...	...
25	31.5	.162	91	.437	.275	1.0	N 14 E	8.4	10.4	36.2	30.0	6.2	...	...	2.5	15.6	.250	15.5
26	22.3	.095	79	.765	.670	0.2	N 35 W	7.6	9.1	30.4	20.7	9.7	...	...	...	...	...	...
27	27.7	.135	87	.640	.502	0.9	S 57 E	2.1	2.6	36.5	12.8	23.7	...	...	S	0.2	S	0.2
28	Sunday						S 80 W	12.3	13.0	41.0	31.8	9.2	...	...	...	...	...	...
29	23.8	.100	82	.795	.689	0.7	N 83 W	7.4	7.5	28.0	23.0	5.0	...	...	S	1.0	S	1.0
	24.3	0.119	82	29.491	29.372	0.7	S 84 W	6.5	10.1	31.5	18.9	12.6	0.397	7.5	9.5	55.6	1.347	63.1

14

TORONTO.
GENERAL METEOROLOGICAL ABSTRACT, MARCH, 1864.

Days.	DAILY MEANS.						WIND.				EXTREMES OF TEMPERATURE.			RAIN.		SNOW.		TOTAL FALL.	
	Temperature of Air.	Pressure of Vapour.	Rel. Humid.	Barometric Pressure.	Pressure of Dry Air.	Clouded Sky.	Resultant Direction.	Resultant Velocity.	Mean Velocity.	Maximum.	Minimum.	Difference.	Depth in Inches.	Approximate duration.	Depth in Inches.	Approximate duration.	Depth in Inches.	Approximate duration.
1	22.2	.100	84	29.622	29.522	0.9	S 86 W	3.0	3.2	28.2	14.6	13.6	...	...	0.2	3.0	0.020	9.7
2	24.4	.101	76	.729	.628	0.8	N 65 W	10.7	10.0	29.8	22.1	7.7	...	...	0.1	0.7	.010	0.7
3	27.2	.129	85	.808	.679	0.1	S 16 E	2.8	4.4	35.5	16.0	19.5	...	...	...	...	...	...
4	39.9	.185	75	.268	.083	0.7	S 54 W	4.2	6.0	50.2	27.0	23.2	0.305	6.2	...	...	.305	6.2
5	31.7	.163	90	.224	.061	1.0	N 16 W	9.8	10.8	36.5	30.6	5.9	.300	3.0	1.0	6.5	.400	9.5
6	Sunday						N 36 W	4.0	4.3	37.0	17.8	19.2	...	...	...	...	...	...
7	32.6	.131	70	.380	.250	0.0	N 48 W	10.7	10.9	42.4	23.0	19.4	...	...	...	...	...	...
8	31.3	.118	68	.514	.396	0.1	N 50 W	3.2	3.8	41.5	23.2	18.3	...	...	...	...	...	...
9	31.8	.136	76	.810	.674	0.7	N 17 E	2.7	6.8	39.4	24.2	15.2	...	...	...	...	...	...
10	34.0	.176	90	.376	.198	1.0	N 85 E	12.2	12.2	38.0	29.8	8.2	.080	9.0	...	...	.080	9.0
11	39.3	.226	93	28.954	28.729	1.0	S 66 W	4.8	9.6	42.0	32.0	10.0	.480	7.7	...	..	.480	7.7
12	33.9	.147	75	29.379	29.232	0.0	N 86 W	7.8	8.4	37.8	31.4	6.4	...	...	...	...	...	...
13	Sunday						N 17 W	8.2	8.5	38.4	26.0	12.4	...	...	S	1.0	S	1.0
14	30.9	.133	76	.654	.521	0.5	S 35 W	4.3	5.0	37.8	22.8	15.0	...	...	0.1	2.0	.010	2.0
15	22.9	.100	87	.622	.513	0.7	N 43 W	12.7	13.0	27.3	24.0	3.3	...	...	S	...	S	...
16	25.9	.116	82	.512	.396	0.9	N 83 W	7.9	8.2	32.8	14.7	18.1	...	...	0.5	12.0	.050	12.0
17	31.7	.147	82	.308	.161	1.0	S 30 W	16.3	16.4	27.4	26.0	11.4	...	...	0.4	2.5	.040	2.5
18	27.2	.121	76	.115	28.994	0.5	S 87 W	16.5	20.7	34.5	28.6	5.9	...	...	S	0.2	S	0.2
19	16.1	.071	79	.429	29.358	0.9	N 79 W	8.0	9.1	22.0	10.5	11.5	...	...	...	...	...	...
20	Sunday						N 65 W	9.0	10.5	18.8	4.7	14.1	...	...	...	...	...	...
21	11.9	.059	79	.801	.742	0.7	N 77 W	8.7	10.0	19.2	3.0	16.2	...	...	...	...	...	...
22	11.7	.049	66	.986	.937	0.1	N 48 E	4.9	6.0	18.0	3.0	15.0	...	...	...	...	...	...
23	21.9	.080	67	.790	.710	0.1	N 21 W	2.0	3.3	33.0	11.1	21.9	...	...	...	...	...	...
24	30.9	.104	62	.706	.602	0.1	S 35 W	4.8	5.0	44.0	15.6	28.4	...	...	...	...	...	...
25	...	...	...	...	...	...	N 69 E	3.3	3.8	41.5	24.4	17.1	.010	0.5	...	...	.010	0.5
26	35.6	.183	87	.607	.423	0.7	S 3 W	0.7	1.8	41.0	33.8	7.2	R	0.2	...	...	R	0.2
27	Sunday						N 49 E	1.3	2.7	39.6	27.2	12.4	...	...	...	...	...	...
28	35.1	.175	85	.644	.469	0.9	N 82 E	18.0	19.0	40.0	29.4	11.2	...	...	...	...	...	...
29	37.3	.195	87	.370	.175	1.0	N 86 E	14.9	15.1	41.8	34.0	7.8	.255	3.0	1.0	2.2	.355	5.2
30	34.7	.162	81	.247	.085	1.0	N 60 E	8.8	9.6	38.0	32.0	6.0	.085	15.5	0.2	2.0	.085	17.5
31	35.2	.199	97	.358	.158	1.0	N 64 E	1.0	1.1	39.4	33.0	6.4	.125	15.0	0.2	3.5	.145	18.5
	29.1	.135	80	29.508	29.373	0.7	N 53 W	2.3	8.4	35.6	22.4	13.2	1.620	60.1	3.7	35.6	1.900	95.7

TORONTO.
GENERAL METEOROLOGICAL ABSTRACT, APRIL, 1864.

Days.	DAILY MEANS.						WIND.			EXTREMES OF TEMPERATURE			RAIN.		SNOW.		TOTAL FALL.	
	Temperature of Air.	Pressure of Vapour.	Rel. Humid.	Barometric Pressure.	Pressure of Dry Air.	Clouded Sky.	Resultant Direction.	Resultant Velocity.	Mean Velocity.	Maximum.	Minimum.	Difference.	Depth in inches.	Approximate duration.	Depth in inches.	Approximate duration.	Depth in inches.	Approximate duration.
1	35.4	0.189	92	29.387	29.198	1.0	N 81 E	7.0	8.0	39.8	31.8	8.0	...	...	...	...	...	...
2	39.9	.204	86	.381	.177	0.9	N 65 E	6.9	7.0	42.5	34.4	8.1	0.045	2.5	..	...	.045	2.5
3	Sunday						N 86 E	3.0	4.7	45.0	36.8	8.2	R	0.5	...	...	R	0.5
4	40.4	.190	70	.543	.353	0.8	N 84 E	10.0	11.2	46.0	35.0	11.0	.100	3.6	...	...	.100	3.6
5	37.4	.178	80	.595	.417	1.0	N 81 E	7.4	7.6	40.8	35.0	5.8	.015	3.5	...	...	.015	3.5
6	40.2	.220	88	.820	.600	1.0	N 87 E	1.1	1.2	48.2	36.0	12.2	.005	3.0	...	...	.005	3.0
7	42.5	.214	79	.844	.630	0.7	N 89 E	3.3	3.5	46.1	38.5	7.3	...	...	...	...	...	...
8	45.2	.220	73	.689	.469	0.9	N 76 E	10.0	10.2	50.0	38.0	12.0	...	...	...	...	...	...
9	39.8	.218	89	.466	.248	1.0	N 80 E	16.5	16.6	44.0	37.5	6.5	1.280	19.5	...	...	1.280	19.5
10	Sunday						N 81 E	10.7	10.8	38.2	33.0	5.2	.160	11.5	1.0	3.0	.260	14.5
11	41.1	.214	81	.549	.335	0.9	N 23 W	1.5	3.2	46.5	34.6	11.9	R	1.0	...	...	R	1.0
12	36.6	.176	81	.544	.368	1.0	N 72 E	11.2	11.4	39.5	33.5	6.3	R	2.1	1.0	3.0	.100	5.1
13	36.5	.187	87	.462	.275	0.9	N 48 W	5.8	6.9	44.0	32.8	11.2	R	0.2	1.5	4.0	.150	4.2
14	39.4	.196	81	.567	.371	1.0	N 62 W	2.6	4.8	45.4	34.5	10.9	.033	1.0	...	...	.033	1.0
15	40.6	.169	67	.443	.274	0.5	N 60 W	0.2	5.2	49.8	34.4	15.4	...	...	...	...	...	...
16	39.3	.161	66	.345	.194	0.1	N 21 W	3.4	8.4	49.0	31.0	18.0	...	...	...	...	...	...
17	Sunday						N 59 W	13.0	13.1	50.2	30.6	19.4	...	...	...	...	...	...
18	30.0	.142	61	.597	.455	0.5	N 18 W	5.8	6.1	49.2	31.2	18.0	...	...	...	...	...	...
19	40.8	.108	66	.714	.547	0.9	N 7 E	2.6	5.0	45.0	34.5	10.5	...	...	...	...	...	...
20	41.5	.166	62	.628	.462	0.8	N 49 W	1.3	4.0	49.8	36.2	13.6	...	...	...	...	...	...
21	43.3	.150	56	.689	.539	0.1	S 17 W	2.2	3.8	56.0	31.6	24.4	...	...	...	...	...	...
22	45.8	.207	69	.668	.461	0.6	S 64 E	3.5	5.9	55.2	32.2	23.0	.175	4.7	...	...	.175	4.7
23	46.2	.286	91	.629	.343	1.0	N 14 W	5.1	5.4	51.0	42.6	5.4	1.010	14.5	...	...	1.010	14.5
24	Sunday						N 75 E	14.7	14.9	49.4	36.5	12.9	...	...	...	...	...	...
25	44.8	.266	89	.453	.157	0.8	N 69 E	2.1	3.6	51.4	40.2	11.2	.490	6.0	...	...	.490	6.0
26	49.3	.278	80	.495	.217	0.8	N 67 W	7.9	9.3	59.4	39.0	20.4	...	...	...	...	...	...
27	37.8	.160	71	.640	.480	0.6	N 28 W	18.5	18.5	44.0	34.6	9.4	.215	2.0	...	...	.215	2.0
28	38.3	.153	66	.867	.714	0.6	N 11 W	9.4	9.8	49.0	28.1	20.9	...	...	...	...	...	...
29	41.4	.135	52	.884	.749	0.3	S 1 W	1.2	5.2	51.0	31.2	19.8	...	...	...	...	...	...
30	43.4	.153	66	.005	.425	0.8	N 36 E	3.5	5.0	48.6	32.4	16.2	.105	3.0	...	...	.105	3.0
	40.0	.194	73	29.597	29.403	0.7	N 41 E	3.4	7.8	47.5	31.6	12.9	3.633	78.6	3.5	10.0	3.983	89.6

TORONTO.
GENERAL METEOROLOGICAL ABSTRACT, MAY, 1864.

Days.	DAILY MEANS.						WIND.			EXTREMES OF TEMPERATURE.			RAIN.		SNOW.		TOTAL FALL.	
	Temperature of Air.	Pressure of Vapour.	Rel. Humid.	Barometric Pressure.	Pressure of Dry Air.	Cloud of Sky.	Resultant Direction.	Resultant Velocity.	Mean Velocity.	Maximum.	Minimum.	Difference.	Depth in inches.	Approximate duration.	Depth in inches.	Approximate duration.	Depth in inches.	Approximate duration.
1	Sunday						S 73 W	3.5	4.9	54.0	36.8	17.2	R	1.0	...	...	R	1.0
2	42.8	0.222	81	29.233	29.011	1.0	N 11 W	2.3	7.7	52.0	36.5	16.5	0.310	9.9	...	...	0.310	9.9
3	40.8	.220	89	.326	.096	0.9	N 43 W	4.9	6.9	47.8	34.5	13.3	.300	9.5	...	...	.300	9.5
4	49.7	.246	87	.663	.417	0.3	N 75 W	6.3	7.3	63.2	37.0	26.1	...	...	...	...	...	...
5	54.4	.286	67	.686	.411	0.2	S 80 W	6.4	6.5	64.0	38.8	25.2	...	...	...	...	...	...
6	55.9	.344	77	.571	.227	1.0	N 48 W	2.9	6.9	71.0	49.0	22.0	.090	2.3	...	...	.090	2.3
7	43.9	.265	93	.553	.288	1.0	N 83 E	3.0	3.1	48.2	42.0	6.2	.200	9.5	...	...	.200	9.5
8	Sunday						S 48 E	0.8	0.8	57.2	43.0	14.2	.258	5.5	...	...	.258	5.5
9	57.6	.383	81	.290	28.908	0.5	S 26 W	3.4	3.5	67.4	45.2	22.2	.225	3.6	...	...	.225	3.6
10	42.6	.251	88	.382	29.131	0.8	N 18 W	11.9	12.2	53.0	42.5	10.5	.620	10.2	...	...	.620	10.2
11	39.6	.169	69	.575	.406	0.9	N 75 E	1.8	1.9	43.5	32.2	11.3	...	...	...	...	...	...
12	45.2	.203	69	.528	.325	0.5	S 40 E	1.8	2.9	54.5	34.0	20.5	.095	2.0	...	...	.095	2.0
13	50.5	.328	59	.483	.155	1.0	N 8 E	0.4	9.5	55.0	41.0	14.0	.445	13.8	...	...	.445	13.8
14	54.8	.396	92	.511	.115	1.0	N 69 E	10.1	10.6	60.8	51.0	9.8	.027	2.3	...	...	.027	2.3
15	Sunday						N 66 E	9.1	9.3	66.2	52.6	13.0	.515	3.8	...	...	.515	3.8
16	61.1	.454	84	.605	.151	0.7	N 80 E	3.4	3.6	69.2	54.2	14.0	R	0.6	...	...	R	0.6
17	66.0	.473	74	.525	.052	0.6	N 17 E	2.3	3.7	74.0	49.8	24.2	...	...	...	...	...	...
18	61.5	.333	61	.535	.203	0.4	N 77 E	1.6	3.3	67.4	55.2	12.4	...	...	...	...	...	...
19	59.1	.287	57	.570	.283	0.4	S 80 E	1.1	2.6	66.8	49.2	17.6	...	...	...	...	...	...
20	60.8	.384	72	.443	.059	0.8	S 89 W	4.2	5.8	69.2	47.4	21.8	...	...	...	...	...	...
21	67.2	.408	70	.306	28.838	0.9	N 52 W	7.0	9.3	79.0	58.2	20.8	R	1.5	...	...	R	1.5
22	Sunday						N 4 W	2.5	4.1	67.0	54.0	13.0	...	...	...	...	...	...
23	55.0	.312	72	.402	29.000	0.0	N 84 E	3.7	4.1	62.0	46.8	15.2	...	...	...	...	...	...
24	63.0	.470	81	.359	28.890	0.8	S 39 W	1.6	5.5	72.4	53.0	19.4	.355	2.1	...	...	.355	2.1
25	60.8	.467	88	.390	28.931	0.7	S 76 E	1.0	1.2	69.0	55.0	13.8	...	...	...	...	...	...
26	61.7	.464	84	.322	28.858	1.0	N 26 W	3.0	4.4	67.0	54.2	12.8	.010	0.3	...	...	.010	0.3
27	62.8	.300	54	.883	29.053	0.4	N 24 W	12.2	12.6	74.0	56.8	17.2	...	...	...	...	...	...
28	50.6	.190	53	.685	.492	0.2	N 22 W	8.9	9.4	59.2	45.0	11.2	...	...	...	...	...	...
29	Sunday						S 32 W	3.8	4.2	58.8	37.0	21.8	.040	1.5	...	...	.040	1.5
30	55.0	.327	75	.433	.106	0.8	S 80 E	3.2	4.0	61.0	46.0	15.0	...	...	...	...	...	...
31	62.9	.402	72	.505	.103	0.6	N 11 W	1.4	3.7	75.0	51.2	23.8	.580	8.2	...	...	.580	8.2
	54.8	0.333	75	29.472	29.139	0.7	N 7 W	1.9	5.6	62.9	46.2	16.7	4.070	87.6	...	...	4.070	87.6

TORONTO.
GENERAL METEOROLOGICAL ABSTRACT, JUNE, 1864.

Days.	DAILY MEANS.						WIND.			EXTREMES OF TEMPERATURE.			RAIN.		SNOW.		TOTAL FALL.	
	Temperature of Air.	Pressure of Vapour.	Rel. Humid.	Barometric Pressure.	Pressure of Dry Air.	Clouded Sky.	Resultant Direction.	Resultant Velocity.	Mean Velocity.	Maximum.	Minimum.	Difference.	Depth in inches.	Approximate duration.	Depth in inches.	Approximate duration.	Depth in inches.	Approximate duration.
1	54.0	0.334	79	29.602	29.268	0.6	N 48 W	2.5	2.7	62.8	51.6	11.2	0.005	1.0	...	...	0.005	1.0
2	54.3	.285	67	.627	.341	0.3	N 63 W	2.4	3.7	63.0	44.2	18.8	...	...	...	...	...	...
3	55.1	.292	67	.070	.378	0.1	S 8 W	2.2	2.6	63.6	42.0	21.6	...	...	...	...	...	...
4	58.6	.319	65	.603	.284	0.0	S 61 E	1.1	1.8	69.8	46.4	23.4	...	...	...	...	...	...
5	Sunday						S 15 E	2.9	3.7	68.2	52.2	16.0	...	...	...	...	...	...
6	53.0	.250	60	.597	.347	0.4	N 40 W	10.6	10.8	63.0	55.8	7.2	R	0.1	...	...	R	0.1
7	52.6	.260	66	.852	.592	0.1	S 22 W	3.5	3.5	64.8	34.8	30.0	...	...	...	...	...	...
8	56.0	.310	70	.535	.225	0.9	S 25 W	2.4	2.9	67.2	48.4	23.8	.120	8.0	...	...	.120	8.0
9	56.9	.370	79	.163	28.784	0.4	N 37 W	10.7	11.5	70.8	52.6	18.2	.305	2.5	...	...	.305	2.5
10	57.4	.185	37	.551	29.366	0.1	N 25 W	9.2	9.3	54.4	42.2	12.2	...	...	...	...	...	...
11	50.6	.207	57	.684	.477	0.5	N 39 W	4.4	5.8	59.0	40.8	18.2	...	...	...	...	...	...
12	Sunday						N 31 W	1.5	5.1	60.0	42.4	17.6	...	...	...	...	...	...
13	57.0	.282	61	.878	.590	0.2	S 75 W	1.4	4.1	63.8	42.0	21.8	...	...	...	...	...	...
14	61.2	.320	59	.739	.419	0.1	S 43 W	1.2	1.4	71.0	45.0	25.8	...	...	...	...	...	...
15	65.5	.290	48	.627	.337	0.1	S 79 W	0.0	1.6	74.2	49.8	24.4	...	...	...	...	...	...
16	70.0	.366	49	.609	.243	0.3	S 24 W	1.0	1.0	83.2	51.5	31.7	...	...	...	...	...	...
17	71.3	.407	52	.683	.276	0.0	Calm.	0.0	0.0	78.6	62.6	16.0	...	...	...	...	...	...
18	68.6	.416	50	.671	.255	0.4	S 65 E	1.5	1.5	76.0	57.6	18.4	...	...	...	...	...	...
19	Sunday						S 20 E	0.6	1.6	81.4	59.0	22.4	...	...	...	...	...	...
20	70.8	.500	66	.746	.246	0.1	S 86 E	1.9	3.4	79.8	60.0	19.8	...	...	...	...	...	...
21	71.6	.530	68	.829	.238	0.5	N 85 E	4.5	4.7	79.2	64.0	15.2	...	...	...	...	...	...
22	74.2	.604	73	.726	.121	0.6	S 83 W	2.1	3.3	87.8	63.5	24.3	...	...	...	...	...	...
23	75.6	.606	69	.665	.050	0.1	N 29 W	2.1	4.1	86.6	63.0	23.6	...	...	...	...	...	...
24	55.5	.627	71	.624	28.997	0.2	S 10 E	0.3	2.7	80.8	60.8	20.0	...	...	...	...	...	...
25	81.8	.625	60	.520	28.896	0.5	S 88 W	0.9	10.3	93.4	70.6	22.8	...	...	...	...	...	...
26	Sunday						N 57 W	8.6	11.6	88.0	71.2	16.8	.050	0.2	...	...	.050	0.2
27	62.2	.314	60	.735	29.391	0.3	N 13 W	9.2	11.5	71.0	52.0	19.0	...	...	...	...	...	...
28	60.3	.244	48	.894	.050	0.0	S 24 E	3.0	4.3	69.2	50.2	19.0	...	...	...	...	...	...
29	51.6	.346	63	.716	.371	0.8	S 87 E	2.5	2.5	70.2	48.2	22.0	...		...	...	...	...
30	73.2	.550	68	.469	29.910	0.4	S 44 W	1.6	2.9	85.0	60.4	24.6	...	...	...	...	...	...
	63.0	0.389	63	29.635	29.274	0.3	N 55 W	1.7	4.5	73.1	52.9	20.2	0.570	11.8	...	...	0.570	11.8

19

TORONTO.
GENERAL METEOROLOGICAL ABSTRACT, JULY, 1864.

Days.	DAILY MEANS.							WIND.			EXTREMES OF TEMPERATURE.				RAIN.		SNOW.		TOTAL FALL.	
	Temperature of Air	Pressure of Vapour.	Rel. Humid.	Barometric Pressure.	Pressure of Dry Air.	Clouded Sky.	Resultant Direction.	Resultant Velocity.	Mean Velocity.	Maximum.	Minimum.	Difference.	Depth in inches.	Approximate duration.	Depth in inches	Approximate duration.	Depth in inches.	Approximate duration.
1	65.1	0.555	81	29.479	28.924	1.0	S 79 E	1.9	2.5	75.0	58.8	16.2	0.440	4.5	...	...	0.440	4.5
2	66.8	.546	83	.407	28.860	0.8	N 71 W	9.8	10.0	77.5	63.5	14.0	.007	1.0	...	...	.007	1.0
3	Sunday						N 65 W	12.7	12.7	73.5	56.2	17.3	...	...	...	...	...	...
4	63.2	.347	59	.622	29.275	0.4	N 49 W	6.6	7.0	73.0	52.2	20.8	...	...	...	...	...	...
5	67.5	.426	64	.677	.251	0.4	S 22 W	4.9	5.7	77.2	49.0	28.2	...	...	...	...	...	...
6	70.6	.513	68	.569	.056	0.8	S 62 W	3.1	4.5	83.8	59.4	24.4	...	...	...	...	...	...
7	65.3	.500	80	.513	.012	1.0	N 47 E	5.1	5.8	70.8	65.2	5.6	.005	3.0	...	...	.005	3.0
8	71.2	.507	69	.683	.176	0.3	S 57 E	0.5	3.5	79.0	61.6	17.4	...	...	...	...	...	...
9	70.2	.516	72	.750	.234	0.1	S 40 E	1.8	2.5	82.0	58.5	23.5	...	...	...	...	...	...
10	Sunday						S 18 E	1.0	1.5	74.2	60.0	14.2	.165	3.0	...	...	.165	3.0
11	72.7	.489	63	.431	28.942	0.2	N 85 W	7.9	10.8	85.0	61.2	23.8	...	...	...	...	...	...
12	68.6	.376	54	.663	29.287	0.1	N 17 W	10.2	10.5	75.6	58.2	19.8	...	...	...	...	...	...
13	68.4	.416	60	.804	.388	0.2	S 60 W	1.6	5.0	76.0	57.5	18.5	...	...	...	...	...	...
14	71.0	.423	57	.761	.338	0.1	S 88 E	3.7	4.5	82.8	57.5	25.3	...	...	...	...	...	...
15	72.2	.512	66	.705	.193	0.2	S 72 E	2.1	3.8	84.4	63.8	20.6	...	...	...	...	...	...
16	76.6	.536	59	.680	.144	0.0	S 1 W	0.8	4.1	88.2	61.4	26.8	...	...	...	...	...	...
17	Sunday						N 79 E	3.9	4.5	81.0	68.8	12.2	...	...	...	...	...	...
18	75.3	.595	69	.795	.200	0.6	S 65 E	3.2	3.7	85.0	65.0	20.0	...	...	...	...	...	...
19	76.7	.552	63	.721	.169	0.2	S 13 W	4.4	4.5	87.0	66.2	20.8	...	...	...	...	...	...
20	73.8	.444	56	.557	.113	0.6	N 48 W	12.0	13.0	88.0	63.8	24.2	...	...	...	...	...	...
21	61.4	.256	49	.712	.456	0.0	N 28 W	13.8	13.9	69.0	53.2	15.8	...	...	...	...	...	...
22	62.7	.235	44	.730	.495	0.3	N 37 W	8.6	8.6	74.6	50.0	24.6	...	...	...	...	...	...
23	66.2	.343	54	.708	.365	0.5	S 73 W	3.7	5.1	82.4	51.2	31.2	...	...	...	...	...	...
24	Sunday						S 51 E	2.2	3.8	78.0	57.0	21.0	...	...	...	...	...	...
25	65.8	.490	78	.546	.056	1.0	N 1 W	3.5	7.8	73.0	61.0	12.0	.330	8.5	...	...	.330	8.5
26	66.8	.556	85	.609	.053	0.8	S 68 W	3.3	5.1	78.8	61.6	17.2	.215	2.7	...	...	.215	2.7
27	71.1	.562	74	.730	.168	0.0	S 65 W	1.9	3.6	81.5	59.0	22.5	...	...	...	...	...	...
28	75.3	.563	67	.552	28.989	0.7	S 80 W	7.1	8.4	88.2	60.5	27.7	.010	0.8	...	...	.010	0.8
29	72.4	.511	65	.486	28.975	0.2	N 37 W	2.1	4.5	80.0	65.5	14.5	...	...	...	...	...	...
30	73.1	.535	66	.464	28.929	0.4	S 16 W	1.4	1.8	81.2	63.0	18.2	...	...	...	...	...	...
31	Sunday						S 18 W	2.5	3.3	80.2	63.6	16.6	.100	1.2	...	...	.100	1.2
	69.7	0.473	66	29.020	29.556	0.4	N 61 W	2.2	6.0	80.0	59.8	20.2	1.332	24.7	...	...	1.332	24.7

TORONTO.
GENERAL METEOROLOGICAL ABSTRACT, AUGUST, 1864.

Days.	DAILY MEANS.						WIND.			EXTREMES OF TEMPERATURE.			RAIN.		SNOW.		TOTAL FALL.	
	Temperature of Air.	Pressure of Vapour.	Rel. Humid.	Barometric Pressure.	Pressure of Dry Air.	Clouded Sky.	Resultant Direction.	Resultant Velocity.	Mean Velocity.	Maximum.	Minimum.	Difference.	Depth in inches.	Approximate duration.	Depth in inches.	Approximate duration.	Depth in inches.	Approximate duration.
1	73.9	0.674	76	29.409	28.735	0.0	S 42 W	5.2	6.3	88.2	67.2	21.0	0.930	9.2	...	...	0.930	9.2
2	70.1	.571	78	.491	28.920	0.8	N 41 E	3.7	5.0	75.0	64.8	10.2	R	1.0	...	...	R	1.0
3	66.4	.459	71	.492	29.033	0.7	N 14 E	4.9	5.4	76.0	64.0	12.0	R	0.4	...	...	R	0.4
4	68.0	.517	76	.485	28.918	0.4	S 35 W	1.0	2.0	76.4	61.4	15.0	...	...	...	...	...	...
5	70.4	.550	74	.597	29.017	0.8	S 53 E	0.9	1.1	79.0	61.2	17.8	...	...	...	...	...	...
6	71.4	.543	71	.703	.160	0.8	S 13 E	1.4	2.4	80.4	64.0	16.4	...	...	...	...	...	...
7	Sunday						S 87 W	2.7	3.9	81.5	61.6	19.9	...	...	...	...	...	...
8	78.8	.563	60	.646	.083	0.0	N 68 W	5.0	6.2	94.0	64.8	29.2	...	...	...	...	...	...
9	77.3	.537	58	.500	28.963	0.8	S 58 W	4.9	5.5	92.0	66.4	25.6	...	...	...	...	...	...
10	80.2	.685	66	.431	28.746	0.9	S 55 W	3.3	3.8	92.8	69.9	22.9	...	...	...	...	...	...
11	76.0	.634	70	.494	28.860	1.0	N 39 E	1.9	2.4	86.0	71.0	15.0	.210	1.2	...	...	.210	1.2
12	72.6	.614	76	.531	28.917	1.0	S 73 W	2.2	3.1	79.8	66.8	13.0	.320	3.1	...	...	.320	3.1
13	72.0	.670	85	.455	28.779	0.4	S 77 W	4.6	5.7	82.0	69.6	12.4	.905	3.0	...	...	.905	3.0
14	Sunday						N 51 W	3.0	4.2	82.5	62.0	20.5	...	...	...	...	...	...
15	70.3	.495	68	.643	29.148	0.3	S 89 E	2.8	3.9	80.0	58.0	22.0	...	...	...	...	...	...
16	71.9	.594	76	.602	.008	0.9	N 28 W	1.4	1.7	81.2	64.0	17.2	...	...	...	...	...	...
17	70.4	.442	60	.610	.168	1.0	N 7 W	8.4	8.8	79.0	68.2	10.8	R	...	...	...	R	..
18	66.4	.400	69	.742	.342	1.0	N 47 E	1.0	2.2	71.2	58.5	12.7	...	...	...	...	...	...
19	64.5	.416	67	.814	.398	1.0	N 50 E	1.4	2.7	74.5	54.5	17.0	.005	0.5	...	...	.005	0.5
20	62.4	.471	83	.741	.270	1.0	N 88 E	9.5	10.3	67.2	60.1	7.1	.905	17.7	...	...	.905	17.7
21	Sunday						S 86 E	2.9	3.4	69.5	59.2	10.3	.300	9.5	...	...	.300	9.5
22	65.0	.538	84	.551	.013	1.0	N 39 W	3.9	4.0	68.8	65.0	3.8	R	0.2	...	...	R	0.2
23	64.3	.500	83	.638	.138	0.5	S 57 W	1.7	2.2	73.0	53.5	19.5	...	...	...	...	...	...
24	70.6	.606	81	.509	28.904	0.7	S 11 W	2.2	2.8	78.2	62.2	16.0	...	...	...	...	...	...
25	69.3	.592	78	.353	28.771	0.5	S 40 W	4.8	5.8	77.2	63.8	13.4	.030	1.0	...	...	.030	1.0
26	63.3	.479	82	.289	28.810	0.7	S 53 E	2.4	5.1	74.0	55.5	18.5	1.325	9.5	...	...	1.325	9.5
27	61.6	.425	79	.149	28.725	0.0	S 53 W	9.5	9.7	70.0	56.8	13.2	.010	0.5	...	...	.010	0.5
28	Sunday						N 82 W	7.1	7.8	58.4	56.0	12.4	.105	0.8	...	...	.105	0.8
29	59.7	.391	76	.455	29.067	0.8	N 70 W	8.1	8.8	67.5	53.8	13.7	...	...	...	...	...	...
30	57.0	.264	57	.617	.088	0.0	N 27 W	7.1	7.7	76.2	53.0	13.2	.015	0.2	...	...	.015	0.2
31	57.2	.398	66	.785	.10	0.0	S 78 W	1.1	2.8	70.0	47.0	19.0	...	...	...	...	...	...
	68.6	0.516	73	29.515	29.029	0.7	N 70 W	1.4	4.8	77.2	61.4	15.8	5.060	57.8	...	...	5.060	57.8

20

TORONTO.
General Meteorological Abstract, September, 1864.

Days.	DAILY MEANS.					WIND.			EXTREMES OF TEMPERATURE.			RAIN.		SNOW.		TOTAL FALL.	
	Temperature of Air.	Pressure of Vapour.	Rel. Humid.	Barometer Pressure.	Pressure of dry Air.	Clouded Sky.	Resultant Direction.	Resultant Velocity.	Mean Velocity.	Maximum.	Minimum.	Difference.	Depth in Inches.	Approximate duration.	Depth in Inches.	Approximate duration.	Depth in Inches.	Approximate duration.
1	59.5	0.362	71	29.773	29.411	0.8	S 47 W	1.0	1.6	71.4	46.0	25.4	...	...	...	...	...	...
2	61.0	.425	77	.641	.216	0.8	N 65 E	1.9	2.0	67.0	55.8	11.2	R	0.6	...	...	R	0.6
3	61.7	.416	76	.519	.103	0.3	N 72 E	2.6	3.8	70.8	54.5	16.3	...	...	...	...	...	...
4	Sunday						N 62 E	4.9	5.5	70.6	54.5	16.1	0.005	0.5	...	...	.005	0.5
5	57.9	.366	76	.702	.336	1.0	N 59 E	9.4	9.7	70.5	55.2	5.3	...	...	...	...	...	...
6	58.3	.336	69	.808	.532	0.2	N 72 E	6.9	7.6	65.0	54.0	11.0	...	...	...	...	...	...
7	59.9	.354	68	.926	.572	0.5	S 80 E	8.0	8.6	67.6	50.6	17.0	.040	0.8	...	...	.040	0.8
8	58.5	.426	57	.773	.347	1.0	S 7 E	3.1	3.6	61.0	56.5	4.5	.005	5.8	...	...	.005	5.8
9	65.4	.519	83	.565	.046	0.8	S 70 W	3.4	4.9	73.0	56.0	17.0	...	...	...	...	...	...
10	60.5	.434	82	.507	.073	0.7	N 88 E	1.0	3.8	67.2	52.4	14.8	.025	1.0	...	...	.025	1.0
11	Sunday						N 23 W	9.0	9.4	66.5	54.2	12.3	...	...	...	...	...	...
12	55.0	.277	64	.680	.403	0.6	N 3 W	8.6	8.7	63.5	46.4	17.1	...	...	...	...	...	...
13	57.1	.251	56	.587	.336	0.0	N 24 W	7.4	7.7	59.8	46.4	13.4	...	...	...	...	...	...
14	55.2	.394	90	.313	25.919	0.8	S 47 W	5.3	7.0	61.5	43.2	18.3	.290	3.8	...	...	.290	3.8
15	55.6	.332	75	.382	29.050	0.4	N 76 W	13.5	13.9	63.0	53.2	9.8	...	...	...	...	...	...
16	52.7	.262	67	.595	.333	0.3	N 40 W	5.1	5.4	64.8	47.0	17.8	...	...	...	...	...	...
17	53.4	.310	76	.589	.280	0.2	S 69 E	2.0	2.9	61.8	37.8	24.0	...	...	...	...	...	...
18	Sunday						S 51 W	5.6	8.0	70.0	51.2	18.8	.835	3.0	...	...	.835	3.0
19	51.1	.264	71	.606	.342	0.7	N 81 W	4.6	4.7	58.8	44.5	14.3	...	...	...	...	...	...
20	55.5	.259	62	.647	.388	0.6	S 82 W	6.6	6.9	69.8	42.8	27.0	...	...	...	...	...	...
21	55.3	.325	75	.682	.357	0.6	N 45 E	4.5	6.4	63.0	44.0	19.0	...	...	...	...	...	...
22	52.2	.334	84	.592	.258	0.8	N 66 E	6.7	6.7	56.8	46.8	10.0	...	...	...	...	...	...
23	63.3	.510	87	.377	28.867	0.8	S 20 W	6.0	6.9	70.0	51.6	18.4	.078	1.5	...	...	.078	1.5
24	57.2	.329	66	.314	28.985	0.8	N 80 W	13.9	14.6	66.0	58.6	7.4	...	...	...	...	...	...
25	Sunday						N 63 W	9.4	9.5	55.4	42.4	13.0	...	...	...	...	...	...
26	49.7	.295	82	.508	29.303	0.6	N 75 E	4.2	5.7	56.0	42.0	14.0	R	R	...	...	R	R
27	60.4	.416	80	.427	.011	0.7	S 58 W	9.3	12.7	68.8	47.0	21.4	.080	7.0	...	...	.080	7.0
28	52.0	.287	74	.785	.489	0.2	N 35 W	3.6	0.8	60.0	49.7	10.3	...	...	...	...	...	...
29	50.9	.331	86	.555	.224	0.5	N 20 W	6.2	11.1	59.6	43.0	16.6	1.150	7.0	...	...	1.150	7.0
30	41.6	.214	73	.850	.636	0.8	N 14 E	4.9	5.2	49.0	41.2	7.8	...	...	...	...	...	...
	56.4	0.347	75	29.610	29.263	0.6	N 38 W	1.9	7.1	73.9	48.9	15.0	2.508	31.0	...	...	2.508	31.0

TORONTO.
GENERAL METEOROLOGICAL ABSTRACT, OCTOBER, 1864.

Days.	DAILY MEANS.						WIND.			EXTREMES OF TEMPERATURE.			RAIN.		SNOW.		TOTAL FALL.	
	Temperature of Air.	Pressure of Vapour.	Rel. Humid.	Barometric Pressure.	Pressure of Dry Air.	Clouded Sky.	Resultant Direction.	Resultant Velocity.	Mean Velocity.	Maximum.	Minimum.	Difference.	Depth in inches.	Approximate duration.	Depth in inches.	Approximate duration.	Depth in inches.	Approximate duration.
1	47.8	0.270	80	29.775	29.506	1.6	N 66 E	11.8	11.9	52.0	43.2	8.8	1.190	13.0	...	...	1.190	13.0
2	Sunday						N 70 E	2.9	3.0	56.0	48.0	8.0	.030	2.7	...	...	.030	2.7
3	54.6	.385	91	.816	.432	1.0	N 57 E	2.1	3.8	58.0	50.0	8.0	.010	1.5	...	...	.010	1.5
4	54.2	.302	86	.825	.463	0.7	N 27 W	1.0	1.5	63.4	53.4	10.0	...	...	...	...	...	...
5	53.8	.371	89	.657	.286	0.6	N 76 E	4.1	4.3	60.4	46.4	14.0	.405	9.2	...	...	.405	9.2
6	56.9	.406	85	.268	28.862	0.4	S 49 W	6.3	8.0	67.0	54.6	12.4	.010	2.5	...	...	.010	2.5
7	52.5	.308	77	.172	28.864	1.0	S 49 W	8.6	9.0	60.0	49.0	11.0	.018	1.8	...	...	.018	1.8
8	38.3	.169	72	.236	29.069	0.9	N 35 W	10.1	16.4	44.5	36.4	8.1	.035	1.5	S	1.0	.035	2.5
9	Sunday						S 73 W	7.0	8.0	48.0	29.8	18.2	...	...	...	...	...	...
10	47.0	.213	67	.394	.181	0.5	N 85 W	10.9	12.7	57.2	36.4	20.8	...	...	...	...	...	...
11	43.2	.215	77	.719	.504	0.6	N 63 W	1.2	3.2	51.8	35.2	16.6	R	0.2	...	...	R	0.2
12	41.9	.236	68	.519	.283	0.7	N 44 W	5.4	5.8	49.2	39.5	9.7	.200	4.2	...	...	.200	4.2
13	39.8	.177	74	.544	.367	0.7	N 33 W	9.1	9.3	48.2	32.0	16.2	.008	3.0	...	...	.008	3.0
14	41.0	.167	66	.481	.314	0.0	N 37 W	7.5	7.8	51.5	32.6	18.9	...	...	...	...	...	...
15	41.9	.181	67	.337	.156	0.2	N 65 W	3.9	5.2	54.0	28.0	26.0	.230	3.0	...	...	.230	3.0
16	Sunday						N 86 W	9.7	10.7	48.2	39.6	8.6	.085	3.5	...	...	.085	3.5
17	39.4	.170	71	.603	.433	0.5	S 86 W	8.4	8.5	48.4	34.0	14.4	...	...	...	...	...	...
18	41.3	.192	74	.433	.241	1.0	S 86 W	6.4	7.3	48.0	28.8	19.2	.020	2.0	...	...	.020	2.0
19	41.9	.206	78	.424	.216	0.9	N 80 W	6.4	6.7	50.5	40.0	10.5	.018	1.2	...	...	.018	1.2
20	42.0	.201	75	.613	.412	0.8	N 71 W	6.3	8.5	50.2	32.4	17.8	...	...	...	...	...	...
21	42.8	.213	79	.656	.442	0.6	N 65 W	3.4	3.9	50.0	39.2	10.8	.012	0.2	...	...	.012	0.2
22	44.9	.216	73	.461	.245	1.0	N 81 W	4.8	5.2	54.0	35.2	18.8	...	...	...	...	...	...
23	Sunday						S 80 W	1.5	3.0	52.8	42.0	10.8	.015	0.5	...	...	.015	0.5
24	42.3	.236	87	.527	.291	1.0	N 8 W	3.6	3.0	44.8	41.6	3.2	R	0.5	...	...	R	0.5
25	42.9	.216	76	.733	.523	0.3	S 77 W	1.2	4.3	51.4	37.2	14.2	...	...	...	...	...	...
26	43.9	.237	82	.668	.431	0.7	N 75 E	7.4	7.7	49.5	34.8	14.7	R	R	...	...	R	R
27	47.2	.306	94	.509	.003	1.0	N 82 E	4.9	5.3	50.0	43.0	7.0	.110	11.0	...	...	.110	11.0
28	48.5	.326	94	.130	28.816	1.0	N 60 W	10.2	10.8	51.5	46.8	4.7	.720	21.0	...	...	.720	21.0
29	45.3	.283	93	.463	29.180	1.0	N 46 W	1.1	1.9	50.2	45.0	6.2	.155	15.5	...	...	.155	15.5
30	Sunday						N 67 W	1.5	3.2	50.0	39.6	10.4	.055	3.0	...	...	.055	3.0
31	39.6	.197	80	.775	.578	0.9	N 11 W	4.3	5.0	43.0	38.0	5.0	...	...	...	...	...	...
	45.2	0.248	80	29.521	29.273	0.7	N 60 W	5.2	6.7	52.0	39.7	12.3	3.321	101.0	S	1.0	3.321	102.0

TORONTO.
GENERAL METEOROLOGICAL ABSTRACT, NOVEMBER, 1864.

Days.	DAILY MEANS.					WIND.			EXTREMES OF TEMPERATURE.			RAIN.		SNOW.		TOTAL FALL.	
	Temperature of Air.	Pressure of Vapour.	Rel. Humid.	Barometric Pressure.	Pressure of Dry Air.	Clouded Sky.	Resultant Direction.	Resultant Velocity.	Mean Velocity.	Maximum.	Minimum.	Difference.	Depth in inches.	Approximate duration.	Depth in inches.	Approximate duration.	Depth in inches.	Approximate duration.
1	34.8	0.137	69	29.972	29.835	0.5	N 21 W	3.4	3.6	42.2	33.5	8.7	...	...	...	...	...	...
2	35.5	.164	79	.887	.723	0.9	N 61 W	1.9	2.5	41.4	26.2	15.2	...	...	...	...	...	...
3	38.3	.162	69	.528	.366	1.0	S 87 E	8.4	9.3	44.0	33.6	10.4	0.620	5.0	...	...	.620	5.0
4	37.8	.202	87	28.867	28.665	0.9	N 47 W	7.8	12.7	43.8	36.0	7.8	.225	9.5	S	S	.225	9.5
5	29.7	.115	70	29.468	29.353	0.3	N 63 W	8.3	8.8	37.0	28.2	8.8	...	...	S	0.5	S	0.5
6	Sunday						S 10 E	5.9	7.7	48.2	24.0	24.2	.065	3.0	...	...	.065	3.0
7	45.3	.246	82	.703	.458	0.3	S 33 W	6.1	6.1	54.0	39.6	14.4	...	...	...	...	...	...
8	40.3	.295	93	.629	.334	1.0	N 82 E	5.8	6.7	55.2	37.8	17.4	.705	20.7	...	...	.705	20.7
9	55.1	.402	92	.083	28.680	0.8	S 35 W	14.0	14.8	60.2	45.1	14.8	.720	11.5	...	...	.720	11.5
10	40.6	.155	62	.183	29.028	0.9	S 60 W	20.2	20.2	47.2	41.0	6.2	...	...	...	...	...	...
11	34.2	.147	75	.312	.164	1.0	S 72 W	10.1	10.3	41.5	33.4	8.1	...	...	...	...	...	...
12	30.3	.125	73	.426	.301	0.7	N 48 W	9.6	10.0	38.8	24.5	14.3	...	...	...	...	...	...
13	Sunday						N 52 W	9.0	9.1	33.0	25.4	7.6	...	...	S	1.0	S	1.0
14	28.2	.111	71	.859	.748	0.8	S 33 W	0.8	6.1	34.6	21.1	13.5	...	...	1.5	3.5	.150	3.5
15	29.2	.129	80	.711	.582	0.9	N 14 W	3.2	6.0	32.0	26.6	5.4	...	...	3.0	4.5	.300	4.5
16	31.8	.146	81	30.028	.882	0.9	S 58 E	3.9	5.3	36.4	23.0	13.4	...	...	...	...	...	...
17	37.8	.204	90	29.714	.510	1.0	S 87 W	3.3	5.5	41.2	32.5	8.7	.005	5.0	...	...	.005	5.0
18	34.8	.147	73	.754	.607	0.4	S 76 W	9.4	9.6	42.5	28.6	13.9	...	...	...	...	...	...
19	34.5	.155	77	.721	.560	0.5	S 26 W	4.0	4.2	40.0	27.9	12.1	...	...	...	...	...	...
20	Sunday						S 32 E	3.9	5.6	43.0	27.0	16.0	.035	0.5	...	...	.035	0.5
21	30.4	.169	73	.273	.114	1.0	S 73 W	8.3	8.8	43.0	36.5	6.5	...	...	...	...	...	...
22	28.5	.115	73	.306	.191	0.9	S 80 W	13.0	13.8	31.4	28.0	3.4	...	...	S	1.5	S	1.5
23	24.5	.087	66	.768	.681	0.5	N 57 W	6.3	7.0	31.0	21.6	9.4	...	...	S	1.0	S	1.0
24	30.7	.143	83	30.015	.872	1.0	S 52 W	2.4	2.5	33.6	21.0	12.6	...	...	S	1.0	S	1.0
25	34.2	.149	76	30.46	.897	0.7	S 13 W	1.8	1.9	39.4	25.8	10.6	...	...	...	...	...	...
26	39.2	.219	91	29.677	.458	1.0	S 8 W	4.9	5.3	42.5	32.2	10.3	.315	11.0	...	...	.315	11.0
27	Sunday						S 56 W	1.3	3.2	45.0	33.6	11.4	...	...	...	...	...	...
28	44.4	.284	96	.373	.089	1.0	S 16 E	2.2	4.7	50.0	33.0	17.6	1.020	24.0	...	...	1.020	24.0
29	50.6	.343	93	.205	28.862	0.5	S 45 W	5.2	5.3	60.2	45.0	15.2	.055	1.5	...	...	.055	1.5
30	46.9	.195	61	.548	29.353	0.3	S 86 W	13.0	13.1	52.5	44.4	8.1	R	R	...	...	R	R
	36.9	.182	78	29.579	29.397	0.8	S 72 W	3.8	7.6	42.8	31.3	11.5	3.765	91.7	4.5	13.0	4.215	104.7

23

TORONTO.
General Meteorological Abstract, December, 1864.

Days.	DAILY MEANS.					WIND.			EXTREMES OF TEMPERATURE.			RAIN.		SNOW.		TOTAL FALL.	
	Temperature of Air.	Pressure of Vapour.	Rel. Humid.	Barometric Pressure.	Pressure of Dry Air.	Clouded Sky.	Resultant Direction.	Resultant Velocity.	Mean Velocity.	Maximum.	Minimum.	Difference.	Depth in inches.	Approximate duration.	Depth in inches.	Approximate duration.	Depth in inches.	Approximate duration.
1	38.9	0.185	78	29.82	29.644	0.7	N 64 W	2.6	4.3	45.0	32.6	12.4	...	...	...	...	...	...
2	38.0	.212	92		.571	.359	1.0	N 78 E	12.6	13.6	43.0	33.8	9.2	1.130	17.8	...	...	1.130	17.8
3	41.5	.205	78		.205	.060	0.8	S 77 W	13.1	14.9	50.4	36.0	14.4	.250	3.5	...	...	.250	3.5
4	Sunday						S 82 W	10.7	10.8	36.8	31.6	5.2	...	...	S	1.0	S	1.0
5	33.9	.155	70	.488	.333	1.0	S 36 E	3.8	4.6	39.0	25.5	13.5	R	0.2	S	1.5	S R	1.8
6	38.0	.189	81	.368	.180	1.0	S 57 W	6.2	6.9	43.4	33.0	10.4	R	1.5	1.0	1.5	.100	3.0
7	31.7	.159	87	.160	.001	1.0	S 80 W	11.6	15.4	37.8	30.8	7.0	.465	8.0	1.8	8.0	.645	16.0
8	11.6	.057	75	.820	.763	0.3	S 74 W	22.3	22.7	16.5	9.6	6.9	...	...	0.1	0.5	.010	0.5
9	18.4	.078	77	30.156	30.078	0.6	S 74 E	9.1	10.7	27.0	6.3	20.7	...	...	4.0	7.2	.400	7.2
10	26.2	.125	87	29.646	29.521	0.8	N 85 E	1.1	6.6	32.4	23.0	9.4	...	...	3.0	7.8	.300	7.5
11	Sunday						S 83 W	10.2	17.2	33.0	18.5	14.6	...	...	5.0	14.2	.500	14.2
12	8.0	.048	74	.697	.649	0.6	N 69 W	10.6	10.7	14.8	9.0	5.8	...	...	...	...	...	...
13	19.8	.098	87	.562	.463	1.0	S 30 W	9.1	11.7	29.1	-1.5	30.6	...	...	1.0	13.0	.100	13.0
14	17.5	.087	80	.567	.480	0.7	N 74 W	9.9	10.8	30.0	23.6	6.4	...	...	0.2	1.5	.020	1.5
15	16.4	.094	87	.779	.695	0.9	S 77 E	1.7	4.6	26.0	-2.5	28.5	...	...	0.1	5.0	.010	5.0
16	27.6	.141	92	.697	.555	1.0	S 85 E	1.9	4.0	35.2	17.7	17.5	R	0.2	0.1	2.7	.010	2.9
17	33.2	.164	85	.795	.634	0.7	N 76 W	5.1	6.4	38.0	26.2	11.8	...	...	...	...	...	...
18	Sunday						N 80 W	6.6	7.9	33.6	19.8	13.8	.175	1.5	...	...	.175	1.5
19	29.4	.121	71	.292	.171	0.7	N 79 W	15.8	16.7	37.5	28.0	9.5	.015	0.2	0.1	0.4	.025	0.6
20	23.0	.096	75	.550	.450	0.8	S 54 W	8.1	8.5	27.2	14.6	12.6	...	...	...	...	...	...
21	21.6	.111	93	.049	28.938	1.0	N 2 E	11.8	15.5	28.6	22.6	5.4	...	...	10.0	18.6	1.000	18.0
22	1.4	.036	78	.696	29.570	0.2	N 87 W	11.7	12.8	11.6	0.8	10.8	...	...	...	...	...	...
23	11.6	.068	88	.625	.560	1.0	S 65 W	10.6	11.0	21.0	-10.4	31.4	...	...	0.1	6.5	.010	6.5
24	25.9	.126	84	.646	.520	1.0	S 53 W	8.8	9.1	32.2	14.6	17.6	...	...	...	...	...	...
25	Sunday						S 33 W	7.8	7.9	38.6	25.0	13.0	...	...	0.2	4.0	.020	4.0
26	...	...	...	...	...	...	S 8 E	0.5	0.9	37.0	32.0	5.0	...	...	...	...	...	...
27	38.1	.206	90	.094	28.888	0.8	S 1 E	3.9	5.2	42.6	34.0	8.1	.010	3.5	...	...	.010	3.5
28	29.9	.136	81	.241	29.105	0.5	S 76 W	9.2	8.1	36.4	28.6	7.8	...	...	...	...	...	...
29	21.7	.085	74	.267	.122	1.0	S 84 W	10.6	11.4	26.0	20.7	5.2	...	...	0.1	1.7	.010	1.7
30	23.0	.109	87	.214	.105	0.7	S 75 W	10.8	11.4	30.6	19.0	11.6	...	...	0.3	1.0	.030	1.0
31	15.0	.060	79	.612	.574	0.7	N 54 W	7.5	7.8	21.2	9.0	12.2	...	...	...	...	...	...
	24.7	0.121	82	29.529	29.399	0.7	S 82 W	4.9	10.0	32.2	19.7	12.5	2.015	36.5	27.1	95.2	4.755	131.7

TORONTO.
GENERAL METEOROLOGICAL ABSTRACT, JANUARY, 1865.

Days.	DAILY MEANS.						WIND.			EXTREMES OF TEMPERATURE			RAIN.		SNOW.		TOTAL FALL.	
	Temperature of Air.	Pressure of Vapour.	Rel. Humid.	Barometric Pressure.	Pressure of dry Air.	Clouded Sky.	Resultant Direction.	Resultant Velocity.	Mean Velocity.	Maximum.	Minimum.	Difference.	Depth in inches.	Approximate duration.	Depth in inches.	Approximate duration.	Depth in Inches.	Approximate duration.
1	Su nday						S 66 W	7.1	8.3	23.2	3.5	19.7	...	...	S	0.2	S	0.2
2	21.6	0.086	74	29.728	29.642	0.3	S 87 W	7.1	7.4	29.0	16.2	12.8	...	...	S	0.2	S	0.2
3	19.3	.088	80	.706	.618	0.5	S 83 W	4.9	5.4	27.0	9.0	15.0	...	...	S	1.0	S	1.0
4	13.5	.058	73	.818	.760	0.3	N 43 W	7.2	10.0	26.4	11.9	14.5	...	...	0.1	0.6	.010	0.6
5	32.6	.144	77	.526	.382	0.9	S 34 W	9.4	9.7	37.2	5.8	31.4	...	...	...	...	...	...
6	28.3	.122	77	.516	.394	1.0	N 2 W	11.8	12.0	36.0	29.2	6.8	...	...	...	...	...	...
7	5.9	.046	79	.765	.719	0.6	N 12 W	13.0	13.2	10.0	3.8	6.2	...	...	S	0.2	S	0.2
8	Su uday						S 14 W	6.0	7.9	28.4	-2.0	30.4	...	...	0.7	5.0	.070	5.0
9	29.3	.139	86	.770	.631	1.0	S 50 W	4.6	5.0	33.5	19.4	14.1	...	...	1.5	5.5	.150	5.5
10	17.6	.087	84	.425	.338	1.0	N 9 W	16.0	17.8	26.0	18.3	7.7	...	...	7.0	15.0	.700	15.0
11	12.4	.069	87	.590	.520	0.7	S 58 W	9.6	9.9	23.0	0.0	23.0	...	...	...	...	...	...
12	25.5	.110	80	.594	.484	0.7	S 63 W	13.8	12.9	29.5	15.7	13.8	...	...	...	...	...	...
13	30.5	.146	85	.492	.346	1.0	S 41 W	4.0	4.0	34.8	23.0	11.8	...	...	2.0	6.3	.200	6.3
14	18.5	.089	83	.308	.219	0.7	N 30 W	8.8	9.5	28.5	16.2	12.3	...	...	0.5	5.0	.050	5.0
15	Su nday						N 16 W	5.2	5.5	18.5	10.5	8.0	...	...	0.2	3.5	.020	3.5
16	6.0	.053	95	.331	.278	0.7	N 84 W	3.7	7.2	15.5	-5.0	20.5	...	...	0.4	6.0	.040	6.0
17	1.8	.041	85	.289	.248	0.7	N 14 W	7.4	7.9	7.2	3.7	3.5	...	...	1.0	8.0	.100	8.0
18	5.3	.045	81	.640	.600	0.1	S 66 W	12.0	12.2	14.8	-9.0	23.8	...	...	...	...	...	...
19	11.0	.062	84	.720	.658	0.7	S 78 W	5.0	5.3	16.0	6.4	9.6	...	...	...	...	...	...
20	17.6	.070	79	.893	.814	0.3	S 65 E	4.5	6.3	26.0	2.5	23.5	...	...	...	...	...	...
21	25.0	.111	83	.674	.563	0.9	N 79 E	13.4	13.9	28.2	17.2	11.0	...	...	...	...	...	...
22	Su nday						N 30 E	1.4	7.0	36.5	20.7	15.8	0.440	10.0	1.0	3.0	.540	13.0
23	27.4	.131	85	.308	.177	1.0	N 66 W	8.4	9.9	36.0	30.0	6.0	...	...	0.2	4.0	.020	4.0
24	17.9	.076	77	.304	.228	0.7	S 79 W	18.1	18.1	23.0	15.6	7.4	...	...	...	...	...	...
25	11.9	.058	77	.371	.314	0.9	S 55 W	16.1	16.1	14.6	10.4	4.2	...	...	...	...	...	...
26	10.4	.057	82	.381	.324	1.0	S 65 W	13.2	13.2	13.0	10.6	2.4	...	...	0.1	1.0	.010	1.0
27	7.4	.049	80	.444	.395	0.7	S 84 W	10.4	10.5	14.8	2.8	12.0	...	...	...	...	...	...
28	16.9	.081	82	.631	.550	1.0	N 44 W	9.0	10.3	23.5	4.6	18.9	...	...	0.1	1.5	.010	1.5
29	Su uday						N 39 W	4.9	5.2	23.0	10.0	13.0	...	...	...	...	...	...
30	17.7	.085	84	30.121	30.036	1.0	S 56 W	4.3	4.5	27.0	4.8	10.0	...	...	...	...	...	...
31	28.4	.132	84	29.950	29.818	0.3	S 63 W	4.3	4.3	32.8	7.0	25.8	...	...	S	0.8	S	0.8
	17.8	0.086	81	29.589	29.502	0.7	N 85 W	4.8	9.4	24.6	10.1	14.5	0.440	10.0	14.8	66.8	1.920	76.8

TORONTO.
GENERAL METEOROLOGICAL ABSTRACT, FEBRUARY, 1865.

Days.	DAILY MEANS.						WIND.			EXTREMES OF TEMPERATURE.			RAIN.		SNOW.		TOTAL FALL.	
	Temperature of Air	Pressure of Vapour	Rel. Humid.	Barometric Pressure	Pressure of Dry Air	Clouded Sky	Resultant Direction	Resultant Velocity	Mean Velocity	Maximum	Minimum	Difference	Depth in inches	Approximate duration	Depth in inches	Approximate duration	Depth in inches	Approximate duration
1	25.3	0.130	82	30.005	29.875	0.7	N 25 W	6.3	6.9	34.8	28.5	6.3	...	...	...	...	...	...
2	18.8	.087	82	30.123	30.037	0.4	N 82 E	8.1	9.5	29.4	9.8	19.6	...	...	...	...	...	...
3	31.3	.154	87	29.645	29.491	1.0	S 82 E	4.8	4.8	34.8	19.7	15.1	0.240	15.8	8	0.2	0.240	16.0
4	34.9	.164	80	.448	.284	1.0	N 84 W	13.9	14.6	40.4	30.4	10.0	.050	2.0	...	...	.050	2.0
5	Sunday						N 56 W	14.6	15.3	25.0	19.1	5.9	...	...	S	1.0	S	1.0
6	16.2	.073	80	.796	.723	1.0	N 5 E	2.7	3.3	20.8	11.2	9.6	...	...	...	...	...	...
7	17.7	.086	89	.589	.503	1.0	N 23 E	9.7	10.2	21.0	15.6	5.4	...	...	2.5	17.0	.250	17.0
8	16.9	.086	93	.200	.113	1.0	N 37 W	17.3	17.4	20.6	16.8	3.8	...	...	6.5	19.0	.650	19.0
9	14.2	.067	91	.427	.360	0.6	N 66 W	9.8	12.8	21.2	9.0	12.2	...	...	...	...	...	...
10	21.8	.090	78	.361	.271	0.9	N 60 W	13.0	14.9	27.8	9.2	18.6	...	...	0.4	3.0	.040	3.0
11	9.6	.057	85	.092	.034	0.7	N 21 E	5.2	5.5	15.0	4.8	10.2	...	...	0.3	6.0	.030	6.0
12	Sunday						N 17 W	8.1	8.3	10.6	0.0	10.6	...	...	...	...	...	...
13	5.4	.047	81	30.090	30.043	0.5	S 74 W	2.8	3.0	16.0	-10.0	26.0	...	...	...	...	...	...
14	13.1	.066	80	29.767	29.701	0.3	N 16 W	1.8	2.0	24.2	0.3	23.9	...	...	...	...	...	...
15	19.2	.094	90	.430	.336	0.0	N 56 E	10.3	10.6	26.0	11.3	14.7	...	...	2.0	10.7	.200	10.7
16	24.3	.116	89	.284	.168	1.0	N 29 E	1.0	1.0	29.0	19.5	9.5	...	...	0.6	3.0	.060	3.0
17	28.7	.130	86	.361	.225	1.0	N 69 E	5.1	5.3	32.8	21.7	11.1	...	...	...	...	...	...
18	29.1	.142	87	.508	.366	1.0	N 78 W	5.2	6.1	34.6	26.6	8.0	...	...	1.5	10.5	.150	10.5
19	Sunday						N 57 W	7.0	7.4	31.3	14.4	16.9	...	...	...	...	...	...
20	21.5	.095	82	30.043	.948	0.0	N 8 W	2.8	2.7	31.4	15.0	16.4	...	...	...	...	...	...
21	27.6	.120	83	30.058	.932	0.1	N 87 E	8.5	8.4	31.9	14.0	17.9	...	...	...	...	...	...
22	35.6	.176	84	29.716	.539	0.0	S 35 W	5.7	7.9	42.2	27.0	15.2	.085	2.2	...	...	.085	2.2
23	29.4	.107	66	.769	.662	0.7	N 80 W	9.3	9.3	45.3	28.6	16.9	...	...	...	...	...	...
24	20.8	.091	79	.963	.872	0.0	S 25 E	0.8	2.6	31.3	14.6	16.4	...	...	...	...	...	...
25	27.8	.134	80	.656	.522	0.7	N 78 E	13.1	13.3	37.0	14.6	22.4	.435	9.1	...	...	.435	9.1
26	Sunday						S 89 W	10.7	13.9	42.2	29.4	12.8	R	0.7	...	...	R	0.7
27	25.4	.090	75	30.026	.930	0.4	N 67 E	7.9	9.6	28.0	19.3	8.7	...	...	1.0	3.0	.100	3.0
28	21.1	.100	87	29.902	.802	1.0	N 15 E	3.7	4.0	27.0	14.0	13.6	...	...	2.0	5.0	.200	5.0
	22.4	0.105	83	29.702	29.597	0.7	N 23 W	4.9	8.2	28.	15.5	13.1	0.810	29.8	46.8	78.4	2.490	108.2

TORONTO.
GENERAL METEOROLOGICAL ABSTRACT, MARCH, 1865.

Days.	DAILY MEANS.						WIND.			EXTREMES OF TEMPERATURE.			RAIN.		SNOW.		TOTAL FALL.	
	Temperature of Air.	Pressure of Vapour.	Rel. Humid.	Barometric Pressure.	Pressure of dry Air.	Clouded Sky.	Resultant Direction.	Resultant Velocity.	Mean Velocity.	Maximum.	Minimum.	Difference.	Depth in inches.	Approximate duration.	Depth in inches.	Approximate duration.	Depth in inches.	Approximate duration.
1	25.1	0.115	85	30.016	29.902	1.0	S 89 E	10.9	11.0	30.0	21.5	8.5	...	...	S	2.0	S	2.0
2	33.2	.176	92	29.651	.475	1.0	S 87 E	5.1	5.5	36.8	24.0	12.5	0.580	13.0	...	...	0.580	13.0
3	34.4	.110	58	.713	.596	1.0	N 22 E	3.7	3.7	39.8	32.3	7.2	...	...	1.0	4.0	.100	4.0
4	25.3	.119	54	.606	.487	0.7	N 33 W	13.8	14.7	31.5	27.0	4.5	...	...	5.0	7.0	.500	7.0
5	Sunday						S 56 E	2.8	2.8	28.8	2.0	26.8	...	...	...	...	...	...
6	26.7	.122	82	.828	.706	0.4	S 23 E	3.3	3.3	35.5	12.0	23.5	...	...	...	...	...	...
7	35.6	.160	75	.490	.330	0.7	S 85 W	4.9	10.6	42.8	22.8	20.0	R	0.2	...	...	R	0.2
8	20.7	.090	80	.796	.706	0.5	N 67 E	12.0	13.5	30.2	11.0	19.2	...	...	2.0	5.0	.200	5.0
9	33.2	.178	94	.324	.146	1.0	S 83 W	3.7	10.0	38.6	21.0	16.4	.100	7.5	5.0	4.3	.600	11.8
10	15.7	.067	74	.611	.544	0.4	S 78 W	11.8	12.0	20.5	11.8	8.7	...	...	...	...	...	...
11	17.9	.078	76	.607	.529	0.7	S 88 W	12.0	16.7	28.0	9.6	18.4	...	...	1.0	4.5	.100	4.5
12	Sunday						S 78 E	6.4	6.7	18.0	-3.5	21.	...	...	2.5	10.0	.250	10.0
13	24.1	.097	75	.874	.777	1.0	N 22 E	5.2	7.8	27.0	10.6	18.4	...	...	1.0	4.8	.100	4.8
14	30.3	.143	84	.789	.646	1.0	N 75 E	7.5	7.0	38.6	21.0	17.0	.025	0.5	...	...	.025	0.5
15	42.2	.249	92	.548	.299	1.0	N 63 E	3.1	3.2	48.0	29.8	18.2	...	...	...	...	...	...
16	41.4	.245	91	.222	28.976	1.0	S 59 W	5.1	10.3	49.0	38.0	11.0	.050	5.5	0.3	2.2	.680	10.7
17	36.3	.176	81	.248	29.072	0.7	S 60 W	11.4	14.1	43.5	20.9	13.0	.050	0.3	S	S	.050	0.3
18	35.4	.140	69	.694	.554	0.3	S 81 W	14.5	14.7	42.2	32.2	10.0	...	...	...	...	...	...
19	Sunday						S 45 W	2.3	2.0	43.5	29.4	14.1	...	...	...	...	...	...
20	38.0	.184	80	.529	.345	0.8	N 72 E	2.0	2.3	43.0	33.5	9.5	.250	1.0	...	...	.250	1.0
21	42.3	.254	93	.094	28.839	1.0	S 25 E	1.8	4.0	50.8	34.5	16.3	.660	9.5	...	...	.660	9.5
22	34.9	.170	83	28.800	28.630	1.0	S 71 W	17.2	18.9	38.0	33.0	5.0	.245	8.5	1.0	9.8	.345	8.5
23	36.6	.108	71	29.005	28.837	0.8	N 85 W	16.1	16.4	44.0	32.0	12.0	...	...	...	...	...	...
24	33.6	.152	79	.232	29.080	1.0	N 56 W	11.3	11.0	37.2	30.0	7.2	...	...	...	...	...	...
25	31.4	.145	82	.561	.416	0.7	N 40 W	11.0	11.1	36.5	30.5	6.0	...	...	0.1	3.1	.010	3.1
26	Sunday						N 58 W	4.9	5.7	39.2	26.0	12.6	...	...	...	...	...	...
27	39.5	.192	78	.902	.710	0.6	S 53 E	1.1	3.7	48.0	27.0	20.4	...	...	...	...	...	...
28	39.8	.162	66	.809	.647	0.0	N 73 E	10.9	10.9	44.8	34.0	10.8	...	...	...	...	...	...
29	41.0	.217	84	.644	.427	1.0	N 59 E	0.9	1.2	52.8	35.5	17.3	.490	10.5	...	...	.490	10.5
30	45.7	.203	67	.451	.248	0.7	N 15 E	6.6	6.9	55.6	38.4	17.2	...	...	...	...	...	...
31	45.8	.161	52	.207	.046	0.7	N 30 W	5.8	8.7	54.8	39.2	15.6	...	...	...	...	...	...
	33.6	0.159	79	29.528	29.369	0.8	N 61 W	2.2	8.8	39.3	25.1	14.2	3.050	59.5	18.9	56.4	4.940	115.9

TORONTO.
GENERAL METEOROLOGICAL ABSTRACT, APRIL, 1865.

Days.	DAILY MEANS.					WIND.			EXTREMES OF TEMPERATURE.			RAIN.		SNOW.		TOTAL FALL.	
	Temperature of Air.	Pressure of Vapour.	Rel. Humid.	Barometric Pressure.	Pressure of Dry Air.	Clouded Sky.	Resultant Direction.	Resultant Velocity.	Mean Velocity.	Maximum.	Minimum.	Difference.	Depth in inches.	Approximate duration.	Depth in inches.	Approximate duration.	Depth in inches.	Approximate duration.
1	39.2	0.165	68	29.405	29.240	0.4	N 60 W	14.8	15.3	47.8	35.2	12.6	...	...	...	...	...	...
2	Sunday						S 69 W	1.9	3.7	49.5	29.4	20.1	...	...	...	...	...	...
3	42.0	.129	47	.847	.719	0.3	N 77 E	0.9	10.2	51.2	31.4	19.8	...	...	...	...	...	...
4	45.3	.230	78	.791	.555	0.7	S 78 E	4.6	5.0	57.0	38.2	18.8	0.330	7.5	...	...	0.330	7.5
5	49.3	.288	81	.667	.378	1.0	S 76 E	3.0	3.2	56.0	41.0	15.0	.080	2.5	...	...	.080	2.5
6	51.9	.313	80	.435	.123	0.7	S 39 W	10.3	10.7	59.8	47.4	12.4	.030	2.0	...	...	.030	2.0
7	38.7	.135	58	.720	.591	0.5	S 79 W	15.9	16.3	47.5	39.2	8.3	...	...	...	...	...	...
8	31.6	.125	71	30.025	.890	0.6	N 71 W	7.5	7.8	38.0	29.4	8.6	...	...	S	0.2	S	0.2
9	Sunday						N 82 E	4.8	5.2	37.0	23.0	14.0	...	...	1.0	2.0	.100	2.0
10	35.4	.181	87	29.792	.611	0.8	N 33 E	2.2	2.3	40.5	30.8	9.7	...	...	1.0	4.0	.100	4.0
11	37.6	.206	91	.635	.429	1.0	N 75 E	8.5	8.6	46.2	30.8	15.4	.500	11.0	...	...	.500	11.0
12	15.5	.219	71	.196	28.977	1.0	S 76 W	17.5	19.4	55.5	37.5	18.0	R	0.5	...	...	R	0.5
13	39.4	.177	73	.647	29.470	0.4	S 44 W	5.8	6.5	48.4	33.0	15.4	R	R	...	...	R	R
14	...	...	...	...	...	...	S 31 W	3.6	3.8	58.0	34.5	23.5	R	R	...	...	R	R
15	45.6	.228	76	.461	.233	0.7	S 42 E	0.3	0.4	56.8	39.8	17.0	.260	4.5	S	0.2	.260	4.7
16	Sunday						N 36 W	11.7	12.3	45.2	32.8	12.4	R	0.2	...	...	R	0.2
17	36.4	.166	70	.706	.540	0.1	S 68 E	3.4	3.9	45.2	25.0	20.2	R	0.2	...	...	R	0.2
18	48.1	.178	58	.409	.231	0.4	N 86 W	13.6	14.4	62.5	32.5	30.0	.025	2.5	...	...	.025	2.5
19	43.0	.192	60	.846	.654	0.7	N 81 E	6.7	7.5	48.4	34.0	14.4	...	...	...	...	...	...
20	39.8	.183	74	.625	.44	1.0	N 72 E	14.7	14.7	43.0	36.2	6.8	.720	19.0	...	...	.720	19.0
21	48.4	.313	92	.335	.022	0.9	N 85 E	2.5	7.3	57.2	36.0	21.2	.270	3.0	...	...	.270	3.0
22	41.9	.165	61	.341	.176	0.8	S 64 W	17.2	17.5	48.8	41.0	7.8	.010	0.8	S	0.2	.010	1.0
23	Sunday						N 89 W	11.5	11.6	44.6	31.2	13.4	...	...	S	S	S	S
24	42.9	.163	59	.813	.650	0.3	S 51 W	3.2	4.4	52.0	32.4	19.6	...	...	...	...	...	...
25	41.1	.184	65	.807	.623	0.0	N 85 E	4.0	4.1	54.0	37.0	17.0	...	...	...	...	...	...
26	51.2	.270	72	.596	.319	0.6	N 80 W	3.0	5.4	69.0	34.4	25.0	.090	0.6	...	...	.090	0.6
27	47.9	.162	49	.073	.511	0.9	N 6 W	3.9	6.3	56.6	41.4	15.2	...	...	...	...	...	...
28	45.0	.253	85	.636	.383	0.9	N 70 E	7.3	8.7	51.0	43.6	7.4	1.600	17.5	...	...	1.600	17.5
29	43.2	.242	84	.887	.145	0.7	N 74 W	10.5	11.7	52.4	39.5	12.0	.057	1.0	...	...	.057	1.0
30	Sunday						S 63 W	1.9	3.5	50.6	30.4	19.6	...	...	...	...	...	...
	43.1	0.203	72	29.617	29.414	0.6	N 81 W	2.1	8.4	50.6	31.9	15.7	3.972	72.8	2.0	0.6	4.172	70.4

TORONTO.
GENERAL METEOROLOGICAL ABSTRACT, MAY, 1865.

Days.	DAILY MEANS.					WIND.			EXTREMES OF TEMPERATURE			RAIN.		SNOW.		TOTAL FALL.	
	Temperature of Air.	Pressure of Vapour.	Rel. Humid.	Barometric Pressure.	Pressure of Dry Air.	Clouded Sky.	Resultant Direction.	Resultant Velocity.	Mean Velocity.	Maximum.	Minimum.	Difference.	Depth in inches.	Approximate duration.	Depth in Inches.	Approximate duration.	Depth in inches.	Approximate duration.
1	41.0	0.198	76	29.558	29.360	0.7	N 40 W	3.4	4.6	47.2	36.4	10.8	0.015	1.5	...	...	0.015	1.5
2	43.4	.151	63	.675	.494	0.2	S 50 E	1.2	2.5	53.0	30.2	22.8	...	...	...	...	...	...
3	44.5	.195	67	.772	.577	0.3	S 47 W	1.6	3.7	55.8	33.0	22.8	...	...	...	...	...	...
4	43.8	.231	81	.605	.374	1.0	N 83 E	6.1	6.7	47.2	38.6	8.6	.185	9.0	...	...	.185	9.0
5	52.0	.300	77	.397	.097	0.4	N 7 E	2.7	3.8	67.0	42.0	25.0	...	...	...	...	...	...
6	48.0	.295	87	.457	.162	0.9	N 39 W	7.0	8.5	53.2	48.2	5.0	.700	12.0	...	...	.700	12.0
7	Sunday						S 37 W	8.6	9.0	57.0	37.2	19.8	...	...	...	...	...	...
8	50.1	.297	74	.345	.018	1.0	N 30 W	4.5	5.6	60.5	45.4	15.1	...	...	...	...	...	...
9	48.4	.235	69	.507	.302	0.5	S 28 E	2.8	5.6	58.0	45.0	13.0	...	...	...	...	...	...
10	45.8	.264	85	.534	.270	1.0	N 15 W	6.2	8.2	58.0	41.2	16.8	.355	7.2	...	...	.355	7.2
11	40.1	.137	55	.670	.533	0.7	N 30 W	8.8	8.9	47.0	37.8	9.2	...	...	...	...	...	...
12	43.4	.162	55	.631	.469	0.2	S 1 W	4.7	5.3	53.0	30.0	23.0	...	...	...	...	...	...
13	50.4	.250	69	.661	.411	0.5	N 7 W	2.3	4.8	58.4	39.0	19.4	...	...	...	...	...	...
14	Sunday						N 17 W	0.2	0.2	53.2	40.8	12.4	.010	2.5	...	...	.010	2.5
15	54.9	.254	60	.931	.677	0.4	N 85 E	2.9	3.0	62.0	41.6	20.4	...	...	...	...	...	...
16	60.1	.367	70	.691	.324	0.3	S 36 W	3.6	3.9	73.0	47.4	25.6	...	...	...	...	...	...
17	59.2	.451	88	.562	.111	0.9	N 73 E	4.8	7.4	74.0	55.0	19.0	2.200	13.0	...	...	2.200	13.0
18	50.4	.270	73	.697	.427	1.0	N 77 E	10.7	10.8	54.0	46.2	7.8	.280	5.1	...	...	.280	5.1
19	52.8	.355	89	.620	.264	0.8	N 68 E	6.4	6.4	60.0	49.0	11.0	.125	1.2	...	...	.125	1.2
20	60.2	.457	88	.507	.050	0.7	N 83 E	3.1	3.4	71.0	50.8	20.2	...	...	...	...	...	...
21	Sunday						N 75 E	2.1	3.5	69.0	48.0	21.0	.030	1.5	...	...	.030	1.5
22	55.7	.340	74	.320	28.981	0.4	N 4 W	7.0	7.5	64.0	51.8	12.2	.105	1.5	...	...	.105	1.5
23	48.3	.255	66	.500	29.275	0.2	N 66 W	3.6	5.3	59.0	37.0	22.0	...	...	...	...	...	...
24	51.8	.273	70	.566	.293	0.8	N 23 W	1.8	3.5	58.0	35.5	22.5	R	0.5	...	...	R	0.5
25	56.9	.308	67	.587	.280	0.1	N 3 E	4.0	5.9	63.8	45.4	18.4	...	...	...	...	...	...
26	54.9	.209	48	.598	.390	0.2	N 13 W	4.6	7.6	64.5	47.0	17.5	...	...	...	...	...	...
27	58.8	.211	43	.453	.242	0.1	N 14 W	7.1	8.1	69.2	48.2	21.0	...	...	...	...	...	...
28	Sunday						S 60 E	2.2	3.0	67.0	49.0	18.0	...	...	...	...	...	...
29	62.1	.291	51	.562	.271	0.3	N 52 W	6.1	8.2	70.5	50.5	20.0	...	...	...	...	...	...
30	63.6	.328	56	.708	.380	0.6	S 79 W	1.5	2.7	72.0	53.6	18.2	...	...	...	...	...	...
31	68.4	.411	57	.683	.272	0.4	N 39 W	1.0	2.3	79.0	52.0	27.0	...	...	...	...	...	...
	52.3	0.278	69	29.585	29.307	0.5	N 3 W	1.6	5.5	61.2	43.6	17.6	4.005	55.0	...	...	4.005	55.0

TORONTO.
General Meteorological Abstract, June. 1865.

Days.	DAILY MEANS.						WIND.			EXTREMES OF TEMPERATURE			RAIN.		SNOW.		TOTAL FALL.	
	Temperature of Air.	Pressure of Vapour.	Humidity	Barometric Pressure.	Pressure of Dry Air.	Clouded Sky.	Resultant Direction.	Resultant Velocity.	Mean Velocity.	Maximum.	Minimum.	Difference.	Depth in inches	Approximate duration	Depth in inches	Approximate duration	Depth in inches	Approximate duration
1	61.7	0.276	19	29.667	29.391	0.7	N 81 E	4.0	4.2	74.8	60.0	7.8	...	...	...	...	...	...
2	58.9	.281	57	.658	.377	0.8	S 83 E	2.9	3.2	65.0	51.4	13.6	...	...	...	...	...	...
3	64.2	.430	71	.600	.170	0.0	S 10 E	0.8	1.0	73.0	55.2	17.8	...	...	...	...	...	...
4	Sunday						S 84 W	2.5	4.0	80.2	61.2	20.0	0.260	3.5	...	...	0.260	3.5
5	64.3	.410	68	.774	.364	0.6	S 83 E	1.4	1.4	69.8	59.8	10.0	...	...	...	...	...	...
6	65.9	.444	69	.741	.297	0.0	S 58 E	1.8	2.8	73.8	56.5	17.3	...	...	...	...	...	...
7	63.9	.525	71	.631	.106	0.6	S 81 W	3.2	6.0	79.0	62.0	17.0	...	...	...	...	...	...
8	66.3	.401	62	.726	.325	0.5	S 78 W	2.1	3.5	75.0	54.5	20.5	...	...	...	...	...	...
9	63.3	.419	72	.647	.228	1.0	N 28 E	1.2	1.4	70.2	59.0	11.2	.200	2.5	...	...	.200	2.5
10	58.5	.386	7	.640	.254	0.4	N 27 W	8.5	8.0	78.8	58.2	10.0	...	...	...	...	...	...
11	Sunday						S 30 E	1.5	1.9	77.0	43.0	34.0	...	...	...	...	...	...
12	69.1	.471	65	.512	.041	0.3	N 67 W	2.5	4.2	82.9	46.0	36.9	...	...	...	...	...	...
13	58.1	.298	61	.711	.413	0.7	N 86 E	4.0	4.3	63.2	57.0	6.2	...	...	...	...	...	...
14	61.4	.270	50	.731	.461	1.0	N 74 E	10.5	10.0	66.8	54.0	12.8	...	...	...	...	...	...
15	59.5	.412	87	.681	.239	0.9	N 79 E	3.2	3.2	65.0	53.3	9.7	.530	8.7	...	...	.530	8.7
16	63.2	.589	85	.676	.087	0.4	S 57 E	1.2	1.3	76.2	57.0	19.2	...	...	...	...	...	...
17	71.4	.677	88	.733	.056	0.5	S 1 E	1.2	1.6	82.5	61.4	21.1	...	...	...	...	...	...
18	Sunday						S 71 E	0.5	0.5	80.0	65.0	15.0	...	...	...	...	...	...
19	70.9	.587	77	.607	.020	0.8	N 26 W	1.9	2.4	81.4	65.0	16.4	...	...	...	...	...	...
20	67.4	.463	71	.611	.178	0.5	S 35 W	3.8	4.2	78.2	59.0	19.2	...	...	...	...	...	...
21	65.0	.395	66	.630	.235	0.5	N 79 W	4.0	4.9	74.0	59.0	15.0	...	...	...	...	...	...
22	61.6	.330	60	.721	.391	0.2	N 35 E	1.1	3.5	70.5	54.0	16.5	...	...	...	...	...	...
23	62.2	.355	63	.822	.467	0.7	S 14 E	2.1	2.0	71.0	49.2	21.8	...	...	...	...	...	...
24	72.1	.552	70	.649	.007	0.0	S 17 W	3.8	4.4	80.2	57.8	22.4	...	...	...	...	...	...
25	Sunday						S 7 W	4.0	4.9	44.5	64.2	20.3	.550	7.5	...	...	.550	7.5
26	66.5	.522	81	.268	29.730	0.8	S 38 W	8.2	8.7	75.0	64.8	10.2	.180	3.8	...	...	.180	3.8
27	55.4	.309	70	.181	29.173	0.7	S 78 W	7.8	8.6	62.0	53.5	8.5	...	...	...	...	...	...
28	58.6	.356	73	.618	.262	0.8	S 25 E	2.0	3.8	57.5	15.0	22.5	.215	0.7	...	...	.215	0.7
29	66.4	.514	79	.377	28.866	0.7	S 34 W	4.0	5.7	79.0	51.0	25.0	.070	2.0	...	...	.070	2.0
30	69.4	.516	72	.508	28.992	0.0	N 85 W	1.2	3.1	76.2	60.0	16.2	...	...	...	...	...	...
	64.5	0.432	70	29.633	29.201	0.6	S 30 W	0.6	4.1	74.2	56.7	17.5	2.005	34.7	...	...	2.005	34.7

TORONTO.
General Meteorological Abstract. July. 1865.

Days.	DAILY MEANS.						WIND.			EXTREMES OF TEMPERATURE.			RAIN.		SNOW.		TOTAL FALL.	
	Temperature of Air	Pressure of Vapour.	Rel Humid.	Barometric Pressure.	Pressure of Dry Air.	Clouded Sky	Resultant Direction	Resultant Velocity.	Mean Velocity.	Maximum.	Minimum.	Difference.	Depth in inches	Approximate duration	Depth in inches	Approximate duration	Depth in inches.	Approximate duration.
1	55.3	.537	86	29.430	28.953	0.7	S 77 E	1.7	3.5	72.0	58.8	13.2	R	0.5	...	...	R	0.5
2	Sunday						S 88 W	7.6	7.8	71.0	57.4	13.6	0.025	0.1	...	...	0.025	0.1
3	56.4	.413	64	.592	.179	0.3	S 40 W	4.3	4.5	74.8	55.5	19.3	...	...	...	...	...	...
4	59.7	.410	57	.632	.222	0.8	N 50 W	4.4	6.2	81.0	59.5	21.5	...	...	...	...	...	...
5	54.8	.338	56	.772	.435	0.8	S 61 W	0.8	2.7	73.0	56.4	16.6	R	0.5	...	...	R	0.5
6	54.9	.416	74	.632	.186	0.4	N 74 E	1.8	3.9	57.4	36.0	21.4	.050	0.5	...	...	.050	0.5
7	71.9	.477	61	.579	.102	0.5	N 60 W	9.9	10.2	81.8	63.0	18.8	...	...	...	...	...	...
8	67.4	.439	76	.605	.166	0.4	S 33 W	3.5	3.9	78.0	59.8	18.2	...	...	...	...	...	...
9	Sunday						N 12 W	4.3	6.0	73.0	53.5	19.5	...	...	...	...	...	...
10	64.6	.309	51	.674	.365	0.9	N 82 E	2.0	2.5	72.0	55.0	17.0	...	...	...	...	...	...
11	66.9	.382	59	.517	.134	0.3	S 10 W	1.4	2.0	76.0	57.4	18.6	...	...	...	...	...	...
12	62.7	.396	57	.483	.097	0.7	N 87 W	6.6	7.5	73.1	54.0	19.1	1.190	4.0	...	...	1.190	4.0
13	56.2	.283	61	.653	.370	0.5	N 57 W	11.3	11.8	67.0	48.4	18.6	...	...	...	...	...	...
14	56.5	.276	62	.705	.432	0.2	N 75 W	4.9	5.0	66.6	46.0	20.6	...	...	...	...	...	...
15	55.8	.297	67	.682	.385	1.0	S 44 E	1.3	1.9	55.8	45.8	20.0	...	...	...	...	...	...
16	Sunday						N 53 E	1.6	2.7	64.2	51.6	12.6	.015	1.1	...	...	.015	1.1
17	63.8	.296	52	.519	.223	0.2	N 41 W	6.1	6.4	73.0	54.2	18.8	...	...	...	...	...	...
18	67.0	.314	47	.432	.119	0.3	S 59 W	8.8	9.2	82.0	53.0	29.0	...	...	...	...	...	...
19	60.7	.447	81	.347	28.930	0.7	S 4 W	1.8	2.1	68.8	53.0	15.8	.120	2.0	...	...	.120	2.0
20	66.1	.494	73	.526	29.055	0.7	S 68 W	4.7	6.8	75.8	51.8	24.0	.090	1.4	...	...	.090	1.4
21	65.7	.437	61	.707	.270	0.7	N 21 E	2.5	4.1	70.0	59.2	11.8	...	...	...	...	...	...
22	64.7	.333	55	.781	.431	0.5	N 46 E	0.9	5.0	71.0	59.4	11.6	...	...	...	...	...	...
23	Sunday						S 72 W	0.7	2.3	78.0	56.8	21.2	...	...	...	...	...	...
24	65.7	.425	68	.679	.251	1.0	S	1.5	2.3	75.0	56.0	19.0	R	0.4	...	...	R	0.4
25	66.0	.518	78	.358	28.340	0.7	S 48 W	8.2	10.7	80.5	62.4	18.1	.910	2.5	...	...	.910	2.5
26	70.8	.482	65	.465	29.982	0.4	N 73 W	12.1	12.5	81.8	63.0	18.8	...	...	...	...	...	...
27	70.4	.481	65	.527	29.040	0.3	S 37 W	1.3	1.4	82.0	59.2	22.8	...	...	...	...	...	...
28	71.5	.551	71	.490	28.944	0.8	S 52 W	1.4	3.4	83.0	62.5	20.5	.070	4.5	...	...	.070	4.5
29	63.3	.372	65	.620	29.304	0.2	N 4 W	4.9	7.2	75.0	56.8	19.2	...	...	...	...	...	...
30	Sunday						S 6 W	1.9	3.5	66.8	51.2	15.6	...	...	...	...	...	...
31	60.4	.321	68	.935	.611	0.0	S 79 E	5.7	6.0	58.8	40.0	19.8	...	...	...	...	...	...
	63.0	0.432	65	29.595	29.193	0.5	N 83 W	2.3	5.3	74.1	55.6	18.5	2.670	17.5	...	...	2.470	17.5

TORONTO.
GENERAL METEOROLOGICAL ABSTRACT, AUGUST, 1865.

Days.	DAILY MEANS.						WIND.			EXTREMES OF TEMPERATURE.				RAIN.		SNOW.		TOTAL FALL.	
	Temperature of Air.	Pressure of Vapour.	Rel. Humid.	Barometric Pressure.	Pressure of Dry Air.	Clouded Sky.	Resultant Direction.	Resultant Velocity.	Mean Velocity.	Maximum.	Minimum.	Difference.		Depth in inches.	Approximate duration.	Depth in inches.	Approximate duration.	Depth in inches.	Approximate duration.
1	67.7	0.509	74	29.908	29.399	0.6	S 89 E	3.7	3.8	75.0	54.0	21.0		...	...	...	...	...	...
2	71.8	.584	74	.835	.251	0.4	S 72 E	3.6	3.8	80.8	64.0	16.8		...	...	...	...	...	...
3	76.7	.675	75	.760	.085	0.5	S 36 W	2.2	3.6	87.8	63.5	24.3		0.085	3.0	...	...	0.085	3.0
4	66.8	.521	79	.772	.251	0.8	N 26 W	1.8	2.0	74.5	66.6	7.9		.130	3.7	...	...	.130	3.7
5	71.1	.508	67	.729	.221	0.4	S 11 E	0.4	3.0	79.8	58.0	21.8		...	...	...	...	...	...
6	Sunday						S 50 W	5.4	7.9	77.5	62.2	15.3		.925	3.5	...	...	.925	3.5
7	65.7	.384	62	.450	.066	0.5	N 75 W	9.1	9.3	75.0	62.0	13.0		...	...	...	...	...	...
8	65.7	.445	70	.650	.214	0.4	S 53 W	2.0	2.2	75.8	54.2	21.6		R	0.7	...	...	R	0.7
9	69.7	.506	70	.626	.120	0.6	S 8 E	2.6	3.4	78.2	54.2	24.0		.165	2.5	...	...	.165	2.5
10	70.0	.513	71	.376	29.863	0.7	N 58 W	12.9	14.9	81.2	65.4	15.6		.445	2.5	...	...	.445	2.5
11	57.6	.360	76	.592	29.233	0.8	N 21 W	8.4	8.8	63.5	56.5	7.0		...	...	...	...	...	...
12	59.8	.345	66	.670	.325	0.0	N 15 W	0.1	1.6	67.8	52.2	15.6		...	...	...	...	...	...
13	Sunday						Calm.	0.0	0.0	73.5	45.4	28.7		...	...	...	...	...	...
14	67.2	.467	70	.664	.197	0.0	S 24 W	1.6	1.6	77.0	55.0	22.0		...	...	...	...	...	...
15	71.3	.458	60	.576	.120	0.2	N 49 W	2.3	4.8	85.5	55.2	30.3		...	...	...	...	...	...
16	63.3	.380	62	.673	.293	0.3	N 7 W	9.4	9.6	74.0	60.4	13.6		...	...	...	...	...	...
17	61.0	.353	65	.774	.421	0.0	S 65 E	3.3	3.9	69.8	53.5	16.3		...	...	...	...	...	...
18	63.7	.407	69	.639	.292	0.2	S 50 E	1.5	1.9	74.0	50.0	24.0		...	...	...	...	...	...
19	67.5	.436	65	.625	.189	0.5	S 45 W	1.8	3.1	79.2	55.6	23.6		...	...	...	...	...	...
20	Sunday						S 47 W	5.2	5.4	77.0	57.8	19.2		.220	3.0	...	...	.220	3.0
21	65.1	.438	71	.435	29.997	1.0	N 18 W	6.8	8.2	75.8	61.5	14.3		.120	1.5	...	...	.120	1.5
22	59.3	.289	59	.533	29.250	0.8	N 14 W	7.1	7.8	65.8	52.8	13.0		...	...	...	...	...	...
23	53.2	.254	64	.663	.400	0.3	N 30 W	3.5	7.2	61.5	46.5	15.0		...	...	...	...	...	...
24	56.8	.307	69	.792	.485	0.1	S 81 W	3.4	5.0	67.2	44.4	22.8		...	...	...	...	...	...
25	63.7	.378	66	.802	.425	0.0	S 45 W	5.1	3.9	75.8	48.0	27.8		...	...	...	...	...	...
26	67.7	.463	60	.696	.223	0.3	S 57 W	8.9	6.8	79.6	52.5	27.1		...	...	...	...	...	...
27	Sunday						N 26 W	3.4	9.0	72.0	57.8	14.2		...	...	...	...	...	...
28	57.9	.319	68	.740	.430	0.2	S 51 E	1.9	4.1	69.0	49.8	19.2		...	...	...	...	...	...
29	60.5	.386	74	.762	.376	0.0	S 40 E	3.9	2.6	69.6	47.0	22.6		...	...	...	...	...	...
30	64.8	.419	74	.813	.394	0.3	S 80 E	3.9	4.6	72.8	55.0	17.8		...	...	...	...	...	...
31	73.6	.592	71	.729	.147	0.5	S 5 W	3.9	4.8	87.8	57.0	30.8		...	...	...	...	...	...
	65.2	0.431	69	29.689	29.216	0.4	N 60 W	1.6	5.1	74.9	55.4	19.5		1.990	20.4	...	...	1.990	20.4

TORONTO.
General Meteorological Abstract, September, 1865.

Days.	DAILY MEANS.					Clouded Sky.	WIND.			EXTREMES OF TEMPERATURE			RAIN.		SNOW.		TOTAL FALL.	
	Temperature of Air.	Pressure of Vapour.	Rel. Humid.	Barometric Pressure.	Pressure of Dry Air.		Resultant Direction.	Resultant Velocity.	Mean Velocity.	Maximum.	Minimum.	Difference.	Depth in inches.	Approximate duration.	Depth in inches	Approximate duration.	Depth in inches	Approximate duration.
1	70.4	0.578	78	29.656	29.077	0.8	S 62 W	1.7	3.0	77.8	68.0	9.8	R	1.0	...	...	R	1.0
2	69.2	.494	69	.571	.077	0.1	N 84 E	3.5	3.8	80.0	60.0	20.0	...	...	...	...	...	...
3	Su	nday					8 51 E	3.3	3.4	83.4	63.4	20.0	...	...	...	...	...	...
4	75.7	.641	73	.580	28.939	0.5	S 23 W	4.9	4.9	85.4	66.0	19.4	...	...	...	...	...	...
5	74.4	.509	62	.542	29.03	0.7	N 40 W	2.1	3.8	86.0	68.4	17.6	0.030	4.7	...	...	0.030	4.7
6	57.4	.444	67	.527	.083	0.4	S 35 W	4.4	5.1	77.1	61.0	16.1	...	...	...	...	...	...
7	70.8	.518	69	.567	.049	0.3	S 65 E	3.6	6.2	81.4	57.0	24.4	...	...	...	...	...	...
8	51.4	.490	89	.518	.028	1.0	N 71 E	10.7	10.8	65.8	58.2	7.6	.500	8.0	...	...	.500	8.0
9	55.7	.582	91	.607	.025	0.8	N 13 E	1.0	3.2	70.0	59.8	10.2	R	1.0	...	...	R	1.0
10	Su	nday					S 22 E	0.9	2.1	76.0	60.0	16.0	R	0.1	...	...	R	0.1
11	69.9	.560	76	.560	.000	0.4	S 67 W	2.1	3.2	79.0	65.0	14.0	.045	1.0	...	...	.045	1.0
12	67.4	.405	61	.760	.355	0.0	S 81 E	2.7	3.4	77.0	52.8	24.2	...	...	...	...	...	...
13	71.2	.434	71	.813	.278	0.1	S 82 E	2.2	2.3	80.8	64.8	16.0	...	...	...	...	...	...
14	75.1	.665	78	.700	.035	0.7	N 82 W	3.6	5.6	90.5	65.6	24.9	.005	0.4	...	...	.005	0.4
15	67.3	.344	54	.865	.521	0.2	N 32 W	2.3	4.1	78.0	61.9	16.1	...	...	...	...	...	...
16	64.7	.411	67	.823	.412	0.0	S 23 E	0.4	0.5	74.0	51.6	22.4	...	...	...	...	...	...
17	Su	nday					N 29 E	5.4	7.0	81.5	60.0	21.5	.940	14.0	...	...	.940	14.0
18	52.3	.222	57	.794	.572	0.2	N 40 E	4.9	5.0	62.8	45.0	17.0	...	...	...	...	...	...
19	54.5	.296	71	.878	.582	0.0	S 25 W	3.2	3.9	65.4	42.0	23.4	...	...	...	...	...	...
20	59.8	.417	81	.780	.363	0.5	S 24 E	3.7	3.8	70.4	49.8	20.6	...	...	...	...	...	...
21	61.2	.451	81	.766	.315	0.8	S 56 W	1.1	1.3	69.0	53.0	16.0	R	0.6	...	...	R	0.6
22	65.1	.523	84	.839	.316	0.6	S 33 E	1.7	2.2	71.4	58.0	13.4	...	...	...	...	...	...
23	64.2	.529	88	.843	.314	0.4	S 84 E	2.3	2.4	70.2	62.0	8.2	...	...	...	...	...	...
24	Su	nday					S 45 W	3.4	3.9	69.5	56.5	13.0	.885	4.5	...	...	.885	4.5
25	51.5	.400	73	.684	.284	0.1	N 32 W	8.2	8.5	71.0	57.0	14.0	...	...	...	...	...	...
26	50.7	.286	78	.912	.626	0.0	S 57 E	2.5	3.9	59.0	44.0	15.0	...	...	...	...	...	...
27	54.6	.338	81	.957	.648	0.0	S 82 E	4.4	4.5	63.0	45.0	18.0	...	...	...	...	...	...
28	58.9	.414	83	.912	.498	0.2	N 87 E	1.9	1.9	69.4	47.8	21.6	...	...	...	...	...	...
29	64.1	.49	84	.680	.184	0.6	S 13 W	3.2	4.4	73.2	51.0	22.2	.045	2.0	...	...	.045	2.0
30	59.5	.352	69	.507	.156	0.8	S 74 W	5.6	5.9	65.0	58.5	6.5	R	2.0	...	...	R	2.0
	64.5	0.458	75	29.718	29.260	0.4	S 56 E	0.5	4.1	74.1	57.1	17.0	2.450	39.3	...	...	2.450	39.3

TORONTO.
GENERAL METEOROLOGICAL ABSTRACT, OCTOBER, 1865.

Days.	DAILY MEANS.					WIND.			EXTREMES OF TEMPERATURE.			RAIN.		SNOW.		TOTAL FALL.	
	Temperature of Air.	Pressure of Vapour.	Rel. Humid.	Barometric Pressure.	Pressure of Dry Air.	Clouded Sky.	Resultant Direction.	Resultant Velocity.	Mean Velocity.	Maximum.	Minimum.	Difference.	Depth in inches	Approximate duration	Depth in inches	Approximate duration	Depth in inches	Approximate duration
1	Sunday						N 80 W	7.0	7.0	64.8	49.0	15.8	0.085	1.0	...	...	0.085	1.0
2	44.0	0.210	77	29.507	29.289	0.3	N 37 W	5.2	5.6	54.5	37.4	17.1	R	0.5	...	...	R	0.5
3	45.4	.218	72	.531	.312	0.9	N 21 W	7.2	7.5	54.0	38.1	15.9	R	1.0	...	...	R	1.0
4	44.0	.235	81	.556	.321	1.0	N 35 W	12.3	12.4	49.2	36.0	13.2	...	...	...	...	...	...
5	46.1	.216	70	.731	.515	0.5	N 33 W	8.2	8.4	53.2	41.8	11.4	...	...	...	...	...	...
6	49.1	.268	76	.820	.562	0.3	S 44 W	3.3	4.1	59.5	38.4	21.1	...	...	...	...	...	...
7	50.6	.406	88	.615	.148	1.0	S 70 W	4.1	5.7	70.0	47.0	23.0	1.275	11.5	...	...	1.275	11.5
8	Sunday						N 57 E	1.7	1.7	5.0	50.6	4.4	.045	1.6	...	...	.045	1.6
9	58.7	.440	88	.537	.092	0.5	S 71 W	6.2	8.2	67.0	43.4	23.0	...	...	...	...	...	...
10	52.4	.439	77	.027	.158	0.6	N 34 E	3.6	5.8	71.4	56.0	15.	...	...	...	...	...	...
11	54.0	.320	75	.587	.207	0.8	N 1 E	3.0	7.0	61.8	46.6	15.2	.045	1.5	...	...	.045	1.5
12	43.4	.169	67	.763	.573	0.4	N 8 W	7.0	7.1	50.5	41.0	9.8	...	...	...	...	...	...
13	40.7	.194	77	.724	.530	0.0	N 78 E	3.2	4.1	49.4	33.8	15.6	...	...	...	...	...	...
14	45.6	.247	80	.339	.092	0.2	N 20 E	3.7	4.6	54.8	36.2	18.0	...	...	...	...	...	...
15	Sunday						N 18 W	12.2	12.5	50.2	42.0	8.2	R	1.0	...	...	R	1.0
16	39.6	.178	74	.680	.507	0.2	N 45 W	7.0	7.2	50.2	30.5	19.7	...	...	...	...	...	...
17	44.8	.208	79	.645	.436	0.7	S 41 E	4.9	6.1	53.2	28.4	24.8	.025	2.0	...	...	.025	2.0
18	53.8	.363	87	.323	28.961	1.0	S 63 E	5.2	0.5	59.0	47.6	11.0	.460	19.0	...	...	.460	19.0
19	51.0	.306	79	28.870	28.563	0.7	N 69 W	16.4	17.0	55.0	52.0	3.0	.160	2.5	...	...	.160	2.5
20	42.2	.181	68	29.167	28.985	0.4	N 73 W	10.1	10.6	49.0	39.8	9.2	.160	2.5	...	...	.160	2.5
21	38.7	.164	71	.609	29.445	0.4	N 72 W	10.2	10.3	48.0	32.6	15.4	...	...	...	...	...	...
22	Sunday						S 89 W	4.7	5.1	53.2	31.2	22.0	.105	2.5	...	...	.105	2.5
23	38.7	.165	7	.808	.705	0.2	N 6 W	4.2	4.3	47.0	30.7	11.3	...	...	...	...	...	...
24	35.4	.138	94	.975	.857	0.1	N 4 E	2.9	3.1	45.0	29.4	15.6	...	...	...	...	...	...
25	39.7	.156	70	.805	.685	0.8	N 45 E	4.9	5.1	47.0	29.0	18.0	...	...	...	...	...	...
26	51.4	.182	91	.860	.683	1.0	N 46 E	10.7	10.7	43.2	35.0	8.2	.125	3.0	2.0	15.0	.325	18.0
27	27.0	.135	88	.691	.550	1.0	N 48 E	9.4	9.5	34.0	24.8	9.2	.102	5.0	1.0	7.5	.202	12.5
28	33.0	.171	90	.358	.187	0.9	N 35 W	5.3	5.6	35.5	28.2	7.3	R	1.0	1.5	5.0	.150	2.5
29	Sunday						S 77 W	3.8	3.4	40.5	21.0	18.0	...	...	...	...	...	...
30	41.3	.211	77	.071	.769	1.0	S 36 E	4.0	5.8	45.5	31.2	12.	.100	6.3	...	...	.100	6.3
31	42.2	.28	77	.878	.649	0.7	N 73 E	2.8	5.	49.0	42.2	7.2	.01	2.0	...	...	.015	2.0
	44.5	0.214	77	29.019	28.870	0.6	N 36 W	3.6	7.2	52.8	8.1	11.	2.700	53.8	4.5	27.5	3.155	91.3

TORONTO.
GENERAL METEOROLOGICAL ABSTRACT, NOVEMBER, 1865.

Days.	DAILY MEANS.					WIND.				EXTREMES OF TEMPERATURE			RAIN	SNOW		TOTAL FALL.
	Temperature of Air.	Pressure of Vapour.	Rel. Humid	Barometric Pressure.	Pressure of Dry Air.	Cloud'd Sky.	Resultant Direction.	Resultant Velocity.	Mean Velocity.	Maximum.	Minimum.	Difference.	Depth in Inches.	Approximate duration	Depth in inches.	Approximate duration.
1	44.2	0.220	77	29.782	29.550	0.9	S 56 E	5.4	6.1	50.0	35.3	14.7	0.050	2.1	...	...	0.050	2.1
2	45.0	.230	78	.606	.370	0.7	S 71 E	7.3	7.6	52.0	44.8	17.2	...	...	...	...	...
3	39.9	.194	79	.667	.473	0.5	S 14 W	3.2	4.2	49.0	31.0	18.0	...	...	...	...	...
4	41.0	.220	80	.338	.118	0.9	N 65 W	6.2	7.7	48.0	36.5	11.5	.335	10.1	...	...	.335	10.1
5	Sunday						N 66 W	13.5	15.9	55.0	30.0	5.0	...	...	0.2	...	.020	5.9
6	37.1	.159	72	.435	.276	1.0	S 87 W	15.5	18.0	40.6	28.4	12.2	.070	1.0	0.2	1.2	.090	1.2
7	27.5	.120	80	30.031	.912	0.0	N 16 W	2.7	5.1	34.2	24.6	9.6	...	...	...	...	...
8	38.7	.179	76	29.800	.621	0.8	S 24 E	3.8	6.1	44.8	3.6	21.2	...	...	...	...	...
9	36.6	.168	75	.945	.780	0.9	N 43 W	8.5	10.5	46.0	34.8	11.2	...	...	...	...	...
10	28.7	.121	77	30.287	30.160	0.9	N 26 E	5.0	5.2	32.8	27.8	5.0	...	...	...	...	...
11	29.1	.120	78	30.222	30.096	0.8	N 54 E	2.2	2.3	31.6	26.8	4.8	...	...	...	...	...
12	Sunday						S 57 W	6.0	6.3	47.0	25.0	22.6	...	...	...	...	...
13	45.7	.213	71	29.614	29.401	0.5	S 62 W	8.2	8.5	57.0	32.8	24.2	...	...	...	...	...
14	47.7	.241	75	.499	.258	0.3	S 42 W	5.5	5.0	54.7	41.0	13.7	...	...	...	...	...
15	46.7	.257	80	.545	.288	0.4	S 53 W	4.0	4.7	60.0	40.0	20.6	...	...	...	...	...
16	46.9	.260	81	.513	.260	0.4	S 6 W	3.4	4.1	55.2	38.4	10.8	...	...	...	...	...
17	48.8	.233	67	.508	.275	0.9	N 88 W	12.9	15.2	53.2	44.6	18.6	...	...	...	...	...
18	38.1	.163	71	.768	.604	1.0	N 11 W	4.0	4.7	43.0	35.8	7.2	...	...	...	...	...
19	Sunday						S 34 W	1.3	4.5	46.2	31.0	15.2	...	...	...	...	...
20	39.8	.177	71	.735	.558	0.6	S 73 E	8.7	9.3	42.5	32.4	10.1	...	...	...	...	...
21	38.3	.209	89	.460	.253	1.0	N 30 E	6.9	9.3	43.6	38.6	5.0	.290	15.0	0.1	3.0	.300	15.1
22	34.2	.177	89	.176	28.999	1.0	N 41 W	14.6	14.8	36.5	32.5	4.0	...	...	0.5	10.5	.050	10.5
23	37.3	.177	80	.512	29.335	0.9	N 22 W	11.4	11.6	41.6	33.4	8.2	...	...	...	...	...
24	36.9	.171	78	.768	.596	0.9	N 62 W	1.9	2.7	39.4	33.2	6.2	...	...	...	...	...
25	40.0	.197	79	.683	.487	1.0	N 67 W	2.7	3.2	44.0	33.8	10.2	...	...	...	...	...
26	Sunday						N 62 W	3.0	3.7	44.2	36.8	7.4	...	...	...	...	...
27	31.9	.137	76	.659	.522	0.6	N 52 W	11.7	12.5	42.0	30.0	12.0	...	...	S	0.5	S	0.5
28	26.9	.119	80	.819	.700	0.9	N 51 E	4.3	5.1	34.0	24.0	10.0	...	...	...	...	...
29	35.8	.155	74	.548	.393	1.0	S 31 E	7.7	8.8	39.8	25.4	14.4	...	...	S	0.2	S	0.2
30	40.5	.193	77	.106	28.913	1.0	S 23 W	11.8	14.0	45.8	35.0	10.8	.230	3.5	0.1	1.0	.240	4.5
	38.6	0.186	77	29.655	29.470	0.8	N 79 W	3.0	7.9	44.8	32.9	11.9	0.975	31.7	1.1	21.4	1.085	53.1

TORONTO.
GENERAL METEOROLOGICAL ABSTRACT, DECEMBER, 1865.

Days.	DAILY MEANS.						WIND.			EXTREMES OF TEMPERATURE.				RAIN.		SNOW.		TOTAL FALL.	
	Temperature of Air.	Pressure of Vapour.	Rel. Humid.	Barometric Pressure.	Pressure of Dry Air.	Clouded Sky.	Resultant Direction.	Resultant Velocity.	Mean Velocity.	Maximum.	Minimum.	Difference.		Depth in inches.	Approximate duration.	Depth in inches.	Approximate duration.	Depth in inches.	Approximate duration.
1	23.4	0.160	84	29.230	29.070	0.9	S 63 W	10.2	10.7	37.2	32.0	5.2		...	...	S	1.0	S	1.0
2	37.7	.160	73	.319	.153	1.0	N 83 E	3.3	5.0	42.2	29.4	12.8		...	...	...	...	...	...
3	Sunday						N 65 E	6.4	6.6	43.5	32.2	11.3		.505	10.5	...	...	.505	10.5
4	41.7	.222	83	.066	.444	1.0	N 59 W	11.5	12.3	54.2	33.4	20.8		.055	0.6	...	...	.055	0.6
5	29.3	.101	63	.987	.856	0.2	S 84 W	5.2	3.9	35.0	24.8	10.2		...	...	...	...	...	...
6	31.6	.130	76	.074	.838	0.4	S 61 W	1.7	2.1	38.0	23.3	14.7		...	...	...	...	...	...
7	28.7	.108	67	.538	.431	0.6	N 55 W	14.8	15.6	37.0	30.9	6.1		...	...	...	...	...	...
8	27.8	.114	70	.923	.809	1.0	S 89 W	4.1	4.2	32.0	20.6	11.4		...	...	0.2	4.5	.020	4.5
9	32.1	.160	88	.017	.457	0.9	S 11 E	4.1	9.1	35.8	25.0	10.8		...	...	1.0	4.0	.100	4.0
10	Sunday						S 35 W	4.8	5.1	40.2	28.4	11.8		...	...	...	...	...	...
11	39.2	.199	83	.539	.340	0.8	S 82 E	4.8	6.3	44.8	33.4	11.4		.045	4.0	...	...	.045	4.0
12	41.6	.232	85	.456	.224	0.7	S 47 W	8.0	13.3	51.6	38.6	13.0		R	1.0	...	...	R	1.0
13	23.7	.087	69	.922	.834	0.7	S 73 W	7.0	7.8	28.2	21.9	6.3		...	...	...	...	...	...
14	15.2	.063	71	.680	.616	0.4	S 74 W	16.1	16.4	21.4	12.6	8.8		...	...	S	0.5	S	0.5
15	12.6	.058	76	.857	.628	0.2	S 84 W	6.6	6.7	20.0	11.1	8.9		...	...	...	...	...	...
16	16.3	.074	78	.769	.715	0.7	S 38 E	3.4	3.9	22.0	6.0	10.0		...	...	0.2	3.5	.020	3.5
17	Sunday						S 54 E	0.8	1.2	29.0	16.0	13.0		...	...	S	3.0	S	3.0
18	31.7	.153	85	.094	.541	0.9	S 58 E	3.2	3.7	38.0	24.8	13.2		.100	2.5	0.2	5.7	.120	8.2
19	35.0	.163	78	.323	.160	0.9	S 89 W	15.6	16.7	42.5	30.8	11.7		...	...	S	1.0	S	1.0
20	19.1	.080	78	.400	.380	0.9	N 27 E	10.0	13.0	22.0	18.8	3.2		...	...	3.5	10.2	.350	10.2
21	15.8	.002	69	.530	.468	0.4	S 88 W	12.2	13.4	21.4	8.2	13.2		...	...	...	...	...	...
22	12.3	.059	77	.849	.790	0.0	S 64 W	5.4	5.5	17.5	10.8	6.7		...	...	...	...	...	...
23	17.1	.082	83	.986	.904	0.6	S 25 W	2.5	3.1	30.3	5.7	30.6		...	...	...	...	...	...
24	Sunday						S 40 W	2.3	2.3	38.0	15.8	22.2		...	...	...	...	...	...
25	...	...	...	...	...	...	S 47 W	1.4	1.4	40.2	33.6	6.6		...	...	...	...	...	...
26	36.4	.205	95	.307	.192	1.0	N 38 E	0.4	0.6	40.0	29.8	10.4		.810	14.0	...	...	.810	14.0
27	31.0	.172	87	.590	.418	0.6	N 31 W	1.8	2.2	30.0	34.4	4.6		.212	1.5	...	...	.212	1.5
28	31.9	.157	87	.730	.573	1.0	N 68 W	5.2	4.7	34.5	27.2	7.3		...	...	0.1	3.2	.010	3.2
29	24.5	.104	78	30.035	.931	0.9	N 23 W	1.8	7.7	28.0	24.1	3.9		...	...	S	3.0	S	3.0
30	23.7	.109	85	29.882	.773	0.8	N 50 E	7.5	7.7	29.4	21.2	0.2		...	...	...	...	...	...
31	Sunday						S 18 W	9.0	10.2	37.8	10.6	18.2		...	...	...	...	...	...
	27.7	.129	79	29.076	29.547	0.7	S 81 W	3.1	7.3	34.7	23.3	11.4		1.727	33.1	5.2	30.6	2.247	72.7

TORONTO.
GENERAL METEOROLOGICAL ABSTRACT, JANUARY, 1866.

Days.	DAILY MEANS.						WIND.			EXTREMES OF TEMPERATURE.			RAIN.		SNOW.		TOTAL FALL.	
	Temperature of Air.	Pressure of Vapour.	Rel. Humid.	Barometric Pressure.	Pressure of Dry Air.	Clouded Sky.	Resultant Direction.	Resultant Velocity.	Mean Velocity.	Maximum.	Minimum.	Difference.	Depth in Inches.	Approximate duration.	Depth in inches.	Approximate duration.	Depth in Inches.	Approximate duration.
1	30.0	0.128	74	30.769	29.643	0.9	S 51 W	10.9	11.4	36.0	32.2	3.8	...	...	...	...	...	...
2	23.1	.098	78	.837	.739	0.5	S 17 W	1.8	1.8	29.6	17.8	11.8	...	...	...	...	...	...
3	26.9	.122	84	.580	.457	1.0	S 71 W	6.2	6.5	31.8	21.1	10.7	...	...	0.1	3.0	0.010	3.0
4	9.8	.061	80	.717	.657	0.4	N 44 W	13.5	14.7	23.2	13.4	9.8	...	...	0.1	1.7	.010	1.7
5	7.6	.053	82	.864	.811	0.7	N 74 W	6.8	10.1	14.8	-7.6	22.4	...	...	S	0.3	S	0.3
6	4.2	.044	83	30.093	30.049	1.0	N 12 E	7.7	8.0	6.0	1.0	5.0	...	...	0.2	7.0	.020	7.0
7	-9.5	.023	77	30.672	30.649	0.1	N 1 W	10.0	10.1	-6.4	-13.0	6.6	...	...	...	...	...	...
8	-0.5	.034	84	30.836	30.801	0.0	N 18 W	5.9	6.1	8.0	-14.0	22.0	...	...	...	...	...	...
9	8.0	.053	89	30.493	30.440	0.1	N 38 W	0.3	0.4	19.0	-2.6	21.6	...	...	...	...	...	...
10	21.6	.108	89	29.917	29.809	0.8	S 42 W	6.1	6.8	28.0	6.8	21.2	...	...	0.4	3.0	.040	3.0
11	30.9	.159	91	.736	.577	1.0	S 29 E	1.6	3.6	34.6	25.0	9.6	...	...	1.2	3.0	.120	3.0
12	31.2	.170	97	.405	.238	1.0	N 75 E	11.3	11.4	35.2	29.6	5.6	0.055	9.0	1.0	6.5	.155	15.5
13	23.8	.123	80	.414	.290	1.0	N 43 W	12.7	14.8	38.0	28.2	9.8	...	...	0.3	4.5	.030	4.5
14	Sunday						N 8 W	7.6	8.2	3.0	-6.5	9.5	...	...	...	...	...	...
15	13.2	.079	93	.782	.703	1.0	S 87 E	15.9	18.5	34.0	-6.8	40.8	...	...	3.0	18.0	.300	18.0
16	26.6	.114	77	.323	.209	0.9	S 53 W	17.2	17.2	35.6	14.2	21.3	...	...	0.2	3.5	.020	3.5
17	26.7	.109	74	.456	.347	1.0	S 57 W	9.2	9.7	32.0	20.4	11.6	...	..	S	0.5	S	0.5
18	27.6	.123	82	.460	.337	0.8	N 20 E	1.2	4.0	36.2	23.2	13.0	...	...	S	0.5	S	0.5
19	32.3	.169	92	.434	.266	1.0	N 75 E	5.9	6.5	44.0	24.8	19.2	.317	5.0	...	...	.317	5.0
20	21.2	.114	78	.535	.421	0.7	S 72 W	24.1	24.4	44.0	15.0	29.0	.085	1.0	S	0.5	.085	1.5
21	Sunday						S 66 W	20.1	20.3	15.0	3.7	11.3	...	...	...	...	...	...
22	12.6	.060	78	.775	.715	0.8	S 80 W	0.1	9.2	18.0	11.0	7.0	...	...	S	2.0	S	2.0
23	15.2	.063	73	.946	.883	0.7	N 63 W	1.6	1.8	22.0	7.0	15.0	...	...	...	...	...	...
24	20.6	.096	84	.859	.763	0.8	N 70 E	12.4	13.1	28.0	10.7	17.3	...	...	2.5	7.5	.250	7.5
25	23.3	.111	88	.458	.347	1.0	N 2 E	4.7	6.5	28.5	17.8	10.7	...	...	1.0	14.1	.100	14.1
26	19.2	.082	80	.629	.547	0.8	N 34 W	5.4	5.0	23.0	16.4	6.6	...	...	0.1	1.0	.010	1.0
27	20.8	.091	81	.792	.701	1.0	N 57 E	2.1	4.5	24.2	17.2	7.0	...	...	...	...	...	...
28	Sunday						S 54 E	3.2	4.1	26.2	21.4	4.6	...	...	...	...	...	...
29	26.9	.129	88	.648	.519	1.0	N 87 E	4.8	5.8	33.4	21.6	11.8	...	...	...	...	...	...
30	31.7	.154	85	.077	.224	0.7	S 79 W	7.7	10.6	38.0	26.4	11.6	.065	5.0	S	0.3	.065	5.3
31	24.9	.095	72	.257	.162	0.4	S 84 W	12.9	13.2	33.2	18.4	14.8	...	...	0.2	2.0	.020	2.0
	20.7	0.101	83	29.718	29.617	0.8	N 75 W	3.0	9.3	26.3	12.7	13.6	0.522	20.0	10.3	78.9	1.552	98.9

TORONTO.
General Meteorological Abstract, February, 1866.

Days.	DAILY MEANS.						WIND.			EXTREMES OF TEMPERATURE			RAIN.		SNOW.		T'TAL FALL.	
	Temperature of Air	Pressure of Vapour.	Rel. Humid.	Barometric Pressure.	Pressure of Dry Air.	Clouded Sky.	Resultant Direction.	Resultant Velocity.	Mean Velocity.	Maximum.	Minimum.	Difference.	Depth in inches.	Approximate duration.	Depth in inches.	Approximate duration.	Depth in inches.	Approximate duration.
1	18.2	0.077	77	29.240	29.163	0.9	N 80 W	13.6	14.0	21.2	18.5	2.7	...	...	...	...	...	...
2	16.2	.073	81	.293	.220	0.7	S 80 W	10.4	10.8	13.0	14.2	8.8	...	...	0.1	2.1	0.010	2.1
3	14.6	.062	73	.414	.352	0.7	S 72 W	16.8	17.0	20.0	10.6	9.4	...	...	...	...	...	...
4	Su	uday					N 69 W	10.2	11.2	13.5	7.2	6.3	...	...	0.2	2.5	.020	2.5
5	9.0	.049	74	30.029	.980	0.8	S 58 W	13.9	14.4	16.2	-3.5	19.7	...	...	...	...	...	...
6	11.4	.051	68	30.166	30.115	0.9	N 4 W	5.1	9.5	18.3	9.2	9.1	...	...	S	2.0	S	2.0
7	23.5	.008	76	29.893	29.795	1.0	S 1 W	2.4	3.1	29.0	8.2	20.8	...	...	...	...	...	...
8	26.4	.126	88	.704	.578	1.0	N 37 E	5.2	6.0	31.0	24.8	6.2	...	...	2.5	11.3	.250	11.3
9	25.7	.120	86	.553	.433	1.0	S 34 E	4.2	5.1	13.2	18.7	16.5	...	...	...	...	...	...
10	34.1	.176	89	.452	.276	1.0	N 40 E	1.6	2.4	39.0	25.2	13.8	0.150	5.0	1.5	5.0	.300	10.0
11	Su	nday					N 15 W	10.7	10.9	35.0	32.2	2.8	...	...	3.5	8.5	.350	8.5
12	23.3	.107	85	.799	.692	0.6	N 6 W	7.8	8.0	26.0	22.8	3.2	...	...	...	...	...	...
13	25.7	.119	84	.772	.653	0.9	S 72 W	2.0	4.2	30.9	15.2	15.7	...	...	0.6	2.5	.060	2.5
14	29.0	.141	87	.240	.099	1.0	S 52 W	12.9	16.0	37.2	23.6	13.6	...	...	1.5	6.5	.150	6.5
15	2.7	.040	79	.710	.670	0.6	N 62 W	7.7	8.7	7.0	3.4	3.6	...	...	...	...	...	...
16	2.6	.044	84	30.053	30.009	0.5	S 51 W	19.2	19.8	16.1	-8.0	24.1	...	...	...	...	...	...
17	26.0	.103	73	29.859	29.786	0.4	S 37 W	16.8	16.9	33.0	2.5	30.5	...	...	...	...	...	...
18	Su	nday					S 21 W	3.1	3.7	32.4	25.0	7.4	...	...	5.0	11.0	.500	11.0
19	29.5	.144	87	.269	.126	1.0	S 74 W	6.0	6.8	35.2	30.2	5.0	...	...	0.5	5.5	.050	5.5
20	19.6	.090	85	.640	.549	0.9	N 87 W	4.9	7.4	31.0	18.5	12.5	...	...	0.5	5.0	.050	5.0
21	23.6	.112	79	.924	.812	0.8	S 6 E	3.7	5.3	39.6	1.5	38.1	...	...	...	...	...	...
22	40.1	.189	76	.782	.593	0.6	S 39 W	7.0	8.8	43.5	28.0	15.6	...	...	...	...	...	...
23	40.6	.204	82	.568	.364	0.9	S 67 E	1.8	4.1	45.0	33.8	11.2	.600	11.0	...	...	.600	11.0
24	33.1	.171	88	.364	.193	0.7	N 75 W	14.3	16.1	45.0	32.0	13.0	.080	4.0	...	...	.080	4.0
25	Su	nday					N 68 W	13.7	14.1	13.4	8.4	5.0	...	...	...	...	...	...
26	10.4	.055	81	30.229	30.174	0.7	S 47 W	5.0	5.6	22.0	-2.0	24.0	...	...	1.0	3.0	.100	3.0
27	15.6	.105	78	30.022	29.917	0.8	S 87 W	3.5	4.1	23.8	14.2	19.6	...	...	...	...	...	...
28	30.5	.142	88	29.961	.818	1.0	N 83 E	8.9	9.0	34.2	20.5	13.7	...	...	...	...	...	...
	22.6	0.108	81	29.707	29.599	0.8	S 80 W	5.1	9.4	43.6	18.1	15.5	0.830	20.0	16.0	64.0	2.520	84.9

TORONTO.
GENERAL METEOROLOGICAL ABSTRACT, MARCH, 1866.

Days	DAILY MEANS.						WIND.			EXTREMES OF TEMPERATURE.			RAIN.		SNOW.		TOTAL FALL.	
	Temperature of Air.	Pressure of Vapour.	Rel. Humid.	Barometric Pressure.	Pressure of Dry Air.	Clouded Sky.	Resultant Direction.	Resultant Velocity.	Mean Velocity.	Maximum.	Minimum.	Difference.	Depth in Inches.	Approximate duration.	Depth in Inches.	Approximate duration.	Depth in Inches.	Approximate duration.
1	36.9	0.188	8	29.748	29.561	0.8	N 60 E	2.5	2.5	42.8	28.4	14.4	).005	0.2	...	...	).005	0.2
2	38.2	.203	88	.654	.451	0.9	N 61 E	4.3	5.2	44.0	34.0	10.0	.055	1.7	...	...	.055	1.7
3	35.6	.140	68	.632	.492	0.4	S 78 W	7.9	11.8	45.8	33.9	11.9	...	...	S	1.0	S	1.0
4	Sunday						N 71 W	20.0	21.1	27.5	19.3	8.2	...	...	S	4.0	S	4.0
5	23.3	.076	63	.820	.744	0.2	N 71 W	21.0	21.2	30.8	17.2	13.6	...	...	...	...	...	...
6	23.7	.091	73	.844	.753	0.1	N 76 W	14.5	14.6	30.9	16.2	14.9	...	...	...	...	...	...
7	19.3	.068	66	.716	.648	0.4	N 64 W	23.0	23.2	23.0	17.5	5.5	...	...	...	...	...	...
8	22.0	.075	64	.793	.718	0.3	N 52 W	12.4	13.1	29.5	17.0	12.5	...	...	S	0.2	S	0.2
9	19.1	.075	74	.763	.688	0.5	N 49 W	11.4	11.9	24.0	15.0	9.0	...	...	0.4	4.0	.040	4.0
10	21.8	.089	73	.864	.778	0.2	S 47 W	5.9	9.3	31.0	9.4	21.6	...	...	3.0	4.0	.300	4.0
11	Sunday						S 56 W	4.0	8.5	38.2	21.5	16.7	.030	3.5	1.5	1.5	.180	5.0
12	33.7	.171	88	.723	.552	1.0	N 20 E	3.7	3.9	38.2	31.5	6.7	...	...	S	1.0	S	1.0
13	33.2	.155	84	.949	.794	1.0	N 55 E	7.5	8.0	37.5	29.8	7.7	.330	8.5	S	1.0	.330	9.5
14	35.0	.196	97	.736	.540	1.0	N 17 E	2.0	5.2	37.5	32.4	5.1	.635	12.5	...	...	.635	12.5
15	34.4	.185	93	.591	.406	1.0	N 35 E	0.6	5.3	36.6	34.0	2.6	.320	6.5	...	...	.320	6.5
16	31.2	.140	77	.304	.164	0.8	S 77 W	15.9	16.7	39.0	32.2	6.8	...	...	0.1	4.0	.010	4.0
17	10.7	.047	66	.608	.561	0.0	N 82 W	20.4	20.6	12.2	10.0	2.2	...	...	...	...	...	...
18	Sunday						S 78 W	10.1	12.2	26.0	7.5	18.5	...	...	0.3	5.0	.030	5.0
19	19.9	.068	62	.701	.633	0.5	N 19 W	6.8	6.9	28.8	14.2	14.6	...	...	...	...	...	...
20	20.7	.089	77	.551	.462	0.9	N 66 E	15.0	15.3	30.0	14.4	15.8	.500	...	0.2	13.	.520	13.0
21	23.2	.103	83	.394	.291	0.7	N 75 W	8.2	9.3	30.4	20.5	19.9	...	...	...	...	...	...
22	28.2	.116	75	.801	.685	0.7	S 9 W	2.4	7.3	34.8	17.9	16.9	...	...	...	...	...	...
23	32.9	.159	84	.466	.307	1.0	N 56 W	5.1	10.5	37.0	30.0	7.0	...	...	0.4	3.0	.040	3.0
24	30.4	.140	82	.430	.290	0.9	S 89 W	12.3	14.3	37.0	28.0	9.0	...	...	0.3	6.0	.030	6.6
25	Sunday						N 73 W	22.6	25.2	16.2	10.6	5.6	...	...	S	3.0	S	3.0
26	19.3	.069	67	.556	.787	0.6	N 57 W	11.2	11.5	29.0	12.0	17.0	...	...	...	...	...	...
27	25.0	.097	73	30.059	.962	0.0	S 75 W	1.5	2.5	34.0	12.9	21.1	...	...	...	...	...	...
28	31.3	.154	86	29.630	.476	1.0	S 57 E	5.6	9.7	35.8	23.0	2.8	.020	1.5	0.6	5.2	.090	5.2
29	31.5	.141	80	.498	.357	0.8	N 76 W	12.6	13.0	36.0	30.2	5.8	...	...	0.2	3.0	.020	3.0
30	...	...	...	...	...	...	S 64 W	6.	8.5	29.0	20.5	18.5	...	...	0.1	1.0	.010	1.0
31	35.6	.177	84	.192	.014	1.0	S 61 W	4.8	8.2	40.4	30.5	9.9	.010	1.0	0.1	2.0	.020	3.0
	27.5	0.124	77	29.667	29.543	0.6	N 73 W	6.8	11.5	33.0	21.7	11.3	1.915	35.7	7.2	62.5	2.035	98.2

TORONTO
GENERAL METEOROLOGICAL ABSTRACT, APRIL, 1866.

Days.	DAILY MEANS.						WIND.			EXTREMES OF TEMPERATURE			RAIN.		SNOW.		TOTAL FALL.	
	Temperature of Air.	Pressure of Vapour.	Hel Humid	Barometric Pressure.	Pressure of Dry Air.	Clouded Sky.	Resultant Direction.	Resultant Velocity.	Mean Velocity.	Maximum.	Minimum.	Difference.	Depth in inches	Approximate duration	Depth in inches	Approximate duration	Depth in inches	Approximate duration
1	Su	nday					N 50 W	5.7	5.9	41.2	34.4	6.8	...	...	...	...	...	...
2	35.3	0.146	71	29.864	29.718	0.4	N 74 E	4.9	5.0	40.0	32.7	7.9	...	...	...	...	...	...
3	39.9	.138	56	.759	.621	0.0	N 74 E	8.2	8.8	44.5	32.4	12.1	...	...	...	...	...	...
4	43.8	.221	77	.632	.411	0.3	N 88 E	3.0	3.1	54.5	37.4	17.1	...	...	...	...	...	...
5	49.7	.281	77	.578	.297	0.0	S 78 W	6.3	7.9	70.0	33.8	36.2	...	...	...	...	...	...
6	46.3	.131	61	.832	.701	1.0	N 83 W	10.4	11.0	41.5	35.4	6.1	...	...	...	...	...	...
7	42.0	.119	67	.854	.734	0.8	N 40 W	6.3	7.9	38.6	30.0	8.0	...	...	...	...	...	...
8	Su	nday					N 38 W	2.5	6.2	40.2	28.8	11.4	...	...	...	...	...	...
9	36.4	.094	46	.931	.837	0.0	S 8 W	1.5	2.0	47.5	28.5	19.0	...	...	...	...	...	...
10	40.5	.151	60	.740	.589	0.7	S 70 E	3.1	4.1	49.5	29.0	20.5	R	0.5	...	...	R	0.5
11	40.2	.203	65	.673	.470	0.0	S 10 W	1.0	1.1	57.4	38.5	18.9	...	...	...	...	...	...
12	51.6	.245	64	.519	.273	0.5	S 54 W	4.5	8.5	63.5	37.0	26.5	0.215	1.7	...	...	.215	1.7
13	42.1	.181	65	.837	.656	0.4	N 64 W	3.5	0.0	51.0	39.4	11.6	...	...	...	...	...	...
14	40.5	.166	65	.610	.444	0.6	N 73 E	2.8	3.9	49.0	35.8	13.2	...	...	...	...	...	...
15	Su	nday					N 56 W	2.0	4.1	48.2	31.6	16.6	...	...	...	...	...	...
16	44.4	.172	59	.868	.690	0.5	N 80 E	11.4	11.5	51.5	34.0	17.5	...	...	...	...	...	...
17	48.9	.259	75	.919	.660	0.3	N 89 E	4.3	4.3	50.4	41.8	19.6	...	...	...	...	...	...
18	53.8	.312	76	.802	.490	0.6	S 71 E	2.7	2.8	62.0	43.2	18.8	.010	0.8	...	...	.010	0.8
19	50.4	.398	87	.737	.339	1.0	N 78 E	6.2	6.9	57.0	51.4	15.6	.160	1.5	...	...	.160	1.5
20	52.5	.324	82	.479	.155	1.0	S 84 E	0.9	1.0	0.8	46.4	14.4	.210	5.0	...	...	.210	5.0
21	56.3	.274	64	.235	28.961	0.7	S 58 W	7.1	9.0	71.0	48.4	22.6	...	...	...	...	...	...
22	Su	nday					N 42 W	4.7	6.7	64.0	40.0	24.0	...	...	...	...	...	...
23	40.6	.213	85	.035	28.822	1.0	N 15 W	21.9	24.3	49.0	39.0	10.0	1.050	10.7	...	...	1.080	10.7
24	39.9	.132	56	.027	28.895	0.0	N 61 W	19.4	20.4	43.0	32.8	16.2	...	...	S	0.6	S	0.6
25	37.6	.114	52	.217	29.103	0.5	N 56 W	13.9	14.3	47.8	30.0	17.8	...	...	...	...	...	...
26	39.2	.135	58	.512	.377	0.4	N 44 W	11.7	11.8	47.0	33.8	13.2	...	...	S	1.0	S	1.0
27	43.9	.170	59	.623	.453	0.5	S 89 W	0.1	2.7	53.0	30.6	22.4	R	0.1	...	...	R	0.1
28	47.5	.190	57	.363	.173	0.4	N 59 W	8.3	12.3	59.0	39.0	20.0	...	...	...	...	...	...
29	Su	nday					N 68 W	18.5	18.7	56.0	35.0	20.0	...	...	...	...	...	...
30	42.0	.115	43	.599	.475	0.0	N 49 W	3.3	5.9	52.0	29.2	22.8	...	...	...	...	...	...
	43.0	0.195	65	29.600	29.414	0.6	N 42 W	3.3	8.0	52.9	36.0	16.9	1.675	20.3	S	1.6	1.675	21.9

TORONTO.
GENERAL METEOROLOGICAL ABSTRACT, MAY, 1866.

Days.	DAILY MEANS.						WIND.		EXTREMES OF TEMPERATURE.				RAIN.		SNOW.		TOTAL FALL.	
	Temperature of Air	Pressure of Vapour.	Rel. Humid.	Barometric Pressure.	Pressure of Dry Air.	Clouded Sky.	Resultant Direction.	Resultant Velocity.	Mean Velocity	Maximum.	Minimum.	Difference.	Depth in inches.	Approximate duration.	Depth in inches.	Approximate duration.	Depth in inches.	Approximate duration.
1	39.1	0.155	65	29.324	29.169	1.0	N 43 E	6.4	10.0	47.0	33.8	10.2	0.075	3.0	...	...	0.075	3.0
2	39.7	.153	63	.463	.310	0.6	N 48 W	14.6	15.3	46.0	35.0	11.0	...	...	...	...	...	...
3	40.8	.115	47	.508	.393	0.6	N 69 W	10.9	11.0	52.0	35.4	16.6	...	...	...	...	...	...
4	47.9	.135	42	.433	.298	0.4	N 53 W	12.3	13.0	58.0	34.4	23.6	...	...	...	...	...	...
5	46.4	.176	57	.520	.344	0.7	N 47 W	9.2	11.0	57.8	34.0	23.8	...	...	...	...	...	...
6	Sunday						N 27 W	12.8	13.1	60.2	37.8	22.4	...	...	...	...	...	...
7	48.1	.160	48	.802	.642	0.3	S 47 E	2.3	2.6	56.0	38.4	17.6	...	...	...	...	...	...
8	50.0	.212	60	.535	.323	0.8	N 37 E	4.6	6.7	56.4	37.2	19.2	.270	7.0	...	...	.270	7.0
9	50.5	.280	76	.426	.146	0.7	S 69 W	4.3	6.1	60.0	44.8	15.2	...	...	...	...	...	...
10	49.8	.248	70	.545	.297	0.4	S 58 E	2.2	3.6	60.0	36.8	23.2	...	...	...	...	...	...
11	56.3	.277	62	.507	.230	0.1	S 66 E	1.4	1.6	70.0	40.5	29.5	...	...	...	...	...	...
12	60.6	.309	60	.454	.145	0.5	S 44 W	5.5	9.8	72.2	44.0	28.2	.165	5.0	...	...	.165	5.0
13	Sunday						N 41 W	12.2	12.4	49.0	44.2	4.8	.315	4.0	...	...	.315	4.0
14	43.3	.149	56	.664	.515	0.0	N 68 W	3.6	5.3	55.0	33.8	21.2	...	...	...	...	...	...
15	46.9	.232	71	.416	.184	0.9	S 14 W	3.2	7.4	55.5	33.4	22.1	.125	5.5	...	...	.125	5.5
16	43.9	.201	69	.541	.340	0.6	N 1 W	4.3	6.9	50.2	43.0	6.6	...	...	...	...	...	...
17	44.4	.169	57	.593	.424	0.4	S 83 E	5.6	5.8	52.4	34.0	18.4	...	...	...	...	...	...
18	51.1	.260	68	.425	.165	0.7	N 80 E	3.8	5.0	59.2	41.5	17.7	...	...	...	...	...	...
19	57.0	.299	63	.463	.164	0.5	S 62 E	2.5	3.7	67.0	43.8	23.2	...	...	...	...	...	...
20	Sunday						N 39 W	4.4	10.6	73.4	45.8	27.6	.180	1.5	...	...	.180	1.5
21	47.0	.170	53	.465	.295	0.7	N 60 W	22.0	22.2	53.8	47.4	6.4	R	1.0	...	...	R	1.0
22	42.9	.142	52	.617	.475	0.5	N 49 W	17.5	17.9	50.5	39.2	11.3	...	...	...	...	...	...
23	45.0	.193	64	.662	.469	0.4	N 64 W	13.2	13.7	57.8	35.0	22.8	...	...	...	...	...	...
24	54.3	.150	39	.585	.435	0.5	S 72 W	10.4	11.3	68.0	36.2	31.8	...	...	...	...	...	...
25	50.0	.231	63	.411	.179	0.6	S 76 W	2.4	4.8	58.0	47.0	11.0	.090	4.0	...	...	.090	4.0
26	51.8	.260	67	.323	.063	0.2	N 71 E	10.2	10.8	56.0	39.8	16.2	R	0.2	...	...	R	0.2
27	Sunday						N 47 E	12.1	14.7	55.0	48.0	7.0	1.290	20.5	...	...	1.290	20.5
28	48.3	.260	77	.135	28.875	0.7	N 48 W	11.2	11.6	55.8	47.0	8.8	.085	4.5	...	...	.085	4.5
29	47.6	.204	79	.268	29.003	0.7	S 84 W	3.7	5.4	58.5	39.4	19.1	.108	0.3	...	...	.108	0.3
30	50.9	.280	75	.321	.041	0.7	N 87 W	5.2	7.4	58.2	39.4	18.8	.115	4.5	...	...	.115	4.5
31	49.0	.233	65	.670	.443	0.4	N 51 W	2.2	6.4	55.0	42.8	15.2	...	...	...	...	...	...
	48.3	0.212	62	29.485	29.273	0.5	N 46 W	4.5	9.3	57.6	30.8	17.8	2.820	60.1	...	...	2.820	60.1

TORONTO.
GENERAL METEOROLOGICAL ABSTRACT, JUNE, 1866.

Days.	DAILY MEANS.					WIND.			EXTREMES OF TEMPERATURE			RAIN.		SNOW.		TOTAL FALL.	
	Temperature of Air.	Pressure of Vapour.	Rel. Humid.	Barometric Pressure.	Pressure of Dry Air.	Clouded Sky.	Resultant Direction.	Resultant Velocity.	Mean Velocity.	Maximum.	Minimum.	Difference.	Depth in inches.	Approximate duration.	Depth in inches.	Approximate duration.	Depth in inches.	Approximate duration.
1	49.9	0.218	66	29.753	29.54	0.4	S 2 W	1.5	2.1	60.4	30.0	30.4	...	...	...	...	...	...
2	55.4	.281	64	.612	.331	0.2	N 67 E	1.4	2.1	65.3	44.6	20.7	...	...	...	...	...	...
3	Sunday						N 76 E	9.4	9.4	65.0	48.5	16.5	R	0.5	...	...	R	0.5
4	56.6	.421	87	.387	28.986	0.9	N 70 E	4.2	4.2	74.0	51.2	12.8	0.14	3.0	...	...	0.14	3.0
5	58.2	.493	95	.410	28.947	1.0	N 86 E	2.1	2.2	55.2	51.4	13.8	.150	8.0	...	...	.150	8.0
6	55.8	.382	86	.237	28.914	0.9	S 23 W	4.3	5.1	77.0	71.0	16.0	.14	4.0	...	...	.14	4.0
7	60.8	.361	73	.403	29.015	0.5	N 78 W	10.1	10.2	89.5	51.5	18.0	...	...	...	...	...	...
8	60.4	.397	75	.551	.160	0.4	N 88 E	6.4	7.8	68.8	51.2	17.6	...	...	...	...	...	...
9	57.3	.395	84	.544	.149	0.5	N 89 E	1.5	2.2	67.5	51.0	16.5	...	...	...	...	...	...
10	Sunday						N 40 W	4.2	6.0	75.2	42.4	25.8	...	...	...	...	...	...
11	57.4	.282	60	.861	.579	0.4	S 36 E	0.6	2.1	65.2	50.8	15.4	...	...	...	...	...	...
12	56.0	.269	60	.677	.408	0.6	N 82 E	9.1	9.1	60.4	50.0	10.4	.710	2.2	...	...	.710	2.2
13	57.1	.424	90	.393	28.963	0.5	S 41 E	0.7	1.2	69.0	47.8	21.2	.100	1.0	...	...	.100	1.0
14	65.2	.348	59	.361	29.013	0.6	S 78 W	6.6	6.8	77.8	57.0	20.8	...	...	...	...	...	...
15	64.2	.33	57	.364	.034	0.6	S 89 W	6.9	7.7	72.4	51.4	21.0	R	0.5	...	...	R	0.5
16	59.8	.366	72	.418	.052	0.3	S 20 W	2.6	3.2	67.8	52.0	15.8	.100	0.5	...	...	.100	0.5
17	Sunday						N 62 E	6.5	7.5	64.5	49.5	15.	.950	15.0	...	...	.950	15.0
18	52.6	.332	83	.037	28.705	1.9	S 29 E	10.3	12.8	57.7	48.8	8.2	.245	17.0	...	...	.245	17.0
19	55.4	.336	75	.453	29.120	0.7	N 76 W	7.7	7.6	65.4	48.4	17.2	R	1.0	...	...	R	1.0
20	52.0	.363	87	.663	.295	0.1	S 30 W	4.3	4.4	73.4	45.4	28.0	...	...	...	...	...	...
21	67.5	.472	66	.524	.052	0.4	S 23 W	6.6	6.9	75.8	52.0	23.8	...	...	...	...	...	...
22	67.0	.443	65	.524	.041	0.2	S 45 W	2.9	3.7	76.2	60.0	16.2	...	...	...	...	...	...
23	65.7	.543	75	.541	28.939	0.7	S 26 W	1.3	1.3	77.0	56.6	20.4	...	...	...	...	...	...
24	Sunday						S 57 E	1.3	2.5	76.8	59.0	17.8	...	...	...	...	...	...
25	74.1	.583	71	.633	29.02	0.5	S 61 W	4.8	5.1	89.3	74.6	23.7	R	0.2	...	...	R	0.2
26	68.3	.537	75	.430	28.89	0.7	S 15 W	7.0	4.8	79.7	57.6	21.3	.08	0.7	...	...	.08	0.7
27	64.8	.462	71	.42	28.997	1.0	N 42 W	4.6	6.7	72.6	63.8	8.8	.13	2.5	...	...	.13	2.5
28	64.4	.275	41	.644	29.367	0.0	N 41 W	1.4	4.2	77.3	55.1	22.2	...	...	...	...	...	...
29	58.7	.251	57	.734	.44	0.2	S 44 E	1.1	2.2	70.4	41.0	29.4	.025	1.0	...	...	.025	1.0
30	58.4	.254	62	.78	.474	0.2	S 25 E	1.4	1.7	76.6	55.6	21.0	...	...	...	...	...	...
	60.2	0.38	70	29.521	29.14	0.4	S 15 W	0.7	5.1	89.3	41.4	14.1	2.720	57.1	...	...	2.720	57.1

TORONTO.
GENERAL METEOROLOGICAL ABSTRACT, JULY, 1866.

Days.	DAILY MEANS.						WIND.			EXTREMES OF TEMPERATURE.			RAIN.		SNOW.		TOTAL FALL.	
	Temperature of Air.	Pressure of Vapour.	Rel. Humid.	Barometric Pressure.	Pressure of Dry Air.	Cloud. d Sky.	Resultant Direction.	Resultant Velocity.	Mean Velocity.	Maximum.	Minimum.	Difference.	Depth in inches.	Approximate duration.	depth in inches.	Approximate duration.	Depth in inches.	Approximate duration.
1	Sunday						S 14 W	3.3	3.4	74.5	47.8	26.7	0.005	1.0	...	...	0.005	1.0
2	65.7	0.487	77	29.756	29.269	0.8	S 22 W	3.4	3.6	74.0	58.8	15.2	R	1.0	...	...	R	1.0
3	69.6	.497	71	.535	.038	1.0	S 24 W	6.2	6.4	78.5	56.0	22.5	.135	3.5	...	...	.135	3.5
4	66.2	.408	79	.350	28.853	0.7	S 08 W	3.2	4.0	76.5	59.2	17.3	.660	4.0	...	...	.660	4.0
5	67.8	.576	85	.530	28.954	0.7	S 28 W	3.2	3.4	80.0	59.2	20.8	.110	4.3	...	...	.110	4.3
6	73.6	.650	81	.550	28.691	0.6	S 32 W	4.1	4.2	83.0	63.4	19.6	...	...	...	...	...	...
7	73.2	.664	81	.509	28.845	0.7	S 39 W	2.2	2.2	81.5	64.0	17.5	.410	3.8	...	...	.410	3.8
8	Sunday						N 45 W	5.1	6.1	79.0	66.0	13.0	.480	2.2	...	...	.480	2.2
9	64.3	.390	65	.824	29.434	0.5	N 25 E	1.0	2.8	71.6	59.0	12.6	...	...	...	...	...	...
10	65.8	.370	61	.844	.468	0.1	S 72 E	1.5	1.8	75.5	54.6	20.9	...	...	...	...	...	...
11	70.8	.498	67	.766	.268	0.1	S 34 W	3.5	3.9	80.0	57.2	22.8	...	...	...	...	...	...
12	74.2	.595	70	.659	.064	0.0	S 48 W	5.1	5.4	88.2	58.0	30.2	...	...	...	...	...	...
13	81.1	.686	67	.536	28.850	0.5	S 79 W	4.6	6.3	94.0	59.0	35.0	.525	0.8	...	...	.525	0.8
14	69.0	.493	68	.617	29.124	0.5	N 85 E	3.8	3.9	75.8	67.0	8.8	.010	0.6	...	...	.010	0.6
15	Sunday						S 48 W	4.0	4.7	91.2	61.0	30.2	...	...	...	...	...	...
16	90.5	.740	72	.637	28.897	0.2	S 36 W	3.2	3.4	92.0	68.6	23.4	R	0.2	...	...	R	0.2
17	75.2	.689	79	.602	28.914	0.4	S 53 W	3.1	5.0	90.2	69.0	21.2	2.345	4.0	...	...	2.345	4.0
18	65.0	.548	80	.536	28.988	0.7	N 20 E	2.9	3.8	72.4	64.5	7.9	.165	4.0	...	...	.165	4.0
19	64.4	.425	71	.715	29.290	0.6	S 83 E	1.8	3.2	71.0	54.5	16.5	...	...	...	...	...	...
20	54.8	.409	93	.688	.278	0.8	N 61 E	4.8	5.0	70.0	54.0	16.0	...	...	...	...	...	...
21	66.4	.546	75	.542	28.996	1.0	N 64 E	4.0	4.4	71.4	61.8	9.6	.145	1.5	...	...	.145	1.5
22	Sunday						N 69 W	1.6	4.3	76.5	61.5	15.0	.365	1.5	...	...	.365	1.5
23	68.1	.516	75	.506	28.990	0.4	N 32 W	4.9	5.5	78.4	60.6	17.8	...	...	...	...	...	...
24	71.7	.536	69	.602	29.060	0.2	S 35 W	1.5	2.1	80.2	56.8	23.4	...	...	...	...	...	...
25	72.8	.521	65	.018	.096	0.4	N 23 W	4.3	5.9	81.0	61.8	19.2	...	...	...	...	...	...
26	72.3	.619	79	.669	.050	0.7	S 49 E	0.1	1.8	80.0	63.4	16.6	...	...	...	...	...	...
27	74.0	.631	76	.606	28.975	0.2	N 84 W	0.6	2.1	80.5	58.4	22.1	...	...	...	...	...	...
28	75.0	.538	63	.476	28.938	0.4	N 18 W	2.7	4.1	86.2	66.2	20.0	...	...	...	...	...	...
29	Sunday						N 27 W	2.5	3.9	80.0	66.2	13.8	R	0.1	...	...	R	0.1
30	69.3	.385	56	.519	29.133	0.4	N 15 W	9.1	9.4	78.4	64.2	14.4	...	...	...	...	...	...
31	69.4	.396	51	.560	.174	0.0	S 5 W	1.4	2.5	77.0	59.2	17.8	.035	1.0	...	...	.035	1.0
	70.4	0.535	72	29.606	29.071	0.5	S 79 W	0.9	4.2	79.6	60.6	19.0	5.390	33.5	...	...	5.390	33.5

TORONTO.
GENERAL METEOROLOGICAL ABSTRACT, AUGUST, 1866.

Days.	DAILY MEANS.					WIND.			EXTREMES OF TEMPERATURE.			RAIN.		SNOW.		TOTAL FALL.	
	Temperature of Air.	Pressure of Vapour.	Rel. Humid.	Barometric Pressure.	Pressure of Dry Air.	Clouded Sky.	Resultant Direction.	Resultant Velocity.	Mean Velocity.	Maximum.	Minimum.	Difference.	Depth in inches.	Approximate duration.	Depth in Inches.	Approximate duration.	Depth in Inches.	Approximate duration.
1	66.3	0.610	85	29.302	28.692	0.6	S 25 W	5.2	5.2	77.0	63.4	13.6	0.165	4.0	...	...	0.165	4.0
2	57.4	.384	64	.428	29.044	0.6	N 89 W	10.4	10.5	71.7	61.5	10.2	...	...	...	...	...	...
3	57.1	.414	77	.566	.152	0.7	S 68 W	2.1	3.2	72.0	52.0	20.0	1.100	13.5	...	...	1.100	13.5
4	56.7	.395	74	.524	.126	0.6	N 35 W	10.2	10.8	72.0	57.8	14.2	.295	3.5	...	...	.295	3.5
5	Sunday						N 59 W	10.1	10.5	71.0	55.0	16.0	...	...	...	...	...	...
6	54.0	.294	55	.636	.342	0.1	N 66 W	10.5	10.6	76.5	53.0	23.5	...	...	...	...	...	...
7	57.0	.347	55	.649	.302	0.2	N 44 W	4.9	5.3	77.0	54.4	22.6	...	...	...	...	...	...
8	58.0	.426	76	.514	.089	0.8	N 48 E	3.5	3.9	71.6	52.5	19.1	.085	5.5	...	...	.085	5.5
9	55.2	.343	63	.475	.133	0.6	N 45 W	9.1	9.4	73.0	56.0	17.0	...	...	...	...	...	...
10	56.4	.373	65	.602	.299	0.2	N 54 W	2.9	4.5	71.5	52.4	19.1	...	...	...	...	...	...
11	55.9	.362	66	.763	.401	0.0	S 27 E	1.2	1.4	73.0	50.0	23.0	...	...	...	...	...	...
12	Sunday						N 79 E	5.5	5.7	70.0	55.0	15.0	2.145	15.0	...	...	2.145	15.0
13	62.4	.550	94	.439	28.890	1.0	N 47 E	4.8	4.0	65.0	60.4	4.6	R	5.5	...	...	R	5.5
14	65.1	.592	80	.490	28.907	0.9	N 35 W	1.1	1.9	73.2	63.0	10.2	.010	0.2	...	...	.010	0.2
15	53.1	.320	61	.780	29.400	0.4	N 13 W	9.6	10.0	66.8	60.0	6.8	...	...	...	...	...	...
16	48.8	.268	61	.905	.637	0.0	S 79 W	0.7	2.4	65.0	46.0	19.0	...	...	...	...	...	...
17	54.3	.355	65	.761	.406	0.0	S 31 W	2.0	2.7	71.3	44.2	27.1	...	...	...	...	...	...
18	60.9	.482	78	.576	.093	0.8	N 1 W	1.0	1.7	72.2	53.0	19.2	.180	6.5	...	...	.180	6.5
19	Sunday						N	2.5	3.4	68.0	58.0	10.0	.355	3.0	...	...	.355	3.0
20	54.7	.373	74	.526	.153	0.6	S 66 W	1.2	3.0	66.8	50.0	16.8	.035	0.5	...	...	.035	0.5
21	54.7	.355	72	.422	.064	0.6	S 60 W	3.1	4.0	70.8	52.5	18.3	.065	2.0	...	...	.065	2.0
22	50.3	.291	67	.438	.144	0.8	N 73 W	8.8	8.9	63.0	42.0	11.0	...	...	...	...	...	...
23	47.1	.258	65	.453	.194	0.3	N 72 W	3.0	3.7	62.4	44.0	18.4	...	...	...	...	...	...
24	47.0	.270	73	.529	.259	0.5	N 76 W	5.8	5.9	63.0	42.4	20.6	R	0.1	...	...	R	0.1
25	49.6	.306	74	.598	.292	0.6	N 89 W	4.2	4.2	63.5	43.5	20.0	...	...	...	...	...	...
26	Sunday						S 40 W	5.5	5.7	68.2	47.0	21.2	.007	0.9	...	...	.007	0.9
27	58.7	.460	80	.505	.040	0.9	S 31 W	3.0	3.6	68.8	51.5	17.5	...	...	...	...	...	...
28	59.1	.456	80	.516	.060	0.5	N 39 E	0.1	2.3	73.0	52.0	21.0	...	...	...	...	...	...
29	55.3	.375	73	.558	.183	0.7	N 44 W	2.2	2.7	70.0	57.2	12.8	...	...	...	...	...	...
30	51.9	.303	82	.537	.143	0.9	S 59 E	1.0	1.7	65.0	42.5	22.5	.015	0.5	...	...	.015	0.5
31	58.1	.430	81	.580	.130	1.0	N 69 E	5.0	6.0	66.4	52.0	14.4	...	...	...	...	...	...
	55.8	0.390	73	29.601	29.171	0.6	N 59 W	2.6	5.2	60.6	52.7	16.9	4.457	60.7	...	...	4.457	60.7

TORONTO.
GENERAL METEOROLOGICAL ABSTRACT, SEPTEMBER, 1866.

Days.	DAILY MEANS.					WIND.			EXTREMES OF TEMPERATURE.			RAIN.		SNOW.		TOTAL FALL.	
	Temperature of Air	Pressure of Vapour.	Rel. Humid.	Barometric Pressure.	Pressure of Dry Air.	Clouded Sky	Resultant Direction.	Resultant Velocity.	Mean Velocity.	Maximum.	Minimum.	Difference.	Depth in inches	Approximate duration	Depth in inches	Approximate duration.	Depth in inches.	Approximate duration.
1	64.4	0.550	91	29.403	28.853	0.6	S 89 E	2.1	2.6	70.2	59.4	10.8	0.080	2.0	...	...	0.080	2.0
2	Sunday						N 79 W	3.2	4.4	80.0	62.8	17.2	...	...	...	...	...	...
3	59.7	.400	76	.001	29.225	0.7	N 28 E	1.5	2.4	71.0	54.0	17.0	...	...	...	...	...	...
4	64.0	.403	69	.542	.139	0.7	N 78 E	3.5	3.8	71.0	54.0	17.0	.470	3.5	...	...	.470	3.5
5	62.1	.401	74	.525	.124	0.5	N 69 W	5.3	5.5	72.0	58.6	13.4	.055	1.5	...	...	.055	1.5
6	51.7	.391	71	.666	.274	0.3	S 63 W	0.7	3.8	71.0	49.8	21.2	...	...	...	...	...	...
7	59.6	.422	86	.469	.047	1.0	N 32 E	5.1	6.2	62.5	57.0	5.5	.860	10.5	...	...	.860	10.5
8	59.2	.362	76	.569	.206	0.6	N 45 W	7.1	7.2	68.4	55.8	12.6	R	1.5	...	...	R	1.5
9	Sunday						N 33 W	5.1	5.4	69.0	48.6	20.4	...	...	...	...	...	...
10	57.4	.377	80	.729	.352	0.4	S 4 E	0.6	1.8	67.2	46.2	21.0	R	0.5	...	...	R	0.5
11	61.0	.509	94	.291	28.782	0.8	S 72 E	2.7	6.4	64.0	56.0	8.0	.675	11.0	...	...	.675	11.0
12	62.5	.437	76	.223	28.786	0.6	S 53 W	9.9	10.3	71.2	60.0	11.2	.077	1.0	...	...	.077	1.0
13	56.6	.275	63	.533	29.258	0.3	S 77 W	6.5	6.5	66.0	52.2	13.8	...	...	...	...	...	...
14	51.6	.280	72	.535	.255	0.4	S 58 W	9.3	9.9	68.0	45.7	22.3	.170	1.0	...	...	.170	1.0
15	45.9	.208	67	.902	.694	0.2	N 85 W	2.1	3.4	57.4	34.8	22.6	...	...	...	...	...	...
16	Sunday						S 73 E	1.1	3.6	64.0	41.4	26.6	.780	17.5	...	...	.780	17.5
17	56.0	.349	77	.596	.246	1.0	N 32 W	5.3	5.3	64.0	52.0	12.0	.020	3.2	...	...	.020	3.5
18	51.1	.294	78	.587	.293	1.0	N 28 E	1.8	1.9	54.0	48.4	5.6	...	...	...	...	...	...
19	51.2	.267	71	.622	.355	0.6	N 40 E	2.6	3.2	57.0	47.0	10.0	R	0.5	...	...	R	0.5
20	48.5	.296	87	.408	.202	1.0	N 25 E	7.5	9.4	52.8	45.0	7.8	.560	14.5	...	...	.560	14.5
21	46.2	.232	73	.573	.341	0.6	N 56 W	6.8	7.1	53.8	45.0	8.8	...	...	...	...	...	...
22	44.6	.226	77	.839	.613	0.2	S 5 W	1.1	3.0	55.5	34.4	21.1	...	...	...	...	...	...
23	Sunday						N 82 E	7.3	7.0	53.5	39.0	14.5	...	...	...	...	...	...
24	53.9	.335	79	.732	.397	0.7	S 87 E	3.3	3.8	60.0	44.3	15.7	R	0.2	...	...	R	0.2
25	52.6	.351	88	.663	.312	1.0	N 3 W	9.1	9.2	57.2	52.2	5.0	1.190	21.0	...	...	1.910	21.0
26	49.7	.278	79	.786	.508	0.6	N 27 W	0.4	1.0	58.4	46.0	12.4	...	...	...	...	...	...
27	51.9	.308	79	.826	.518	0.0	S 31 W	1.6	1.6	63.5	42.0	21.5	...	...	...	...	...	...
28	53.7	.367	87	.890	.523	0.0	S 45 W	0.5	0.7	65.5	41.0	24.5	...	...	...	...	...	...
29	54.1	.359	80	.860	.501	0.2	N 29 W	0.1	0.2	64.0	44.0	20.0	...	...	...	...	...	...
30	Sunday						N 8 E	1.7	2.4	68.0	45.4	22.6	...	...	...	...	...	...
	55.2	0.349	78	29.621	29.372	0.6	N 33 W	1.4	4.0	64.0	48.7	15.3	5.657	89.4	...	...	5.657	89.4

TORONTO.
GENERAL METEOROLOGICAL ABSTRACT, OCTOBER, 1866.

Days.	DAILY MEANS.						WIND.			EXTREMES OF TEMPERATURE			RAIN.		SNOW.		TOTAL FALL.	
	Temperature of Air.	Pressure of Vapour.	Rel. Humid.	Barometric Pressure.	Pressure of Dry Air.	Clouded Sky.	Resultant Direction.	Resultant Velocity.	Mean Velocity.	Maximum.	Minimum.	Diffrence.	Depth in inches	Approximate duration.	Depth in inches	Approximate duration.	Depth in inches	Approximate duration.
1	52.2	0.349	80	29.751	29.401	0.1	S 88 E	0.5	0.8	67.1	50.0	17.0	...	...	...	...	...	...
2	54.8	.400	80	.517	.147	0.6	N 68 W	4.4	8.1	71.0	46.2	24.8	R	0.1	...	...	R	0.1
3	42.2	.219	72	.712	.492	0.4	N 14 W	6.4	6.7	55.0	43.0	12.0	...	...	...	...	...	...
4	36.0	.150	59	.954	.805	0.3	N 26 E	3.0	3.5	50.5	35.6	14.9	...	...	...	...	...	...
5	30.6	.101	64	30.151	.990	0.2	N 79 E	1.5	3.1	47.5	33.4	14.1	...	...	...	...	...	...
6	43.3	.230	74	29.989	.753	0.0	S 21 E	0.7	1.1	58.0	35.8	22.2	...	...	...	...	...	...
7	Sunday						S 34 W	2.4	2.4	45.8	41.5	24.3	...	...	...	...	...	...
8	37.0	.439	97	.682	.243	0.4	S 17 W	0.8	1.2	71.0	50.6	20.4	...	...	...	...	...	...
9	34.5	.411	93	.658	.247	1.0	N 76 E	9.0	9.1	60.0	53.2	6.8	.895	5.8	...	...	.895	5.8
10	53.4	.383	67	.690	.297	1.0	N 73 E	9.4	9.4	58.0	54.4	3.6	.015	1.0	...	...	.015	1.0
11	51.8	.346	90	.704	.358	0.8	N 57 E	3.8	4.1	61.0	53.0	8.0	...	...	...	...	...	...
12	49.2	.266	65	.684	.418	0.1	N 40 E	2.9	3.8	59.0	49.0	10.0	...	...	...	...	...	...
13	49.4	.298	77	.761	.463	0.2	N 6 W	4.0	5.1	58.2	48.4	9.8	...	...	...	...	...	...
14	Sunday						N 4 W	6.2	6.9	58.0	42.4	15.6	...	...	...	...	...	...
15	49.2	.245	59	30.071	.826	0.0	N 13 W	7.8	7.9	57.0	45.6	21.4	...	...	...	...	...	...
16	50.0	.297	68	29.923	.626	0.0	N 50 W	1.1	2.2	57.0	50.5	16.5	...	...	...	...	...	...
17	51.0	.337	79	.715	.378	0.3	S 50 W	0.6	0.8	67.0	43.4	23.6	...	...	...	...	...	...
18	49.5	.312	76	.716	.404	0.0	S 40 E	0.5	0.8	65.0	45.0	20.0	...	...	...	...	...	...
19	51.4	.341	79	.678	.337	0.8	S 54 W	1.4	3.9	56.5	43.8	22.7	.160	3.4	...	...	.160	3.4
20	52.2	.365	86	.748	.383	0.9	N 70 E	2.3	2.4	50.0	49.0	11.0	...	...	...	...	...	...
21	Sunday						S 8 W	5.8	6.1	57.0	54.0	13.0	.150	2.0	...	...	.150	2.0
22	47..	.221	47	.305	.084	0.3	S 45 W	14.6	14.8	52.2	55.0	7.2	R	0.3	...	...	R	0.3
23	38.6	.160	55	.416	.256	0.5	S 63 W	9.5	0.7	52.5	44.2	8.3	...	...	...	...	...	...
24	34.4	.165	75	.601	.430	0.7	N 49 W	9.1	9.4	45.0	31.8	13.2	...	...	...	...	...	...
25	32.8	.142	66	.830	.688	0.9	S 70 E	4.4	4.8	42.8	32.6	10.2	.095	4.0	...	...	.095	4.0
26	39.7	.231	90	.575	.344	0.9	S 29 E	3.4	4.4	45.0	35.4	9.6	.320	11.5	...	...	.320	11.5
27	47.4	.190	76	.793	.603	0.9	N 24 W	3.4	5.8	45.8	38.2	7.6	...	...	...	...	...	...
28	Sunday						S 89 E	10.5	10.8	50.8	36.3	14.5	.360	13.5	...	...	.360	13.5
29	37.1	.310	91	.406	.083	1.0	N 62 W	4.0	7.4	51.9	44.0	7.9	.475	17.5	...	...	.475	17.5
30	39.7	.219	82	.341	.122	0.6	S 89 W	6.2	6.4	47.8	41.0	6.8	R	0.4	...	...	R	0.4
31	30.9	.131	66	.675	.515	0.6	N 75 W	8.1	8.2	41.0	32.4	8.6	...	...	S	0.2	S	0.2
	45.5	0.272	75	29.706	29.431	0.5	N 30 W	0.8	5.5	57.5	43.8	13.7	2.470	59.5	S	0.2	2.670	59.7

TORONTO
GENERAL METEOROLOGICAL ABSTRACT, NOVEMBER, 1866.

Days.	DAILY MEANS.					WIND.			EXTREMES OF TEMPERATURE.			RAIN.		SNOW.		TOTAL FALL.	
	Temperature of Air.	Pressure of Vapour.	Rel. Humid.	Barometric Pressure.	Pressure of Dry Air.	Clouded Sky.	Resultant Direction.	Resultant Velocity.	Mean Velocity.	Maximum.	Minimum.	Difference.	Depth in inches.	Approximate duration.	Depth in inches.	Approximate duration.	Depth in inches.	Approximate duration.
1	43.3	0.195	68	29.499	29.304	1.0	S 50 W	10.8	14.2	48.0	31.8	16.2	R	1.0	...	...	R	1.0
2	37.3	.101	73	.734	.573	0.0	N 75 W	5.5	5.8	42.0	37.2	4.8	...	...	...	...	...	...
3	34.6	.140	75	.955	.809	0.8	N 82 W	3.1	3.4	41.0	28.7	12.3	...	...	S	0.7	S	0.7
4	Sunday						N 1 E	4.5	4.6	36.4	30.2	6.2	...	...	...	...	...	...
5	28.6	.117	76	30.319	30.202	0.0	N 24 W	1.4	1.6	36.4	23.3	13.1	...	...	...	...	...	...
6	33.8	.140	73	30.131	29.991	0.1	S 35 W	2.6	2.7	44.2	23.0	21.2	...	...	...	...	...	...
7	39.9	.163	67	29.847	.685	0.3	S 44 W	3.8	4.0	53.0	31.8	21.2	...	...	...	...	...	...
8	43.6	.219	77	.689	.470	0.7	S 61 W	3.8	4.0	54.2	30.0	24.2	...	...	...	...	...	...
9	43.7	.236	82	.680	.445	0.2	S 52 W	4.3	5.9	51.8	37.0	14.8	...	...	...	...	...	...
10	42.2	.209	78	.075	.460	0.6	S 85 E	4.9	7.0	51.0	35.0	16.0	.230	1.5	...	...	.230	1.5
11	Sunday						S 38 W	9.0	10.9	49.6	42.0	7.6	R	0.2	...	...	R	0.2
12	38.7	.167	72	.819	.652	0.3	N 77 W	5.1	5.8	47.5	32.8	14.7	...	...	...	...	...	...
13	38.8	.185	77	.975	.790	0.4	S 83 E	5.2	5.5	44.8	28.4	10.4	...	...	...	...	...	...
14	45.3	.244	81	.702	.459	0.9	S 51 E	5.2	6.4	50.0	35.8	14.2	.275	10.5	...	...	.275	10.5
15	43.2	.259	92	.192	28.933	1.0	N 60 W	4.6	7.7	46.0	42.0	4.0	.875	19.5	...	...	.875	19.5
16	35.3	.198	85	28.971	28.773	1.0	S 83 W	15.0	15.1	41.0	36.6	4.4	.465	10.0	...	...	.465	10.0
17	39.3	.180	75	29.417	29.237	0.8	S 67 W	7.6	8.2	43.6	35.2	8.4	.023	1.0	...	...	.023	1.0
18	Sunday						S 53 W	2.6	3.5	47.5	39.0	8.5	.080	4.0	...	...	.080	4.0
19	43.9	.255	89	.260	.005	1.0	S 83 E	4.5	6.8	46.0	41.0	5.0	.320	10.5	...	...	.320	10.5
20	39.7	.216	88	.251	.034	0.9	N 45 W	17.9	18.3	44.0	39.3	4.7	.055	4.0	...	...	.055	4.0
21	31.9	.140	80	.514	.369	0.9	N 48 W	8.9	10.0	35.0	32.7	2.3	...	...	...	...	...	...
22	27.5	.129	86	.469	.340	1.0	N 31 E	9.0	9.9	30.0	25.0	5.0	...	...	2.0	13.0	.200	13.0
23	27.4	.130	87	.672	.542	0.9	N 44 W	4.0	4.7	33.0	24.0	9.0	...	...	...	...	...	...
24	28.0	.126	82	.666	.540	0.8	N 78 W	7.8	9.2	33.2	25.0	8.2	...	...	0.2	3.5	.020	3.5
25	Sunday						S 20 W	2.1	2.4	34.2	21.8	12.4	...	...	...	...	...	...
26	37.9	.189	82	.744	.555	0.8	S 28 W	3.2	3.2	43.4	24.2	19.2	...	...	...	...	...	...
27	44.1	.230	82	.032	.396	0.9	S 44 E	2.8	3.3	47.8	37.2	10.6	.060	4.5	...	...	.060	4.5
28	48.3	.324	96	.358	.034	1.0	S 12 E	1.2	2.8	53.8	44.4	9.4	.520	12.0	...	...	.520	12.0
29	43.6	.262	92	.335	.073	1.0	N 57 W	4.3	5.1	47.4	43.8	3.6	.060	3.0	...	...	.060	3.0
30	35.2	.174	74	.412	.258	1.0	N 86 W	15.5	16.9	39.0	36.8	2.2	...	...	S	1.4	S	1.4
	38.4	0.192	80	29.612	29.421	0.7	N 68 W	3.1	7.0	43.8	33.2	10.6	2.963	81.7	2.2	18.6	3.183	100.3

TORONTO.
GENERAL METEOROLOGICAL ABSTRACT, DECEMBER, 1866.

Days.	DAILY MEANS.						WIND.			EXTREMES OF TEMPERATURE.			RAIN.		SNOW.		TOTAL FALL.	
	Temperature of Air.	Pressure of Vapour.	Rel. Humid.	Barometric Pressure.	Pressure of Dry Air.	Clouded Sky.	Resultant Direction.	Resultant Velocity.	Mean Velocity.	Maximum.	Minimum.	Difference.	Depth in inches.	Approximate duration.	Depth in inches.	Approximate duration.	Depth in inches.	Approximate duration.
1	25.8	0.117	73	29.791	29.674	0.8	N 64 W	7.0	7.9	31.3	25.0	6.3	...	...	...	...	...	...
2	Sunday						S 22 W	4.6	4.8	38.0	24.8	13.2	...	...	...	...	...	...
3	38.6	.152	65	.612	.460	0.7	S 58 E	5.6	6.3	13.2	27.8	15.4	0.200	3.0	...	...	0.200	3.0
4	40.0	.222	90	.357	.135	0.7	S 62 W	5.3	7.0	44.0	38.0	6.0	.420	9.0	...	...	.420	9.0
5	36.4	.181	84	.847	.666	0.4	S 75 W	2.8	3.8	45.8	34.0	11.8	...	...	...	...	...	...
6	39.2	.220	92	.741	.521	1.0	N 71 E	2.0	4.3	43.2	31.0	12.2	.035	2.5	...	...	.035	2.5
7	41.2	.219	85	.593	.374	0.2	S 3 W	3.5	6.8	49.2	37.0	12.2	.045	1.5	...	...	.045	1.5
8	43.2	.207	74	.695	28.588	0.5	S 48 W	14.3	18.2	51.0	35.0	16.0	1.120	6.2	0.1	0.5	1.130	6.3
9	Sunday						S 71 W	10.4	10.7	34.0	37.6	6.4	...	...	...	...	...	...
10	17.6	.005	68	.492	29.427	0.3	S 73 W	15.9	16.1	21.0	15.2	5.8	...	...	...	...	...	...
11	19.3	.077	74	.576	.500	0.4	S 72 W	11.8	11.8	26.4	17.0	9.4	...	...	...	...	...	...
12	17.6	.004	68	.678	.614	0.4	S 73 W	14.7	14.7	23.0	14.2	8.8	...	...	...	...	...	...
13	17.9	.073	74	.771	.698	0.4	N 54 W	9.9	12.8	24.0	15.5	8.5	...	...	S	0.3	S	0.3
14	9.6	.054	80	30.081	30.027	0.2	N 20 W	7.5	7.0	13.2	5.0	8.2	...	...	...	...	...	...
15	13.9	.060	71	30.027	29.967	0.5	N 50 E	6.4	6.9	22.5	4.6	18.5	...	...	...	...	...	...
16	Sunday						N 64 E	12.4	14.2	28.0	14.2	13.8	...	...	0.0	20.0	.600	20.0
17	23.0	.109	88	29.512	.403	1.0	N 54 W	7.1	7.2	27.0	19.0	8.0	...	...	0.5	2.0	.050	2.0
18	26.1	.112	78	.745	.633	0.9	S 50 W	8.2	8.4	32.0	15.8	16.2	...	...	...	...	...	...
19	25.1	.121	83	.723	.602	0.9	N 18 W	8.2	11.0	34.0	28.0	6.0	...	...	2.0	8.0	.200	8.0
20	1.9	.030	80	30.200	30.221	0.4	N 21 E	6.8	7.7	13.5	-5.0	18.5	...	...	1.0	2.5	.100	2.5
21	19.2	.079	75	30.007	29.928	0.7	S 33 B	6.4	7.5	31.8	-2.0	33.8	...	...	...	...	...	...
22	34.2	.159	80	29.557	.398	1.0	S 21 E	6.1	6.3	37.8	20.0	17.8	.130	8.0	S	1.5	.130	9.5
23	Sunday						S 76 W	3.4	5.3	41.0	31.8	9.2	.840	16.0	...	...	.840	16.0
24	34.1	.184	93	.123	28.939	1.0	S 64 W	0.2	6.0	37.2	34.6	2.6	...	...	0.3	2.6	.030	2.6
25	...	...	...	...	...	...	S 60 W	11.1	11.8	29.0	26.0	3.0	...	...	0.1	3.5	.010	3.5
26	27.0	.135	91	.415	29.280	0.8	S 69 W	4.8	8.2	32.0	16.2	15.8	...	...	5.0	11.5	.500	11.5
27	19.8	.083	75	.312	.229	0.6	N 61 W	24.9	25.1	26.2	21.0	5.2	...	...	...	...	...	...
28	16.4	.067	72	.428	.361	0.9	N 68 W	24.4	24.8	20.0	11.4	8.6	...	...	S	1.5	S	1.5
29	16.2	.071	78	.676	.605	0.5	W	9.6	10.4	21.2	13.0	8.2	...	...	0.4	2.3	.040	2.3
30	Sunday						S 36 W	2.9	4.7	21.8	11.0	10.8	...	...	0.1	3.5	.010	3.5
31	20.6	.087	70	.754	.667	0.7	S 4 E	1.0	2.6	25.0	15.2	9.8	...	...	...	...	...	...
	25.1	0.118	79	29.647	29.529	0.6	S 86 W	5.0	0.9	51.2	20.0	11.2	2.700	46.2	16.5	59.7	4.340	1.050

TORONTO.
GENERAL METEOROLOGICAL ABSTRACT, JANUARY, 1867.

Days.	DAILY MEANS.						WIND.		EXTREMES OF TEMPERATURE.			RAIN.		SNOW.		TOTAL FALL.	
	Temperature of Air	Pressure of Vapour.	Rel. Humid.	Barometric Pressure.	Pressure of Dry Air.	Cloud Sky.	Resultant Direction.	Resultant Velocity.	Mean Velocity.	Maximum.	Minimum.	Difference.	Depth in Inches.	Approximate duration.	Depth in inches	Approximate duration.	Depth in inches	Approximate duration.
1	20.8	0.008	86	29.858	29.760	0.8	N 89 W	5.2	5.2	27.0	15.5	11.5	...	...	...	...	...	...
2	17.1	.076	81	.795	.719	0.5	S 65 W	5.0	6.1	20.2	14.6	5.6	...	...	...	...	...	...
3	18.8	.077	72	.704	.627	0.1	S 51 W	3.2	3.2	27.0	5.0	22.0	...	...	...	...	...	...
4	30.0	.147	88	.660	.513	1.0	S 5 W	0.5	2.1	35.2	21.8	13.4	...	...	0.5	2.5	0.050	2.5
5	31.1	.143	81	.237	.094	1.0	N 58 E	3.8	6.8	35.0	28.5	6.5	...	...	0.2	6.0	.020	6.0
6	Sunday						N 80 W	8.3	9.4	32.0	26.8	5.2	...	...	0.1	5.0	.010	5.0
7	18.2	.074	76	.552	.478	0.7	N 72 W	7.2	7.3	22.2	13.2	9.0	...	...	0.1	3.0	.010	3.0
8	17.9	.072	73	.416	.344	0.6	N 40 W	4.4	4.4	22.2	16.4	5.8	...	...	0.1	3.5	.010	3.5
9	21.0	.104	88	.232	.128	1.0	N 15 W	0.3	0.5	22.2	13.0	14.0	...	...	1.5	20.0	.150	20.0
10	19.7	.081	77	.133	.052	8.0	N 49 W	1.4	2.0	27.0	16.8	6.6	...	...	0.5	6.0	.050	6.0
11	16.4	.067	73	.457	.389	0.7	N 67 W	5.0	5.6	23.4	14.2	10.0	...	...	0.1	1.0	.010	1.0
12	9.6	.049	74	.899	.850	0.7	N 7 W	6.1	7.0	24.2	7.0	8.0	...	...	0.5	2.0	.050	2.0
13	Sunday						N 46 E	9.4	10.0	15.0	5.8	11.0	...	...	4.0	18.0	.400	18.0
14	9.3	.052	77	.619	.567	0.6	N 22 E	4.2	4.2	16.8	8.0	5.8	...	...	...	...	...	...
15	3.1	.036	72	.758	.722	0.3	N 11 W	3.8	3.9	13.8	-2.2	12.2	...	...	S	0.5	S	0.5
16	17.7	.093	92	.502	.410	1.0	N 77 E	2.0	5.4	10.0	-4.8	23.8	...	...	6.0	17.0	.600	17.0
17	12.2	.066	86	.602	.536	0.7	N 20 W	13.7	14.1	24.0	12.8	4.2	...	...	2.0	10.0	.200	10.0
18	3.0	.041	80	.842	.801	0.1	N 39 W	15.7	16.0	17.0	-3.0	11.0	...	...	...	...	...	...
19	5.8	.048	84	.573	.525	0.0	S 89 W	4.1	4.2	8.0	-3.5	17.5	...	...	...	...	...	...
20	Sunday						N 66 E	9.2	9.6	14.0	-3.2	26.2	...	...	15.0	17.0	1.500	17.0
21	17.1	.084	90	.196	.112	1.0	N 33 E	5.2	5.6	23.0	13.2	6.0	...	...	3.0	13.5	.300	13.5
22	18.4	.087	87	.503	.416	1.0	N 61 W	3.0	3.6	19.8	14.0	9.0	...	...	...	...	...	...
23	24.0	.101	79	.745	.644	0.7	N 52 W	8.9	9.2	23.0	18.5	9.7	...	...	S	0.1	S	0.1
24	26.3	.122	86	.942	.820	1.0	N 25 W	1.3	1.7	28.2	21.8	7.2	...	...	...	...	...	...
25	25.0	.129	90	.401	.272	1.0	S 80 E	9.2	11.5	29.0	15.5	17.5	...	...	6.0	8.5	.600	8.5
26	26.0	.119	84	28.991	28.872	1.0	S 75 W	14.1	14.8	33.0	24.8	5.2	...	...	1.0	18.0	.100	18.0
27	Sunday						N 64 W	11.5	11.7	30.0	15.4	6.6	...	...	0.2	3.0	.020	3.0
28	16.4	.075	81	29.800	29.526	0.8	S 68 W	12.6	12.9	22.0	13.8	8.2	...	...	...	...	...	...
29	8.3	.052	82	.704	.651	0.7	N 88 W	7.4	7.9	12.2	5.5	6.7	...	...	1.0	9.0	.100	9.0
30	10.5	.062	86	.920	.858	0.9	S 46 W	3.0	4.3	20.1	2.5	17.6	...	...	0.2	1.5	.020	1.5
31	20.1	.155	9	.484	.329	1.0	S 43 W	6.2	7.0	43.8	12.2	31.6	R	1.0	...	...	R	1.0
	17.0	0.086	82	29.568	29.48	0.7	N 55 W	3.3	7.0	23.2	11.6	11.5	R	1.0	42.0	165.1	4.200	166.1

TORONTO.
GENERAL METEOROLOGICAL ABSTRACT, FEBRUARY, 1867.

Days.	DAILY MEANS.						WIND.			EXTREMES OF TEMPERATURE			RAIN.		SNOW.		TOTAL FALL.	
	Temperature of Air.	Pressure of Vapour.	Rel. Humid.	Barometric Pressure.	Pressure of Dry Air.	Cloud'd Sky.	Resultant Direct'n.	Resultant Velocity.	Mean Velocity.	Maximum.	Minimum.	Difference.	Depth in inches.	Approximate duration.	Depth in inches	Approximate duration.	Depth in inches	Approximate duration.
1	33.6	0.142	73	29.445	29.303	0.8	N 78 W	9.2	10.0	41.8	29.0	12.8	...	...	...	...	...	...
2	28.5	.135	88	.175	.037	1.0	N 82 E	14.3	15.6	35.0	22.6	12.4	0.076	4.0	2.0	4.5	0.276	6.0
3	Su	nday					S 66 W	9.5	10.9	34.0	25.2	8.8	...	...	2.5	7.5	.250	7.5
4	30.2	.148	87	.275	.127	0.8	N 72 E	7.8	9.1	32.8	22.6	10.2	...	...	3.0	11.5	.300	11.5
5	28.4	.129	83	.417	.298	1.0	N 60 W	4.0	5.6	32.0	24.8	7.2	...	...	0.1	9.0	.010	9.0
6	28.3	.135	87	.773	.638	0.6	S 50 W	6.9	7.0	32.2	24.2	8.0	...	...	...	...	...	...
7	29.2	.126	79	.878	.752	0.5	S 18 W	3.7	4.0	38.0	21.5	16.5	...	...	...	...	...	...
8	32.4	.132	73	.569	.437	0.7	N 71 E	1.5	1.6	40.0	20.0	20.0	R	1.0	...	...	R	1.0
9	25.9	.131	91	.245	.114	1.0	N 49 W	17.1	18.1	36.4	27.7	8.7	...	...	2.5	15.0	.250	15.0
10	Su	nday					N 74 W	9.3	10.4	15.0	0.2	14.8	...	...	...	...	...	...
11	24.3	.087	67	30.127	30.040	1.0	S 35 W	12.9	13.0	13.4	5.8	27.6	...	...	...	...	...	...
12	35.3	.175	83	29.986	29.811	1.0	S 32 W	4.2	4.2	40.4	26.4	14.0	.082	2.7	...	...	.082	2.7
13	39.3	.220	95	.543	.414	0.9	S 51 W	5.0	7.4	44.0	32.2	11.8	.630	8.5	...	...	.630	8.5
14	32.1	.148	80	.915	.767	1.0	N 2 E	8.6	9.9	35.0	32.6	2.4	...	...	S	0.5	S	0.5
15	25.0	.107	78	.974	.867	0.8	N 82 E	12.6	12.8	36.2	18.0	18.2	.155	4.0	...	...	.155	4.0
16	39.4	.162	70	.315	.153	0.9	S 60 W	13.2	16.7	44.0	24.8	19.2	.250	5.0	...	...	.250	5.0
17	Su	nday					S 83 W	8.6	9.5	38.0	34.0	3.4	...	...	...	...	...	...
18	31.7	.155	87	.586	.431	0.9	N 30 E	3.8	6.2	35.5	27.2	8.3	...	...	0.2	1.2	.020	1.2
19	23.3	.084	66	.811	.727	1.0	N 58 E	8.9	10.2	28.0	21.5	6.5	...	...	0.5	3.0	.050	3.0
20	21.6	.107	90	.681	.574	1.0	N 68 E	10.3	10.7	29.4	9.2	20.2	...	...	1.0	12.0	.100	12.0
21	26.7	.124	85	.529	.406	1.0	N 17 E	7.2	10.9	31.0	23.5	7.5	...	...	1.5	11.3	.150	11.3
22	21.2	.056	74	.813	.727	0.8	N 56 W	5.4	10.1	27.0	20.9	6.1	...	...	S	0.5	S	0.5
23	32.6	.165	85	.256	.096	1.0	S 75 E	1.9	8.1	38.0	14.2	23.6	.110	4.2	0.1	2.2	.120	2.2
24	Su	nday					N 63 W	11.2	12.5	31.4	27.7	3.7	...	...	...	...	...	...
25	19.7	.084	77	.784	.705	0.9	N 59 E	3.5	3.7	24.5	10.4	14.1	...	...	S	2.0	S	2.0
26	27.2	.104	72	.892	.788	0.1	N 85 W	4.9	5.6	37.0	15.8	21.2	...	...	...	...	...	...
27	26.7	.124	81	30.025	.995	0.0	S 86 E	2.7	3.4	34.0	17.5	16.5	...	...	...	...	...	...
28	32.3	.152	82	29.680	.524	1.0	N 79 E	1.2	1.3	37.0	24.4	12.6	.025	1.2	...	...	.025	1.2
	28.9	0.132	81	29.658	29.526	0.8	N 57 W	7.6	8.8	34.3	21.6	12.7	1.328	30.6	13.4	80.2	2.668	110.8

TORONTO
GENERAL METEOROLOGICAL ABSTRACT, MARCH, 1867.

Days.	DAILY MEANS.						WIND.			EXTREMES OF TEMPERATURE			RAIN.		SNOW.		TOTAL FALL.	
	Temperature of Air.	Pressure of Vapour.	Rel Humid.	Barometric Pressure.	Pressure of Dry Air.	Clouded Sky.	Resultant Direction.	Resultant Velocity.	Mean Velocity.	Maximum.	Minimum.	Difference.	Depth in inches.	Approximate duration.	Depth in inches.	Approximate duration.	Depth in inches.	Approximate duration.
1	33.1	0.160	80	29.211	29.042	0.9	N 51 E	0.9	6.2	44.2	31.0	13.2	0.050	5.5	...	...	0.050	5.5
2	24.7	.122	83	.377	.255	0.9	N 52 W	10.2	17.4	38.5	20.8	17.7	...	...	...	...	...	...
3	Sunday						N 64 E	10.7	11.9	21.5	8.0	13.5	...	..	1.0	13.0	.100	13.0
4	21.2	.088	77	.587	.499	0.8	N 36 W	2.8	3.1	26.9	13.2	13.7	...	...	0.5	2.5	.050	2.5
5	26.0	.105	76	.935	.829	0.3	N 79 W	5.3	8.4	31.8	22.0	9.8	...	...	...	...	...	...
6	23.8	.103	79	.967	.864	0.9	N 75 E	12.4	13.8	31.5	15.0	15.9	...	...	2.0	8.0	.200	8.0
7	23.1	.106	83	.758	.651	0.0	N 18 E	4.5	6.3	31.0	21.0	10.0	...	...	1.0	6.0	.100	6.0
8	25.7	.113	84	30.052	.934	1.0	N 64 E	3.4	4.8	33.0	7.8	25.2	...	...	...	...	...	...
9	28.8	.123	73	29.851	.728	0.8	N 69 E	4.7	5.0	33.8	24.2	9.6	...	...	...	...	...	...
10	Sunday						N 60 E	1.4	8.4	42.8	27.2	15.6	.135	8.0	...	...	.135	8.0
11	34.3	.156	69	.715	.558	1.0	N 22 W	4.9	5.7	37.4	34.8	2.6	...	...	0.2	1.0	.020	1.0
12	30.9	.146	84	.567	.422	1.0	N 18 E	4.3	4.7	36.0	27.3	8.7	...	...	1.0	5.0	.100	5.0
13	27.1	.129	84	.525	.399	0.6	S 78 W	12.4	14.3	35.8	28.4	7.2	R	1.5	0.2	4.1	.020	5.6
14	14.7	.058	69	.833	.774	0.4	S 75 W	11.3	11.5	21.4	11.1	10.3	...	...	...	...	...	...
15	17.8	.070	72	30.003	.933	0.4	S 63 W	5.8	5.9	26.8	9.6	17.2	...	...	...	...	...	...
16	23.1	.102	81	29.709	.607	1.0	S 82 E	12.8	13.0	27.0	13.0	14.0	...	...	5.5	14.2	.550	14.2
17	Sunday						S 60 W	14.0	14.6	32.2	23.0	9.2	...	...	1.5	9.0	.150	9.0
18	15.4	.061	68	.700	.630	0.5	S 78 W	7.9	7.9	24.0	9.0	15.0	...	...	...	...	...	...
19	20.0	.084	74	.921	.837	0.1	N 4 W	1.0	1.1	30.6	3.0	27.0	...	...	...	...	...	...
20	28.0	.101	71	30.065	.961	0.4	N 75 E	5.7	6.0	34.0	15.5	18.5	...	...	...	...	...	...
21	32.5	.158	85	29.777	.619	0.9	N 85 E	14.6	14.7	36.0	24.8	11.2	...	...	15.0	16.5	1.500	16.5
22	32.8	.158	85	.773	.615	1.0	S 69 E	3.2	3.4	35.5	30.0	5.5	...	...	1.5	6.0	.150	6.0
23	34.7	.171	85	.842	.670	1.0	N 73 E	4.6	4.6	37.4	31.6	5.8	.007	1.0	...	...	.007	1.0
24	Sunday						S 41 E	0.9	3.1	38.0	32.6	5.4	.070	10.0	1.5	4.0	.200	14.0
25	30.0	.126	76	.828	.702	1.0	N 68 W	12.2	13.2	35.0	30.0	5.0	...	...	...	...	...	...
26	25.2	.111	82	.855	.744	0.9	N 70 E	4.1	6.2	30.5	18.2	12.3	...	...	0.5	2.5	.050	2.5
27	28.0	.127	89	.425	.298	1.0	N 18 E	6.3	8.2	29.8	23.4	6.4	...	...	2.0	15.5	.200	15.5
28	26.0	.095	63	.476	.388	0.3	N 49 W	14.1	14.7	34.0	20.5	13.5	...	...	...	...	...	...
29	29.5	.107	68	.440	.333	0.0	N 74 W	14.4	14.5	41.6	17.6	24.0	...	...	...	...	...	...
30	37.0	.132	62	.326	.194	0.0	S 81 W	8.2	8.6	45.8	28.0	17.8	...	...	...	...	...	...
31	Sunday						S 60 W	0.9	3.2	46.8	32.0	14.8	.355	5.0	...	...	.355	5.0
	26.6	0.116	78	29.712	29.596	0.7	N 34 W	72.1	8.5	33.9	21.1	12.8	0.617	31.0	33.4	107.3	3.057	136.3

TORONTO.
GENERAL METEOROLOGICAL ABSTRACT, APRIL, 1867.

Days.	DAILY MEANS.						WIND.			EXTREMES OF TEMPERATURE.			RAIN.		SNOW.		TOTAL FALL.	
	Temperature of Air.	Pressure of Vapour.	Rel. Humid.	Barometric Pressure.	Pressure of Dry Air.	Clouded Sky.	Resultant Direction.	Resultant Velocity.	Mean Velocity.	Maximum.	Minimum.	Difference.	Depth in inches.	Approximate duration.	Depth in inches.	Approximate duration.	Depth In inches.	Approximate duration.
1	36.7	0.188	87	29.043	28.855	1.0	S 80 W	12.9	13.2	40.6	34.0	6.6	0.140	6.5	...	...	0.140	6.5
2	34.7	.126	82	.529	29.404	0.8	N 75 W	12.9	13.1	41.0	34.0	7.0	...	...	...	...	...	...
3	34.0	.127	64	.802	.674	0.5	N 82 E	4.3	5.1	42.5	27.4	15.1	...	...	...	...	...	...
4	38.3	.201	87	.408	.207	1.0	N 71 E	6.2	6.5	48.0	34.2	13.8	1.155	15.7	...	...	1.155	15.7
5	33.2	.155	81	.171	.016	0.8	N 69 W	6.5	8.6	38.5	32.6	5.9	...	...	2.2	8.5	.220	8.5
6	35.7	.144	69	.392	.248	0.7	S 51 W	7.1	8.0	43.0	26.8	16.2	...	...	...	...	...	...
7	Sunday						S 88 W	7 0	8.5	48.2	37.0	11.2	...	...	...	...	...	...
8	37.8	.177	76	.046	.409	0.6	N 49 W	4.4	6.3	43.0	35.4	7.6	.175	4.0	...	...	.175	4.0
9	35.3	.148	71	.813	.665	0.3	S 12 W	0.3	1.4	45.8	29.4	16.4	...	...	...	...	...	...
10	35.3	.166	80	.457	.291	1.0	N 25 W	5.1	5.7	39.0	31.0	8.0	.100	5.3	...	...	.100	5.3
11	33.5	.126	65	.521	.396	0.6	N 64 W	5.1	7.2	45.0	25.4	19.6	...	...	...	...	...	...
12	44.8	.184	62	.456	.272	0.0	S 73 W	1.1	4.1	59.0	31.8	27.2	...	...	...	...	...	...
13	37.2	.157	71	.696	.539	0.2	N 87 E	6.6	6.9	41.0	35.0	6.0	...	...	...	...	...	...
14	Sunday						N 74 E	5.3	5.7	51.5	33.8	17.7	...	...	...	...	...	...
15	47.0	.230	80	.422	.192	1.0	S 58 E	0.6	1.2	53.0	39.4	13.6	.205	11.0	...	...	.205	11.0
16	45.3	.301	88	.333	.082	0.8	N 8 W	10.0	10.4	57.0	45.0	12.0	...	...	...	...	...	...
17	47.7	.129	43	.023	.494	0.0	N 40 W	15.3	15.9	60.5	37.8	22.7	...	...	...	...	...	...
18	40.7	.125	50	.929	.834	0.4	N 31 W	3.0	4.1	51.2	37.2	14.0	...	...	...	...	...	...
19	...	...	...	...	...	...	N 84 E	4.6	4.8	49.4	34.5	14.9	.007	0.3	...	...	.007	0.3
20	46.8	.233	72	.271	.038	0.7	N 90 W	8.7	10.0	65.5	38.5	27.0	.060	1.3	...	...	.060	1.3
21	Sunday						N 64 W	6.2	8.5	51.5	40.0	11.5	...	...	0.5	3.0	.050	3.0
22	35.3	.177	85	.316	.139	1.0	N 30 W	11.3	12.7	41.2	32.8	8.4	R	0.5	3.5	6.0	.350	6.5
23	34.9	.133	67	.763	.630	0.8	N 56 W	4.6	5.8	42.4	31.8	10.6	...	...	S	0.1	S	0.1
24	33.4	.169	88	.782	.013	0.7	N 83 E	1.1	6.5	40.0	30.6	9.2	...	...	1.0	9.5	.100	9.5
25	43.2	.242	86	.744	.502	0.8	S 21 W	6.9	7.0	50.4	31.6	18.8	R	0.8	...	...	R	0.8
26	47.3	.187	59	.477	.290	0.6	S 36 W	10.2	13.1	56.0	33.5	22.5	.055	2.0	...	...	.055	2.0
27	33.4	.114	69	.672	.559	0.4	N 31 W	11.7	12.2	41.2	30.	10.8	...	...	...	...	...	...
28	Sunday						N 88 E	7.9	8.0	40.1	27.3	13.1	...	...	...	...	...	...
29	42.0	.229	82	.565	.301	0.9	S 70 E	5.1	6.5	48.0	33.4	15.0	R	0.9	...	...	R	0.9
30	48.5	.291	86	.393	.099	1.0	N 4 W	4.6	7.5	58.0	42.4	15.6	.250	8.0	...	...	.250	8.0
	39.5	0.181	63	29.628	29.347	0.6	N 51 W	2.7	7.9	47.7	33.8	13.9	2.147	56.3	7.2	27.1	2.867	83.4

TORONTO.
GENERAL METEOROLOGICAL ABSTRACT, MAY, 1867.

Days.	DAILY MEANS.						WIND.			EXTREMES OF TEMPERATURE.			RAIN.		SNOW.		TOTAL FALL.	
	Temperature of Air.	Pressure of Vapour.	Rel. Humid.	Barometric Pressure.	Pressure of Dry Air.	Clouded Sky.	Resultant Direction.	Resultant Velocity.	Mean Velocity.	Maximum.	Minimum.	Difference.	Depth in inches.	Approximate duration.	Depth in Inches.	Approximate duration.	Depth in Inches.	Approximate duration.
1	40.2	0.212	85	29.336	29.124	0.7	N 51 W	19.9	21.0	49.0	37.0	12.0	0.235	4.5	...	...	0.235	4.5
2	31.4	.116	65	.790	.674	0.5	N 75 W	11.4	11.4	37.5	29.8	7.7	...	...	S	1.0	S	1.0
3	33.7	.123	64	30.032	.910	0.3	S 78 E	6.1	6.7	40.0	24.6	15.4	...	...	...	...	...	...
4	41.3	.194	68	29.081	.486	1.0	N 87 E	8.8	9.0	49.8	32.4	17.4	.055	4.0	...	...	.055	4.0
5	Su	nday					S 24 W	3.2	3.7	60.0	43.4	16.6	R	1.5	...	...	R	1.5
6	44.8	.253	85	.493	.240	0.8	S 39 W	4.1	4.8	49.0	44.4	4.6	.190	7.2	...	...	.190	7.2
7	43.8	.200	71	.475	.275	0.9	N 48 W	3.6	7.2	52.2	36.0	16.2	...	...	...	...	...	...
8	46.2	.194	63	.258	.064	1.0	N 19 W	20.2	20.8	55.0	36.5	18.5	R	1.5	...	...	R	1.5
9	47.0	.192	59	.216	.024	0.7	N 48 W	13.7	14.1	55.5	43.2	12.3	...	...	...	...	...	...
10	48.7	.236	66	.384	.148	0.2	N 76 W	7.0	7.6	63.5	37.2	26.3	...	...	...	...	...	...
11	47.8	.197	58	.547	.350	0.2	N 61 W	7.3	9.8	60.0	34.5	25.5	...	...	...	...	...	...
12	Su	nday					N 61 W	2.6	5.4	61.0	40.2	20.8	...	...	...	...	...	...
13	44.9	.235	79	.406	.173	1.0	N 60 E	7.7	8.9	48.0	38.0	10.0	.255	6.5	...	...	.255	6.5
14	46.9	.265	82	.152	28.870	1.0	S 77 W	8.9	9.3	53.0	42.0	11.0	.035	2.6	...	...	.035	2.6
15	46.1	.229	74	.210	28.931	1.0	N 60 W	11.0	11.4	51.8	42.0	9.8	R	3.5	...	...	R	3.5
16	49.1	.246	71	.421	29.170	0.6	N 59 W	4.1	6.7	59.0	38.0	21.0	...	...	...	...	...	...
17	48.3	.210	63	.572	.363	0.6	N 52 W	8.3	10.7	59.0	40.0	19.0	...	...	...	...	...	...
18	49.6	.236	58	.775	.572	0.6	N 31 W	11.0	11.0	58.8	42.6	16.2	...	...	...	...	...	...
19	Su	nday					S 49 E	0.7	2.8	55.4	39.8	15.6	.055	1.5	...	...	.055	1.5
20	47.7	.253	77	.543	.290	0.6	N 85 E	4.0	4.7	55.8	43.4	12.4	...	...	...	...	...	...
21	49.5	.240	70	.256	.010	0.9	N 67 E	12.5	12.7	55.0	41.0	14.0	1.090	15.0	...	...	1.090	15.0
22	47.5	.286	87	.052	28.766	1.0	S 12 W	6.0	7.5	51.5	43.8	7.7	.140	5.6	...	...	.140	5.6
23	45.1	.245	82	.218	28.973	0.9	N 80 W	8.1	9.1	51.2	41.6	9.6	.080	5.0	...	...	.080	5.0
24	48.8	.255	74	.528	29.273	0.5	S 1 W	2.3	5.3	57.6	38.0	19.6	.310	1.3	...	...	.310	1.3
25	49.5	.280	80	.389	.106	0.3	S 14 W	4.5	5.8	56.2	43.5	12.7	.345	3.0	...	...	.345	3.0
26	Su	nday					N 61 W	7.6	8.1	60.0	42.8	17.2	...	...	...	...	...	...
27	49.3	.211	60	.726	.515	0.4	N 33 W	1.4	2.9	57.5	36.4	21.1	R	0.2	...	...	R	0.2
28	48.6	.272	70	.613	.341	1.0	N 60 E	4.5	4.7	53.0	42.5	10.5	.270	4.6	...	...	.270	4.6
29	55.0	.363	84	.486	.123	0.7	S 86 W	1.0	2.4	65.0	46.5	18.5	R	0.4	...	...	R	0.4
30	52.0	.285	73	.571	.286	0.9	N 71 W	8.9	11.4	58.5	49.0	9.5	.160	1.0	...	...	.160	1.0
31	51.2	.291	77	.750	.459	0.0	N 64 W	1.4	3.4	59.0	42.0	17.0	...	...	...	...	...	...
	46.5	0.233	72	29.477	29.244	0.7	N 51 W	3.5	6.4	54.8	39.8	15.0	3.220	68.9	S	1.0	3.220	68.9

TORONTO.
GENERAL METEOROLOGICAL ABSTRACT, JUNE, 1867.

Days.	Temperature of Air.	Pressure of Vapour.	Rel. Humid.	Barometric Pressure.	Pressure of Dry Air.	Clouded Sky.	Resultant Direction.	Resultant Velocity.	Mean Velocity.	Maximum.	Minimum.	Difference.	Depth in inches.	Approximate duration.	Depth in inches.	Approximate duration.	Depth in inches.	Approximate duration.
1	56.9	0.308	67	29.017	29.309	0.9	N 77 E	4.5	4.7	64.8	44.0	20.8	0.020	1.5	...	...	0.020	1.5
2	Sunday						S 74 E	1.1	1.3	64.0	52.0	12.0	.520	11.5	...	...	.520	11.5
3	58.0	.368	77	.203	28.834	0.6	S 72 W	7.2	7.7	65.8	53.0	12.8	...	...	...	...	...	...
4	61.2	.300	67	.488	29.127	0.2	N 51 W	2.2	3.4	71.5	51.8	19.7	...	...	...	...	...	...
5	60.1	.333	65	.635	.305	0.2	S 21 E	0.9	1.8	69.0	48.6	20.4	...	...	...	...	...	...
6	61.2	.420	70	.518	.092	0.1	S 15 W	0.7	0.9	75.0	50.5	24.5	...	...	...	...	...	...
7	68.1	.533	77	.588	.055	0.6	N 52 E	0.2	4.1	79.8	59.0	20.8	...	...	...	...	...	...
8	64.0	.299	51	.717	.418	0.3	N 61 E	4.2	4.6	71.8	55.8	16.0	...	...	...	...	...	...
9	Sunday						N 77 E	1.2	1.9	71.8	57.6	14.2	...	...	...	...	...	...
10	62.0	.344	62	.772	.428	0.2	N 76 E	3.2	3.4	69.0	54.0	15.0	...	...	...	...	...	...
11	61.0	.321	60	.688	.367	0.6	S 70 E	3.0	3.1	67.2	50.0	17.2	.080	1.0	...	...	.080	1.0
12	68.2	.472	69	.584	.112	0.7	S 40 W	2.8	3.5	76.4	57.6	18.8	...	...	...	...	...	...
13	68.2	.439	64	.663	.225	0.3	S 59 E	0.6	2.8	77.0	56.4	20.6	...	...	...	...	...	...
14	64.8	.458	74	.618	.160	0.5	N 88 E	1.9	3.2	72.8	57.0	15.8	...	...	...	...	...	...
15	68.5	.493	69	.506	.011	0.8	S 10 W	3.2	3.8	76.2	59.0	17.2	R	0.5	...	...	R	0.5
16	Sunday						N 14 W	1.3	2.3	81.2	62.4	18.8	...	...	...	...	...	...
17	64.2	.540	90	.505	.055	0.9	N 88 E	1.9	2.0	72.6	58.0	14.6	.105	1.0	...	...	.105	1.0
18	64.2	.378	63	.647	.269	0.4	N 66 W	11.5	11.4	73.0	60.8	12.2	...	...	...	...	...	...
19	61.4	.350	68	.770	.421	0.2	S 20 W	3.3	3.5	72.0	47.2	24.8	...	...	...	...	...	...
20	60.7	.416	79	.825	.409	0.7	N 66 E	4.0	4.6	67.0	52.4	14.6	...	...	...	...	...	...
21	61.5	.394	71	.618	.424	0.1	N 85 E	3.7	4.6	68.8	54.0	14.8	...	...	...	...	...	...
22	66.2	.409	74	.716	.247	0.8	S 70 E	1.5	1.6	77.5	53.8	23.7	...	...	...	...	...	...
23	Sunday						S 83 E	1.0	1.8	78.8	56.0	22.8	...	...	...	...	...	...
24	69.0	.530	72	.539	.000	0.1	N 85 E	3.6	3.8	77.8	59.5	18.3	...	...	...	...	...	...
25	70.9	.568	75	.483	28.915	0.4	N 73 E	8.7	8.7	76.8	63.5	13.3	R	0.2	...	...	R	0.2
26	66.6	.565	88	.561	28.996	0.9	N 83 E	3.3	3.4	73.0	61.8	11.2	.110	3.0	...	...	.110	3.0
27	68.2	.555	80	.512	28.950	0.6	N 10 E	1.0	5.7	74.0	63.8	10.2	.050	0.3	...	...	.050	0.3
28	61.9	.383	69	.719	29.330	0.2	S 69 W	2.9	4.4	72.5	57.8	14.7	...	...	...	...	...	...
29	60.7	.419	65	.642	.223	0.2	S 21 W	6.5	7.1	75.0	47.0	28.0	...	...	...	...	...	...
30	Sunday						N 88 W	5.3	9.2	88.6	61.0	24.6	...	...	...	...	...	...
	64.3	0.429	71	29.617	29.188	0.4	S 84 E	0.5	4.1	73.4	55.0	17.8	0.885	19.0	...	...	0.885	19.1

TORONTO.
General Meteorological Abstract, July, 1867.

Days.	DAILY MEANS.						WIND.			EXTREMES OF TEMPERATURE.			RAIN.		SNOW.		TOTAL FALL.	
	Temperature of Air.	Pressure of Vapour.	Rel. Humid.	Barometric Pressure.	Pressure of Dry Air.	Clouded Sky.	Resultant Direction.	Resultant Velocity.	Mean Velocity.	Maximum.	Minimum.	Difference.	Depth in inches.	Approximate duration.	Depth in inches.	Approximate duration.	Depth in inches.	Approximate duration.
1	...	...	...	...	...	...	N 64 E	1.0	5.0	74.0	52.2	21.8	...	...	...	...	...	...
2	68.4	0.426	63	29.581	29.155	0.2	S 8 W	2.8	3.1	75.3	55.0	20.2	...	...	...	...	...	...
3	76.9	.588	65	.491	28.903	0.4	S 36 W	2.2	2.6	90.2	61.0	29.2	R	0.7	...	...	R	0.7
4	71.9	.598	76	.436	28.839	0.9	N 65 E	2.8	4.7	81.5	64.4	17.1	.225	1.5	...	...	.225	1.5
5	63.8	.487	82	.449	28.902	1.0	N 84 E	5.6	5.0	67.5	60.4	7.1	.120	3.5	...	...	.120	3.5
6	70.8	.515	69	.400	28.885	0.4	N 46 W	5.9	6.4	81.4	63.0	18.4	.070	3.0	...	...	.070	3.0
7	Sunday						N 70 W	7.1	7.5	79.2	58.4	20.8	R	0.2	...	...	R	0.2
8	63.7	.353	61	.692	29.339	0.7	S 45 W	0.9	2.9	74.0	50.0	24.0	.370	5.0	...	...	.370	5.0
9	60.8	.378	71	.707	.329	0.5	S 5 W	0.8	2.3	68.5	55.0	13.5	...	...	...	...	...	...
10	63.7	.418	71	.087	.269	0.8	S 20 W	5.1	5.3	72.0	48.9	23.6	R	0.1	...	...	R	0.1
11	69.2	.530	74	.468	28.938	0.9	S 99 W	4.0	6.1	80.0	61.4	18.6	.005	0.2	...	...	.005	0.2
12	62.0	.350	64	.634	29.277	0.5	N 14 W	9.1	9.4	70.5	60.8	10.0	...	...	...	...	...	...
13	60.1	.277	54	.870	.593	0.0	S 52 E	2.5	4.6	68.0	51.6	16.4	...	...	...	...	...	...
14	Sunday						N 87 E	6.2	6.4	71.0	50.8	20.2	...	...	...	...	...	...
15	65.8	.507	80	.663	.156	0.7	N 7 W	2.0	7.8	71.0	56.0	15.0	1.110	4.2	...	...	1.110	4.3
16	62.3	.322	55	.720	.398	0.1	N 38 W	5.4	6.5	74.0	56.5	17.5	...	...	...	...	...	...
17	64.8	.398	62	.791	.403	0.5	N 25 W	1.6	3.9	76.0	50.4	25.6	...	...	...	...	...	...
18	68.3	.380	55	.765	.385	0.2	N 1 W	4.0	6.0	79.0	56.0	23.0	...	...	...	...	...	...
19	64.9	.407	65	.752	.346	0.2	S 68 E	0.6	3.6	71.0	56.8	14.2	...	...	...	...	...	...
20	68.5	.435	62	.609	.264	0.2	N 25 W	2.8	5.5	75.5	58.4	17.1	...	...	...	...	...	...
21	Sunday						N 24 W	10.8	11.0	85.8	59.0	26.8	...	...	...	...	...	...
22	77.1	.473	51	.440	28.966	0.2	N 32 W	4.3	6.2	90.5	63.2	27.3	...	...	...	...	...	...
23	76.5	.536	59	.531	28.935	0.3	S 20 W	2.3	2.5	88.0	62.2	25.8	...	...	...	...	...	...
24	80.4	.584	58	.506	28.922	0.6	S 83 W	3.7	4.4	94.0	65.2	28.8	...	...	...	...	...	...
25	73.5	.632	77	.430	28.904	0.9	S 75 W	1.6	2.0	79.8	71.6	8.2	R	1.3	...	...	R	1.3
26	71.0	.580	76	.486	28.906	0.6	S 55 E	2.1	2.6	77.5	67.2	10.3	...	...	...	...	...	...
27	74.6	.618	72	.495	28.877	0.3	S 50 E	2.3	3.8	80.0	61.5	18.5	...	...	...	...	...	...
28	Sunday						S 62 W	6.0	8.9	83.2	69.0	14.2	R	R	...	...	R	R
29	64.3	.310	53	.613	29.303	0.1	N 41 W	12.9	13.3	76.8	63.2	13.6	...	...	...	...	...	...
30	63.7	.337	59	.785	.448	0.0	S 13 W	2.1	4.6	78.0	52.0	26.0	...	...	...	...	...	...
31	66.1	.464	73	.643	.179	0.9	S 56 E	3.5	4.2	73.0	51.4	21.6	.005	1.7	...	...	.005	1.7
	68.2	0.458	66	29.605	29.147	0.5	N 42 W	1.1	5.4	77.6	58.4	19.2	1.905	21.5	...	...	1.905	21.5

TORONTO.
GENERAL METEOROLOGICAL ABSTRACT, AUGUST, 1867.

Days.	DAILY MEANS.					WIND.			EXTREMES OF TEMPERATURE.			RAIN.		SNOW.		TOTAL FALL.	
	Temperature of Air.	Pressure of Vapour.	Rel. Humid.	Barometric Pressure.	Pressure of Dry Air.	Clouded Sky.	Resultant Direction.	Resultant Velocity.	Mean Velocity.	Maximum.	Minimum.	Difference.	Depth in Inches.	Approximate duration.	Depth in inches.	Approximate duration.	Depth in inches.	Approximate duration.
1	66.1	0.553	86	29.470	28.916	1.0	S 4 E	3.5	3.8	72.2	62.0	10.2	0.145	2.2	...	...	0.145	2.2
2	67.1	.465	71	.484	29.019	0.6	N 40 W	5.1	5.7	75.8	62.0	13.8	...	...	...	...	...	...
3	64.4	.372	61	.691	.319	0.1	N 45 W	1.9	3.7	74.0	56.0	18.0	...	...	...	...	...	...
4	Sunday						S 15 W	4.0	4.1	81.5	50.0	31.5	...	...	...	...	...	...
5	74.0	.585	69	.780	.195	0.6	S 31 W	1.1	2.2	85.4	62.5	22.9	R	0.4	...	...	R	0.4
6	70.4	.612	83	.741	.129	0.7	S 37 W	1.2	1.9	83.0	61.4	21.6	.700	5.2	...	...	.700	5.2
7	73.6	.593	73	.724	.131	0.7	S 33 W	0.2	0.2	84.0	65.8	18.2	...	...	...	...	...	...
8	75.0	.604	70	.661	.057	0.1	S 3 W	1.0	1.1	83.8	64.5	19.3	...	...	...	...	...	...
9	75.7	.682	78	.595	28.913	0.4	S 8 E	1.6	2.8	86.0	64.4	21.6	...	...	...	...	...	...
10	72.5	.408	53	.734	29.326	0.3	N 19 W	10.6	11.0	81.0	69.8	11.2	...	...	...	...	...	...
11	Sunday						S 39 E	10.9	3.3	76.8	59.5	17.3	...	...	...	...	...	...
12	70.8	.516	69	.500	28.984	0.3	S 7 E	3.1	4.1	81.2	56.4	24.4	.220	2.0	...	...	.220	2.0
13	69.3	.540	78	.376	28.836	0.8	N 32 W	4.8	4.9	77.8	64.8	13.0	R	2.2	...	...	R	2.2
14	68.0	.493	73	.629	29.136	0.2	N 40 W	1.3	3.8	77.4	57.8	19.6	...	...	...	...	...	...
15	68.7	.343	50	.734	.301	0.1	N 56 E	3.4	5.8	77.5	59.6	17.9	...	...	...	...	...	...
16	70.7	.382	51	.576	.194	0.6	N 22 E	4.3	5.9	80.8	60.0	20.8	...	...	...	...	...	...
17	72.9	.503	61	.424	28.922	0.5	S 15 W	3.7	4.8	82.4	62.0	20.4	...	...	...	...	...	...
18	Sunday						N 80 W	8.0	9.3	95.2	63.5	31.7	...	...	...	...	...	...
19	64.6	.305	56	.600	.205	0.8	N 73 W	6.5	6.7	73.5	59.0	14.5	...	...	...	...	...	...
20	56.0	.162	71	.656	.194	0.7	N 85 W	1.0	4.1	75.0	53.0	21.6	...	...	...	...	...	...
21	56.7	.450	70	.620	.170	0.2	S 13 E	1.7	3.1	77.5	57.8	19.7	...	...	...	...	...	...
22	57.0	.454	68	.549	.095	0.3	N 87 E	2.7	3.4	78.0	57.4	20.6	...	...	...	...	...	...
23	70.0	.548	75	.434	28.880	0.6	S 26 E	0.8	4.7	79.8	59.5	20.3	.040	1.7	...	...	.040	1.7
24	65.3	.350	57	.557	29.207	0.3	N 37 W	9.0	9.8	77.0	61.2	15.8	...	...	...	...	...	...
25	Sunday						S 12 W	2.8	3.1	77.0	49.8	27.2	...	...	...	...	...	...
26	67.1	.422	63	.707	.286	0.4	S 68 E	1.1	1.7	79.6	53.0	26.6	...	...	...	...	...	...
27	74.0	.645	77	.489	28.846	0.7	S 3 W	4.2	5.2	82.0	63.6	18.4	.210	2.0	...	...	.210	2.0
28	70.0	.502	69	.354	28.852	0.6	N 73 W	5.7	6.8	81.0	67.8	16.2	.010	2.0	...	...	.010	2.0
29	59.3	.310	65	.555	29.243	0.4	N 78 W	3.8	4.4	70.4	53.0	17.6	.105	3.6	...	...	.105	3.6
30	53.2	.264	65	.760	.276	0.2	N 58 W	3.8	4.8	63.5	44.2	19.3	...	...	...	...	...	...
31	57.2	.359	76	.584	.225	0.8	S 19 W	3.1	3.7	67.8	42.2	25.6	.95	13.5	...	...	.050	13.5
	68.1	0.475	8	29.592	29.117	0.5	N 76 W	1.2	4.5	78.7	58.8	19.9	2.410	31.7	...	...	2.440	34.7

TORONTO.
General Meteorological Abstract, September, 1867.

Days.	DAILY MEANS.					WIND.			EXTREMES OF TEMPERATURE.			RAIN.		SNOW.		TO AL FALL.	
	Temperature of Air.	Pressure of Vapour.	Rel. Humid.	Barometric Pressure.	Pressure of Dry Air.	Clouded Sky.	Resultant Direction.	Resultant Velocity.	Mean Velocity.	Maximum.	Minimum.	Difference.	Depth in inches.	Approximate duration.	Depth in inches.	Approximate duration.	Depth in inches.	Approximate duration.
1	Sunday						N 10 W	8.3	8.4	4.5	56.0	8.5	...	...	...	...	...	...
2	55.7	0.312	70	29.679	29.336	0.2	N 81 E	4.1	4.4	63.5	43.5	20.0	...	...	...	...	...	...
3	60.1	.440	83	.576	.136	0.8	S 41 W	3.4	3.9	68.8	51.6	17.2	0.170	3.0	...	...	0.170	3.0
4	59.2	.363	72	.670	.313	0.0	S 79 E	1.4	2.8	68.2	50.0	18.2	...	...	...	...	...	...
5	63.7	.490	81	.535	.039	0.0	S 87 E	2.6	3.1	72.4	53.0	19.4	.010	0.2	...	...	.010	0.2
6	60.9	.368	65	.582	.213	0.5	N 41 W	6.3	9.0	75.8	60.6	15.2	.010	0.6	...	...	.010	0.6
7	57.2	.318	69	.935	.617	0.1	N 78 E	3.4	5.0	66.0	48.0	18.0	...	...	...	...	...	...
8	Sunday						N 82 E	4.5	4.9	66.2	50.0	16.2	...	...	...	...	...	...
9	64.5	.482	78	.576	.094	0.9	S 85 W	5.0	8.8	76.0	57.8	18.2	.191	3.0	...	...	.191	3.0
10	53.4	.211	61	.700	.460	0.4	N 34 W	5.5	5.7	64.0	45.0	19.0	...	...	...	...	...	...
11	55.5	.301	69	.678	.377	0.0	S 18 W	5.3	5.5	68.5	38.5	20.7	...	...	...	...	...	...
12	62.2	.399	72	.510	.111	0.4	S 30 W	6.5	6.3	75.3	47.2	28.1	...	...	...	...	...	...
13	57.4	.389	81	.514	.125	0.7	N 33 W	5.4	7.5	74.0	57.0	17.4	.355	3.2	...	...	.355	3.2
14	48.4	.209	62	.925	.719	0.4	S 81 E	4.8	5.5	56.2	41.4	14.8	...	...	...	...	...	...
15	Sunday						S 85 E	3.1	3.2	64.0	46.6	17.4	...	...	...	...	...	...
16	64.0	.508	82	.758	.250	0.5	S 28 W	1.3	1.3	72.0	54.8	17.2	.120	1.0	...	...	.12	1.0
17	72.1	.646	83	.791	.145	0.3	S 26 W	1.8	1.9	85.5	62.0	23.5	...	...	...	...	...	...
18	72.3	.638	81	.746	.108	0.6	N 70 W	4.0	6.2	87.0	64.4	22.6	.280	0.5	...	...	.280	0 5
19	64.0	.464	78	.787	.323	0.2	S 77 E	1.8	2.3	39.8	59.5	10.3	...	...	...	...	...	...
20	61.5	.430	78	.670	.240	0.2	N 68 W	6.2	7.0	83.0	59.6	23.4	.020	1.0	...	...	.02	1.0
21	56.9	.328	72	.830	.503	0.5	S 78 W	0.8	1.7	59.0	39.0	20.0	...	...	...	...	...	...
22	Sunday						N 40 W	5.7	8.4	76.4	48.0	28.4	...	...	...	...	...	...
23	46.8	.199	63	30.070	.871	0.0	N 86 E	2.1	3.0	56.2	41.6	14.6	...	...	...	...	...	...
24	57.3	.302	70	29.790	.428	0.0	S 17 W	2.7	3.6	69.3	40.0	29.3	...	...	...	...	...	...
25	56.9	.290	62	.693	.403	0.2	N 34 W	13.6	14.3	65.2	57.0	8.2	...	...	...	...	...	...
26	47.5	.22	70	.819	.596	0.2	N 13 W	14.5	4.7	58.0	39.5	18.5	...	...	...	...	...	...
27	49.6	.257	80	.666	.379	0.0	S 85 W	2.1	3.5	51.8	36.6	25.2	...	...	...	...	...	...
28	59.1	.370	75	.523	.153	0.0	S 26 W	5.2	5.5	71.2	43.2	28.0	...	...	...	...	...	...
29	Sunday		...				N 2 W	9.9	10.0	61.8	49.4	12.4	.070	0.7	...	...	.070	0.7
30	40.9	.139	56	.827	.689	0.2	N 23 W	3.8	4.9	53.0	31.8	21.2	...	...	...	...	...	...
	57.9	0.360	73	29.714	29.345	0.3	N 37 W	1.5	5.4	68.7	49.4	19.3	1.226	13.2	...	...	1.226	13.2

TORONTO.
GENERAL METEOROLOGICAL ABSTRACT, OCTOBER, 1867.

Days.	DAILY MEANS.					WIND.			EXTREMES OF TEMPERATURE			RAIN.		SNOW.		TOTAL FALL.	
	Temperature of Air	Pressure of Vapour	Rel. Humid.	Barometric Pressure.	Pressure of Dry Air.	Clouded Sky.	Resultant Direction.	Resultant Velocity.	Mean Velocity	Maximum.	Minimum.	Difference.	Depth in inches.	Approximate duration.	Depth in inches.	Approximate duration.	Depth in inches.	Approximate duration.
1	45.6	0.249	68	29.587	29.338	0.1	S 21 W	5.1	5.8	62.8	31.0	31.8	R	0.1	...	...	R	0.1
2	58.6	.335	68	.300	28.965	0.0	N 83 W	8.1	10.2	69.5	50.6	18.9	1.075	0.8	...	...	1.075	0.8
3	45.3	.171	57	.626	29.455	0.3	N 11 W	4.8	6.0	55.0	45.0	10.0	...	...	...	...	...	...
4	48.4	.246	72	.675	.429	0.5	S 88 E	8.2	9.2	56.0	34.8	21.2	1.070	7.8	...	...	1.070	7.8
5	47.5	.287	80	.502	.215	0.7	N 33 W	9.7	10.3	52.8	49.7	3.1	.095	4.0	...	...	.095	4.0
6	Sunday						N 26 W	7.9	7.9	55.0	37.8	17.2	...	...	...	...	...	...
7	41.1	.102	64	30.130	.968	0.1	N 43 E	0.4	2.2	50.4	35.0	15.4	...	...	...	...	...	...
8	47.0	.214	66	29.891	.677	0.7	S 31 E	1.5	1.9	55.0	33.0	22.0	...	...	...	...	...	...
9	52.3	.336	85	.372	.036	1.0	S 6 W	5.8	7.3	67.8	42.0	15.8	.285	3.5	...	...	.285	3.5
10	51.5	.331	86	.113	28.782	1.0	S 27 W	2.7	2.8	57.5	49.0	8.5	.340	8.0	...	...	.340	8.0
11	50.8	.326	88	.281	28.955	1.0	N 46 E	1.3	2.7	56.8	45.7	11.1	.005	0.5	...	...	.005	0.5
12	48.4	.297	87	.515	29.220	0.9	N 23 E	2.8	3.0	52.0	47.2	4.8	.035	7.0	...	...	.035	7.0
13	Sunday						N 65 W	7.9	8.0	51.0	40.4	20.0	...	...	...	...	...	...
14	50.8	.280	76	.616	.336	0.5	S 59 W	4.1	5.1	50.2	33.0	22.2	...	...	...	...	...	...
15	49.6	.239	69	.649	.410	0.2	N 43 W	6.8	6.0	61.0	44.4	16.6	...	...	...	...	...	...
16	51.0	.308	80	.740	.432	0.1	S 32 E	1.3	2.7	61.0	36.5	24.5	...	...	...	...	...	...
17	59.8	.428	81	.522	.094	0.4	S 42 W	6.8	7.5	69.8	50.4	19.4	...	...	...	...	...	...
18	60.0	.349	60	.517	.168	0.1	S 58 W	4.9	5.2	75.4	53.8	21.6	...	...	...	...	...	...
19	51.6	.391	72	.646	.256	0.6	N 56 E	0.6	2.4	71.2	50.0	21.2	...	...	...	...	...	...
20	Sunday						N 81 E	2.9	3.2	67.0	54.4	12.6	...	...	...	...	...	...
21	60.7	.403	77	.641	.241	0.0	S 61 W	3.8	7.0	71.9	51.0	20.9	.030	1.5	...	...	.030	1.5
22	47.6	.253	76	.739	.525	0.7	N 41 W	9.4	9.6	53.6	50.0	3.6	...	...	...	...	...	...
23	41.2	.182	71	30.050	.867	0.2	N 73 W	1.5	4.1	51.0	34.8	16.2	...	...	...	...	...	...
24	42.0	.181	67	30.100	.919	0.0	S 18 W	3.4	4.0	53.0	32.0	21.0	...	...	...	...	...	...
25	43.4	.174	60	30.041	.870	0.0	N 59 E	2.4	1.2	53.2	32.0	21.2	...	...	...	...	...	...
26	41.3	.194	65	29.978	.784	0.0	N 18 W	0.8	3.0	54.8	38.4	16.4	...	...	...	...	...	...
27	Sunday						N 57 E	3.1	4.0	57.8	36.0	21.8	...	...	...	...	...	...
28	49.3	.392	86	.888	.585	1.0	N 74 E	7.6	7.9	53.6	42.0	11.6	.035	6.8	...	...	.035	6.8
29	51.4	.242	64	.634	.392	0.7	N 23 E	7.2	7.9	59.5	48.0	11.5	R	0.2	...	...	R	0.2
30	43.8	.252	70	.492	.241	0.5	N 18 W	4.3	6.2	57.0	42.0	15.0	...	...	...	...	...	...
31	43.5	.203	72	.653	.450	0.0	N 36 W	7.7	8.5	51.8	43.0	8.8	...	...	...	...	...	...
	49.9	0.272	73	29.965	29.393	0.5	N 45 W	4.5	5.7	59.8	42.5	16.3	1.970	40.2	...	...	1.970	40.2

TORONTO.
General Meteorological Abstract, November, 1867.

Days.	DAILY MEANS.					WIND.				EXTREMES OF TEMPERATURE			RAIN.		SNOW.		T'TAL FAL'.	
	Temperature of Air.	Pressure of Vapour.	Hel. Humid.	Barometric Pressure.	Pressure of Dry Air.	Clouded Sky.	Resultant Direction.	Resultant Velocity.	Mean Velocity.	Maximum.	Minimum.	Difference.	Depth in inches.	Approximate duration.	Depth in inches.	Approximate duration.	Depth in inches.	Approximate duration.
1	32.6	0.255	63	29.361	29.106	0.8	S 41 W		3.3	42.1	12.3	59.2	36.4	22.8	...	...	...	...	...
2	40.1	.200	57	.317	.117	0.7	N 75 W		9.7	10.8	59.0	50.2	8.8	0.020	0.4	...	...	0.020	0.4
3	80	uday					S 32 W		5.2	16.0	60.4	41.0	19.4	.795	8.0	...	...	.795	8.0
4	37.9	.164	75	.601	.407	0.6	S 89 W		7.9	8.3	46.0	38.4	7.6	R	0.7	S	0.2	R	0.9
5	38.5	.143	63	.808	.666	0.5	S 87 W		12.9	14.2	51.0	31.4	19.6	...	...	S	S	S	...
6	32.5	.141	77	.911	.770	0.4	S 79 E		3.4	3.7	39.0	27.5	11.5	...	...	...	...	...	...
7	37.6	.180	90	.626	.446	0.8	N 84 E		11.0	11.3	42.5	29.5	13.0	...	...	...	...	...	...
8	50.6	.283	70	.342	.059	0.7	S 5 E		3.2	4.0	58.5	36.0	22.5	.030	1.0	...	...	.030	1.0
9	51.3	.251	65	.389	.138	0.4	S 44 W		6.4	6.7	59.4	51.0	8.4	...	...	...	...	...	...
10	Su	nday					S 38 W		4.8	5.1	53.0	40.0	13.0	...	...	...	...	...	...
11	37.1	.143	65	.621	.478	0.6	N 83 W		3.0	3.4	41.0	37.6	6.4	...	...	...	...	...	...
12	32.7	.139	75	.651	.512	0.7	N 48 W		9.2	9.7	38.8	25.5	13.3	...	...	0.3	3.9	.030	3.9
13	30.5	.138	82	.519	.381	0.7	N 42 W		4.1	4.3	36.4	27.0	9.4	...	...	0.2	2.5	.020	2.5
14	32.9	.121	65	.389	.268	0.8	N 45 W		10.5	11.2	43.5	27.6	15.9	...	...	S	0.2	S	0.2
15	32.1	.147	77	.709	.562	0.6	S 53 W		6.7	8.4	41.6	21.5	20.1	...	...	...	...	...	...
16	33.8	.142	73	.516	.373	0.6	N 69 W		15.6	16.1	41.5	30.5	10.7	...	...	0.1	3.5	.010	3.5
17	Su	nday					N 43 W		10.1	12.7	43.0	25.8	16.2	...	...	S	2.0	S	2.0
18	29.9	.080	71	.706	.629	0.7	N 65 W		5.0	5.8	27.4	15.0	12.4	...	...	...	...	...	...
19	25.2	.096	70	.793	.697	1.0	S 61 W		5.2	5.5	36.5	12.8	23.7	...	...	0.1	3.1	.010	3.1
20	38.1	.155	60	.634	.479	0.8	S 80 W		5.8	6.7	47.8	27.6	20.2	...	...	...	...	...	...
21	35.4	.188	80	.791	.603	1.0	N 87 E		4.1	4.1	47.5	29.8	17.7	...	...	...	...	...	...
22	38.8	.208	85	.646	.438	1.0	N 86 E		0.3	0.3	45.0	33.5	11.5	...	...	...	...	...	...
23	41.0	.235	91	.679	.444	1.0	S 88 E		0.7	1.0	50.0	37.4	12.6	R	0.1	...	...	R	0.1
24	Su	nday					S 66 E		1.0	1.6	50.4	35.6	14.8	.305	2.3	...	...	.305	2.3
25	48.1	.308	91	.409	.101	1.0	S 45 W		6.3	8.5	52.5	47.9	4.6	.095	2.7	...	...	.095	2.7
26	37.7	.143	63	.715	.574	0.9	N 70 W		7.4	7.5	45.0	36.4	8.6	...	...	...	...	...	...
27	37.0	.176	80	.732	.556	1.0	S 6 W		0.6	0.6	40.4	31.2	9.2	...	...	...	...	...	...
28	39.1	.210	88	.622	.413	1.0	S 5 W		2.1	2.8	42.2	36.0	6.2	...	...	...	...	...	...
29	35.6	.191	84	.122	28.931	0.9	N 66 W		11.0	18.3	43.0	39.0	4.0	.590	11.5	0.2	2.0	.610	13.5
30	12.3	.062	82	.599	29.529	0.4	N 64 W		10.7	12.1	17.4	12.0	5.4	...	...	...	...	...	...
	36.9	0.173	75	29.584	29.411	0.7	N 87 W		4.0	7.8	45.4	32.4	13.0	1.835	26.7	0.9	17.4	1.925	44.1

TORONTO
GENERAL METEOROLOGICAL ABSTRACT, DECEMBER, 1867.

Days.	Temperature of Air	Pressure of Vapour	Bar. at Humid	Barometric Pressure	Pressure of Dry Air	Clouded Sky	Resultant Direction	Resultant Velocity	Mean Velocity	Maximum	Minimum	Difference	Depth in inches (Rain)	Approximate duration	Depth in inches (Snow)	Approximate duration	Depth in inches (Total)	Approximate duration
1	Sunday						S 43 W	10.4	11.0	31.0	9.6	21.4	...	...	0.1	2.3	0.010	2.3
2	31.5	0.141	79	29.603	29.462	1.0	S 70 W	7.5	7.9	34.2	21.2	13.0	...	...	0.1	2.5	.010	2.5
3	32.4	.125	69	.564	.439	0.8	W	7.2	11.9	36.6	27.8	9.0	...	...	8	0.5	8	0.5
4	37.7	.071	72	.422	.351	0.9	N 67 W	5.5	5.6	35.0	8.6	16.4	...	...	8	0.2	8	0.2
5	23.8	.100	84	.456	.356	0.8	S 83 W	5.7	8.1	32.0	19.7	12.3	...	...	0.2	2.0	.020	2.0
6	15.7	.185	88	.061	28.875	1.0	"	...	...	46.4	18.6	27.8	...	...	0.2	1.5	.020	1.5
7	21.6	.063	55	.491	29.425	0.4	S 86 W	...	15.6	30.0	22.6	7.4	...	...	8	1.0	8	1.0
8	Sunday						N 68 W	...	4.5	23.0	12.0	11.0	...	...	2.5	8.0	.250	8.0
9	11.9	.07	84	.711	.640	1.6	N 78 W	...	3.4	29.0	-1.0	30.0	...	...	0.5	5.5	.050	5.5
10	15.5	.072	72	.503	.431	0.6	N 43 W	...	3.6	23.5	8.8	14.7	...	...	8	1.0	8	1.0
11	13.2	.059	72	.664	.605	0.9	N 21 E	...	8.8	29.0	9.4	10.6	...	...	...	...	...	...
12	-5.0	.023	96	.835	.782	0.9	N 26 E	...	11.7	-1.6	-9.2	7.6	...	...	...	...	...	...
13	0.2	.034	73	.915	.881	0.4	N 12 E	...	6.2	0.8	-12.8	22.0	...	...	...	...	...	...
14	12.5	.063	88	.748	.679	1.0	N 46 E	...	11.4	17.2	2.0	15.2	...	...	0.5	9.0	.030	9.0
15	Sunday						N 47 E	...	1.5	22.0	14.0	8.0	...	...	2.0	10.0	.200	10.0
16	21.1	.098	87	.498	.400	1.0	"	...	...	25.8	15.7	10.1	...	...	0.1	4.0	.010	4.0
17	22.5	.108	80	.369	.261	0.9	"	...	...	27.5	19.0	8.5	R	4.5	...	...	R	4.5
18	11.4	.06	82	.867	.808	0.5	N 22 W	6.5	6.7	17.0	8.2	8.8	...	...	...	...	...	...
19	13.2	.057	90	30.069	30.051	0.7	S 66 E	3.9	5.9	21.8	1.0	23.8	...	...	0.5	4.0	.050	4.0
20	29.0	.131	8	29.703	29.575	1.0	S 78 W	9.8	11.0	35.0	11.2	20.8	R	1.5	0.8	3.5	.080	5.0
21	29.5	.11	90	.834	.684	1.0	S 89 E	9.9	10.1	38.2	21.4	13.8	0.553	4.0	3.0	8.5	.853	12.5
22	Sunday						S 71 W	16.4	18.7	41.0	29.4	14.9	.090	1.0	...	...	.090	1.0
23	21.9	.104	74	.759	.649	0.7	N 72 W	11.7	14.5	35.2	21.7	8.5	...	...	8	8	8	8
24	25.1	.155	91	.654	.499	1.0	S 40 W	7.5	9.0	37.6	21.0	14.6	.035	1.0	0.3	3.5	.065	4.5
25	...	...	...	...	...	...	S 21 E	1.7	15.0	19.5	28.0	21.5	.475	12.5	...	...	.475	12.5
26	37.2	.162	74	.564	.402	1.0	S 85 W	4.2	8.2	41.5	34.2	9.3	...	...	...	...	...	...
27	38.4	.225	76	.267	28.981	0.5	N 72 W	7.4	8.6	48.0	32.5	15.5	.255	6.0	...	...	.225	6.0
28	31.5	.107	72	.658	29.552	0.1	W	9.4	19.7	33.8	28.0	5.8	...	...	...	...	...	...
29	Sunday						S 83 W	15.1	15.2	26.0	21.0	5.0	...	...	8	1.5	8	1.5
30	15.5	.064	71	30.115	30.085	0.4	N 40 W	4.6	10.4	21.6	17.6	4.0	...	...	8	0.5	8	0.5
31	23.1	.083	72	29.922	29.842	0.5	S 85 E	9.2	10.3	31.2	7.4	23.8	...	...	3.0	7.5	.300	7.5
	21.6	0.101	77	29.617	29.516	0.8	S 81 W	4.8	10.5	29.1	15.3	14.1	1.408	30.5	13.6	76.5	2.768	107.0

TORONTO.
GENERAL METEOROLOGICAL ABSTRACT, JANUARY, 1868.

Days.	Temperature of Air	Pressure of Vapour	Rel. Humid.	Barometric Pressure	Pressure of Dry Air	Clouded Sky	Resultant Direction	Resultant Velocity	Mean Velocity	Maximum	Minimum	Difference	Depth in inches	Approximate duration	Depth in inches	Approximate duration	Depth in inches	Approximate duration
				DAILY MEANS			WIND			EXTREMES OF TEMPERATURE			RAIN		SNOW		TOTAL FALL	
1	29.9	0.151	91	29.119	28.968	1.0	S 30 E	4.0	0.7	32.0	23.5	8.5	...	...	1.5	18.5	.150	18.5
2	32.2	.163	89	.161	28.998	1.0	S 55 W	3.0	4.0	35.2	26.0	9.2	...	...	...	...	...	...
3	31.0	.155	89	.302	29.147	0.9	N 73 E	2.3	5.4	38.0	28.6	9.4	...	...	1.0	5.5	.100	5.5
4	27.0	.132	80	.356	.225	1.0	N 42 E	5.9	6.1	31.5	26.8	4.5	...	...	0.8	7.0	.050	7.0
5	Sunday						N 35 E	4.0	4.0	18.2	14.2	4.0	...	...	...	...	...	...
6	20.5	.090	81	.813	.723	0.9	N 51 E	9.7	10.0	28.0	12.8	15.2	...	...	S	1.0	S	1.0
7	22.0	.101	88	.673	.569	1.0	N 5 E	3.6	4.0	27.5	16.5	11.0	R	0.5	0.2	1.7	.020	1.5
8	25.9	.115	84	.580	.462	1.0	N 85 W	5.8	6.0	32.4	22.0	10.4	...	...	0.4	4.5	.010	4.5
9	7.7	.037	51	.490	.453	0.4	S 77 W	20.3	20.5	10.5	5.3	5.2	...	...	...	...	...	...
10	9.4	.054	77	.438	.384	0.0	S 61 W	14.1	14.1	15.0	1.8	13.2	...	...	S	3.5	S	3.5
11	11.3	.065	57	.485	.421	0.0	N 64 W	8.6	9.0	17.2	9.0	8.2	...	...	S	0.5	S	0.5
12	Sunday						S 75 W	8.2	9.1	14.8	-7.0	21.8	...	...	...	...	...	...
13	12.8	.062	70	30.066	30.004	0.0	S 80 W	10.8	10.2	17.0	10.4	6.6	...	...	...	...	...	...
14	14.8	.074	80	29.908	29.834	1.0	N 43 E	11.4	12.0	18.6	10.0	8.6	...	...	6.0	18.5	.600	18.5
15	16.8	.077	80	.497	.42	0.7	S 75 W	7.6	8.9	26.2	10.0	16.2	...	...	0.1	5.0	.010	5.0
16	13.5	.066	81	.448	.382	0.7	S 64 W	10.2	10.5	18.5	9.2	9.3	...	...	0.1	3.0	.010	3.0
17	16.1	.074	80	.548	.474	0.9	S 73 W	6.6	6.9	22.0	5.2	18.8	...	...	...	...	...	...
18	13.9	.072	85	.675	.603	0.7	S 58 W	6.4	6.5	19.5	14.7	4.8	...	...	0.2	5.5	.025	5.5
19	Sunday						S 32 W	9.4	9.8	30.0	0.0	30.0	...	...	S	0.4	S	0.4
20	29.9	.139	84	.602	.463	1.0	N 22 E	3.0	4.3	33.0	23.0	10.6	...	...	0.2	3.8	.020	3.8
21	21.4	.089	70	.653	.569	0.4	N 13 W	7.7	8.2	28.5	25.0	3.5	...	...	...	...	...	...
22	30.1	.099	51	.913	.814	0.7	S 74 E	3.8	6.1	33.4	4.0	29.4	...	...	...	...	...	...
23	34.4	.169	84	.363	.194	0.9	S 49 W	16.0	17.7	39.0	23.0	16.0	R	2.0	0.2	1.0	.020	3.0
24	23.9	.007	74	.552	.455	1.0	S 60 W	15.0	15.1	28.2	25.3	2.9	...	...	0.1	2.2	.010	2.2
25	20.3	.088	81	.655	.570	1.0	N 70 W	8.3	7.4	25.0	17.2	7.8	...	...	2.0	12.5	.200	12.5
26	Sunday						N 12 W	9.5	10.0	10.4	4.9	5.5	...	...	1.5	8.0	.150	8.0
27	3.1	.043	83	.684	.641	0.1	N	3.3	3.3	13.5	-5.6	19.1	...	...	0.1	2.0	.010	2.9
28	11.5	.061	82	.659	.598	0.8	N 17 E	1.5	5.6	22.8	-3.0	25.8	...	...	0.1	9.0	.010	9.0
29	13.4	.071	57	.606	.535	0.9	S 83 W	6.2	6.3	20.1	3.5	16.6	...	...	...	...	...	...
30	12.6	.061	89	.795	.734	0.0	S 58 W	9.6	10.1	19.8	6.0	13.8	...	...	...	...	...	...
31	17.9	.073	75	30.044	.971	0.6	S 60 W	11.6	12.5	23.0	7.0	16.0	...	...	0.1	1.1	.010	1.1
	19.0	0.092	82	29.536	29.504	0.6	S 83 W	4.0	8.9	24.1	11.0	12.3	R	2.5	14.6	114.0	1.460	116.5

TORONTO.
General Meteorological Abstract, February, 1868.

Days	DAILY MEANS.						WIND.			EXTREMES OF TEMPERATURE.				RAIN.		SNOW.		TOTAL FALL.	
	Temperature of Air	Pressure of Vapour	Rel. Humid.	Barometric Pressure	Pressure of Dry Air	Clouded Sky	Resultant Direction	Resultant Velocity	Mean Velocity	Maximum	Minimum	Difference	Depth in inches	Approximate duration	Depth in inches	Approximate duration	Depth in inches	Approximate duration
1	18.9	.082	81	30.073	29.990	0.4	S 50 W	13.6	13.7	26.2	12.0	14.2	...	...	...	...	...	...
2	Sunday						N 40 W	10.8	12.1	23.0	13.6	9.4	...	...	...	...	...	...
3	4.1	.047	84	30.117	30.068	0.7	S 39 W	10.6	11.5	18.4	-10.6	29.0	...	...	...	...	...	...
4	18.3	.076	75	29.990	29.824	0.5	S 75 W	5.8	6.2	24.1	7.8	16.3	...	...	...	...	...	...
5	27.4	.124	82	.512	.387	1.0	S 10 W	5.9	6.4	33.5	9.5	24.0	...	...	0.5	6.2	.040	6.2
6	18.2	.089	85	.328	.239	0.8	N 78 W	16.6	17.4	31.0	20.0	11.0	...	...	0.5	0.5	.050	2.5
7	2.2	.039	81	.956	.917	0.1	N 46 W	3.8	4.0	17.0	-6.8	23.8	...	...	...	...	...	...
8	23.2	.106	82	.679	.573	0.9	S S W	11.8	12.0	33.8	-4.4	38.2	...	...	4.0	5.9	.400	5.9
9	Sunday						N 49 W	12.0	16.5	36.0	24.2	11.8	0.040	3.0	...	...	.040	3.0
10	-1.5	.035	83	.983	.948	0.4	N 22 W	5.1	5.1	5.2	-10.0	15.2	...	...	...	...	...	...
11	0.6	.058	84	.927	.869	0.7	S 67 W	7.6	8.2	19.8	-4.2	24.0	...	...	S	0.5	S	0.5
12	15.0	.070	82	.912	.842	1.0	N 52 W	2.3	5.8	26.2	9.0	17.2	...	...	S	4.5	S	4.5
13	20.6	.091	81	.730	.639	0.6	N 67 W	12.6	13.9	32.2	14.0	18.2	...	...	...	...	...	...
14	12.3	.075	84	.791	.716	0.7	S 38 W	7.8	9.2	31.5	-7.2	38.7	...	...	0.5	5.1	.050	5.1
15	26.7	.118	80	.638	.519	0.8	N 25 W	8.5	8.6	34.0	13.4	20.6	...	...	1.5	5.0	.150	5.0
16	Sunday						S 22 W	5.7	7.0	32.0	13.0	19.0	...	...	4.0	8.0	.400	8.0
17	25.1	.119	80	.496	.377	0.6	N 40 W	16.5	18.7	36.5	20.0	16.5	...	...	1.0	4.0	.100	4.7
18	15.5	.074	78	.628	.554	0.0	S 50 W	8.5	10.2	32.0	-4.6	36.6	...	...	...	...	...	...
19	31.9	.128	81	.486	.357	0.3	S 82 W	7.2	7.8	39.2	16.8	22.4	...	...	...	...	...	...
20	32.1	.133	74	.348	.215	0.8	S 75 W	4.6	6.9	45.0	20.5	24.5	...	...	...	...	...	...
21	12.0	.058	72	.774	.716	0.4	N 9 W	11.2	11.5	19.7	13.8	5.9	...	...	S	0.5	S	0.5
22	-2.4	.032	78	30.299	30.168	0.0	N 5 W	8.7	8.9	5.8	-9.8	15.6	...	...	...	...	...	...
23	Sunday						N 73 E	10.4	12.4	16.2	-11.5	27.7	...	...	1.0	3.0	.100	3.0
24	18.2	.092	83	30.084	29.992	1.0	S 81 E	23.7	23.8	22.6	6.2	15.8	...	...	12.0	21.0	1.200	24.0
25	21.3	.108	91	29.990	.852	1.0	N 79 E	16.2	16.9	24.8	18.0	6.8	...	...	6.0	16.0	.600	16.0
26	22.8	.115	94	.861	.746	0.9	N 67 E	19.7	19.8	28.8	17.9	10.6	...	...	0.8	3.0	.080	3.0
27	26.1	.129	94	.334	.205	0.7	N 88 W	5.2	7.2	39.0	23.6	6.4	...	...	1.0	12.5	.100	1.0
28	29.8	.083	71	.303	.220	0.9	N 61 W	13.2	13.8	27.0	21.0	6.0	...	...	...	...	...	...
29	10.6	.053	82	.579	.526	0.6	N 45 W	6.6	7.1	20.0	10.6	9.4	...	...	0.1	1.0	.010	1.0
	17.2	0.086	81	29.711	29.658	0.7	N 69 W	3.2	10.8	26.5	8.2	18.3	0.040	3.0	32.8	102.4	1.320	105.4

TORONTO.
GENERAL METEOROLOGICAL ABSTRACT, MARCH, 1868.

Days.	DAILY MEANS.					WIND.				EXTREMES OF TEMPERATURE.			RAIN.		SNOW.		TOTAL FALL.
	Temperature of Air.	Pressure of Vapour.	Rel. Humid.	Barometric Pressure.	Pressure of Dry Air.	Clouded Sky.	Resultant Direction.	Resultant Velocity.	Mean Velocity.	Maximum.	Minimum.	Difference.	Depth in inches.	Approximate duration.	Depth in inches.	Approximate duration.	Depth in inches.	Approximate duration.
1	Sunday						N 53 E	11.8	12.4	20.0	-4.4	24.4	...	...	1.5	5.0	0.159	5.0
2	1.2	0.035	75	29.325	29.290	0.7	N 12 W	14.3	17.3	9.0	1.8	7.2	...	...	2.5	6.0	.250	6.0
3	-2.3	.034	79	.708	.675	0.	N 68 W	8.8	9.0	7.5	-15.0	23.1	...	...	S	1.0	S	1.0
4	9.8	.050	72	.980	.930	0.2	N 54 W	6.0	6.1	25.0	-3.0	28.0	...	...	...	...	...	...
5	20.0	.098	83	30.070	.978	0.7	S 75 E	5.2	6.3	33.4	-1.2	34.0	R	1.0	...	...	R	1.0
6	35.6	.202	97	29.615	.413	1.0	S 20 W	10.4	10.0	58.2	24.8	13.4	0.540	18.5	...	...	.540	18.5
7	38.5	.229	98	.540	.311	1.0	S 13 W	5.1	7.0	41.5	35.2	6.3	.770	14.5	...	...	.770	14.5
8	Sunday						S 74 W	7.3	7.4	43.2	37.0	6.2	...	...	...	...	...	...
9	33.9	.159	82	.96	.801	1.0	S 60 W	1.4	4.4	39.5	27.6	1.9	...	...	...	...	...	...
10	35.9	.109	80	.853	.683	0.9	N 41 W	4.0	4.8	41.8	32.8	9.0	...	...	...	...	...	...
11	28.4	.124	79	30.200	30.070	0.5	N 76 E	8.1	9.3	33.4	29.1	4.3	...	...	...	...	...	...
12	32.9	.180	95	29.562	29.382	1.0	N 80 E	4.8	6.1	40.2	24.6	15.6	.560	7.0	...	...	.560	7.0
13	40.2	.207	84	.334	.127	1.	S 77 W	5.6	5.7	48.0	33.4	14.6	...	...	...	...	...	...
14	37.2	.197	88	.366	.169	0.7	N 76 E	5.2	6.0	44.4	31.3	13.1	.205	3.0	...	...	.205	3.0
15	Sunday						N 59 E	0.8	3.3	55.2	31.2	24.0	...	...	...	...	...	...
16	39.6	.237	97	.427	.190	1.0	N 72 E	6.8	7.0	45.0	25.0	10.0	.540	8.0	...	...	.540	8.0
17	47.4	.280	86	.173	28.893	1.0	S 55 W	13.7	15.8	55.0	37.8	17.8	.045	2.0	...	...	.045	2.0
18	30.4	.117	69	.804	29.087	0.4	N 73 W	12.4	12.7	35.5	28.0	7.5	...	...	0.1	0.6	.010	3.0
19	30.4	.127	75	.813	.686	0.8	N 79 E	7.4	8.2	34.0	22.9	11.1	...	...	0.1	0.6	.010	1.0
20	33.9	.151	77	.593	.442	0.9	N 33 W	14.4	14.7	37.2	30.0	7.2	...	...	...	...	...	...
21	24.0	.086	66	.554	.468	0.5	N 27 W	28.0	28.0	29.0	21.1	7.9	...	...	...	...	...	...
22	Sunday						W	5.5	18.8	36.3	16.6	19.7	...	...	...	...	...	...
23	39.9	.154	64	.417	.293	0.4	N 35 W	4.4	8.7	48.8	12.4	16.4	...	...	...	...	...	...
24	31.9	.113	62	.750	.637	0.1	N 80 E	6.0	7.0	38.0	31.6	6.4	...	...	...	...	...	...
25	32.2	.111	62	.856	.745	0.4	N 73 E	9.4	9.8	37.0	24.8	12.2	...	...	...	...	...	...
26	39.7	.103	64	.904	.801	0.2	S 62 E	2.2	5.0	36.4	25.5	10.9	...	...	...	...	...	...
27	35.8	.034	10	.567	.473	0.5	N 37 W	1.8	4.0	45.0	23.8	21.2	...	...	...	...	...	...
28	41.3	.118	46	.651	.533	0.6	N 62 E	3.2	4.9	51.0	31.6	19.4	...	...	...	...	...	...
29	Sunday						S 77 E	4.1	4.9	51.0	34.9	16.1	...	...	...	...	...	...
30	41.3	.124	46	.746	.612	0.1	S 88 W	4.1	8.1	59.0	27.0	32.0	...	...	...	...	...	...
31	41.5	.131	51	.590	.459	0.0	S 76 E	2.0	3.3	53.0	34.0	19.0	...	...	...	...	...	...
	31.3	0.140	74	29.669	29.529	0.6	N 21 W	2.1	8.0	39.1	23.9	15.2	2.660	54.0	4.2	16.0	3.080	70.0

TORONTO.
GENERAL METEOROLOGICAL ABSTRACT, APRIL, 1868.

	DAILY MEANS.					WIND.			EXTREMES OF TEMPERATURE.			RAIN.		SNOW.		TOTAL FALL.	
Days.	Temperature of Air.	Pressure of Vapour.	Rel. Humid.	Barometric Pressure.	Pressure of Dry Air.	Clouded Sky.	Resultant Direction.	Resultant Velocity.	Mean Velocity.	Maximum.	Minimum.	Difference.	Depth in inches.	Approximate duration.	Depth in inches.	Approximate duration.	Depth in inches.	Approximate duration.
1	46.8	0.202	66	29.326	29.124	0.7	N 34 W	7.8	9.0	63.8	32.7	31.1	...	...	...	...	...	...
2	32.0	.124	67	.445	.322	0.7	N 41 W	8.9	9.3	40.2	32.6	7.6	...	...	0.2	4.0	.020	4.0
3	31.9	.114	64	.415	.301	0.0	S 51 W	3.1	5.1	40.0	22.5	17.5	...	...	0.2	1.0	.020	1.0
4	25.8	.108	77	.334	.226	0.7	N 59 W	7.4	10.2	35.2	25.0	10.2	...	...	2.0	6.5	.200	6.5
5	Sunday						N 82 W	8.7	8.9	29.5	9.2	20.3	...	...	0.1	1.4	.010	1.5
6	29.7	.101	63	.650	.549	0.8	S 48 W	6.3	7.3	41.0	14.6	26.4	...	...	0.1	1.0	.010	1.0
7	31.0	.152	89	.223	.071	0.8	N 38 W	2.4	5.4	36.8	30.6	6.8	...	...	0.5	4.7	.050	4.7
8	22.9	.080	65	.429	.349	0.6	N 68 W	17.5	17.8	31.0	20.0	11.0	...	...	0.2	3.2	.020	3.2
9	24.8	.082	62	.946	.867	0.4	S 61 E	2.7	8.5	34.0	17.4	16.7	...	...	...	...	...	...
10	...	...	...	...	...	...	N 86 E	5.4	6.4	33.1	21.1	9.0	...	...	...	...	...	...
11	35.8	.175	83	.360	.185	0.7	S 79 W	6.0	13.0	45.0	25.3	19.7	0.225	3.5	...	...	.225	3.5
12	Sunday						N 11 W	11.4	11.0	34.0	21.5	12.5	...	...	...	...	...	...
13	29.9	.109	60	.990	.803	0.0	S 27 E	4.3	5.0	38.0	19.0	19.0	...	...	...	...	...	...
14	37.3	.181	70	.585	.405	0.8	S 89 E	6.9	7.1	42.0	26.3	15.7	.025	6.0	...	...	.025	6.0
15	50.6	.274	75	.121	28.847	0.7	S 45 E	5.5	8.3	61.0	37.0	27.0	.105	2.0	...	...	.105	2.0
16	49.2	.253	74	.120	29.865	0.7	S 39 W	15.3	15.2	58.2	43.5	14.7	...	...	...	...	...	...
17	43.2	.200	70	.375	29.175	0.7	S 73 W	17.1	18.4	56.5	40.0	15.9	.005	0.5	S	2.0	.105	0.5
18	39.0	.124	52	.824	.700	0.9	N 87 W	10.9	11.0	47.9	32.0	15.9	...	...	...	...	...	...
19	Sunday						S 24 W	3.6	4.1	51.5	31.0	20.5	.020	1.0	...	...	.020	1.0
20	40.8	.209	82	.701	.492	0.7	"	...	4.0	50.0	37.6	12.4	...	...	...	...	...	...
21	46.8	.190	59	.659	.469	0.3	"	...	9.0	60.0	31.0	29.0	...	...	...	...	...	...
22	38.3	.114	44	.858	.710	0.7	N	9.6	10.4	47.0	35.5	11.5	...	...	1.5	7.0	.150	7.5
23	31.8	.140	76	.954	.807	0.2	N 14 W	8.0	9.0	44.5	32.4	12.1	...	...	0.5	1.5	.050	1.5
24	41.0	.132	54	.986	.854	0.7	S 7 E	2.5	3.2	51.0	24.8	26.2	...	...	...	...	...	...
25	41.1	.204	78	.890	.686	0.8	N 79 E	4.8	6.5	48.0	37.0	11.0	...	...	...	...	...	...
26	Sunday						N 55 W	2.4	6.8	57.0	33.0	24.0	...	...	...	...	...	...
27	39.3	.171	71	.776	.604	0.6	N 78 E	9.2	9.4	45.0	39.0	6.0	...	...	...	...	...	...
28	41.4	.211	80	.855	.644	0.2	N 76 E	10.9	11.2	48.0	32.0	16.0	...	...	...	...	...	...
29	46.0	.277	88	.457	.181	1.0	S 71 E	6.0	8.4	51.0	40.6	10.4	.610	7.2	...	...	.610	7.2
30	40.0	.275	76	.390	.115	0.8	N 66 W	11.9	15.4	60.0	44.6	15.4	R	1.0	...	...	R	1.0
	38.0	0.170	70	29.557	29.417	0.6	N 63 W	2.4	9.2	46.1	29.7	16.4	0.930	21.2	5.3	32.9	1.520	54.1

TORONTO.
GENERAL METEOROLOGICAL ABSTRACT, MAY, 1868.

Days.	DAILY MEANS.							WIND.			EXTREMES OF TEMPERATURE.			RAIN.		SNOW.		TOTAL FALL.	
	Temperature of Air.	Pressure of Vapour.	Rel. Humid.	Barometer Pressure.	Pressure of Dry Air.	Clouded Sky.	Resultant Direction.	Resultant Velocity.	Mean Velocity.	Maximum.	Minimum.	Difference.	Depth in Inches.	Approximate duration.	Depth in inches.	Approximate duration.	Depth in Inches.	Approximate duration.
1	37.8	0.187	82	29.740	29.502	0.7	S 86 E	4.8	6.6	44.8	33.2	11.6	0.380	9.0	...	...	0.380	9.0
2	42.3	.219	51	.590	.371	0.8	N 64 W	6.3	7.6	49.0	33.4	15.6	.010	0.2	...	...	.010	0.2
3	Su	nday					S 45 E	1.7	4.1	53.8	35.8	23.0	...	...	...	...	...	...
4	50.5	.269	73	.513	.244	0.6	N 86 E	3.7	4.3	60.6	41.0	19.6	.630	2.5	...	...	.630	2.5
5	52.7	.320	82	.273	28.944	0.8	N 32 W	4.3	9.5	67.2	44.5	22.7	1.410	2.5	...	...	1.410	2.5
6	46.7	.208	65	.466	29.258	0.8	N 16 W	8.4	9.9	54.5	42.2	12.3	...	...	...	...	...	...
7	43.6	.220	80	.356	.187	1.0	N 71 E	3.9	5.7	47.0	39.0	8.0	...	...	...	...	...	...
8	45.2	.189	61	.416	.257	0.2	N 36 W	10.6	10.7	56.5	40.0	16.5	...	...	...	...	...	...
9	47.8	.144	45	.546	.402	0.2	N 29 W	8.1	9.7	59.0	33.6	25.4	...	...	...	...	...	...
10	Su	nday					S 42 E	1.2	5.4	54.6	41.5	13.1	...	...	...	...	...	...
11	46.8	.196	61	.880	.684	0.0	N 88 E	5.3	6.0	55.2	38.0	17.2	...	...	...	...	...	...
12	50.6	.196	53	.712	.516	0.4	N 80 E	13.6	13.6	56.0	41.4	14.6	...	...	...	...	...	...
13	45.5	.284	89	.470	.186	1.0	N 62 E	17.8	18.2	54.0	42.5	11.5	2.220	21.0	...	...	2.220	21.0
14	52.9	.364	90	.267	28.902	0.9	N 59 E	5.8	8.9	62.8	43.5	19.3	.620	6.5	...	...	.620	6.5
15	51.2	.337	80	.508	29.171	1.0	N 79 E	7.0	7.0	56.0	43.8	12.2	.035	5.0	...	...	.035	5.0
16	53.2	.355	87	.530	.184	1.0	N 79 E	3.0	3.3	59.8	47.0	12.8	.760	7.9	...	...	.760	7.9
17	Su	nday					N 15 E	6.7	7.3	60.0	45.4	14.6	.620	13.5	...	...	.620	13.5
18	50.9	.169	48	.617	.448	0.4	N 4 E	8.9	9.2	62.0	43.8	18.2	...	...	...	...	...	...
19	51.2	.240	64	.737	.497	0.5	S 48 E	1.6	3.0	57.8	43.0	14.8	...	...	...	...	...	...
20	50.4	.262	71	.731	.469	0.8	N 70 E	3.5	4.9	55.0	45.0	10.0	...	...	...	...	...	...
21	55.6	.342	78	.503	.161	0.9	N 24 W	7.9	8.4	59.4	47.8	11.6	.270	16.0	...	...	.270	16.0
22	55.3	.378	85	.414	.041	1.0	N 89 E	2.1	2.6	59.0	52.4	6.6	.150	8.5	...	...	.150	8.5
23	54.4	.370	87	.532	.162	0.7	N 74 E	3.4	4.1	61.0	49.0	12.0	R	0.5	...	...	R	0.5
24	Su	nday					N 9 W	0.8	3.2	63.0	48.0	15.0	.405	2.2	...	...	.405	2.2
25	51.8	.305	71	.594	.100	0.1	S 32 W	0.7	2.7	69.0	53.2	15.8	...	...	...	...	...	...
26	52.0	.412	75	.555	.143	0.1	N 79 E	2.8	3.4	73.0	50.6	22.4	...	...	...	...	...	...
27	62.6	.451	79	.335	28.881	0.8	N 73 E	5.1	5.5	73.0	53.4	19.6	.010	1.0	...	...	.010	1.0
28	60.1	.447	86	.367	28.920	0.9	N 83 E	2.4	2.9	67.0	55.0	12.0	.000	1.6	...	...	.030	1.6
29	57.0	.429	92	.339	29.010	1.0	N 81 E	4.2	4.8	65.0	52.0	13.0	...	...	...	...	...	...
30	57.3	.330	77	.485	29.115	1.0	N 80 W	11.6	12.1	65.0	51.4	13.6	...	...	...	...	...	...
31	Su	nday					N 60 W	5.5	7.8	66.4	48.2	18.2	R	0.2	...	...	R	0.2
	51.8	0.299	75	29.521	29.222	0.7	N 38 E	3.2	6.9	59.7	44.5	15.2	7.670	98.1	...	...	7.670	98.1

TORONTO:
GENERAL METEOROLOGICAL ABSTRACT, JUNE, 1868.

Days.	DAILY MEANS.						WIND.			EXTREMES OF TEMPERATURE.			RAIN.		SNOW.		TOTAL FALL.	
	Temperature of Air.	Pressure of Vapour.	Rel. Humid.	Barometric Pressure.	Pressure of Dry Air.	Clouded Sky.	Resultant Direction.	Resultant Velocity.	Mean Velocity.	Maximum.	Minimum.	Difference.	Depth in inches.	Approximate duration.	Depth in inches.	Approximate duration.	Depth in inches.	Approximate duration.
1	54.7	0.315	72	29.696	29.381	0.4	N 10 W	5.7	6.4	64.2	47.8	16.4	0.010	0.5	...	...	0.010	0.5
2	52.2	.253	64	.773	.520	0.2	N 37 E	0.8	5.2	58.0	44.2	13.8	...	...	...	...	...	...
3	52.0	.211	62	.807	.566	0.9	N 66 E	7.3	7.6	56.0	41.4	14.6	...	...	...	...	...	...
4	57.6	.365	76	.774	.411	0.9	N 82 E	4.3	4.7	64.0	47.0	17.0	.440	4.0	...	...	.440	4.0
5	56.8	.427	92	.545	.118	0.9	S 3 E	2.0	4.9	68.0	51.0	17.0	.825	9.5	...	...	.825	9.5
6	57.4	.404	81	.550	.146	1.0	N 31 W	0.2	0.0	68.8	54.7	14.1	.540	5.5	...	...	.540	5.5
7	Sunday						S 44 E	2.7	4.2	56.5	42.6	13.9	...	...	...	...	...	...
8	53.9	.334	79	.754	.419	0.6	S 66 W	2.2	7.1	65.8	39.0	26.8	.020	3.0	...	...	.020	3.0
9	50.9	.267	71	.806	.539	0.4	N 53 W	1.7	4.4	61.4	42.0	19.4	...	...	...	...	...	...
10	53.9	.310	75	.872	.562	0.1	S 1 W	1.2	4.3	63.0	38.0	25.0	...	...	...	...	...	...
11	55.4	.293	67	.777	.484	0.6	N 64 E	2.6	4.4	62.8	44.0	18.8	...	...	...	...	...	...
12	53.9	.421	71	.654	.233	0.2	N 68 W	2.6	4.7	74.2	47.0	27.2	R	0.2	...	...	R	0.2
13	64.4	.462	76	.688	.226	1.0	S 79 E	1.9	3.2	73.0	59.2	13.8	R	0.7	...	...	R	0.7
14	Sunday						N 88 E	3.0	3.4	73.8	58.8	15.0	...	...	...	...	...	...
15	63.3	.458	79	.605	.147	1.0	N 57 E	0.4	3.2	73.0	56.2	16.8	.275	3.3	...	...	.275	3.3
16	69.6	.612	84	.614	.002	0.4	N 45 W	3.3	5.3	77.5	55.4	22.1	...	...	...	...	...	...
17	72.4	.617	77	.597	28.980	0.1	N 81 W	2.3	4.5	82.0	62.0	20.0	...	...	...	...	...	...
18	72.0	.541	67	.507	28.066	0.1	S 23 W	4.8	5.2	84.2	64.0	20.2	...	...	...	...	...	...
19	72.7	.638	79	.335	28.697	0.6	S 23 W	6.8	7.2	81.5	58.0	23.5	...	...	...	...	...	...
20	67.5	.450	71	.389	28.909	0.7	N 17 W	8.6	9.5	77.0	63.0	14.0	...	...	...	...	...	...
21	Sunday						N 1 W	5.8	7.4	67.0	57.0	10.0	.040	1.0	...	...	.040	1.0
22	62.3	.419	74	.615	29.196	0.9	S 76 W	1.1	4.5	70.2	56.8	13.4	.022	1.0	...	...	.022	1.0
23	62.0	.382	69	.633	.251	0.7	N 55 W	2.5	5.2	74.0	50.8	23.2	.045	2.0	...	...	.045	2.0
24	61.9	.411	74	.758	.346	0.1	N 77 E	4.5	5.6	67.6	51.8	15.8	...	...	...	...	...	...
25	64.1	.432	74	.812	.376	0.0	N 81 E	4.0	4.9	72.0	54.4	17.6	...	...	...	...	...	...
26	68.0	.449	66	.673	.224	0.2	S 83 W	0.9	4.3	78.0	54.6	23.4	...	...	...	...	...	...
27	71.1	.501	65	.549	.048	0.4	N 29 W	7.5	8.0	82.0	55.0	27.0	...	...	...	...	...	...
28	Sunday						S 32 E	2.3	3.2	72.5	61.2	11.3	...	...	...	...	...	...
29	65.0	.432	70	.693	.202	0.6	S 81 E	3.6	3.8	74.0	55.4	18.6	...	...	...	...	...	...
30	64.3	.496	77	.602	.166	0.5	S 81 E	2.0	2.5	76.0	57.2	18.8	...	...	...	...	...	...
	62.0	0.422	71	29.659	29.237	0.5	N 16 E	0.6	5.3	70.6	52.3	18.3	2.217	30.7	...	...	2.217	30.7

TORONTO.
GENERAL METEOROLOGICAL ABSTRACT, JULY, 1868.

Days.	DAILY MEANS.					WIND.			EXTREMES OF TEMPERATURE.			RAIN.		SNOW.		TOTAL FALL.	
	Temperature of Air.	Pressure of Vapour.	Rel. Humid.	Barometric Pressure.	Pressure of Dry Air.	Clouded Sky.	Resultant Direction.	Resultant Velocity.	Mean Velocity	Maximum.	Minimum.	Difference.	Depth in inches.	Approximate duration.	Depth in inches.	Approximate duration.	Depth in inches.	Approximate duration.
1	75.6	0.679	78	29.695	29.016	0.4	S 6 W	4.0	4.1	88.0	60.6	27.4	...	...	...	...	...	...
2	76.1	.705	79	.724	.019	0.5	S 10 E	1.9	2.9	87.5	64.8	22.7	...	...	...	...	...	...
3	76.7	.725	79	.720	28.995	0.8	S 81 E	1.4	2.5	85.5	67.0	18.5	...	...	...	...	...	...
4	82.4	.708	70	.024	28.856	0.6	S 63 W	3.9	8.6	93.0	70.0	23.0	...	...	...	...	...	...
5	Sunday						N 14 W	7.9	8.3	86.0	70.8	15.2	...	...	...	...	...	...
6	71.9	.556	72	.663	29.107	1.0	S 84 E	4.2	4.4	79.0	63.5	15.5	0.000	0.4	...	...	0.000	0.4
7	73.6	.072	82	.465	28.793	0.7	N 51 E	1.3	4.1	85.5	66.0	19.5	.245	1.6	...	...	.245	1.6
8	74.3	.616	72	.550	28.934	0.3	N 30 W	2.4	5.4	84.0	64.4	19.6	...	...	...	...	...	...
9	73.3	.599	73	.636	29.037	0.2	N 86 E	4.6	5.3	81.0	66.8	14.2	...	...	...	...	...	...
10	75.1	.617	72	.663	.046	0.1	S 73 E	3.5	3.8	84.0	66.0	18.0	...	...	...	...	...	...
11	78.2	.602	63	.661	.059	0.3	S 6 E	2.6	2.7	89.2	64.0	25.2	...	...	...	...	...	...
12	Sunday						S 14 E	2.2	2.4	90.0	67.5	22.5	...	...	...	...	...	...
13	84.0	.732	64	.667	28.935	0.0	S 35 E	2.3	2.6	93.4	69.6	23.8	...	...	...	...	...	...
14	84.5	.770	65	.615	28.845	0.2	S 6 E	0.9	4.2	93.0	71.4	21.6	...	...	...	...	...	...
15	82.4	.806	72	.548	28.742	0.4	N 34 W	6.5	8.5	92.0	76.0	16.0	...	...	...	...	...	...
16	73.6	.538	65	.613	29.075	0.2	S 60 E	3.5	5.1	82.0	68.4	13.6	...	...	...	...	...	...
17	75.1	.517	61	.613	.096	0.1	S 25 E	2.9	3.0	86.0	62.0	24.0	...	...	...	...	...	...
18	81.1	.720	67	.557	28.837	0.8	S 60 W	0.6	5.4	90.6	66.0	24.6	.030	0.3	...	...	.030	0.3
19	Sunday						S 87 E	3.3	5.0	86.4	73.0	13.4	...	...	...	...	...	...
20	76.2	.513	57	.636	29.123	0.1	N 86 E	5.7	6.0	83.0	69.4	13.6	...	...	...	...	...	...
21	76.7	.680	74	.534	28.854	0.7	S 76 E	0.3	2.0	86.0	67.5	18.5	...	...	...	...	...	...
22	75.8	.682	76	.499	28.817	0.7	N 72 E	4.0	4.8	84.0	66.8	17.2	...	...	...	...	...	...
23	71.3	.506	65	.455	28.949	1.0	N 56 E	3.2	4.4	78.0	65.6	12.4	R	3.7	...	...	R	3.7
24	75.3	.555	65	.385	28.830	1.0	N 17 W	4.1	6.1	85.6	67.0	18.6	...	...	...	...	...	...
25	69.4	.456	63	.555	29.009	0.9	N 1 W	1.8	6.2	80.2	64.8	15.4	...	...	...	...	...	...
26	Sunday						N 42 E	0.8	2.9	80.0	59.0	21.0	...	...	...	...	...	...
27	70.4	.507	67	.694	.187	1.0	S 78 E	3.1	3.4	78.8	60.0	18.8	...	...	...	...	...	...
28	74.2	.595	59	.660	.165	1.0	N 2 E	1.4	5.6	85.2	60.6	24.6	...	...	...	...	...	...
29	71.6	.506	67	.674	.165	1.0	N 22 W	2.7	2.7	82.0	63.4	18.6	...	...	...	...	...	...
30	72.9	.505	62	.655	.150	1.0	S 10 W	1.5	3.0	83.4	61.5	21.9	...	...	...	...	...	...
31	74.9	.608	81	.447	28.784	0.9	S 34 W	8.8	9.0	85.0	67.6	17.4	.175	5.5	...	...	.175	5.5
	75.8	0.619	69	29.600	28.981	0.6	S 87 E	0.7	4.7	85.4	66.2	19.2	.510	11.5	...	...	0.510	11.5

TORONTO.
GENERAL METEOROLOGICAL ABSTRACT, AUGUST, 1868.

Days.	DAILY MEANS.						WIND.		EXTREMES OF TEMPERATURE.			RAIN.		SNOW.		TOTAL FALL.	
	Temperature of Air.	Pressure of Vapour.	Rel. Humid.	Barometric Pressure.	Pressure of Dry Air.	Clouded Sky.	Resultant Direction.	Resultant Velocity.	Mean Velocity.	Maximum.	Minimum.	Difference.	Depth in inches.	Approximate duration.	Depth in inches.	Approximate duration.	Depth in inches.	Approximate duration.
1	71.1	0.608	79	29.268	23.660	0.6	S 77 W	3.8	4.6	81.0	68.8	12.2	0.075	2.5	...	...	0.075	2.5
2	Sunday						N 51 W	7.5	8.9	84.0	59.5	24.5	...	...	...	...	..	...
3	67.6	.462	68	.559	.097	0.5	N 19 E	2.6	6.8	77.0	60.4	16.6	...	...	...	...	...	...
4	68.8	.432	62	.744	.312	0.6	E	4.8	6.3	78.0	61.0	17.0	...	...	...	...	...	...
5	69.7	.465	63	.876	.411	0.0	S 59 E	2.0	5.7	80.0	62.5	17.5	...	...	...	...	...	...
6	71.0	.436	58	.800	.364	0.0	S 68 E	4.2	5.4	81.0	57.8	23.2	...	...	...	...	...	...
7	71.9	.524	67	.500	28.976	0.8	S 68 E	5.4	7.5	78.0	58.0	20.0	R	0.1	...	...	R	0.1
8	71.7	.557	72	.294	28.738	0.8	S 39 W	9.0	10.5	81.8	66.5	15.3	R	0.1	...	...	R	0.1
9	Sunday						N 86 W	8.8	9.2	72.0	58.0	14.0	...	...	...	...	...	...
10	62.7	.392	69	.631	.239	0.9	S 44 W	1.7	5.4	71.5	53.0	18.5	.020	8.7	...	...	.020	8.7
11	60.3	.418	80	.636	.218	0.9	N 32 W	3.4	5.5	68.0	56.5	11.5	.100	3.0	...	...	.100	3.0
12	60.2	.326	64	.750	.424	0.3	N 37 W	7.5	8.3	70.8	53.4	17.4	R	0.1	...	...	R	0.1
13	66.1	.307	51	.740	.433	0.3	N 73 E	8.5	8.5	80.5	46.8	33.7	...	...	...	...	...	...
14	69.0	.381	55	.666	.285	0.8	S 74 W	5.7	6.7	84.4	54.0	30.4	...	...	...	...	...	...
15	69.3	.413	61	.588	.175	0.6	N 79 W	6.4	9.3	82.5	60.6	21.9	.020	0.5	...	...	.020	0.5
16	Sunday						S 61 E	2.3	4.1	69.0	55.0	14.0	...	...	...	...	...	...
17	59.1	.349	70	.815	.466	0.3	E	5.9	6.0	66.4	52.0	14.4	...	...	...	...	...	...
18	65.6	.523	83	.569	.046	0.8	S 4 W	4.7	7.2	72.0	54.4	17.6	.225	2.0	...	...	.225	2.0
19	69.4	.506	83	.534	28.937	0.7	S 17 W	5.6	5.7	79.0	62.4	16.6	R	0.2	...	...	R	0.2
20	65.0	.508	81	.625	29.120	0.7	N 27 W	4.8	6.2	75.8	63.8	12.0	.350	1.5	...	...	.350	1.5
21	63.9	.397	67	.803	.406	0.3	N 36 W	0.4	4.8	71.8	58.0	13.0	...	...	...	...	...	...
22	64.5	.424	71	.815	.391	0.1	S 44 E	1.3	2.6	77.0	56.2	20.8	...	...	...	...	...	...
23	Sunday						S 30 E	1.8	2.2	78.0	53.2	24.8	...	...	...	...	...	...
24	66.1	.438	70	.645	.207	0.7	S 52 E	1.8	2.1	78.0	55.0	23.0	...	...	...	...	...	...
25	68.9	.480	71	.658	.172	0.0	S 16 E	3.1	3.1	82.8	55.2	27.6	...	...	...	...	...	...
26	71.2	.478	64	.734	.356	0.5	N 44 E	1.5	3.9	83.5	59.8	23.7	...	...	...	...	...	...
27	62.1	.480	68	.874	.494	0.3	N 86 E	5.4	5.6	68.5	57.5	11.0	...	...	..	...	...	...
28	72.5	.562	74	.642	.080	0.5	S 6 W	0.6	7.2	84.0	59.0	25.0	.070	1.5	...	...	.070	1.5
29	72.0	.601	74	.507	28.900	0.9	S 33 W	5.6	8.5	82.4	66.5	15.9	.040	1.0	...	...	.040	1.0
30	Sunday						N 48 W	1.3	5.0	74.2	60.5	13.7	...	...	...	...	...	...
31	66.8	.567	80	.467	28.899	0.9	N 53 W	0.6	7.6	72.0	58.0	14.0	.602	5.2	...	...	.602	5.2
	67.2	0.463	70	29.644	29.181	0.5	S 58 W	1.0	6.1	76.0	58.2	18.7	1.502	20.4	...	...	1.502	20.4

TORONTO.
GENERAL METEOROLOGICAL ABSTRACT, SEPTEMBER, 1868.

Days.	DAILY MEANS.					WIND.			EXTREMES OF TEMPERATURE.			RAIN.		SNOW.		TOTAL FALL.	
	Temperature of Air.	Pressure of Vapour.	Rel. Humid.	Barometric Pressure.	Pressure of Dry Air.	Clouded Sky.	Resultant Direction.	Resultant Velocity.	Mean Velocity.	Maximum.	Minimum.	Difference.	Depth in inches.	Approximate duration.	Depth in inches.	Approximate duration.	Depth in inches.	Approximate duration.
1	64.2	0.523	86	29.620	29.097	0.8	N 35 W	4.9	5.3	69.4	60.9	8.5	...	...	...	...	...	...
2	63.5	.414	76	.719	.275	0.4	N 39 E	6.6	7.4	71.2	54.3	17.0	...	...	...	...	...	...
3	67.7	.540	80	.047	.109	1.0	S 55 E	6.9	7.8	74.0	62.0	12.0	.207	0.5	...	...	0.207	0.5
4	66.2	.482	75	.585	.103	0.6	S 46 W	3.9	5.7	75.0	61.0	14.0	...	...	...	...	...	...
5	62.0	.331	61	.612	.281	0.0	N 81 W	8.6	9.0	72.0	54.5	17.5	...	...	...	...	...	...
6	Sunday						N 67 E	4.5	7.3	68.0	53.0	15.0	1.080	7.5	...	...	1.080	7.5
7	62.3	.133	77	.602	.169	0.5	N 35 W	1.0	5.2	70.0	56.8	13.2	...	...	...	...	...	...
8	63.3	.504	80	.506	.002	0.7	S 26 E	5.7	6.7	70.5	51.2	19.3	1.585	6.0	...	...	1.58	6.0
9	66.9	.507	77	.449	28.942	0.7	N 67 W	4.1	4.4	75.5	63.0	12.5	...	...	...	...	...	...
10	64.0	.483	80	.524	29.041	0.9	N 82 E	2.6	2.7	69.8	52.6	17.2	R	0.2	...	...	R	0.2
11	67.7	.620	91	.669	.049	0.7	N 83 E	3.3	3.7	71.2	62.8	8.4	...	...	...	...	...	...
12	68.7	.640	92	.614	28.965	0.7	N 78 E	2.7	3.7	74.0	65.8	8.2	R	0.7	...	...	R	0.7
13	Sunday						N 34 W	9.9	10.0	69.5	62.0	7.5	...	...	...	...	...	...
14	56.7	.327	72	.837	29.509	0.1	N 83 E	4.5	5.6	65.0	46.6	18.4	...	...	...	...	...	...
15	63.7	.488	82	.578	.090	0.9	S 60 W	2.1	10.4	68.0	54.0	14.0	.210	2.5	...	...	.210	2.5
16	47.0	.223	68	.751	.528	0.3	N 61 W	12.6	12.6	60.0	48.5	11.5	...	...	...	...	...	...
17	46.3	.209	67	.865	.656	0.2	N 86 W	6.1	6.3	57.5	36.6	20.0	...	...	...	...	...	...
18	50.0	.254	71	.939	.685	0.2	S 23 W	5.7	6.0	63.0	36.6	26.4	...	...	...	...	...	...
19	55.6	.376	83	.817	.441	1.0	S 5 E	7.6	8.5	63.0	43.5	19.5	.285	11.8	...	...	.255	11.8
20	Sunday						N 85 W	6.6	9.9	64.2	55.8	8.4	.055	2.2	...	...	.055	2.2
21	44.1	.201	70	.750	.549	0.2	N 89 W	3.8	4.4	52.0	36.6	15.4	...	...	...	...	...	...
22	53.8	.350	84	.445	.094	0.9	S 86 E	3.4	3.6	59.0	42.2	16.8	.085	4.0	...	...	.085	4.0
23	50.3	.263	71	.677	.414	0.5	N 68 W	8.0	8.4	58.8	50.8	8.0	R	0.2	...	...	R	0.2
24	47.3	.234	73	.806	.571	1.0	N 74 E	5.1	7.2	55.0	39.0	16.0	.255	9.5	...	...	.255	9.5
25	44.6	.254	86	.565	.311	1.0	N 19 E	3.4	3.5	48.8	41.4	7.4	R	0.2	...	...	R	0.2
26	48.7	.268	78	.686	.418	0.2	S 57 E	6.0	6.5	56.0	38.2	17.8	...	...	...	...	...	...
27	Sunday						S 7 E	4.5	5.9	57.0	47.4	9.6	.385	8.5	...	...	.385	8.5
28	52.0	.300	78	.557	.257	0.9	S 82 W	7.2	7.6	60.0	50.0	10.0	.012	0.3	...	...	.012	0.3
29	45.5	.217	72	.690	.473	0.9	N 86 W	7.5	8.5	57.2	40.6	16.6	.020	1.5	...	...	.020	1.5
30	43.1	.264	76	.646	.392	0.8	N 63 W	2.7	6.1	54.4	36.0	18.4	R	0.2	...	...	R	0.2
	56.6	0.375	77	29.660	29.285	0.6	N 74 W	0.9	6.7	64.3	50.1	14.2	4.239	55.8	...	...	4.239	55.8

TORONTO.
GENERAL METEOROLOGICAL ABSTRACT, OCTOBER, 1868.

Days.	DAILY MEANS.					WIND.			EXTREMES OF TEMPERATURE.			RAIN.		SNOW.		TOTAL FALL.	
	Temperature of Air	Pressure of Vapour.	Rel. Humid.	Barometric Pressure.	Pressure of Dry Air.	Clouded Sky	Resultant Direction.	Resultant Velocity.	Mean Velocity.	Maximum.	Minimum.	Difference.	Depth in inches.	Approximate duration.	Depth in inches	Approximate duration.	Depth in inches.	Approximate duration.
1	49.7	0.173	68	29.928	29.755	0.1	N 80 E	6.4	6.9	46.8	34.0	12.8	...	...	...	...	...	...
2	45.9	.223	72	.867	.644	0.8	N 78 E	2.2	3.0	55.2	36.2	19.0	...	...	...	...	...	...
3	44.6	.192	65	.941	.749	0.0	N 66 E	3.8	5.4	54.0	40.0	14.0	...	...	...	...	...	...
4	Sunday						S 85 E	3.4	3.1	53.8	36.0	17.8	...	...	...	...	...	...
5	52.1	.318	81	.349	.031	0.8	S 72 W	6.0	6.9	62.0	42.5	19.5	R	R	...	...	R	R
6	50.6	.280	70	.610	.330	0.7	S 8 W	2.6	5.6	58.0	43.0	15.0	...	...	...	...	...	..
7	39.5	.405	79	.306	28.901	0.9	S 29 W	8.7	12.0	67.6	49.4	18.2	0.120	2.5	...	...	.120	2.5
8	40.0	.188	74	.660	29.481	0.9	N 84 W	10.1	11.3	45.0	39.0	6.0	...	...	...	...	...	...
9	43.7	.212	73	.752	.540	0.8	S 2 E	5.4	5.8	51.0	33.4	17.0	...	...	...	...	...	...
10	50.0	.243	69	.595	.352	0.7	S 21 E	5.3	6.1	56.4	44.0	12.4	...	...	...	...	...	...
11	Sunday						S 82 W	7.9	8.8	62.5	47.0	15.5	...	...	...	...	...	...
12	45.4	.190	65	.634	.644	0.1	N 77 W	8.0	8.2	57.0	39.6	17.4	...	...	...	...	...	...
13	43.3	.230	84	.872	.637	1.0	N 72 W	2.2	2.8	49.0	35.0	14.0	.025	2.0	...	...	.025	2.0
14	42.4	.219	80	.784	.565	0.1	S 68 E	2.0	3.6	51.0	35.5	15.5	...	...	...	...	...	...
15	40.9	.224	86	.661	.437	0.0	S 24 E	2.1	2.7	54.0	31.8	22.2	...	...	...	...	...	...
16	39.7	.199	81	.096	.407	1.0	N 22 W	7.0	8.4	47.0	33.0	14.0	R	0.7	S	S	R S	0.7
17	30.7	.115	89	30.070	.955	0.2	N 51 W	9.9	10.7	38.8	28.8	10.0	...	...	...	...	...	...
18	Sunday						S 33 W	2.8	3.7	45.0	24.2	20.8	R	3.0	...	...	R	3.0
19	39.3	.204	85	29.664	.460	0.9	S 78 W	7.2	7.5	45.4	34.5	10.9	...	...	...	...	...	...
20	42.6	.217	80	.804	.587	1.0	N 55 W	2.3	4.8	48.0	34.8	13.2	.020	2.0	...	...	.020	2.0
21	36.1	.191	59	.695	.504	1.0	N 41 E	8.5	10.0	38.0	36.4	1.6	.180	15.0	2.0	0.8	.020	0.8
22	31.1	.142	81	.870	.728	1.0	N 30 W	12.3	12.5	33.2	30.0	3.2	...	...	S	3.0	S	3.0
23	30.7	.132	78	30.096	.964	0.4	S 69 W	1.2	2.0	37.7	24.0	13.7	...	...	...	...	...	...
24	39.5	.195	79	29.892	.697	0.9	S 9 W	4.6	4.9	45.7	27.0	18.7	...	...	...	...	...	...
25	Sunday						N 27 W	3.5	6.5	50.8	42.0	8.8	.155	3.0	...	...	.155	3.0
26	45.8	.245	79	.805	.560	0.9	S 54 E	1.6	4.0	50.4	45.0	5.4	...	...	...	...	...	...
27	50.1	.291	80	.398	.107	0.8	S 28 W	6.6	10.3	58.0	40.8	17.2	R	1.0	...	...	R	1.0
28	38.6	.191	79	.729	.539	0.3	N 06 W	11.9	12.0	44.0	39.0	5.0	...	...	...	...	...	...
29	31.4	.127	73	30.096	.969	0.8	N 75 E	4.8	6.0	39.0	26.5	12.5	...	...	...	...	...	...
30	41.7	.193	68	29.976	.793	0.0	N 89 E	14.3	14.3	47.1	30.2	16.9	...	...	...	...	...	...
31	46.6	.289	91	.467	.118	1.0	S 36 W	7.4	9.5	52.0	40.5	11.5	.865	13.3	...	...	.865	13.3
	42.4	0.216	77	29.757	29.541	0.6	N 89 W	1.3	7.1	49.8	36.2	13.6	1.365	42.5	2.0	0.8	1.565	52.3

TORONTO
GENERAL METEOROLOGICAL ABSTRACT, NOVEMBER, 1868.

Days.	DAILY MEANS.						WIND.			EXTREMES OF TEMPERATURE			RAIN.		SNOW.		TOTAL FALL.	
	Temperature of Air.	Pressure of Vapour.	Rel. Humid.	Barometric Pressure.	Pressure of Dry Air.	Clouded Sky.	Resultant Direction.	Resultant Velocity.	Mean Velocity.	Maximum.	Minimum.	Difference.	Depth in inches.	Approximate duration.	Depth in Inches	Approximate duration.	Depth in Inches	Approximate duration.
1	Sunday						N 37 W	13.4	14.0	40.5	36.0	4.5	R	R	S	1.5	R	1.5
2	32.2	0.139	77	29.822	29.683	0.6	N 29 W	3.5	13.6	38.0	32.2	5.8	...	...	...	...	...	...
3	34.9	.174	83	.599	.425	0.1	S 11 E	3.2	3.4	48.0	24.6	23.2	...	...	...	...	...	...
4	40.7	.217	85	.469	.252	0.7	N 59 E	4.0	4.9	47.2	31.6	15.6	0.260	7.0	...	...	.260	7.0
5	40.2	.210	83	.573	.363	0.8	N 76 W	14.4	14.8	49.0	39.0	10.0	.015	3.1	...	...	.015	3.1
6	33.2	.140	77	.974	.828	1.0	N 72 W	5.5	6.1	38.0	30.2	7.8	...	...	...	...	...	...
7	35.2	.171	82	.953	.782	1.0	N 82 E	11.9	12.2	42.0	29.0	13.0	.190	5.0	S	0.5	.190	5.5
8	Sunday						N 81 E	2.6	2.6	45.5	35.8	9.7	.600	20.0	...	...	.600	20.0
9	40.6	.233	92	.675	.442	1.0	N 64 E	8.3	9.2	42.1	38.0	4.1	1.210	20.0	...	...	1.210	20.0
10	38.9	.212	89	.523	.311	1.0	S 51 E	2.5	9.5	42.0	36.8	5.2	.030	6.0	...	...	.030	6.0
11	34.1	.127	64	.604	.477	0.7	S 67 W	12.8	12.9	38.0	34.2	3.8	...	...	S	0.4	S	0.4
12	34.7	.168	84	.917	.749	0.9	S 47 W	6.3	7.0	40.4	29.0	11.4	...	...	...	...	...	...
13	41.1	.190	74	.863	.673	0.1	S 68 W	5.5	5.8	50.5	33.0	17.5	...	...	...	...	...	...
14	37.4	.178	79	.935	.757	0.6	N 84 E	4.7	5.1	45.0	29.4	15.6	...	...	...	...	...	...
15	Sunday						N 51 E	8.4	8.6	36.9	31.0	5.6	...	...	...	...	...	...
16	32.2	.147	80	.921	.774	1.0	N 80 E	16.6	17.0	39.5	25.5	14.0	.005	1.0	...	...	.005	1.0
17	40.9	.239	92	.468	.229	1.0	S 84 E	9.3	13.2	43.0	33.0	10.0	2.230	21.0	...	...	2.230	21.0
18	36.5	.185	95	.453	.269	0.9	S 43 E	1.4	2.6	39.8	33.5	6.3	.075	4.0	S	0.5	.075	4.5
19	35.5	.162	78	.492	.330	0.8	N 55 W	2.4	2.7	40.2	33.0	7.2	R	1.0	1.2	5.0	.120	6.0
20	34.0	.166	85	.547	.381	1.0	N 7 W	4.7	4.9	38.0	32.0	6.0	...	...	1.0	5.0	.100	5.0
21	34.0	.170	87	.601	.431	1.0	N 33 W	15.8	16.0	39.0	32.0	6.0	...	...	S	1.0	S	1.0
22	Sunday						N 34 W	9.7	9.7	37.0	26.5	10.5	...	...	...	...	...	...
23	37.7	.155	69	.786	.621	0.4	S 74 W	7.7	8.4	47.0	27.8	19.2	...	...	...	...	...	...
24	37.0	.167	77	.800	.633	0.4	N 82 W	5.9	6.0	45.0	32.0	13.0	...	...	...	...	...	...
25	39.8	.210	85	.490	.250	1.0	S 50 E	3.2	4.5	43.8	32.8	11.0	.480	12.2	...	...	.480	12.2
26	39.5	.173	73	.438	.254	0.9	N 71 W	11.4	12.0	42.0	39.0	3.0	R	1.5	S	1.5	R	3.0
27	32.7	.241	76	.722	.581	0.7	S 83 W	2.1	2.6	36.8	32.0	4.8	...	...	...	...	...	...
28	37.4	.192	80	.335	.146	0.9	S 63 W	7.1	9.7	43.0	28.0	15.0	.055	4.0	...	...	.055	4.0
29	Sunday						N 56 W	3.6	7.1	35.0	32.0	3.0	...	...	2.0	9.5	.200	9.5
30	24.3	.111	84	.261	.150	1.0	N 18 W	7.6	7.8	31.3	21.9	9.4	...	...	0.1	3.0	.010	3.0
	36.1	0.175	81	29.649	29.474	0.8	N 35 W	2.1	8.2	41.4	31.7	9.7	5.150	105.8	4.3	27.9	5.580	133.7

TORONTO.
GENERAL METEOROLOGICAL ABSTRACT, DECEMBER, 1868.

Days.	DAILY MEANS.					WIND.			EXTREMES OF TEMPERATURE.			RAIN.		SNOW.		TOTAL FALL.	
	Temperature of Air.	Pressure of Vapour.	Rel. Humid.	Barometric Pressure.	Pressure of Dry Air.	Clouded Sky	Resultant Direction.	Resultant Velocity.	Mean Velocity.	Maximum.	Minimum.	Difference.	Depth in Inches.	Approximate duration.	Depth in Inches.	Approximate duration.	Depth in inches.	Approximate duration.
1	19.4	0.083	79	29.432	29.349	0.9	N 54 W	7.8	8.6	23.8	17.4	6.4	...	...	S	3.0	S	3.0
2	22.0	090	83	.743	.644	0.9	N 60 W	4.1	4.3	25.5	15.4	10.1	...	...	S	1.0	S	1.0
3	29.2	.134	84	.996	.861	1.0	N 50 W	3.8	4.2	32.0	23.9	8.1	...	...	...	...	...	...
4	25.9	.127	90	.729	.602	1.0	N 55 E	12.0	13.0	29.5	19.5	10.0	...	...	4.0	11.0	0.400	11.0
5	25.7	.124	89	.641	.517	1.0	N 33 E	5.2	5.2	28.0	21.5	6.5	...	...	3.5	9.5	.350	9.5
6	Sunday						S 84 E	8.0	8.7	33.0	25.0	8.0	...	...	...	...	...	...
7	9.7	.157	94	.053	28.896	1.0	N 74 E	2.9	12.5	35.0	27.0	8.0	...	...	3.0	17.7	.300	17.7
8	21.2	.034	7	.062	28.968	0.9	N 70 W	17.9	18.3	30.0	24.6	5.4	...	...	...	...	...	...
9	17.8	.076	78	.528	29.452	0.4	S 86 W	9.8	10.8	21.0	15.0	6.0	...	...	0.1	0.5	.010	0.5
10	12.8	.058	74	.571	.512	0.5	S 76 W	9.4	9.5	18.5	10.6	7.9	...	...	...	...	...	...
11	14.7	.067	82	.515	.448	0.6	S 88 W	9.2	9.3	24.0	2.0	22.0	...	...	S	1.0	S	1.0
12	18.5	.087	86	.796	.709	0.3	S 79 W	14.9	15.0	21.0	16.0	8.0	...	...	...	...	...	...
13	Sunday						S 78 W	5.5	5.6	23.0	9.8	13.2	...	...	...	...	...	...
14	26.4	.124	86	.530	.406	0.7	S 85 W	6.3	7.5	31.0	19.0	12.0	...	...	0.4	8.5	.045	8.5
15	27.2	.132	89	.816	.684	0.9	N 63 E	2.0	4.4	29.0	23.0	6.0	...	...	...	...	...	...
16	25.6	.116	83	.350	.234	0.6	S 78 W	1.1	6.3	34.5	19.7	14.8	...	...	...	...	...	...
17	31.8	.153	76	28.986	28.832	0.7	N 80 W	12.4	14.0	39.0	22.4	16.6	...	...	S	0.3	S	0.3
18	29.4	.096	85	29.673	29.577	0.3	N 32 W	9.2	9.6	27.0	23.2	3.8	...	...	S	1.0	S	1.0
19	18.4	.002	55	.866	.774	0.2	S 85 E	13.1	14.5	36.2	3.5	32.7	...	...	0.1	1.8	.010	1.8
20	Sunday						S 57 W	8.2	10.3	11.2	20.7	23.5	0.005	0.5	...	...	.005	0.5
21	32.3	.161	87	.467	.306	1.0	S 81 W	13.2	13.4	35.6	32.0	3.6	...	...	0.2	3.8	.020	3.8
22	27.4	.124	84	.628	.504	0.9	N 86 W	6.8	8.2	31.4	27.0	4.4	...	...	0.5	17.5	.050	17.5
23	11.5	.059	77	.727	.668	0.6	N 32 W	13.2	13.6	17.0	12.4	4.6	...	...	0.2	3.5	.050	3.5
24	7.6	.052	85	.721	.669	0.5	N 78 W	8.3	11.0	17.0	-3.2	20.2	...	...	...	...	...	...
25	...	...	...	...	...	...	N 86 W	8.2	13.3	25.8	4.5	21.3	...	...	0.5	6.5	.050	6.5
26	17.9	.088	82	.906	.826	0.9	N 86 E	5.7	7.2	27.0	9.0	18.0	...	...	0.1	5.0	.010	5.0
27	Sunday						S 41 E	9.8	11.7	32.8	11.5	18.3	...	...	2.5	13.0	.250	13.8
28	27.4	.118	79	.84	.77	1.0	S 51 W	6.3	7.3	31.8	25.8	9.0	...	...	0.4	3.2	.01	3.2
29	29.5	.132	79	.688	.556	0.8	N 58 W	9.2	11.2	34.5	23.8	10.7	...	...	...	...	...	...
30	17.8	.078	81	.918	.83	0.7	N 31 E	5.1	5.4	26.5	12.5	11.6	...	...	...	...	...	...
31	23.5	.104	85	.917	.808	0.9	N 46 E	8.1	9.5	30.5	11.5	19.0	...	...	...	...	...	...
	22.3	1.105	82	29.049	29.514	0.7	N 71 W	4.0	9.8	39.1	17.1	12.0	0.005	0.5	15.5	108.6	1.555	109.1

TORONTO.
GENERAL METEOROLOGICAL ABSTRACT, JANUARY, 1869.

Days.	DAILY MEANS.					WIND.				EXTREMES OF TEMPERATURE			RAIN.		SNOW.		TOTAL FALL.	
	Temperature of Air	Pressure of Vapour.	R. Humid.	Barometric Pressure.	Pressure of Dry Air.	Clouded Sky	Resultant Direction.	Resultant Velocity.	Mean Velocity.	Maximum.	Minimum.	Difference.	Depth in Inches	Approximate duration	Depth in inches	Approximate duration	Depth in Inches.	Approximate duration.
1	11.5	0.061	83	29.873	29.812	1.0	N 66 E	16.6	17.0	23.0	19.0	19.0	...	...	4.5	24.0	0.450	24.0
2	29.7	.148	88	.525	.377	1.0	S 15 W	3.8	10.0	35.0	9.0	26.0	...	...	4.6	10.2	.400	10.2
3	Sunday						S 3 W	3.5	4.8	37.0	30.9	6.1	...	...	...	...	...	...
4	38.9	.191	81	.318	.124	0.8	S 48 W	5.2	7.3	43.0	33.8	9.2	...	...	...	...	...	...
5	32.8	.147	78	.376	.229	0.8	N 83 W	11.8	12.0	36.2	33.0	3.2	...	...	S	0.1	S	0.1
6	32.5	.141	77	.519	.378	0.5	S 60 W	7.0	7.1	38.8	28.0	10.8	...	...	...	...	...	...
7	39.3	.173	72	.566	.392	0.1	S 60 W	5.9	6.3	45.0	30.2	14.8	...	...	...	...	...	...
8	34.8	.170	84	.654	.485	1.0	N 89 E	9.0	9.4	39.8	34.2	5.6	0.625	8.0	0.2	2.8	.645	10.8
9	38.9	.204	85	.233	.029	1.0	S 68 W	7.6	9.4	45.0	33.1	11.9	.055	1.5	...	...	.055	1.5
10	Sunday						N 43 W	3.8	4.0	35.0	29.2	5.8	...	...	S	0.5	S	0.5
11	28.4	.134	86	.646	.512	1.0	N 34 E	8.0	9.9	34.2	28.0	6.2	...	...	0.4	12.0	.040	12.0
12	24.3	.091	70	.694	.603	0.2	N 27 W	6.1	6.4	30.3	23.0	7.5	...	...	...	...	...	...
13	20.1	.125	77	.774	.649	0.0	S 46 W	8.7	9.0	35.4	18.2	17.2	...	...	...	...	...	...
14	32.9	.159	84	.604	.445	0.1	S 59 W	8.2	8.5	40.4	26.0	14.4	...	...	...	...	...	...
15	30.7	.122	77	.505	.380	0.7	N 26 W	9.8	10.0	38.5	29.8	8.7	...	...	...	...	...	...
16	34.1	.096	74	.785	.692	0.6	S 83 W	2.5	3.4	34.0	16.7	17.3	...	...	...	...	...	...
17	Sunday						N 69 E	8.0	9.0	33.2	20.0	13.2	...	...	...	...	...	...
18	19.9	.075	70	.813	.737	1.0	N 39 E	4.0	4.0	22.5	17.5	5.0	...	...	S	6.0	S	6.0
19	27.3	.115	77	.608	.493	1.0	S 59 W	8.8	10.1	32.0	20.0	12.0	...	...	0.1	3.2	.010	3.2
20	25.8	.120	81	.458	.338	1.0	N 54 W	9.9	11.2	37.0	27.0	10.0	...	...	0.2	4.0	.020	4.0
21	25.7	.108	75	.420	.312	1.0	N 40 W	8.9	13.9	37.2	18.5	18.7	...	...	S	0.5	S	0.5
22	12.4	.059	77	.715	.656	0.4	N 89 W	5.6	8.2	25.5	6.6	18.7	...	...	...	...	...	...
23	32.9	.140	76	.286	.146	0.1	S 68 W	11.1	11.7	43.6	10.0	33.6	...	...	...	...	...	...
24	Sunday						N 45 W	9.7	12.0	36.5	19.0	17.5	...	...	...	...	...	...
25	6.7	.047	79	.683	.636	0.2	N 27 W	8.9	10.0	13.6	-1.0	14.6	...	...	...	...	...	...
26	16.6	.080	86	.780	.700	0.7	S 80 W	7.5	7.7	24.0	7.0	17.0	...	...	S	0.2	S	0.2
27	26.2	.123	84	.567	.444	0.8	S 84 W	5.2	5.4	34.4	13.0	21.4	...	...	...	...	...	...
28	23.3	.147	78	.592	.445	0.9	S 71 W	5.2	5.4	39.0	28.6	10.4	...	...	...	...	...	...
29	34.8	.177	88	.476	.299	1.0	N 85 E	10.7	10.8	39.0	29.5	8.5	.165	6.0	...	...	.165	6.0
30	31.5	.154	85	.248	.094	1.0	N 80 W	13.6	15.1	40.0	34.0	6.0	.042	2.0	0.4	5.0	.082	7.0
31	Sunday						N 49 W	14.4	14.5	25.0	17.3	7.7	...	...	...	...	...	...
	27.7	0.127	80	29.586	29.439	0.7	N 72 W	3.4	9.2	34.6	22.0	12.6	0.887	17.5	9.8	68.5	1.867	86.0

TORONTO.
General Meteorological Abstract, February, 1869.

	DAILY MEANS.					WIND.			EXTREMES OF TEMPERATURE.			RAIN.		SNOW.		TOTAL FALL.	
Days.	Temperature of Air.	Pressure of Vapour.	Rel. Humid.	Barometric Pressure.	Pressure of Dry Air.	Clouded Sky.	Resultant Direction.	Resultant Velocity.	Mean Velocity.	Maximum.	Minimum.	Difference.	Depth in inches.	Approximate duration.	Depth in Inches.	Approximate duration.	Depth in inches.	Approximate duration.
1	20.4	0.077	72	30.037	29.980	0.1	N 21 W	4.7	7.5	29.0	15.0	14.0	...	...	...	...	...	...
2	24.4	.111	84	29.837	.725	1.0	E	16.3	16.8	30.5	15.0	15.5	...	...	6.0	11.0	.600	11.0
3	24.9	.116	85	.240	.120	1.0	N 21 E	16.5	18.4	30.0	23.4	6.0	...	...	4.0	6.0	.400	6.0
4	14.9	.071	83	.160	.039	1.0	N 24 W	23.4	25.1	19.4	10.0	9.4	...	...	0.3	4.0	.030	4.0
5	20.3	.072	66	.574	.502	0.2	N 54 W	9.9	11.7	28.4	11.0	17.4	...	...	...	...	...	...
6	27.2	.118	79	.779	.661	0.7	N 63 W	0.6	9.5	32.8	20.5	12.5	...	...	...	...	...	...
7	Sunday						N 62 E	3.6	4.5	21.0	8.2	15.8	...	...	...	...	...	...
8	27.0	.133	82	.840	.701	1.0	N 73 E	1.6	1.6	31.2	12.8	18.4	...	...	0.5	5.0	.050	5.0
9	31.4	.152	87	.685	.533	1.0	N 85 E	3.2	3.5	35.0	27.2	7.8	...	...	...	...	...	...
10	33.7	.160	85	.616	.156	1.0	S 41 W	2.5	6.1	37.9	30.0	7.0	...	...	0.2	0.3	.020	0.3
11	34.8	.135	65	.752	.617	0.5	N 56 W	8.4	8.5	42.6	31.6	11.0	...	...	...	...	...	...
12	17.8	.151	80	.634	.446	0.9	S 59 W	1.7	3.9	16.0	26.8	19.2	...	...	...	...	...	...
13	36.3	.118	83	.628	.451	1.0	N 55 E	5.6	7.0	41.0	32.2	8.8	.100	6.0	0.4	12.0	.200	18.0
14	Sunday						N 78 E	16.9	6.9	34.0	21.1	12.9	...	...	5.0	19.0	.500	19.0
15	34.0	.169	87	.113	28.974	0.9	N 82 W	5.2	7.1	41.2	23.5	17.7	...	...	0.2	4.0	.020	4.0
16	27.4	.124	83	.305	29.179	0.7	N 88 W	9.1	9.4	31.2	26.0	5.2	...	...	0.2	6.0	.020	6.0
17	32.5	.163	89	.018	28.835	1.0	N 82 W	9.3	14.5	36.0	24.4	11.6	.005	1.0	0.2	7.0	.025	8.0
18	22.3	.091	76	.104	29.013	0.7	N 59 W	6.6	8.7	29.0	16.2	12.8	...	...	0.7	2.5	.070	2.5
19	20.7	.082	75	.294	.212	0.4	N 87 W	13.1	13.9	27.0	18.5	8.5	...	...	0.2	0.8	.020	0.8
20	23.3	.092	72	.560	.468	1.0	N 13 W	5.0	6.9	32.0	18.7	13.3	...	...	0.1	1.8	.010	1.8
21	Sunday						N 13 E	7.2	7.4	17.0	14.2	2.8	...	...	5.5	9.2	.550	9.2
22	18.6	.080	79	.589	.509	0.7	N 20 E	5.6	6.1	24.0	12.0	12.0	...	...	5.0	5.0	.500	5.0
23	15.2	.075	86	.181	.106	0.7	N 27 W	11.5	13.7	21.0	14.2	6.8	...	...	9.0	6.5	.900	6.5
24	17.7	.066	70	.677	.611	0.5	S 86 W	10.3	10.9	25.0	5.4	19.6	...	...	0.2	3.5	.020	3.5
25	17.7	.081	80	.854	.773	0.8	S 30 W	6.2	9.5	31.8	3.0	28.8	...	...	3.5	12.0	.350	12.0
26	28.6	.138	86	.517	.179	0.9	S 65 W	9.3	14.1	35.2	19.3	15.9	...	...	0.5	8.0	.050	8.0
27	8.6	.051	78	.550	.493	0.5	N 44 W	17.5	17.6	14.0	7.8	6.2	...	...	...	...	...	...
28	Sunday						N 70 W	2.8	3.2	22.0	-1.0	23.0	...	...	...	...	...	...
	23.0	0.111	80	29.516	29.402	0.8	N 34 W	4.2	10.0	35.3	20.3	15.0	0.165	7.0	39.7	123.0	4.135	130.6

TORONTO.
General Meteorological Abstract, March, 1869.

Days.	DAILY MEANS.						WIND.			EXTREMES OF TEMPERATURE.			RAIN.		SNOW.		TOTAL FALL.	
	Temperature of Air.	Pressure of Vapour.	Rel. Humid.	Barometric Pressure.	Pressure of Dry Air.	Clouded Sky.	Resultant Direction.	Resultant Velocity.	Mean Velocity.	Maximum.	Minimum.	Difference.	Depth in inches.	Approximate duration	Depth in inches	Approximate duration	Depth in inches.	Approximate duration.
1	16.8	0.074	79	29.945	29.571	0.8	S 24 W	3.7	4.1	24.5	8.4	16.1	...	...	0.1	3.0	0.010	3.0
2	25.2	.122	89	.681	.259	1.0	W	1.0	2.5	31.4	15.0	16.4	...	...	1.0	12.0	.100	12.5
3	30.6	.141	82	.587	.450	0.4	S 79 W	7.2	11.0	36.2	25.0	11.2	...	...	...	...	...	...
4	5.1	.045	80	.771	.726	0.2	N 53 W	7.4	8.4	12.6	3.5	8.5	...	...	...	...	...	...
5	9.2	.059	84	.510	.451	0.6	S 51 W	9.2	9.3	16.1	-5.4	21.5	...	...	0.1	2.0	.010	2.0
6	13.8	.062	75	.592	.530	0.6	N 55 W	12.7	13.8	21.0	13.2	7.8	...	...	...	...	...	...
7	Sunday						S 61 W	8.0	8.7	22.5	2.0	19.9	...	...	...	...	...	...
8	26.1	.101	72	.841	.740	0.7	S 78 W	3.6	3.8	31.8	18.0	13.8	...	...	...	...	...	...
9	30.0	.138	82	.729	.591	0.8	S 72 W	1.3	4.7	7.0	21.0	16.0	...	...	S	1.0	S	1.0
10	18.1	.096	89	.427	.331	1.0	N 19 W	10.7	13.0	31.5	16.1	15.4	...	...	8.0	16.5	.800	16.5
11	11.7	.050	78	.754	.694	0.5	S 84 W	1.6	1.7	22.0	0.0	22.0	...	...	...	...	...	...
12	18.7	.081	77	.468	.387	0.9	S 35 W	6.7	8.5	26.6	-1.0	27.0	...	...	2.5	7.0	.250	7.5
13	22.8	.092	76	.442	.350	0.6	S 53 W	6.0	7.1	30.0	17.0	13.0	...	...	...	...	...	...
14	Sunday						N 78 W	13.4	16.5	39.0	17.4	21.0	...	...	...	...	...	...
15	15.4	.061	71	.848	.787	0.6	N 26 W	7.1	7.1	3.2	16.0	7.2	...	...	...	...	...	...
16	13.9	.052	64	.872	.820	0.1	S 72 W	5.8	4.0	26.2	1.3	24.9	...	...	...	...	...	...
17	15.3	.065	73	.801	.736	0.4	W	5.7	5.9	25.9	4.5	19.9	...	...	...	...	...	...
18	23.8	.086	69	.931	.845	0.1	S 77 W	3.7	4.2	35.0	10.0	25.0	...	...	...	...	...	...
19	26.5	.132	90	.590	.458	1.0	N 57 E	3.7	14.2	32.2	15.2	17.0	...	...	1.2	12.0	.120	12.0
20	24.3	.106	77	.493	.387	0.4	N 21 W	13.8	8.7	34.0	26.6	7.4	...	...	0.1	2.5	.010	2.5
21	Sunday						N 2 W	3.4	13.2	20.0	-0.5	20.5	...	...	...	...	...	...
22	24.2	.103	77	.812	.710	0.9	S 76 E	12.0	5.9	30.0	5.5	24.5	...	...	2.0	4.5	.200	4.5
23	28.8	.120	81	.711	.582	0.4	N 88 W	4.0	3.9	38.0	21.8	16.2	...	...	...	...	...	...
24	24.5	.090	69	.923	.833	0.6	N 17 W	3.7	8.1	37.6	23.8	13.8	...	...	...	...	...	...
25	27.6	.107	71	.927	.820	0.6	N 78 E	7.6	6.0	36.2	15.5	20.7	...	...	...	...	...	...
26	...	...	.	...	...	...	N 78 E	2.7	3.7	39.0	29.4	9.6	.215	4.2	...	...	.215	4.2
27	38.9	.182	78	.632	.450	0.3	S 81 W	2.2	13.0	16.8	34.9	11.9	...	...	...	...	...	...
28	Sunday						N 71 E	12.8	8.4	41.0	30.0	11.0	...	...	...	...	...	...
29	37.3	.214	94	.361	.147	1.0	N 61 E	8.0	12.3	41.2	36.8	4.4	.660	23.0	...	...	.660	23.0
30	38.5	.212	90	.237	.025	1.0	N 47 W	11.6	12.3	43.0	35.0	8.0	.110	4.8	...	...	.110	4.8
31	31.6	.130	72	.596	.466	0.3	N 30 W	14.5	14.9	36.2	30.8	5.4	...	...	...	...	...	...
	23.1	0.105	78	29.650	29.544	0.6	N 52 W	2.9	8.0	31.2	15.7	15.5	0.985	32.0	15.0	61.5	2.485	93.5

75

TORONTO.
GENERAL METEOROLOGICAL ABSTRACT, APRIL, 1869.

Days.	DAILY MEANS.					WIND.			EXTREMES OF TEMPERATURE.			RAIN.		SNOW.		TOTAL FALL.	
	Temperature of Air.	Pressure of Vapour.	Hct. Humid.	Barometric Pressure.	Pressure of Dry Air.	Clouded Sky.	Resultant Direction.	Resultant Velocity.	Mean Velocity.	Maximum.	Minimum.	Difference.	Depth in Inches.	Approximate duration.	Depth in Inches.	Approximate duration.	Depth in Inches.	Approximate duration.
1	27.1	0.110	74	29.486	29.376	0.8	N 82 E	11.0	11.7	33.4	24.1	9.3	...	...	0.0	4.2	0.030	4.2
2	31.9	.145	82	.346	.197	1.0	N 68 W	8.3	10.1	38.2	26.5	13.6	...	...	S	0.1	S	0.1
3	24.9	.096	72	.500	.412	0.8	N 75 W	13.4	13.9	28.8	21.0	7.8	...	...	S	2.5	S	2.5
4	Sunday						S 80 W	10.7	11.2	32.8	21.5	11.3	...	...	0.1	4.5	.010	4.5
5	36.5	.172	50	.155	28.983	0.6	S 77 W	9.0	9.2	46.0	27.0	19.0	...	...	...	...	...	...
6	35.3	.126	62	.253	29.127	0.6	N 75 W	9.0	9.3	42.2	33.5	8.7	...	...	...	...	...	...
7	36.7	.132	63	.413	.280	0.9	S 65 W	6.9	8.5	44.0	28.4	15.0	...	...	S	1.0	S	1.0
8	33.3	.136	72	.567	.431	0.4	N 55 W	11.4	11.6	41.6	29.4	12.2	...	...	...	...	...	...
9	33.4	.124	67	.085	.561	0.5	N 33 W	7.4	7.8	42.0	26.8	15.2	...	...	...	...	...	...
10	34.4	.115	70	.752	.637	0.1	N 9 W	8.7	9.0	42.8	28.4	14.4	...	...	...	...	...	...
11	Sunday						N 17 W	2.6	4.7	42.2	27.0	15.2	...	...	...	...	...	...
12	31.7	.131	66	.623	.492	0.9	N 23 W	4.8	6.6	41.2	30.0	11.2	...	...	0.1	1.8	.010	1.8
13	34.0	.099	56	.663	.564	0.5	N 28 W	10.5	10.9	42.8	29.4	13.4	...	...	...	...	...	...
14	38.2	.108	50	.818	.710	0.4	N 60 W	5.7	6.8	48.0	28.0	20.0	...	...	...	...	...	...
15	38.7	.159	68	.830	.671	0.2	S 35 E	3.6	4.2	49.0	16.0	32.4	...	...	...	...	...	...
16	18.7	.190	61	.530	.340	0.8	S 51 W	5.9	7.5	63.0	34.4	28.6	0.240	7.2	...	...	.240	7.2
17	45.0	.230	70	.432	.202	0.6	N 80 W	9.6	11.4	54.0	41.0	13.0	R	0.1	...	...	R	0.1
18	Sunday						N 71 E	9.3	9.6	45.0	33.5	11.5	1.490	7.2	...	...	1.490	7.2
19	44.7	.272	91	.201	28.929	1.0	N 78 E	6.2	6.9	56.0	40.0	16.0	R	0.5	...	...	R	0.5
20	49.8	.321	88	.011	28.691	0.9	S 59 W	3.0	10.1	59.8	41.0	18.8	.635	5.5	...	...	.63	5.5
21	41.1	.172	65	.266	29.095	1.0	N 88 W	18.3	18.7	46.8	41.0	5.8	R	R	...	...	R	R
22	42.6	.196	71	.840	.644	0.0	N 71 W	3.6	7.3	52.4	35.4	17.0	...	...	...	...	...	...
23	42.6	.200	77	.675	.469	0.6	N 81 E	6.8	8.4	46.8	36.0	10.8	R	0.3	...	...	R	0.3
24	47.7	.213	62	.622	.400	0.4	N 59 W	10.4	11.3	58.0	36.5	21.7	.010	0.6	...	...	.010	0.6
25	Sunday						N 66 W	10.1	11.3	58.5	37.8	20.7	...	...	...	...	...	...
26	50.9	.235	53	.599	.361	0.4	N 57 W	7.3	7.6	72.2	40.5	31.7	...	...	...	...	...	...
27	43.2	.239	76	.562	.323	0.8	N 24 E	2.2	3.2	59.8	41.2	18.6	.590	2.0	...	...	.590	2.0
28	51.7	.267	70	.470	.208	0.8	N 17 E	5.0	7.2	58.7	42.0	16.7	...	...	...	...	...	...
29	41.4	.185	71	.589	.406	0.4	N 32 E	3.4	7.0	46.4	39.5	6.9	...	...	...	...	...	...
30	40.7	.005	37	.618	.555	0.0	S 79 E	3.1	4.7	48.5	32.2	16.3	...	...	...	...	...	...
	19.1	0.173	64	29.522	29.349	0.6	N 45 W	2.0	8.0	48.0	32.3	12.8	2.965	23.4	0.5	14.1	3.015	37.5

TORONTO.
GENERAL METEOROLOGICAL ABSTRACT, MAY, 1869.

Days.	DAILY MEANS.						WIND.			EXTREMES OF TEMPERATURE			RAIN.		SNOW.		TOTAL FALL.
	Temperature of Air.	Pressure of Vapour.	Rel. Humid.	Barometric Pressure.	Pressure of Dry Air.	Clouded Sky.	Resultant Direction.	Resultant Velocity.	Mean Velocity.	Maximum.	Minimum.	Difference.	Depth in inches.	Approximate duration.	Depth in inches.	Approximate duration.	Depth in inches. Approximate duration.
1	37.5	0.174	78	29.290	29.110	1.0	N 67 E	12.2	13.1	61.0	50.4	3.0	.810	18.5	S	S	.810	18.5
2	Sunday						N 26 W	12.2	13.7	47.8	31.4	16.4	.100	6.0	...	...	.100	6.0
3	41.5	.117	45	.283	.166	0.5	N 48 W	18.2	18.1	19.0	35.0	14.0	...	...	...	...	...	...
4	44.9	.136	46	.483	.347	0.5	N 29 W	15.1	15.3	54.0	25.4	18.6	...	...	...	...	...	...
5	44.8	.190	62	.626	.436	0.5	S 88 E	2.6	4.9	52.0	35.0	17.0	...	...	...	...	...	...
6	49.6	.200	57	.685	.485	0.6	N 51 E	5.0	8.0	65.2	51.2	14.0	...	...	...	...	...	...
7	52.7	.197	49	.705	.508	0.9	N 19 W	4.6	7.5	59.0	46.2	12.8	...	...	...	...	...	...
8	52.9	.272	66	.601	.419	0.0	S 78 W	0.5	3.5	60.0	40.4	19.6	R	0.4	...	...	R	0.4
9	Sunday						S 24 W	0.6	2.3	64.0	46.2	18.0	...	...	...	...	...	...
10	52.1	.218	56	.520	.302	0.0	S 80 E	3.5	3.8	57.0	45.2	11.8	R	1.0	...	...	R	1.0
11	60.0	.318	61	.371	.053	0.5	S 44 W	3.9	6.0	74.2	43.8	30.4	...	...	...	...	...	...
12	58.6	.346	72	.317	28.971	0.7	S 89 E	4.5	4.0	75.8	52.1	21.4	.040	0.5	...	...	.040	0.5
13	51.4	.317	84	.133	28.810	1.0	N 68 E	6.7	6.3	62.0	44.2	17.8	.120	1.8	...	...	.120	1.8
14	54.1	.343	82	.079	28.730	0.7	S 57 E	1.5	2.5	62.8	47.0	15.8	R	0.1	...	...	R	0.1
15	51.6	.317	83	.121	28.804	1.0	W	2.5	4.1	60.0	46.5	13.5	R	0.2	...	...	R	0.2
16	Sunday						N 75 W	9.5	11.1	54.0	47.2	6.8	.720	6.2	...	...	.720	6.2
17	44.9	.231	78	.405	29.177	0.7	N 73 W	9.7	9.8	50.2	42.5	7.7	R	0.3	...	...	R	0.3
18	45.6	.223	73	.527	.302	0.8	N 56 W	4.1	4.4	53.5	37.0	16.5	...	...	...	...	...	...
19	47.2	.246	75	.483	.235	1.0	N 29 W	6.7	6.9	54.0	42.6	11.4	R	1.7	...	...	R	1.7
20	49.2	.216	60	.623	.406	0.0	N 40 W	4.4	5.8	57.2	41.0	13.2	...	...	...	...	...	...
21	46.0	.178	57	.531	.416	0.3	N 23 W	1.9	5.0	54.0	37.4	16.6	...	...	...	...	...	...
22	51.1	.165	44	.527	.362	0.1	N 49 W	5.2	6.8	60.0	39.4	20.6	...	...	...	...	...	...
23	Sunday						S 32 W	1.7	1.8	57.4	40.5	26.9	...	...	...	...	...	...
24	58.1	.344	72	.543	.199	0.3	S 24 W	4.3	4.4	70.2	44.8	25.4	...	...	...	...	...	...
25	62.9	.372	65	.459	.087	0.7	S 56 W	3.5	5.0	72.0	48.0	24.0	.240	2.5	...	...	.240	2.5
26	52.8	.321	76	.536	.215	1.0	N 4 W	7.1	8.0	65.8	52.0	13.8	.015	1.5	...	...	.015	1.5
27	48.1	.174	52	.785	.610	0.8	N 80 E	5.8	6.1	52.0	40.0	12.0	...	...	...	...	...	...
28	40.1	.298	83	.575	.287	1.0	N 73 E	7.6	7.8	53.0	46.0	7.0	.320	9.2	...	...	.320	9.
29	53.3	.337	82	.640	.305	0.7	N 83 W	0.7	1.4	60.5	45.4	15.1	...	...	...	...	...	...
30	Sunday						S 81 E	3.0	3.1	60.0	44.2	15.8	.020	1.5	...	...	.020	1.5
31	58.9	.476	94	.526	.050	0.0	S 61 W	0.5	0.6	67.8	48.0	19.8	.420	6.0	...	...	.420	.0
	50.8	0.258	67	29.482	29.224	0.9	N 20 W	2.4	6.6	59.8	42.7	16.1	2.805	57.4	S	S	2.805	57.4

TORONTO.
GENERAL METEOROLOGICAL ABSTRACT, JUNE, 1869.

	DAILY MEANS.					WIND.			EXTREMES OF TEMPERATURE.			RAIN.		SNOW.		TOTAL FALL.	
Days.	Temperature of Air.	Pressure of Vapour.	Rel. Humid.	Barometric Pressure.	Pressure of Dry Air.	Clouded Sky.	Resultant Direction.	Resultant Velocity.	Mean Velocity.	Maximum.	Minimum.	Difference.	Depth in inches.	Approximate duration.	Depth in inches.	Approximate duration.	Depth in inches.	Approximate duration.
1	62.1	0.455	82	29.673	29.218	0.6	S 28 W	2.0	3.1	72.2	55.8	16.4	...	...	...	...	...	...
2	60.5	.436	83	.760	.324	0.3	S 25 E	0.4	0.6	72.0	49.8	22.2	...	...	...	...	...	...
3	62.4	.419	75	.726	.307	0.2	S 19 E	1.0	1.4	75.0	50.4	24.6	...	...	...	...	...	...
4	61.1	.452	84	.456	.014	1.0	N 5 W	2.7	4.5	64.4	43.0	14.4	0.890	5.7	...	...	0.890	5.7
5	51.8	.304	76	.483	.179	0.7	N 41 W	11.1	11.3	59.0	54.2	4.8	.075	4.0	...	...	.075	4.0
6	Sunday						N 29 W	0.3	2.7	55.0	36.4	18.6	R	0.2	...	...	R	0.2
7	50.4	.263	72	.845	.581	0.4	S 65 W	1.0	5.9	59.8	37.2	22.6	.175	1.0	...	...	.175	1.0
8	51.1	.275	73	.894	.619	0.8	N 19 W	1.7	2.8	59.0	43.4	15.6	...	...	...	...	...	...
9	52.8	.279	71	.604	.525	0.7	S 85 E	8.1	8.1	58.4	43.0	15.4	.450	6.1	...	...	.450	6.1
10	55.8	.370	85	.495	.124	0.0	N 86 W	4.5	5.9	60.8	48.0	21.8	.375	9.5	...	...	.375	9.5
11	50.6	.256	68	.451	.195	0.7	N 73 W	9.5	9.8	60.0	45.5	14.5	...	...	...	...	...	...
12	52.9	.289	72	.453	.164	0.6	S 73 E	1.5	3.4	63.0	42.0	21.0	R	1.5	...	...	R	1.5
13	Sunday						S 21 W	6.6	7.1	5.6	49.5	16.1	.050	9.0	...	...	.050	9.0
14	57.8	.357	79	.114	28.757	0.6	S 40 W	8.5	8.9	66.2	50.4	15.8	...	...	...	...	...	...
15	52.2	.308	79	.326	29.018	0.9	N 82 W	4.8	4.9	59.0	49.8	9.2	.060	4.5	...	...	.060	4.5
16	55.7	.284	65	.563	.280	0.7	N 74 W	6.7	7.1	64.5	49.0	15.5	.033	0.5	...	...	.033	0.5
17	59.1	.314	60	.728	.414	0.5	S 60 E	2.5	3.3	69.2	45.4	23.8	.010	0.6	...	...	.010	0.6
18	62.8	.448	71	.565	.160	0.8	N 54 W	3.3	5.8	51.0	52.4	8.6	...	...	...	...	...	...
19	59.9	.415	81	.716	.295	0.8	N 81 E	2.6	4.9	66.0	57.2	8.8	.375	4.7	...	...	.375	4.7
20	Sunday						N 52 W	5.2	6.9	76.2	52.0	24.2	.050	1.2	...	...	.050	1.2
21	62.7	.431	77	.489	.058	0.9	S 61 E	2.2	2.8	69.0	58.2	10.8	.005	1.2	...	...	.005	1.2
22	62.9	.427	73	.448	.025	0.6	S 8 W	3.9	4.6	72.0	54.0	18.0	.075	0.4	...	...	.075	0.4
23	63.0	.371	60	.537	.166	0.5	S 88 W	7.1	7.9	71.8	56.2	15.6	...	...	...	...	...	...
24	60.9	.350	65	.683	.333	0.7	S 87 W	3.8	6.1	69.5	49.0	20.5	R	0.2	...	...	R	0.2
25	55.0	.299	67	.820	.521	0.7	S 47 E	0.4	3.2	64.4	46.2	18.2	...	...	...	...	...	...
26	56.8	.308	67	.691	.383	1.0	N 69 E	1.6	2.2	63.2	50.4	12.8	.925	11.5	...	...	.925	11.5
27	Sunday						S 68 E	1.6	2.2	61.0	50.0	11.0	.690	15.5	...	...	.690	15.5
28	65.8	.455	72	.452	28.907	0.4	N 58 W	5.3	6.5	77.0	53.4	23.6	R	0.1	...	...	R	0.1
29	67.1	.572	80	.539	28.967	0.8	S 67 W	4.0	5.1	81.4	56.4	25.0	.125	3.6	...	...	.125	3.6
30	64.4	.436	71	.510	29.104	0.8	N 13 W	9.0	9.2	73.8	63.0	10.6	.010	2.5	...	...	.010	2.5
	58.4	0.367	71	29.557	29.220	0.7	N 80 W	1.8	5.2	87.4	50.0	17.3	1.373	83.5	...	...	1.373	83.5

78

TORONTO.
GENERAL METEOROLOGICAL ABSTRACT, JULY, 1869.

Days.	DAILY MEANS.					WIND.			EXTREMES OF TEMPERATURE.			RAIN.		SNOW.		TOTAL FALL.	
	Temperature of Air.	Pressure of Vapour.	Rel. Humid.	Barometric Pressure.	Pressure of Dry Air.	Clouded Sky.	Resultant Direction.	Resultant Velocity.	Mean Velocity.	Maximum.	Minimum.	Difference.	Depth in inches.	Approximate duration.	Depth in inches.	Approximate duration.	Depth in inches.	Approximate duration.
1	68.3	0.382	70	24.674	29.292	1.0	S 27 W	2.2	2.5	81.8	52.5	12.3	...	...	...	...	...	...
2	65.6	.513	81	.483	28.967	0.7	S 20 W	3.3	3.5	76.0	52.2	23.8	0.140	2.0	...	...	0.140	2.0
3	73.8	.656	79	.289	28.626	0.7	S 84 W	3.7	5.3	42.0	62.8	19.2	.020	0.4	...	...	.020	0.4
4	Sunday						N 49 W	8.8	10.6	75.0	64.0	11.0	...	...	...	...	...	...
5	59.5	.339	68	.861	29.522	0.2	S 27 W	1.7	3.0	68.0	52.2	15.8	...	...	...	...	...	...
6	61.0	.362	67	.865	.503	0.9	S 46 E	1.3	2.4	70.0	49.8	20.2	...	...	...	...	...	...
7	63.0	.459	80	.659	.200	0.7	S 87 E	2.7	3.0	71.4	54.2	17.2	.400	2.3	...	...	.400	2.3
8	67.1	.589	80	.512	28.932	1.0	S 39 W	2.9	3.0	74.2	60.0	14.2	.140	5.0	...	...	.140	5.0
9	67.4	.536	80	.454	28.918	0.5	S 74 W	1.4	3.5	75.0	61.8	13.2	...	...	...	...	...	...
10	60.6	.552	76	.345	28.793	0.4	N 73 W	9.1	10.0	77.8	59.0	18.8	.240	1.0	...	...	.240	1.0
11	Sunday						N 73 W	10.0	11.0	75.0	66.0	9.0	...	...	...	...	...	...
12	62.9	.370	65	.694	29.324	0.5	N 51 W	1.0	5.8	70.0	50.8	19.2	...	...	...	...	...	...
13	62.4	.412	70	.67	.261	0.8	N 76 E	7.2	7.5	57.4	59.0	8.4	...	...	...	...	...	...
14	64.2	.503	84	.563	.063	1.0	N 78 E	4.9	5.0	69.2	58.5	9.7	.055	1.3	...	...	.055	1.3
15	72.8	.636	80	.470	28.833	0.7	S 2 E	1.8	2.7	84.0	60.8	24.1	1.600	2.5	...	...	1.600	2.5
16	74.2	.604	73	.456	28.851	0.7	S 77 W	7.7	8.1	82.6	67.0	15.0	...	...	...	...	...	...
17	68.5	.480	69	.579	29.019	0.6	S 83 W	1.2	4.5	75.8	58.0	17.8	...	...	...	...	...	...
18	Sunday						N 35 W	1.6	5.1	76.0	61.4	14.6	...	...	...	...	...	...
19	64.2	.401	67	.576	.175	0.2	S 82 E	2.9	2.4	70.2	59.0	11.2	...	...	...	...	...	...
20	63.5	.510	86	.355	28.846	0.7	S 59 E	3.1	4.7	70.4	55.5	14.9	.420	1.5	...	...	.420	1.5
21	59.7	.383	75	.439	29.056	0.8	S 83 W	9.2	9.7	64.0	59.0	5.0	.040	2.7	...	...	.040	2.7
22	61.6	.384	69	.656	.270	0.3	S 61 W	1.9	2.7	71.0	55.0	16.0	...	...	...	...	...	...
23	61.1	.453	84	.638	.185	1.0	S 31 W	4.1	4.2	70.8	53.8	17.0	.060	3.0	...	...	.060	3.0
24	64.1	.531	89	.548	.017	1.0	S 44 W	2.6	2.6	70.0	58.6	11.4	...	...	...	...	...	...
25	Sunday						S 27 W	4.4	4.9	78.0	59.0	19.0	...	...	...	...	...	...
26	67.2	.554	83	.417	28.863	0.7	S 34 W	3.7	3.9	76.5	61.8	14.7	.005	1.0	...	...	.005	1.0
27	66.4	.513	79	.470	28.957	0.5	S 42 W	4.0	4.5	78.0	57.0	21.0	.210	2.5	...	...	.210	2.5
28	72.2	.502	88	.448	28.946	1.0	S 80 W	3.5	6.5	69.8	57.4	12.4	1.280	5.3	...	...	1.280	5.3
29	58.5	.384	78	.543	29.159	0.7	N 73 W	8.2	8.3	66.5	56.8	9.7	...	...	...	...	...	...
30	62.4	.344	63	.738	.394	0.5	N 62 W	3.9	4.2	74.0	51.6	22.4	...	...	...	...	...	...
31	59.5	.333	56	.925	.592	0.5	S 23 E	0.9	1.2	71.8	51.5	20.3	...	...	...	...	...	...
	64.5	0.470	77	29.568	29.098	0.7	S 67 W	2.0	5.1	73.1	57.6	15.5	4.610	30.1	...	...	4.610	30.1

TORONTO
GENERAL METEOROLOGICAL ABSTRACT, AUGUST, 1869.

Days.	DAILY MEANS.					Cloulded Sky.	WIND.			EXTREMES OF TEMPERATURE			RAIN.		SNOW.		TOTAL FALL.	
	Temperature of Air.	Pressure of Vapour.	Rel Humid.	Barometric Pressure.	Pressure of Dry Air.		Resultant Direction.	Resultant Velocity.	Mean Velocity.	Maximum.	Minimum.	Difference.	Depth in inches.	Approximate duration.	Depth in inches	Approximate duration.	Depth in inches	Approximate duration.
1	Su	nday					S 45 E	1.3	1.4	73.5	54.8	19.7	...	...	...	...	...	...
2	65.7	0.550	87	29.562	29.012	0.9	S 51 W	6.7	8.3	73.0	57.4	15.6	0.610	4.0	...	...	0.610	4.0
3	66.9	.482	67	.531	.098	0.4	N 65 W	6.6	6.8	76.8	54.0	22.8	.025	0.7	...	...	.025	0.7
4	55.7	.402	90	.465	.064	0.8	N 5 E	1.8	2.2	61.2	55.0	6.2	.155	3.5	...	...	.155	3.5
5	57.8	.310	66	.052	.330	0.3	N 6 W	8.3	8.4	65.8	49.4	16.4	...	...	...	...	...	...
6	56.9	.28	62	.854	.571	0.3	N 18 W	7.7	7.8	65.2	43.5	21.7	...	...	...	...	...	...
7	56.5	.311	68	.898	.587	0.1	N 40 W	2.6	5.2	66.5	48.8	17.7	...	...	...	...	...	...
8	Su	nday					S 26 W	3.0	3.4	69.0	45.0	24.0	...	...	...	...	...	...
9	63.2	.428	74	.719	.291	0.4	S 33 W	3.5	3.6	73.2	50.0	23.2	...	...	...	...	...	...
10	66.6	.504	78	.614	.110	0.6	S 35 W	2.9	3.1	73.8	53.0	19.8	.155	3.5	...	...	.155	3.5
11	69.3	.536	76	.672	.135	0.5	N 11 W	5.6	6.0	78.0	62.2	15.8	...	...	...	...	...	...
12	64.7	.452	75	.716	.254	0.2	N 77 E	2.8	3.9	71.0	58.6	12.4	.471	1.5	...	...	.471	1.5
13	66.7	.519	79	.089	.101	0.7	N 25 W	3.8	6.1	77.0	58.6	18.4	...	...	...	...	...	...
14	61.4	.396	73	.063	.267	0.8	S 88 E	6.8	7.6	65.0	54.8	10.2	.700	3.3	...	...	.700	3.3
15	Su	nday					N 83 W	9.1	10.3	75.4	58.0	17.4	...	...	...	...	...	...
16	61.5	.456	82	.582	.132	1.0	S 40 E	0.7	1.8	66.5	57.5	9.0	...	...	...	...	...	...
17	64.0	.471	79	.698	.237	0.4	N 82 W	1.1	2.8	73.5	58.0	15.5	...	...	...	...	...	...
18	66.2	.504	78	.675	.170	0.5	S 14 W	2.0	2.4	75.0	55.8	19.2	...	...	...	...	...	...
19	69.7	.635	88	.530	28.895	0.7	S 26 W	4.3	5.3	78.0	60.0	18.0	...	...	...	...	...	...
20	75.2	.672	76	.477	28.805	0.8	N 29 W	4.1	7.3	89.0	68.4	20.6	R	0.2	...	...	R	0.2
21	54.5	.493	81	.625	29.130	1.0	N 60 E	3.8	4.4	68.0	61.0	7.0	1.150	3.6	...	...	1.150	3.0
22	Su	nday					S 81 E	1.0	2.4	71.0	62.4	8.6	...	...	...	...	...	...
23	64.8	.435	72	.859	.424	0.5	N 68 E	2.3	3.0	72.2	56.4	15.8	...	...	...	...	...	...
24	66.7	.55	84	.763	.210	0.6	S 72 E	1.3	1.7	74.8	58.0	16.8	...	...	...	...	...	...
25	8.9	.519	75	.594	.054	0.3	N 46 W	7.1	8.5	82.2	61.8	19.4	.030	0.3	...	...	.030	3.0
26	61.6	.387	71	.789	.335	0.4	N 56 W	0.2	2.5	70.0	58.0	12.0	...	...	...	...	...	...
27	62.0	.432	77	.077	.245	0.7	N 80 E	3.0	3.2	69.0	50.0	19.0	.517	2.0	...	...	.517	2.0
28	55.6	.612	87	.458	28.845	0.7	N 65 W	2.8	3.2	79.2	60.0	19.2	.460	1.0	...	...	.460	1.0
29	Su	nday					N 56 W	10.4	10.5	71.0	53.2	18.8	...	...	...	...	...	...
30	58.8	.337	68	.715	29.378	0.3	N 53 W	9.5	9.7	66.8	50.5	16.3	...	...	...	...	...	...
31	51.2	.239	65	.845	.605	0.2	N 23 W	6.8	6.9	60.8	45.0	15.8	...	...	...	...	...	...
	63.6	0.458	76	29.665	29.218	0.5	N 42 W	2.0	5.1	72.1	55.6	16.5	4.273	25.0	...	...	4.273	23.0

TORONTO
GENERAL METEOROLOGICAL ABSTRACT, SEPTEMBER, 1869.

Days.	DAILY MEANS.						WIND.			EXTREMES OF TEMPERATURE			RAIN.		SNOW.		TOTAL FALL.	
	Temperature of Air.	Pressure of Vapour.	Rel. Humid.	Barometric Pressure.	Pressure of dry Air.	Clouded Sky.	Resultant Direction.	Resultant Velocity.	Mean Velocity.	Maximum.	Minimum.	Diff-rence.	Depth in Inches.	Approximate duration.	Depth in Inches	Approximate duration.	Depth in Inches	Approximate duration.
1	54.3	0.256	62	29.926	29.670	0.0	N 9 W	6.8	7.0	64.0	43.4	20.6	...	...	...	...	...	...
2	55.4	.313	71	.999	.686	0.0	S 40 E	1.4	2.3	64.0	48.3	15.7	...	...	...	...	...	...
3	58.0	.301	78	.837	.440	0.2	S 5 W	2.4	2.8	68.5	46.4	22.1	...	...	...	...	...	...
4	63.7	.485	82	.606	.211	0.0	S 14 W	3.6	3.7	74.5	52.2	22.3	...	...	...	...	...	...
5	Sunday						S 18 W	5.2	5.8	75.2	55.0	20.2	...	...	...	...	...	...
6	67.9	.540	80	.606	.060	0.8	S 9 W	4.4	4.8	76.2	60.0	16.2	2.350	20.0	...	...	2.350	20.0
7	63.2	.535	91	.464	28.929	1.0	N 14 W	7.2	9.5	67.0	63.0	4.0	.470	10.3	...	...	.470	10.3
8	56.8	.417	90	.395	28.978	1.0	N 22 W	11.5	12.3	59.8	55.8	4.0	...	...	...	...	...	...
9	54.8	.325	76	.617	29.289	0.9	N 32 W	7.0	7.4	59.5	53.0	6.5	...	...	...	...	...	...
10	58.1	.383	79	.735	.352	0.2	N 7 W	0.5	2.7	68.0	50.8	17.2	R	0.1	...	...	R	0.1
11	62.5	.421	73	.739	.315	0.0	S 32 W	2.5	2.7	72.2	48.0	24.2	...	...	...	...	...	...
12	Sunday						S 34 E	1.4	2.4	74.5	57.8	16.7	...	...	...	...	...	...
13	65.1	.492	80	.881	.388	0.0	S 79 E	2.0	3.2	72.0	57.6	14.4	...	...	...	...	...	...
14	65.1	.461	75	.888	.428	0.7	S 83 E	4.1	4.3	70.6	55.2	15.4	R	0.5	...	...	R	0.5
15	65.7	.511	81	.703	.192	0.7	S 79 E	2.7	2.5	71.2	60.2	11.0	.410	4.8	...	...	.410	4.8
16	67.0	.563	86	.620	.057	0.6	S 38 E	2.0	3.1	73.6	62.6	11.0	...	...	...	...	...	...
17	63.0	.446	78	.778	.332	0.5	S 68 W	0.7	2.3	72.0	60.0	12.0	...	...	...	...	...	...
18	62.3	.483	85	.869	.386	0.3	S 63 E	1.6	1.9	70.5	50.4	20.1	...	...	...	...	...	...
19	Sunday						S 40 W	2.1	2.3	79.4	56.8	22.6	.195	1.5	...	...	.195	1.5
20	68.7	.569	81	.705	.196	0.8	N 82 E	0.4	2.4	81.0	62.0	19.0	...	...	...	...	...	...
21	64.6	.404	67	.798	.394	0.8	N 23 W	6.9	7.3	71.2	63.0	8.2	...	...	...	...	...	...
22	62.1	.454	82	.854	.399	0.4	S 86 E	1.2	2.2	71.2	57.8	13.4	...	...	...	...	...	...
23	62.8	.471	83	.910	.440	0.5	N 61 E	3.5	3.0	69.0	56.0	13.0	...	...	...	...	...	...
24	66.6	.556	90	.810	.224	0.6	S 51 E	2.2	3.2	74.8	58.0	16.8	.540	9.7	...	...	.540	9.7
25	64.5	.548	89	.632	.084	0.8	N 53 W	4.5	7.6	77.5	64.4	13.1	.062	1.0	...	...	.062	1.0
26	Sunday						N 30 W	12.0	12.0	58.0	51.0	7.0	...	...	...	...	...	...
27	42.0	.193	73	.764	.570	0.3	N 46 W	8.1	8.5	52.0	35.4	16.6	...	...	...	...	...	...
28	49.5	.245	70	.852	.607	0.5	S 65 W	6.3	6.8	58.0	34.4	23.6	...	...	...	...	...	...
29	54.9	.314	73	.865	.551	0.1	S 43 W	5.3	5.6	66.4	49.0	17.4	...	...	...	...	...	...
30	57.7	.364	77	.859	.495	0.2	S 40 W	4.6	5.0	68.8	48.0	20.8	...	...	...	...	...	...
	60.7	0.430	79	29.764	29.334	0.5	N 53 W	1.2	4.9	69.4	53.9	15.5	4.027	47.9	...	...	4.027	47.9

TORONTO.
GENERAL METEOROLOGICAL ABSTRACT, OCTOBER, 1869.

Days.	DAILY MEANS.						WIND.			EXTREMES OF TEMPERATURE				RAIN.		SNOW.		TOTAL FALL.	
	Temperature of Air	Pressure of Vapour.	Rel. Humid.	Barometric Pressure.	Pressure of Dry Air.	Clouded Sky	Resultant Direction.	Resultant Velocity.	Mean Velocity.	Maximum.	Minimum.	Difference.	Depth in inches.	Approximate duration.	Depth in inches	Approximate duration	Depth in inches.	Approximate duration.
1	57.4	0.372	79	29.745	29.373	0.4	S 68 E	1.2	2.3	69.8	47.5	22.3	...	...	...	...	...	...
2	59.6	.410	82	.568	.149	0.9	S 79 W	2.9	6.1	68.0	52.2	15.8	0.150	8.0	...	...	0.150	8.0
3	Sunday						N 82 E	1.6	3.5	50.5	43.5	16.0	...	...	...	...	...	...
4	52.7	.253	64	.331	.078	0.7	N 27 W	12.7	13.3	59.0	45.0	14.0	...	...	...	...	...	...
5	47.1	.263	80	.021	.358	0.3	N 41 W	11.1	11.2	55.4	47.2	8.2	...	...	...	...	...	...
6	44.6	.220	78	.719	.490	0.2	S 17 W	1.7	4.2	56.0	33.6	22.4	...	...	...	...	...	...
7	50.8	.311	84	.773	.462	0.1	S 71 E	1.6	3.7	63.0	40.0	23.0	...	...	...	...	...	...
8	50.1	.350	79	.793	.443	0.0	N 79 E	2.7	3.7	65.2	45.0	20.2	...	...	...	...	...	...
9	58.5	.381	77	.613	.233	0.5	S 37 E	3.3	6.9	65.5	48.4	17.1	...	...	...	...	...	...
10	Sunday						S 51 W	3.8	4.1	55.0	50.2	4.8	...	...	...	...	...	...
11	44.9	.212	72	.369	.157	0.8	W	3.8	4.6	56.4	35.0	18.4	.085	0.3	...	...	.085	0.3
12	43.4	.187	70	.368	.181	0.4	N 79 W	5.9	7.0	55.0	37.0	18.0	...	...	...	...	...	...
13	38.7	.173	75	.432	.259	0.3	N 57 W	5.8	6.9	51.0	31.4	19.6	...	...	...	...	...	...
14	41.4	.247	83	.254	.007	0.7	S 9 W	5.1	7.4	50.0	32.0	18.0	.096	5.5	...	...	.096	5.5
15	42.3	.213	79	.477	.264	0.5	N 69 W	6.5	7.3	50.0	38.1	11.4	...	...	...	...	...	...
16	39.9	.182	74	.556	.375	0.3	S 32 W	2.8	3.1	51.5	30.4	21.1	...	...	...	...	...	...
17	Sunday						N 67 W	10.0	10.3	53.8	35.5	18.3	...	...	...	...	...	...
18	36.6	.159	74	.653	.494	0.5	N 71 W	6.6	6.8	45.2	31.2	14.0	...	...	...	...	...	...
19	34.7	.156	78	.631	.475	0.3	N 83 W	7.7	8.0	44.0	31.2	12.8	R	R	S	0.6	R S	0.6
20	33.0	.105	71	.557	.389	0.5	S 54 W	7.7	7.8	47.0	27.0	20.0	...	...	S	0.3	S	0.3
21	37.4	.177	79	.467	.290	0.8	S 32 W	6.1	6.3	44.8	30.0	14.8	...	...	...	...	...	...
22	41.5	.215	83	.589	.371	0.9	N 65 E	3.1	4.1	45.8	33.8	12.0	.114	10.0	...	...	.114	10.0
23	40.2	.219	87	.300	.081	1.0	N 40 W	9.5	10.6	44.2	40.0	4.2	.465	8.5	...	...	.465	8.5
24	Sunday						S 85 W	8.7	9.0	40.0	29.0	11.0	...	...	S	2.0	S	2.0
25	32.3	.120	86	.053	.853	0.5	S 80 W	7.7	7.9	39.8	27.2	12.6	...	...	...	...	...	...
26	29.6	.128	78	.800	.672	0.8	N 68 W	7.1	8.2	34.0	28.5	5.5	...	...	2.0	5.0	.200	5.0
27	38.9	.131	83	.729	.595	0.7	N 87 W	2.0	2.9	36.5	18.7	17.8	...	...	0.2	3.0	.020	3.0
28	34.2	.181	91	.241	.060	1.0	S 60 W	3.1	3.1	38.0	29.2	8.8	.052	1.0	0.1	5.0	.062	6.0
29	33.9	.158	81	.464	.306	1.0	N 20 W	13.8	14.0	37.0	33.0	4.0	R	R	...	...	R	R
30	30.4	.128	75	.820	.701	0.9	N 16 W	8.2	8.4	34.0	26.2	7.8	...	...	8	0.5	S	0.5
31	Sunday						S 61 W	5.8	6.1	38.0	25.2	9.8	...	...	...	...	...	...
	42.3	0.221	78	29.571	29.350	0.6	N 73 W	3.7	6.7	50.1	35.8	14.3	0.962	33.3	2.3	16.4	1.192	49.7

TORONTO.
General Meteorological Abstract, November, 1869.

Days	DAILY MEANS.						WIND.			EXTREMES OF TEMPERATURE			RAIN.		SNOW.		TOTAL FALL.	
	Temperature of Air.	Pressure of Vapour.	Rel. Humid.	Barometric Pressure.	Pressure of Dry Air.	Clouded Sky.	Resultant Direction.	Resultant Velocity.	Mean Velocity.	Maximum.	Minimum.	Difference.	Depth in inches.	Approximate duration.	Depth in Inches.	Approximate duration.	Depth in Inches.	Approximate duration.
1	39.6	0.188	78	29.695	29.507	0.6	N 61 W	4.8	5.2	50.5	32.4	18.1	...	...	...	...	...	...
2	37.9	.207	89	.857	.651	0.9	S 21 E	1.1	1.4	45.2	30.6	14.6	...	...	...	...	...	...
3	42.8	.221	82	.724	.500	0.3	S 87 W	2.8	2.9	55.0	33.4	24.0	...	...	...	...	...	...
4	46.5	.262	81	.455	.193	0.7	S 13 W	4.5	5.7	55.8	33.4	22.4	0.140	5.2	...	...	0.140	5.2
5	40.2	.197	79	.206	.008	0.9	S 66 W	14.0	14.5	49.0	41.4	6.6	.045	1.0	S	1.0	.045	2.0
6	31.2	.153	87	.423	.270	1.0	N 39 W	7.7	8.2	34.0	31.6	2.4	...	...	0.2	14.0	.020	14.6
7	Sunday						N 57 W	18.0	19.0	30.4	21.5	8.9	...	...	0.1	7.0	.010	7.0
8	30.0	.141	84	.386	.245	1.0	N 71 W	13.4	13.6	33.8	25.2	8.6	...	...	0.4	15.0	.049	15.0
9	31.6	.148	83	.453	.305	0.8	S 84 W	8.4	8.4	36.0	27.0	9.0	...	...	S	1.0	S	1.0
10	29.3	.123	76	.527	.405	0.7	N 64 W	7.0	7.2	38.0	25.0	13.0	...	...	0.1	3.0	.010	3.0
11	30.1	.129	77	.593	.464	0.7	N 75 W	9.9	10.8	37.0	24.8	12.2	...	...	...	...	...	...
12	32.4	.138	76	.657	.519	0.9	N 75 W	7.3	7.6	35.0	27.4	10.6	...	...	S	0.4	S	0.4
13	28.2	.134	87	.678	.544	0.9	N 37 E	7.5	8.0	35.0	24.8	10.8	...	...	0.5	7.5	.050	7.5
14	Sunday						N 9 W	4.8	5.1	31.8	24.8	7.0	...	...	...	...	...	...
15	27.2	.130	87	.744	.614	0.9	N 22 W	1.2	1.4	31.4	20.8	10.6	...	...	S	1.5	S	1.5
16	32.9	.160	85	.605	.445	1.0	S 86 E	13.8	14.2	36.6	26.0	10.6	1.400	7.0	3.0	5.3	1.700	12.3
17	34.7	.163	79	28.867	28.704	1.0	S 52 W	16.8	20.3	41.0	31.0	10.0	.015	2.5	S	1.2	.045	3.7
18	30.6	.128	75	29.379	29.251	0.9	S 79 W	7.9	9.1	37.0	27.8	9.2	...	...	0.1	1.5	.010	1.5
19	34.8	.183	90	.373	.190	1.0	S 70 E	6.3	8.2	37.0	27.0	10.0	.350	8.0	0.2	4.1	.370	12.1
20	33.5	.166	86	.206	.041	1.0	N 69 W	11.4	11.9	40.2	32.0	8.2	R	1.0	0.1	4.0	.010	5.0
21	Sunday						N 63 W	6.2	6.5	32.5	26.2	6.3	...	...	S	0.5	S	0.5
22	25.5	.125	90	.685	.560	0.7	N 85 E	7.2	11.2	32.0	20.0	12.0	...	...	5.5	12.4	.550	12.4
23	24.8	.144	85	.678	.564	0.9	N 4 W	5.4	5.0	27.8	21.5	6.3	...	...	...	...	...	...
24	20.6	.083	76	30.058	.975	0.1	N 3 W	0.7	0.8	30.0	13.0	17.0	...	...	...	...	...	...
25	27.2	.134	89	29.988	.854	0.9	S 67 E	3.3	3.6	33.5	13.0	20.5	...	...	...	...	...	...
26	30.3	.151	90	.774	.623	1.0	N 43 E	0.9	2.2	34.4	27.6	6.8	R	0.3	...	...	R	0.3
27	33.3	.157	83	.622	.465	0.9	S 80 W	9.6	10.1	37.0	30.0	7.0	...	...	S	1.5	S	1.5
28	Sunday						S 72 W	5.3	5.7	34.4	27.0	7.4	...	...	...	...	...	...
29	35.0	.180	88	.476	.296	1.0	S 62 W	4.2	4.8	42.8	26.0	16.8	.180	15.5	S	2.0	.180	17.5
30	40.8	.234	91	.197	28.962	1.0	N 85 W	9.9	11.0	48.0	34.6	13.4	.380	5.5	...	...	.380	5.5
	32.7	0.160	84	29.550	29.390	0.8	N 78 W	3.7	8.1	38.3	26.9	11.4	2.540	46.0	10.2	83.5	3.560	129.5

TORONTO.
General Meteorological Abstract, December, 1869.

Days	DAILY MEANS.					WIND.			EXTREMES OF TEMPERATURE.			RAIN.		SNOW.		TOTAL FALL.	
	Temperature of Air.	Pressure of Vapour.	Rel. Humid.	Barometric Pressure.	Pressure of Dry Air.	Clouded Sky.	Resultant Direction.	Resultant Velocity.	Mean Velocity.	Maximum.	Minimum.	Difference.	Depth in inches.	Approximate duration.	Depth in inches.	Approximate duration.	Depth in inches.	Approximate duration.
1	21.0	0.114	87	29.759	29.645	0.7	N 47 W	9.8	11.7	32.5	23.0	8.5	...	...	0.1	2.0	0.010	2.0
2	21.0	.099	87	.656	.558	0.9	N 19 W	3.6	8.2	25.8	18.0	7.8	...	...	2.0	12.0	.200	12.0
3	14.4	.068	79	.876	.808	0.5	S 27 W	1.8	7.0	29.1	6.4	22.7	...	...	0.3	2.0	.030	2.0
4	32.7	.166	88	.467	.301	1.0	S 63 W	8.3	11.7	36.5	13.0	23.5	0.040	2.0	...	...	.040	2.0
5	Sunday						N 15 E	9.1	9.4	29.8	23.5	6.0	...	...	...	...	...	...
6	9.5	.051	76	.020	.868	0.2	N 8 W	5.1	5.2	14.3	6.0	8.3	...	...	...	...	...	...
7	10.2	.099	89	.906	.807	1.0	N	0.3	1.5	25.0	7.8	17.2	...	...	0.2	7.2	.020	7.2
8	27.0	.116	76	30.083	.967	0.7	N 48 W	1.6	3.0	32.8	22.6	10.2	...	...	...	...	...	...
9	32.1	.135	75	30.046	.911	0.9	S 30 W	9.5	9.5	39.5	23.0	15.1	...	...	...	...	...	...
10	37.1	.196	89	29.900	.704	1.0	S 37 W	5.2	5.8	39.0	29.5	9.5	R	0.2	...	...	R	0.2
11	37.0	.213	96	.695	.485	1.0	N 85 E	6.4	6.5	40.0	33.8	6.2	.200	8.0	...	...	.200	8.0
12	Sunday						N 21 W	5.4	7.5	45.0	35.4	9.6	R	3.0	...	...	R	3.0
13	22.4	.103	85	30.168	30.065	1.0	N 12 E	6.9	7.1	24.6	21.4	3.2	...	...	...	...	...	...
14	26.1	.127	89	30.031	29.904	1.0	N 77 E	7.1	7.9	32.0	20.3	11.7	...	...	...	...	...	...
15	33.9	.180	92	29.586	.406	0.9	S 86 E	12.0	12.0	38.0	26.5	11.5	1.405	18.5	...	...	1.405	18.5
16	36.1	.187	88	.451	.264	1.0	S 37 W	7.9	11.1	41.2	34.0	7.2	.050	3.7	...	...	.050	3.7
17	32.4	.147	79	.688	.542	1.0	"	"	"	37.8	31.4	6.4	...	...	...	...	...	...
18	30.6	.140	81	.383	.243	1.0	S 37 W	9.8	12.3	32.4	29.2	3.2	...	...	S	0.5	S	0.5
19	Sunday						S 79 W	12.1	12.3	33.2	23.5	9.7	...	...	...	...	...	...
20	21.3	.104	79	.812	.708	0.9	S 74 W	10.0	10.1	26.2	23.2	3.0	...	...	S	4.0	S	4.0
21	25.8	.113	80	.949	.836	1.0	S 67 E	8.5	10.4	34.9	21.5	13.4	.360	0.5	3.5	11.0	.710	11.5
22	34.3	.167	83	.245	.078	0.5	S 58 W	12.0	16.0	43.0	26.0	17.0	.070	6.0	...	...	.070	6.0
23	34.0	.086	66	742	.656	0.6	S 64 W	15.1	15.1	27.8	21.4	6.4	...	...	S	1.0	S	1.0
24	27.0	.112	72	.947	.835	0.4	S 53 W	9.2	9.4	34.0	17.2	16.8	...	...	...	...	...	...
25	...	...	...	...	...	...	S 32 W	0.4	2.1	36.0	25.5	10.5	...	...	...	...	...	...
26	Sunday						N 51 E	4.1	4.3	40.0	23.3	16.7	.005	3.0	...	...	.005	3.0
27	30.2	.200	97	.507	.298	1.0	N 85 E	4.5	7.0	39.0	34.0	5.0	.400	9.0	...	...	.400	9.0
28	35.1	.187	90	.492	.304	1.0	S 67 W	5.6	5.8	36.5	34.0	2.5	...	...	...	...	...	...
29	33.6	.164	85	.488	.324	0.9	S 55 W	9.0	9.2	36.8	33.0	3.8	...	...	1.0	3.5	.100	3.5
30	34.5	.159	79	.358	.201	0.8	S 77 W	0.0	0.1	37.0	31.4	5.6	...	...	...	...	...	...
31	33.6	.153	80	.659	.506	0.7	S 36 E	1.1	4.4	37.0	31.8	5.2	...	...	...	...	...	...
	28.7	0.138	83	29.724	29.586	0.8	S 90 W	2.3	8.4	34.1	21.3	0.8	2.500	53.9	7.1	43.2	3.300	97.1

TORONTO.
GENERAL METEOROLOGICAL ABSTRACT, JANUARY, 1870.

Days.	DAILY MEANS.						WIND.			EXTREMES OF TEMPERATURE.			RAIN.		SNOW.		TOTAL FALL.	
	Temperature of Air.	Pressure of Vapour.	Rel. Humid.	Barometric Pressure.	Pressure of Dry Air.	Clouded Sky.	Resultant Direction.	Resultant Velocity.	Mean Velocity.	Maximum.	Minimum.	Difference.	Depth in inches.	Approximate duration.	Depth in inches.	Approximate duration.	Depth in inches.	Approximate duration.
1	31.9	0.149	82	29.534	29.385	1.0	N 78 E	12.7	12.8	36.5	29.5	6.7	...	...	4.0	9.3	0.400	9.3
2	Sunday						S 88 E	5.5	18.4	38.4	28.0	10.4	1.000	11.0	1.0	3.0	1.100	14.0
3	27.0	.101	66	23.909	23.868	1.0	S 62 W	13.8	13.8	38.0	28.8	9.2	...	...	0.2	4.5	.020	4.5
4	28.5	.103	81	29.321	29.218	0.6	N 76 W	5.7	6.1	28.8	22.0	6.8	...	...	S	1.1	S	1.1
5	23.3	.091	71	.637	.545	0.8	S 52 W	12.5	13.5	34.5	3.5	31.0	...	...	0.5	7.5	.050	7.3
6	25.5	.118	81	.580	.462	0.8	N 71 W	11.9	12.6	34.5	22.3	12.2	...	...	0.1	1.0	.010	1.0
7	16.3	.073	81	.688	.615	0.8	S 76 W	5.1	6.5	22.4	11.2	11.2	...	...	4.0	10.5	.400	10.0
8	14.4	.067	79	.597	.530	0.5	N 65 W	10.9	11.7	23.0	10.0	13.0	...	...	0.3	1.5	.030	1.5
9	Sunday						S 47 W	10.5	10.9	20.5	-3.2	23.7	...	...	0.2	14.0	.020	14.0
10	27.6	.120	79	.510	.390	1.0	S 67 W	6.9	8.6	34.2	14.8	19.4	...	...	0.1	4.1	.010	4.1
11	29.6	.140	82	.790	.650	0.7	S 78 W	4.5	4.8	35.0	21.0	14.0	.385	10.0	0.2	1.8	.405	11.5
12	31.9	.169	92	.503	.424	1.0	N 9 E	6.7	7.0	37.8	30.8	7.0	.315	8.7	2.0	5.5	.515	14.2
13	6.6	.054	89	.916	.862	0.9	N 16 E	11.0	11.8	15.0	6.0	9.0	...	...	2.0	7.0	.200	7.0
14	10.7	.075	90	.976	.901	1.0	N 61 E	10.6	11.3	34.2	-2.0	36.2	.270	8.0	4.0	16.0	.670	24.0
15	36.6	.198	92	.353	.155	1.0	S 76 W	8.5	8.8	40.0	4.0	36.0	.172	10.0	...	...	.172	10.0
16	Sunday						S 76 E	7.3	8.5	42.8	29.4	13.4	.350	10.5	...	...	.350	10.5
17	35.8	.199	84	.347	.148	0.7	S 63 W	11.4	13.4	45.0	31.4	13.0	.500	11.0	...	...	.500	11.0
18	18.0	.071	72	30.047	.976	0.3	"	"	"	22.5	17.0	5.5	...	...	...	...	...	...
19	20.3	.076	71	30.010	.934	0.3	"	"	"	26.8	11.4	15.4	...	...	...	...	...	...
20	30.1	.130	78	29.653	.523	1.0	"	"	"	34.5	21.5	13.0	...	...	...	...	...	...
21	21.9	.095	79	.888	.793	0.4	"	"	"	25.9	23.1	2.8	...	...	...	...	...	...
22	31.5	.161	87	.690	.529	0.8	"	"	"	40.8	13.7	27.1	.420	11.5	...	...	.420	11.5
23	Sunday						"	"	"	32.7	27.0	5.7	...	...	...	...	...	...
24	16.7	.078	83	.824	.746	1.0	"	"	"	23.0	10.8	12.2	...	...	1.5	10.0	.150	10.0
25	25.3	.119	85	.213	.094	0.9	"	"	"	34.8	16.2	18.0	...	...	1.0	7.5	.100	7.5
26	32.2	.151	83	.532	.381	0.9	S 61 W	4.0	4.0	38.0	24.2	13.8	...	...	0.2	7.0	.020	7.0
27	24.2	.100	76	.830	.730	0.2	S 65 W	3.3	3.4	30.2	22.5	7.7	...	...	...	...	...	...
28	21.4	.091	78	.803	.712	0.1	S 4 E	2.1	3.3	28.8	9.6	18.2	...	...	...	...	...	...
29	28.9	.127	79	.400	.273	0.9	N 83 W	7.7	8.0	35.0	19.5	15.5	...	...	S	1.2	S	1.2
30	Sunday						N 40 W	1.9	2.9	33.0	24.0	9.0	...	...	...	...	...	...
31	24.0	.108	84	.494	.386	0.8	N 56 W	3.3	3.5	30.2	15.7	14.5	...	...	...	...	...	...
	24.4	0.115	82	29.624	29.509	0.8	S 89 W	2.6	9.0	32.2	17.6	14.6	3.412	80.7	21.3	112.0	5.542	192.7

TORONTO.
General Meteorological Abstract, February, 1870.

Days.	DAILY MEANS.							WIND.			EXTREMES OF TEMPERATURE.			RAIN.		SNOW.		TOTAL FALL.
	Temperature of Air.	Pressure of Vapour.	Rel. Humid.	Barometric Pressure.	Pressure of Dry Air.	Clouded Sky.	Resultant Direction.	Resultant Velocity.	Mean Velocity.	Maximum.	Minimum.	Difference.	Depth in inches.	Approximate duration.	Depth in inches.	Approximate duration.	Depth in inches.	Approximate duration.
1	22.6	0.089	73	29.646	29.557	0.8	S 69 W	1.7	7.4	25.0	17.7	7.3	...	...	2.5	6.5	0.250	5.0
2	25.1	.114	84	.582	.468	0.9	N 30 E	3.5	6.9	29.6	21.0	8.6	...	...	2.0	16.0	.200	16.0
3	13.6	.064	89	.996	.932	0.8	N 33 E	6.4	6.5	17.8	10.0	7.8	...	...	0.2	3.0	.020	3.0
4	15.2	.077	89	30.044	.967	0.8	N 43 E	8.2	9.2	22.4	10.0	12.4	...	...	0.5	10.0	.050	10.0
5	22.1	.102	85	29.848	.746	0.8	N 19 W	0.3	0.6	32.0	14.0	18.0	...	...	...	...	...	...
6	Sunday						S 83 W	0.9	0.9	32.2	14.4	17.8	...	...	...	...	...	...
7	25.9	.116	83	.708	.652	0.8	S 2 E	1.4	4.5	31.0	21.0	10.0	...	...	...	...	...	...
8	28.3	.125	81	.428	.303	1.0	N 10 E	5.9	6.6	31.6	24.0	7.6	...	...	...	...	...	...
9	28.9	.132	84	.255	.122	1.0	N 80 W	2.8	2.9	34.8	24.8	10.0	...	...	0.2	6.5	.020	6.5
10	22.7	.102	80	.562	.460	0.8	N 41 W	7.6	7.8	29.0	23.5	5.5	...	...	8	0.7	8	0.5
11	26.3	.117	81	.333	.216	0.9	S 62 E	5.9	8.0	36.0	10.6	25.2	...	...	0.1	0.5	.010	0.5
12	25.1	.080	56	.365	.285	0.7	N 69 W	20.1	20.9	37.5	23.7	13.8	...	...	8	0.3	8	0.3
13	Sunday						S 65 E	4.4	5.5	31.2	5.0	26.2	...	...	8	1.5	8	1.5
14	32.9	.173	92	.191	.018	1.0	S 40 W	0.6	3.3	35.2	14.8	20.4	...	...	0.8	5.8	.080	5.8
15	27.6	.115	75	.597	.482	0.3	N 20 W	6.4	6.7	33.4	26.8	6.6	...	...	...	...	...	...
16	27.4	.118	78	.905	.787	0.5	S 51 E	2.7	4.3	35.8	16.6	19.2	...	...	...	...	...	...
17	34.8	.181	89	.530	.349	0.7	N 58 W	0.6	8.5	40.6	27.5	13.1	0.520	9.2	3.0	7.5	.820	16.7
18	15.5	.077	85	.393	.316	0.8	N 36 W	19.1	19.2	23.8	14.2	9.6	...	...	1.0	5.0	.100	5.0
19	11.0	.062	83	.543	.481	0.5	N 49 E	8.3	9.9	14.0	3.7	10.3	...	...	3.5	6.2	.350	6.2
20	Sunday						N 40 W	10.1	10.6	13.0	9.5	3.5	...	...	...	...	...	...
21	2.9	.041	82	.625	.584	0.6	N 83 W	11.8	12.3	9.0	-6.6	15.6	...	...	0.3	3.7	.030	3.7
22	11.6	.055	74	.474	.419	0.5	S 72 W	12.7	12.9	17.2	4.0	13.2	...	...	...	...	...	...
23	17.1	.077	80	.285	.208	0.5	S 82 W	6.2	7.1	26.4	9.0	17.4	...	...	...	...	...	...
24	9.4	.054	78	.452	.398	0.5	N 34 W	10.7	10.9	16.8	9.0	7.8	...	...	8	6.8	8	0.8
25	22.0	.085	81	.355	.270	0.6	S 86 W	8.0	9.0	31.0	0.8	30.2	...	...	...	...	...	...
26	21.4	.103	79	.426	.323	0.8	N 75 E	4.7	5.6	31.0	15.0	16.0	...	...	1.5	3.0	.150	3.0
27	Sunday						N 81 E	14.0	15.0	30.2	24.8	5.4	R	0.5	4.5	15.0	.450	15.5
28	24.1	.116	88	.152	.036	0.7	N 50 W	3.3	3.5	34.0	23.6	10.4	...	...	8	4.5	8	4.5
	21.5	0.099	80	29.531	29.432	0.7	N 29 W	2.8	8.1	28.0	14.7	13.3	0.520	9.7	29.1	96.3	2.530	100.0

TORONTO.
GENERAL METEOROLOGICAL ABSTRACT, MARCH, 1870.

Days.	Temperature of Air.	Pressure of Vapour.	Rel. Humid.	Barometric Pressure.	Pressure of Dry Air.	Clouded Sky.	Resultant Direction.	Resultant Velocity.	Mean Velocity.	Maximum.	Minimum.	Difference.	Depth in Inches.	Approximate duration.	Depth in Inches.	Approximate duration.	Depth in Inches.	Approximate duration.
1	22.7	0.103	83	29.361	29.258	0.8	N 59 W	9.9	10.9	30.8	16.5	14.3	...	...	0.2	0.7	0.020	0.7
2	14.1	.066	81	.648	.582	0.4	N 45 W	12.3	12.9	20.0	12.4	7.6	...	...	S	1.0	S	1.0
3	11.2	.060	70	.912	.852	0.2	N 25 W	3.9	4.5	24.8	5.2	19.6	...	...	...	...	...	...
4	22.9	.109	88	.664	.556	1.0	N 67 E	8.2	8.5	27.4	11.5	15.9	...	...	0.3	5.5	.030	5.5
5	25.8	.116	84	.784	.668	0.9	N 55 W	2.2	4.1	31.5	18.5	13.0	...	...	S	2.8	S	2.8
6	Sunday						N 71 E	11.7	12.6	30.2	20.4	9.8	...	...	2.5	9.5	.250	9.5
7	25.4	.115	84	.441	.326	1.0	N 22 E	4.9	5.5	29.8	20.5	9.3	...	...	0.2	10.0	.020	10.0
8	21.5	.095	81	.629	.534	0.5	N 34 W	6.9	7.0	30.0	19.9	10.1	...	...	...	...	...	...
9	22.5	.093	77	.703	.610	0.7	N 72 W	5.7	7.3	34.0	11.0	23.0	...	...	0.5	9.5	.050	9.5
10	22.0	.100	81	.613	.513	0.8	N 13 W	8.4	9.5	29.6	22.0	7.6	...	...	1.5	5.2	.150	5.2
11	12.8	.067	85	.611	.544	1.0	N 42 E	10.1	10.2	17.0	9.0	8.0	...	...	0.5	10.0	.050	10.0
12	17.0	.082	86	.324	.243	1.0	N 59 E	17.5	17.7	24.0	10.4	13.6	...	...	6.0	12.5	.600	12.5
13	Sunday						N 40 E	10.6	11.7	27.8	15.5	12.3	...	...	9.0	11.0	.900	11.0
14	25.7	.096	70	.708	.612	0.4	N 52 E	3.2	4.5	33.4	22.2	11.2	...	...	...	...	...	...
15	28.0	.136	87	.533	.397	0.7	N 86 E	13.5	17.0	35.8	15.0	20.8	...	...	10.0	8.2	1.000	8.2
16	17.0	.087	89	.161	.074	1.0	N 81 W	9.3	12.3	24.2	13.2	11.0	...	...	10.0	18.5	1.000	18.5
17	32.6	.135	73	.275	.140	0.6	N 10 W	14.0	14.9	41.8	15.2	26.6	...	...	1.5	4.0	.150	4.0
18	26.4	.083	58	.704	.621	0.0	N 42 W	8.1	8.5	38.0	22.5	15.5	...	...	...	...	...	...
19	28.6	.110	66	.774	.665	0.6	S 28 W	1.8	2.8	37.4	11.0	26.4	...	...	...	...	...	...
20	Sunday						S 62 E	3.9	4.9	40.2	29.6	10.6	0.205	9.2	...	...	.205	9.2
21	36.4	.183	84	.411	.229	1.0	S 84 W	8.0	8.5	40.8	35.0	5.8	...	...	...	...	...	...
22	31.2	.142	81	.683	.541	0.8	N 54 W	11.6	12.1	36.0	32.0	4.0	...	...	0.2	1.8	.020	1.8
23	26.2	.093	67	.954	.861	0.3	N 42 W	19.4	19.5	32.6	20.9	11.7	...	...	...	...	...	...
24	29.2	.090	56	30.118	30.028	0.0	N 14 W	8.6	9.2	38.2	23.6	14.6	...	...	...	...	...	...
25	26.0	.103	72	30.092	29.989	0.5	N 80 E	8.4	8.6	29.8	17.4	12.4	...	...	...	...	...	...
26	32.5	.144	78	29.725	.581	0.8	N 81 E	15.9	15.9	37.2	25.2	12.0	.550	7.0	3.5	6.0	.900	13.0
27	Sunday						N 79 E	15.9	16.2	35.0	30.0	5.0	...	...	16.0	20.0	1.600	20.0
28	35.7	.176	84	.304	.128	1.0	N 28 W	9.4	9.8	39.0	30.5	8.5	...	...	0.5	5.3	.050	5.3
29	36.4	.174	81	.680	.506	0.6	N 21 W	1.9	1.9	44.0	33.8	10.2	...	...	...	...	...	...
30	36.3	.185	86	.768	.583	0.7	N 78 E	12.9	12.9	37.8	30.2	7.6	...	...	...	...	...	...
31	39.7	.193	79	.805	.612	0.7	N 77 E	12.7	12.7	44.0	34.2	9.8	...	...	...	...	...	...
	26.3	0.116	78	29.644	29.528	0.7	N 18 E	4.7	10.1	33.0	20.5	12.5	0.755	16.2	62.4	141.5	6.995	157.7

TORONTO.
GENERAL METEOROLOGICAL ABSTRACT, APRIL, 1870.

Days.	DAILY MEANS.					WIND.			EXTREMES OF TEMPERATURE.			RAIN.		SNOW.		TOTAL FALL.	
	Temperature of Air.	Pressure of Vapour.	Rel. Humid.	Barometric Pressure.	Pressure of Dry Air.	Clouded Sky.	Resultant Direction.	Resultant Velocity.	Mean Velocity.	Maximum.	Minimum.	Difference.	Depth in Inches.	Approximate duration.	Depth in inches.	Approximate duration.	Depth in Inches.	Approximate duration.
1	43.4	0.115	41	29.773	29.658	0.6	N 66 E	12.0	12.1	48.8	38.0	10.8	...	...	...	...	...	...
2	46.7	.107	33	.683	.576	0.5	N 40 E	8.7	9.8	53.0	38.4	14.6	...	...	...	...	...	...
3	Sunday						N 7 E	7.5	7.7	48.8	34.8	14.0	...	...	...	...	...	...
4	45.9	.120	58	.699	.579	0.6	N 3 W	8.4	9.0	44.0	30.8	13.2	...	...	0.1	1.5	0.010	1.5
5	36.9	.163	73	.610	.447	0.9	N 4 W	5.6	5.8	40.0	33.0	7.0	0.080	7.5	S	1.7	.080	9.2
6	40.3	.107	78	.649	.452	1.0	N 57 W	1.0	2.1	47.4	35.8	11.6	...	...	...	...	...	...
7	42.7	.152	58	.645	.493	0.3	N 27 W	6.1	6.2	54.8	35.0	19.8	...	...	...	...	...	...
8	43.7	.169	50	.752	.582	0.1	S 79 W	1.9	2.3	57.0	29.6	27.4	...	...	...	...	...	...
9	45.3	.160	55	.747	.587	0.1	N 73 E	4.3	5.0	59.6	31.6	28.0	...	...	...	...	...	...
10	Sunday						N 72 E	8.1	8.2	53.5	39.0	14.5	...	...	...	...	...	...
11	41.4	.220	75	.587	.367	0.7	N 30 E	3.4	3.8	54.0	35.2	18.8	...	...	...	...	...	...
12	42.4	.161	61	.666	.505	0.1	N 31 W	12.5	12.8	52.0	37.5	14.5	...	...	...	...	...	...
13	40.9	.187	72	.614	.427	0.8	N 79 E	3.8	4.4	48.5	30.0	18.5	...	...	...	...	...	...
14	52.8	.315	75	.525	.210	0.9	S 57 W	2.6	3.7	67.0	38.8	28.2	.025	4.5	...	...	.025	4.5
15	...	...	...	...	...	...	N 81 E	13.7	13.8	50.0	45.0	5.0	...	...	...	...	...	...
16	47.4	.244	74	.547	.303	1.0	N 81 E	8.8	9.4	53.0	39.0	14.0	.030	4.0	...	...	.030	4.0
17	Sunday						N 78 E	17.0	17.2	48.0	36.8	11.2	.720	17.5	...	...	.720	17.5
18	51.6	.323	84	.292	28.969	1.0	N 61 E	16.4	16.4	58.2	38.5	19.7	.460	13.0	...	...	.460	13.0
19	45.0	.281	93	.302	29.021	1.0	N 84 E	5.6	5.8	52.2	43.2	9.0	.120	4.5	...	...	.120	4.5
20	41.1	.240	93	.314	.074	1.0	S 78 E	1.5	1.9	45.0	37.8	7.2	.260	11.3	...	...	.260	11.3
21	42.1	.229	85	.489	.259	0.8	S 88 E	0.6	1.9	47.4	39.0	8.2	...	...	...	...	...	...
22	45.9	.236	77	.559	.323	0.8	S 54 E	1.2	2.8	56.2	35.8	20.4	...	...	...	...	...	...
23	48.0	.253	76	.614	.361	0.3	S 59 E	0.9	1.6	60.0	37.8	22.2	...	...	...	...	...	...
24	Sunday						N 23 E	7.4	8.8	66.0	39.0	27.0	.450	6.0	...	...	.450	6.0
25	43.3	.140	50	.921	.781	0.0	N 9 W	5.8	7.1	54.8	37.4	17.4	...	...	...	...	...	...
26	47.0	.204	64	.812	.608	0.1	S 29 W	4.8	5.0	61.0	31.4	29.6	...	...	...	...	...	...
27	49.6	.202	56	.493	.292	0.6	S 18 W	2.7	4.1	63.4	36.5	26.9	R	R	...	...	R	R
28	45.4	.180	59	.563	.383	0.1	N 41 W	13.4	14.0	54.0	44.0	9.4	...	...	...	...	...	...
29	42.9	.160	58	.752	.592	0.2	S 42 E	1.2	3.3	50.0	33.8	16.2	...	...	...	...	...	...
30	48.4	.201	59	.611	.410	0.2	S 23 W	3.6	4.3	57.8	32.0	25.8	...	...	...	...	...	...
	44.6	0.198	67	29.609	29.411	0.6	N 40 E	3.5	7.0	53.5	36.5	17.0	2.145	68.3	0.1	3.2	2.155	71.5

TORONTO.
General Meteorological Abstract, May, 1870.

Days.	DAILY MEANS.						WIND.			EXTREMES OF TEMPERATURE.			RAIN.		SNOW.		TOTAL FALL.	
	Temperature of Air.	Pressure of Vapour.	Rel. Humid.	Barometric Pressure.	Pressure of Dry Air.	Clouded Sky.	Resultant Direction.	Resultant Velocity.	Mean Velocity.	Maximum.	Minimum.	Difference.	Depth in inches.	Approximate duration.	Depth in inches.	Approximate duration.	Depth in inches.	Approximate duration.
1	Su nday						N 32 W	7.6	7.9	67.5	39.0	28.7	...	...	...	...	...	...
2	52.3	0.292	52	29.801	29.599	0.2	S 78 E	2.4	2.6	63.8	43.6	20.2	...	...	...	...	...	...
3	55.7	.276	62	.171	.195	0.0	N 40 W	1.0	3.5	65.0	35.8	29.2	...	...	...	...	...	...
4	62.1	.295	54	.430	.132	0.6	N 3 W	7.7	10.2	74.0	53.5	20.5	...	...	...	...	...	...
5	52.5	.208	52	.561	.358	0.9	N 83 E	4.6	4.8	57.0	46.4	10.6	...	...	...	...	...	...
6	51.8	.204	55	.256	.052	0.9	N 74 E	8.1	8.5	57.8	49.0	8.8	0.350	12.7	...	...	0.350	12.5
7	47.4	.211	64	.176	28.965	0.7	N 31 E	2.2	2.3	53.8	44.5	9.3	.050	0.6	...	...	.050	0.6
8	Su nday						S 87 E	0.7	2.4	60.0	42.0	18.0	...	...	...	...	...	...
9	55.1	.280	65	.354	29.074	0.9	N 56 E	0.6	2.4	67.4	46.5	20.9	.080	2.0	...	...	.080	2.0
10	47.1	.292	90	.424	.132	0.7	S 84 E	1.3	1.9	59.0	43.6	15.4	.090	3.5	...	...	.090	3.5
11	48.3	.282	83	.486	.204	0.9	S 58 E	3.2	4.5	57.5	41.0	16.5	...	...	...	...	...	...
12	49.5	.252	70	.525	.213	0.8	S 51 W	2.6	4.6	58.0	44.2	13.8	.130	2.9	...	...	.130	2.9
13	60.1	.192	40	.545	.346	0.2	N 29 W	12.7	12.9	70.8	40.0	30.8	...	...	...	...	...	...
14	64.5	.292	49	.591	.299	0.5	S 80 W	5.7	6.4	81.2	53.2	28.0	...	...	...	...	...	...
15	Su nday						S 59 W	5.1	5.4	81.0	51.8	29.2	...	...	...	...	...	...
16	51.5	.390	72	.519	.129	0.9	N 83 E	2.8	5.4	77.8	51.8	26.0	R	0.2	...	...	R	0.2
17	54.6	.272	64	.693	.427	0.5	S 45 E	2.9	3.2	64.0	48.0	16.0	...	...	...	...	...	...
18	58.5	.379	77	.705	.325	0.0	S 76 E	4.2	4.4	69.2	47.0	22.2	...	...	...	...	...	...
19	65.1	.379	63	.705	.326	0.7	N 84 W	1.2	4.3	76.2	52.0	24.2	...	...	...	...	...	...
20	64.0	.293	51	.762	.469	0.6	S 42 E	2.1	3.5	74.8	53.2	21.6	...	...	...	...	...	...
21	54.4	.267			.459	0.7	N 84 E	2.9	3.0	64.0	52.0	12.0	.010	0.3	...	...	.010	0.3
22	Su nday						S 73 E	3.8	4.7	59.2	47.6	11.7	.240	2.0	...	...	.240	2.0
23	49.7	.311	87	.511	.200	1.0	N 86 E	3.9	4.5	62.0	45.4	16.6	.290	2.3	...	...	.290	2.3
24	58.5	.369	76	.400	.031	1.0	N 85 W	11.4	11.7	66.8	47.9	18.9	...	...	...	...	...	...
25	52.1	.267	68	.578	.311	0.7	N 46 W	8.3	10.1	59.0	51.5	7.5	...	...	...	...	...	...
26	50.7	.227	61	.676	.449	0.4	N 80 E	5.7	7.7	57.0	44.2	12.8	...	...	...	...	...	...
27	57.5	.248	62	.667	.419	0.1	N 70 E	7.1	8.8	63.2	45.4	17.8	...	...	...	...	...	...
28	59.1	.259	51	.542	.283	0.3	S 6 E	1.2	5.6	66.2	47.0	19.2	...	...	...	...	...	...
29	Su nday						N 21 W	2.1	6.0	75.2	48.4	26.8	...	...	...	...	...	...
30	68.5	.291	49	.760	.469	0.7	N 67 W	2.0	3.8	78.0	54.4	23.6	R	0.1	...	...	R	0.1
31	62.3	.344	63	.763	.419	0.9	S 83 E	2.6	2.7	71.4	55.8	15.6	...	...	...	...	...	...
	56.3	0.282	63	29.563	29.281	0.6	N 23 E	1.1	5.5	66.5	47.4	19.1	1.150	26.4	...	...	1.150	26.4

TORONTO.
GENERAL METEOROLOGICAL ABSTRACT, JUNE, 1870.

Days.	DAILY MEANS.					WIND.			EXTREMES OF TEMPERATURE.			RAIN.		SNOW.		TOTAL FALL.	
	Temperature of Air.	Pressure of Vapour.	Rel. Humid.	Barometric Pressure.	Pressure of Dry Air.	Clouded Sky.	Resultant Direction.	Resultant Velocity.	Mean Velocity.	Maximum.	Minimum.	Difference.	Depth in inches.	Approximate duration.	Depth in inches.	Approximate duration.	Depth in inches.	Approximate duration.
1	60.6	0.405	77	29.664	29.259	0.7	S 63 E	0.5	0.0	71.0	50.2	20.8	...	...	...	...	...	...
2	65.4	.412	67	.550	.137	0.5	Calm.	0.0	0.0	74.8	50.0	24.8	...	...	...	...	...	...
3	63.5	.475	76	.558	.083	0.4	N 82 E	4.0	4.8	72.4	55.8	16.0	...	...	...	...	...	...
4	57.5	.522	77	.587	.065	0.5	S 84 E	5.1	5.5	75.0	54.8	20.2	R	0.3	...	...	R	0.3
5	Sunday						S 69 E	2.3	3.4	70.0	57.4	12.6	).500	6.1	...	...	).500	6.1
6	55.7	.480	76	.533	.050	0.2	S 13 E	3.3	5.6	74.8	57.2	17.6	...	...	...	...	...	...
7	64.3	.464	77	.627	.163	0.7	N 47 E	2.5	5.8	72.0	54.2	17.8	...	...	...	...	...	...
8	66.7	.425	63	.594	.160	0.8	N 89 E	1.8	5.4	76.6	54.0	22.6	R	0.1	...	...	R	0.1
9	62.9	.481	84	.428	28.947	1.0	N 56 E	2.2	6.5	70.2	59.0	11.2	.390	12.1	...	...	.390	12.1
10	57.4	.413	87	.401	28.988	1.0	N 11 W	7.3	7.7	61.0	55.2	5.8	.050	7.0	...	...	.050	7.0
11	53.2	.440	91	.424	28.984	1.0	N 59 E	3.3	3.6	65.0	55.0	10.0	2.360	3.2	...	...	2.360	3.2
12	Sunday						N 82 E	6.5	7.8	67.5	52.5	15.0	.350	6.0	...	...	.350	6.0
13	61.6	.438	81	.463	29.028	0.7	S 10 W	5.4	6.4	68.4	54.4	14.0	.060	1.7	...	...	.060	1.7
14	61.7	.439	70	.419	28.950	0.9	S 5 W	7.0	7.2	70.0	53.8	16.8	.260	4.2	...	...	.260	4.2
15	61.3	.440	82	.440	28.991	0.5	S 29 E	2.4	3.1	69.5	58.2	11.3	R	0.4	...	...	R	0.4
16	65.2	.484	77	.600	29.116	0.5	N 32 W	1.6	2.5	73.4	52.4	21.0	...	...	...	...	...	...
17	74.0	.476	56	.640	.164	0.0	N 19 W	5.4	6.0	85.8	54.0	31.8	...	...	...	...	...	...
18	77.1	.595	55	.658	.153	0.1	N 36 W	4.7	5.4	88.4	59.6	28.8	...	...	...	...	...	...
19	Sunday						S 66 W	4.1	5.0	87.0	60.6	26.4	...	...	...	...	...	...
20	69.2	.417	57	.517	.039	0.3	N 33 W	10.3	11.5	82.6	62.0	20.6	.010	0.3	...	...	.010	0.3
21	59.7	.242	46	.760	.518	0.1	N 25 W	10.8	11.0	68.8	50.8	18.0	...	...	...	...	...	...
22	64.7	.351	59	.822	.470	0.3	S 48 W	4.2	5.0	75.0	51.8	23.2	...	...	...	...	...	...
23	70.2	.540	72	.791	.252	0.6	S 52 W	3.2	3.9	83.0	56.0	27.0	...	...	...	...	...	...
24	75.5	.593	67	.750	.157	0.1	S 50 W	1.9	2.7	87.5	55.8	31.7	...	...	...	...	...	...
25	72.1	.652	83	.706	.054	0.6	S 52 W	1.6	3.2	84.0	64.0	20.0	.090	1.2	...	...	.090	1.2
26	Sunday						S 31 E	1.9	3.6	83.0	69.0	14.0	.750	0.8	...	...	.750	0.8
27	77.6	.743	80	.599	28.853	0.4	S 43 W	1.8	4.1	87.8	65.6	22.3	.070	2.8	...	...	.070	2.8
28	77.7	.711	75	.545	28.834	0.5	N 12 E	0.8	5.4	85.0	67.4	17.6	R	1.0	...	...	R	1.0
29	70.5	.458	61	.521	29.063	0.0	N 85 E	4.1	4.3	76.0	69.0	7.0	...	...	...	...	...	...
30	71.8	.611	78	.307	28.696	0.8	S 69 E	1.9	7.5	85.8	61.8	24.0	2.000	3.5	...	...	2.000	3.5
	67.5	0.485	72	29.573	29.088	0.5	N 17 E	0.4	5.1	76.4	57.4	19.0	8.000	50.7	...	...	8.000	50.7

TORONTO.
GENERAL METEOROLOGICAL ABSTRACT, JULY, 1870.

Days.	Temperature of Air.	Pressure of Vapour.	Rel. Humid.	Barometric Pressure.	Pressure of Dry Air.	Clouded Sky.	Resultant Direction.	Resultant Velocity.	Mean Velocity.	Maximum.	Minimum.	Difference.	Depth in inches.	Approximate duration.	Depth in inches	Approximate duration.	Depth in inches	Approximate duration.
1	61.9	0.374	68	29.553	29.179	0.7	N 63 E	3.4	4.3	70.2	58.4	11.8	...	...	...	...	...	...
2	63.9	.305	52	.627	.321	0.6	N 61 E	3.4	4.0	70.0	53.0	17.0	...	...	...	...	...	...
3	Sunday						S 21 E	1.8	2.1	74.0	55.6	18.4	...	...	...	...	...	...
4	68.7	.551	79	.481	28.930	0.7	S 3 W	0.7	4.4	78.0	55.8	22.2	0.372	3.5	...	...	0.372	3.5
5	69.6	.519	70	.519	29.001	0.4	S 37 W	2.9	3.9	79.2	61.0	18.2	...	...	...	...	...	...
6	70.2	.537	72	.506	28.960	0.8	S 86 E	1.9	4.4	77.2	59.6	17.6	.020	2.8	...	...	.020	2.8
7	65.7	.565	89	.242	28.677	0.9	S 85 W	2.2	3.1	70.0	65.2	4.8	.520	4.5	...	...	.520	4.5
8	63.3	.359	63	.474	29.115	0.4	N 54 W	6.1	6.2	72.2	56.0	16.2	...	...	...	...	...	...
9	66.5	.448	76	.601	.153	0.1	S 46 W	3.4	3.5	77.2	53.2	24.0	...	...	...	...	...	...
10	Sunday						S 32 W	3.3	3.3	80.0	57.2	22.8	...	...	...	...	...	...
11	66.9	.564	86	.498	28.934	1.0	N 62 E	2.6	4.9	70.8	58.0	12.8	.030	8.5	...	...	.030	8.5
12	68.1	.556	81	.419	28.863	0.5	S 61 W	4.9	5.0	78.5	61.4	17.0	.010	1.0	...	...	.010	1.0
13	70.4	.564	76	.413	28.849	0.8	S 72 W	2.9	5.9	80.0	57.0	23.0	...	...	...	...	...	...
14	65.9	.409	64	.495	29.089	0.2	N 58 W	2.0	4.9	74.8	58.0	16.8	...	...	...	...	...	...
15	60.7	.379	71	.626	.247	0.5	N 85 W	1.1	3.1	68.0	48.0	20.0	.010	2.0	...	...	.010	2.0
16	65.8	.548	86	.526	28.977	0.8	N 7 E	1.2	3.4	76.8	57.4	19.4	.150	2.5	...	...	.150	2.5
17	Sunday						S 62 W	2.6	4.8	86.4	64.0	22.4	R	0.5	...	...	R	0.5
18	74.3	.657	77	.538	28.881	0.5	N 71 W	2.4	5.9	85.2	67.4	17.8	...	...	...	...	...	...
19	73.9	.580	70	.577	28.997	0.3	S 79 E	2.9	3.1	81.8	67.0	14.8	...	...	...	...	...	...
20	74.7	.670	78	.510	28.840	0.7	S 50 W	0.3	7.7	85.0	65.0	20.0	.110	3.8	...	...	.110	3.8
21	68.8	.393	58	.672	29.279	0.0	N 24 W	7.0	7.4	78.2	61.6	17.2	...	...	...	...	...	...
22	70.3	.558	75	.616	.055	0.7	S 20 W	3.9	5.4	78.8	56.0	22.8	.010	2.2	...	...	.010	2.2
23	75.6	.663	74	.502	28.899	0.5	S 13 W	4.6	5.6	87.4	67.0	20.4	...	...	...	...	...	...
24	Sunday						S 50 W	4.5	5.0	82.0	67.0	15.0	.045	2.5	...	...	.045	2.5
25	74.9	.595	70	.650	29.055	0.7	N 62 W	1.6	4.0	84.0	65.4	18.6	...	...	...	...	...	...
26	72.6	.645	81	.580	28.944	0.5	S 60 W	0.8	3.2	78.2	63.8	14.4	.145	2.8	...	...	.145	2.8
27	71.5	.704	91	.567	28.862	0.7	S 6 W	1.1	1.7	78.8	68.5	10.3	.030	1.0	...	...	.030	1.0
28	72.2	.632	80	.410	28.778	1.0	S 67 W	3.8	6.1	80.0	66.6	13.4	R	0.5	...	...	R	0.5
29	63.9	.446	75	.491	29.045	0.8	N 59 W	10.2	10.4	71.2	59.6	12.1	.010	0.2	...	...	.010	0.2
30	68.9	.380	57	.701	.315	0.2	N 44 W	5.1	6.0	77.8	54.8	23.4	...	...	...	...	...	...
31	Sunday						S 32 W	5.4	5.6	76.0	52.0	24.0	.034	0.5	...	...	.034	0.5
	68.8	0.523	74	29.533	29.010	0.6	S 78 W	1.6	4.8	77.7	60.0	17.7	1.896	38.8	...	...	1.896	38.8

TORONTO.
GENERAL METEOROLOGICAL ABSTRACT, AUGUST, 1870.

Days.	DAILY MEANS.						WIND.			EXTREMES OF TEMPERATURE.			RAIN.		SNOW.		TOTAL FALL.	
	Temperature of Air	Pressure of Vapour.	Rel. Humid.	Barometric Pressure.	Pressure of Dry Air.	Clouded Sky.	Resultant Direction.	Resultant Velocity.	Mean Velocity.	Maximum.	Minimum.	Difference.	Depth in inches	Approximate duration	Depth in inches	Approximate duration	Depth in inches.	Approximate duration.
1	71.0	0.537	72	29.548	29.011	0.7	N 64 W	3.2	6.3	81.0	61.4	22.6	...	...	...	...	...	...
2	77.3	.470	71	.554	.078	0.3	S 63 E	2.2	3.8	74.5	58.6	15.9	0.040	1.0	...	...	0.040	1.0
3	70.3	.544	75	.444	28.900	0.6	N 75 W	3.8	6.8	83.0	59.8	23.2	.240	3.5	...	...	.240	3.5
4	66.9	.417	76	.478	29.039	0.2	N 77 W	4.5	7.0	77.4	52.0	25.4	...	...	...	...	...	...
5	68.7	.564	81	.414	29.850	0.5	S 45 W	5.2	4.5	78.8	59.8	19.0	1.490	2.8	...	...	1.490	2.2
6	71.7	.582	76	.455	28.878	0.7	S 23 W	3.4	4.8	80.0	60.8	19.2	...	...	...	...	...	...
7	Sunday						N 52 E	4.3	4.7	78.2	62.0	16.2	.590	5.0	...	...	.590	5.0
8	73.1	.698	80	.540	28.842	0.6	S 35 W	3.2	4.1	82.5	64.4	18.1	.265	1.5	...	...	.265	1.5
9	72.8	.645	80	.628	28.983	0.9	N 37 W	1.8	2.9	81.0	67.4	13.6	R	0.1	...	...	R	0.1
10	71.9	.568	74	.695	29.130	0.3	S 18 E	1.0	3.4	79.8	61.0	18.8	...	...	...	...	...	...
11	71.7	.460	59	.094	.235	0.6	N 61 E	3.1	4.1	79.5	61.0	18.5	...	...	...	...	...	...
12	78.4	.460	57	.079	.210	0.8	N 63 W	7.5	7.8	83.8	65.6	18.2	...	...	...	...	...	...
13	70.4	.421	60	.700	.273	0.7	N 89 W	3.1	4.3	70.0	53.0	17.0	.020	3.8	...	...	.020	3.8
14	Sunday						N 40 W	9.9	10.4	76.5	52.4	24.1	...	...	...	...	...	...
15	65.1	.433	69	.655	.222	0.1	S 75 E	1.5	4.9	73.0	51.0	19.0	...	...	...	...	...	...
16	66.5	.424	66	.481	.057	0.2	S 20 W	4.0	4.5	77.0	53.0	24.0	...	...	...	...	...	...
17	70.5	.480	66	.315	28.830	0.2	S 35 W	10.3	10.3	81.0	60.4	20.6	R	0.1	...	...	R	0.1
18	70.7	.572	77	.509	28.937	0.4	S 25 E	2.8	3.5	80.0	60.8	19.2	...	...	...	...	...	...
19	72.4	.635	81	.500	28.862	0.7	S 74 W	5.8	10.8	82.0	62.0	20.0	.080	1.0	...	...	.080	1.0
20	69.9	.295	58	.792	29.497	0.2	N 22 W	7.6	7.9	71.5	53.4	18.1	...	...	...	...	...	...
21	Sunday						N 14 W	4.7	5.2	73.0	48.0	25.0	...	...	...	...	...	...
22	61.7	.381	69	.863	.482	0.6	N 79 W	2.7	5.0	71.0	49.8	21.2	...	...	...	...	...	...
23	62.7	.463	81	.620	.157	1.0	N 80 E	6.5	7.2	65.8	57.4	8.4	.135	10.5	...	...	.135	10.5
24	67.7	.612	91	.419	28.837	0.7	N 73 E	4.6	4.8	74.8	60.0	14.8	.065	2.2	...	...	.065	2.2
25	70.6	.530	72	.467	28.937	0.5	N 54 W	10.8	13.5	82.8	62.0	20.8	.402	0.7	...	...	.402	0.7
26	64.8	.227	55	.910	29.083	0.0	N 16 W	7.8	7.4	65.8	48.0	17.8	...	...	...	...	...	...
27	67.5	.301	63	.876	.572	0.3	S 86 E	1.6	3.3	70.8	40.0	30.8	...	...	...	...	...	...
28	Sunday						S 85 E	1.0	1.3	71.6	51.8	19.8	.130	4.0	...	...	.130	4.0
29	72.2	.570	84	.340	28.776	0.6	S 46 W	6.1	7.1	79.2	62.0	17.2	.025	0.2	...	...	.025	0.2
30	63.2	.280	68	.550	29.170	0.1	S 72 W	6.8	6.5	74.0	52.0	22.0	...	...	...	...	...	...
31	68.1	.480	76	.545	.063	0.1	N 74 W	3.4	5.7	80.4	57.0	23.4	...	...	...	...	...	...
	67.1	0.488	72	29.552	29.094	0.5	N 75 W	1.8	5.9	76.8	57.1	19.7	3.422	36.6	...	...	3.422	36.0

TORONTO.
GENERAL METEOROLOGICAL ABSTRACT, SEPTEMBER, 1870.

Days.	Temperature of Air.	Pressure of Vapour.	Rel. Humid.	Barometric Pressure.	Pressure of Dry Air.	Clouded Sky.	Resultant Direction.	Resultant Velocity.	Mean Velocity.	Maximum.	Minimum.	Difference.	Depth in inches.	Approximate duration.	Depth in inches.	Approximate duration.	Depth in inches.	Approximate duration.
				DAILY MEANS.			WIND.			EXTREMES OF TEMPERATURE.			RAIN.		SNOW.		TOTAL FALL.	
1	68.8	0.515	73	29.519	29.004	0.3	S 3 E	3.0	5.9	78.0	53.8	19.2	...	...	...	...	...	...
2	58.1	.544	79	.462	28.918	0.5	N 26 W	3.4	6.7	77.8	61.8	16.0	...	...	...	...	...	...
3	59.8	.447	87	.110	28.002	1.0	N 15 W	7.5	7.9	66.0	57.2	8.8	0.725	8.7	...	...	0.725	8.7
4	Sunday						N 46 W	8.8	8.9	69.5	57.8	11.7	...	...	...	...	...	...
5	59.1	.375	73	.729	29.354	0.5	S 86 W	1.8	2.4	70.0	48.2	21.8	...	...	...	...	...	...
6	61.1	.422	78	.824	.402	0.7	S 40 E	0.9	1.1	69.5	52.0	7.5	.285	3.0	...	...	.285	3.0
7	63.0	.429	85	.832	.333	0.4	N 74 E	5.3	6.1	69.7	59.0	10.7	.200	2.0	...	...	.200	2.0
8	65.0	.519	83	.842	.323	0.3	N 70 E	4.5	4.9	72.0	59.2	12.9	...	...	...	...	...	...
9	58.4	.606	87	.721	.115	1.0	N 16 W	2.9	4.7	77.0	58.8	18.2	.510	2.9	...	...	.510	2.9
10	51.0	.325	61	.811	.486	0.1	N 7 E	7.1	7.1	69.5	58.4	11.1	...	...	...	...	...	...
11	Sunday						N 7 W	1.8	3.4	63.8	46.4	17.4	...	...	...	...	...	...
12	57.8	.342	73	.953	.611	0.0	N 74 E	2.2	5.6	66.0	47.8	18.2	...	...	...	...	...	...
13	53.9	.302	63	.932	.630	0.0	N 59 E	4.4	5.1	67.8	48.8	19.3	...	...	...	...	...	...
14	52.4	.435	77	.811	.376	0.5	N 87 E	3.2	3.7	70.0	51.4	18.6	...	...	...	...	...	...
15	67.2	.568	80	.066	.098	1.0	S 39 W	0.7	3.2	74.8	59.0	15.8	2.285	11.6	...	...	2.285	11.6
16	60.1	.464	88	.771	.307	1.0	N 48 E	5.3	5.8	63.8	59.0	4.8	.230	4.5	...	...	.230	4.5
17	61.5	.441	80	.818	.370	0.8	N 19 E	4.3	5.3	68.0	54.0	14.0	...	...	...	...	...	...
18	Sunday						N 2 E	8.4	8.7	72.0	59.4	12.6	...	...	...	...	...	...
19	56.0	.308	69	.922	.614	0.0	N 11 W	0.6	3.0	65.4	49.0	16.4	...	...	...	...	...	...
20	59.2	.326	66	.933	.607	0.1	N 58 E	1.9	3.5	69.8	45.8	24.0	...	...	...	...	...	...
21	61.0	.377	71	.930	.553	0.0	S 61 E	2.3	3.8	70.5	52.0	18.5	...	...	...	...	...	...
22	61.7	.435	79	.810	.375	0.4	S 15 W	2.0	2.8	71.2	51.4	19.8	.105	6.5	...	...	.105	6.5
23	64.9	.533	75	.656	.122	0.8	S 68 W	1.4	1.7	71.8	54.2	17.1	.850	10.3	...	...	.850	10.3
24	62.1	.510	91	.589	.079	0.0	N 3 E	1.5	1.7	64.0	61.0	3.0	.150	4.5	...	...	.150	4.5
25	Sunnay						N 4 W	3.8	4.1	68.0	56.0	12.0	...	...	...	...	...	...
26	57.4	.408	86	.806	.398	0.4	N 88 W	0.5	3.0	66.0	49.8	16.2	...	...	...	...	...	...
27	62.7	.434	75	.743	.309	0.4	N 4 E	2.0	5.5	70.0	49.0	20.2	...	...	...	...	...	...
28	65.0	.385	83	.749	.364	0.4	N 60 E	4.6	5.3	63.2	50.8	12.4	...	...	...	...	...	...
29	61.7	.409	90	.701	.292	0.9	N 82 E	7.3	7.6	67.0	52.4	14.6	.254	12.6	...	...	.254	12.0
30	59.7	.460	91	.566	.099	1.0	N 58 E	8.9	11.3	64.0	59.0	5.0	1.200	19.5	...	...	1.200	19.5
	61.8	0.442	79	29.751	29.309	0.5	N 29 E	2.3	5.0	69.2	54.3	14.9	8.794	85.5	...	...	6.794	85.5

TORONTO.
GENERAL METEOROLOGICAL ABSTRACT, OCTOBER, 1870.

Days.	DAILY MEANS.					WIND.			EXTREMES OF TEMPERATURE.			RAIN.		SNOW.		TOTAL FALL.	
	Temperature of Air.	Pressure of Vapour.	Rel. Humid.	Barometric Pressure.	Pressure of Dry Air.	Clouded Sky.	Resultant Direction.	Resultant Velocity.	Mean Velocity.	Maximum.	Minimum.	Difference.	Depth in inches.	Approximate duration.	Depth in inches.	Approximate duration.	Depth in Inches.	Approximate duration.
1	49.4	0.439	83	29.624	29.185	0.5	N 17 E	2.6	3.6	68.5	55.8	12.7	...	...	...	...	...	...
2	Sunday						S 83 E	6.3	7.1	68.0	52.8	15.2	0.380	5.0	...	...	0.380	5.0
3	57.5	.436	92	.312	28.876	0.8	S 23 E	4.3	7.0	62.6	55.5	7.1	.340	6.0	...	...	.340	6.0
4	56.8	.385	84	.309	29.014	0.8	N 11 W	7.6	8.5	62.8	52.4	10.4	...	...	...	...	...	...
5	54.5	.316	74	.799	.483	0.8	N 32 E	3.9	4.0	58.4	51.2	7.2	...	...	...	...	...	...
6	54.8	.311	72	.980	.669	1.0	N 47 E	4.0	4.7	59.5	49.0	10.5	...	...	...	...	...	...
7	50.5	.289	78	30.022	.733	0.2	N 54 E	4.5	6.2	58.0	44.6	13.4	...	...	...	...	...	...
8	42.7	.301	76	29.975	.674	0.2	N 49 W	2.8	4.8	63.5	40.2	23.3	...	...	...	...	...	...
9	Sunday						S 51 W	2.6	3.8	64.0	43.4	20.0	...	...	...	...	...	...
10	55.1	.371	85	.671	.300	0.8	S 62 E	1.3	1.7	62.5	43.4	19.1	.100	2.5	...	...	.100	2.5
11	59.2	.414	82	.306	28.892	0.8	S 27 W	3.8	4.4	67.4	53.2	14.2	.050	3.0	...	...	.050	3.0
12	54.0	.346	82	.266	28.920	0.4	S 60 W	4.6	4.9	61.8	51.4	10.4	.105	2.0	...	...	.105	2.0
13	49.2	.268	77	.378	.110	0.5	West	7.2	7.8	58.2	39.4	18.8	.010	0.5	...	...	.010	0.5
14	50.5	.293	80	.571	.275	0.7	S 37 W	3.7	4.0	60.0	38.4	21.6	.040	4.0	...	...	.040	4.0
15	57.7	.368	77	.682	.313	0.8	S 36 W	4.5	5.0	65.5	46.6	18.9	...	...	...	...	...	...
16	Sunday						S 41 W	8.8	9.1	66.8	53.0	13.8	...	...	...	...	...	...
17	60.0	.436	87	.501	.155	1.0	S 78 W	7.4	8.5	63.0	54.8	8.2	.225	14.5	...	...	.225	14.5
18	42.2	.191	71	.649	.455	0.3	N 38 W	12.7	12.9	49.0	41.0	8.0	...	...	...	...	...	...
19	42.7	.208	75	.478	.270	0.7	S 44 E	1.6	5.8	51.5	30.2	21.3	.250	12.0	...	...	.250	12.0
20	43.6	.237	80	.105	28.868	0.8	N 72 W	5.2	6.4	51.2	40.0	11.2	.005	0.4	...	...	.015	0.4
21	44.0	.238	82	.359	29.121	0.3	S 43 W	4.5	4.8	55.0	35.0	20.0	.005	0.3	...	...	.005	0.3
22	42.1	.208	70	.815	.607	0.1	N 84 W	6.0	8.9	54.0	33.8	20.2	...	...	...	...	...	...
23	Sunday						N 85 E	6.7	7.1	52.0	34.2	17.8	...	...	...	...	...	...
24	51.5	.297	78	.803	.506	0.7	S 42 W	6.3	6.5	62.0	38.8	23.2	...	...	...	...	...	...
25	47.4	.280	84	.604	.414	0.8	N 30 W	7.0	8.9	60.8	46.8	14.0	.110	4.0	...	...	.110	4.0
26	58.8	.167	70	.959	.822	0.4	S 73 E	8.8	9.8	41.7	34.0	10.7	...	...	...	...	...	...
27	48.9	.286	81	.533	.247	0.8	N 81 W	8.0	10.7	66.0	36.6	29.4	R	3.2	...	...	R	3.2
28	43.9	.211	74	.701	.490	0.7	N 65 W	5.7	6.1	50.6	38.2	12.4	R	0.2	...	...	R	0.2
29	41.0	.166	65	.841	.675	0.3	N 25 W	6.2	6.7	49.0	35.2	13.8	...	...	...	...	...	...
30	Sunday						S 40 E	6.1	15.6	48.0	31.8	16.2	.930	6.4	...	...	.930	6.4
31	41.1	.203	78	.369	.167	0.5	West	14.2	14.7	47.2	38.0	9.2	.040	1.7	...	...	.040	1.7
	50.0	0.295	79	29.612	29.317	0.4	N 85 W	1.9	7.1	58.4	43.2	15.2	2.690	65.7	...	...	2.690	65.7

TORONTO.
GENERAL METEOROLOGICAL ABSTRACT, NOVEMBER, 1870.

Days	DAILY MEANS.						WIND.			EXTREMES OF TEMPERATURE.			RAIN.		SNOW.		TOTAL FALL.	
	Temperature of Air.	Pressure of Vapour.	Rel. Humid.	Barometric Pressure.	Pressure of Dry Air.	Clouded Sky.	Resultant Direction.	Resultant Velocity.	Mean Velocity.	Maximum.	Minimum.	Difference.	Depth in inches.	Approximate duration.	Depth in inches.	Approximate duration.	Depth in inches.	Approximate duration.
1	42.9	0.213	77	29.501	29.288	0.2	S 25 W	5.8	6.0	51.8	37.5	14.3	...	...	...	...	...	...
2	40.6	.254	71	.266	.012	0.2	S 30 W	6.6	8.0	57.2	34.5	22.7	...	...	...	...	...	...
3	42.1	.176	67	.492	.316	0.3	N 67 W	12.4	12.6	50.2	37.8	12.4	...	...	...	...	...	...
4	41.2	.209	86	.607	.397	0.8	S 51 W	3.2	4.1	50.0	30.0	20.0	...	...	...	...	...	...
5	40.8	.170	68	.860	.690	0.0	N 9 W	9.7	11.2	48.8	37.4	11.4	...	...	...	...	...	...
6	Sunday						N 67 E	4.7	6.4	43.8	30.5	13.3	...	...	...	...	...	...
7	37.7	.169	75	.890	.720	0.7	S 74 E	2.8	5.8	44.5	30.2	14.3	...	...	...	...	...	...
8	18.4	.291	84	.361	.070	1.0	S 15 W	7.2	9.0	56.4	35.0	21.4	0.424	13.5	...	...	0.424	13.5
9	44.4	.244	60	.365	.121	0.8	N 88 W	16.1	17.1	53.5	45.0	8.5	.090	2.3	0.1	2.0	.100	4.3
10	33.9	.137	71	.977	.840	0.2	N 65 W	5.2	5.2	43.0	29.8	13.2	...	...	...	...	...	...
11	34.1	.160	81	.772	.612	0.5	S 30 E	2.4	3.6	42.2	23.2	19.0	...	...	...	...	...	...
12	38.6	.193	82	.523	.330	0.4	N 88 W	2.6	3.8	48.8	28.2	20.0	...	...	...	...	...	...
13	Sunday						N 74 W	7.8	8.1	49.8	31.0	18.8	.060	2.0	...	...	.060	2.0
14	34.0	.170	88	.360	.181	0.7	N 36 W	4.7	5.7	38.8	34.0	4.8	.020	2.5	...	...	.020	2.5
15	32.0	.136	76	.399	.263	0.6	N 81 W	5.5	5.8	41.0	27.0	14.0	...	...	S	S	S	S
16	34.6	.138	69	.522	.384	0.0	S 61 W	9.1	9.2	42.2	25.2	17.0	...	...	...	...	...	...
17	38.9	.195	82	.507	.402	1.0	S 52 W	10.4	14.2	43.4	31.2	12.2	R	0.5	...	...	R	0.5
18	29.2	.125	80	.657	.532	0.9	N 41 W	14.8	15.2	33.5	27.5	6.0	...	...	S	2.0	S	2.0
19	27.6	.118	78	.630	.513	0.0	N 68 W	8.6	10.6	38.0	20.8	17.2	...	...	...	...	...	...
20	Sunday						S 44 W	11.3	11.9	43.4	23.8	19.0	...	...	...	...	...	...
21	30.4	.140	81	.787	.647	0.7	N 47 W	9.1	9.9	37.8	32.4	5.4	...	...	...	...	...	...
22	27.4	.131	86	.658	.527	0.9	N 54 E	13.6	14.3	35.0	19.4	15.0	...	...	3.0	11.5	.300	11.5
23	28.4	.134	85	.367	.234	1.0	N 72 W	10.4	11.9	34.2	25.2	9.0	...	...	S	1.0	R	1.0
24	34.2	.163	83	.620	.457	0.6	S 63 W	7.0	7.1	40.8	24.4	16.4	...	...	...	...	...	...
25	33.2	.156	82	.481	.325	0.3	S 46 W	8.9	9.0	40.7	26.4	14.3	...	...	...	...	...	...
26	36.8	.182	83	.245	.063	0.8	S 51 W	10.6	10.7	41.0	28.2	12.8	...	...	...	...	...	...
27	Sunday						S 63 W	4.9	4.9	50.8	36.0	14.8	...	...	...	...	...	...
28	39.4	.213	86	.661	.448	0.7	N 46 E	4.3	4.9	44.0	31.5	12.5	R	2.0	...	...	R	2.0
29	37.1	.164	73	.840	.676	0.7	N 8 W	7.0	7.1	41.8	36.8	5.0	...	...	...	...	...	...
30	33.6	.154	79	.957	.803	0.4	S 50 W	7.8	8.8	37.8	25.4	12.4	...	...	...	...	...	...
	36.6	0.175	79	29.592	29.417	0.6	N 89 W	4.4	8.7	44.2	30.2	14.0	0.594	22.8	3.1	16.5	0.904	39.3

TORONTO.
GENERAL METEOROLOGICAL ABSTRACT, DECEMBER, 1870.

	DAILY MEANS.					WIND.			EXTREMES OF TEMPERATURE				RAIN.		SNOW.		TOTAL FALL.	
Days	Temperature of Air	Pressure of Vapour	Rel. Humid.	Barometric Pressure	Pressure of Dry Air	Clouded Sky	Resultant Direction	Resultant Velocity	Mean Velocity	Maximum	Minimum	Difference	Depth in inches	Approximate duration	Depth in inches	Approximate duration	Depth in inches	Approximate duration
1	7.8	.157	69	29.514	29.356	1.0	S 58 W	7.1	7.2	13.0	3.2	12.8	...	...	...	...	...	...
2	7.8	.167	74	.381	.213	0.5	N 84 W	10.7	11.1	45.0	29.5	15.5	...	...	...	...	...	...
3	37.0	.177	78	.526	.349	0.7	S 59 W	6.1	6.8	44.0	30.0	14.0	...	...	...	...	...	...
4	Sunday						N 82 W	1.5	5.3	45.0	34.5	10.5	...	...	...	...	...	...
5	38.30	.219	94	.154	28.935	1.0	S 83 E	8.1	15.5	45.2	32.8	12.7	1.950	14.3	...	...	1.950	14.3
6	31.9	.173	85	.385	29.212	0.8	N 58 W	11.8	12.0	39.8	13.0	6.2	...	...	...	...	...	...
7	36.5	.187	87	.297	.110	1.0	S 65 E	2.7	11.8	42.2	27.8	14.4	.180	12.0	...	...	.180	12.0
8	22.	.154	85	.504	.351	1.0	N 35 W	16.7	16.8	35.0	21.5	3.5	...	...	S	0.2	S	0.2
9	27.3	.129	84	.831	.762	1.0	N 7 W	5.9	6.0	30.0	26.5	3.5	...	...	...	...	...	...
10	26.7	.129	87	30.004	.878	0.7	N 19 W	6.6	7.4	31.5	26.2	5.2	...	...	...	...	...	...
11	Sunday						N 68 E	14.2	14.7	34.0	18.0	16.0	...	...	6.0	8.7	.600	8.5
12	36.5	.200	95	29.580	.374	1.0	S 40 E	7.9	9.1	39.8	20.4	19.4	.200	10.5	0.1	1.0	.270	11.5
13	35.5	.184	87	.476	.292	1.0	S 59 W	7.6	7.8	39.5	34.4	5.1	.040	3.5	0.2	2.5	.060	6.0
14	31.3	.151	85	.415	.294	1.0	N 76 W	18.1	19.1	35.0	30.0	5.0	...	...	...	...	...	...
15	21.2	.095	81	.784	.689	0.7	N 45 W	12.4	13.1	26.2	19.4	6.8	...	...	0.2	6.0	.020	6.0
16	22.1	.095	78	.848	.750	0.8	N 67 W	18.0	10.0	28.0	15.4	12.6	...	...	S	3.0	S	3.0
17	29.7	.133	82	.480	.352	0.9	S 71 W	11.1	12.2	32.5	20.0	12.5	...	...	0.3	1.5	.030	1.5
18	Sunday						N 18 E	2.2	4.2	30.5	21.4	8.1	...	...	S	1.5	S	1.5
19	31.5	.151	83	.315	.164	1.0	S 36 E	6.0	11.0	36.0	26.0	10.0	R	1.5	2.0	8.0	.200	8.0
20	32.5	.151	82	.122	28.970	1.0	S 65 W	13.0	13.1	35.0	27.0	9.0	...	...	0.1	2.0	.010	2.0
21	15.6	.069	73	.593	29.524	0.4	S 67 W	17.6	17.6	22.5	18.4	4.4	...	...	...	...	...	...
22	1.5	.027	77	.777	.726	0.2	S 78 W	10.7	11.1	18.0	7.0	11.0	...	...	...	...	...	...
23	10.6	.050	77	.758	.602	0.5	S 88 W	10.2	10.8	15.2	6.4	8.8	...	...	...	...	...	...
24	8.0	.035	85	.829	.773	0.6	N 45 W	6.0	6.3	16.0	1.4	12.2	...	...	0.2	2.0	.020	2.0
25	Sunday						S 40 W	13.7	11.7	20.5	5.0	15.5	...	...	2.0	16.0	.200	16.0
26	...	...	...	...	...	...	S 62 W	16.5	16.0	34.2	14.2	10.0	...	...	...	...	...	...
27	21.8	.091	77	.561	.467	0.7	S 60 W	14.2	15.7	28.2	19.4	17.8	...	...	0.2	2.0	.020	2.0
28	11.1	.046	81	.563	.498	0.6	N 16 W	13.4	13.6	20.0	13.0	7.0	...	...	0.1	2.5	.010	2.5
29	0.7	.037	85	.665	.628	0.1	N 65 W	5.3	8.1	20.5	-5.8	20.3	...	...	...	...	...	...
30	27.9	.125	86	.199	28.965	1.0	S 16 W	13.9	15.7	35.8	-0.2	30.0	R	0.3	4.0	12.5	.490	12.9
31	25.1	.131	81	.380	29.255	1.0	N 73 W	8.0	9.7	30.2	25.8	4.4	...	...	0.6	6.5	.050	6.5
	20.5	0.129	82	29.532	29.193	0.8	S 89 W	5.0	11.5	32.0	20.5	11.5	2.430	43.1	15.0	76.3	4.020	110.4

TORONTO.
General Meteorological Abstract, January, 1871.

Days	DAILY MEANS.						WIND.			EXTREMES OF TEMPERATURE.			RAIN.		SNOW.		TOTAL FALL.	
	Temperature of Air.	Pressure of Vapour.	Hel. Humid.	Barometric Pressure.	Pressure of Dry Air.	Clouded Sky.	Resultant Direction.	Resultant Velocity.	Mean Velocity.	Maximum.	Minimum.	Difference.	Depth in inches.	Approximate duration.	Depth in inches.	Approximate duration.	Depth in inches.	Approximate duration.
1	Sunday						S 54 W	10.2	11.4	37.5	23.0	14.5	...	...	S	1.0	S	1.0
2	26.8	0.106	72	29.425	29.319	0.5	S 71 W	20.8	21.2	35.2	26.0	12.2	...	...	0.2	1.0	0.020	1.0
3	14.6	.071	79	.625	.554	0.4	S 85 W	12.3	13.4	34.6	14.2	9.4	...	...	0.5	3.5	.050	3.5
4	12.7	.069	86	.746	.677	0.7	S 31 W	5.7	9.4	35.0	0.4	34.6	...	...	2.5	5.0	.250	5.0
5	30.4	.149	69	.158	.008	0.9	S 49 W	14.7	15.2	41.4	10.6	30.8	R	0.5	S	3.0	R	3.5
6	21.9	.093	75	.580	.441	0.5	N 77 W	10.5	12.4	30.4	25.8	4.6	...	...	0.1	1.2	.010	1.2
7	12.7	.071	86	.845	.774	0.6	S 64 E	2.8	6.3	21.0	1.2	9.8	...	...	0.3	4.0	.030	4.0
8	Sunday						N 36 E	10.1	12.6	22.2	15.0	7.2	...	...	6.5	7.8	.050	7.8
9	14.9	.006	77	30.022	.956	0.9	N 74 W	2.1	4.6	3.6	-0.8	23.8	...	...	...	...	...	...
10	24.9	.110	85	29.748	.633	1.0	S 28 E	9.3	10.6	31.5	13.1	21.1	...	...	4.5	8.0	.450	8.0
11	26.0	.102	80	.509	.377	1.0	S 20 E	1.9	2.0	39.0	23.0	16.0	...	...	...	...	...	...
12	39.2	.211	81	.854	.643	0.6	N 65 E	3.5	3.7	44.2	34.8	9.7	...	...	...	...	...	...
13	30.7	.210	84	.956	.738	0.5	N 12 E	3.3	5.8	46.3	32.0	14.4	...	...	...	...	...	...
14	32.2	.150	80	30.000	.847	1.0	N 31 E	11.0	12.0	37.3	34.5	2.9	0.050	4.5	...	...	.056	4.5
15	Sunday						N 17 W	8.4	10.0	33.8	24.8	9.0	.400	11.0	0.2	1.0	.420	12.0
16	17.3	.088	87	29.740	.657	1.0	N 46 W	11.4	11.7	9.7	13.2	6.5	...	...	2.5	7.1	.250	7.1
17	19.3	.090	88	.859	.768	0.8	S 78 W	4.7	6.0	23.8	5.9	20.5	...	...	0.1	3.5	.010	3.5
18	19.5	.089	84	30.128	30.037	0.8	N 34 E	7.4	8.2	31.0	29.0	4.0	...	...	S	9.5	S	9.5
19	25.0	.110	84	30.077	29.961	0.7	S 56 E	2.4	4.6	31.4	15.2	16.2	...	...	0.1	5.0	.010	5.0
20	32.6	.108	88	29.767	29.604	1.0	S 57 W	5.7	6.3	36.2	22.5	13.7	R	2.0	...	...	R	2.0
21	27.3	.130	83	.479	.349	0.8	N 48 W	10.1	12.5	32.5	29.0	3.5	...	...	4.0	13.5	4.0	13.5
22	Sunday						N 11 W	7.0	8.2	0.8	-6.8	7.6	...	...	...	...	...	...
23	-5.7	.032	90	.787	.755	1.0	N 23 E	14.7	14.7	1.0	-13.2	14.2	...	...	4.5	14.0	.450	14.0
24	10.3	.062	84	.848	.786	0.5	N 60 W	3.3	5.7	20.0	-6.7	20.7	...	...	S	1.0	S	1.0
25	-1.6	.033	84	30.310	30.281	1.4	N 20 E	14.2	15.0	4.0	-7.4	12.0	...	...	5.0	11.0	.500	11.0
26	2.4	.040	91	29.858	29.812	1.0	N 22 E	8.7	11.7	18.7	-7.8	26.5	...	...	6.0	13.5	.600	13.5
27	18.7	.077	75	.711	.634	0.8	N 87 W	9.2	11.4	37.2	3.7	23.5	...	...	0.1	2.0	.010	2.0
28	11.0	.057	79	.772	.714	0.5	N 46 E	12.0	13.0	20.0	6.8	13.2	...	...	6.0	17.5	.600	17.5
29	Sunday						S 46 W	5.7	8.4	33.2	6.0	27.2	...	...	0.3	3.0	.030	3.0
30	30.7	.158	91	.686	.528	1.0	S 89 E	3.6	4.2	34.2	26.4	7.8	.100	6.5	0.2	3.5	.120	10.0
31	36.4	.194	91	.225	.029	0.9	S 62 W	8.9	10.9	12.2	31.3	10.8	.314	4.0	...	...	.314	4.0
	21.3	0.110	84	29.759	29.649	0.8	N 49 W	2.6	9.8	23.4	13.4	15.0	0.864	25.5	43.6	140.2	5.224	109.7

TORONTO.
GENERAL METEOROLOGICAL ABSTRACT, FEBRUARY, 1871.

Days.	DAILY MEANS.					WIND.			EXTREMES OF TEMPERATURE.			RAIN.		SNOW.		TOTAL FALL.	
	Temperature of Air.	Pressure of Vapour.	Rel Humid.	Barometric Pressure.	Pressure of Dry Air.	Clouded Sky.	Resultant Direction.	Resultant Velocity.	Mean Velocity.	Maximum.	Minimum.	Difference.	Depth in inches.	Approximate duration.	Depth in inches.	Approximate duration.	Depth in inches.	Approximate duration.
1	31.5	.144	80	29.625	29.481	1.0	S 44 W	6.0	7.5	34.4	29.0	5.4	...	...	...	...	...	...
2	26.6	.115	75	.510	.395	0.7	N 74 W	16.3	18.4	37.3	28.0	9.2	...	...	0.3	2.5	0.030	2.5
3	30.0	.117	69	.304	.187	0.9	N 85 W	21.3	23.7	38.6	15.4	23.2	...	...	...	...	...	...
4	3.5	.041	72	.717	.677	0.7	N 14 W	13.5	13.7	17.2	1.5	15.7	...	...	...	...	...	...
5	Sunday						N 1 W	9.5	9.5	-1.2	-15.8	14.0	...	...	...	...	...	...
6	5.8	.04	78	.998	.952	0.5	N 4 W	6.0	6.7	14.6	-5.4	20.0	...	...	...	...	...	...
7	20.4	.090	84	.525	.728	1.0	N 68 E	9.1	9.7	29.8	8.0	21.8	...	...	0.3	4.5	.030	4.5
8	30.0	.119	88	.572	.423	1.0	S 49 E	1.5	2.2	34.8	20.1	14.7	...	...	1.0	4.0	.100	4.0
9	30.4	.145	81	.457	.292	1.0	S 73 W	13.8	15.4	37.0	30.9	6.1	...	...	1.5	8.0	.150	8.0
10	18.4	.075	75	.881	.809	0.7	S 80 W	16.0	16.1	22.0	16.8	5.2	...	...	0.1	2.0	.010	2.0
11	17.8	.068	70	.037	.960	0.7	N 58 W	2.9	6.7	23.4	16.0	7.4	...	...	0.1	1.0	.010	1.0
12	Sunday						N 21 E	10.7	11.8	19.2	12.2	7.0	...	...	6.0	17.5	.600	17.5
13	14.2	.069	82	.809	.631	0.5	S 59 W	0.1	3.4	22.5	4.5	18.0	...	...	...	...	...	...
14	20.3	.09	82	.695	.604	0.9	N 58 W	3.9	5.3	24.8	12.2	12.6	...	...	...	...	...	...
15	27.8	.128	81	.535	.410	0.9	S 23 E	5.4	9.3	38.8	11.8	27.0	...	...	...	...	...	...
16	32.9	.129	69	.528	.39	0.4	N 81 W	10.2	10.6	38.5	31.0	7.5	...	...	0.1	1.0	.010	0.1
17	29.9	.142	81	.414	.272	0.7	E	5.2	6.5	34.5	23.4	11.1	0.040	0.5	12.0	10.7	1.240	11.2
18	24.9	.110	79	.106	28.99	0.6	N 63 W	12.7	13.3	36.0	21.4	11.4	...	...	1.0	3.0	.100	3.0
19	Sunday						S 70 W	8.2	9.1	32.8	15.0	17.8	...	...	8	1.5	8	1.5
20	21.8	.092	76	.716	29.024	1.0	N 17 W	6.9	7.3	29.4	23.0	6.4	...	...	8	1.5	8	1.5
21	14.3	.065	77	.940	.855	0.2	N 22 E	3.3	3.0	22.4	7.2	15.2	...	...	...	...	...	...
22	19.1	.080	78	.055	.971	0.5	N 68 E	6.1	6.5	26.5	10.0	16.5	...	...	8	1.5	8	1.5
23	29.3	.132	79	.790	.658	0.8	N 79 E	3.6	4.0	10.2	16.4	23.8	...	...	...	...	...	...
24	12.4	.217	80	.271	.057	0.4	S 56 W	11.4	12.8	18.0	30.0	18.0	R	0.2	...	...	8	0.2
25	35.7	.137	60	.473	.33	0.0	S 82 W	6.3	7.0	41.2	35.8	5.4	...	...	...	...	...	...
26	Sunday						N 2 E	5.9	9.3	16.8	30.0	6.8	R	5.0	0.3	9.5	.030	13.5
27	26.3	.107	74	.359	.232	1.0	N 66 W	15.2	15.8	29.6	26.4	3.2	...	...	0.3	0.9	.030	0.9
28	30.4	.122	72	.542	.420	0.8	S 19 W	8.3	10.9	41.0	21.9	19.1	...	...	...	...	...	...
	21.3	0.109	77	29.631	29.522	0.7	N 70 W	4.3	9.9	30.4	17.0	13.4	0.040	5.7	23.0	03.1	2.340	74.8

TORONTO.
GENERAL METEOROLOGICAL ABSTRACT, MARCH, 1871.

Days.	DAILY MEANS.						WIND.			EXTREMES OF TEMPERATURE.			RAIN.		SNOW.		TOTAL FALL.	
	Temperature of Air.	Pressure of Vapour.	Rel. Humid.	Barometric Pressure.	Pressure of Dry Air.	Clouded Sky.	Resultant Direction.	Resultant Velocity.	Mean Velocity.	Maximum.	Minimum.	Difference.	Depth in inches.	Approximate duration.	Depth in inches.	Approximate duration.	Depth in inches.	Approximate duration.
1	31.1	0.114	58	29.494	29.380	0.9	S 89 W	10.4	12.1	38.8	30.0	8.8	...	...	1.5	3.0	0.150	3.0
2	33.2	.169	88	.473	.304	1.0	N 57 E	4.8	5.4	38.8	26.8	12.0	.060	9.7	8	0.2	.600	9.9
3	29.9	.144	85	.404	.259	0.5	N 43 W	11.4	11.5	39.4	27.0	11.4	.150	4.0	0.2	1.5	.170	5.5
4	23.8	.130	81	.669	.539	0.5	S 41 W	2.1	2.8	34.5	19.7	14.8	...	...	...	...	...	...
5	Sunday						N 35 E	1.4	3.4	40.0	28.0	12.0	...	...	...	...	...	...
6	33.6	.155	80	.664	.509	0.6	N 57 W	13.7	13.8	40.8	32.4	8.4	...	...	...	...	...	...
7	33.1	.144	76	.664	.520	0.8	N 87 E	5.2	6.0	38.8	23.3	15.5	...	...	...	...	...	...
8	42.2	200	74	.463	.263	0.8	N 56 E	6.0	6.2	47.4	32.4	15.0	...	...	...	...	...	...
9	45.0	.233	78	.323	.090	0.8	S 26 E	3.4	9.0	58.7	39.0	19.5	.060	4.7	...	...	.060	4.7
10	42.3	.158	60	.576	.418	0.5	S 31 W	7.7	8.1	51.0	36.4	14.0	...	...	...	...	...	...
11	38.1	.195	81	.578	.383	1.0	N 2 E	5.3	6.8	45.0	33.0	12.0	1.050	16.5	1.0	2.0	1.150	18.5
12	Sunday						N 51 W	10.7	11.2	41.2	33.4	7.8	...	...	0.0	4.7	.060	4.7
13	32.4	.154	83	.502	.478	0.5	S 52 W	1.9	4.5	40.0	26.8	13.2	...	...	0.2	4.0	.020	4.0
14	32.0	.130	72	.775	.645	0.7	N 69 E	5.2	6.2	38.0	24.4	13.0	...	...	1.5	4.8	.150	4.3
15	32.8	.166	89	.651	.485	1.0	N 68 E	12.6	12.0	34.4	30.4	4.0	.570	12.0	...	...	.570	12.0
16	37.2	.205	91	.437	.232	1.0	N 62 E	4.7	5.7	41.8	31.0	13.2	.294	12.0	...	...	.294	12.6
17	38.5	.194	82	.469	.275	1.0	S 84 W	7.4	8.0	43.0	36.8	6.2	.008	2.5	...	...	.008	2.5
18	36.8	.169	76	.683	.531	0.4	N 41 W	2.1	8.0	44.0	30.8	13.2	...	...	...	...	...	...
19	Sunday						N 60 E	8.9	11.8	35.5	26.0	9.9	...	...	...	...	...	...
20	39.0	.179	73	.491	.392	1.0	N 69 E	5.5	12.7	43.4	28.2	20.2	.050	2.0	...	...	.050	2.0
21	34.1	.141	72	.327	.185	1.0	S 87 W	13.0	13.8	38.0	34.0	3.4	...	...	S	0.1	S	0.1
22	30.9	.131	78	.455	.321	1.0	N 85 W	7.3	8.7	35.0	25.4	6.0	...	...	2.0	7.8	.200	7.8
23	25.7	.117	84	.444	.327	0.7	N 58 W	6.7	8.5	29.8	23.8	6.0	...	...	0.2	8.0	.020	8.0
24	27.8	.104	70	.768	.663	0.2	N 73 W	9.0	9.8	39.5	17.0	21.8	...	...	...	...	...	...
25	33.4	.110	58	.853	.743	0.0	N 61 W	2.4	5.4	42.0	25.4	16.0	...	...	...	...	...	...
26	Sunday						N 68 E	10.9	11.5	37.2	26.0	11.2	...	...	5.0	10.8	.500	10.5
27	34.2	.155	79	.305	.150	1.0	N 42 W	11.0	11.1	39.2	30.0	8.0	...	...	0.8	3.9	.086	3.9
28	33.1	.123	60	.727	.604	0.5	N 41 W	6.7	7.2	40.5	27.4	13.1	...	...	...	...	...	...
29	34.5	.144	72	.753	.610	0.3	S 52 E	2.3	3.7	42.2	22.5	19.7	...	...	...	...	...	...
30	39.9	.162	66	.622	.460	0.9	N 19 W	7.0	8.0	49.4	32.0	17.4	...	...	...	...	...	...
31	32.8	.133	72	.710	.578	0.3	N 44 E	1.4	3.4	40.0	30.0	9.4	...	...	...	...	...	...
	34.6	0.154	76	29.569	29.415	0.7	N 31 W	2.6	8.3	41.1	28.9	12.2	2.782	64.0	13.0	49.8	4.082	113.5

TORONTO.
GENERAL METEOROLOGICAL ABSTRACT, APRIL, 1871.

	DAILY MEANS.					WIND.				EXTREMES OF TEMPERATURE			RAIN.		SNOW.		TOTAL FALL.	
Days.	Temperature of Air	Pressure of Vapour.	R-l. Humid.	Barometric Pressure.	Pressure of Dry Air.	Clouded Sky	Resultant Direction.	Resultant Velocity.	Mean Velocity.	Maximum.	Minimum.	Difference.	Depth in inches	Approximate duration	Depth in inches	Approximate duration	Depth in Inches.	Approximate duration.
1	13.3	0.159	8.	29.43	29.274	0.9	N 48 E	5.8	8.1	35.8	26.8	9.0	0.040	1.5	1.2	7.0	0.160	8.5
2	Sunday						N 73 E	4.6	7.4	41.5	30.2	11.3	.070	6.5	...	...	.070	6.5
3	41.1	.222	8.	.22	.002	0.8	N 21 W	5.0	7.7	45.8	33.4	12.4	.165	6.0	...	...	.165	6.0
4	14.5	.170	70	.425	.250	0.7	N 76 W	10.4	19.0	51.5	31.0	30.5	...	...	...	...	...	...
5	32.2	.114	52	.704	.593	0.7	N 2 W	1.0	5.5	40.8	26.4	14.4	...	...	...	...	...	...
6	36.8	.141	67	.51	.373	0.4	N 69 E	5.5	6.7	49.0	28.4	20.6	...	...	...	...	...	...
7	...	...	...	...	...	...	4 30 W	5.5	6.2	64.8	33.5	31.3	...	...	...	...	...	...
8	58.2	.399	3	.493	.124	0.6	S 39 W	7.2	7.5	72.8	47.0	25.8	...	...	...	...	...	...
9	Sunday						S 74 W	9.0	12.1	72.4	49.4	23.0	...	...	...	...	...	...
10	39.7	.175	72	.551	.376	0.4	N 85 E	8.1	10.1	52.2	31.2	21.0	.510	11.6	...	...	.510	11.6
11	42.8	.209	75	.090	28.881	0.5	S 61 W	7.5	13.2	53.2	36.0	17.2	.080	3.0	...	...	.080	3.0
12	41.8	.154	59	.251	29.097	0.6	S 84 W	11.9	12.4	52.5	36.0	16.5	R	0.2	0.1	0.5	.010	0.7
13	42.9	.177	71	.317	.140	0.4	N 60 W	4.0	5.5	51.4	31.5	20.9	.100	1.5	...	...	.100	1.5
14	37.4	.147	66	.373	.225	0.6	N 46 W	6.4	8.8	47.0	28.4	18.8	...	...	...	...	...	...
15	37.0	.130	60	.430	.360	0.8	N 43 W	10.5	10.9	41.2	33.0	11.2	...	...	...	...	...	...
16	Sunday						N 53 W	6.3	8.4	47.4	27.2	20.2	...	...	...	...	...	...
17	42.3	.150	55	.731	.584	0.1	N 42 W	6.0	9.1	52.2	32.0	20.2	...	...	...	...	...	...
18	44.7	.148	50	.680	.532	0.3	N 74 E	13.8	11.0	51.0	43.4	17.6	R	1.0	...	...	R	1.0
19	45.3	.231	83	.334	.082	0.7	N 70 E	13.0	13.9	50.6	41.8	8.8	.040	6.3	...	...	.040	6.3
20	51.4	.251	60	.237	28.986	0.9	S 70 W	5.5	7.3	63.0	41.0	22.0	R	0.4	...	...	R	0.4
21	43.2	.215	77	.570	29.455	0.9	S 74 W	2.8	3.2	50.0	40.0	10.0	.008	7.0	...	...	.008	7.0
22	40.4	.199	79	.517	.310	0.8	N 72 W	11.3	11.0	46.0	28.4	7.6	.010	3.2	...	...	.010	3.2
23	Sunday						N 65 W	10.7	11.9	54.4	32.0	22.4	...	...	...	...	...	...
24	43.6	.155	55	.960	.891	0.6	S 89 E	4.4	5.3	52.8	38.4	14.4	...	...	...	...	...	...
25	46.5	.214	65	.663	.449	0.6	N 25 W	2.4	4.9	58.0	37.6	20.4	.070	2.7	...	...	.070	2.7
26	46.3	.141	45	.715	.574	0.5	N 74 E	13.5	13.7	54.0	36.0	18.0	.520	4.5	...	...	.520	4.5
27	45.7	.304	94	.357	.050	1.0	N 69 E	8.6	9.0	51.8	40.4	11.4	1.025	12.5	...	...	1.025	12.5
28	48.8	.252	74	.304	.051	0.8	S 25 W	5.2	6.4	59.0	42.8	16.2	R	0.2	...	...	R	0.2
29	46.1	.273	87	.307	.031	1.0	S 24 W	3.2	3.8	52.0	42.2	10.4	.080	8.6	...	...	.080	8.0
30	Sunday						N 75 W	3.1	4.9	56.0	42.0	13.4	...	...	...	...	...	...
	42.9	0.194	68	29.458	29.264	0.7	N 48 W	1.9	8.8	52.8	35.6	17.2	3.318	76.1	1.3	7.5	3.448	83.6

TORONTO.
GENERAL METEOROLOGICAL ABSTRACT, MAY, 1871.

Days.	DAILY MEANS.						WIND.			EXTREMES OF TEMPERATURE			RAIN.		SNOW.		TOTAL FALL.	
	Temperature of Air.	Pressure of Vapour.	Rel. Humid.	Barometric Pressure.	Pressure of Dry Air.	Clouded Sky.	Resultant Direction.	Resultant Velocity.	Mean Velocity.	Maximum.	Minimum.	Difference.	Depth in inches.	Approximate duration.	Depth in inches.	Approximate duration.	Depth in inches.	Approximate duration.
1	50.1	0.245	67	29.556	29.311	0.6	S 79 W	1.3	4.4	59.0	42.2	16.8	...	...	...	...	...	...
2	52.0	.259	66	.659	.380	0.8	N 79 E	10.4	10.8	58.2	42.0	16.2	...	...	...	...	...	...
3	49.7	.195	51	.606	.421	1.0	N 65 E	17.6	17.7	58.0	48.6	9.4	0.012	8.0	...	...	0.012	8.0
4	43.1	.259	93	.437	.177	1.0	N 61 E	20.3	20.3	45.0	39.0	6.6	1.500	17.9	...	...	1.500	17.9
5	41.6	.205	90	.399	.195	1.0	N 49 E	3.7	4.8	48.8	49.6	8.2	.010	4.0	...	...	.010	4.0
6	46.3	.229	70	.429	.200	0.7	N 37 W	13.5	14.0	54.0	43.2	10.8	R	1.0	...	...	R	1.0
7	Sunday						N 55 W	15.2	15.5	52.8	36.0	16.8	...	...	...	...	...	...
8	41.3	.160	62	.575	.415	0.5	N 52 W	11.2	11.4	49.2	33.2	17.0	...	...	...	...	...	...
9	44.8	.173	59	.686	.513	0.4	N 40 W	7.5	8.4	53.2	34.0	19.2	...	...	...	...	...	...
10	47.5	.186	57	.710	.524	0.1	N 32 W	8.5	8.6	57.0	36.8	20.2	...	...	...	...	...	...
11	51.7	.246	63	.597	.351	0.2	S 24 W	4.9	5.1	63.0	38.0	25.0	...	...	...	...	...	...
12	57.5	.243	52	.592	.259	0.2	N 13 W	3.4	4.8	58.0	30.4	28.0	...	...	...	...	...	...
13	47.9	.166	49	.677	.511	0.0	N 29 W	8.6	11.3	55.8	44.4	11.4	...	...	...	...	...	...
14	Sunday						N 61 W	6.6	8.4	58.5	37.0	21.5	...	...	...	...	...	...
15	47.7	.186	57	.585	.400	0.2	S 30 W	3.1	3.8	59.2	32.4	26.8	...	...	...	...	...	...
16	54.4	.295	69	.363	.068	0.4	S 73 W	6.6	8.9	66.0	36.4	29.6	.030	2.0	...	...	.030	2.0
17	46.6	.169	54	.651	.482	0.2	N 40 W	11.6	12.6	54.2	41.0	13.2	...	...	...	...	...	...
18	49.1	.230	59	.824	.616	0.2	S 48 E	1.5	1.8	57.5	37.6	19.9	...	...	...	...	...	...
19	55.4	.286	60	.710	.424	0.5	S 16 W	4.6	4.7	68.8	38.0	30.8	...	...	...	...	...	...
20	57.6	.421	62	.636	.215	0.3	S 29 W	3.8	4.3	79.2	47.0	32.2	...	...	...	...	...	...
21	Sunday						S 42 W	2.3	4.0	77.8	55.2	22.6	...	...	...	...	...	...
22	59.9	.275	54	.532	.257	0.6	N 51 W	8.7	10.0	71.2	53.8	17.4	...	...	...	...	...	...
23	51.6	.157	44	.744	.587	0.5	N 34 W	8.1	8.4	61.5	42.0	19.5	...	...	...	...	...	...
24	52.2	.201	51	.904	.703	0.5	S 85 E	2.9	4.6	61.8	37.6	24.2	...	...	...	...	...	...
25	61.4	.404	71	.674	.270	0.7	S 30 W	2.7	5.1	73.2	43.0	30.2	.750	2.5	...	...	.750	2.5
26	57.6	.470	72	.682	.211	0.6	N 87 W	3.5	4.5	79.2	61.0	18.2	...	...	...	...	...	...
27	55.9	.232	51	.795	.563	0.4	N 72 E	5.7	6.4	62.8	53.4	9.4	...	...	...	...	...	...
28	Sunday						S 20 E	1.0	1.9	72.4	45.2	27.2	...	...	...	...	...	...
29	70.7	.562	75	.615	.053	0.1	South.	2.4	3.7	83.0	56.5	26.5	...	...	...	...	...	...
30	74.6	.618	73	.565	28.949	0.8	S 48 W	2.0	3.6	85.0	61.4	23.6	R	R	...	...	R	R
31	70.7	.554	74	.614	29.060	0.5	N 70 E	4.0	5.1	78.8	65.8	13.0	...	...	...	...	...	...
	54.1	0.283	63	29.618	29.335	0.5	N 23 W	2.5	7.7	63.7	43.9	19.8	2.302	35.4	...	...	2.302	35.4

TORONTO.
GENERAL METEOROLOGICAL ABSTRACT, JUNE, 1871.

Days.	DAILY MEANS.					Clouded Sky.	WIND.			EXTREMES OF TEMPERATURE.			RAIN.		SNOW.		TOTAL FALL.	
	Temperature of Air.	Pressure of Vapour.	Rel. Humid.	Barometric Pressure.	Pressure of Dry Air.		Resultant Direction.	Resultant Velocity.	Mean Velocity.	Maximum.	Minimum.	Difference.	Depth in inches.	Approximate duration.	Depth in inches.	Approximate duration.	Depth in inches.	Approximate duration.
1	69.0	0.533	75	29.657	29.124	0.0	S 66 E	2.3	3.1	80.2	59.0	21.2	...	...	...	...	...	...
2	72.0	.58	75	.619	.032	0.2	S 47 E	1.5	2.8	83.0	57.4	25.6	...	...	...	...	...	...
3	72.3	.634	80	.89	28.966	0.6	S 36 W	4.0	5.7	81.6	61.0	20.6	...	...	...	...	...	...
4	Sunday						N 12 W	4.2	6.1	83.0	64.2	18.8	...	...	...	...	...	...
5	67.8	.334	40	.614	.270	0.2	N 74 E	4.3	5.4	73.4	63.8	9.6	...	...	...	...	...	...
6	69.5	.509	71	.380	28.877	0.4	S 43 E	3.4	7.1	75.0	57.2	17.8	0.440	8.5	...	...	0.440	8.5
7	70.0	.473	66	.270	28.803	0.3	S 84 W	8.0	8.3	79.4	66.6	12.8	...	...	...	...	...	...
8	59.0	.314	62	.582	29.217	0.4	N 73 W	12.6	13.1	70.0	55.2	14.8	...	...	...	...	...	...
9	55.6	.309	70	.709	.461	0.4	S 47 W	2.6	5.9	61.6	13.2	20.8	...	...	...	...	...	...
10	61.1	.450	84	.487	.030	0.7	S 28 W	3.2	5.2	73.8	44.2	29.6	.570	1.1	...	...	.570	1.1
11	Sunday						S 86 W	5.1	6.3	73.8	53.6	20.2	R	0.5	...	...	R	0.5
12	56.1	.306	69	.272	28.966	0.5	N 81 W	11.3	12.4	64.2	46.5	17.7	.060	2.5	...	...	.060	2.5
13	53.8	.308	74	.241	28.933	0.4	N 89 W	13.4	13.6	66.0	50.5	15.4	...	...	...	...	...	...
14	56.9	.290	67	.488	29.180	0.6	N 77 W	5.8	6.7	70.4	43.2	27.2	.040	0.2	...	...	.040	0.2
15	54.4	.285	68	.616	.320	0.2	N 12 W	4.4	6.8	65.6	43.8	21.8	.005	2.0	...	...	.005	2.0
16	53.2	.276	68	.727	.452	0.1	N 14 E	0.9	6.8	64.6	42.2	21.8	...	...	...	...	...	...
17	57.3	.259	55	.603	.344	0.8	N 64 E	11.2	11.6	62.8	44.2	18.4	.250	7.0	...	...	.250	7.0
18	Sunday						N 47 E	1.1	3.3	69.5	54.0	15.4	.010	3.0	...	...	.010	3.0
19	65.2	.479	77	.480	.001	0.0	S 55 W	3.0	4.9	77.0	51.4	25.6	...	...	...	...	...	...
20	58.6	.346	69	.565	.219	0.5	N 74 W	5.0	6.4	66.4	55.2	11.2	.220	5.5	...	...	.220	5.5
21	58.9	.309	59	.758	.455	0.5	N 33 W	0.7	4.7	68.0	51.4	16.6	...	...	...	...	...	...
22	61.0	.370	65	.620	.251	0.6	S 36 W	3.5	6.5	70.4	45.8	24.6	...	...	...	...	...	...
23	61.0	.370	67	.589	.219	0.9	N 61 E	2.6	4.8	69.5	55.4	14.1	.505	6.0	...	...	.505	6.0
24	55.9	.350	78	.554	.201	0.7	N 54 E	5.8	7.6	67.8	51.8	16.0	.270	4.5	...	...	.270	4.5
25	Sunday						S 15 W	0.9	2.5	72.8	51.2	21.6	...	...	...	...	...	...
26	63.4	.447	65	.641	.191	0.4	S 24 W	2.5	3.1	77.2	48.8	28.4	...	...	...	...	...	...
27	66.6	.511	78	.463	28.892	0.4	S 47 W	4.5	6.1	78.0	59.0	19.0	.880	1.0	...	...	.880	1.0
28	61.3	.345	65	.312	28.997	0.5	N 69 W	7.4	8.5	73.0	52.4	20.6	...	...	...	...	...	...
29	53.0	.246	63	.582	29.336	0.5	N 47 W	6.7	6.7	60.0	51.8	8.2	R	0.5	...	...	R	0.5
30	56.8	.274	66	.706	.452	0.6	S 31 E	2.8	5.4	65.0	41.2	23.8	...	...	...	...	...	...
31																		
	61.4	0.382	69	29.513	29.161	0.5	N 80 W	2.6	6.6	71.5	52.2	19.0	1.340	42.3	...	...	3.340	42.3

TORONTO.
GENERAL METEOROLOGICAL ABSTRACT, JULY, 1871.

Days	DAILY MEANS.						WIND.			EXTREMES OF TEMPERATURE			RAIN.		SNOW.		TOTAL FALL.	
	Temperature of Air.	Pressure of Vapour.	Rel. Humid.	Barometric Pressure.	Pressure of Dry Air.	Clouded Sky.	Resultant Direction.	Resultant Velocity.	Mean Velocity.	Maximum	Minimum	Difference.	Depth in inches.	Approximate duration.	Depth in inches.	Approximate duration.	Depth in inches.	Approximate duration.
1	64.5	0.394	65	29.577	29.183	0.4	S 15 E	3.8	5.2	73.5	51.2	22.3	...	...	...	...	...	...
2	Sunday						S 63 W	1.3	2.4	78.4	57.2	21.2	...	...	...	...	...	...
3	66.6	.382	59	.625	.246	0.4	E	3.2	5.2	76.4	53.0	23.4	0.100	1.0	...	...	0.100	1.0
4	62.1	.459	82	.357	28.990	0.6	S 54 W	3.0	7.3	72.5	57.8	14.7	.415	3.5	...	...	.415	3.5
5	57.6	.531	79	.551	29.020	0.2	S 17 W	4.7	5.0	76.0	53.2	22.8	...	...	...	...	...	...
6	66.0	.541	83	.359	28.818	0.8	S 41 W	2.8	8.1	73.2	59.0	14.2	.455	1.5	...	...	.455	1.5
7	57.6	.376	58	.515	29.139	0.6	N 67 W	11.0	11.1	78.2	60.0	18.2	...	...	...	...	...	...
8	68.4	.437	63	.618	.177	0.4	S 4 E	2.3	2.4	80.4	52.4	28.0	...	...	...	...	...	...
9	Sunday						N 40 W	7.8	8.4	88.4	63.5	24.9	...	...	...	...	...	...
10	64.3	.402	66	.568	.106	0.8	N 82 E	3.3	4.5	70.4	59.8	10.6	.010	2.3	...	...	.010	2.3
11	65.9	.479	76	.423	28.944	0.5	S 12 W	2.1	2.4	75.0	59.0	16.0	R	0.2	...	...	R	0.2
12	73.1	.495	65	.536	29.042	0.1	N 76 W	4.2	5.5	85.2	59.5	25.7	...	...	...	...	...	...
13	75.4	.530	64	.570	.057	0.5	S 22 E	1.5	3.2	87.5	60.5	27.0	...	...	...	...	...	...
14	74.9	.582	67	.488	28.905	0.4	N 71 W	2.2	5.8	86.0	61.0	25.0	.015	0.1	...	...	.015	0.1
15	73.8	.434	53	.437	29.000	0.6	S 53 W	4.5	5.4	83.8	61.8	22.0	...	...	...	...	...	...
16	Sunday						N 41 W	1.6	3.0	72.4	59.2	13.2	R	0.1	...	...	R	0.1
17	63.9	.292	5	.409	.117	0.4	N 63 E	4.9	5.4	74.0	53.5	20.5	...	...	...	...	...	...
18	65.4	.347	50	.227	28.980	0.7	S 65 W	4.4	7.0	79.8	51.2	28.6	R	0.2	...	...	R	0.2
19	57.5	.316	56	.41	29.094	0.7	N 48 W	3.0	4.2	66.0	48.4	17.6	...	...	...	...	...	...
20	59.0	.334	66	.559	.219	0.5	S 53 W	2.6	3.9	71.0	48.0	23.0	...	...	...	...	...	...
21	59.5	.306	62	.598	.293	0.6	N 58 W	4.0	6.8	70.0	50.2	19.8	...	...	...	...	...	...
22	60.8	.301	60	.693	.392	0.4	N 53 W	8.5	9.1	69.8	49.8	19.0	...	...	...	...	...	...
23	Sunday						S 51 W	2.5	6.0	73.0	50.0	23.0	...	...	...	...	...	...
24	63.3	.337	60	.813	.475	0.0	S 77 E	2.1	5.2	73.0	47.8	25.2	...	...	...	...	...	...
25	65.9	.371	59	.771	.400	0.0	N 74 E	4.6	5.9	76.2	52.6	23.6	...	...	...	...	...	...
26	68.2	.428	63	.554	.127	0.6	S 24 E	3.5	6.0	78.2	52.5	25.7	.050	1.5	...	...	.050	1.5
27	65.4	.456	77	.547	.057	0.7	N 77 W	5.0	6.4	76.0	62.0	14.0	.210	0.8	...	...	.210	0.8
28	62.9	.452	80	.724	.262	0.9	N 29 W	2.3	4.3	71.0	56.2	14.8	...	...	...	...	...	...
29	65.5	.445	71	.765	.320	0.7	S 74 E	2.2	3.7	72.0	59.2	12.8	...	...	...	...	...	...
30	Sunday						S 39 W	1.3	6.8	76.8	56.2	20.0	R	1.0	...	...	R	1.0
31	7.5	.503	75	.612	.100	0.8	N 23 W	4.0	8.1	77.0	60.0	17.0	...	...	...	...	...	...
	66.0	0.422	72	29.555	29.133	0.5	N 88 W	1.5	5.7	76.1	55.7	20.4	1.255	12.2	...	...	1.255	12.2

TORONTO.
GENERAL METEOROLOGICAL ABSTRACT, AUGUST, 1871.

Days.	DAILY MEANS.						WIND.			EXTREMES OF TEMPERATURE.			RAIN.		SNOW.		TOTAL FALL.	
	Temperature of Air.	Pressure of Vapour.	Rel. Humid.	Barometric Pressure.	Pressure of Dry Air.	Clouded Sky.	Resultant Direction.	Resultant Velocity.	Mean Velocity.	Maximum.	Minimum.	Difference.	Depth in inches.	Approximate duration.	Depth in inches.	Approximate duration.	Depth in inches.	Approximate duration.
1	65.0	0.463	74	29.64	29.175	0.1	N 81 E	4.5	5.5	73.5	57.6	15.9	...	...	...	...	...	...
2	70.1	.491	68	.068	.177	0.6	S 31 E	3.6	3.9	82.6	58.6	24.0	...	...	...	...	...	...
3	72.8	.570	71	.562	28.986	0.7	S 5 E	3.1	3.9	84.0	60.2	23.8	...	...	...	...	...	...
4	76.1	.670	75	.380	28.710	0.6	S 46 W	3.5	6.2	85.5	65.4	20.1	...	...	...	...	...	...
5	69.9	.313	50	.412	29.069	0.3	N 48 W	6.7	7.2	81.0	62.0	19.0	...	...	...	...	...	...
6	Sunday						N 56 W	2.2	5.3	88.4	59.0	29.4	...	...	...	...	...	...
7	72.0	.548	70	.544	28.993	0.7	S 72 E	3.2	4.7	82.8	61.5	19.3	0.120	0.2	...	...	0.120	0.2
8	74.0	.567	62	.372	28.865	0.6	S 89 W	10.7	12.0	89.4	66.4	23.0	...	...	...	...	...	...
9	67.5	.412	52	.624	29.204	0.0	N 46 W	4.6	7.0	78.2	57.0	21.2	...	...	...	...	...	...
10	66.1	.379	53	.64	.267	0.3	S 59 E	2.4	4.2	77.2	53.2	24.0	...	...	...	...	...	...
11	63.8	.520	72	.549	.023	0.8	N 12 W	4.5	7.3	81.5	54.4	27.1	...	...	...	...	...	...
12	62.6	.352	62	.770	.418	0.0	N 38 E	2.9	7.0	71.0	58.8	12.2	...	...	...	...	...	...
13	Sunday						N 55 E	6.0	8.1	73.5	54.0	19.5	...	...	...	...	...	...
14	63.5	.462	68	.634	.172	0.4	N 87 E	2.8	4.8	79.7	56.6	23.1	...	...	...	...	...	...
15	70.8	.618	82	.502	28.973	1.0	S 41 E	0.5	2.7	82.0	63.4	18.6	.330	3.6	...	...	.330	3.0
16	70.9	.491	66	.538	29.042	0.5	N 64 W	9.8	10.8	80.5	57.4	22.1	...	...	...	...	...	...
17	64.7	.372	52	.68	.317	0.6	N 69 W	4.0	6.8	75.8	53.4	22.4	...	...	...	...	...	...
18	64.7	.265	51	.573	.281	9.0	N 83 W	10.9	11.7	76.0	52.0	24.0	...	...	...	...	...	...
19	63.5	.312	55	.636	.357	0.4	S 8 E	1.7	5.9	74.5	46.0	28.5	...	...	...	...	...	...
20	Sunday						N 50 E	7.8	10.7	70.0	59.0	11.0	.270	5.0	...	...	.270	5.0
21	59.1	.491	78	.668	.264	0.8	N 15 E	2.7	3.9	67.4	52.4	15.0	...	...	...	...	...	...
22	67.6	.544	80	.783	.212	0.7	N 75 E	4.3	5.2	74.5	56.0	18.5	...	...	...	...	...	...
23	72.0	.611	74	.742	.123	0.8	S 14 E	1.6	3.7	83.2	63.8	19.4	.040	1.0	...	...	.040	1.0
24	70.1	.422	50	.687	.264	0.2	N 57 W	3.9	6.6	81.8	61.4	23.4	...	...	...	...	...	...
25	62.8	.331	59	.705	.371	0.5	N 1 W	1.6	5.9	74.5	49.0	25.5	...	...	...	...	...	...
26	61.6	.447	80	.564	.117	1.0	N 29 E	6.2	7.2	67.0	57.2	9.8	1.030	13.0	...	...	1.030	13.0
27	Sunday						N 18 W	4.6	5.9	72.0	60.0	12.0	.020	1.0	...	...	.020	1.0
28	61.2	.481	79	.549	.068	0.6	N 79 E	7.9	9.0	69.0	54.8	14.2	.100	1.6	...	...	.100	1.6
29	67.8	.589	80	.198	28.698	0.5	S 15 W	10.8	11.3	75.2	64.2	11.0	.884	4.8	...	...	.884	4.8
30	61.4	.398	67	.227	28.820	0.6	S 59 W	11.3	12.0	72.8	59.5	13.3	...	...	...	...	...	...
31	57.5	.301	66	.633	28.339	0.4	N 84 W	5.4	5.7	65.5	52.6	12.6	...	...	...	...	...	...
	67.4	0.458	68	29.578	29.120	0.5	N 52 W	1.1	6.8	77.4	57.9	19.5	2.800	29.6	...	...	2.809	29.6

TORONTO.
GENERAL METEOROLOGICAL ABSTRACT. SEPTEMBER, 1871.

Days.	DAILY MEANS.						WIND.			EXTREMES OF TEMPERATURE			RAIN.		SNOW.		TOTAL FALL.	
	Temperature of Air	Pressure of Vapour.	Rel. Humid.	Barometric Pressure.	Pressure of Dry Air.	Clouded Sky	Resultant Direction.	Resultant Velocity.	Mean Velocity.	Maximum	Minimum	Difference	Depth in inches	Approximate duration	Depth in inches	Approximate duration	Depth in inches.	Approximate duration.
1	57.7	0.353	75	29.875	29.522	0.2	S 19 E	1.2	1.2	69.5	46.0	23.5	...	...	...	...	...	...
2	63.1	.391	68	.885	.494	0.8	S 19 E	3.3	3.5	71.0	49.2	21.8	...	...	...	...	...	...
3	Sunday						S 40 E	1.4	2.0	56.3	36.3	20.0	...	...	...	...	...	...
4	67.5	.575	86	.682	.104	0.7	S 26 E	1.9	1.9	78.0	61.4	16.6	...	...	...	...	...	...
5	70.6	.543	73	.573	.030	0.2	S 9 W	5.2	5.4	81.8	60.0	21.8	...	...	...	...	...	...
6	67.8	.465	66	.461	28.996	0.6	N 86 W	8.4	10.4	78.0	44.4	33.6	...	...	...	...	...	...
7	55.9	.267	61	.774	29.507	0.1	N 18 W	4.5	5.0	65.0	45.8	19.8	...	...	...	...	...	...
8	58.0	.296	61	.913	.617	0.3	S 70 E	6.1	7.4	4.2	48.2	16.6	...	...	...	...	...	...
9	65.1	.449	72	.824	.364	0.5	S 59 W	2.4	8.0	74.8	51.4	23.4	0.030	2.5	...	...	0.050	2.5
10	Sunday						N 2 W	6.5	7.8	65.4	57.4	8.0	...	...	...	...	...	...
11	58.7	.315	64	30.002	.687	0.7	N 57 E	1.2	4.5	68.0	49.8	8.2	...	...	...	...	...	...
12	58.4	.290	61	29.920	.630	0.1	S 62 E	0.4	9.3	69.4	48.8	20.4	...	...	...	...	...	...
13	55.6	.212	51	.858	.646	0.7	N 26 W	6.8	6.8	70.4	46.4	23.0	...	...	...	...	...	...
14	48.4	.220	62	.994	.774	0.9	N 82 E	5.3	5.8	3.0	58.8	14.5	R	0.2	...	...	R	0.2
15	52.7	.344	80	.670	.326	0.8	S 76 E	4.3	7.2	65.2	48.8	6.4	.425	10.0	...	...	.425	10.0
16	57.0	.372	80	.556	.183	1.0	S 70 W	2.4	2.9	63.0	50.4	12.6	.100	1.5	...	...	.100	1.5
17	Sunday						N 44 W	10.2	10.4	57.0	0.4	6.8	...	...	...	...	...	...
18	49.5	.267	74	.722	.455	0.7	S 54 E	3.5	4.9	58.2	36.2	22.0	.005	1.0	...	...	.005	1.0
19	53.9	.316	74	.512	.19	0.8	N 49 W	7.7	8.2	64.0	52.0	12.0	...	...	...	...	...	...
20	42.7	.174	65	.807	.633	0.3	N 30 W	5.4	5.8	54.8	36.0	18.8	...	...	...	...	...	...
21	41.8	.179	67	.975	.796	0.0	N 33 E	0.8	2.0	52.4	34.0	18.4	...	...	...	...	...	...
22	50.9	.276	74	.741	.465	0.4	S 9 E	3.1	3.7	62.2	34.6	27.6	...	...	...	...	...	...
23	64.3	.450	74	.385	28.935	0.6	S 42 W	6.8	7.2	71.0	45.2	25.8	...	...	...	...	...	...
24	Sunday						N 26 W	7.5	7.0	59.4	57.6	11.8	...	...	...	...	...	...
25	53.8	.297	72	.520	29.232	0.9	S 82 W	2.1	3.0	55.8	42.4	13.4	.650	8.5	...	...	.650	8.5
26	47.9	.263	79	.347	.084	0.7	S 77 W	5.9	6.0	56.8	47.0	9.8	.030	1.0	...	...	.030	1.0
27	46.9	.273	84	.332	.060	0.9	S 66 W	5.3	5.7	52.8	38.5	14.3	.030	3.0	...	...	.030	3.0
28	44.3	.226	77	.572	.346	0.8	N 60 W	10.2	10.3	53.0	38.2	14.8	...	...	...	...	...	...
29	44.0	.196	69	.901	.705	0.3	N 55 W	5.9	6.0	63.8	35.5	18.3	...	...	...	...	...	...
30	48.4	.244	77	.939	.695	0.4	S 66 W	1.2	2.0	61.0	36.0	21.4	...	...	...	...	...	...
	54.8	0.317	71	29.720	29.103	0.6	N 74 W	1.7	5.8	64.5	46.9	17.6	1.290	27.7	...	...	1.290	27.7

TORONTO.
GENERAL METEOROLOGICAL ABSTRACT, OCTOBER, 1871.

Days	DAILY MEANS.						WIND.			EXTREMES OF TEMPERATURE			RAIN.		SNOW.		TOTAL FALL.	
	Temperature of Air.	Pressure of Vapour.	Rel. Humid.	Barometric Pressure.	Pressure of Dry Air.	Clouded Sky.	Resultant Direction.	Resultant Velocity	Mean Velocity.	Maximum.	Minimum.	Difference.	Depth in inches.	Approximate duration.	Depth in inches.	Approximate duration.	Depth in inches.	Approximate duration.
1	Su	nday					S 31 W	3.5	3.0	66.0	41.2	24.8	R	R	...	...	R	R
2	56.3	.343	70	9.550	29.29	0.8	S 10 W	4.8	5.2	67.4	45.3	22.1	0.100	2.0	...	...	0.100	2.0
3	55.8	.318	77	.260	28.917	0.9	S 71 W	8.4	9.2	61.8	51.8	10.0	R	0.0	...	...	R	0.0
4	53.1	.244	83	.152	29.208	0.6	S 88 W	5.7	8.7	65.0	47.6	17.4	...	...	...	...	...	...
5	56.7	.324	72	.380	.050	0.5	S 26 W	4.1	6.7	68.4	41.8	23.6	R	0.2	...	...	R	0.2
6	50.0	.241	65	.506	.262	0.8	N 61 W	10.8	11.0	58.5	50.2	8.3	...	...	...	...	...	...
7	39.0	.16	71	.774	.609	0.0	S 20 W	1.6	2.4	48.2	31.0	17.2	...	...	...	...	...	...
8	Su	nday					S 25 W	5.2	5.4	40.4	35.0	25.4	...	...	...	...	...	...
9	6.1	.313	70	.633	.288	0.5	S 18 W	7.8	7.8	58.2	41.2	24.0	...	...	...	...	...	...
10	55.9	.30	50	.430	.137	0.0	S 37 W	8.0	9.3	65.0	52.0	13.0	.115	2.0	...	...	.115	2.0
11	16.7	.244	77	.674	.430	0.8	S 80 W	2.5	2.9	56.0	40.8	15.2	R	0.5	...	...	R	0.5
12	15.1	.202	56	.81	.615	0.7	S 83 W	1.0	3.1	55.0	36.4	19.2	...	...	...	...	...	...
13	48.7	.228	71	.925	.690	0.2	S 19 E	5.0	5.7	59.5	35.4	24.1	...	...	...	...	...	...
14	54.1	.366	80	.478	.318	1.0	S 15 W	8.3	9.0	64.0	48.8	15.2	.035	2.2	...	...	.035	2.2
15	Su	nday					S 77 W	14.7	15.5	62.8	52.9	9.9	...	...	...	...	...	...
16	43.8	.202	67	.655	.483	0.0	S 69 W	6.6	7.0	56.4	39.4	17.0	...	...	...	...	...	...
17	42.4	.208	77	.677	.469	0.0	S 73 W	5.0	7.8	50.0	33.8	16.2	R	1.0	...	...	R	1.0
18	39.0	.157	66	.801	.644	0.7	N 62 W	7.4	9.2	45.8	37.2	8.0	.060	2.0	...	...	.060	2.0
19	48.8	.207	61	.467	.260	0.0	N 88 W	13.5	17.4	64.2	33.4	30.8	...	...	...	...	...	...
20	38.0	.157	67	.975	.817	0.2	N 27 W	4.3	8.5	49.0	35.4	13.6	...	...	...	...	...	...
21	47.9	.237	71	.730	.493	0.3	S 35 W	5.0	6.3	58.4	29.4	29.0	...	...	...	...	...	...
22	Su	nday					S 15 W	9.5	9.6	72.2	44.8	27.4	...	...	...	...	...	...
23	56.0	.331	71	.579	.248	0.8	N 48 W	4.6	7.8	67.2	52.0	15.2	...	...	...	...	...	...
24	43.1	.196	70	.870	.673	0.2	N 62 E	6.1	6.7	49.5	39.4	10.1	...	...	...	...	...	...
25	47.3	.264	78	.781	.517	1.0	N 72 E	10.3	10.7	54.0	36.2	17.8	.050	1.0	...	...	.050	1.0
26	53.5	.354	86	.520	.166	0.8	S 5 E	3.7	7.9	62.2	48.5	13.7	.510	3.0	...	...	.510	3.0
27	44.1	.225	78	.557	.164	0.8	S 68 W	7.5	9.2	56.0	42.2	13.8	.065	4.0	...	...	.005	4.0
28	39.0	.165	65	.546	.381	0.9	S 84 W	14.7	12.1	45.2	35.4	9.8	...	...	...	...	...	...
29	Su	nday					N 23 W	1.9	5.1	46.0	36.2	9.8	...	...	...	...	...	...
30	45.4	.211	65	.779	.568	0.8	N 78 E	1.1	4.9	53.0	34.4	18.0	...	...	...	...	...	...
31	44.7	.235	70	.622	.386	1.0	N 66 E	4.8	7.0	50.1	28.6	21.5	.250	11.7	...	...	.250	11.7
	48.3	0.250	7.	29.633	29.383	0.7	S 66 W	3.7	7.8	58.3	40.8	17.5	1.185	30.2	...	...	1.185	30.2

TORONTO.
GENERAL METEOROLOGICAL ABSTRACT, NOVEMBER, 1871.

Days	DAILY MEANS.						WIND.			EXTREMES OF TEMPERATURE.			RAIN.		SNOW.		TOTAL FALL.	
	Temperature of Air.	Pressure of Vapour.	Rel. Humid.	Barometric Pressure.	Pressure of Dry Air.	Cloud'd Sky.	Resultant Direction.	Resultant Velocity.	Mean Velocity.	Maximum.	Minimum.	Difference.	Depth in Inches.	Approximate duration.	Depth in inches.	Approximate duration.	Depth in Inches.	Approximate duration.
1	41.1	0.192	73	29.479	29.287	0.9	N 65 W	13.0	13.7	47.1	40.4	6.7	...	...	...	...	...	...
2	40.9	.157	73	.615	.427	0.9	N 84 W	5.6	7.4	46.5	37.4	9.1	R	0.5	...	...	R	0.5
3	35.8	.136	97	.853	.713	0.4	N 19 E	1.5	2.7	43.0	29.0	13.4	...	...	...	...	...	...
4	37.9	.169	74	.696	.527	0.7	N 70 E	8.5	9.0	42.8	31.8	11.0	...	...	...	...	...	...
5	Sunday						N 22 W	5.0	5.0	41.5	31.0	10.5	...	...	...	...	...	...
6	27.6	.113	75	.883	.770	0.9	N 45 W	7.1	7.8	32.0	24.2	7.8	...	...	S	S	S	S
7	34.3	.111	60	.696	.585	0.4	S 85 W	7.7	8.1	43.0	22.2	20.8	...	...	...	...	...	...
8	38.2	.144	63	.480	.336	0.8	N 57 W	8.7	8.8	44.8	33.4	11.4	...	...	...	...	...	...
9	36.7	.145	66	.521	.376	0.0	N 88 E	7.8	8.8	43.2	28.2	15.0	0.050	1.7	...	...	.050	1.5
10	37.9	.194	84	.292	.098	1.0	N 45 W	5.6	11.2	42.8	32.0	10.8	.195	3.2	S	0.1	.195	3.3
11	32.5	.135	73	.994	.859	0.3	N 43 W	10.7	11.0	33.2	31.0	4.2	...	...	S	0.5	S	0.5
12	Sunday						N 68 E	4.0	4.0	34.0	19.2	14.7	...	...	...	...	...	...
13	33.7	.163	69	.777	.614	0.7	N 83 E	13.5	13.0	43.8	26.8	17.0	...	...	...	...	...	...
14	41.6	.229	87	.166	28.937	1.0	N 47 E	11.4	15.9	44.6	38.0	6.6	2.310	22.0	0.2	2.0	2.330	24.0
15	26.8	.124	84	.269	29.145	1.0	N 40 W	32.1	32.4	34.5	26.7	7.8	...	...	2.0	19.0	.200	19.0
16	23.6	.103	82	.672	.568	0.1	N 37 W	13.4	13.8	26.8	19.2	7.6	...	...	...	...	...	...
17	23.0	.143	90	.967	.524	0.8	N 18 W	5.3	5.8	34.8	23.8	10.7	...	...	...	...	...	...
18	31.9	.158	87	30.031	.873	1.0	N 68 E	4.4	7.0	36.0	28.0	8.0	...	...	...	...	...	...
19	Sunday						S 57 E	6.4	8.0	45.2	29.5	15.7	.040	1.5	...	...	.040	1.5
20	39.0	.186	77	29.614	.428	1.0	S 62 W	11.7	11.8	44.0	39.4	4.6	R	0.3	...	...	R	0.3
21	33.9	.149	76	.428	.270	1.0	S 57 W	12.0	12.8	36.0	32.0	4.0	...	...	S	4.0	S	4.0
22	28.3	.119	76	.280	.161	0.0	S 81 W	11.0	12.8	34.5	28.2	6.3	...	...	0.2	0.6	.020	0.6
23	27.1	.100	65	.631	.530	0.8	S 24 E	8.0	10.7	34.5	15.5	19.0	...	...	0.2	3.0	.020	3.0
24	34.9	.165	80	.387	.222	1.0	S 42 W	10.3	14.0	41.4	27.4	14.0	R	0.5	1.5	5.0	.150	5.5
25	33.1	.130	73	.795	.659	1.0	S 2 E	2.5	5.4	39.6	30.6	9.0	R	2.0	...	...	R	2.0
26	Sunday						N 64 W	7.0	9.1	45.0	30.0	15.0	.060	9.0	...	...	.060	9.0
27	17.1	.070	73	.734	.664	0.7	N 23 W	12.0	12.8	24.5	15.7	8.8	...	...	S	2.0	S	2.0
28	8.9	.054	84	.728	.674	0.7	N 17 E	10.2	10.7	13.2	4.8	8.4	...	...	0.4	5.0	.040	5.0
29	9.3	.055	84	.771	.715	0.4	N 47 W	9.1	9.6	16.2	4.5	11.7	...	...	S	0.5	S	0.5
30	9.4	.056	83	.870	.815	0.4	N 76 W	5.8	6.4	16.0	0.0	16.0	...	...	...	...	...	...
	30.6	0.136	76	29.640	29.503	0.8	N 45 W	4.1	10.4	37.0	26.1	10.9	2.655	40.5	4.5	41.7	3.105	82.2

TORONTO.

General Meteorological Abstract, December, 1871.

Days	Temperature of Air	Pressure of Vapour	Rel. Humid.	Barometric Pressure	Pressure of Dry Air	Clouded Sky	Resultant Direction	Resultant Velocity	Mean Velocity	Maximum	Minimum	Difference	Depth in inches	Approximate duration	Depth in inches	Approximate duration	Depth in inches	Approximate duration
1	17.7	0.079	81	29.705	29.62	1.0	S 83 W	4.8	6.7	25.4	7.7	17.7	...	...	0.2	1.3	1.020	1.5
2	25.5	.112	78	.679	.567	0.8	S 40 W	10.6	10.9	35.2	9.4	25.8	...	...	...	...	...	...
3	Sunday						S	9.5	10.1	11.0	28.0	13.0	.010	2.0	...	...	.010	2.0
4	26.6	.126	8	.140	.013	0.8	S 87 W	19.1	20.3	33.0	30.2	8.8	...	...	0.1	0.2	.010	0.2
5	11.6	.054	77	.532	.478	0.6	N 89 W	15.7	16.2	14.8	8.6	6.2	...	...	S	1.6	S	1.0
6	20.7	.097	82	.362	.235	0.2	S 35 W	17.9	18.9	29.1	7.8	21.3	...	...	0.5	6.5	.050	6.5
7	30.2	.131	78	.211	.080	1.0	S 70 W	13.1	13.4	32.0	20.0	12.0	...	...	1.5	5.8	.150	5.8
8	21.7	.085	76	.447	.355	0.1	S 64 W	16.8	17.0	26.2	20.1	6.1	...	...	0.1	4.6	.010	4.5
9	18.9	.076	74	.80	.721	0.8	S 69 W	12.8	13.0	23.8	14.4	9.4	...	...	...	...	...	...
10	Sunday						S 54 W	13.6	13.6	29.5	15.8	13.7	...	...	...	...	...	...
11	31.1	.148	84	.417	.269	1.0	S 78 W	5.7	7.3	34.5	24.1	10.4	...	...	0.1	2.7	.010	2.7
12	23.9	.125	78	.593	.468	1.0	S 64 E	7.5	8.0	33.5	20.3	13.2	...	...	2.0	7.5	.200	7.5
13	21.2	.119	85	.425	.306	0.5	N 64 W	8.3	10.4	33.0	25.0	8.0	...	...	1.0	12.0	.100	12.0
14	11.8	.069	81	.681	.612	1.0	N 70 W	7.2	8.1	19.5	10.6	8.9	...	...	0.1	1.5	.010	1.5
15	19.5	.081	76	.652	.571	1.0	S 2 E	4.5	6.9	26.4	8.8	17.6	...	...	0.1	3.0	.010	3.0
16	30.2	.132	79	.156	.318	1.0	S 18 W	14.6	16.5	37.0	20.0	17.0	...	...	1.0	2.7	.100	2.7
17	Sunday						S 78 W	9.9	11.0	37.2	28.8	8.4	...	...	0.1	1.0	.010	1.0
18	26.0	.112	80	.721	.609	0.7	N 76 W	5.9	7.5	31.7	23.1	8.4	...	...	0.3	12.5	.030	12.5
19	17.3	.079	80	.385	.306	1.0	S 72 W	13.3	13.5	24.6	20.2	4.3	...	...	1.0	6.5	.100	6.5
20	-3.8	.03	84	.379	.346	1.0	N 62 W	2.7	14.2	9.0	-1.0	10.0	...	...	0.1	0.7	.010	0.5
21	-2.6	.02	83	.86	.83	0.3	S 70 W	7.1	7.3	10.0	-21.0	31.0	...	...	S	2.5	S	2.5
22	18.0	.092	89	.875	.78	0.4	S 83 E	7.7	8.9	34.8	0.7	34.3	...	...	6.5	13.2	.350	13.2
23	27.5	.181	79	.28	.09	1.0	S 47 W	9.2	17.0	48.2	17.0	31.2	.380	3.6	...	...	.380	3.5
24	Sunday						S 25 W	3.2	4.9	39.0	30.0	9.0	...	...	...	...	...	...
25	...	...	...	...	...		N 41 W	9.6	10.5	35.2	27.0	8.2	...	...	...	...	...	...
26	11.7	.064	85	.68	.62	1.0	N 10 W	5.7	7.2	22.5	3.5	19.0	...	...	1.5	14.0	.150	11.0
27	14.1	.063	75	.672	.609		S 70 W	21.5	21.5	20.8	13.0	7.8	...	...	1.0	3.0	.100	3.0
28	9.9	.051	74	.93	.88	0.7	S 58 W	9.7	9.7	28.0	2.0	26.0	...	...	...	...	...	...
29	19.7	.078	74	.77	.691	0.5	N 10 E	2.6	3.7	26.0	9.4	16.0	...	...	...	...	...	...
30	27.9	.138	88	.728	.590	1.0	N 76 E	11.0	11.0	33.0	15.0	21.0	.230	11.3	...	...	.230	11.3
31	Sunday						N 39 W	8.8	9.0	41.4	21.5	16.9	.320	7.0	...	...	.320	7.0
	16.9	1.031	0	29.577	29.479	8.8	S 70 W	6.9	11.5	29.6	14.9	14.7	0.94	21.8	11.2	102.7	1.360	125.9

www.ingramcontent.com/pod-product-compliance
Lightning Source LLC
Chambersburg PA
CBHW021403230426
43666CB00006B/627